Scalability Experts, Inc.

Microsoft® SQL Server 2005

Changing the Paradigm

(SQL Server 2005 Public Beta Edition)

Microsoft SQL Server 2005: Changing the Paradigm

International Standard Book Number: 0-672-32778-3

Library of Congress Catalog Card Number: 2005901837

Printed in the United States of America

First Printing: September 2005

08   07   06   05   4   3   2   1

Trademarks

Warning and Disclaimer

Bulk Sales

Sams Publishing offers excellent discounts on this book when ordered in quantity for bulk purchases or special sales. For more information, please contact

   U.S. Corporate and Government Sales
   1-800-382-3419
   corpsales@pearsontechgroup.com

For sales outside of the U.S., please contact

   International Sales
   international@pearsoned.com

Publisher
Paul Boger

Acquisitions Editor
Neil Rowe

Development Editor
Mark Renfrow

Managing Editor
Charlotte Clapp

Senior Project Editor
Matthew Purcell

Copy Editor
Kitty Jarrett

Indexer
Tim Wright

Proofreader
Suzanne Thomas

Technical Editor
Ross Mistry

Publishing Coordinator
Cindy Teeters

Multimedia Developer
Dan Scherf

Designer
Gary Adair

Page Layout
Kelly Maish

Contents at a Glance

Table of Contents

Foreword

This book represents a major milestone in a journey that began a few months before the second beta release of SQL Server 2005, which at the time was code-named Yukon. It began with a new model for working with developers. We called this new model Ascend, and it represented a refinement of best practices that my colleague Roger Doherty and I had created or borrowed from others over the past 10 years at Microsoft.

In the beta 1 time frame, we focused most of our energy on helping developers get a leg up on the programmability aspects in this latest release of Microsoft's next-generation data management and analysis software. This included working with the common language runtime (CLR) and .NET integration, native XML, X-Query, and user-defined types. As we approached the second beta release, it was obvious that we needed to expand on our early success with developers and reach out to the DBA community as well as to application developers. Feedback from the first wave of customers and partners working with us in Ascend indicated that we needed to offer high-quality training on the fundamental architecture, administration, and components of SQL Server 2005. That is where Scalability Experts entered the picture. Don Petersen, another long-time colleague of Roger and me, was working on the SQL Server 2005 marketing team. He recommended that Scalability Experts help us build the DBA course for Ascend. After a meeting or two, it was clear that this was a winning strategy, so we plowed forward and built a five-day, deep-dive training workshop for DBAs. This book represents much of what was covered in that course, with the added value of having refined the material over 30 deliveries of our training workshop worldwide.

Organizations today face numerous data challenges—for example, the need for faster and more data-driven decisions, increasing the productivity and flexibility of development staff, and pressure to reduce overall information technology budgets. At the same time, requirements for scaling the infrastructure are constantly increasing. Much of this challenge falls squarely on the shoulders of DBAs. Like the workshop the material was drawn from, this book will help DBAs and application developers learn how to apply the new capabilities of SQL Server 2005 and understand why it will provide greater value and more flexibility, and how it will make enterprise-level features more affordable, scalable, and secure. This book will also help architects understand and better leverage the significant improvements in SQL Server 2005 to design more efficient, more scalable, and more secure solutions.

As this book's title suggests, SQL Server 2005 represents a major change in the way data management and analysis software are viewed—and the critical role of the DBA in managing that change. The skill and commitment to quality we experienced while working with Scalability Experts really shows in this book. It is sure to be one of the DBA's best guides to the workings of this exciting new product. Enjoy.

Andy Gammuto
Group Manager, Evangelism Programs
Microsoft Corporation

P.S. Congratulations to Scalability Experts on winning the Microsoft Advanced Infrastructure Solutions–Data Management specialization excellence award two years in a row (2004 and 2005).

About the Author

Scalability Experts, Inc., focuses on the backbone of business success—the integrity and reliability of your Microsoft SQL Server system. Scalability Experts core competencies include consolidation, Business Intelligence, upgrade, migrations and database assessments. SE's specialized approach allows it to provide SQL Server users with the most experienced, innovative and intelligent SQL Server consultants and trainers to help them reach higher goals in less time than expected. Its SQL Server Master Series workshops focus on 300-400 level education in scalability, high availability, security, performance tuning, and database migration. By combining consulting, analysis and knowledge transfer Scalability Experts offers unique solutions that allow SQL Server users to dramatically increase the productivity and dependability of their current and future Microsoft SQL Server implementations.

We Want to Hear from You!

As the reader of this book, *you* are our most important critic and commentator. We value your opinion and want to know what we're doing right, what we could do better, what areas you'd like to see us publish in, and any other words of wisdom you're willing to pass our way.

As publisher for Sams Publishing, I welcome your comments. You can email or write me directly to let me know what you did or didn't like about this book—as well as what we can do to make our books better.

Please note that I cannot help you with technical problems related to the topic of this book. We do have a User Services group, however, where I will forward specific technical questions related to the book.

When you write, please be sure to include this book's title and author as well as your name, email address, and phone number. I will carefully review your comments and share them with the author and editors who worked on the book.

Email: feedback@samspublishing.com

Mail: Paul Boger
         Publisher
         Sams Publishing
         800 East 96th Street
         Indianapolis, IN 46240 USA

For more information about this book or another Sams Publishing title, visit our website at www.samspublishing.com. Type the ISBN (excluding hyphens) or the title of a book in the Search field to find the page you're looking for.

Changes in the Database Paradigm: How SQL Server 2005 Redefines the Role of a DBA

Microsoft SQL Server 2005 represents the completion of Microsoft SQL Server's transformation into a leading database management system. The changes are extensive, completing the capabilities required for the most demanding enterprise applications and introducing a new application paradigm that affects how many new SQL Server applications will be implemented and deployed.

A major upgrade such as SQL Server 2005 brings many benefits to customers. It greatly improves classic "abilities," such as availability, scalability, reliability, and so on. It introduces powerful new application development capabilities. Many of the rough spots in earlier versions of SQL Server have been polished. And many of the items long requested by the SQL Server community are now provided. SQL Server 2005 has something for everyone.

With any major advance comes challenges. In the case of SQL Server 2005, the challenge for a DBA is adapting to numerous changes from previous versions. Some of these changes fundamentally alter the mechanics of how DBAs interact with SQL Server; others are features with deep, long-term impact on how database applications are built and the demands they place on DBAs.

Before discussing the impact of these changes on DBAs, let's review the SQL Server philosophy and history. Then we'll look at the impact of some key changes in SQL Server 2005 on the DBA. Finally, we'll take a holistic look at these changes as part of the new application architecture.

SQL Server Philosophy

SQL Server 2005, like SQL Server 7.0 and SQL Server 2000, was driven by five major philosophical forces: enterprise suitability, developer friendliness, cost of ownership, completeness, and ubiquity.

Enterprise Suitability

The ability of SQL Server to handle the most demanding enterprise applications has been a key philosophy since SQL Server 7.0 development began. The focus has been on classic attributes such as quality, performance and scalability, availability, platform integration, and manageability as well as on key functionality required by enterprise customers. With SQL Server 2005 the enterprise suitability push is particularly strong, most notably in the focus on high availability.

Developer Friendliness

While earlier versions of SQL Server focused on developers, with a special emphasis on independent software vendor (ISV) application developers, SQL Server 2005 is a developer's paradise. Deep integration of the Microsoft .NET common language runtime (CLR), extensive XML support, enhanced Transact-SQL (T-SQL) support, new development tools, and many other enhancements make SQL Server 2005 *the* database system for developers.

Cost of Ownership

SQL Server has always been inexpensive compared with the competition. Since SQL Server 7.0, Microsoft has focused on lowering the overall cost of ownership. While 7.0 was somewhat revolutionary in that regard, SQL Server 2005 is more evolutionary. SQL Server 2005 continues the tradition of reducing or automating most of the traditional tuning requirements of database systems. New management tools, supportability enhancements, and platform integration further address lowering the cost of ownership.

Completeness

Prior to SQL Server 7.0, a database management system product generally consisted of a relational database engine, a client/server communications mechanism, and some rudimentary tools. Good management tools, powerful data-loading tools, replication, analytic tools, and so on were extra-cost options, if available at all. SQL Server 7.0 changed that by including most of what was necessary to build and deploy database applications in the base product. SQL Server 2005 continues this philosophy through the inclusion of an end-user component for Reporting Services, better integration of Analysis Services and the relational engine, fleshed out data mining support, and the new Service Broker.

Ubiquity

One of the goals of SQL Server 7.0 was to replace the need for multiple different data stores with a single technology base. This required SQL Server to be capable of running while embedded within an application on a desktop as well as being a standalone database server running on the largest enterprise server hardware. It also required compatible technology to run on handheld devices. This resulted in the creation of MSDE and SQL Server CE. SQL Server 2005 makes a further push toward ubiquity by replacing those earlier technologies with SQL Server 2005 Express Edition and SQL Server 2005 Mobile Edition.

History

After a late 1993 decision to become a mainstream database management system vendor, Microsoft began work on its first in-house–developed version of SQL Server. Prior to that point, Microsoft was a porting partner for Sybase SQL Server, adapting it to Microsoft operating systems and enhancing it with tools more suitable for the workgroup and departmental environments that used Microsoft-based servers. In 1995 Microsoft shipped SQL Server 6.0, and followed it up with SQL Server 6.5 in 1996. These two releases, developed entirely in-house, based on the Sybase architecture and code, allowed Microsoft to push beyond its original workgroup and departmental markets into some enterprise applications. But even before SQL Server 6.0 shipped, work had begun on a revolutionary new SQL Server. A new query processor, cursor engine, database API (OLE DB), and other database management system components were already under development. And initial discussions to acquire OLAP technology had already taken place.

SQL Server's transformation was planned as three releases. The first release would focus on the basic re-architecture of SQL Server and making it suitable for enterprise use. The second release would be a quick-turnaround release to address key customer concerns and plug any critical competitive holes that had emerged. And the third release would be the one where Microsoft could fully exploit the new architecture to address a broad range of new customer requirements.

With the first release, SQL Server 7.0, Microsoft successfully ripped out the internals it had inherited from Sybase and replaced them with the new technology it had developed in-house. This approach, rather than building a new database system completely from scratch, was employed to retain compatibility for the thousands of applications already running on SQL Server. Customers experienced major improvements in reliability, scalability, performance, and manageability. SQL Server also became the first database product to incorporate all the tools necessary for building data warehouses when it included both extraction, transformation, and loading (ETL) tools and an online analytical processing (OLAP) engine. With its Distributed Query feature and OLE DB architecture, it also became the first database system to make heterogeneous data access a standard integrated capability. Replication, a SQL Server strong-suit since version 6.0, underwent a major upgrade in capabilities. Perhaps most importantly, SQL Server 7.0 focused on automating or eliminating many of the tuning and management demands that had historically been required of database systems.

The second release, SQL Server 2000, was a refinement of SQL Server 7.0. XML was just emerging as an interesting topic in computing, and the SQL Server team became convinced that adding support for XML was critical. Materialized (a.k.a. indexed) views, originally envisioned as a feature for the third release, had become a hot requirement as a result of the then-popular TPC-D benchmark. And numerous modest performance, scalability, and availability improvements were incorporated to enable SQL Server to continue to meet enterprise requirements. Subsequently to the initial release of SQL Server 2000, SQL Server was enhanced with better support for mainframe-class servers such as the HP Superdome, Unisys ES/7000, and 64-bit Intel Itanium-based servers; a major security update; new XML capabilities; and new Reporting Services and Notification Services modules. The new Reporting Services feature, along with major OLAP upgrades and new data mining capabilities included in the initial SQL Server 2000 release, and various server upgrades such as materialized views, made SQL Server 2000 a leading data warehousing platform.

Work on SQL Server 2005 began late in 2000, with a goal of delivering on most of the remaining capabilities envisioned in the original three-release plan. Leading the priorities, the original vision of "Visual Basic stored procedures" had evolved to be full support for the Microsoft .NET CLR (and thus all CLR languages). As anticipated with SQL Server 2000, XML had indeed become a major force in the application development world, and it would become core to nearly all new work in SQL Server 2005. Along with these technology shifts, new features such as direct HTTP access and subsystems such as Service Broker would enable a greatly enhanced SQL Server application model. On the data warehousing front, Analysis Services would receive a major overhaul, and SQL Server's Data Transformation Services would be replaced by a new enterprise-class ETL tool. At the same time, nearly every other area of SQL Server would receive major upgrades.

SQL Server 2005 and Database Administrators

Initially, many DBAs will see SQL Server 2005 as little more than an evolutionary release with many new features and management capabilities that they will need to master. Over time, most DBAs will come to see SQL Server 2005 as a new application platform that dramatically changes how the applications are built and how they work, as well as the skills DBAs must master to support these applications. In the following sections, we'll look at SQL Server 2005 from the evolutionary standpoint and then concentrate on it as a revolutionary new application platform.

One Small Step for a DBA

You, the DBA for several SQL Server databases, are suddenly handed the DVD for SQL Server 2005 and told to prepare for an upgrade. What should you expect? Just upgrading an application from SQL Server 7.0 or SQL Server 2000 doesn't require much effort on the part of DBAs or developers. After installation, nearly all applications just run as before. Evolving applications to take advantage of new SQL Server 2005 features, or deploying new applications developed specifically for SQL Server 2005, is a different story. But for now, let's focus on straightforward upgrades of existing systems. In most regards, this is more straightforward than the upgrade that occurred between SQL Server 6.5 and 7.0, but there are a few twists for DBAs.

Unlike with the 6.5 to 7.0 upgrade, SQL Server 2005 retains the same basic on-disk structures as the previous version, and thus there is no requirement for a database migration. And while all feasible measures have been taken to ensure the near-complete application compatibility, with APIs continuing to work and T-SQL compatibility maintained (via a Compatibility Level setting in some cases), you need to be aware that there might be some application compatibility challenges. But while application compatibility generally shouldn't be an issue, DBAs will find that how they interact with SQL Server 2005 is substantially different than in the past.

The first substantial change that a DBA will notice is that the toolset for SQL Server 2005 has been completely replaced. Gone are the familiar SQL Enterprise Manager and Query Analyzer tools; they have been replaced by SQL Server Management Studio. SQL Server Management Studio also takes on some of the capabilities that were present in Analysis Manager. Although OSQL.exe is still provided, it has been deprecated in favor of the new sqlcmd.exe utility. The Client Network Utility, Server Network Utility, and SQL Service Manager have been replaced by the SQL Server Configuration Manager MMC snap-in. And a new tool, Business Intelligence Development Studio, is introduced for building business intelligence applications. These toolset changes represent a major departure from earlier versions of SQL Server and require immediate attention from DBAs.

Why such a dramatic change in the toolset? There are many reasons, but let's start with the basic truth about DBAs. While much of the IT world has a clear split between developers and operational personnel, the DBA role encompasses development, system management, and operational activities. The previous SQL Enterprise Manager/Query Analyzer split meant you, as a DBA, had to constantly switch between two different tools with completely different user interface styles to perform your job. The new SQL Server Management Studio allows you to performance all aspects of your job by using one tool. DBAs with a strong development focus will easily embrace SQL Server Management Studio, with its Visual Studio .NET–based user interface, as a superior replacement for the earlier tools. System management–focused DBAs may find the transition less natural and take some time to become fond of the new tools.

Another reason for the toolset change was the growing complexity of the overall SQL Server product. In order to build a business intelligence application, should there be separate tools for the relational database, the analysis engine, the ETL service, and the reporting service? Or should there be one tool for building the business intelligence application and another for managing all the underlying services? With SQL Server's new toolset, Microsoft chose the latter approach.

Both development- and system management–oriented DBAs will find that the new toolset offers considerable new functionality and a far more powerful DBA environment than was available in previous releases of SQL Server.

In addition to its new toolset, SQL Server 2005 has a number of other new developments. Perhaps the most glaring is that Microsoft has replaced SQL Server 7.0/2000's Data Transformation Services (DTS) with SQL Server Integration Services (SSIS). Although it is possible to continue to run DTS packages in SQL Server 2005, there are no tools to support further development of those packages. When you need to do new development, you have to migrate your DTS packages to SSIS, with the help of the Data Transformation Services Migration Wizard. It is important to keep in mind that even minor maintenance of existing DTS packages forces a DBA to deal with this change.

As a DBA works with SQL Server 2005, he or she will begin to notice considerable differences in other core aspects of SQL Server 2005. For example, the classic system tables have been largely replaced by the system catalog, whose primary access is through a set of catalog views. For compatibility, the system tables remain, implemented as a set of compatibility views over the system catalog. In addition, usage of the master database has been split in two. The Microsoft-shipped system objects now reside in a read-only (and generally hidden) Resource database. For DBAs used to having the ability to modify the Microsoft-shipped system objects such as system stored procedures, this represents a substantial change.

There are solid reasons for these changes, and DBAs are sure to welcome them once an initial adjustment period has passed. The new system catalog cleans up the metadata mess introduced with SQL Server 7.0. In SQL Server 6.5 and earlier, the system tables exposed considerable information about the implementation of SQL Server. Applications relied on this information. With the re-architecture of SQL Server 7.0, the internals changed in ways that couldn't be compatibly represented in the system tables. Although the tables were cobbled together to preserve as much application compatibility as possible, Microsoft started to recommend that customers not reference them directly. Various alternatives were suggested, but none fully met the needs of users. Changes in SQL Server 2005, such as the support for partitioning, once again require major changes in the system tables. Therefore, Microsoft came up with the new system catalog. The catalog views isolate new applications from future changes to the system catalog, and the compatibility views isolate existing applications from the new metadata design. This should provide a far superior design moving forward.

Likewise, the Resource database solves a number of problems, most importantly the ability to roll back service packs. This highly requested feature has previously proven impractical to implement because applying a service pack almost always results in changes to system objects, such as system stored procedures. With these changes in the master database, and applied via scripts, there is no straightforward way to undo them (without losing user information stored in the master database). By moving them to the resource database, you can undo them simply by copying the older version of the resource database back onto the system.

So far we've focused on changes that are somewhat disruptive, and you may be questioning the wisdom of upgrading to SQL Server 2005. Of course, we haven't looked at many of the benefits that even a simple upgrade can bring. For example, in addition to the new catalog views, SQL Server 2005 provides dynamic management views, which give a DBA extensive insight into what is happening inside SQL Server 2005 and can be used to troubleshoot performance and other problems. And the Dedicated Administrative Console feature allows a DBA to get into a server that is overloaded or otherwise appears hung, to diagnose and correct problems. And a DBA can take advantage of the new plan guides (sp_create_plan_guide) to use query hints to tune specific queries without modifying any application code. In addition, SQL Server 2005 provides the ability to perform nearly all operations, such as index creation, online. It also provides the ability to easily maintain in your network a mirror copy of a database that's on another server. These are just a few examples of the many immediate benefits DBAs gain when upgrading to SQL Server 2005.

DBAs will also find SQL Server 2005 a compelling option for new hardware platforms their organizations deploy. SQL Server 2005 has added support for AMD and Intel's 64-bit extensions to the x86 architecture, full support for Itanium 64-bit systems, and extensions for tuning NUMA (non-uniform memory access, the memory architecture used to build many high-end servers) systems. Microsoft performed modest tuning to SQL Server 2000 for new hardware using service packs, but SQL Server 2005 is the first release really designed for the computer systems of 2005 and beyond rather than for those of 2000. These changes allow for greatly increased scalability with little impact on the DBA. In some cases, the DBA's workload will decrease as the need to tune around 32-bit memory limitations is eliminated.

Although most applications easily upgrade to SQL Server 2005, you need to invest in upgrading your skills even for straightforward upgrades. And depending on which features of SQL Server applications use, it may make more sense to make substantial changes as part of the upgrade process.

A Giant Leap for DBA-kind

Every aspect of SQL Server 2005 has received new capabilities. Many of the largest changes in SQL Server 2005 reflect new features for application developers. In the database world, when a developer sneezes, it means the DBA is about to catch a cold. But first we'll explore some of the more significant classic database features that have changed. The following sections focus on the new features in SQL Server 2005 that have a major impact on DBAs.

The More Things Change, the More They Stay the Same

SQL Server 2005 has a true toy-chest of wonderful capabilities for DBAs. One that I've already mentioned is database mirroring, which is the ability to maintain an exact (and, if desired, fully synchronous) copy of a database on another server for high availability purposes. This is an alternative to using Microsoft Clustering Services (MSCS), and it offers numerous benefits (for example, easier to set up, no special hardware required, very fast failover time) and some limitations (for example, only individual application databases failover—not the entire environment). Database mirroring is particularly useful in conjunction with MSCS because you can use MSCS to provide high availability within your data center and database mirroring to provide a copy in a different physical location, in case of a disaster (for example, power grid outage, earthquake, terrorist attack). Database mirroring is a more integrated, real-time (or synchronous) version of the log shipping that was available in SQL Server 2000.

One change that will please DBAs (and developers) who work with both SQL Server and Oracle is support for snapshot isolation. Snapshot isolation brings to SQL Server Oracle-like "readers don't block writers" and "writers don't block readers" style concurrency. With SQL Server 2005, it is also possible to specify that all read committed transactions (the default transaction isolation mode) should use snapshot isolation. With traditional locking, read committed transactions already have the property that readers don't block writers. Specifying that read committed transactions should use snapshot isolation for reads also means that writers can't block readers.

For those with larger databases, particularly data warehouses, SQL Server now supports table and index partitioning. Partitioning is generally used to make maintenance easier. For example, in a data warehouse you could load the data for a new month into a table independently of its final destination and then do a rapid switch of that table into a partition of the larger table. Or you could independently rebuild an index partition rather than an entire index.

As mentioned earlier, DTS has been replaced by SSIS. Whereas DTS was a basic ETL tool, SSIS is an enterprise-class ETL and data integration tool, offering a more powerful programming model and very high performance through extensive parallelization.

The security architecture of SQL Server 2005 has been enhanced. The new endpoint-based authentication mechanism allows you to easily manage and secure access to SQL Server. Windows authentication is still the preferred authentication mechanism, but for applications that require SQL authentication, a lot of work has been done to strengthen the SQL authentication. SQL Server now allows granular permissions, and it has fixed ownership chaining issues, introduced the notion of "real" schemas and separated them from the users, and added cryptography support. Microsoft has gone to great lengths to ensure that a problem the magnitude of W32.Slammer does not happen again. Examples of this initiative include the "off by default" features and the new Surface Area Configuration tool, which lets you protect your SQL Server 2005 environment by reducing the attack-able area of a system.

These are just a few of the substantial improvements to classic database functionality in SQL Server 2005 that DBAs will be taking advantage of.

You Call This a Relational Database Management System?

The biggest changes in SQL Server 2005 relate to its new features for developers. These changes are not on the same level as changes in previous versions, such as adding a new client API like OLE DB. These are major fundamental changes to how the database server portion of an application is written. And they affect the DBA just as strongly as they affect developers. These developer features include ability to natively store, index, query, and modify XML data, writing stored procedures and functions using .NET languages, and implementing asynchronous messaging inside the database.

The Ubiquity of XML   In a few short years, XML has gone from being a curiosity that might better enable the interchange of data between disparate applications to being the most important application building block of our time. SQL Server 2000 introduced support of XML at the level of mapping XML documents back and forth to relational tables. SQL Server 2005 treats XML as a fundamental data type. This means that SQL Server 2005 can now natively store, index, and manipulate XML data. SQL Server 2005 handles the XQuery query language, not just SQL. It also means that SQL Server 2005 uses XML itself in places where complex information must be communicated. For example, query notification and event notification both format their notification messages in XML. The new Service Broker returns its errors messages as XML strings. And Analysis Services 2005 uses XML for Analysis as its native protocol.

XML has become a native protocol for talking to the SQL Server 2005 database engine. In earlier versions of SQL Server, the only protocol support by the database engine was Tabular Data Stream (TDS). Microsoft provided several native APIs, all of which spoke TDS to the server. SQL Server 2005 provides an alternative: native HTTP SOAP access to the server. By using HTTP SOAP and without using any client database API, an application can formulate a request to the database server, have it natively handled by the server (without the need for IIS or any other intermediary), and have the data returned formatted as XML. This is particularly useful when a non-Windows system (such as Unix or Linux) for which Microsoft doesn't provide a client API needs to make a request to SQL Server 2005. But it can be used for any application on any platform, including Windows, and with the broad support for XML documents on most platforms, many applications may choose to bypass traditional database APIs in favor of HTTP SOAP.

DBAs who have already made XML a key part of their environments will take very naturally to these new capabilities in SQL Server 2005. Even if an installation doesn't yet make use of XML for application data, DBAs (and developers) need to become XML experts in order to use many of the new features in SQL Server 2005.

To .NET or Not to .NET?   No feature of SQL Server 2005 is more powerful or more controversial to the DBA community than its support for the Microsoft .NET CLR. At its basic level, CLR support enables the writing of stored procedures in programming languages such as C# and VB.NET. The SQL Server and .NET teams have gone to great lengths to ensure that these stored procedures run with the same level of safety and integrity as those written in T-SQL. For truly data-intensive processing, T-SQL remains a better choice, but for code that does complex computation or need access to resources external to SQL Server 2005 itself, a CLR language is the appropriate choice.

CLR support is much more than just new languages for writing stored procedures. With SQL Server 2005's support for user defined types, user defined functions, user defined aggregates, indexes on computed columns, and so on, CLR support is a core means of extending the server's functionality to support applications not easily handled by purely relational systems. It could be used for something as simple as adding a new Date data type (to handle the Arabic calendar, for example) to integrating support for spatial data into SQL Server.

Another popular use of CLR support is as a replacement for extended stored procedures. Extended stored procedures have a reputation for negatively affecting the reliability of a server and for making it very difficult to diagnose seemingly unrelated server problems. Most extended stored procedures can be replaced by CLR stored procedures running with SAFE or EXTERNAL_ACCESS permissions, neither of which allow the integrity of the server to be compromised. The few that require UNSAFE permission have the potential to cause the same problems as extended stored procedures and require similar care to prevent problems. However, they are written for an environment that makes it easier to find, diagnose, and correct problems than exists for extended stored procedures.

So why all the controversy around CLR support? It all goes back to the fundamental nature of DBAs. Some DBAs are purely responsible for operational aspects of the server. Most are responsible for data modeling and the design and maintenance of the database schema. Many DBAs also write T-SQL stored procedures that are then called by applications. Often, these DBAs are responsible for reviewing T-SQL stored procedures written by developers before putting them into production. And, of course, DBAs are the ones who are called in the middle of the night to diagnose a problem when the database server breaks. But only a few DBAs are themselves developers, expert in programming languages such as C# and VB.NET. If their installation allows—or worse, requires—that database server logic be written using the CLR, these DBAs fear they will be forced to become developers or be unable to carry out their job responsibilities. And even those without this concern wonder if a C# stored procedure really can be as safe to run in the server as T-SQL.

SQL Server isn't, of course, the first database system to face the question of whether a traditional programming language can be used inside the database system itself. Multiple database products have supported and emphasized the use of Java to write stored procedures for a number of years. So the basic concept is proven.

SQL Server 2005 lets a DBA decide whether the CLR is to be supported at all in an installation, and it can't slip in behind the DBA's back. Most conservative organizations are likely to avoid the use of CLR in the database server for now. But given the growing popularity of the CLR in application development, DBAs will eventually find themselves pressured into supporting this environment. And given the choice of allowing an extended stored procedure or a CLR stored procedure into the database server, even the most skeptical DBA should opt for the CLR route.

Are You Being Served?   After XML and .NET CLR support, the most significant developer enhancement to SQL Server 2005 is the new Service Broker. Service Broker is a messaging system, similar to message-oriented middleware, that is fully integrated into the database engine. This gives SQL Server an integrated asynchronous distributed programming model that can work within a single instance or across instances on multiple computer systems. The queues for Service Broker are fully implemented in SQL Server, allowing them to participate in SQL Server transactions without the need for two-phase commit. This yields higher performance and greater scalability than transactional queuing implemented outside the database system. Also, because Service Broker is fully integrated, it is managed using SQL Server 2005 facilities (for example, part of SQL Server's security model, managed with SQL Server Management Studio, backed up as part of the database backup, and so on). Finally, because Service Broker is an integral part of the database engine, it is also used as a system communication facility for features such as event notifications and query notifications.

As a standalone feature, Service Broker will have a dramatic impact on how SQL Server applications are built in the future. Take a current system in which two applications must communicate information such as a shopping cart application shipping an order to an order processing application. Because the shopping cart application is generally running on one or more servers outside the normal production world, it wouldn't be possible for those servers to share databases. In traditional application development, the shopping cart application would read the order from its database and use RPC, a web service interface (for modern, synchronous applications), a batch file, or message-oriented middleware (for asynchronous applications) to ship the orders to the order processing application. The order processing application would accept the orders and place them in its database. With Service Broker, this process is greatly simplified. The shopping cart application would simply send to the order processing application a message that contains the order information as part of the SQL transaction finalizing the customer's order request. SQL Server Service Broker would take care of getting the message to the order processing database, where it would be picked up by the order processing application.

Of course, you can use Service Broker for even simple scenarios, such as communicating work requests between two modules of the same application. And it is a more robust and flexible solution than using two-phase commit for solving the problem of applications that need to update two or more databases (in separate instances) in the same transaction.

One of the most interesting scenarios is Service Broker's ability to enable very high, even continuous, availability. For example, an application might normally function with requests between systems being completed immediately. However, if a back-end server were to fail (or be taken offline for maintenance), the front end could continue to accept requests and queue them until the back-end server was restored. Further, Service Broker would transparently route requests to a mirror database should it take over as the principal database. This ability to hide transient failures, as well as longer-term planned and unplanned outages, makes Service Broker a key tool in creating systems whose availability exceeds that possible with a single computer.

Because Service Broker doesn't come into play unless developers build applications that use it, the initial impact on DBAs may be low. On the other hand, because Service Broker takes full advantage of the skills and expertise of the DBA community, DBAs may want to encourage developers to use Service Broker rather than alternatives such as message-oriented middleware. Either way, over time, DBAs should expect Service Broker to become a major means of interconnecting databases.

Where No One Has Gone Before

From the late 1960s though the mid-1980s, database systems were essentially pure data repositories residing on the same computer systems as the applications that used them. In the mid-1980s, client/server computing became popular, with applications residing on desktop computers talking to databases running on servers. For client/server computing to work properly, database systems had to evolve from being pure data repositories to having support for protecting the integrity of the data they held from being damaged by the client. This required database systems to create their own application model. Sybase SQL Server was the first to do so, offering features such as stored procedures and triggers. As this feature set evolved, it became known as TP-Lite because it subsumed many of the capabilities traditionally provided by transaction processing monitors such as CICS, ACMS, and Tuxedo. In the mid-1990s, the client/server model gave way to the n-tier model. In the n-tier model, the database system continues to live on its own server, the application itself resides on a separate tier of servers (often front-ended by a tier of web servers), and the client is yet another tier that interacts through the web tier. The n-tier model is particularly popular for high-performance transaction processing.

In the mid-2000s, the application model is once again evolving based on the notion of Web Services. You could take a very simple view of Web Services and say that it is simply replacing the HTML front end exposed by the web servers with an interface specification that uses XML instead. But it really goes deeper. Web Services encourages the development of applications that are partitioned into a set of services with published service interfaces. This encourages applications that are scalable (because each service can run on a separate system), distributable, reusable, and so on. So there is both a design philosophy difference in how to think about building an exposing application functionality and a change in the technology for exposing that functionality. This affects primarily the application server level, but imagine if you took it to the database level.

SQL Server 2005 encourages taking Web Services to the database server level and implementing databases as database services. The extensive support for XML, a key technology for constructing Web Services applications; the support for native HTTP SOAP access, another key technology for Web Services; and the availability of the CLR, which allows SQL Server 2005 to host complex application functionality make SQL Server 2005 an ideal platform for building Web Services applications. With the addition of Service Broker, with its ability to reliably tie together distributed database services, SQL Server 2005 represents a new-generation database application platform.

The benefits of building applications on database services fall into many areas. For a DBA, two of the major benefits are availability and scalability. As discussed earlier, by using Service Broker to tie together the various database services, it is possible to achieve very high availability across a broad range of unplanned and planned outages. By breaking an application into several Database Services, it is possible to achieve extremely high scalability. For example, an application might initially host database services for order entry, order verification, credit verification, distribution, shipping, and so on—on a single server. As the application outgrows the server, individual database services can be transparently moved to other servers. In the extreme, an installation could allocate a 64-way server to each database service, resulting in the ability to handle several million transactions per minute—more than required for any currently known application.

Is this the future of databases? With SQL Server 2005, that certainly is possible.

Summary

The feature-rich SQL Server 2005 release changes the database paradigm by introducing .NET CLR integration, deep XML support, asynchronous messaging, HTTP SOAP access, a new toolset, enhanced business intelligence capabilities, and more. At the same time, a lot of work has been done to enhance the availability, scalability, security, and reliability of the server. This paradigm shift opens up unlimited opportunities for application developers, enabling them to architect and build applications in a way never done before. On the other side, it brings challenges and a new learning curve for DBAs.

This chapter discusses how SQL Server 2005 continues on SQL Server's basic philosophy to be a database management system that can handle the most demanding enterprise applications, be developer friendly, reduce the total cost of ownership, be feature-rich and complete, and be able to run as a lightweight database engine and run on handheld devices.

This chapter also details the upgrades and new features introduced in SQL Server 2005, the challenges it brings, and how to deal with them. Chapter 2, "SQL Server 2005 Architecture and Components," looks at the SQL Server 2005 architecture in more detail.

SQL Server 2005 Database Engine Architectural Changes

S QL Server 2005 is loaded with features related to scalability, reliability, performance, high availability, programmability, security, and manageability. These features and enhancements are the primary drivers for the major overhauls in several areas of the database engine to accommodate a seamless integration throughout. Microsoft has made changes to SQL Server's memory management, thread scheduling, statistics management, parallelism, system metadata management, query optimization and execution, transactions, and other areas to better support new hardware architectures.

SQL Server has a single code base that can scale a small application that supports a few users to a large and complex enterprise application that supports multi-terabyte databases and thousands of concurrent users. While the foundation for the architecture that can achieve such linear scalability was laid in SQL Server 7.0 and further enhanced in SQL Server 2000, SQL Server 2005 offers significant changes and enhancements, taking SQL Server further into mission-critical enterprise database space.

This chapter provides an overview of the architectural changes made to the SQL Server 2005 database engine. If you are interested only in the functional operations of SQL Server 2005 and want to consider engine behavior as a black box operation, you can safely skip this chapter. If you want to first understand new features and enhancements introduced in this release, you can come back to this chapter after you have become more familiar with SQL Server 2005's functionality. This chapter covers the relational database engine architecture details only. Systems such as Analysis Services, Reporting Services, SQL Server Integration Services (formerly known as Data Transformation Services), and Notification Services have their own architectural enhancements, which are beyond the scope of this chapter.

The SQL Server Operating System (SQLOS)

An instance of a running application, known as a *process*, is merely a container for one or more threads that are scheduled to run on a processor for a time slice determined by the operating system. Threads allow applications to make more effective use of a CPU, even on a computer that has a single CPU. Windows is a preemptive, multitasking operating system. That means in order to run application code, the operating system grants a time slice to the thread. And when the time slice is over or when a high-priority thread needs to run, the operating system saves the contextual information for the current thread, preempts or stops the running thread, and loads the contextual information of the other thread so the other thread can run. This approach is designed to keep a single application from taking over the system and to provide even performance across the system.

User Mode Scheduler (UMS)

SQL Server efficiently leveraged the previously discussed Windows scheduling facility up through SQL Server 6.5. However, this general-purpose, one-size-fits-all scheduling approach limited the scalability heights that SQL Server was trying to achieve. The Windows preemptive scheduling approach results in context switches (stopping one thread and running another thread), which are expensive operations and involve switching from user mode to kernel mode. In a process such as SQL Server that makes use of a lot of threads, excessive context switching has a negative impact on the overall performance of and limits the scalability of SQL Server. This is why the SQL Server team decided that SQL Server should handle its own scheduling. SQL Server knows its own scheduling needs better than Windows does. Therefore, SQL Server can do a better job than Windows of implementing efficient thread scheduling and avoiding context switching.

SQL Server 7.0 first introduced the notion of User Mode Scheduler (UMS), which is a thin layer above the operating system, whose primary job is to optimize SQL Server thread management by minimizing the context switches and keeping as much of the SQL Server scheduling process as possible in user mode. UMS functionality is provided in a file named `ums.dll` under the `binn` folder. In addition to taking over scheduling from Windows, UMS also abstracts operating system–dependent features such as fibers and asynchronous I/O. But how does UMS take over scheduling from the preemptive operating system? UMS has Windows believe that all threads except the one that UMS wants to run are not viable. If a thread is in an infinite wait state, that means if a thread calls `WaitForSingleObject` and passes `INFINITE` for the timeout value, Windows considers the thread not viable for scheduling purposes and ignores it. The only way to awaken such a sleeping thread is to signal the thread's event object. To the operating system, only one SQL Server thread per processor generally appears to be active at a time. So, even though the server may have hundreds of worker threads at any given time, only one of them for each processor on the server appears to Windows to be actually doing anything.

The Windows scheduler is a preemptive scheduler. UMS, on the other hand, follows the cooperative model and is a non-preemptive scheduler. UMS relies on threads to yield voluntarily. UMS takes this approach to keep from involving the Windows kernel any more than absolutely necessary. UMS cooperative scheduling requires more careful coding on the part of SQL Server development team, but it can actually be more efficient than a preemptive model because the scheduling process can be tailored to the specific needs of the application. When a thread yields—either because it has finished the task at hand or because it has executed code with an explicit call to one of the UMS yield functions—it checks the list of threads that are ready to run and signals the first thread in the list that it can run. This way, everything happens in user mode, avoiding a switch to kernel mode.

When SQL Server starts, one UMS scheduler is created for each processor in the machine. Each scheduler maintains the following five lists:

- **Worker list**—This is a list of available threads or fibers. The number of available threads is based on the max worker threads sp_configure configuration value. If you set max worker threads to 255 on an eight-processor machine, each processor, and hence each UMS scheduler, can host a maximum of approximately 32 workers. A single UMS worker can service multiple user connections or SPIDs.

- **Runnable list**—This is a list of UMS workers that are ready to execute an existing work request. When any UMS worker yields, as part of yielding it checks the scheduler's runnable list for a ready worker and signals that worker's event so that it can run.

- **Resource waiter list**—When a UMS worker requests a resource that is owned by another worker, it puts itself on the waiter list for the resource and enters an infinite wait state. When the worker that owns the resource is ready to release it, it scans the waiter list for workers that are waiting on the resource and moves them to the runnable list. When the worker owning the resource yields, it signals the event object of the first worker on the runnable list.

- **I/O List**—This is a list of outstanding asynchronous I/O requests.

- **Timer List**—This is a list of UMS timer request that encapsulate a timed work request, such as waiting on a resource for a specific amount of time before timing out.

In SQL Server 7.0 and 2000, you used the DBCC SQLPERF(umsstats) undocumented statement to monitor the health of each visible scheduler on the system. In SQL Server 2005, you can access the sys.dm_os_schedulers dynamic management view (DMV) to list statistics for both visible and hidden schedulers on the system. DMVs are a new type of metadata views provided for monitoring and troubleshooting purposes. They essentially provide a real-time snapshot of internal memory structures, indicating the server state. DMVs are discussed in Chapter 9, "Performance Analysis and Tuning."

Introducing SQLOS

The UMS-based thread management architecture made SQL Server self-managing and easy to scale as new CPUs are added to the machine. During the SQL Server 7.0 rewrite, when UMS was introduced, the memory manager, storage engine, and relational engine were also upgraded to have built-in adaptive algorithms and self-tuning capabilities. When SQL Server 7.0 was shipped in 1998, it truly was the first enterprise database engine that was capable of automatic configuration and dynamic self-tuning—a concept that other database vendors initially downplayed as "not for the enterprise" but are now aggressively pursuing.

In SQL Server 2005, Microsoft has taken the self-managing and self-tuning paradigm to a much higher level. As a result, a component named SQLOS was born. SQLOS is a layer that sits on top of the underlying operating system and is responsible for managing operating system resources that are specific to SQL Server. SQLOS gives SQL Server the ability to serve its internal resource requirements much more efficiently and comprehensively. Each component within SQLOS is dedicated to performing specific functions as well as working with other components in a harmonious manner, providing large-scale performance with the ease of adapting to different hardware configurations, such as 32-bit, 64-bit, x64, dual core chips, and large memory addressability. In other words, no configuration changes are necessary within SQL Server in order for SQLOS to adapt to hardware resources while providing unprecedented scalability.

You will notice that SQL Server 2005 does not ship `ums.dll` anymore. UMS is now referred to as the "Non Preemptive Scheduler," and it is one of the components of SQLOS. Figure 2.1 shows various SQLOS components.

As Figure 2.1 shows, the two big components of SQLOS are non-preemptive scheduling (formerly known as UMS) and memory management. Other components include the resource monitor, exception handler, and hosting subsystems. SQLOS brings all these system components together and provides a cohesive API that the SQL Server development team can use to easily exploit hardware and operating system features.

Non-Preemptive Scheduling

The non-preemptive scheduling component of SQLOS is used for scheduling and synchronizing concurrent tasks without having to call the Windows kernel. It is responsible for scheduling Windows threads or fibers effectively. The scheduler is responsible for managing the scheduling process and for ensuring that only one thread processor is active at any given time. The `sys.dm_os_schedulers` DMV can be used to view a list of schedulers. A collection of schedulers that provides an abstraction layer over a group of CPUs is called a *scheduling node*. The term *task* refers to a unit of work that is scheduled by SQL Server. A Transact-SQL (T-SQL) statement batch can map to one or more tasks. For instance, a parallel query is executed by multiple tasks. The tasks are executed by worker threads. A worker thread represents a logical thread in SQL Server that is internally mapped (1:1) to either a Windows thread or, if lightweight pooling is on, to a fiber. The worker thread-to-Windows thread mapping is maintained until the worker thread is deallocated either because of memory pressure or because it has been idle for a long time. Worker threads are executed and managed by system threads.

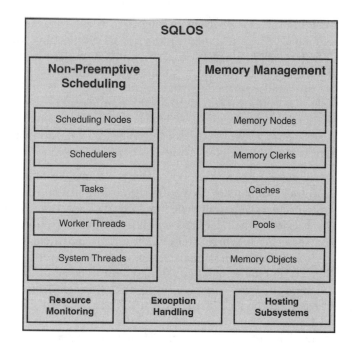

FIGURE 2.1   SQLOS is a user mode operating system layer that sits between the SQL Server engine and the operating system and provides services such as thread management, memory management, and hosting services.

The max worker threads Option   Each instance of SQL Server maintains a pool of either Windows threads or fibers for processing user queries. This thread pool helps optimize performance when large numbers of clients are connected to the server. The maximum size of this pool is controlled by the max worker threads server configuration option.

The minimum and default values for the max worker threads advanced option have changed in SQL Server 2005. In SQL Server 2000, the minimum value that can be set for the max worker threads option is 32; it is 128 in SQL Server 2005. In SQL Server 2000, the max worker threads option defaults to 255. In SQL Server 2005, this option is by default set to 0, which allows SQL Server to automatically configure the number of worker threads at startup. If the max worker threads option is left at the default of 0, SQL Server 2005 uses the formula shown in Table 2.1 to set the max worker threads configuration value.

TABLE 2.1   The max worker threads Formula

Number of Processors	max worker threads (32-Bit Platform)	max worker threads (64-Bit Platform)
≤4	256	512
>4	256+((CPUs−4)*8)	512+((CPUs−4)*16)

For instance, on an eight-processor 32-bit machine, max worker threads defaults to 256+((8–4)*8), which equals 288. On an eight-processor 64-bit machine, max worker threads defaults to 512+((8–4)*16), which equals 576. It is important to note that SQL Server does not actually create all the threads, but it reserves the memory required for creating the number of threads specified by the max worker threads option. When the actual number of user connections is smaller than the number set in max worker threads, one thread handles each connection. However, when the actual number of connections exceeds the number set in max worker threads, SQL Server pools the worker threads so that the next available worker thread can handle the request.

Routing Tasks to a Scheduler   SQL Server 2000 chose the scheduler in a round-robin fashion at connection time. All batches on a connection were run on the same scheduler, which could lead to imbalances, especially with long-lived connections. In SQL Server 2005, the decision to choose a scheduler is based on how busy the scheduler is. In other words, unlike in SQL Server 2000, where a task was routed to a particular scheduler, in SQL Server 2005, the routing decision is made based on the load on the scheduler. At connection time, SQL Server chooses a scheduler based on the load on the schedulers. Each subsequent batch on the same connection uses the same algorithm, and a new scheduler is chosen based on the load, with a bias toward the current scheduler for the connection. That is, if the load on the current scheduler (where the last batch for the connection was executed) is not appreciably higher than the average load, SQL Server does not look for a new scheduler; instead, it utilizes the warm cache and minimizes the CPU cycles used to find the least loaded scheduler. The columns such as load_factor and runnable_tasks_count in sys.dm_os_schedulers can be used to determine how busy a scheduler is.

Memory Management
On a 32-bit x86 platform, Windows gives all processes a 4GB virtual address space (VAS), which is divided into two partitions of 2GB each: the user mode partition and the kernel mode partition. If an application demands more than 2GB of user mode VAS, you can place a /3GB switch in the system's BOOT.INI file to limit the kernel VAS to 1GB and provide 3GB of user mode VAS to the application. Windows XP and Windows 2003 support an additional /USERVA switch in the BOOT.INI file that provides a finer degree of control by allowing you to specify exactly how much address space to set aside for user mode access. If even 3GB memory is not sufficient, you can use a Pentium Pro or later processor, place the /PAE switch in your BOOT.INI file, and leverage the Address Windowing Extensions (AWE) facility provided by Windows to access up to 64GB of physical memory. Note that by reducing the kernel portion of VAS to 1GB, you reduce the space available to support internal management structures. If there is more than 16GB of physical memory available on a computer, the operating system needs 2GB of process address space for system purposes and therefore can support only a 2GB user mode address space. In order for AWE to use the memory range above 16GB, you need to be sure that the /3GB parameter is not in the BOOT.INI file. If it is, the operating system cannot address any memory above 16GB.

SQL Server divides its VAS into two regions: the buffer pool and reserved address space. The buffer pool, also known as the BPool, is a primary memory allocation source for SQL Server, and it is used as a data and index page cache and for memory allocations smaller than 8KB. The BPool size is governed by the `min server memory` and `max server memory` configuration options. The BPool never drops its memory allocation below the level specified in `min server memory`, and it never acquires more memory than the level specified in `max server memory`. Objects that use the BPool include the buffer cache, the procedure cache, system-level structures, locks, log caches, and connection contexts.

The second region in SQL Server VAS is often called *MemToLeave*, which actually is an incorrect term; the correct term for this memory region is reserved address space. The reserved address space region is used for internal SQL Server allocations that exceed 8KB of contiguous space and for allocations made by external consumers, such as extended stored procedures, OLE DB providers, in-process COM objects, SQLCLR (.NET common language runtime integration with SQL Server) assemblies, and so on. The reserved address space is a contiguous allocation of memory of size 256MB+(`max worker threads`*512KB). For instance, if `max worker threads` is set to 256, the reserved address space size is 256MB+(256*512KB), which equals 384MB.

As shown in Figure 2.1, the SQL Server 2005 memory management architecture consists of several components, such as memory nodes, memory clerks, caches, pools, and memory objects. The memory node component is responsible for providing the locality of allocations. It consists of the single-page allocator, the multi-page allocator, the large page allocator, the reserved page allocator, the virtual allocator, and the shared memory allocator. Memory clerks, which are the key to granular memory management in SQL Server 2005, enable SQLOS to track and control the amount of memory consumed by a component. The `sys.dm_os_memory_clerks` DMV can be used to figure out memory distribution and to see a list of active memory clerks and the amounts of different kinds of memory allocated by each clerk. For example, the following query uses the `sys.dm_os_memory_clerks` DMV to list each type of memory clerk along with the sum of reserved virtual memory, committed virtual memory, and single and multi-pages allocated by each clerk:

```
SELECT [type],
    SUM(virtual_memory_reserved_kb) AS TotalVirMemReservedKB,
    SUM(virtual_memory_committed_kb) AS TotalVirMemCommittedKB,
    SUM(multi_pages_kb) AS TotalMultiPagesKB,
    SUM(single_pages_kb) AS TotalSinglePagesKB
  FROM sys.dm_os_memory_clerks
  GROUP BY [type]
  ORDER BY TotalVirMemCommittedKB DESC, TotalVirMemReservedKB DESC,
      TotalMultiPagesKB DESC, TotalSinglePagesKB DESC;
```

You can use the `sys.dm_os_virtual_address_dump` DMV to obtain detailed information about the VAS.

In addition to the architectural change just discussed, the following are some more changes that have been introduced to memory management in SQL Server 2005:

- **Dynamic AWE**—As described earlier, the AWE mechanism allows 32-bit systems to access memory over 4GB. Instances of SQL Server 2000 running in AWE memory mode allocated the full amount of memory specified in `max server memory` on server startup. This has changed in SQL Server 2005. During startup, SQL Server 2005 running under Windows Server 2003 now reserves only a small portion of AWE mapped memory. As additional AWE mapped memory is required, the operating system dynamically allocates it to SQL Server. Dynamic AWE enables the buffer pool to dynamically manage AWE mapped memory to balance SQL Server memory use with the overall system requirements.

  It is important to note that when AWE is enabled, SQL Server 2005 always attempts to use the AWE mechanism to allocate its memory. In other words, in AWE mode, most allocations are made through the AWE mechanism. Another important point to remember is that although SQL Server can dynamically release AWE mapped memory, the current amount of allocated AWE mapped memory cannot be swapped out to the page file. This means that, unless the objects are released and AWE mapped memory is freed, this memory cannot be swapped out to the page file and made available to the operating system or to other instances on the system. AWE mapped memory can never be swapped out to a page file. Therefore, you may consider setting `max server memory` for SQL Server to guarantee additional memory for other applications operating on the computer.

- **Hot add memory**—Dynamic AWE also allows SQL Server to increase memory if additional memory is added to a computer that supports hot add memory. Available in Windows Server 2003, Enterprise and Datacenter Editions, hot add memory allows memory to be added while the computer is running. Hot add memory is only available for 64-bit SQL Server and for 32-bit SQL Server when AWE is enabled. Hot add memory is not available for 32-bit SQL Server when AWE is not enabled. Hot add memory is only available for Windows Server 2003, Enterprise and Datacenter Editions. It also requires special hardware supported by the hardware vendor. To use hot add memory, when you start SQL Server 2005, you must use the `-h` option. Note that removing physical memory from the system still requires you to restart the server. Dynamic AWE is not supported on SQL Server 2005 Standard, Workgroup, and Express Editions.

- **The common caching framework**—SQL Server 2000 included two types of caches: the data page cache and the procedure cache. These two caches were tightly coupled, and each relied on the other cache's eviction mechanism to control its size. SQL Server 2005, on the other hand, supports a lot more types of caches in order to better support new features and new requirements. You can use the `type` column in the `sys.dm_os_memory_cache_*` DMVs (such as `sys.dm_os_memory_cache_entries`) to see some of the cache types. To better support these new caches, SQL Server 2005 introduces the notion of the common caching framework, which controls the behavior of multiple caches. This framework provides a uniform caching mechanism and common costing policies to cache different types of data.

- **The resource monitor**—In SQL Server 2005, the lazy writer is responsible for freeing data pages only. SQL Server 2005 introduces a new thread, called the resource monitor, that manages the caches and clerks. The resource monitor responds to memory pressure by broadcasting the notification to appropriate memory clerks. In addition, the resource monitor also ensures that a single cache does not monopolize the buffer pool and that the overall cache memory does not exceed 75% of the buffer pool.

Another important function that the resource monitor performs is to respond to VAS pressure. In SQL Server 2000, it was hard for the server to recover once it got into VAS pressure. Server restart was the only option in such a scenario. In SQL Server 2005, if a memory node fails to allocate a region of 4MB or less, or when the resource monitor's probe to VAS for a 4MB region fails, the resource monitor sends a notification that all the memory clerks that have the opportunity to do so should shrink. For instance, when such a broadcast notification is sent, a CPU node might try to shrink its threads, a CLR clerk might unload appdomains that are currently not in use, network libraries might shrink their network buffers, and so on.

Non-Uniform Memory Access (NUMA) Architecture Support

Today's critical enterprise applications demand a larger number of processors, with increased clock speed. In the past, hardware vendors provided the support for more and faster CPUs, but with a single system bus and the memory latency, the additional processing power was not fully utilized. Such an architecture, where all memory accesses are posted to the same shared memory bus, is known as *symmetric multiprocessing (SMP)*. To circumvent this, the concept of a large on-chip L3 cache was introduced, but it was also a limited solution. NUMA is designed to overcome the scalability limitations of SMP architecture.

NUMA hardware architecture includes more than one system bus, each serving a small set of processors. Each group of processors has its own memory and, possibly, its own I/O channels. Each group is called a *NUMA node*. For example, a 16-processor machine may have 4 NUMA nodes, each node having 4 CPUs, its own system bus, and, possibly, its own I/O channels. This allows for a greater memory locality for that group of schedulers when tasks are processed on the node. Note that each CPU can, however, access memory associated with other groups in a coherent way. *Non-uniform memory access* means that it takes longer to access some regions of memory (for example, remote memory on a different node) than others (for example, local memory on the same node). The main benefit of NUMA is scalability for high-end machines (generally eight or more processors). In summary, NUMA reduces memory contention by having several memory buses and only a small number of CPUs competing for a shared memory bus.

SQL Server 2005 is NUMA-aware. This means it can perform better on NUMA hardware without special configuration. When a thread running on a specific NUMA node has to allocate memory, SQL Server's memory manager tries to allocate memory from the memory associated with the NUMA node for locality of reference. Each NUMA node has an associated I/O completion port that is used to handle network I/O. SQLOS, SQL Server startup, network binding, and BPool management have been designed to make effective use of NUMA.

SQL Server Configuration Manager allows you to associate a TCP/IP address and port to a single or multiple NUMA nodes. You can configure NUMA affinity so that clients can connect to specific nodes. NUMA affinity is configured as a server setting in SQL Server Configuration Manager. To set a TCP/IP address and port to a single or multiple nodes, you append a node identification bitmap (an affinity mask) in square brackets after the port number. Nodes can be specified in either decimal or hexadecimal format. For instance, both 1453[0x3] and 1453[3] map port 1453 to NUMA nodes 0 and 1. The affinity mask value [3] translates to binary 00000011, and because the 0th and 1st bits are set, the client requests on port 1453 are served on 0th and 1st NUMA nodes. Let's look at another example. 1453[0x11] and 1453[17] both map the port 1453 to NUMA nodes 0 and 4 because the binary representation of hex 11 or decimal 17 is 00010001 and the 0th and 4th bits are set. The default node identification bitmap is -1, which means listen on all nodes. To configure a TCP/IP port to one or more NUMA nodes, you follow these steps:

1. Start SQL Server Configuration Manager.

2. Expand SQL Server 2005 Network Configuration.

3. Expand Protocols for <instance_name> and then click TCP/IP.

4. In the details pane, right-click the IP address to configure and then click Properties.

5. Specify the NUMA node identifier in brackets after the port numbers in the TCP Port box (for example, `1600[-1]`, `1460[0x11]`, `1400[4]`). This maps port 1600 to all NUMA nodes, port 1460 to NUMA nodes 0 and 4, and port 1400 to NUMA node 2.

Setting the NUMA affinity and having different clients served by different NUMA nodes is an easy-to-manage alternative to traditional multi-instance-based server consolidation and load balancing approaches.

Query Optimization and Execution

Query processing, which involves parsing, compiling, optimizing, and execution, is one of the most critical functions of a relational database engine. SQL Server 2005 continues to build on the award-winning cost-based optimizer of SQL Server 2000, and it introduces several new features to improve the overall query performance. The following sections discuss the new enhancements made to SQL Server's query optimization and execution.

Statistics Management in SQL Server 2005

SQL Server automatically creates and updates statistics. The query optimizer uses these statistics during query execution to determine things such as whether using an index would speed up a query and to develop an optimal query execution plan. The statistics include information such as cardinality (number of unique values), density (uniqueness of values within a dataset), selectivity (number of rows that will be returned by a particular query criterion), and so on, for one or more columns. In SQL Server 2000, the statistics were saved in the statblob column in the sysindexes system table. In SQL Server 2005, these statistics are now saved in an internal system table, sys.sysobjvalues. Therefore, the statblob column in the sys.sysindexes backward-compatibility view is now always returned as NULL.

NOTE

You cannot access system internal tables in multiuser mode. You have to start SQL Server in single-user mode, make the Resource database (discussed later) the current database, and then use the three-part naming convention (for example, AdventureWorks.sys.sysobjvalues) to view the system table contents.

Missing or out-of-date statistics can have a negative impact on the query optimizer's ability to choose the most efficient plan. Out-of-date or missing statistics are indicated as warnings (with the table name in red text) when the execution plan of a query is graphically displayed in SQL Server Management Studio.

SQL Server 2005 introduces several enhancements that improve the management of statistics and also help the query optimizer choose the most efficient query plan for a broader range of queries. Here are some of these enhancements:

- **Column-level change tracking**—In SQL Server 2000, statistics update was determined by the number of row changes. SQL Server 2005, on the other hand, tracks the data changes at the column level and avoids the automatic update of statistics on columns that have not changed enough to warrant a statistics update. This reduces the instances of automatic update statistics and hence may improve query performance.

- The **AUTO_UPDATE_STATISTICS_ASYNC database option**—In SQL Server 2000, if a query caused an automatic statistics update, the query was blocked until the statistics were refreshed. This sometimes caused query timeout errors and unpredictable query response times. For such scenarios, SQL Server 2005 provides a databasewide option called AUTO_UPDATE_STATISTICS_ASYNC that, when turned on, results in statistics being updated in the background, without blocking the query. The query that caused the statistics update proceeds with the old statistics, while SQL Server starts a new thread to update the statistics. This provides more predictable query response time for some workloads. The AUTO_UPDATE_STATISTICS_ASYNC database option is turned off by default. It is recommended that you perform enough analysis and testing before turning this option on to ensure that it does not adversely affect the query performance or any other part of the engine. You can use the is_auto_update_stats_async_on column in the sys.databases catalog view to determine whether the AUTO_UPDATE_STATISTICS_ASYNC database option is turned on or off.

- **Parallelism**—SQL Server 2005 supports creating full scan statistics in parallel for both partitioned and non-partitioned tables. This can potentially lead to much faster statistics creation times.

- **String statistics**—For character columns, SQL Server now gathers information about the frequency distribution of substrings. In other words, SQL Server 2005 gathers a new kind of statistics called "tries" that aid the optimizer in better estimating the selectivity of conditions that use the LIKE operator. In addition, SQL Server now allows columns of large object types such as text, ntext, image, nvarchar(max), varchar(max), and varbinary(max) to be specified as statistics columns.

- **Computed columns**—SQL Server 2000 only partially supported (and did not document) creating and updating statistics on computed columns. SQL Server 2005 now fully supports and documents computed column statistics.

- **A change in the sampling size formula**—As in earlier releases, to minimize the cost of automaticstatistical update, SQL Server samples the data instead of analyzing all the data. For tables that have more than 1,024 pages (that is, tables over 8MB), SQL Server 2005 now ensures that a minimum of 8MB of data is sampled during statistics gathering.

- **Statistics on up to 32 columns**—The limit on the number of columns in a statistics object has been increased to 32, from 16.

- **Enhanced DBCC SHOW_STATISTICS results**—The DBCC SHOW_STATISTICS statement provides the option to restrict the output to header, density vector, histogram, or a combination of these. If no options are specified, all three result sets are returned. In addition, the output has been enhanced to display the name of statistics object being displayed and whether it is a string index.

Statement-Level Recompilation

Before a query, batch, stored procedure, trigger, prepared statement, or dynamic SQL statement (henceforth, "batch") begins execution on a SQL Server database, the batch is compiled into a plan. The plan is then executed for its effects or to produce results. Such compiled plans are stored in a part of SQL Server's memory called the *plan cache*. If SQL Server is later able to reuse a compiled plan from the plan cache, it avoids the compilation costs, which improves the overall performance.

NOTE

The area of memory where compiled plans are cached is sometimes referred as the *procedure cache*. However, the term *plan cache* is more accurate because this cache stores plans of other queries in addition to those of stored procedures.

When a cacheable batch is submitted to SQL Server 2005 for execution, it is compiled, and a query plan for it is put in the plan cache. A *query plan* is a read-only reentrant structure that is shared by multiple users. There are at most two instances of a query plan at any time in the plan cache: One for all the serial executions and one for all the parallel executions. Each user concurrently executing a batch has an *execution context* that holds data (such as parameter values) specific to his or her execution. Although execution contexts are reused, they are not reentrant (that is, they are single threaded). That is, at any point of time, an execution context can be executing only one batch submitted by a session, and while the execution is happening, the context is not given to any other session or user. A query plan and multiple associated execution contexts can coexist in the plan cache. However, just an execution context (without an associated query plan) cannot exist in the plan cache. Whenever a query plan is removed from the plan cache, all the associated execution contexts are also removed along with it. Also, query plan reuse does not necessarily imply execution context reuse. Execution contexts for parallel plans are not cached. An *execution plan* is a combination of a query plan and an execution context. You can query the sys.dm_exec_cached_plans DMV or sys.syscacheobjects backward-compatibility view to obtain information about the query execution plans that are cached by SQL server.

Before executing a query plan, SQL Server checks the correctness and optimality of that query plan. If one of the checks fails, the statement corresponding to the query plan or the entire batch is compiled again, and possibly a different query plan is produced. This process is known as *recompilation*. Recompilations are often performed for good reasons. However, sometimes excessive recompilations can degrade performance. In such cases, it becomes necessary to analyze the reasons for recompilations and try to reduce the occurrences of recompilations.

When a batch was recompiled in SQL Server 2000, all the statements in the batch were recompiled—not just the one that triggered the recompilation. SQL Server 2005 improves on this behavior by compiling only the statement that caused the recompilation—not the entire batch. This *statement-level recompilation* feature improves SQL Server 2005's recompilation behavior when compared to that of SQL Server 2000. In particular, SQL Server 2005 spends less CPU time and memory during batch recompilations, and it obtains fewer compile locks. You can use a new Profiler trace event called SQL:StmtRecompile under the T-SQL event class to trace statement-level recompilations.

Calculating Query Plan Cost

In addition to stored procedures and triggers, SQL Server can cache the query plans for dynamic SQL, prepared queries, sp_executesql queries, ad hoc queries, auto-parameterized queries, and other batches. Every query plan and execution context has a cost associated with it. When the cost reaches 0, the plan or context becomes a candidate for deletion from the plan cache. In other words, the cost partially controls how long the plan or context lives in the plan cache. These costs are calculated and manipulated differently in SQL Server 2005 than they were in SQL Server 2000.

In SQL Server 2000, costs were calculated and manipulated as follows:

```
Query plan cost c = f(cpuTime, pagesRead, pagesWritten) / pagesUsedInMem
```

In SQL Server 2000, the query plan cost was a mathematical function that used four factors: CPU time spent generating the plan, number of pages read from disk, number of pages written to disk, and number of memory pages occupied by the query plan of the batch. In SQL Server 2000, the lazy writer thread occasionally swept through the plan cache and decremented costs by dividing them by 4. In case of memory pressure, query plans and execution contexts with costs of 0 were deleted from the plan cache. When a query plan or an execution context was reused, its cost was reset back to its compilation (or execution context generation) cost.

In SQL Server 2005, costs are calculated and manipulated as follows:

```
Query plan cost c = I/O cost + context switch cost + memory cost
```

In SQL Server 2005, the query plan cost is calculated in terms of the number of ticks, with a maximum of 31 ticks. It is a sum of the following:

- **I/O cost**—Two I/Os cost 1 tick, with a maximum of 19 ticks

- **Context switch cost**—Two context switches cost 1 tick, with a maximum of 8 ticks

- **Memory cost**—Sixteen memory pages (128KB) cost 1 tick, with a maximum of 4 ticks

In SQL Server 2005, the lazy writer does not decrement costs. Instead, as soon as the size of the plan cache reaches 50% of the BPool size, the next plan cache access decrements the ticks of all the plans by 1 each. If the sum of the sizes of all the caches in SQL Server 2005 reaches or exceeds 75% of the BPool size, a dedicated resource monitor thread gets activated, and it decrements the tick counts of all the objects in all the caches. As in SQL Server 2000, query plan reuse causes the query plan cost to be reset to its initial value.

Parallel Query Processing

Depending on factors such as available memory, type and estimated cost of query, number of schedulers on the server, load on the schedulers, and so on, SQL Server might decide to execute a query in parallel. You can use the `max degree of parallelism` `sp_configure` option to limit the number of processors to use in parallel plan execution. The default value of `0` uses all available processors. In addition to queries, SQL Server 2005 considers parallel execution plans for index DDL operations and static and keyset-driven cursor population. You can override the `max degree of parallelism` value in queries by specifying the `MAXDOP` query hint in the query statement.

The relational engine has been enhanced to perform more types of tasks in parallel. As mentioned earlier, SQL Server can now update statistics in parallel. Another example of improved support for parallelism is parallel index operations. In SQL Server 2005 Enterprise Edition, indexes can be created or rebuilt in parallel. DDL statements such as `CREATE/ALTER/DROP INDEX` and `ALTER TABLE` now accept a `MAXDOP` setting that you can provide to override the `max degree of parallelism` value.

SQL Server 2005 avoids the intra-query deadlock bug (see Microsoft Knowledge Base article 837983) present in SQL Server 2000. SQL Server 2000 Service Pack 3 first fixed this problem (see Microsoft Knowledge Base article 315662) by detecting a deadlock that involves the threads that are used by the same parallel query and returning error message 8650. SQL Server 2005 is designed so that intra-query deadlock will not happen.

Row Versioning

The SQL Server 2005 database engine implements a new functionality called *row versioning* that is designed to improve performance by avoiding reader-writer blocking. Whenever a transaction modifies a row, SQL Server uses the `tempdb` system database to maintain a copy of the original (that is, before image of the) row. If multiple transactions modify a row, multiple versions of the row are stored in a version chain. The versioning information is saved in 14 bytes of the row header. These 14 bytes include transaction sequence number (TXN) and are added to the header when the row is modified for the first time. Because a transaction can read the before versions of a row from the version store in `tempdb`, the reader does not block the writer.

The following are some of the new features in SQL Server 2005 that depend on row versioning functionality:

- **Snapshot isolation level**—This is a new transaction isolation level that provides functionality similar to that of the REPEATABLE READ isolation level, without the issue of readers blocking writers.

- **New implementation of the read-committed isolation level**—SQL Server 2005 provides a new database option called READ_COMMITED_SNAPSHOT that, when turned on, uses row versioning to provide the same functionality as the READ COMMITTED (the default) isolation level, without the issue of readers blocking writers.

- **Multiple active result sets (MARS)**—MARS is an ADO.NET 2.0 feature that is supported by SQL Server 2005 to allow the execution of multiple statements on a single connection. Row versioning is used to version the rows affected by data modification statements issued by a MARS session.

- **Online index operation**—This is a new high-availability feature introduced in SQL Server 2005 that allows you to create, rebuild, and drop indexes, while allowing concurrent access to the underlying table or clustered index data and any associated nonclustered indexes.

Row versioning is turned off by default. You can enable it by turning on the ALLOW_SNAPSHOT_ISOLATION database option and using the new snapshot isolation feature or by turning on the READ_COMMITED_SNAPSHOT database option and using the default READ COMMITTED isolation level. When row versioning is enabled, you must ensure that the `tempdb` database has adequate space to hold the version store.

You can monitor row versioning usage by using DMVs such as `sys.dm_tran_current_transaction`, `sys.dm_tran_top_version_generators`, sys.dm_tran_version_store, sys.dm_tran_active_snapshot_database_transactions, and sys.dm_tran_transactions_snapshot, as well as various Performance Monitor counters—such as Free Space in tempdb, Snapshot Transactions, and Version Store Size—under the SQLServer:Transactions object. The database engine periodically removes from the version store in tempdb rows that are no longer needed to support snapshot or read-committed transactions.

More details on row versioning and snapshot isolation can be found in Chapter 9.

System Metadata Access and the Security Architecture

System metadata refers to information such as the number and names of tables or views in a database, information about columns in a table, details on constraints and indexes defined for a table, users and login information, and so on. Many applications and scripts access this system metadata information for various purposes. SQL Server 2000 supported rich metadata exposure through SQL-92 INFORMATION_SCHEMA views, system tables at the server and database level, and system stored procedures. However, there were some limitations, such as the following:

- Although it was not recommended, SQL Server 2000 did allow direct updates to system objects.

- Even if a user did not have any permission on the object, the user could still see the object metadata by using one of the previously mentioned metadata access mechanisms.

- Developers and DBAs spent a lot of time understanding the strange bitmasks used in system tables.

- Last, but definitely not the least, upgrades and service packs involved dropping and re-creating system objects. This process was very time-consuming, and, more importantly, it made rolling back a service pack very difficult, if not impossible.

Metadata access and management has been completely redesigned and rethought in SQL Server 2005. The following section explains a new system database called the Resource database and the role it plays. Next, you will learn about how the new security architecture restricts access to system metadata. Finally, the following section discusses the concept of schemas, which is a major change in the SQL Server security architecture.

The Resource Database

The SQL Server 2005 database rengine makes use of a new system database called the Resource database (with database ID 32767). This is a hidden, read-only database that contains all the system objects that are included with SQL Server 2005. These system objects were present in the master database in previous releases. The Resource database consists of definitions of system stored procedures, views, functions, assemblies, and so on. The system objects are persisted in the resource database, but they logically appear in every database. These system objects are present in a schema named sys. (The concept of schemas is discussed later in this chapter.) The Resource database does not show up in graphical tools or when you access the sys.databases catalog view (discussed later in this chapter). The resource database files (that is, mssqlsystemresource.mdf and mssqlsystemresource.ldf) are present in the same folder where the master database files reside.

CAUTION

Do not move or rename the Resource database file, or SQL Server will not start. Also, do not put the Resource database in either compressed or encrypted NTFS file system folders. Doing so hinders performance and prevents upgrades.

Note that the Resource database does not contain any user data or user metadata. The system-level information for an instance of SQL Server is still saved in the master database. Therefore, it is not necessary to backup the Resource database (unless some changes are made to the Resource database to apply a Quick Fix Engineering (QFE) based on instructions from a Microsoft Customer Support Services specialist).

The Resource database makes upgrading to a new version of SQL Server an easier and faster procedure. In earlier versions, upgrading involved dropping and creating system objects. Because the Resource database file contains all system objects, an upgrade is accomplished by copying the single Resource database file to the local server. This copy method also means that all that is required to roll back a service pack is an overwrite operation of the current version of the Resource database with the identified older version.

You can access the ResourceVersion and ResourceLastUpdateDateTime server properties to determine the Resource database version and the date and time that the Resource database was last updated:

```
SELECT SERVERPROPERTY('ResourceVersion');
SELECT SERVERPROPERTY('ResourceLastUpdateDateTime');
```

The only way to access the Resource database is to start SQL Server in single-user admin mode (using the -m startup parameter) and then run the USE mssqlsystemresource SQL statement. After you have connected to a SQL Server 2005 instance in single-user admin mode and changed the database context to Resource database by running the USE mssqlsystemresource SQL statement, you can then directly query the system base tables, such as master.sys.sysdbreg, in the master database or the sys.sysidxstats system table in any user database. You need to ensure that the Resource database is the current database in the context, and then you can query system tables in any user database or in the master database. Note that these system tables are not the ones available in previous releases. The system tables from previous releases have been replaced with backward-compatibility views, as explained in the next section. These system base tables are used by the SQL Server 2005 database engine and by Microsoft personnel during the troubleshooting process.

NOTE

When DBCC CHECKDB is executed against the master database, a second CHECKDB is also run internally on the Resource database. This means that running DBCC CHECKDB on the master database can return extra results. The command returns extra result sets when no options are set or when either the PHYSICAL ONLY or ESTIMATE ONLY option is set.

Metadata Access and Visibility

The new system metadata architecture in SQL Server 2005 is designed to meet the following goals:

- Provide a simple, consistent, secure, and efficient way to access system metadata

- Disallow direct updates to system tables

- Provide maximum backward compatibility

- Restrict access to metadata and provide a permission-based solution to allow viewing the metadata

To meet these design goals, SQL Server 2005 introduces the changes described in the following sections.

Introducing Catalog Views

All the system tables available in previous releases are now shipped as backward-compatibility views, and their use is discouraged. SQL Server 2005 introduces the notion of catalog views, and using them is the preferred way to access system metadata. There are four different types of views in SQL Server 2005: catalog views, backward-compatibility views, DMVs, and information schema views. Using catalog views is the most efficient and recommended approach to access system metadata, and it is the only way to access metadata for new features such as Service Broker. System tables available in previous releases have been completely removed, and views having the same names as the system tables are provided for backward compatibility. The backward-compatibility views and information schema are not available for new features introduced in SQL Server 2005.

There are about 286 system metadata views, which include catalog views, DMVs, information schema views, and backward-compatibility views. You can run the following query to obtain a list of all the system metadata views available in SQL Server 2005:

```
SELECT * FROM sys.all_views
    WHERE is_ms_shipped = 1
    ORDER BY [name];
```

All the system metadata objects belong to the sys or INFORMATION_SCHEMA schemas. Catalog views use a naming convention wherein sys.% views describe a user's metadata, sys.system_% describes system objects, sys.all_% is the union of system objects and user objects, and sys.server_% views describe server-level metadata. Consider the following SQL statements:

```
USE [AdventureWorks];
SELECT * FROM sysobjects ORDER BY [name];
SELECT * FROM dbo.sysobjects ORDER BY [name];
SELECT * FROM sys.sysobjects ORDER BY [name];
SELECT * FROM sys.objects ORDER BY [name];
SELECT * FROM sys.all_objects ORDER BY [name];
SELECT * FROM sys.system_objects ORDER BY [name];
```

The first SELECT statement should look familiar. However, note that sysobjects is no longer a system table; rather, it is a backward-compatibility view. The next two statements continue to use the sysobjects backward-compatibility view but illustrate that you can use the dbo or sys schema while accessing the backward-compatibility views. The next SELECT statement uses the sys.objects catalog view, which returns a list of user-defined objects and base system tables present in the database. The sys.all_objects catalog view returns system objects in addition to user-defined objects. These system objects are persisted in the Resource database but are accessible in every database. Finally, the sys.system_objects catalog view returns only the system objects.

Catalog views are designed using the inheritance model, where the base or parent view (such as sys.objects) contains a subset of columns and a superset of rows, while the derived or child views (such as sys.tables and sys.views) return a superset of columns and a subset of rows. The inheritance hierarchy is illustrated in Figure 2.2.

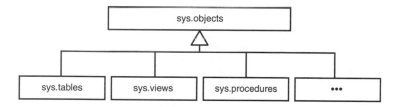

FIGURE 2.2   The catalog views design is based on the inheritance model.

Try out the following SQL statements and notice that sys.objects returns a subset of columns and a superset of rows, whereas sys.tables, sys.views, and sys.procedures return a superset of columns but a subset of rows:

```
USE AdventureWorks;
SELECT * FROM sys.objects;
SELECT * FROM sys.tables;
SELECT * FROM sys.procedures;
SELECT * FROM sys.views;
```

Catalog Security

SQL Server 2005 implements a metadata catalog security system that is similar in spirit to what the ANSI SQL-99 specification calls for. The basic idea is pretty simple: You can see metadata for objects you have access to; you get back an empty set for objects you don't have access to. A new security layer has been added over the persisted system metadata. All the metadata access mechanisms go through this security layer. Therefore, if a user does not have permission on an object, metadata information for that object is not returned when the catalog is accessed.

For instance, let's say a user X is created in the AdventureWorks sample database and no permissions are assigned to this user. If this user X tries to access the sys.objects catalog view, the sys.sysobjects backward compatibility view, or the INFORMATION_SCHEMA.TABLES view, an empty result set is returned. Let's now assume that user X is granted SELECT or VIEW DEFINITION permission on the Sales.Store table. Now, when the same metadata query is run by user X, the results containing metadata for Sales.Store are returned. In other words, metadata information is filtered and made visible only on a need-to-know basis; that is, catalog security returns rows for objects on which the user has some permission. This is a huge change from previous releases, where metadata information was available to all users, regardless of whether they had permission on the object.

Note that sa has access to all the systemwide metadata, and dbo has access to all the databasewide metadata. Also, some metadata is accessible by all database users. Typically, this is for things such as filegroups that have no grantable permissions. Therefore, anyone can query the sys.filegroups catalog view and obtain the database filegroups information. Figure 2.3 shows the new metadata architecture.

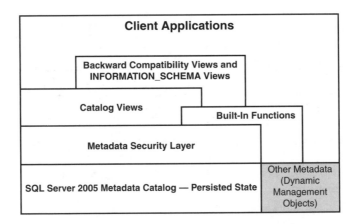

FIGURE 2.3 A new security layer on top of persisted metadata ensures that the metadata access mechanism, such as catalog views, backward-compatibility views, and so on, get the filtered rows based on permissions assigned to the user.

More details on metadata security can be found in Chapter 7, "SQL Server 2005 Security."

The allow updates **Option**

Because direct updates to system tables are not supported, the system configuration option allow updates is meaningless in SQL Server 2005.

User–Schema Separation

User–schema separation is another important change to the security and management architecture of SQL Server. As per the ANSI SQL-92 standard, the purpose of a schema is to act like a namespace to group related database entities and to avoid name collisions. For instance, if you want to group related objects, such as all the sales objects or all the human resources objects, or if you want to have two objects with the same name, the SQL-92 standard's answer is to use database schemas.

In earlier versions of SQL Server, a database user was used to form a namespace and to avoid name collision. The name of the owner of the object was used, along with the object name, to uniquely identify an object (for example userX.table1, userY.table1). This approach of treating users as schemas caused of lot of database management headaches. For instance, let's assume that you wanted to drop a user. Before you did that, either you had to drop all the objects that the user owned or assign the object ownership to a different user. Dropping objects was often not a practical solution, and changing the owner often required change in the application (for example, the application had to be updated to access userY.table1 instead of userX.table1). Applications often used the dbo user as the object owner, but that approach had its own problems (as discussed in Chapter 7).

SQL Server 2005 breaks the tight coupling between users and schemas, and it does not treat users as schemas. SQL Server 2005 introduces support for database schemas as per the SQL-92 standard. Therefore, object names in SQL Server 2005 no longer follow the <owner_name>.<object_name> pattern; rather, object names in SQL Server 2005 are <schema_name>.<object_name>, where <schema_name> is created by using the CREATE SCHEMA DDL statement, and schemas are owned by database users. Database users who have schema creation permissions can create schemas by using CREATE SCHEMA DDL statements. Database users who have object creation permissions can create objects in a schema. Now, if you have to drop a user, all that is required to be done is to just assign the schemas that the user owns to other users. No application change is required because the application will continue to access the objects as <schema_name>.<object_name>, no matter who the schema owner is. Also, instead of changing the object ownership of hundreds of database objects, as before, now you have to just change the ownership of very few database schemas. Figure 2.4 shows the old and new approaches to naming objects.

Every database user has a default schema that is used for name resolution. If you do not specify one, SQL Server 2005 assigns dbo as the default schema for the new user. When the object is not fully qualified, SQL Server looks for the object in the user's default schema. If SQL Server does not find the object, it looks for the object in the dbo schema.

User–schema separation is discussed in detail in Chapter 7.

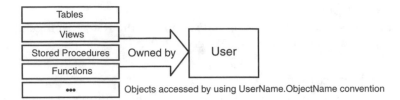

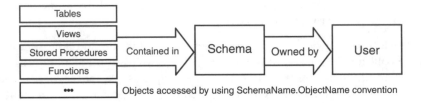

FIGURE 2.4   SQL Server 2005 introduces true support for database schemas, simplifying the security and management architecture.

Storage Engine and I/O Changes

The storage engine is an integral component of the SQL Server architecture, and it is responsible for managing database files, building and reading physical pages, controlling concurrency, handling logging and recovery, carrying out physical I/O, handling table and index traversal, and so on. SQL Server 2005 introduces several enhancements to the storage engine and physical I/O. Here is an overview of these enhancements:

- **Instant file initialization**—On Windows XP and Windows Server 2003, SQL Server 2005 can instantly initialize data files, without filling the reclaimed disk space with zeros. This can be a huge time saver when you're creating very large databases (for instance, while creating databases for a restore operation). This feature is discussed in detail in Chapter 8, "Reliability and High Availability in the Database Engine."

- **Data file autogrow**—In SQL Server 2000, the default FILEGROWTH setting for data files was 10%. SQL Server 2005 changes this to 1MB. The log file FILEGROWTH setting of 10% remains unchanged.

- **Efficient read-ahead**—The read-ahead algorithm has been updated to dynamically detect whether read-ahead is required, despite bad estimates from the optimizer.

- **Multi-path I/O (MPIO)** —SQL Server 2005 leverages the Windows Server 2003 MPIO capability, which allows multiple host bus adapters (HBAs) to be used for concurrent data access. MPIO enables applications to diversify requests to storage in order to circumvent a single point of failure. MPIO dynamically balances the I/O workload.

- **Allocation units (AUs)**—The SQL Server 2000 storage engine made use of index application map (IAM) pages to find out about the extents (that is, groups of eight pages) used by a heap (that is, a group of tables with no clustered index) or an index. A heap or an index had at least one IAM for each file on which it had allocated extents. The storage engine could read the IAM chain to build a sorted list of the disk addresses that needed to be read. There was a single IAM chain per heap/index in SQL Server 2000.

In SQL Server 2005, each heap or index can have multiple IAM chains. This change has been made to support large object (LOB) data types, such as varchar(max), and also to support row overflow data exceeding 8KB. SQL Server 2005 relaxes the restriction of a maximum of 8060 bytes per row for columns containing varchar, nvarchar, varbinary, sql_variant, or CLR user-defined type columns. Therefore, the following batch would fail in SQL Server 2000, but it succeeds in SQL Server 2005:

```
USE tempdb;
CREATE TABLE dbo.tblTest(
    c1 varchar(4000),
    c2 varchar(4000),
    c3 varchar(4000));
GO
INSERT INTO dbo.tblTest VALUES
    (REPLICATE('*', 4000), REPLICATE('*', 4000), REPLICATE('*', 4000));
GO
```

In other words, a SQL Server 2005 table row can contain more than 8,060 bytes. To support this and to support LOB types, SQL Server 2005 introduces two additional IAM chains. SQL Server also introduces a new term called *allocation unit* that refers to a set of pages owned by an IAM chain. These are the three types of allocation units:

- An allocation unit of type IN_ROW_DATA is used to manage data or index rows that contain all data except LOB data.

- An allocation unit of type LOB_DATA is used to manage LOB data of types text, ntext, image, xml, varchar(max), nvarchar(max), varbinary(max), or CLR user-defined data types.

- An allocation unit of type ROW_OVERFLOW_DATA is used to manage variable-length data stored in varchar, nvarchar, varbinary, or sql_variant columns that exceed the 8,060-byte row size limit.

You can use the sys.allocation_units and sys.system_internals_allocation_units catalog views to obtain information about each allocation unit in a database. Note that sys.system_internals_allocation_units is for internal use only and may change in the future.

- **Table and index partitioning**—You can significantly enhance the manageability and scalability of large tables and indexes by horizontally partitioning the data or index into multiple partitions. This feature supersedes the partitioned views functionality available in earlier releases.

  Partitioning enables index and table data to be spread across multiple filegroups in partitions. A *partition function* defines how the rows of a table or an index are mapped to a set of partitions based on the values of certain columns, referred to as *partitioning columns*. A *partition scheme* maps each partition specified by the partition function to a filegroup. This lets you develop archiving strategies that enable tables to be scaled across filegroups and, therefore, physical devices. In some situations, partitioning may also improve performance. Partitioned tables and indexes are supported in the Enterprise and Developer Editions of SQL Server 2005 only.

  SQL Server 2005 introduces new DDL statements, such as CREATE PARTITION FUNC-TION and CREATE PARTITION SCHEME, and enhances existing DDL statements for creating tables and indexes, to allow you to set up table/index partitioning. A complete description of partitioning is beyond the scope of this chapter. Refer to SQL Server 2005 Books Online and whitepapers on the Microsoft website for more details.

Summary

SQL Server 2005 is a significant step up from its predecessors when it comes to database engine architecture enhancements. This chapter covers SQL Server 2005's architectural enhancements and innovations. The chapter begins with an explanation of a core SQL Server engine component called SQLOS, followed by information on NUMA support in SQL Server 2005. The chapter then discusses query processing and optimization enhancements, followed by the new scalability and performance functionality called row versioning. Next, changes to the metadata and security architectures are discussed. The final section in this chapter presents an overview of storage engine enhancements.

It is important that you understand the feature and enhancements that necessitated the architectural changes discussed in this chapter. Chapter 3, "SQL Server 2005 Setup and Deployment," covers information related to installing and upgrading SQL Server. The rest of the book explores new features introduced in SQL Server 2005.

SQL Server 2005 Setup and Deployment

Setup and deployment are integral to a product, and they are two of the important factors that determine the user experience and customer satisfaction. Setup is the "first date" with the product; as you will see in this chapter, Microsoft has gone to great lengths to make SQL Server 2005 setup as "romantic" as possible. A successful installation and the ease of deployment add value to the product and increase the overall customer satisfaction.

Responding to the feedback received from customers and SQL Server product support services professionals, Microsoft has done a lot of work to make SQL Server 2005 setup more robust and user friendly, to reduce the instances of setup failures, to better handle error conditions, and to help users deploy multiple features or components from the SQL Server 2005 family.

In this chapter, you'll learn about the various editions of SQL Server 2005, hardware and software requirements for SQL Server 2005, new setup and deployment experience and features, deprecated and discontinued features, breaking and behavior changes to the database engine, and upgrading from previous releases. Let's begin by looking at various SQL Server 2005 editions.

SQL Server 2005 Editions

One of the tasks in planning a SQL Server deployment is choosing the right combination of SQL

Server editions, based on your application's scalability, availability, performance, and advanced analysis requirements. You can choose from the following SQL Server 2005 editions:

- **Enterprise Edition**—This edition includes the complete set of SQL Server data management and analysis features and is uniquely characterized by several features that make it the most scalable and available edition of SQL Server 2005. This edition has no limit on the number of processors or amount of memory or database size. It includes all the performance, scalability, high-availability, security, manageability, programmability, integration and interoperability, and business intelligence features, making it a comprehensive data and analysis platform for large, mission-critical business applications.

- **Standard Edition**—This edition is a complete data and analysis platform, and it is designed for medium-sized businesses. It places no limit on the amount of memory or the database size, but the number of processors is limited to four. Standard Edition includes high-availability features such as database mirroring and failover clustering, but it does not support online indexing or online page or file restores. Some of the business intelligence features, such as proactive caching and text mining, are turned off in Standard Edition. Standard Edition does not support partitioning or parallel index operations.

- **Workgroup Edition**—In February 2005, Microsoft announced a new addition to both the SQL Server 2000 and SQL Server 2005 families, called Workgroup Edition. Workgroup Edition is an affordable, easy-to-use, and simple-to-manage database solution designed specifically for small to medium-sized organizations. SQL Server 2005 Workgroup Edition places no limit on the size of the database. However, it is limited to two processors and 3GB of RAM. (SQL Server 2000 Workgroup Edition limits the amount of RAM to 2GB.) Workgroup Edition does not support high-availability features such as database mirroring, clustering, and online indexing, and it lacks most of the other editions' business intelligence features.

- **Express Edition**—SQL Server 2005 Express Edition supersedes Microsoft SQL Server 2000 Desktop Engine (MSDE). Like MSDE 2000, SQL Server 2005 Express Edition is a no-cost, freely redistributable version. Unlike MSDE 2000, which does not provide any graphical tools, SQL Server 2005 Express Edition provides graphical tools such as Express Manager and SQL Server Configuration Manager. Unlike MSDE 2000, SQL Server 2005 Express Edition does not implement a "concurrent workload throttle" mechanism to limit the application's scalability under heavy load. Express Edition limits the database size to 4GB, a single processor, and up to 1GB of server memory. Express Edition does not support many features, such as database mirroring, failover, partitioning, and online index operations, and it does not bundle tools such as SQL Server Management Studio and Profiler.

- **Mobile Edition**—Microsoft SQL Server 2000 Windows CE 2.0, also known as SQL Server CE, is being superseded by SQL Server 2005 Mobile Edition. This edition can run on table PCs and smart devices, including any device that runs Microsoft

Windows CE 5.0, Microsoft Mobile Pocket PC 2003, Microsoft Mobile Version 5.0 Pocket PC, or Microsoft Mobile Version 5.0 Smart Phone. SQL Server 2005 Mobile Edition includes a set of relational database features while maintaining a compact footprint. This edition contains several significant advancements over SQL Server CE.

- **Evaluation Edition**—This time-limited trial version, which contains the same features as Enterprise Edition, is available only for testing and evaluation purposes and should not be deployed in production.

- **Developer Edition**—This edition contains the same features as Enterprise Edition, but it is intended only for development purposes and should not be deployed in production.

As you can see, SQL Server 2005 provides the flexibility to acquire the right combination of SQL Server technologies to meet your needs. Once you know which SQL Server editions you need, the next step is to figure out the hardware and software requirements for installing each edition.

Hardware and Software Requirements for Installing SQL Server 2005

SQL Server 2005 can run on 32-bit platforms as well as on 64-bit platforms based on Itanium or x64 64-bit architectures. The hardware and software requirements on the 32-bit platform are different than the requirements for the 64-bit platform. Different editions of SQL Server 2005 have different hardware and software requirements. In addition, different SQL Server 2005 components, such as Reporting Services, have additional requirements. SQL Server 2005 setup includes a startup process called System Configuration Checker (SCC) that checks whether the system meets the minimum hardware and software requirements, in addition to performing other configuration checks. (Note that SCC warns the user but does not block the setup if the processor speed or the available system memory does not meet the requirement. SCC is discussed later in this chapter.)

The following sections list the hardware and software requirements of SQL Server 2005 Enterprise Edition on 32-bit and 64-bit platforms. You can find complete details on SQL Server 2005 requirements at www.microsoft.com/sql and in Books Online.

SQL Server 2005 Enterprise Edition 32-Bit Requirements

SQL Server 2005 Enterprise Edition 32-bit has the following hardware requirements:

- Pentium III–compatible processor or higher

- 500MHz or faster processor

- 512MB of RAM

- 42MB of hard disk space, up to approximately 735MB of hard disk space

SQL Server 2005 Enterprise Edition 32-bit has the following operating system requirements:

- Windows 2000 Advanced or Datacenter Edition with Service Pack 4 or higher

- Windows 2003 Enterprise or Datacenter Edition or Windows Small Business Server 2003 Service Pack 1 Standard or Premium Edition

- x64 systems running Windows 2003 Service Pack 64-bit X64 Standard, Enterprise, or Datacenter Edition

- SQL Server 2005 32-bit will run in Windows on Windows (WOW64) mode on x64 platform

SQL Server setup, which is run by Microsoft Windows Installer 3.0, has the following software requirements:

- SQL Server setup installs Microsoft Windows .NET Framework 2.0 and Microsoft SQL Server Native Client, which are required by the product.

- Microsoft Internet Explorer 6.0 Service Pack 1 or later is required for all installations of SQL Server 2005. However, if you are installing client components only and you will not connect to a server that requires encryption, Internet Explorer 4.01 with Service Pack 2 is sufficient.

NOTE

SQL Server Express Edition does not install .NET Framework 2.0. Before installing Express Edition, you must download and install.NET Framework 2.0 from the Microsoft website.

- SQL Server 2005 Reporting Services requires Internet Information Services (IIS) 5.0 or higher. The IIS web server must be in the running state if you want SQL Server 2005 setup to configure the Report Server.

- For systems running Windows 2000, Reporting Services has a dependency on MDAC 2.8. SQLXML depends on MDAC 2.6 for systems running Windows 2000.

- Notification Services has a dependency on SQLXML, so MDAC 2.6 or higher is required to run Notification Services on Windows 2000.

SQL Server 2005 Enterprise Edition 64-Bit Requirements

SQL Server 2005 Enterprise Edition 64-bit has the following hardware requirements:

- Itanium processor (IA64) or higher or x64 processors such as AMD Opteron, AMD Athlon 64, Intel Xenon with Intel EM64T support, or Intel Pentium IV with EM64T support

- 733MHz or faster Itanium processor or1GHz or faster x64 processor

- 512MB of RAM

SQL Server 2005 Enterprise Edition 64-bit has the following operating system requirements:

- On the IA64 platform, Windows 2003 Service Pack 1 64-bit Itanium Enterprise or Datacenter Edition

- On the x64 platform, Windows 2003 Service Pack 1 64-bit x64 Standard, Enterprise, or Datacenter Edition

SQL Server 2005 Setup Enhancements

Let's now explore some of the enhancements introduced in SQL Server 2005 setup. SQL Server 2005 setup has been redesigned and re-architected from scratch to provide a flexible, unified, easy-to-use, robust, and secure setup experience. The following are some of the new setup features:

- **Windows Installer–based setup**—Instead of using proprietary InstallShield-based setup, SQL Server 2005 now uses the latest Windows Installer (MSI) technology, which provides the most reliable, secure, customizable, and self-healing installation experience.

- **Enhanced user experience**—Microsoft has invested a lot of time and resources in simplifying the installation process and at the same time giving complete control over the installation to the users. Microsoft has done a lot of work to improve the setup usability and user experience. It has redesigned all the setup dialogs, and beta customers and usability engineers have evaluated them several times. Also, Microsoft has improved the setup documentation to serve as a better setup reference and a troubleshooting guide.

- **System Configuration Checker (SCC)**—The SCC routines scan the destination computer for conditions that may block setup. In other words, SCC checks for conditions that would prevent a successful SQL Server installation. Before setup starts the SQL Server 2005 Installation Wizard, the SCC retrieves the status of each check item, compares the result with required conditions, and provides guidance for removal of any blocking issues. SCC checks can run on a local computer, as well as in remote and cluster situations. For clusters, SCC runs on all nodes of the virtual server. As shown in Figure 3.1, SCC checks include operating system minimum level requirements, minimum hardware requirements, any pending reboot requirement, any system administrator privilege requirement, any WMI service requirement, any MSXML requirement, and so on.

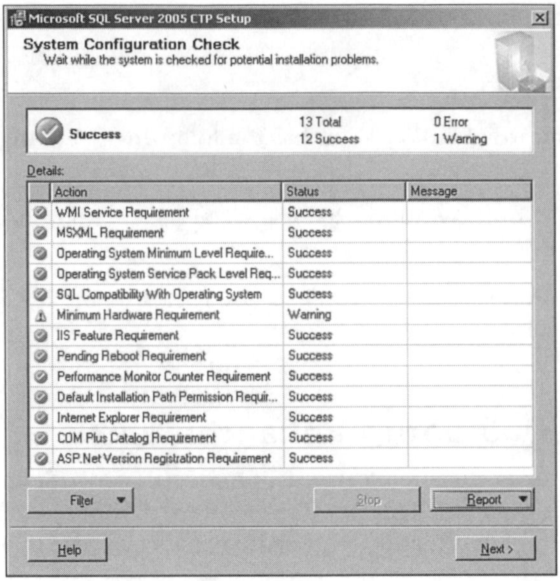

FIGURE 3.1   SCC verifies whether the system meets the minimum requirements and also performs other checks to increase the chances of a successful setup.

- **Integrated setup experience**—SQL Server 2005 setup provides a single feature tree for installation of one or more SQL Server 2005 components, including the database engine, Analysis Services, Reporting Services, Notification Services, Integration Services, replication, management tools, documentation, and samples. Figure 3.2 shows the feature selection tree that provides a unified way to selectively install various SQL Server 2005 components. For each selected component, you can specify a disk folder that the component should be installed in to.

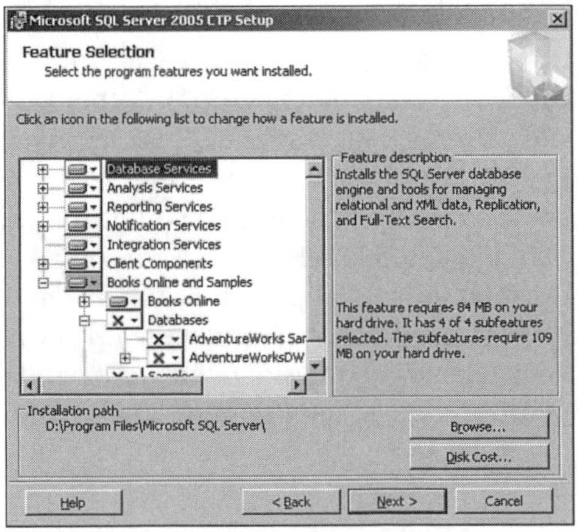

FIGURE 3.2   SQL Server 2005 setup provides a single feature tree to install one or more SQL Server components.

- **Improved logging and error handling**—As discussed previously, SCC minimizes the setup failure instances. However, if a setup still fails, then the improved detailed logging and error-handling mechanism introduced with SQL Server 2005 setup helps you quickly troubleshoot and resolve the setup issue. A setup summary file is generated at `%ProgramFiles%\Microsoft SQL Server\90\Setup Bootstrap\LOG\Summary.txt`, and detailed log files are generated in the `%ProgramFiles%\Microsoft SQL Server\90\Setup Bootstrap\LOG\Files` folder.

TIP

Microsoft provides a tool called `Wilogutl.exe` that you can use to analyze the log files generated by a Windows Installer–based installation, such as SQL Server 2005 setup. You can find more information about this tool at http://msdn.microsoft.com/library/en-us/msi/setup/wilogutl_exe.asp.

Figure 3.3 shows the Setup Progress dialog. When the setup for a component is finished, the text under the Status column becomes a link that can be clicked to open the setup log file for that component.

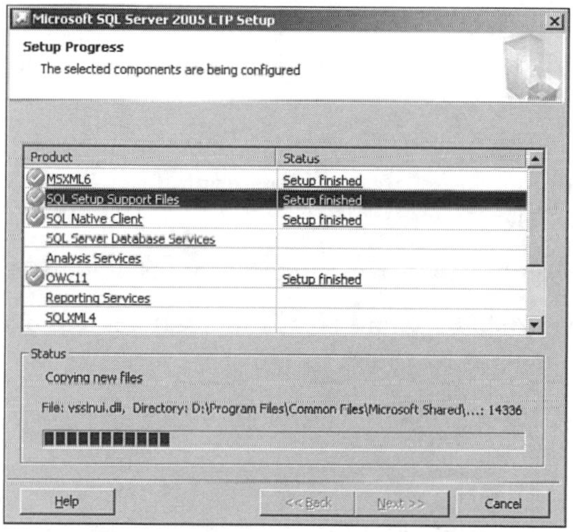

FIGURE 3.3   The Setup Progress dialog box lists each component as it is being installed and configured.

- **Cluster setup enhancements**—SQL Server 2005 setup has been enhanced to better support the installation and configuration of failover clustering. The setup establishes real-time communication between the host computer and secondary nodes during the installation. This facilitates integrated logging, progress reporting, and achieving consistent installation states across all cluster nodes to make the installation more reliable and robust. In addition, unlike in previous releases, SQL Server 2005 setup now provides an ability to selectively install components such as

Full-Text Search and Analysis Services. SQL Server 2005 clustered installations can be scripted for unattended installation.

SQL Server 2005 includes configuration tools such as Surface Area Configuration, Reporting Services Configuration, SQL Server Error and Usage Reporting, and SQL Server Configuration Manager that let you alter some of the settings originally configured using SQL Server setup.

Upgrading to SQL Server 2005

SQL Server 2005 allows you to upgrade from SQL Server 7.0 Service Pack 4 and SQL Server 2000 Service Pack 3 and above. Direct upgrade from SQL Server 6.5 is not supported; you need to first upgrade from SQL Server 6.5 to SQL Server 7.0 Service Pack 4 and then use the SQL Server 2005 setup to upgrade to SQL Server 2005.

Upgrading requires careful planning and execution. You have to consider upgrading your data, Data Transformation Services (DTS) packages, agent jobs, logins, replication setup, failover clustering setup, Analysis Services objects, Full-Text Search objects, Reporting Services configuration, Notification Services configuration, and so on. To help you with the upgrade process, SQL Server 2005 provides a tool called Upgrade Advisor that analyzes the system and installed SQL Server 2000 or SQL Server 7.0 components and then generates a report that identifies issues you must or should address before or after upgrading to SQL Server 2005.

SQL Server 2005 setup has been enhanced to simplify the upgrade process and to reduce the server downtime during the upgrade. Before upgrading the database engine, you need to make sure to do the following:

* Review hardware and software requirements for installing SQL Server 2005.

* Review SQL Server 2005 backward compatibility notes and make appropriate changes to your application and scripts.

* Run the Upgrade Advisor tool to prepare for upgrades and resolve any upgrade blocking issues.

* Back up all SQL Server database files from the instance to be upgraded, so you can completely restore them, if necessary.

* Run the appropriate DBCC commands on databases to be upgraded to ensure that they are in a consistent state.

* Ensure that existing SQL Server system databases—master, model, msdb, and tempdb—are configured with the autogrow setting and ensure that they have adequate hard disk space.

* Disable all startup stored procedures because the upgrade process will stop and start services on the SQL Server instance being upgraded. Stored procedures processed at startup time may block the upgrade process.

* Stop replication and make sure that the replication log is empty.

After you have gone through this pre-upgrade checklist, you can run the setup and install an instance of SQL Server 2005. When SQL Server 2005 is installed, you can move user databases to a SQL Server 2005 instance by using the backup and restore or the detach and attach functionalities in SQL Server 2005. You can then register your server, repopulate any full-text catalogs, update the statistics, and run the Surface Area Configuration tool to reduce the attackable surface.

Before we look at Upgrade Advisor, let's review some changes in SQL Server 2005 that you should be aware of to better prepare for the upgrade process.

Deprecated and Discontinued Database Engine Functionality

Deprecated features in SQL Server 2005 include features that will be removed in the future product releases. Some of the deprecated features will be removed in the next product release, while others will be removed in the releases following that one. The following are some of the deprecated features, which you should try to replace with the recommended items:

NOTE

You can use the SQL Profiler event class Deprecation to trace the usage of these deprecated features.

- The DUMP and LOAD statements are being deprecated, and the recommended approach is to instead use the BACKUP and RESTORE statements, respectively.

- The SETUSER statement is being deprecated, and the recommended approach is to instead use the EXECUTE AS statement.

- sp_addtype is being deprecated; instead, you should use CREATE TYPE. You should also avoid using the sp_attach_db and sp_attach_single_file_db stored procedures; instead, you should use the CREATE DATABASE statement with the FOR ATTACH or FOR ATTACH_REBUILD_LOG option.

- You should avoid using sp_renamedb, sp_dboption, and sp_resetstatus stored procedures; instead, you should use the ALTER DATABASE statement.

- You should avoid full-text search stored procedures, such as sp_fulltext_catalog; instead, you should use the CREATE/ALTER/DROP FULLTEXT CATALOG and CREATE/ALTER/DROP FULLTEXT INDEX statements.

- You should avoid using security stored procedures such as sp_addlogin, sp_adduser, and so on; instead, you should use statements such as CREATE LOGIN, CREATE USER, CREATE ROLE, and so on.

- System tables are being replaced with backward compatibility views. The recommended approach is to use the new system catalog views. Direct updates to system tables are no longer allowed.

SQL Server 2005 does not support some of the features present in the earlier releases:

- SQL Server 2005 no longer includes English Query.

- Tools such as `isql.exe` and `rebuildm.exe` are also not included; you should instead use `sqlcmd.exe` and `setup.exe`. If you need to rebuild the `master` database or rebuild the registry, you should run SQL Server 2005's `setup.exe` from the command prompt and provide the appropriate parameters.

- The `Northwind` and `Pubs` sample databases are being replaced with a new sample database, `AdventureWorks`.

- The `allow updates` option of `sp_configure` is present but because direct updates to system tables are not supported, this option is meaningless.

- Meta Data Services 3.0 is a component of Microsoft SQL Server 2000 that is no longer available in SQL Server 2005. Upgrading does not delete the existing repository tables in the `msdb` database. However, the repository engine that reads and updates the tables will not be available after you upgrade, and the repository tables will no longer be accessible. To remove the unused tables, you can manually delete them. Repository tables have the `Rtbl` prefix.

Breaking and Behavior Changes to the Database Engine

Wherever possible, SQL Server 2005 provides backward compatibility so that applications can be easily migrated to SQL Server 2005. However, in order to better support some new features and to better position the product, Microsoft has introduced some breaking and behavioral changes in SQL Server 2005 that might require changes to your applications:

- SQL Server 2005 adds `trigger_schema` as the last column in the result set returned by the `sp_helptrigger` system stored procedure.

- In SQL Server 2000, the `WITH` keyword to specify table hints is optional. However, in SQL Server 2005, `WITH` is mandatory for table hints, except for single-word hints. For instance, the query `SELECT * FROM master.dbo.sysobjects (TABLOCK, HOLDLOCK)` works in SQL Server 2000 but not in SQL Server 2005. To make this query work in SQL Server 2005, you need to either specify the `WITH` clause or just keep a single table hint.

- In SQL Server 2000, column names in the `ORDER BY` clause are resolved to columns listed in the `SELECT` list, regardless of whether they are qualified. However, in SQL Server 2005, qualified column names and aliases in the `ORDER BY` clause are resolved to columns of tables listed in the `FROM` clause. Consider the following Transact-SQL script:

```
USE [Tempdb];
GO

IF OBJECT_ID('dbo.dblTest') IS NOT NULL
    DROP TABLE dbo.dblTest;
GO
```

```
CREATE TABLE dbo.dblTest (col1 int, col2 varchar(20));
GO

INSERT INTO dbo.dblTest SELECT 1, 'X';
INSERT INTO dbo.dblTest SELECT 2, 'U';
INSERT INTO dbo.dblTest SELECT 3, 'A';
GO

SELECT col1 AS 'col2'
FROM dbo.dblTest a
ORDER BY a.col2;
GO
```

If you run this script in SQL Server 2000 and SQL Server 2005, you will get different output with SQL Server 2000 than with SQL Server 2005. SQL Server 2000 ignores the table alias and maps the a.col2 specified in the ORDER BY clause to the column alias in the SELECT list and hence returns 1, 2, and 3. On the other hand, SQL Server 2005 honors the table alias and sorts the results on col2 in the dbo.tblTest table and hence returns 3, 2, and 1.

SQL Server 2005 Upgrade Advisor

As mentioned earlier, you can use the Upgrade Advisor tool to analyze the system and installed SQL Server 2000 or SQL Server 7.0 components and identify issues that you must or should address before or after upgrading to SQL Server 2005. The Upgrade Advisor tool consists of two components:

- **Analysis Wizard**—Analysis Wizard analyzes a system and saves the results into an XML file. Analysis Wizard does not modify your data or change settings on your computer.

- **Report Viewer**—Report Viewer reads the results XML file generated by Analysis Wizard and displays the results of the analysis. It also allows you to sort and filter the results. Each upgrade issue listed on the Report Viewer screen contains a Tell Me More About This Issue and How to Resolve It link that you can click to obtain more information about the upgrade issue and the steps you need to take to resolve it.

The Upgrade Advisor documentation consists of a section on resolving upgrade issues, with categories such as Analysis Services Upgrade Issues, DTS Upgrade Issues, and Database Engine Upgrade Issues.

Note that the Upgrade Advisor tool is not installed as part of SQL Server 2005 setup. You have to separately install it from the setup splash screen (splash.hta) by clicking the Install SQL Server Upgrade Advisor link. Figure 3.4 shows the Microsoft SQL Server Upgrade Advisor tool in the background, with Analysis Wizard in the foreground.

FIGURE 3.4   The Upgrade Advisor tool is designed to analyze the existing SQL Server environment and identify and resolve any issues that might block the upgrade process.

Summary

SQL Server 2005 setup is designed to minimize installation failures and improve the overall setup experience. This chapter introduces the concepts related to SQL Server 2005 setup and deployment.

The chapter begins with an overview of SQL Server 2005 editions, giving you the information you need to choose the appropriate edition to suit your needs. The chapter also discusses the hardware and software requirements for SQL Server 2005. The subsequent section lists the improvements made to the setup process itself.

The second part of this chapter discusses the upgrade process. It outlines the issues you should be aware of and describes the Upgrade Advisor tool, to better prepare for upgrading to SQL Server 2005.

Chapter 4, "A Tour of New Features in SQL Server 2005," provides an introduction to the new features introduced in this biggest SQL Server release ever.

A Tour of New Features in SQL Server 2005

CHAPTER **4**

For over 11 years, Microsoft SQL Server has been delivering an enterprise-ready, scalable, reliable, and cost-effective data management platform. SQL Server 2005 takes this premise to the next level by introducing several innovative features related to enterprise data management, developer productivity, and business intelligence. This chapter provides an overview of all these new features, which are then discussed in great detail throughout rest of the book.

Setup Enhancements

As discussed in Chapter 3, "SQL Server 2005 Setup and Deployment," SQL Server 2005 setup is based on Windows Installer 3.0 (MSI) technology. Here are some of the benefits offered by the MSI-based setups:

- **Rollback support**—Windows Installer setups are transaction based; a rollback occurs if an installation fails for any reason.

- **Logging and troubleshooting**—Windows Installer technology gives unprecedented control over the level of detail for logging and the name and location for the log file. A verbose setup log can be generated to troubleshoot setup issues.

- **Self-healing**—This MSI feature ensures that all the files installed by the setup are available for the application to run. If any of the installed files are removed by accident, Windows Installer reinstalls the files.

- **Reliable installation and uninstallation**—Windows Installer provides consistent and reliable version rules, which prevent newer files from being overwritten by old files. MSI features systemwide management of shared resources (files and registry keys) that Windows Installer–based applications use. This ensures that when you uninstall a product, Windows Installer does not remove any component that has other applications in its client list.

- **Ease of customizing and command-line control**—An administrator can create MSI Transforms (MSTs) to customize the Windows Installer setup. Also, a large number of command-line switches are available with the MSI setup execution engine (`msiexec.exe`), and they can be used to customize the setup behavior.

By using Windows Installer technology for the setup, SQL Server 2005 leverages all these features.

SQL Server 2005 setup reduces the likelihood of setup failures by introducing a startup process known as Setup Configuration Checker (SCC). This process ensures that all the prerequisites for the installation are met before the actual process of installation kicks off.

The SQL Server 2000 CD includes separate setups for the relational engine and Analysis Services. In addition, the Notification Services and Reporting Services add-ons for SQL Server 2000 have their own setup interface. SQL Server 2005 changes that by introducing a unified, integrated setup environment that presents all the components in a single feature tree. SQL Server 2005 setup offers granular control over individual components that you can install or uninstall.

SQL Server 2005 setup is enhanced to support up to 50 instances each of SQL Server, Analysis Services, Notification Services, and Reporting Services.

In case of a setup error, the Internet Help feature introduced in SQL Server 2005 allows you to click the Help button on the setup error dialog and browse to the documentation page on the Microsoft website for more details on the error and to get some troubleshooting guidelines.

One of the common causes of setup failure and reboots with SQL Server 2000 has to do with MDAC version incompatibilities. SQL Server 2005 avoids these problems by not installing MDAC on the server. The new data access application programming interface (API), known as SQL Native Client (SNAC) is the key to breaking the dependency on a particular version of MDAC. This is discussed in more detail in Chapter 3.

SQL Server 2005 setup supports scripted cluster installation. It also allows you to selectively install the features in a clustered environment, rather than a canned feature set, as is the case with SQL Server 2000 clustered setup.

Database Administration and Management

SQL Server is well known for its graphical management tools that allow administrators, developers, and business intelligence professionals to easily manage data and to monitor and tune servers. These graphical tools and wizards make database professionals more productive and leveraged. Hence these tools are one of the key elements to reducing the total cost of ownership (TCO).

However, there are a few issues with the tools in releases prior to SQL Server 2005:

- Database administrators and developers have to use multiple tools to get a job done. For instance, they need to use Query Analyzer to run queries, Enterprise Manager to manage the server, Service Manager to manage services, separate client and server network utilities, and so on.

- Enterprise Manager suffers performance issues with servers that have a large number of databases and database objects.

- All the dialog boxes in Enterprise Manager are modal. Hence if you open a dialog, such as the Server Properties dialog, you cannot go back to Enterprise Manager until you close that dialog.

- The Profiler tool only allows tracing activity on the relational server; it does not have any knowledge of Analysis Services.

- The tools do not offer project/solution management or integration with source code control system.

- SQL Server 2000 Query Analyzer allows editing and running Transact-SQL (T-SQL) queries only. There is no built-in editor (other than the MDX sample application) to run Analysis Services Multidimensional Expressions (MDX) queries.

Some of the design goals of SQL Server 2005 are to address these problems; to give more power to DBAs, developers, and information workers; and to simplify the management of SQL Server by providing integrated tools.

Introducing SQL Server Management Studio

SQL Server Management Studio is a new integrated tool that combines the functionality of three tools: Query Analyzer, Enterprise Manager, and Analysis Manager. In addition, it allows you to manage all other components, such as Reporting Services, SQL Server Integration Services (SSIS; formerly known as DTS), Notification Services, and SQL Server Mobile.

SQL Server Management Studio defers loading all databases and database objects in the tree, and it expands the nodes asynchronously. This is very useful if you are working on a server with a large number of databases and database objects. In addition, Management Studio allows filtering of the database objects in the tree by name, schema, and creation date. All the dialog boxes in Managed Studio are non-modal, resizable, schedulable, and scriptable.

In addition to T-SQL queries, the Query Editor in Management Studio allows you to work with MDX, Data Mining Prediction (DMX), and XML for Analysis (XMLA) queries.

Management Studio supports the notion of solutions and projects and provides full integration with source code control system such as Microsoft Visual SourceSafe.

Figure 4.1 shows various windows inside the Management Studio, such as Registered Servers, Object Explorer, Query Editor, Solution Explorer, Execution Plan, and Properties.

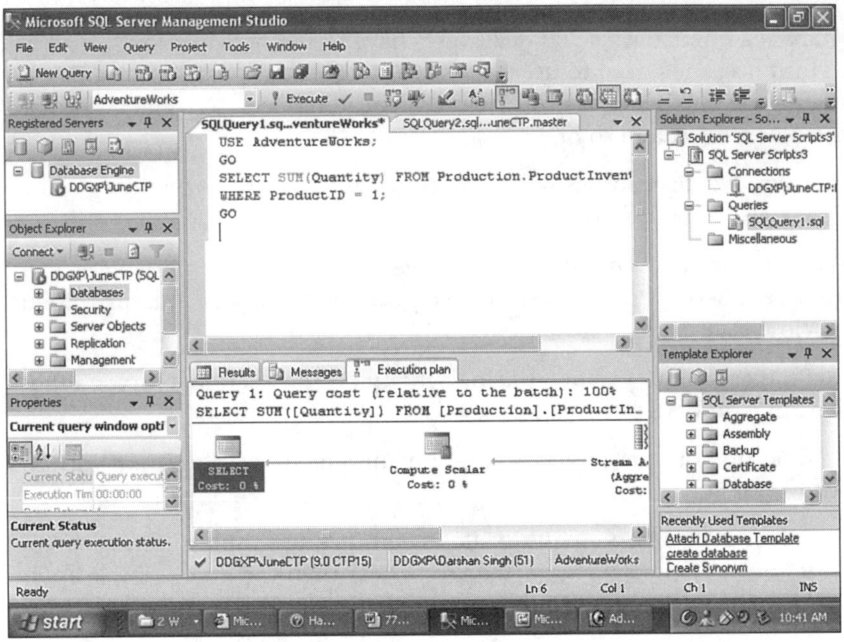

FIGURE 4.1   SQL Server 2005 Management Studio is a new integrated management environment.

In a nutshell, Management Studio is an integrated environment for accessing, configuring, managing, and administering all components of SQL Server. Management Studio and other tools are discussed in more detail in Chapter 5, "SQL Server 2005 Tools and Utilities."

SQL Server Configuration Manager

SQL Server Configuration Manager is an MMC snap-in (like Enterprise Manager in SQL Server 2000) that is intended to replace Server Network Utility, Client Network Utility, and Service Manager. SQL Server Configuration Manager was referred to as SQL Computer Manager in earlier SQL Server 2005 beta builds.

As shown in Figure 4.2, SQL Server Configuration Manager can be used to manage SQL Server 2005 services and service accounts, including Analysis Services, Agent, Reporting Services, Notification Services, SQL Server Browser, and full-text search. It can also be used to manage client and server network connectivity options.

SQL Server Configuration Manager ships with all SQL Server 2005 editions, including Express Edition.

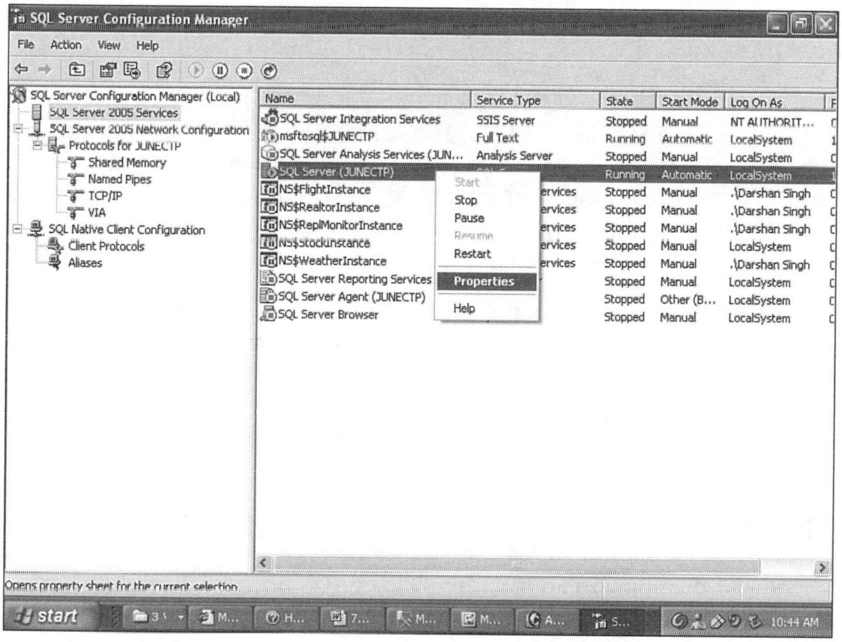

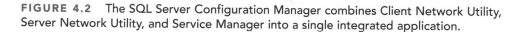

FIGURE 4.2   The SQL Server Configuration Manager combines Client Network Utility, Server Network Utility, and Service Manager into a single integrated application.

SQLCMD and Dedicated Administrator Connection

SQLCMD is DOS command-prompt utility introduced in SQL Server 2005 that supersedes `isql.exe` and `osql.exe`. Like ISQL and OSQL, `SQLCMD.exe` can be used to execute T-SQL statements and scripts. Unlike ISQL and OSQL, SQLCMD has extensive support for scripting and variables. `SQLCMD.exe` uses OLE DB to connect and execute the T-SQL batches.

You can use the `-A` switch with `SQLCMD.exe` in situations where SQL Server is not responding or is otherwise unavailable. This switch establishes a dedicated administrator connection with SQL Server 2005 and can be very helpful while troubleshooting.

DDL Triggers and Event Notifications

With SQL Server 2000, the only way to audit the activity at the server level or at the database level for DDL events (such as `CREATE/DROP/ALTER TABLE`) was to use SQL Profiler. However, no DBA would prefer running SQL Profiler all the time on the production server as an auditing solution.

SQL Server 2005 introduces two solutions to this problem: DDL triggers and event notifications.

Almost all RDBMSs, including SQL Server, support DML triggers. You can write a T-SQL module called a trigger that will automatically execute if an `INSERT`, `DELETE`, or `UPDATE` occurs on a table on which the trigger is defined. This trigger executes synchronously in the scope of the same transaction as the action that caused the trigger to fire, and if you decide to, you can roll back the entire transaction.

DDL triggers are new in SQL Server 2005. You can define a DDL trigger at the database level or at the server level. A database-level DDL trigger allows you to capture events such as CREATE/ALTER/DROP TABLE, VIEW, USER, ROLE, and other DDL statements. The server-level DDL trigger allows you to respond to events such as CREATE/ALTER/DROP LOGIN, CERTIFICATE, and other server-level DDL statements.

Much like DML triggers, DDL triggers are also created by using CREATE TRIGGER T-SQL statements, and they also execute in the same transaction context as the action that started it. You can roll back an entire transaction from the trigger, and you can nest DDL triggers. You can use the EVENTDATA() function inside a DDL trigger to access the information about the event that fired the DDL trigger. The inserted and deleted tables are not created or available inside DDL triggers.

However, in case you would like to respond to DDL events asynchronously or process them on a different or remote server, SQL Server 2005 introduces an alternative to DDL triggers: event notifications. In addition to DDL events, you can also use the event notification mechanism to respond to various profiler trace events. For instance, an event notification mechanism can be set up to notify a DBA whenever a LOCK_DEADLOCK trace event is raised, indicating a deadlock scenario.

Unlike DDL triggers, event notifications can be processed asynchronously and, if required, on a different server. The CREATE EVENT NOTIFICATION T-SQL statement is used to set up an event notification to respond to DDL or trace events or event groups. When an event notification is raised, a message is posted to a Service Broker queue. Service Broker is discussed later in this chapter and in detail in Chapter 15, "SQL Server 2005 Service Broker." Note that because an event notification is not executed in the same transaction scope as the action that raised it, the transaction cannot be rolled back. You can use the EVENTDATA() function to access the details about an event.

Database Mail

The SQL Mail functionality in SQL Server 2000 can be used to send and receive emails from within T-SQL code. However, it has few limitations:

- SQL Mail uses extended MAPI and requires the Microsoft Outlook 2000 client or later to be installed on the SQL Server machine. (Refer to Microsoft KB Articles 263556 and 281293 for more information about this.) This poses extra configuration headaches. But more than that, having an email client installed on a SQL Server box is considered a security risk.

- SQL Mail is not supported on 64-bit platforms.

- SQL Mail does not scale well.

- SQL Mail does not impose any restriction on attachment file size or attachment file extensions.

SQL Server 2005 fixes all these problems by introducing a new SMTP-based emailing solution called Database Mail. Database Mail was referred as SQLiMail in earlier SQL Server 2005 beta builds.

Database Mail does not require MAPI or Outlook to be installed; rather, it uses SMTP to send emails. Database Mail is scalable because it uses Service Broker to send emails asynchronously. The `MaxFileSize` and `ProhibitedExtensions` parameters in the `msdb..sysmail_configuration` table govern the attachment file size and prohibited attachment file extensions. Management Studio provides a user interface to tune these settings. Database Mail is supported on both 32-bit and 64-bit platforms. However, note that Database Mail is not a 100% replacement for SQL Mail in this release because it does not support reading emails. Chapter 5 covers Database Mail in great detail.

Management APIs: SMO, RMO, AMO, and WMI

SQL Server 2000 included two options to programmatically administering SQL Server: using COM-based SQL Distributed Management Objects (SQL-DMO) and using the Windows Management Instrumentation (WMI) API.

SQL-DMO was first introduced in SQL Server 6.5, where it was called SQLOLE; it was then renamed SQL-DMO in SQL Server 7. Enterprise Manager in SQL Server 7 and SQL Server 2000 internally uses SQL-DMO, and hence you could use SQL-DMO to automate all the functionality provided by Enterprise Manager.

SQL-DMO is still supported, but it has been deprecated in SQL Server 2005. It has not been updated to support the new features in this release. SQL-DMO is being superseded by a new .NET-based class library called SQL Server Management Objects (SMO). Administrators can use SMO to programmatically administer SQL Server 7, 2000, and 2005. SQL Server Management Studio internally uses SMO, and hence you can use SMO to automate all the functionality provided by Management Studio to manage a relational server.

In addition to providing maximum coverage of SQL Server 2005 features, the SMO API contains several other improvements over SQL-DMO. These changes include a cached object model, delayed instantiation of objects for improved scalability and performance, enhanced scripting capabilities, and improved ease of use. Further details on the SMO can be found in Chapter 5.

The replication part of the management API is now available in a separate .NET object library called Replication Management Objects (RMO). RMO allows you to programmatically configure and manage the replication architecture.

As mentioned earlier, SQL Server Management Studio internally uses the SMO API to provide server administration and management functionality. To manage Analysis Services, it uses another .NET-based object library called Analysis Management Objects (AMO). AMO is also used by the Business Intelligence Studio tool. AMO is the successor of the COM-based API called Decision Support Objects (DSO), which is available in previous releases. DSO is still available in SQL Server 2005, but AMO is the recommended API for programmatically managing Analysis Services.

WMI Overview

WMI is a component of the Microsoft Windows operating system. WMI provides an industry-standard programming interface for managing an enterprise environment. WMI is based on the Web-Based Enterprise Management (WBEM) initiative. WBEM is a set of standard technologies designed to allow administrators to use a consistent method of managing different systems in an enterprise. The standards that comprise WBEM are developed by the Distributed Management Task Force (DMTF; www.dmtf.org).

An entity managed through WMI is called a *managed object*. A managed object can be a hardware entity, such as memory or a disk drive, or a software entity, such as a user account or SQL Server. WMI provides a consistent way to monitor and control managed objects, regardless of the type of object. For instance, you can use WMI to monitor the amount of free space on a disk drive, to change the permissions for files on the disk drive, to manage virtual directories and permissions on an IIS Web server, and so on. You can access the WMI API from various programming languages, such as VBScript, C++, Visual Basic, and .NET Framework languages, and you can create applications and scripts to automate administrative tasks.

WMI, like SQL-DMO, is a COM API. The WMI API communicates with the WMI Windows Service, which in turn interacts with various WMI providers, such as the SQL Server Administration provider, the Active Directory provider, the NT Event Log provider, and so on. A WMI *provider* is a COM object that monitors a managed object for the WMI. For instance, you can write a VBScript that uses the NT Event Log WMI provider to monitor Application event log entries that are from SQL Server. For instance, as soon as SQL Server logs anything in the Application log, your VBScript can then send an email or a pager notification.

The WMI API also supports a querying language, WMI Query Language (WQL). By using WQL queries, you can request only the data of interest from the provider rather than incur the overhead of enumerating over all the objects.

WMI and SQL Server 2000

SQL Server 2000 was the first release to introduce the WMI API support. The WMI SQL Administration provider can be used to automate various administration tasks and monitor SQL Server events.

SQL Server WMI support is not installed by default. The SQL Server 2000 CD contains the setup files you need in order to use the WMI to administer SQL Server. After you have run the WMI setup, you can then run WMI scripts and applications to automate and monitor SQL Server.

WMI and SQL Server 2005

WMI support in enabled by default in SQL Server 2005, and it is further extended to support SQL Server 2005 features such as Reporting Services. SQL Server Configuration Manager internally uses the WMI API. Hence you can use WMI to automate all the functionality provided by SQL Server Configuration Manager. The WMI may seem like a complex API to use, but the new SMO .NET object library provides an object-oriented wrapper around WMI that is simpler to use. Finally, the WMI enhancements introduced in SQL Server 2005 allow you to generate SQL Server agent alerts in response to WMI events. For instance, you can write a T-SQL script to monitor WMI disk events, and if disk space on a particular drive drops below the specified size, a SQL Server Agent alert can be raised, which in turn notifies the administrator and may also start shrinking the database or log files.

WMI support in SQL Server 2005 is discussed in more detail, with examples, in Chapter 5.

Database Engine Enhancements

The two primary components of the SQL Server database engine are the relational engine and storage engine. The relational engine parses and processes the query, optimizes the execution plan, talks with the storage engine to obtain the results, and formats the results to be sent to the client. The other database engine component, storage engine, is responsible for physical I/O and concurrency control. The storage engine manages the database files and physical data pages. SQL Server 2005 contains significant changes to these two engine components to support new functionality and to improve on existing functionality.

The New xml Data Type

SQL Server 2000 first introduced support for XML by allowing turning a relational rowset into XML by using the FOR XML clause with the SELECT statement and converting XML into a relational rowset by using the OPENXML function. The support for XML in SQL Server 2000 was further extended with the SQLXML Web releases. However, if you need to store XML data inside a database table, the only option with SQL Server 2000 was to use the char/nchar/varchar/nvarchar or text/image data types. In addition, there is no built-in support for working with XML text stored in the database. For instance, if you store XML data in a varchar column, there is no way to execute XPath or XQuery queries to locate data inside XML or to efficiently update XML data.

SQL Server 2005 fills this gap by introducing a new data type called xml. In SQL Server 2005 you can have columns, variables, and parameters of xml data type. There are methods available to query and update XML data. You can store up to 2GB of XML data in a column. A typed XML column is one that has an XML Schema (XSD) associated with it; otherwise, it is called an untyped XML column.

Here is some sample T-SQL code that illustrates the xml data type:

```
USE TempDB;
GO

CREATE TABLE dbo.tblTest(id INT IDENTITY(1,1) PRIMARY KEY NOT NULL,
    logtext xml not null);
GO

INSERT INTO dbo.tblTest (logtext) VALUES ('<log result="1" />');
GO
```

```
DECLARE @varTest xml;
SET @varTest = '<log result="0" />';
INSERT INTO dbo.tblTest (logtext) VALUES (@varTest);
GO

SELECT * FROM dbo.tblTest;
GO

SELECT * FROM dbo.tblTest
WHERE logtext.value('(/log/@result)[1]', 'int') = 1;
GO

DROP TABLE dbo.tblTest;
GO
```

This T-SQL script first creates a table that contains a column of xml data type. It then inserts some sample data by directly providing the XML text string and then by using an xml type variable. The final statement illustrates querying xml type column. If you run this code in the Management Studio Query Editor and view the results in Grid mode, you can see that the xml type column is shown as a hyperlink, and if you click it, you see formatted XML data in a new window.

XML Indexes

To optimize access to XML data, you can create indexes on xml type columns. Without an index, when a query is run on an xml type column, all the XML data is shredded at runtime to evaluate the query. This can be a significant performance hit and can cause queries to run more slowly. Indexes on an xml type column are a little different from those on other columns. First, you have to create a primary index on an xml type column, which is essentially a shredded representation of XML data, and then if you like, you can create secondary indexes to optimize XPath and XQuery queries on the xml type columns.

In addition to using standard XML querying mechanisms using XPath and XQuery, you can also define full-text search on xml type columns and run full-text queries.

In addition to the XML standard, SQL Server 2005 supports various other W3C standards, such as XPath, XQuery, XML namespaces, and XML Schema (XSD).

The xml data type and XQuery are discussed in complete detail in Chapter 10, "XML and Web Services Support in SQL Server 2005."

Large Value Data Types

With SQL Server 2000, if you stored more than 8000 bytes of text or binary data in a column, the only option was to use text or image data types. However, these two data types are not easy to work with because they require different programming techniques than the other text or binary types, such as varchar and varbinary, and they have some very serious limitations (for example, many string functions do not work on text/image columns, you cannot define a variable of type text/image, and so on). To fix this, SQL Server 2005 introduces a new max specifier. The max specifier can be used with varchar, nvarchar, and varbinary types, and it allows you to store up to 2GB of data into a column, variable, or parameter, without any different handling requirements.

Here is an example of T-SQL code that illustrates the use of the max specifier:

```
USE TempDB;
GO


CREATE TABLE dbo.tblTest(id INT IDENTITY(1,1) PRIMARY KEY NOT NULL,
    logtext varchar(max) not null);
GO


DECLARE @char varchar(max);
DECLARE @varTest varchar(max);
SET @char = '-';
SET @varTest = REPLICATE(@char, 100000);
INSERT INTO dbo.tblTest (logtext) VALUES (@varTest);
GO


SELECT * FROM dbo.tblTest;
SELECT LEFT(logtext, 10) FROM dbo.tblTest;
SELECT SUBSTRING(logtext, 99990, 1) FROM dbo.tblTest;
SELECT LEN(logtext) FROM dbo.tblTest;
GO


DROP TABLE dbo.tblTest;
GO
```

This T-SQL batch first creates a table containing a column of type varchar(max). It then inserts 100,000 characters into this column, using a varchar(max) type column, and uses some string functions to illustrate that varchar(max) is no different from other text type columns. In addition, SQL Server 2005 also relaxes the 8060-bytes per row restriction. The following script will not work in SQL Server 2000, but runs successfully in SQL Server 2005:

```
USE tempdb;
CREATE TABLE dbo.tblTest(
    c1 varchar(4000),
    c2 varchar(4000),
    c3 varchar(4000));
GO
INSERT INTO dbo.tblTest VALUES
    (REPLICATE('*', 4000), REPLICATE('*', 4000), REPLICATE('*', 4000));
GO
```

.NET Framework Integration

One of the biggest features introduced in SQL Server 2005 is the .NET Framework integration, better known as SQLCLR. The SQL Server 2005 database engine hosts the .NET Framework CLR, and hence it allows .NET code to run from within the T-SQL script. SQLCLR integration enables developers to extend the T-SQL programming language and type system. The SQLCLR integration allows developers to write stored procedures, triggers, and user-defined functions, and to create new types and aggregates by using .NET.

.NET Framework Overview

The Microsoft .NET Framework, introduced in July 2000, is a development platform that allows the building of Windows, web, and mobile applications. To rapidly build and deploy .NET applications, developers can use Visual Studio .NET tools and a programming language of their choice, such as Visual Basic .NET, C#, C++, or J#, to make use of thousands of classes provided by the .NET Framework Base Class Library.

The .NET programming model is simplified by an execution engine, known as the common language runtime (CLR), which handles a lot of tasks that developers had to do previously. These tasks include allocating and managing memory, thread management, lifetime management or garbage collection, security, and enforcement of type safety.

The code written in .NET languages and executed by the CLR is called *managed code*. Developers can still use legacy COM objects or call a Win32 API from within .NET code, but because the COM objects and Win32 functions are not controlled by the CLR, they are referred to as *unmanaged code*. The .NET Framework code is compiled into intermediate language (IL) and saved into DLLs or EXEs known as assemblies.

Introducing SQLCLR

In SQL Server 2000, the only way to extend T-SQL was to write extended stored procedures, which required C++ programming knowledge and understanding of the Open Data Services (ODS) API. In addition, a poorly written extended stored procedure could potentially cause a number of unpredictable problems with SQL Server.

The SQLCLR integration in SQL Server 2005 allows developers to write stored procedures, triggers, and functions and to extend the type system and aggregates by using any of the .NET languages and the familiar ADO.NET programming model. The .NET security framework, the CLR, and the SQLCLR hosting layer security make sure that the managed code running inside SQL Server does not compromise the integrity of the SQL Server process.

SQLCLR easily outperforms T-SQL in scenarios such as doing a lot of procedural coding (looping, branching, and so on), string manipulation, or computational tasks in T-SQL code. However, for data access, using T-SQL is still the best approach. The SQLCLR assembly that is imported into the database contains compiled .NET code in IL format. When this code is executed, it is just-in-time (JIT) compiled into machine language. T-SQL is an interpreted language. The compiled code always executes faster than interpreted code.

Developers can use Visual Studio .NET and any of the .NET Framework languages to build assemblies, which are compiled .NET code that can be imported into a SQL Server database by using the CREATE ASSEMBLY T-SQL statement. Depending on what the assembly implements, a T-SQL stored procedure, function, trigger, user-defined type, or aggregate can be mapped to .NET code in the assembly.

Let's say a developer gives you a .NET assembly called `Payroll.dll` that contains a managed stored procedure that accepts employee ID and year as the parameters, does some complex calculation, and returns a rowset that contains complete tax details. Here is how you would import the assembly, map a T-SQL stored procedure to the .NET method, and then eventually call the stored procedure:

```
CREATE ASSEMBLY [CLR_Payroll]
    FROM 'F:\FromDev\Payroll.dll'
    WITH PERMISSION_SET = SAFE;
GO


CREATE PROCEDURE dbo.usp_GetTaxDetails
(
    @EmployeeID INT,
    @Year INT
)
AS EXTERNAL NAME [CLR_Payroll].[StoredProcedures].[GetTaxDetails]
GO


EXEC dbo.usp_GetTaxDetails 10, 2004;
GO
```

The important point to note in this sample script is the WITH PERMISSION_SET = SAFE keyword. You as a DBA can control what an imported assembly can or cannot do by using one of the three permission buckets that SQL Server 2005 provides: SAFE, EXTERNAL_ACCESS, and UNSAFE.

SQLCLR Permission Buckets: SAFE, EXTERNAL_ACCESS, and UNSAFE
The assemblies that are imported with SAFE permission set can work with data and use some of the CLR utility classes, but they cannot access external resources (such as the file system or the network), the code must be verifiably type safe by the CLR, and things like COM-interop, PInvoke (Win32 API access), and multithreading are not allowed. This is the default permission set.

The assemblies imported with EXTERNAL_ACCESS are the same as those imported with SAFE, but they also allow access to external sources such as the file system, using the .NET Framework class library.

The assemblies imported with UNSAFE can do virtually anything. They can even call unmanaged code such as COM objects and Win32 functions. It is recommended that UNSAFE permissions be granted only to highly trusted assemblies by experienced developers or administrators. Only members of the sysadmin fixed server role can create UNSAFE assemblies.

The SQLCLR is the subject of Chapter 11, "SQL Server 2005 and .NET Integration." Refer to that chapter for more details and examples of using the .NET integration features.

The New Catalog Views

With SQL Server 2000, the two ways to access SQL catalog or metadata were by using system tables or SQL-99 INFORMATION_SCHEMA views. SQL Server 2000 even allowed updating of system tables, which was not recommended but possible. In general, it is not recommended to access system tables directly. In addition, in SQL Server 2000 there was no real security implemented on metadata access. This meant that even though a database user did not have permissions to see the data, the user could still see what objects existed in the database (sysobjects) or see the structure of objects (sp_help).

With SQL Server 2005, the system tables are deeply hidden inside, and direct access to them is not allowed. They are not visible at all. The recommended way to access SQL metadata is to use the new *catalog views*. For backward compatibility, SQL Server provides *compatibility views* that have the same name and return the same data as the system tables in previous releases. In other words, system tables from previous releases are now compatibility views.

To summarize, SQL Server 2005 completely hides the system tables. There are three ways to access SQL metadata: through catalog views, compatibility views, and SQL-99 INFORMA-TION_SCHEMA views. Of these three features, only catalog views are available for all the features introduced in SQL Server 2005. For example, there is no INFORMATION_SCHEMA or compatibility view available to explore Service Broker objects. In addition, using catalog views is the most efficient way to access system metadata. Because SQL Server 2005 restricts access to base system tables, the allow updates sp_configure option in SQL Server 2005 is meaningless.

SQL Server 2005 implements a security layer on top of metadata views that is used for permission-based metadata access. For example, if a user executes a SELECT statement on a sysobjects compatibility view, a sys.objects catalog view, or a INFORMATION_SCHEMA. Tables view, SQL Server only returns the objects on which a user has access to select or modify the data, unless special VIEW DEFINITION permission is granted to the object.

The Resource Database

SQL Server 2005 also introduces the Resource database. It is an actual .mdf and .ldf file–based SQL Server 2005 database (mssqlsystemresource.mdf and mssqlsystemre-source.ldf), but it is not visible in Management Studio or through metadata views. In previous SQL Server releases, the metadata (schema definitions, system stored procedure text, and so on) for system objects was stored in the master database, and user database–specific system objects were stored in the user database. This posed major issues during upgrade and patching of SQL Server metadata. To expedite and simplify the upgrade process, Microsoft decided to store the system objects metadata inside a hidden Resource database. With this approach, instead of running multiple scripts, the upgrade and rollback process is as simple as copying new or old Resource database files.

The Resource database contains metadata for all system objects, but the system objects logically appear in each database under the sys schema. The master database still holds the actual instance-level data; the user databases still hold the database-specific information, and so on. However, the system objects' schema/metadata and system stored procedure text are stored in the Resource database.

The new metadata architecture is discussed in Chapters 2, "SQL Server 2005 Database Engine Architectural Changes," and 7, "SQL Server 2005 Security."

Scalability, Performance, and Reliability Enhancements

Scalability refers to the ability of a system to maintain and possibly improve performance as the load increases in a predictable manner. SQL Server 2005 introduces several enhancements to the database engine and other subsystems to make sure that the platform scales and performs well even with terabytes of data and thousands of users. In the following sections, you will see some of these new features, and you'll learn more details about them in Chapters 8, "Reliability and High Availability in the Database Engine," and 9, "Performance Analysis Tuning."

Row Versioning and the Snapshot Isolation Level

SQL Server 2000 supports all four isolation levels defined by SQL-92 standard: READ UNCOMMITTED, READ COMMITTED, REPEATABLE READ, and SERIALIZABLE. The default isolation level in SQL Server 2000 and SQL Server 2005 is READ COMMITTED, which ensures that statements cannot read modified data that is not committed yet and hence prevents dirty reads.

Isolation Levels   READ UNCOMMITED is the lowest isolation level. It allows statements to read data that has been modified by other transactions but not yet committed. SERIALIZABLE is the highest isolation level, and it completely isolates two transactions, avoiding all the concurrency issues such as dirty reads, nonrepeatable reads, and phantom reads. In between these two are the READ COMMITTED and REPEATABLE READ levels. Like the READ COMMITTED isolation level, the REPEATABLE READ isolation level also avoids dirty reads by disallowing reading data that is updated but not committed. In addition, it makes sure that no transaction can modify the data that has been read by the current transaction, and hence *readers* can block *writers*. The REPEATABLE READ isolation level avoids dirty reads and nonrepeatable reads, but it can still result in phantom reads.

Snapshot Isolation   SQL Server 2005 introduces a new isolation level called snapshot isolation that is like REPEATABLE READ without the issue of *readers* blocking the *writers*. In other words, while the snapshot isolation level prevents dirty reads and nonrepeatable reads, other transactions can continue to update the data that is read by the current transaction. How does SQL Server achieve this? The answer is row versioning.

Row Versioning in Detail   *Row versioning* is an alternative technique to locking to ensure the integrity of transactions and to maintain the consistency of data when multiple users are accessing the data at the same time. With row versioning, SQL Server uses tempdb to maintain a version of each row that is modified. Whenever a transaction modifies a row,

SQL Server copies the original row in the tempdb database. This technique is used to enable REPEATABLE READ behavior without the issue of readers blocking writers, as readers can now read the original row from the tempdb database. By avoiding blocking, snapshot isolation enables applications to scale and perform better. The applications with more read activity than writes benefit the most from the snapshot isolation level.

To see snapshot isolation in action, you can start two query window sessions in Management Studio and execute the following two T-SQL batches, which create the blocking scenario by using the REPEATABLE READ and READ COMMITTED isolation levels:

Connection 1:

```
USE [AdventureWorks];
SET TRANSACTION ISOLATION LEVEL REPEATABLE READ;
BEGIN TRANSACTION;
SELECT * FROM Sales.Store;
```

Connection 2:

```
USE [AdventureWorks];
SET TRANSACTION ISOLATION LEVEL READ COMMITTED;
BEGIN TRANSACTION;
UPDATE Sales.Store SET SalesPersonID = 280 WHERE SalesPersonID = 281;
```

Notice that the UPDATE statement is blocked because some other transaction in the REPEATABLE READ isolation level has already read the data.

Run the ROLLBACK TRANSACTION statement in the first connection and then in the second Query Editor window.

Let's now see how using the snapshot isolation level instead of repeatable read fixes the blocking problem. You need to change the T-SQL in the connection 1 window to use the snapshot isolation level:

Connection 1:

```
ALTER DATABASE AdventureWorks SET ALLOW_SNAPSHOT_ISOLATION ON;
GO

USE [AdventureWorks];
GO

SET TRANSACTION ISOLATION LEVEL SNAPSHOT;
BEGIN TRANSACTION;
SELECT * FROM Sales.Store;
```

Next, you should run this script in connection 1 and run the same UPDATE statement inside a transaction in connection 2. Note that this time the UPDATE statement is not blocked. If you switch back to connection 1 and run just the SELECT statement again, you should notice that it still shows the original values, which are similar to the REPEATABLE

READ behavior. You should roll back the transactions in both the connections and close the query windows.

You can use a T-SQL statement similar to the following in order to find out whether snapshot isolation is enabled on the database:

```
SELECT snapshot_isolation_state, snapshot_isolation_state_desc
FROM sys.databases WHERE name = 'AdventureWorks';
```

Note that there is a cost involved with using snapshot isolation and with row versioning in general. Because versions of rows are stored in `tempdb`, you have to make sure that you have sufficient space available in the `tempdb` database, and you also need to consider the performance impact of `tempdb` I/O that is caused because of row versioning. Updates and deletes can be a little slow because UPDATE might cause `tempdb` activity. While reading the data, SQL Server has to traverse the version history to determine where to read the row from.

In addition to snapshot isolation level, SQL Server 2005 also introduces a new flavor of the READ COMMITTED isolation level that makes use of row versioning to avoid blocking. This is achieved by turning on the READ_COMMITTED_SNAPSHOT option on the database, as discussed in detail in Chapter 8.

Service Broker
Service Broker is a new scalability technology introduced in SQL Server 2005 that allows you to build reliable, asynchronous queued database applications. All you have to worry about is sending and receiving messages using T-SQL, while the rest of messaging framework, including routing and security, is built into the database engine.

Asynchronous Messaging   One of the important aspects of building scalable applications is performing parts of the operations asynchronously. For example, when an order is submitted, you want to process inventory, shipping, and accounting. If these three tasks are performed synchronously when an order record is inserted, the order submission process takes longer, and the application will not scale. However, if these three tasks are done asynchronously, the order process finishes very quickly, and the application can scale. When an order record is inserted, it just posts a message and returns; this message is later retrieved asynchronously and then the inventory, shipping, and accounting tables are updated appropriately.

This asynchronous messaging breaks the tight coupling between components and allows application to perform better, scale out, distribute the load, and defer the things for batch processing. However, the challenge with asynchronous messaging is that someone should guarantee that the message is delivered for sure, delivered once and only once, and delivered in the order in which it was sent in a batch of messages.

On the application and middle tiers, these services are provided by specialized technologies such as Microsoft Message Queuing (MSMQ), IBM WebSphere MQ (formerly MQSeries), and so on. The SQL Server Service Broker brings these services into the database engine so that you can do asynchronous messaging at the database level.

For example, you can use Service Broker to implement asynchronous triggers. In other words, when a trigger is fired, it posts a message into a queue and returns immediately. This message is later received and processed by a Service Broker application, which can be a T-SQL or SQLCLR stored procedure or an external application.

More details on Service Broker can be found in Chapter 14.

Nonclustered Indexes with Included Columns

Designing and using proper indexes is one of the keys to maximizing query performance. One of the recommendations for designing indexes is to keep the index size small, which tends to be efficient. On the other hand, having all the data required by the query obtained from the covering index without touching the clustered index or table data page results in lesser I/O and better query throughput.

You might wonder whether you should include more columns in the index to maximize the covered query instances or whether you should keep the index key size small and efficient. With SQL Server 2000, you had to choose between these two choices, based on your performance benchmark results. SQL Server 2005 introduces the concept of including non-key columns in the index; this is designed to provide the best of both worlds: smaller key size and at the same time more success of an index being a covering index.

You can use the INCLUDE keyword along with a list of one or more columns and the CREATE INDEX statement to indicate that you want one or more non-key columns to be saved in the leaf level of an index. This way, there are more chances that the query will find all it needs in the index pages itself, without any further lookups. However, you should carefully design and determine when and what columns should be included. Including non-key columns as part of indexes increases the disk space requirement, fewer index rows can fit on index pages, and data is stored and updated twice (once in the base table and then as part of an index at the leaf level). More details on this can be found in Chapter 9.

Persisted Computed Columns

A computed column's value is calculated from an expression by using other columns in the same table. With SQL Server 2000, computed columns are always virtual columns, not physically stored in the table. Their value is determined at runtime, based on the columns in the expression and the expression itself.

SQL Server 2005 introduces the ability to persist the computed column values. The PERSISTED keyword can be specified with the computed column definition in the CREATE TABLE or ALTER TABLE statement to indicate that a computed column's value must be physically stored and updated if any column in the expression is updated. If a computed column is persisted in the data pages, it can speed retrieval for computing-intensive columns. In addition, persisted computed columns allow defining indexes in cases where virtual computed columns prohibit creation of indexes. For instance, if an expression is of type float or real, an index cannot be created on such virtual computed columns, but an index can be created on persisted computed columns. If computed columns are persisted, you can create NOT NULL, FOREIGN KEY, and CHECK constraints in addition to UNIQUE and PRIMARY KEY constraints.

<u>**NOTE**</u>

The persisted computed columns feature is not available in SQL Server 2005 Mobile Edition.

Here is a sample T-SQL script that illustrates persisted computed columns:

```
USE TempDB;
GO


CREATE TABLE dbo.tblTest(id INT IDENTITY(1,1) PRIMARY KEY NOT NULL,
    price float not null,
    qty float not null,
    cost as price * qty);
GO


INSERT INTO dbo.tblTest (price, qty) VALUES (100, 100);
INSERT INTO dbo.tblTest (price, qty) VALUES (200, 200);
GO


SELECT * FROM dbo.tblTest WHERE cost < 40000;
GO


--next stmt will fail; index can't be created on imprecise computed column
CREATE INDEX idTest ON dbo.tblTest(cost);
GO


DROP TABLE dbo.tblTest;
GO


CREATE TABLE dbo.tblTest(id INT IDENTITY(1,1) PRIMARY KEY NOT NULL,
    price float not null,
    qty float not null,
    cost as price * qty PERSISTED NOT NULL CHECK (cost > 0));
GO


INSERT INTO dbo.tblTest (price, qty) VALUES (100, 100);
INSERT INTO dbo.tblTest (price, qty) VALUES (200, 200);
GO
--next stmt will fail; CHECK constraint violation
INSERT INTO dbo.tblTest (price, qty) VALUES (200, -1);
GO


SELECT * FROM dbo.tblTest WHERE cost < 40000;
GO
--next stmt will succeed; index can be created on imprecise
```

```
--but persisted computed column
CREATE INDEX idTest ON dbo.tblTest(cost);
GO

SELECT * FROM dbo.tblTest WHERE cost < 40000;
GO

DROP TABLE dbo.tblTest;
GO
```

This script begins by creating a table containing a virtual computed column of float data type. SQL Server 2000 and 2005 do not allow creating an index on such a column because the computed column is not precise. But if the computed column is PERSISTED, SQL Server 2005 allows creating an index on that column, as well as defining other constraints such as a CHECK constraint, as illustrated in this script.

Partitioned Tables and Indexes

Partitioning of data and indexes is not a new concept. Especially for very large databases (VLDBs), partitioning of data and indexes has been one of the design strategies. Table and index partitioning is a performance, scalability, and manageability feature. Data in a partitioned table is horizontally split into physical units, which may be spread across more than one filegroup in a database.

What's new in SQL Server 2005 is the simplicity and ease with which you can implement and manage partitioned tables and indexes. You can provide a function and scheme for a table, and SQL Server will make sure to route rows automatically to appropriate partitions, based on the partition key. SQL Server 2005 also supports range partitions, where the partition key is the customized ranges of data. This subject is discussed in more detail, with examples, in Chapter 8.

Miscellaneous Performance Improvement Techniques

To wrap up this section, the following are some other performance-related changes introduced in SQL Server 2005.

DATE_CORRELATION_OPTIMIZATION   SQL Server 2005 introduces a new database option, DATE_CORRELATION_OPTIMIZATION, which can improve the performance of queries that perform an equi-join between two tables whose datetime columns are correlated and that specify a date restriction in the query predicate. This option is turned off by default. When you turn on this option, SQL Server maintains correlation statistics between any two tables in the database that have datetime columns and are linked by a foreign key constraint. These statistics are later used during query optimization to improve performance. You can use an ALTER DATABASE statement to turn on or off this option and the is_date_correlation_on field in the sys.databases catalog view to find out whether this option is turned off or on.

AUTO_UPDATE_STATISTICS_ASYNC   With SQL Server 2000, if the query optimizer determined that the statistics are stale, it started the statistics update and used the updated statistics to generate the best query plan. However, whenever this happened, that query ran more slowly than usual, and sometimes client requests experience timeouts. SQL Server 2005 introduces a database-level option that guarantees predictable query response time. When the AUTO_UPDATE_STATISTICS_ASYNC option is turned on, if the query optimizer determines that statistics are outdated, SQL Server uses the worker thread to start updating the statistics asynchronously. The current query continues to use existing statistics, which might not produce the most efficient query plan, but the query might execute quickly because it does not have to wait for update statistics to finish. The subsequent queries are then able to make use of the updated statistics when the worker thread finishes. You can use ALTER DATABASE statement to turn on this option and the is_auto_update_stats_async_on field in the sys.databases catalog view to find out whether this option is turned off or on.

RECOMPILE and OPTIMIZE FOR Hints   SQL Server supports specifying the WITH RECOMPILE option while creating stored procedures. This option tells SQL Server to discard the stored procedure plan and recompile the stored procedure every time it is invoked. With SQL Server 2000, it was all or nothing; however, with SQL Server 2005, you can use a RECOMPILE hint with the query inside a stored procedure to have only that query recompiled every time a stored procedure is called instead of recompiling entire stored procedure.

If you know that a parameter will often have a certain value, you can give this hint to SQL Server by using an OPTIMIZE FOR hint so that SQL Server will generate the most efficient plan, using the value specified.

NUMA, Hyperthreading, 64-Bit Support, and Indexed Views   To maximize the performance on high-end systems (those with eight or more processors), the SQL Server 2005 engine has been architected to leverage non-uniform memory access (NUMA) and hyperthreading. With Symmetric multiprocessing (SMP), all memory accesses are posted to the same shared memory bus. This works fine for a relatively small number of CPUs, but the problem with the shared bus appears when you have a larger number of CPUs competing for access to the shared memory bus. NUMA alleviates these bottlenecks by limiting the number of CPUs on any one memory bus and connecting the various nodes by means of a high-speed interconnection. SQL Server 2005 understands this technology and does all it can to avoid making the CPU travel on the interconnect bus in order to reduce the contention. NUMA support is discussed in detail in Chapter 2. SQL Server 2000 64-bit is supported only on Itanium 2 processors. SQL Server 2005 supports both Itanium 2 and x64 processor platforms. SQL Server 2005 includes many improvements for indexed views. SQL Server 2005 extends the list of constructs that can be used for indexed views. Indexed views and other performance improvements are discussed in Chapter 8.

Mirrored Backup Media Sets and Enhanced Error Detection
SQL Server 2005 can back up simultaneously to a maximum of four devices. It increases the reliability of a system by having extra copies of backup in case a backup media set goes bad. In addition, SQL Server 2005 supports database and backup checksums, to ensure the reliability of the media set. Finally, unlike SQL Server 2000, in SQL Server 2005, RESTORE VERIFYONLY guarantees that the backup is good as it checks everything to ensure that the data is correct.

XML Web Services Support

As mentioned earlier, basic XML support was first introduced in SQL Server 2000, providing the capability to retrieve a relational rowset as XML or to turn an XML string into a relational rowset. The XML support was further extended in SQLXML web releases. One of the features in SQLXML web releases is the ability to quickly expose a stored procedure or function as a web service method. If you are not familiar with XML web services, think of them as an integration API that can work over the Internet. The XML web services support in SQL Server 2005 is functionally similar to that provided by SQLXML web services, but it is more efficient, native, and secure, and it does not have any dependency on a web server such as IIS.

SQL Server 2005 allows you to expose stored procedures and functions as Web service methods. The Web services support in SQL Server 2005 does not require IIS, as it uses the new HTTP listener process (`http.sys`) that is available on Windows XP Service Pack 2 and Windows Server 2003 platforms. Hence, web services in SQL Server 2005 will only work on Windows XP Service Pack 2 and Window Server 2003.

The `CREATE ENDPOINT` T-SQL statement can be used to define a web service and web methods. After you define a service and web methods that map to stored procedures or functions, you can invoke those methods from any platform or any language over the Internet by just using HTTP and SOAP.

Native web services support in SQL Server 2005 is discussed in the second half of Chapter 10.

SQL Server 2005 Express and Mobile Editions

SQL Server 2005 Express Edition is the successor of MSDE, and SQL Server Mobile Edition is the successor of SQL Server CE Edition.

Like MSDE, SQL Server 2005 Express Edition is free, and it is intended to be used for personal or simple data-driven applications. The Express Edition contains several enhancements over MSDE. Some of the enhancements include availability of graphical tools (such as SQL Server Configuration Manager and Express Manager), XCopy deployment, 4GB database size, and removal of concurrent worker throttle mechanism that restricted the scalability under heavy load.

SQL Server Mobile Edition supports more platforms than SQL Server CE, hence the name change. It supports all the mobile devices, including Pocket PCs, Tablet PCs, Embedded CE devices, and smart phones. There are several significant improvements to this edition. Some of the new features introduced in Mobile Edition include integration with Management Studio and Visual Studio .NET 2005; synchronization changes, including configurable compression levels, progress status, column-level sync tracking, and support for multiple subscriptions; multiuser support and `SQLCEResultSet` for efficient data access; and SSIS support.

T-SQL Enhancements

Now that SQL Server 2005 allows the writing of stored procedures, functions, triggers, and other database objects using .NET code, is T-SQL going away? Absolutely not! T-SQL is still the premier language for writing SQL Server data access batches, stored procedures, and so on. Even with SQLCLR or any other data-access API, the query language used is still T-SQL. SQL Server 2005 introduces some very cool enhancements to T-SQL that allow you to write better queries and modules. The following sections introduce some of these enhancements, and Chapter 6, "Transact-SQL Enhancements," discusses each of these new T-SQL features in detail.

Recursive and Non-recursive Common Table Expressions (CTEs)

You can think of CTEs as a simple yet more powerful alternative to derived tables. In some cases, CTEs may be used in places where you are currently using temporary tables, table variables, or views. The three important motivations for introducing CTEs in SQL Server 2005 are recursion; to provide alternative, simplified, readable, and manageable syntax for complex SQL statements, possibly making use of derived tables; and ANSI SQL-99 compliance (CTEs are defined in SQL-99).

A CTE can be defined as a temporary named result set, which is derived from a simple query and defined within the execution scope of a SELECT, INSERT, UPDATE, or DELETE statement. It is important to note that the scope of a CTE is just the statement in which it is declared. The CTE named result set is not available after the statement in which it is declared and used.

Here is a simple example that uses a CTE to count number of direct reports for each manager in the AdventureWorks sample database:

```
USE AdventureWorks ;
GO
WITH DirReps(ManagerID, DirectReports) AS
(
    SELECT ManagerID, COUNT(*)
    FROM HumanResources.Employee AS e
    WHERE ManagerID IS NOT NULL
    GROUP BY ManagerID
)
SELECT * FROM DirReps ORDER BY ManagerID
GO
```

In the scope of a SELECT statement, this query declares a result set named DirReps, and then the outer SELECT statement retrieves everything from that result set. Nothing fancy here—just a simple example to give you a taste of CTE syntax.

The following CTE example that is a bit more involved. This query is used to trend the sales data; for every year, it gets the total sales amount and compares it with the previous year's sales:

```
WITH YearlyOrderAmtCTE(OrderYear, TotalAmount)
AS
(
    SELECT YEAR(OrderDate), SUM(OrderQty*UnitPrice)
    FROM Sales.SalesOrderHeader AS H JOIN Sales.SalesOrderDetail AS D
        ON H.SalesOrderID = D.SalesOrderID
    GROUP BY YEAR(OrderDate)
),
SalesTrendCTE(OrderYear, Amount, AmtYearBefore, AmtDifference, DiffPerc)
AS
(
 SELECT thisYear.OrderYear, thisYear.TotalAmount,
        lastYear.TotalAmount,
          thisYear.TotalAmount - lastYear.TotalAmount,
          (thisYear.TotalAmount/lastYear.TotalAmount - 1) * 100
 FROM YearlyOrderAmtCTE AS thisYear
      LEFT OUTER JOIN YearlyOrderAmtCTE AS lastYear
      ON thisYear.OrderYear = lastYear.OrderYear + 1
)
SELECT * FROM SalesTrendCTE
GO
```

This query essentially defines two CTEs. The first CTE, called `YearlyOrderAmtCTE`, groups the total sales by year. This CTE is then used in the second CTE, called `SalesTrendCTE`, and the outer or main query selects all the rows from `SalesTrendCTE`. Notice how `SalesTrendCTE` uses `YearlyOrderAmtCTE` to get the current and previous years' total sales figures.

In the previous example, the second CTE refers to the previous CTE. If a CTE refers to itself, it is then called a *recursive CTE,* and this is where CTEs get interesting. Without any further ado, here is an example of a recursive CTE:

```
WITH MgrHierarchyCTE(EmployeeID, EmployeeName, ManagerID, Level)
AS
(
   SELECT e.EmployeeID, c.FirstName + ' ' + c.LastName, e.ManagerID, 0
   FROM HumanResources.Employee AS e
        JOIN Person.Contact AS c
        ON c.ContactID = e.ContactID
   WHERE e.EmployeeID = 111

   UNION ALL

   SELECT mgr.EmployeeID, co.FirstName + ' ' + co.LastName, mgr.ManagerID,
          Level + 1
```

```
    FROM HumanResources.Employee AS mgr
        JOIN Person.Contact AS co
        ON co.ContactID = mgr.ContactID
        JOIN MgrHierarchyCTE AS cte
        ON cte.ManagerID = mgr.EmployeeID
)
SELECT * FROM MgrHierarchyCTE;
GO
```

This recursive CTE example illustrates traversing up the management hierarchy all the way up to the topmost manager for the employee with the ID 111. The query returns a result set that contains a row for each manager in the hierarchy, starting with the immediate manager and going up to the top-level manager.

The first SELECT statement within the CTE definition finds the immediate manager details. This row is then combined, using UNION ALL, with another SELECT statement that self-references the CTE to traverse the management hierarchy.

The most common problem with recursion is infinite loops. SQL Server solves this problem by defining a serverwide recursion level limit setting called MAXRECURSION, which defaults to 100. You can also specify a MAXRECURSION hint in your CTE query to limit the recursion level for that query.

CTEs are discussed in more detail in Chapter 6.

Improved Error Handling

In previous releases, the error handling inside T-SQL scripts was done by using @@ERROR at multiple places and by using GOTO and RETURN statements. SQL Server 2005 adopts the modern structured error handling by introducing the TRY...CATCH construct. If you are familiar with Visual Basic .NET or C# .NET, you can think of this as being equivalent to try...catch blocks; however, there is no equivalent to finally blocks.

Here is an example of the modern error handling paradigm in SQL Server 2005:

```
USE AdventureWorks
GO
BEGIN TRY
    -- Generate a constraint violation error.
    DELETE FROM Production.Product WHERE ProductID = 980;
END TRY
BEGIN CATCH
    SELECT ERROR_NUMBER() AS ErrorNumber,
           ERROR_SEVERITY() AS ErrorSeverity,
           ERROR_STATE() as ErrorState,
           ERROR_MESSAGE() as ErrorMessage;
END CATCH
GO
```

To better handle errors, all you have to do is put T-SQL statements inside BEGIN TRY and END TRY, and if an error occurs, you can obtain detailed error information by using various ERROR_XXXX functions. In addition to the previously mentioned functions, you can also use the ERROR_LINE() and ERROR_PROCEDURE() functions inside a module to find the exact line where the error occurred and the name of the module.

Limiting a Result Set by Using TOP and TABLESAMPLE

The TOP keyword is not new to SQL Server 2005. It has been available since SQL Server 7 and can be used to limit a result set to a specified exact number or percentage of rows. However, it is enhanced in this edition so that TOP can be used for DML statements (INSERT, UPDATE, and DELETE). In addition, you no longer have to hard-code the number of rows or percentage value; the TOP keyword now also accepts an expression.

In addition to TOP, SQL Server 2005 introduces the new keyword TABLESAMPLE, which you use to limit the number of rows returned. Unlike TOP, TABLESAMPLE returns a random set of rows from throughout the set of rows processed by the query, and TABLESAMPLE cannot be used with a view. As with TOP, you can specify an exact number of rows or a percentage number.

This sampling technique can be used to get better performance for queries on large databases where absolutely exact results are not desired. For example, if you want to find an approximate estimate for the average employee salary, you can use TABLESAMPLE to do aggregation on a sample of data rather than on an entire large dataset.

The SQL:2003 proposal includes two sampling methods: BERNOULLI and SYSTEM. SQL Server 2005 supports only the SYSTEM sampling method.

Here is an example script that passes a variable to the TOP keyword and illustrates the new TABLESAMPLE keyword:

```
USE AdventureWorks
GO

DECLARE @var INT;
SET @var = 3;
SELECT TOP (@var) * FROM Sales.Store;
GO

SELECT AVG(SickLeaveHours) FROM HumanResources.Employee
TABLESAMPLE SYSTEM (20 PERCENT)
REPEATABLE(3);
GO
```

Like all other T-SQL topics, TOP and TABLESAMPLE are also further discussed in Chapter 6.

Ranking Functions

SQL Server 2005 introduces four very useful functions—ROW_NUMBER(), RANK(), DENSE_RANK(), and NTILE()—that can be used to rank the rows in a partition. For example, you can generate a sequence number, generate a different number for each row, or rank rows based on some partition criteria:

- **ROW_NUMBER()**—You can use this function to generate sequential row numbers. This can be very handy when you're implementing scenarios such as paging in web pages.

- **RANK()**—You can use this function to rank the rows within the partition of a result set. The rank of a row is 1 plus the number of ranks that precede the row in question.

- **DENSE_RANK()**—This function is similar to RANK() except that it does not leave any gaps in ranking. The rank of a row is 1 plus the number of distinct ranks that precede the row in question.

- **NTILE()**—You can use this function to distribute the rows in an ordered partition into a specified number of groups.

Here is an example of a T-SQL statement that makes use of all four of the ranking functions:

```
USE AdventureWorks;
GO
SELECT ROW_NUMBER() OVER(ORDER BY ListPrice DESC) as RowNum,
       ProductID, Name, ProductNumber, ListPrice,
       RANK() OVER (ORDER BY ListPrice DESC) as Rank,
       DENSE_RANK() OVER (ORDER BY ListPrice DESC) as DenseRank,
       NTILE(10) OVER (ORDER BY ListPrice DESC) as NTile_10,
       NTILE(20) OVER (ORDER BY ListPrice DESC) as NTile_20
FROM Production.Product;
```

If you try out this query in the Query Editor in Management Studio, you should notice that the first column, RowNum, is a sequential number starting with 1; the Rank column starts with 1 and when the price changes, the value for Rank column in the next row is 1 plus the number of rows having rank as 1, and so on. When the price column value changes, the DenseRank column value changes to 2, then 3, and so on. The NTile_10 and NTile_20 columns contain values starting from 1 through 10 and 1 through 20, dividing the result set into 10 and 20 groups, respectively.

PIVOT and UNPIVOT

PIVOT and UNPIVOT are two new keywords introduced in SQL Server 2005 that can be used with the SELECT statement. In simple terms, PIVOT can be used to turn rows into columns, and UNPIVOT can be used to turn columns into rows.

Let's begin by looking at an example of the PIVOT keyword:

```
SELECT [316] AS Blade, [331] AS [Fork End]
FROM
    (SELECT ProductID, Quantity FROM Production.ProductInventory) AS pinv
    PIVOT
    (
        SUM (Quantity)
        FOR ProductID IN ([316], [331])
    ) AS pvt;
GO
```

This query essentially generates cross-tabulation reports to summarize the quantity for two products. You should run the query by using the Query Editor in Management Studio and notice that it returns two columns, named Blade and Fork End, and a single row that contains the total quantity available for these two products.

The counterpart of PIVOT is UNPIVOT, which can be used to turn columns into rows. Here is an example of UNPIVOT:

```
CREATE TABLE dbo.tblGrades
    (StudentID int NOT NULL PRIMARY KEY,
    Term1 CHAR(1) NOT NULL,
    Term2 CHAR(1) NOT NULL,
    Term3 CHAR(1) NOT NULL,
    Term4 CHAR(1) NOT NULL);
GO

INSERT INTO dbo.tblGrades SELECT 1, 'A', 'B', 'C', 'D';
INSERT INTO dbo.tblGrades SELECT 2, 'D', 'C', 'B', 'A';
GO

SELECT * FROM dbo.tblGrades;
GO

SELECT StudentID, Term, Grade
FROM
    (SELECT StudentID, Term1, Term2, Term3, Term4 FROM dbo.tblGrades) p
    UNPIVOT
        (Grade FOR Term IN
        (Term1, Term2, Term3, Term4)
)AS unpvt
GO

IF OBJECT_ID('dbo.tblGrades') IS NOT NULL
```

```
BEGIN
    DROP TABLE dbo.tblGrades;
END
GO
```

This sample T-SQL code begins by creating a table that stores student grades for four terms. Each term is a column in the table. The UNPIVOT statement is then used to turn term grade columns into rows. Figure 4.3 shows the power of the UNPIVOT keyword.

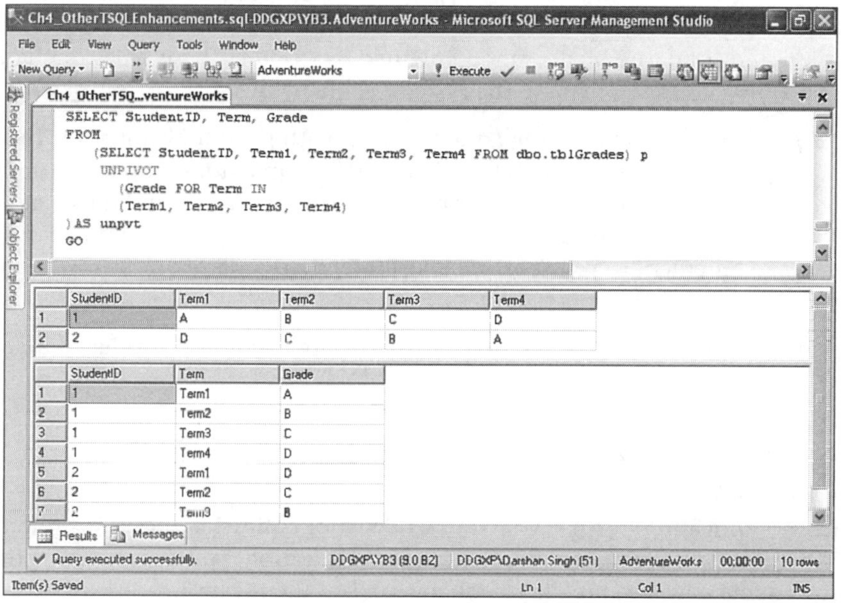

FIGURE 4.3   The UNPIVOT keyword can be used to convert columns into rows.

SQL Server 2005 introduces several other T-SQL enhancements, such as the APPLY keyword to invoke a table valued function for each row in the rowset; the OUTPUT keyword to retrieve rows affected by DML statements; referential integrity enhancements to set a default value or null when a row is deleted from the parent table; and enhancements to FOR XML and OPENXML. Refer to Chapter 6 for complete details on these enhancements.

SQL Server 2005 Security

Microsoft's dedication to trustworthy computing is clearly visible in SQL Server 2005. SQL Server 2005 is secure by design, secure by default, and secure by deployment.

To make sure that SQL Server 2005 is *secure by design*, every team member on the SQL Server 2005 product attended the security training, and each component/feature, such as

Service Broker and SQLCLR, has gone through threat analysis and testing. Code reviews, penetration testing, use of automated code tools, scenario-based testing, and low privileged testing are some other techniques that the SQL Server team used to ensure that the product is secure by design. All existing features have been reevaluated to make them more secure, and every new feature has undergone thorough scrutiny to make sure it meets the security standards.

Secure by default means that when an administrator first installs SQL Server 2005, the data environment is in its most locked-down state, with secure settings for all configuration options. SQL Server 2005 setup installs only the necessary components, features such as SQLCLR are not enabled by default, services such as Agent and Full-Text Search are set to manual start, and Database Mail is not configured by default. These types of changes minimize the attack surface, making the system secure by default.

Secure by deployment means providing administrators with good tools for security assessment, auditing and reducing the attack surface, assisting in automating monitoring, and following the principle of least privilege. The SQL Server Management Studio and Surface Area Configuration tools, DDL triggers, the new auditing capabilities, and departure from the sysadmin requirement to run tools such as Profiler are certainly steps toward making SQL Server solutions secure by deployment.

Let's now briefly look at some of the new security-related features introduced in SQL Server 2005.

Password Policy Enforcement and Strengthening of SQL Authentication

Windows Authentication is still the recommended authentication mechanism in SQL Server 2005. However, if you have to use SQL authentication, you should know that two big improvements have been made to enhance SQL authentication.

SQL Server 2005 makes sure that you specify a strong password when creating a SQL login. For instance, the CREATE LOGIN statement will fail if you specify a blank password, specify a password that is the same as the login name, or use words such as "Admin" or "Administrator." None of the following statements will succeed:

```
CREATE LOGIN TEST1 WITH PASSWORD = '';
GO
CREATE LOGIN TEST1 WITH PASSWORD = 'TEST1';
GO
CREATE LOGIN TEST1 WITH PASSWORD = 'Admin';
GO
CREATE LOGIN TEST1 WITH PASSWORD = 'SA';
GO
CREATE LOGIN TEST1 WITH PASSWORD = 'Administrator';
GO
```

All these statements fail, with the "Password validation failed" error.

In addition, if you are running on Windows Server 2003, which is, by the way, the recommended platform for SQL Server 2005, the same complexity and expiration policies used in Windows Server 2003 can be used for SQL authenticated logins.

The second enhancement is that SQL Server 2005 encrypts the login packets. In other words, unlike in previous releases, SQL Server 2005 never sends SQL authentication details in clear text. If SSL is available, SQL Server uses it; otherwise, it generates a 512-bit certificate and uses it for encryption.

User–Schema Separation

According to the ANSI SQL-92 standard, the sole purpose of a schema is to act as a namespace, to group related objects under one umbrella. However, SQL Server 2000 and previous releases did not differentiate between a schema and a user. A user was essentially treated as a schema. If an administrator wanted to delete a user, he or she needed to delete all the objects owned by that user or change the owner of all the objects owned by the user being deleted. Changing the object owner very often required changing the application code.

SQL Server 2005 breaks the user–schema tight coupling, treating schemas as per the ANSI SQL-92 standard—as meaningful names that can be used to group related objects. For example, in the AdventureWorks sample database, objects are grouped under schemas named Sales, HumanResources, Person, and so on.

Schemas are owned by users, such as dbo or some user UserX. Now, if an administrator wanted to drop the user UserX, all the administrator would have to do is change the schema owner and delete the user. As long as that user does not own any schemas and is not used for the EXECUTE AS context (discussed later in this chapter), the administrator should be able to delete the user. The applications still continue to access the objects by using schema names, such as Sales.Store or HumanResources.Employee.

With SQL Server 2005, every user has a default schema, and if the user has appropriate permissions, he or she can create and own multiple schemas. Each schema can then contain zero or more objects. While resolving the object name, SQL Server follows a simple rule to look for the object under the user's default schema, and if it is not found, SQL Server uses dbo as the schema name.

Note that many users can have the same schema as their default schema. No two objects in a schema can have the same name. However, it is possible to have tables with the same name in different schemas. When you create a new database, SQL Server 2005 creates several schemas in the database, such as schemas named dbo, INFORMATION_SCHEMA, sys, and guest; and also a schema is created for every database role. All the catalog views, dynamic management objects, and system-stored procedures reside in the sys schema. User–schema separation is discussed in more detail, with examples, in Chapter 7.

Encryption Support

SQL Server 2005 provides native support for symmetric keys, asymmetric keys, and certificates that can be used to encrypt and decrypt data. Keys and certificates can be stored inside the database and later used for various purposes, such as authentication and encryption/decryption. SQL Server 2005 provides functions such as `EncryptByKey`, `EncryptByPassPhrase`, `EncryptByAsmKey`, `EncryptByCert`, and their decryption counterparts to encrypt and decrypt data by using keys, certificates, or pass phrases.

Refer to Chapter 7 for more details on keys, certificates, and encryption support in SQL Server 2005.

Module Execution Context and Impersonation

With previous SQL Server releases, if a user had `EXECUTE` permission on a module, SQL Server did not check permission on the objects accessed in the module, as long as the referred objects were owned by the same user as the module owner. This concept is known as *ownership chaining*. As soon as a module refers to an object that is owned by a different user than the module owner, the ownership chain breaks, and SQL Server checks whether the user executing the module has permission on the object being accessed.

SQL Server 2005 introduces a new T-SQL construct, `EXECUTE AS`, that can be used in defining the modules (stored procedures, functions, triggers, and queues) to specify the execution context that the module should run under. SQL Server 2005 uses the specified context to impersonate and run the module. The default `EXECUTE AS` context is `CALLER`. This ensures that the engine behaves as in the previous release, supporting the ownership chain concept. However, the module creator can specify whether the module should run under the context of `SELF`, `OWNER`, or a specific user.

In addition to using `EXECUTE AS` while defining the modules, you can also use `EXECUTE AS USER = '<username>'` within T-SQL batches to change the execution context, and you can use `REVERT` to change the execution context back to the user used to connect to the instance.

SQL Server 2005 introduces several other security-related features, such as granular permissions control, metadata or catalog security, and SQLCLR security. Chapter 7 is dedicated to SQL Server 2005 security and auditing.

In summary, the enhanced security model, granular permission control, secure-by-default deployment, password policy enforcement, and data encryption make SQL Server 2005 a secure and reliable platform for database and analytical applications.

Performance Monitoring and Tuning Enhancements

In SQL Server 2000, SQL Profiler and PerfMon were the two primary tools used to monitor and troubleshoot performance issues. Some other ways to monitor performance included using system stored procedures such as `sp_who2` and `sp_lock`, DBCC statements such as `DBCC INPUTBUFFER` and `DBCC OPENTRAN`, and current activity monitor in Enterprise

Manager. As far as performance tuning is concerned, the only tool available in SQL Server 2000 was the Index Tuning Wizard.

For SQL Server 2005, Microsoft has invested a lot of time and resources in improving the existing tools and introducing new tools to monitor and tune the performance. These include the following:

- Several improvements and new features have been introduced in the Profiler tool.

- The Index Tuning Wizard has been replaced with a full-fledged application called Database Engine Tuning Advisor that does a better job of making recommendations on physical database design, works well with large databases and large workloads, contains more functionality, and is more manageable.

- There are new dynamic management views (DMVs) and dynamic management functions (DMFs) to view the current state of the SQL Server 2005 system.

- There are new ways to monitor and avoid blocking and deadlocking.

- SQL Server 2005 provides new Performance Monitor counters.

The following sections present an overview of these changes, which are discussed in great detail in Chapter 9.

Profiler Enhancements

SQL Profiler is still the primary tool for monitoring the activity on a SQL Server instance. The change in SQL Server 2005 is that Profiler now supports tracing of Analysis Services and Integration Services events, in addition to SQL Server.

A new feature called Performance Counters Correlation allows the correlating of Performance Monitor counter data, with the Profiler trace collected at the same time.

SQL Server 2005 Profiler defines a new event called a deadlock graph, which can be captured to monitor and view deadlock data as a picture. Figure 4.4 shows a deadlock graph as traced by the Profiler.

Several new event categories and events have been added to Profiler to support the tracing of the new functionality, such as Service Broker and online index operation. Profiler also defines event classes to trace OLE DB events and deprecated features.

Profiler allows capturing of a showplan and saving it as XML. This XML showplan can be later analyzed using Query Editor in Management Studio. Third-party applications might be available in the future to allow various other operations, such as comparisons, using an XML showplan.

Profiler includes new replay options that allow the controlling of things such as maximum number of replay threads. Refer to Chapter 9 for more details on changes introduced in SQL Profiler.

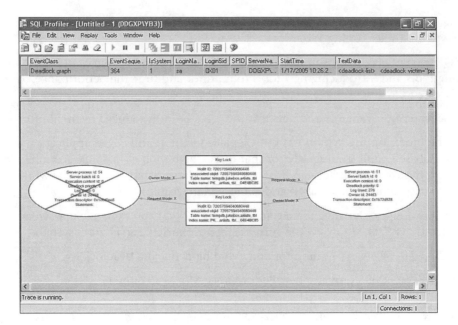

FIGURE 4.4   SQL Server 2005 Profiler provides several new events, such as deadlock graph.

Database Engine Tuning Advisor

The Index Tuning Wizard from previous releases of SQL Server is now being replaced with a full-fledged GUI application (`dtashell.exe`) named Database Engine Tuning Advisor (DTA). DTA can also be invoked from the DOS command prompt (`dta.exe`). It can be used to tune the physical database design to maximize performance and to aid in manageability.

Tuning is generally an iterative process. With the Index Tuning Wizard in previous releases, it was a little difficult to go through the steps multiple times and review the results, and there was no way to compare and do what-if analysis. DTA is a full-blown application that provides the notion of sessions, which makes it is easier to iterate the tuning process, review and evaluate the recommendations, and view reports. Figure 4.5 shows DTA in action.

Here is a summarized list of some of the important tuning advancements introduced in SQL Server 2005:

- In addition to providing recommendations regarding indexes and indexed views, DTA can make several other recommendations, such as how to range partition the data, indexes, and indexed views; including non-key columns with nonclustered indexes; XML indexes; and index rebuilding/reorganization suggestions to reduce the cost of index scans and seeks.

- The Index Tuning Wizard is restricted to workload on a single database and can tune a single database at a time. DTA, on the other hand, supports a workload that spans multiple databases, and in each DTA session, you can choose multiple databases to be considered for tuning.

- It is not recommended to run DTA on a production server during business hours. Depending on the workload and size of the database, DTA might impose significant tuning overhead on the server being tuned. The nice thing is that you can tell DTA when to stop. (Refer to Figure 4.5 and notice the very first option on the Tuning Options tab.)

- DTA session definition and tuning recommendation results can be exported as an XML document. The session definition XML file can later be provided to DTA at the command line (dta.exe) or as a GUI (dtashell.exe) application. The use of XML by DTA opens the door for third-party vendors to provide solutions that integrate with DTA to enhance and support additional functionality. The XSD schema for input and output XML is the same and is available in a file named dtaschema.xsd under the folder C:\Program Files\Microsoft SQL Server\90\Tools\Binn\schemas\sqlserver\2003\03\dta. The month and year in the path might change when SQL Server is released.

- DTA allows you to evaluate recommendations, and when you are satisfied with recommendations, you can specify which ones to implement.

- Unlike Index Tuning Wizard, which only sysadmin server role members can use, DTA can be executed by any members of the db_owner database role.

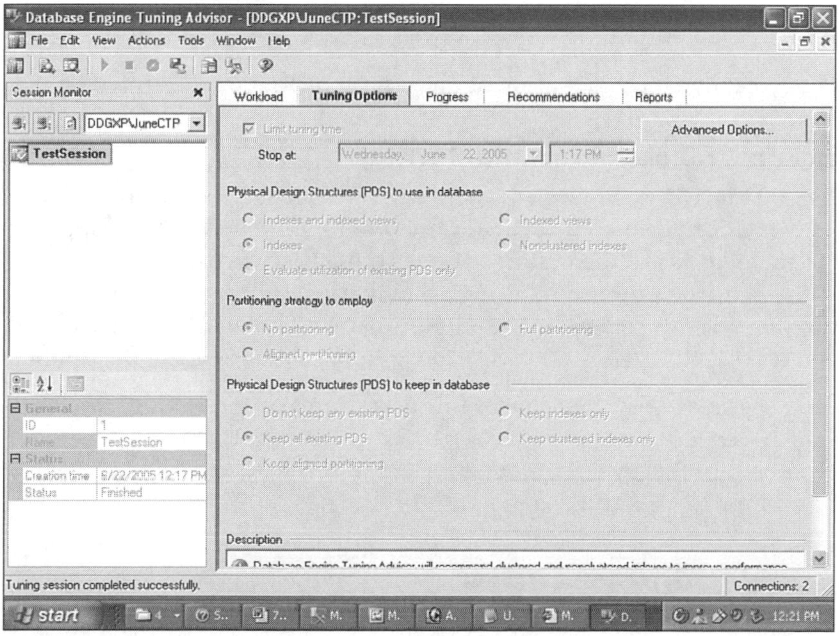

FIGURE 4.5   DTA contains significant improvements over the Index Tuning Wizard in terms of functionality, quality of recommendations, and ability to handle large databases and work-loads.

DTA is discussed in detail in Chapter 9.

Dynamic Management Objects

SQL Server 2005 provides several dynamic management views and functions that essentially provide a real-time snapshot of internal memory structures that indicate the server state. In addition to Profiler and PerfMon, dynamic management objects are an essential tool for proactively monitoring SQL Server. If you run the following query in the Management Studio's Query Editor, you should see a list of all the available DMVs and DMFs:

```
SELECT name, type_desc FROM sys.system_objects WHERE name like 'dm_%';
```

Like catalog views, dynamic management objects also belong to the sys schema.

Here is a sample T-SQL script that illustrates a DMV and a DMF:

```
USE AdventureWorks;
GO

SELECT * FROM sys.dm_tran_locks;
GO

SELECT * FROM sys.dm_db_index_physical_stats
    (DB_ID(), OBJECT_ID('Sales.Store'), NULL, 0, 'DETAILED');
GO
```

Further details on dynamic management objects can be found in Chapter 9.

The Blocked Process Threshold Setting

SQL Server 2005 introduces a new advanced sp_configure setting called blocked process threshold, which can be used to generate an event as soon as blocking happens on the server. The value of this configuration setting is initially set to 0, indicating that this feature is disabled. You can turn on the sp_configure show advanced options setting, change the value of this parameter to a number between 1 and 86400 (indicating 24 hours), and run RECONFIGURE WITH OVERRIDE to immediately activate the option.

Let's say you specified 10 as the value of this new configuration setting. Now if there is a blocking for 10 seconds, SQL Server 2005 generates an event that can be seen in Profiler and also can be captured by using the new event notification mechanism. Refer to Chapter 9 for more details and a demo of this feature.

High-Availability Features

Minimizing the maintenance window, avoiding unnecessary or unscheduled downtimes, and maximizing server availability are top priorities of the administrators. SQL Server 2000 supported three high-availability solutions: failover clustering, transactional replication, and log shipping. SQL Server 2005 builds on these proven technologies and introduces a few new features to assist DBAs in increasing server availability.

Failover Clustering Changes

A SQL Server 2000 cluster allowed a maximum of four nodes. SQL Server 2005 on Windows Server 2003 Enterprise or Datacenter Edition allows up to eight nodes in a cluster. In addition, SQL Server 2005 Analysis Services and Full-Text Search can now be clustered. The cluster setup now allows you to choose which components you want to install. Dynamic AWE memory is another big improvement in SQL Server 2005 clustering. In an active-active cluster scenario, SQL Server 2005 on Windows Server 2003 dynamically adjusts AWE memory usage after failover. Other clustering-related changes include mount point support, script-based setup, and other setup changes for clustering. These changes are discussed in Chapter 8.

Database Mirroring and Snapshot

Unlike failover clustering, which is a high-availability solution at the server level, log shipping is the database-level high-availability solution available in SQL Server 2000. Database mirroring is the successor to log shipping. Mirroring differs from log shipping in two ways: With database mirroring, changes are reflected in real-time on the standby server and the failover is automatic.

A database mirror is made of three instances of SQL Server 2005: the *principal* database resides on the production server; the *mirror* database resides on the second hot-standby server, and the *witness* server is one that monitors the state of the principal and mirror servers.

All the SQL Server 2005 components such as Service Broker and Database Mail support database mirroring. The data access API is updated to support transparent client redirection in case the mirror server takes the role of the principal server.

Database snapshot, a new feature introduced in SQL Server 2005, allows you to create a new database that is a read-only, static view of some other (source) database. The most common application of the database snapshot feature is in conjunction with database mirroring. The mirror database is always in a recovering state and never available for client connections. However, SQL Server 2005 allows creating database snapshots of the mirror database. These snapshots can then be used as the reporting databases, to separate OLTP from reporting.

Database mirroring and snapshot are discussed in great detail in Chapter 8.

Online Index Operations

Index fragmentation is one of the main reasons for performance degradation in SQL Server query execution. To fix the fragmented indexes in SQL Server 2000, there were three options: drop and re-create the indexes manually, rebuild the indexes by using DBCC DBREINDEX, or defragment the indexes by using DBCC INDEXDEFRAG. Most DBAs chose to use DBCC DBREINDEX or INDEXDEFRAG. The problems with DBREINDEX are that it is an atomic operation, so if you cancel it, the rollback might take a long time and that while the index is being built, table data cannot be updated. INDEXDEFRAG is an online index operation and can be cancelled; however, it does not utilize parallelism and can take a very long time to complete if an index is highly fragmented.

SQL Server 2005 supports the same three options as SQL Server 2000 for fixing index fragmentation. It introduces three new options as well: ALTER INDEX...REORGANIZE to defragment the index, ALTER INDEX...REBUILD to rebuild the index, and ALTER INDEX...REBUILD WITH (ONLINE = ON) for online index rebuilding.

Online index rebuilding allows concurrent modifications to the underlying table or index. SQL Server 2005 Profiler has a new event class that can be used to track the progress of online index operation.

Online index operation and other features related to indexes are discussed in more detail in Chapter 8.

Instant File Initialization

Let's say you have to restore a 500GB database from a backup. You begin by creating a new blank database that is 500GB or larger in size. With SQL Server 2000, this step itself could take few hours because SQL Server reserved the space and initialized the data file by filling it with zeros. SQL Server 2005 introduces a new feature called instant file initialization, which skips the second step of zeroing out the file bytes; therefore, even large databases are created instantly. Note that instant file initialization works for data files only, and not for log files.

Online, Piecemeal, and Page Restore

SQL Server 2005 introduces new features so that in case of recovery, a database can be made available as soon as possible. If a database contains multiple filegroups, as soon as the primary filegroup is restored, you can bring the database online and in the background restore other filegroups. The page restore is designed to restore torn pages or pages that a checksum shows to be corrupt.

More discussion on high-availability features can be found in Chapter 8.

Replication

SQL Server Replication is a commonly used technology for copying and distributing data and database objects from one database to another, possibly on a different server, and then synchronizing between databases to maintain consistency. SQL Server 2000 supported 3 replication topologies or models: Snapshot, Transactional, and Merge. SQL Server 2005 builds on this solid foundation and introduces about 30 new features that extend the replication platform to provide new capabilities, simplify configuration and monitoring, and give better control to administrators. The following sections briefly discuss some new features, which are then discussed in more detail, along with other replication enhancements, in Chapter 8.

Replication of Schema Changes

With SQL Server 2000, administrators thought that replication was best suited for static environments, where there were no schema changes on the publisher. This was because SQL Server 2000 provided very limited support for making schema changes once an object is published. In some cases, administrators cannot afford to resynchronize the subscription to apply schema changes on the subscribers. The only two stored procedures available to accommodate schema changes on published objects are `sp_repladdcolumn` and `sp_repldropcolumn`. A combination of these two store procedure can be used to implement some other column schema changes (such as changing the data type), in addition to adding or dropping the column in a published object.

SQL Server 2005 contains broader support for allowing schema changes to be made on the published object, without any need for running a specialized stored procedure such as `sp_repladdcolumn`. SQL Server 2005 makes use of DDL triggers mechanism to capture events such as `ALTER TABLE`, `ALTER VIEW`, and so on and then applies the publisher schema changes on the subscribers.

Oracle Publishing
In snapshot and transactional replication topologies, SQL Server 2005 now supports bringing data from Oracle version 8.0.5 and above that resides on any operating system. It does not require anything to be installed on the Oracle server. You can configure and administer everything from SQL Server tools, and you don't necessarily need to have Oracle knowledge to configure Oracle publisher.

Peer-to-Peer Transactional Replication
Peer-to-peer transactional replication is essentially an efficient way to implement scalable and highly available SQL Server solutions. Each node in the topology, a peer, can update the data, and data is synchronized to other peers, making sure all peers have the same copy of the data. Workload can therefore be distributed among peers or fail over to another peer. Unlike merge replication, peer-to-peer transactional replication does not provide the ability for conflict detection and resolution. It is designed for environments where peers update different parts of data, but same databases have to be available on all the nodes.

Merge Replication over HTTPS
Merge replication subscribers getting data over the Internet by using IIS on the server is not new. The SQL Server CE subscribers could always do that. However, if a subscriber was not a SQL Server CE Edition, then it was not possible for the subscriber to connect to the publisher over HTTPS. SQL Server 2005 fixes this and allows both Mobile and Server Editions to connect to the publisher over HTTPS.

There are many other replication improvements in SQL Server 2005 related to functionality, security, performance, monitoring, programming (RMO), and administration. Refer to Chapter 8 for more details.

Business Intelligence Redefined
Business intelligence refers to tools and techniques that support better decision making. By using these tools and techniques, you can turn raw data into insight. Data from possibly disparate source systems can be intelligently integrated to build a foundation for reporting, analysis, data mining, prediction, and expert systems.

SQL Server 7 first introduced OLAP Services, a data warehouse engine for online analytical processing. To continue the evolution of the business intelligence platform, SQL Server 2000 introduced several significant advancements to OLAP Services and renamed the technology Analysis Services.

Analysis Services 2000, in conjunction with data mining models and Data Transformation Services (DTS), which is Microsoft's premier Extract-Transform-Load (ETL) tool, was a platform of choice for building data warehousing and business intelligence solutions.

SQL Server 2005 revolutionizes and redefines the business intelligence platform by introducing completely redesigned ETL and integration platform known as SQL Server Integration Services (SSIS; formerly known as DTS), and it adds several new features to Analysis Services 2005 by introducing new data mining models, a Web-based reporting solution, and integrated management and development tools.

The main theme of business intelligence in SQL Server 2005 is integrate, analyze, and report: You use SSIS for integration, Analysis Services 2005 and Data Mining for analyzing, and Reporting Services and Report Builder for presentation and delivery of reports. Figure 4.6 shows the core components of the SQL Server 2005 business intelligence framework.

FIGURE 4.6   SQL Server 2005 provides new tools and technologies to build business intelligence solutions.

The business intelligence framework in SQL Server 2005 is based on a solid foundation of a relational engine, and it is supported by innovative development and management tools.

SSIS has been redesigned from scratch, and it goes a step beyond being just an ETL tool. The new SSIS is designed to be an ultimate solution to integrate data from various sources, massage it, and send it to one or more destinations. SSIS is discussed in more detail in Chapter 12, "SQL Server Integration Services Overview."

Microsoft really listened to the feedback it received on Analysis Services 2000, and it combined that with innovative techniques to make Analysis Services 2005 a highly scalable, available, and secure platform for building multidimensional solutions. Analysis Services 2000 is single-instance and cluster-unaware, whereas Analysis Services 2005 supports up to 50 instances and 8-node (32-bit) or 4-node (64-bit) failover clusters. Several enhancements have been made to the Analysis Services engine, cube and dimension handling, new data mining models, a new .NET Framework–based object model from programming, and native support for the XML for Analysis (XMLA) 1.0 specification. As you will see in Chapter 13, "What's New in SQL Server Analysis Services 2005," Analysis Services 2005 is loaded with new features as well as improvements to existing functionality.

In January 2004, Microsoft announced SQL Server 2000 Reporting Services, an enterprise reporting platform that supports a full reporting life cycle, including authoring, management, and delivery. Reporting Services can be used for both paper-oriented and interactive, Web–based reports. Reporting Services is now one of the core subsystems in SQL Server 2005. It incorporates feedback that Microsoft received on SQL Server 2000 reporting services, plus it has tighter integration with SQL Server 2005 and Analysis Services 2005. SQL Server Management Studio, Business Intelligence Development Studio, and other tools have been enhanced to support Reporting Services. SQL Server 2005 Reporting Services supports rich client printing, multivalued parameters, and interactive sorting, and it contains an enhanced expression editor.

SQL Server 2005 also introduces a new ad hoc report design tool targeted at business users. This tool, known as SQL Server 2005 Reporting Services Report Builder, is based on business intelligence technology acquired from ActiveViews Inc. in April 2004. Business users can very easily create reports based on data in a SQL Server relational database or Analysis Services OLAP cubes, without understanding or writing any T-SQL or MDX queries. The reports created using Report Builder can be published to Reporting Services or SharePoint Server.

Introducing Business Intelligence Development Studio

In much the same way as SQL Server Management Studio integrates Enterprise Manager and Query Analyzer into one shell, Business Intelligence Development Studio is an integrated environment for designing and building end-to-end business intelligence solutions. Business Intelligence Development Studio is a single tool that information workers can use to define new Analysis Services data sources, cubes, dimensions, and data mining models; design ETL packages; build reports; and deploy an entire solution to a test or production environment. Essentially, it combines Analysis Manager and DTS Designer, and it adds several new capabilities.

Like Management Studio, Business Intelligence Development Studio is also based on Visual Studio .NET, and it allows you to work with projects and solutions with complete SourceSafe integration. Figure 4.7 shows the Business Intelligence Development Studio environment, with an Analysis Services project being developed.

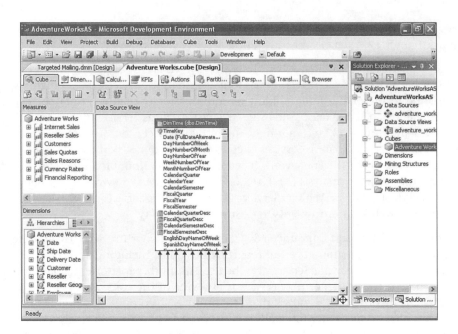

FIGURE 4.7   Business Intelligence Development Studio is an integrated IDE for building and deploying business intelligence solutions.

You might wonder when to use SQL Server Management Studio versus Business Intelligence Development Studio. If you are developing or maintaining business intelligence solutions, such as designing SSIS packages, reporting services reports, or Analysis Services objects, you should use Business Intelligence Development Studio. However, if you are responsible for developing and administrating relational database objects or administrating and configuring already deployed solutions that use business intelligence technologies, you should use SQL Server Management Studio.

Notification Services

Like Reporting Services, the Notification Services technology was also first introduced as an add-on to SQL Server 2000. Released in August 2002, Notification Services is a highly scalable solution for monitoring for events and sending alerts to millions of subscribers. It is a programming framework for building applications that generate and send notifications to subscribed users. MSN Alerts and *New York Times* are some examples where this technology is already being used to send alerts to subscribers. This platform is now tightly integrated into SQL Server 2005. The installation of Notification Services is now integrated with SQL Server 2005 setup. SQL Server 2005 Notification Services supports the 64-bit platform. The SQL Server 2005 Management Studio now provides a user interface for deploying and administering Notification Services instances instead of you doing it by using command-line tools, as in Notification Services for SQL Server 2000.

Full-Text Search Enhancements

Full-Text Search has been available since SQL Server 7. It is designed to allow fast and flexible indexing and querying of unstructured data in a database. SQL Server 2005 Full-Text Search enhancements are mainly related to performance and integration.

Full-Text Search now supports having multiple instances installed on the server. The engine has been optimized for faster indexing and querying. According to Microsoft, indexing of 20 million rows now takes about 10 hours to populate, whereas it used to take about 14 days. The full-text queries run 30% to 50% faster than in previous releases. New full-text DDL statements simplify configuration and administration. Running Full-Text Search queries over a linked server and searching across multiple selected columns are some of the new querying capabilities. Finally, the biggest improvement is that if you back up, restore, attach, or detach the database, the full-text catalogs can be part of it. There are several other new features, such as thesaurus support, XML data type support, and accent sensitivity/insensitivity.

Documentation Improvements

SQL Server Books Online is the first resource that database professionals and information workers refer to for any clarification or to understand SQL Server concepts. SQL Server 2005 Books Online has been significantly enhanced for better usability, searching, and organization of information. It is an integrated resource for both the relational engine and Analysis Services. The new tabbed interface, ability to save searches, improved full-text searching capabilities, new tutorials and samples, and search integration with the MSDN and Codezone Community websites are some of the features that enhance the usability of Books Online to quickly locate relevant information.

Summary

SQL Server 2005 includes hundreds of new features related to security, scalability, high availability, performance, monitoring and maintenance, developer productivity, standards compliance, business intelligence, and database administration. This chapter sets the stage for the rest of the book by giving an overview of these features. In Chapter 5, you will learn about new tools and utilities that you can use as a DBA to administer and manage SQL Server technologies.

SQL Server 2005 Tools and Utilities

Microsoft SQL Server was the first RDBMS to provide graphical management and diagnostic tools bundled with the product, in addition to several command-prompt utilities. Since then, the existing tools have evolved, and new tools have been introduced in every SQL Server release. The SQL Server 2005 release is no different. As a matter of fact, because it is the biggest SQL Server release to date, with hundreds of new features, it was very important for Microsoft to deliver a suite of integrated graphical tools, command-prompt utilities, and new management programming APIs that simplify database administration, management, authoring, and operations. This chapter provides an in-depth look at the new tools and utilities introduced in SQL Server 2005.

Tools and Utilities Overview

With SQL Server 2000, tools are kind of disjointed and sometimes have overlapping capabilities. For instance, you have to use Enterprise Manager for common administration and DTS-related tasks; Query Analyzer as a query and authoring tool; separate client network, server network, and service management tools; Analysis Manager to administer and develop Analysis Services objects; and so on. SQL Server 2000 offers minimal tool integration by providing main menu options to launch one tool from another.

When the SQL Server 2005 team started building the new toolset, it devised two primary guiding principles: integration and "no secrets." *Integration* refers to tools consolidation so that administrators do not have to deal with multiplicity of tools in order to get things done. The new SQL Server Management Studio, Business Intelligence Development Studio, and SQL Server Configuration Manager are examples of this:

- **SQL Server Management Studio**—This is an integrated management and authoring graphical tool that combines the functionality of Enterprise Manager, Query Analyzer, and the administration part of Analysis Manager.

- **Business Intelligence Development Studio**—This is a new integrated graphical tool to design and develop business intelligence applications using SQL Server Integration Services (SSIS; formerly DTS), Analysis Service, and Reporting Services.

- **SQL Server Configuration Manager**—This is a graphical tool that consolidates Client and Server Network Utilities and Service Manager into a single interface.

With SQL Server 2000, you can find developers and administrators running SQL Profiler to find out about what Enterprise Manager is doing behind the scenes to perform a particular function. The "no secrets" design guideline for SQL Server 2005 tools development was devised to fix this. The scriptable dialogs in Management Studio and the new management objects APIs (SMO, RMO, and AMO) are examples of this. Every management dialog in SQL Server Management Studio provides a Script toolbar button that can be used to generate a script for the task performed by that dialog. Everything that you can do using graphical tools can be automated by using new .NET-based management object libraries such as SQL Management Objects (SMO), Replication Management Objects (RMO), and Analysis Management Objects (AMO).

The SQL Server 2005 tools and utilities can be grouped into four categories:

- **Management and authoring**—This category includes SQL Server Management Studio, Business Intelligence Development Studio, and Express Manager.

- **Performance monitoring, tuning, and optimization**—This category includes Profiler, Database Engine Tuning Advisor, and several new performance monitor counters.

- **Operations and configuration**—This category includes the new SQLCMD command-prompt tool, SQL Server Configuration Manager, Database Mail, SQL Agent and maintenance wizard enhancements, other command-prompt utilities and enhancements (such as XML format file for `bcp.exe`), and the Microsoft Operations Manager (MOM) management pack for SQL Server 2005.

- **Management application development APIs**—This category includes the enhanced WMI support and the new managed object libraries, such as SMO, RMO, and AMO.

Table 5.1 maps SQL Server 2000 tools to their equivalents in SQL Server 2005.

TABLE 5.1   SQL Server 2000 Tools and Their SQL Server 2005 Equivalents

SQL Server 2000 Tool	SQL Server 2005 Tool
Enterprise Manager	SQL Server Management Studio
Query Analyzer	Query Editor in SQL Server Management Studio
Index Tuning Wizard	Database Engine Tuning Advisor
Service Manager	SQL Server Configuration Manager
Server Network Utility	SQL Server Configuration Manager
Client Network Utility	SQL Server Configuration Manager
DTS Designer in Enterprise Manager	SSIS in Business Intelligence Development Studio
Analysis Manager	Administer using SQL Server Management Studio and design/develop using Analysis Server Project in Business Intelligence Development Studio
MDX Sample Application	Query Editor in SQL Server Management Studio
Reporting Services Report authoring using Visual Studio .NET	Report Project in Business Intelligence Development Studio or Report Builder
Command-line tools to manage Notification Services applications	Notification Services folder in the Object Explorer tree in SQL Server Management Studio

Management and Authoring

The management aspect of SQL Server 2005 administration refers to tasks such as creating new databases and database objects, performing backups and restores; managing logins, users, and other security settings; scheduling jobs and reviewing job history; importing and exporting data; and processing Analysis Services objects such as cubes and dimensions. Authoring, on the other hand, refers to the ability to write and execute queries and scripts, design new SSIS packages, design and create new Analysis Services objects such as cubes and dimensions, and create new reports. SQL Server Management Studio and Business Intelligence Development Studio are the two tools that provide the management and authoring capabilities in SQL Server 2005. SQL Server 2005 Express Edition includes Express Manager, which can be considered a highly trimmed-down version of Management Studio for managing and authoring relational database objects.

SQL Server Management Studio

SQL Server Management Studio can be used to manage SQL Server versions 7, 2000, and 2005, Analysis Services version 2005, Report Servers 2005, SQL Server 2005 Mobile Edition (formerly SQL CE) databases, and SSIS (formerly DTS) servers. Management Studio also extends the management capabilities to support other SQL Server subsystems, such as notification services, Service Broker, and Database Mail.

The following are some of the features of Management Studio:

- You no longer have to use different tools to manage SQL Server and Analysis Services, author and test queries, and manage reports. A single integrated application provides a consistent interface to manage servers and create queries across all SQL Server components.

- All the management dialog boxes in Management Studio are non-modal, resizable, scriptable, and schedulable. Each such dialog includes the link View Connection Properties that can be used to see the server (operating system and hardware), instance (SQL Server version, language, and collation), connection, and authentication details. If you launch a dialog or wizard in Management Studio, because the dialogs are non-modal, you can still go back and do other things in Management Studio, unlike in Enterprise Manager, where dialogs are modal and you have to either close a dialog or launch a new Enterprise Manager instance. Another nice improvement to these dialogs is a progress indicator. If a dialog is performing some lengthy operation, it shows a progress indicator along with the percentage complete.

- Because Management Studio uses SMO, it leverages all the new enhancements made in the API. This includes the cached object model, optimized instantiation, capture mode, and unique resource name (URN) reference. These features are discussed later in this chapter. Because of these SMO enhancements, Management Studio offers better user interface response and performance, facilitates doing multiple, non-blocking actions, and includes advanced scripting support. Management Studio was designed from the ground up to better support a large number of servers, databases, database objects, and records.

- Much like Visual Studio .NET, Management Studio also offers the capability to work with solutions and projects, and it offers complete SourceSafe integration. The first time you launch Management Studio, the interface might look like Visual Studio .NET to you. But note that you do not need to learn, license, or install Visual Studio .NET in order to use Management Studio. A SQL Server Management Studio *solution* is a collection of one or more SQL Server Management Studio projects. A SQL Server Management Studio *project* is a set of connection definitions and queries that provide a convenient way to organize related queries and connection information.

- With SQL Server 2000 Query Analyzer, you cannot edit queries unless you connect to a server. The Query Editor does not show up unless a connection is made to the server. The Query Editor inside Management Studio introduces a new feature called *disconnected editing* that lets you write and edit queries without connecting to any server. If you try to run a query, however, you are prompted to connect to the server.

- With SQL Server 2000, if you needed help on any Transact-SQL (T-SQL) construct, you had to switch back and forth between Query Analyzer and Books Online. The Dynamic Help feature introduced in SQL Server 2005 displays the context-sensitive help topics as you type T-SQL in the Query Editor. Management Studio provides the option to show the help inside it when you select a help topic from the dynamic help window. This way, you don't have to leave the Query Editor to get help on a topic.

- The new tabbed interface for queries and the ability to split the current query window to see different parts of the same query file improve the usability experience. Management Studio includes several other usability enhancements. For example, a disabled trigger shows up with a different icon than an enabled trigger in Object Explorer; the XML column value shows up as a hyperlink that you can click in order to view formatted XML in a new tab window; and word wrap and line numbering functionality are provided in Query Editor.

- The new Template Explorer window in Management Studio provides hundreds of built-in T-SQL, Multidimensional Expressions (MDX), Data Mining Prediction (DMX), and XML for Analysis (XMLA) templates for SQL Server, Analysis Services, and SQL Mobile. You can also create your own folders and templates to standardize the query authoring throughout your development team or organization. You can press Ctrl+Alt+T or select View | Template Explorer to view the Template Explorer window. As in the Registered Servers window, the toolbar buttons on the top of the Template Explorer window allow switching the context between SQL Server, Analysis Server, and SQL Mobile. The right-click menu in Template Explorer provides options for creating a new folder, creating a template, or searching.

- In case of any error, the error or informational dialog box now displays much more and more detailed information, and it allows you to easily copy the information to the clipboard or email the error details.

- The Profiler integration with Management Studio allows you to capture deadlock graphs and XML showplans in Profiler and then view and analyze them inside Management Studio.

- Activity Monitor and Log File Viewer now support filtering. The Activity Monitor also support automatic refresh.

- Management Studio supports running queries in SQLCMD mode to enable scripting support.

Figure 5.1 shows Management Studio in action. The Registered Servers window shows a SQL Server 2005 instance and a SQL Server 2000 instance; the Object Explorer window shows a connection to an instance of SQL Server 2005, Analysis Services 2005, SQL Mobile Database, SSIS Server, and a SQL Server 2000 instance; the Properties window shows the current query window options; typing the T-SQL word BEGIN in the Query Editor brings up the related help topics in the Dynamic Help Window; Template Explorer shows the SQL Server templates and a list of recently used templates; finally, the Solution Explorer window shows a project open.

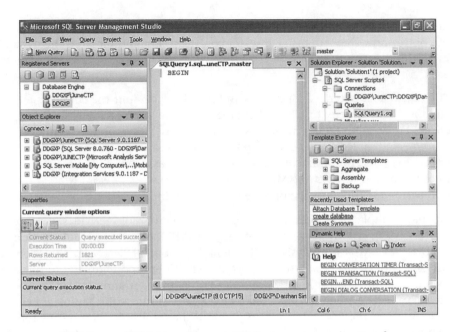

FIGURE 5.1   SQL Server 2005 Management Studio is a new application for managing servers and authoring queries.

The SQL Server Management Studio windows are discussed in detail in the following sections.

Registered Servers

The Registered Servers window allows you to register SQL Server, Analysis Server, Report Server, SQL Mobile Database, and SSIS Server. For each type of server, it lets you create a new server group; add, edit, and remove server registration; and connect Object Explorer or Query Editor to the selected registered server. The icon next to each server indicates whether the server is running. You can export the server registration details into an XML file and import it onto another server by using the Registered Servers window (by right-clicking in the window and selecting either Import or Export). You can double-click a registered server to connect and view the selected server in the Object Explorer window.

Object Explorer

A hierarchical tree view allows you to interact with the objects on the server. For SQL Server, the tree looks similar to the one shown by SQL Server 2000 Enterprise Manager; it contains databases, tables, views, replication, security, and so on. For Analysis Server, the tree looks similar to one shown in Analysis Manager; it contains data sources, cubes, dimensions, and so on. For Report Server, Object Explorer provides options similar to the Report Manager web interface. This includes managing reports and report folders, security, schedules, and jobs. For Mobile Database, Object Explorer allows you to manage tables, views, and Merge Replication subscriptions. For SSIS Server, Object Explorer can be used to view the status of running packages and enables you to work with packages stored in the file system and the msdb system database.

Unlike Enterprise Manager, Object Explorer is designed to handle and work well with a large number of servers, databases, and database objects. When you expand a tree node or folder, Object Explorer asynchronously retrieves only the information required for that node and not for child nodes. Object Explorer allows you to filter the nodes based on various parameters, such as name, creation date, and schema. The Object Explorer tree is limited to 65,536 objects. If you have more than 65,536 objects, Object Explorer does not list them, and the only way to see those objects is to use filtering.

The Connect button on the Object Explorer toolbar allows you to connect to a server that is not registered. After you connect to the server, you can right-click it and select Register to add that server to the Registered Servers list.

For SQL Server, Object Explorer groups system databases in one folder, group database snapshots under another folder, and lists all other user databases in the tree. Unlike Enterprise Manager, which lists the objects on the right side in a grid view, Management Studio shows all the tables, views, and other database objects as tree nodes. If you need to script more than one object, you can right-click a database and select Tasks | Generate Scripts. This brings up the Generate SQL Server Scripts Wizard, in which you can select a database and database objects that you want to script. Pressing the F7 key or by selecting View | Summary brings up a read-only report on the right side for the currently selected item in Object Explorer. Depending on the item selected in the Object Explorer tree, the Summary tab may provide more than one reports. The Report toolbar button on the top of the Summary tab can be used to navigate between multiple reports.

TIP

Object Explorer does not allow you to select multiple items. The multi-select support is provided via the Summary page. On Summary page, you can select multiple tables, views, columns, users, schemas, and other objects, and then you can right-click and select Delete to remove the selected objects.

The stored procedures, database-level DDL triggers, functions, .NET assemblies, types, rules, and defaults are grouped under the Programmability node. The full-text catalog and partitioning schemes and functions are shown under the Storage node. The database users, roles, schemas, and symmetric keys are under the Security node.

TIP

To hide or show system objects in Object Explorer, select Tools | Options and check or clear the Hide System Objects in Object Explorer check box after you select Environment | General.

In addition to databases, these are the other nodes in the Object Explorer tree:

- **Security**—This node allows you to manage logins, server roles, and credentials.

- **Server Objects**—This node allows you to manage backup devices, linked servers, and server-level DDL triggers.

- **Notification Services**—This node allows you to manage notification services applications.

- **Replication**—This node allows you to configure and manage publications and subscriptions. Unlike Enterprise Manager, which shows the Replication Monitor as part of the tree, Management Studio launches a separate application (`sqlmonitor.exe`) when you right-click the Replication or Local Publications node and select Launch Replication Monitor.

- **Management**—This folder allows you to configure and view SQL Server error logs, create and manage maintenance plans, monitor server activity, and configure SMTP-based Database Mail. The Legacy folder under the Management node allows you to configure MAPI-based SQL Mail, open and migrate SQL Server 2000 DTS packages, and view the database maintenance plans history.

- **SQL Server Agent**—This node allows you to manage Agent jobs, alerts, operators, and proxies, and it lets you view Agent error logs.

The Filter icon on the Object Explorer toolbar is enabled when you select nodes such as Tables, Views, or Stored Procedures. Figure 5.2 show the Object Explorer and Summary windows inside Management Studio. Note that system objects are hidden in Object Explorer, the tables list is filtered, and that you can select multiple objects on the Summary tab.

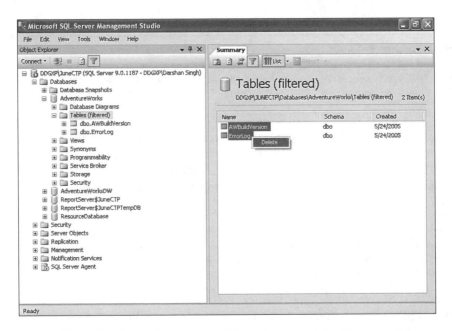

FIGURE 5.2   Object Explorer allows you to filer objects, and the Summary tab supports multi-selection.

The Query Editor

SQL Server Management Studio includes a rich Query Editor that can be used to author and edit T-SQL, MDX, DMX, XMLA, and SQL Server Mobile Edition queries. Much like Query Analyzer, the Query Editor window in Management Studio provides syntax coloring; can output results to a grid, text, or file; and can display estimated or actual execution plan and client statistics.

TIP

You can split the Query Editor window into two parts by using the splitter control above the scrollbar. This can be useful when you want to simultaneously view different parts of the same file.

The Options dialog box provides various settings that you can change to tune the Query Editor environment. You can view query, results, messages, and other windows as tabbed or MDI child windows; view line numbers and enable word wrapping; set query execution options such as various SET options; set query result options such as maximum number of characters displayed in a grid cell or a text column; switch between SQL Server 2005 and SQL Server 2000 keyboard schemes; and so on.

TIP

You can press Shift+Alt+Enter or select View | Full Screen to view Query Editor in full-screen mode and maximize the query editing area. You press Alt+U or Shift+Alt+Enter again to switch back to normal mode.

You can select the File | New (or press Ctrl+N) to start a new query window, or you can right-click the server in Registered Servers select Connect | New Query to launch a new query window. Selecting File | New | Project (or pressing Ctrl+Shift+N) allows you to create a new project and a new solution or add a new project to an existing solution. The three project types available include SQL Server Scripts, Analysis Server Script, and SQL Mobile Scripts. After you create a new project, you can use the Solution Explorer window to define new connections and create new queries.

You might have noticed that if any Microsoft Office product, such as Word or Excel, shuts down abnormally, the next time you launch the application, you are prompted to recover the document you were working on. The SQL Server Management Studio supports a similar feature. Let's say you were working on a bunch of script files and did not save all the changes you made. Now, if somehow the Management Studio tool shuts down unexpectedly, the next time you launch Management Studio, it will allow you to recover the script files that you were working on, preserving the changes you made in the last session.

TIP

Management Studio contains a built-in web browser. You can launch the web browser by pressing Ctrl+Alt+R or by selecting View | Web Browser | Show Browser. Try typing a Web address (such as http://www.microsoft.com) in the Query Editor window, and you should notice that the editor turns the text into a hyperlink. You can press Ctrl+click the URL to launch the web page in a web browser inside Management Studio. The General page after you select Tools | Options | Text Editor | All Languages or Plain Text or XML provides an option to enable or disable this single-click URL navigation feature.

Table 5.2 lists few useful keyboard shortcuts that you can use while working in Query Editor.

TABLE 5.2   Query Editor Keyboard Shortcuts

Shortcut	Action
Ctrl+N	Opens a new query window with the current connection.
Ctrl+I	Performs an incremental search. This is a very useful feature. Press Ctrl+I and begin typing; press Esc or arrow keys to cancel searching.
Ctrl+U	Sets the focus on the available databases combo box. You can then press the up and down arrow keys or the first few letters of the database you want to make your current database.
Shift+Alt+Enter	Switches between full-screen and normal window mode.
Ctrl+Shift+U	Converts selected text to uppercase.
Ctrl+Shift+L	Converts selected text to lowercase.
Ctrl+K followed by Ctrl+C	Comments the selected text block. Uses -- (two dashes) for T-SQL, // (two forward slashes) for MDX and DMX, and <!-- & --> for XMLA and XML.
Ctrl+K followed by Ctrl+U	Uncomments the selected text block.
Ctrl+K followed by Ctrl+K	Sets or clears the bookmark. Bookmarks are useful when you want to remember certain lines in a large script file and go back to those lines quickly.
Ctrl+K followed by Ctrl+N	Views the next bookmark line.
Ctrl+K followed by Ctrl+P	Views the previous bookmark location.
Ctrl+K followed by Ctrl+L	Removes all bookmarks.
Ctrl+K followed by Ctrl+W	Views the bookmarks window.
Ctrl+D or Ctrl+T	Sends the results to a grid or text.
F5 or Ctrl+E or Alt+X	Executes the selected query or the entire text in the query window if nothing is selected.
Ctrl+F5	Parses the query.
Ctrl+R	Hides or shows the results window.

Microsoft has removed some of the functionality from Management Studio Query Editor that is available in Query Analyzer. For example, you can play a .wav sound file when the query finishes executing in Query Analyzer. The Results tab of the Options dialog in SQL Server 2000 Query Analyzer provides an option to play a Windows message beep or a .wav file when a query finishes. No such feature is available in Management Studio.

The other windows in Management Studio include Template Explorer, which can be used to access commonly used T-SQL, MDX, DMX, XMLA, and Mobile queries; Solution Explorer, which lets you manage multiple scripts and connections as a SourceSafe integrated project; the Properties window, which shows the context-specific metadata; and Help windows, which include dynamic help, an index, and the contents.

The General tab of the Options dialog in SQL Server 2000 Query Analyzer provided an option to change the template file location used by the Templates window in Query Analyzer. However, to create a new template folders and template files, you had to go to the file explorer and create folders and files there, and then you had to press F5 or right-click and select the Refresh menu item in the Templates window for the new folders/files to appear in the tree. In other words, the Templates window did not provide any option to add or remove template files and folders. With SQL Server 2005, the template folder for the Template Explorer window is fixed to %ProgramFiles%\Microsoft SQL Server\90\Tools\Binn\VSShell\Common7\IDE\sqlworkbenchnewitems, and Template Explorer right-click menu options are provided for creating and removing template folders and files.

Common Administration Tasks

The goal of the following sections is to show you how to perform some common administration tasks by using SQL Server Management Studio. First, you need to start SQL Server Management Studio and try out the following to see how to get things done using Management Studio.

Registering a Server   Following are the steps to register a SQL Server instance:

1. Press Ctrl+Alt+G or select View | Registered Servers to bring up the Registered Servers window, if it is not already visible.

2. Make sure that the Registered Servers window is showing servers of type Database Engine. If it is not, click the first toolbar button on the Registered Servers window or select View | Registered Server Types | Database Engine.

3. Right-click the Microsoft SQL Servers node in the tree. Select New | Server Group if you would like to create a new group; otherwise, select New | Server Registration to register a server.

4. On the New Server Registration dialog box that appears, type the server name, including the instance name, or select a server from the combo box and provide the authentication details. Use the Connection Properties tab to set other connection properties, such as the default database, the client network protocol to use, the network packet size, the connection and execution timeout values (in seconds), and whether the connection should be encrypted. Click the Test button to verify the connection and click Save when you're done.

Viewing and Changing Server Properties   Following are the steps for viewing or changing SQL Server instance properties:

1. Right-click the SQL Server instance in the Registered Servers window and select Connect | Object Explorer or simply double-click a registered server to connect to an instance in the Object Explorer window.

2. Right-click the server in Object Explorer and select Properties.

3. Note the changes in this dialog compared to the Server Properties dialog in Enterprise Manager. This dialog is non-modal (that is, you can go back to Management Studio without closing the dialog), is resizable, allows you to schedule or script the changes you make instead of applying them immediately, and contains a progress indicator to show status if applying the change takes a long time. Some other changes on this dialog include the new Permissions page, which allows you to manage the new server-level security settings, such as allowing or denying the ability to create/alter endpoints; and the new Advanced page, which can be used to view and set various `sp_configure` settings.

Similarly, you can right-click the SQL Server Agent folder in Object Explorer and select Properties to view and set agent properties such as job history, log size limit, SQL Server event forwarding, and so on.

Creating a New Database   Following are the steps for creating a new SQL Server database:

1. Connect to a SQL Server instance in Object Explorer mode.

2. Right-click Databases and select the New Database menu item.

3. Use the General tab to specify the database name, owner, collation, and recovery model; add or remove database files; and set file properties such as autogrowth, file size, and filegroup.

4. Use the Filegroups page to create or remove filegroups and to set the default filegroup.

5. Use the Options page to view and set various database options such as Auto Create Statistics and Auto Update Statistics.

6. Click OK to create the database immediately, Schedule to create a job that will create the database later on, at a scheduled time, or Script to generate the script to create the database. If you schedule or script the task, you can click the Cancel button on the New Database dialog to avoid action being performed immediately.

Backing Up or Restoring a Database   Following are the steps for backing up an existing database:

1. Connect to a SQL Server instance in Object Explorer mode.

2. Expand the Databases folder in the Object Explorer tree, right-click the database you would like to back up and select Tasks | Back Up. The Backup Database dialog appears.

3. The Backup Database dialog in Management Studio is very similar to one in the Enterprise Manager, except it now shows the database recovery model and provides option to perform a checksum before writing to the media in order to produce reliable backups. Depending on the recovery model of the database, you can perform full or differential database or backups of files/filegroups or the transaction log. Select the backup type, give a name to the backup set, select the backup destination, and set the various media, reliability, and transaction log settings on the Options page and click OK to immediately perform the backup operation, click Schedule to create a job, or click Script to generate a script to perform the backup.

Similarly, to restore a database or transaction log, you follow these steps:

1. Right-click a particular database and select Tasks | Restore or right-click the Databases node and select Restore Database.

2. In the Restore Database dialog that appears, select to restore replication settings or to restore to a particular point in time.

The right-click Tasks menu on any user database allows other operations as well, including attaching, detaching, copying a database, shrinking, importing/exporting data, and generating scripts.

Managing Indexes, Triggers, and Constraints on a Table   Under each database, Object Explorer shows folders such as Database Diagrams, Tables, Views, Synonyms, Programmability, Service Broker, Storage, and Security. All the user tables are shown under the Tables folder. If you expand a table node, you see folders such as Columns, Keys, Constraints, Triggers, Indexes, and Statistics. You can expand each such folder to see existing objects and right-click a folder to create a new item of the selected type. For example, you can right-click Triggers and select the New Trigger menu item to launch Query Editor window to create a new trigger. Let's create a table, and then create an index and a constraint on this new table:

1. With the Object Explorer window open and while you are connected to a SQL Server 2005 instance, expand a database folder node, right-click Tables, and select the New Table menu item.

2. The Table Designer appears as a tabbed window inside Management Studio. Specify the first column name as RecordID and the data type as int, uncheck Allow Nulls, and turn on the Identity property for this column, using the Column Properties tab. Right-click this column row and select the Set Primary Key menu item. Add two more columns, named PostType and MemberID, of data type int, and uncheck the Allow Nulls check box. Add two more columns, PostTitle (as nvarchar(100)) and PostText (as ntext).

3. Press Ctrl+S or select File | Save and name the table `tblPosts`. The Table Designer toolbar (which you open by selecting View | Toolbars | Table Designer) provides various buttons for managing relationships, indexes and keys, check constraints, and full-text indexes. Try them out if you like.

4. The `tblPosts` table should now appear in Object Explorer under the `Tables` node. If it does not, refresh the tree.

5. Next, create a nonclustered index and include one non-key column in this index. To do this, expand the `tblPosts` table, right-click Indexes, and select the New Index menu item. Type the index name as `ncIdxMember`; leave the type as Nonclustered, click the Add button for the Index Key Columns group, and add the MemberID column. The Options page on the New Index dialog lets you enable or disable the index, set the fill factor, control the locking mechanism, and select an index as online or offline. Click the Include Columns page and add the PostTitle column. The Storage page lets you choose the filegroup on which the index should be created. Click OK to immediately create the index. This new index should appear under the Indexes folder.

6. Double-click the `ncIdxMember` index or right-click and select Properties and note that the index properties dialog now includes a new page called Fragmentation that shows details similar to the results returned by running `DBCC SHOWCONTIG` or accessing the `sys.dm_db_index_physical_stats` dynamic management function. As a matter of fact, when this page is accessed, Management Studio runs a query against the `sys.dm_db_index_physical_stats` dynamic management function to obtain the index fragmentation details.

7. Next, create a new constraint that `PostType` must have a value between 1 and 5. Right-click Constraints and select New Constraint. The Table Designer and Check Constraints windows appear. On the Check Constraints dialog, type the constraint name as `chkPostType`, type the expression as `[PostType] > 0 AND [PostType] < 6`, and click Close. Press Ctrl+S or select File | Save tblPosts and close the Table Designer.

8. Refresh the Constraints node in Object Explorer, and you should see `chkPostType` there. If you need to modify or view this constraint, you can right-click it and select the Modify menu item.

9. Start the Query Editor, select the database in which you created the `tblPosts` table, and run the following queries:

```
INSERT INTO tblPosts VALUES (1, 1, N'Test 1', N'Test 1');
GO
INSERT INTO tblPosts VALUES (0, 1, N'Test 2', N'Test 2');
GO
INSERT INTO tblPosts VALUES (6, 1, N'Test 3', N'Test 3');
GO
SELECT * FROM tblPosts;
GO
```

The first INSERT should succeed, and the next two INSERT statements should fail because they violate the chkPostType check constraint.

Viewing SQL Server and Agent Error Logs   The Log File Viewer in SQL Server Management Studio has been enhanced to consistently show SQL Server and Agent log files, as well as Windows event logs. A single screen allows you to view zero or more SQL Server log files, zero or more Agent log files, and all the Windows event log sources. It also allows filtering, searching, exporting, and loading of log files. You can rearrange the columns shown, but the first column, the Date column, is fixed, and if you scroll to the right, the Date column does not scroll, so you can continue to see the date while viewing the other columns on the right side.

Figure 5.3 shows the Log File Viewer screen with the current SQL Server log, current Agent log, and System Windows NT event log source selected, and the log rows are filtered for text containing the word SQL. Different icons in front of the Date column value and the Source column indicate the type and source of the log file row.

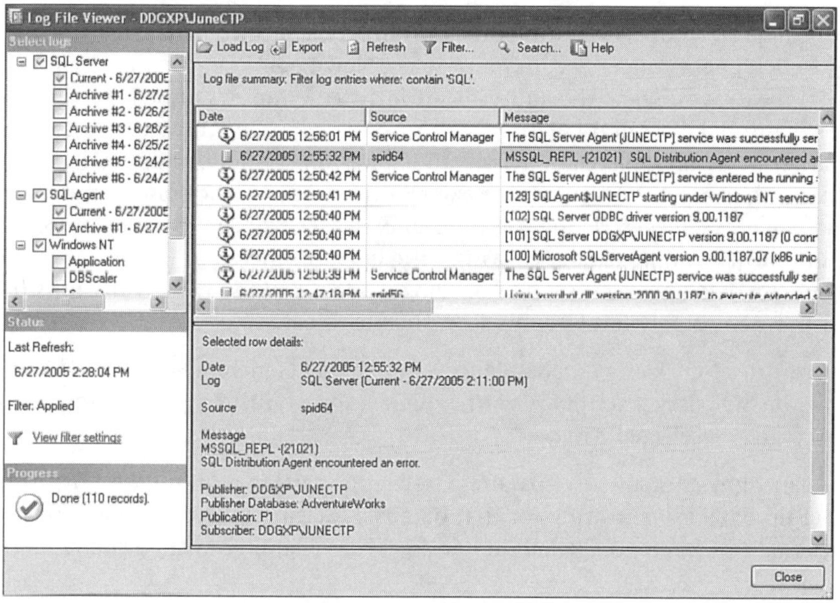

FIGURE 5.3   The Log File Viewer in SQL Server Management Studio shows SQL Server and Agent log files and Windows NT event log data, on a single screen.

You can use the SQL Server Logs folder under the Management folder, or the Error Logs folder under the SQL Server Agent node in Object Explorer to launch the Log File Viewer. Once the Log File Viewer window is open, using it to view, filter data, and so on is very intuitive. The blue filter icon on the toolbar means no filter has been applied, and the green filter icon means rows are filtered based on the provided conditions.

By default, SQL Server keeps the last six log files. You can change this number by right-clicking SQL Server Logs and selecting Configure. Similarly, you can right-click Error Logs under SQL Server Agent and select Configure to set Agent log properties such as the error log file location and the kind of information to log.

Some Miscellaneous Administration Tasks   Before concluding this section, let's look at some other things that you can do by using Object Explorer in Management Studio:

- To view the current server activity that includes processes and locks information, you can expand the Management folder and double-click the Activity Monitor node. The Activity Monitor shows the active processes. You can right-click a process and select Details to view the DBCC INPUTBUFFER value for that process or to kill that process. The two other views shown by the Activity Monitor dialog are Locks by Process and Locks by Object. The top-level combo box allows you to select a process or an object, and the grid shows all the locks acquired by that process or on that object, respectively. By default, Activity Monitor filters system processes. You can click the Filter toolbar button to set Show System Processes to True to view all processes.

- To create a new login account, you can right-click Security and select New | Login or right-click Logins under Security and select New Login. On the new login dialog that appears, you select the authentication type (Windows or SQL Server) and select the default database and language. If it's a SQL Server login, you need to determine whether password policy and password expiration should be applied to this login. You use the Server Roles page to make this new login part of one or more server roles, such as dbcreator. You use the Database Access page to create a user for this login in one or more databases, assign the default schema in that database, and assign the database roles, such as db_datareader. You use the Permissions page to grant or deny server-level permissions such as Create Endpoint.

- You can right-click any database and select Tasks | Generate Scripts to launch the Generate SQL Server Scripts Wizard, which walks you through scripting one or more objects in the selected database.

- You can right-click any user database, select Properties, and use the Mirroring page to set up database mirroring for that database. Setting up database mirroring is discussed in Chapter 8, "Reliability and High Availability in the Database Engine."

Business Intelligence Development Studio

As mentioned in Chapter 4, "A Tour of New Features in SQL Server 2005," Microsoft's strategy for business intelligence in SQL Server 2005 is to integrate, analyze, and report. The Business Intelligence (BI) Development Studio is a new integrated application that supports this strategy. The BI Development Studio tool can be used to build and deploy end-to-end business intelligence solutions.

Like SQL Server Management Studio, BI Development Studio also borrows the Visual Studio .NET shell and supports working with SourceSafe integrated solutions and projects.

BI Development Studio allows you to create SSIS projects, SQL Server Analysis Services 2005 (SSAS) projects, and SQL Server 2005 Reporting Services (SSRS) projects. You can create a BI Development Studio solution containing a mix of projects of type SSIS, SSAS, and SSRS and then deploy the entire business intelligence solution to a test or a production environment. Figure 5.4 shows the BI Development Studio environment with an open solution containing an SSIS project, an SSAS project, and an SSRS project.

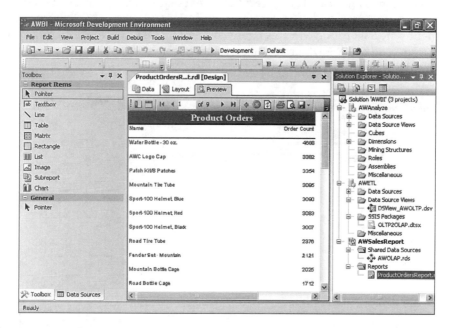

FIGURE 5.4   BI Development Studio supports designing, developing, and deploying end-to-end business intelligence solutions.

Integration Using SSIS

As mentioned previously, in SQL Server 2005, the DTS platform has been renamed SSIS. It is a new platform that lets you bring data from various sources such as file systems, databases, XML files, and web services; transform and integrate the data; and send the data to various types of destinations, such as file systems, databases, mobile devices, analysis and reporting servers, and so on.

You can author SSIS packages by creating an Integration Services Project in BI Development Studio. The SSIS package designer inside BI Development Studio provides an enhanced interface that simplifies the authoring and debugging of the SSIS packages. The packages created using the SSIS designer are saved as XML files with the .dtsx file extension. You can right-click a package and select View Code to see the XML for an SSIS package definition.

The SSIS designer now separates control flow, which includes process-oriented and discrete tasks, from data flow, which includes data-oriented tasks. Examples of control flow tasks include For and Foreach Loop Container tasks, the File System task, the

Send Mail task, the Execute SQL task, and so on. You can either convert your DTS 2000 packages by building new SSIS packages from scratch and making use of the new SSIS features, or you can use the Execute DTS 2000 Package Task control flow task and execute a SQL Server 2000 DTS package from within an SSIS package. The data flow tasks are categorized in three groups: source, transformation, and destination. Examples of data flow tasks include Flat File Source, XML Source, OLE DB Source, Fuzzy Grouping, Lookup Transform, Sort Transform, Flat File Destination, SQL Server Mobile Destination, DataReader Destination, and so on. Figure 5.5 shows the new SSIS designer environment. The SSIS package in this figure contains an OLE DB source, a data conversion transform, and an OLE DB destination. The data conversion error rows are directed to a flat-file destination.

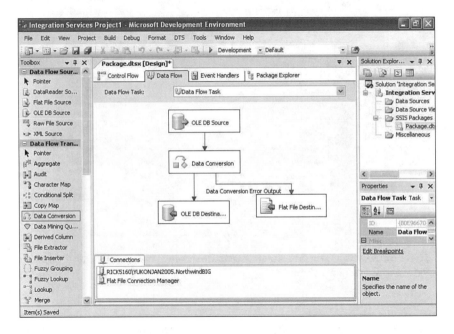

FIGURE 5.5   The new SSIS package designer inside BI Development Studio separates control flow from data flow, provides several built-in task controls, and allows you to send erroneous rows to a different route.

SSIS provides a very robust debugging environment. You can set breakpoints at various steps in the extraction, transformation, and loading (ETL) process and view data as it is flowing through the steps. SSIS also offers you the flexibility to route erroneous rows to one path and all other rows to another path. The SSIS designer in BI Development Studio includes several built-in control and data flow tasks that you can use in your SSIS package. If you don't find a task control that suits your need, you can use the SSIS.NET-based extensibility programming model to build custom control and data flow task controls. The enhanced configuration and logging support in SSIS facilitates building and troubleshooting complex SSIS packages. See Chapter 12, "SQL Server Integration Services Overview," for more details on SSIS.

Analysis Using Analysis Services 2005

The things that business intelligence information workers used to do in Analysis Manager with SQL Server 2000 are now available inside BI Development Studio, with several usability and user experience enhancements. After you create a new Analysis Service project, you can use various wizards and templates provided by BI Development Studio to create the rest of the Analysis Services objects, such as data sources, data source views, cubes, dimensions, mining models, and so on, to be deployed in a single Analysis Services database. You can either create a new solution for the project or add the project to an existing solution. Figure 5.6 shows an Analysis Services project open inside BI Development Studio.

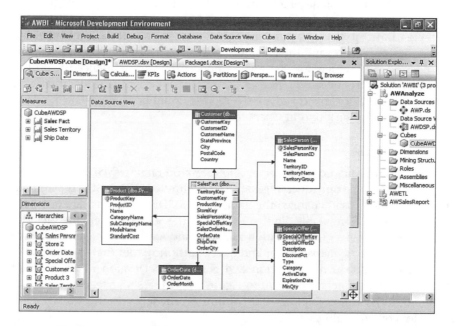

FIGURE 5.6 The SQL Server 2000 Analysis Manager functionality is now available inside BI Development Studio, with several user interface and usability enhancements, as well as support for new Analysis Services 2005 features.

As shown in Figure 5.6, the Analysis Services project contains items such as data sources, data source views, cubes, dimensions, and so on. You can right-click Data Source and select New Data Source to launch the Data Source Wizard; similarly, you can right-click Cubes and select New Cube to launch the Cube Wizard. Analysis Services is discussed in further detail in Chapter 13, "What's New in SQL Server Analysis Services 2005."

Building Reports Using Reporting Services

The final major component of BI Development Studio is the ability to author and edit reports. Prior to this, you had to use Visual Studio .NET to author the Reporting Services reports. Now, because reporting is an integral part of the business intelligence development life cycle, it is integrated into BI Development Studio. You can add reports to your business intelligence solution by creating a new report project, and you can either add it to the current solution or create a new solution for the project.

When you select a project of type Report Project, BI Development Studio presents an empty environment. You start by defining data sources, and then you create new reports, update the project properties to specify the deployment report server, and so on. BI Development Studio also contains another project type, called Report Project Wizard, that walks you through defining a data source, creating a report, and specifying the deployment server information. When you finish that wizard, you have a report ready for preview and deployment.

The report designer in BI Management Studio is very similar to the Visual Studio .NET report designer. It has a Toolbox window from which you can drag and drop items onto the designer, a Data tab that lets you define the source for report data, a Layout tab that is the primary design surface, and the Preview tab that lets you view your report in action. (Refer to Figure 5.4 to see a report in preview mode.) You can right-click the project node in the Solution Explorer tree and select Properties; then, under the General tab you can set the `TargetServerURL` property where the report should be deployed. More details on Reporting Services can be found in Chapter 13.

Express Manager

As you might know, Microsoft SQL Server 2000 Desktop Engine (MSDE) does not include any graphical tools. The only querying tool that is bundled with MSDE is `osql.exe`. With SQL Server 2005, Microsoft changed the name from MSDE to SQL Server 2005 Express Edition. This free, redistributable, limited edition of the SQL Server engine includes two graphical tools: SQL Server Configuration Manager and Express Manager. Express Manager is a lightweight database management and query authoring tool that can be used to manage SQL Server 2005 Express Edition, SQL Server 2005 Developer Edition, and SQL Server 2000 MSDE instances. As shown in Figure 5.7, Express Manager shows a Management Studio Object Explorer–like window on the left side and a T-SQL Query Editor window on the right side.

The Express Manager application limits you to connecting to only one SQL Server instance at a time. However, you can have multiple instances of Express Manager running, and each can connect to a different server.

The Express Manager executable (`xm.exe`) accepts various command-line parameters that you can use to connect to a particular instance and to open one or more files into the editor. For instance, the following command connects to a local SQL Server 2005 Express Edition named instance (`-S` parameter) by using a trusted connection (`-E`), and it opens two script files (`-f`):

```
"C:\Program Files\Microsoft SQL Server 2005 Express Manager\xm.exe "
➥ -S .\SQLEXPRESS -E -f c:\1.sql, c:\2.sql
```

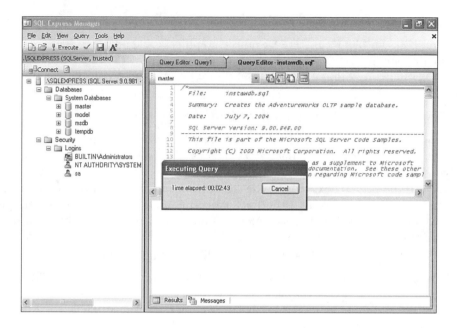

FIGURE 5.7 SQL Server 2005 Express Edition includes graphical tools for managing SQL Server instance and services and for authoring T-SQL queries.

Performance Monitoring, Tuning, and Optimization Tools

SQL Server 2005 provides a number of tools you can use to proactively monitor SQL Server, perform trend analysis, troubleshoot performance issues, and maximize the SQL Server performance.

The SQL Profiler and PerfMon (also known as System Monitor) are still the primary tools for tracing and monitoring the SQL Server performance and system throughout. These two tools have been upgraded to support new SQL Server 2005 features and to provide more useful information to aid in troubleshooting performance issues.

In addition to using Profiler and PerfMon, other performance monitoring techniques include running system stored procedures such as sp_who2, sp_monitor, and sp_lock; running DBCC commands such as DBCC MEMORYSTATUS; accessing dynamic management views (DMVs) and dynamic management functions (DMFs) to view the current state of the SQL Server 2005 system; generating client statistics and execution plans by using Query Editor in SQL Server Management Studio; using Activity Monitor inside Management Studio; implementing DDL triggers and the event notification–based monitoring system; and using command-line tools such as SQLDiag.exe to obtain detailed system information. These techniques are discussed in detail in Chapter 9, "Performance Analysis and Tuning."

SQL Server 2005 Profiler

SQL Server 2005 Profiler (`Profiler90.exe`) is a graphical tool you use to trace T-SQL or MDX queries being submitted to the server. You can use Profiler to find out about slow-performing queries and stored procedures, to trace locking and deadlocking issues, and to audit SQL Server activity.

The following are some of the new features introduced in Profiler:

- **Support for SSAS**—As mentioned earlier, Profiler now allows you to connect to an Analysis Server instance to trace MDX queries being submitted to the server. When you launch Profiler and start a new trace, you can select Analysis Server from the Server Type combo box, provide the credentials, and click Connect. After you click the Connect button, you see the Trace Properties dialog and Analysis Server–specific trace events in the Events Selection tab. You can select the events you want to monitor and other settings, such as the trace name, the trace template, whether to save to a file or table, and so on and click Run to begin tracing.

- **Saving a trace as an XML file**—After capturing a trace, you can select File | Save As | Trace XML File to save the captured trace data as an XML file. You can edit this XML file and then use it later for replay. Having trace data available as XML opens up opportunities for third-party application vendors.

- **XML-based trace definitions**—SQL 2005 Profiler uses XML-based trace definitions to show different events for different types of servers. For instance, if you connect to SQL Server 7, Profiler shows one set of events on the Events Selection tab in the Trace Properties dialog. If you connect to a SQL Server 2000 instance, you see a different set of events that you can capture. Similarly, for SQL Server 2005 and Analysis Services 2005, you see different trace definitions. These trace definition XML files are stored in the `Program Files\Microsoft SQL Server\90\Tools\Profiler\TraceDefinitions` folder. If you are not running the Profiler on the server itself, these XML files are downloaded to the client machine from where you are running the Profiler tool. This ensures that you have up-to-date trace definition events data from which you can select the events to monitor.

- **Capturing of the showplan for queries executed on the server**—The showplan is shown graphically in the Profiler, and you can also save that as XML, which you can later load and analyze in Query Editor in Management Studio to view the showplan graphically without connecting to the server. To use this feature, you select the Showplan XML event under the Performance event class in the Events Selection tab on the Trace Properties dialog. After you select this event, a third tab, named Events Extraction Settings, appears, and in it you can optionally select the file in which the Showplan XML event should be saved. This is discussed in detail in the next section.

- **Performance Monitor integration with Profiler**—This integration allows you to correlate Performance Monitor counter data with the Profiler trace collected at the same time. You select File | Import Performance Data to use this performance counters correlation feature.

- **Enhanced trace replay**—If you have multiple rollover files, Profiler can now automatically play them one after the other continuously and in order. Profiler also provides options to control the replay options, such as the number of reply threads. Look for these options under Tools | Options.

- **Improved Trace Properties dialog**—When you connect to a server instance, Profiler brings up the Trace Properties dialog, which allows you to select events to monitor, columns to show, filters to set, and options for saving a trace to a file or a table. The Trace Properties dialog in SQL Server 2000 Profiler contains four tabs: General, Events, Data Columns, and Filters. It is very cumbersome to move back and forth among the Events, Data, and Columns tabs to select and view the events settings. SQL Server 2005 combines these three tabs under a single screen called Events Selection. This dialog now allows you to use a single screen to select events to monitor and columns to view and to set column filters. In addition, the ability to see only selected events and selected columns is a great usability enhancement. You can click the column header or click the Column Filters button to view or edit the column filter settings. When you click the column header, in addition to the filter settings, you can also specify whether Profiler should exclude rows that do not contain any value for that column. Figure 5.8 shows the new Events Selection tab.

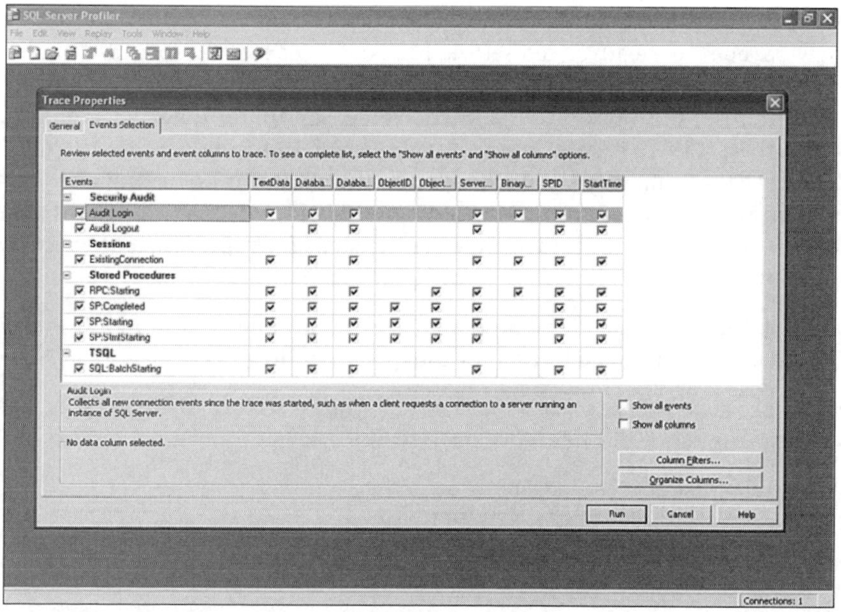

FIGURE 5.8   The new Events Selection tab is a single easy-to-use screen that allows you to select events to monitor and columns to view and to set column filters.

- **New trace events**—Profiler contains several new trace events that either support new features or provide better tracing functionality. For instance, you can use the Broker event class to trace Server Broker activity, the Deprecation events to capture features that are deprecated and might not be available at all in future releases, the Progress Report event class to see the status of tasks such as online index building, OLEDB events to capture events raised by any feature (such as linked servers) that makes use of OLEDB, database mirroring events, several new events for full-text searching under the Performance and Full text event classes, new Server trace events such as Mount Tape, new CLR events such as Assembly Load, and so on.

Let's now look at using some of the new Profiler features. The following section shows three examples: how to detect blocking by using SQL Profiler, how to detect deadlock by using Profiler and viewing the deadlock graph, and how to obtain the query showplan as XML by using Profiler.

NOTE

The Duration column in the Profiler results shows the amount of time taken by the event. Whereas the SQL Server 2000 Profiler outputs this value in milliseconds, the SQL Server 2005 Profiler outputs this value in microseconds.

The Blocked Process Report Profiler Event

SQL Server 2005 introduces a new feature called blocked process report, which is provided via the new `sp_configure` advanced setting `blocked process threshold`. This setting has a default value of `0`, which means the feature is turned off. You can enable advanced options and then set this option to a numeric value, say `10`, to indicate the number of seconds, and then if there is blocking on the server for 10 seconds, SQL Server 2005 will raise an event at that time and every 10 seconds after that until blocking is not resolved. This event can be captured by using the event notification mechanism to run some T-SQL code and also can be seen in Profiler. Here are the steps for capturing a blocked process report event by using Profiler:

1. Start SQL Server Management Studio and open two query windows. Connect to a SQL Server 2005 instance in each of the query windows.

2. Set the `blocked process threshold` `sp_configure` setting to 10 seconds. Execute the following script in one of the query windows:

```
EXEC sp_configure 'show advanced options', 1;
GO
RECONFIGURE WITH OVERRIDE;
GO
EXEC sp_configure 'blocked process threshold', 10;
GO
RECONFIGURE WITH OVERRIDE;
GO
EXEC sp_configure;
/*
--When done with the demo, execute following T-SQL to clean up
```

```
EXEC sp_configure 'blocked process threshold', 0;
GO
RECONFIGURE WITH OVERRIDE;
GO
EXEC sp_configure 'show advanced options', 0;
GO
RECONFIGURE WITH OVERRIDE;
GO
*/
```

3. Verify that the run value for `blocked process threshold` is `10`. Clear the query text and type the following T-SQL into in the first query window:

```
USE [AdventureWorks];
GO


SET TRANSACTION ISOLATION LEVEL READ COMMITTED;
GO


BEGIN TRANSACTION;
GO


UPDATE Production.ProductInventory SET Quantity = Quantity - 1
WHERE ProductID = 1;
GO
-- Execute till above line first
-- And then run query in second connection
-- Finally, To end blocking in other window, execute following code
------------------------------------------------------------


ROLLBACK TRANSACTION;
GO


SELECT @@TRANCOUNT;
GO
```

4. Type the following T-SQL into in the second query window:

```
USE [AdventureWorks];
GO


SET TRANSACTION ISOLATION LEVEL READ COMMITTED;
GO


BEGIN TRANSACTION;
GO
```

```
SELECT SUM(Quantity) FROM Production.ProductInventory
WHERE ProductID = 1;
GO

ROLLBACK TRANSACTION;
GO

SELECT @@TRANCOUNT;
GO
```

Do not run the queries yet. You need to first set up Profiler to capture the blocking event.

5. Start SQL Profiler by running `Profiler90.exe` or by selecting Start | All Programs | Microsoft SQL Server 2005 | Performance Tools | SQL Server Profiler.

6. Click the New Trace toolbar button or select File | New Trace.

7. Connect to a SQL Server 2005 instance.

8. In the Trace Properties dialog box, select Blank from the Use the Template combo box.

9. Click the Events Selection tab, expand the Errors and Warnings event class, and check the Blocked Process Report event. Click Run to start tracing.

10. In the first query window, execute the queries up to the UPDATE statement. Then execute the entire batch in the second query window. Because the first connection updates the data without committing it and the second connection is trying to access the same data in READ COMMITTED isolation mode, the query blocks on the SELECT statement in the second window. Note that the query in the second connection will not be blocked if the READ_COMMITTED_SNAPSHOT database option is turned on. You can turn off the READ_COMMITTED_SNAPSHOT database option by running the ALTER DATABASE statement.

11. Switch to the Profiler window and wait 10 seconds, and you should see the blocked process report event in the Profiler. The event is generated again every 10 seconds.

12. Switch to the first Query Editor window and roll back the transaction in which the UPDATE statement was executed. This should end the blocking in the second query window, the SELECT statement should execute, and even that transaction should be rolled back. You should not see Blocked Process Report events in the Profiler after this.

13. Reset the sp_configure settings by running the commented query block in the `ProfilerSP_Configure.sql` script file. Close the Profiler and Management Studio tools.

Deadlock Graphs

A deadlock occurs when two connections have permanently blocked each other because each connection has a lock on a resource that the other connection is trying to acquire. SQL Server 2000 Profiler contains two events related to deadlocks under the Locks event class: Lock:Deadlock and Lock:Deadlock Chain. The former indicates that the engine has detected a deadlock, and the later results in printing the SPIDs involved in the deadlock. Neither of these events provides any useful information for troubleshooting deadlocks. SQL Server 2005 fixes this by providing detailed deadlock information in the form of XML and also as a graphical picture. Refer to Figure 4.4 in Chapter 4 to see a deadlock graph generated by the Profiler.

Here are the steps for generating a deadlock scenario by simultaneously running two query batches in Query Editor windows and by monitoring the Deadlock Graph event in the Profiler:

1. Start SQL Server Management Studio and open two query windows. Connect to the same SQL Server 2005 instance in both query windows.

2. Type the following script into the first query window:

```
--Connection 1
USE [tempdb];
GO


CREATE SCHEMA Forums;
GO


CREATE TABLE Forums.tblPosts
    (PostID INT IDENTITY(1,1) PRIMARY KEY,
     Title NVARCHAR(256) NOT NULL,
     Question NTEXT NOT NULL DEFAULT '');
GO


INSERT INTO Forums.tblPosts VALUES(N'Post 1', N'Question 1');
INSERT INTO Forums.tblPosts VALUES(N'Post 2', N'Question 2');
GO


DECLARE @RetryCount INT
SET @RetryCount = 5
WHILE (@RetryCount > 0)
BEGIN
    BEGIN TRY
        BEGIN TRANSACTION

        UPDATE Forums.tblPosts SET Title = N'Session 1 Post 1'
            WHERE PostID = 1
```

```
        WAITFOR DELAY '00:00:10'
        UPDATE Forums.tblPosts SET Title = N'Session 1 Post 2'
            WHERE PostID = 2

        SET @RetryCount = -1 --Update successful, break
    END TRY
    BEGIN CATCH
        IF (ERROR_NUMBER() = 1205)
            SET @RetryCount = @RetryCount - 1 --retry
        ELSE --Some other error, break
            SET @RetryCount = -1

        IF (@@TRANCOUNT > 0)
                ROLLBACK TRANSACTION
    END CATCH
END

IF (@@TRANCOUNT > 0)
    COMMIT TRANSACTION


DROP TABLE Forums.tblPosts;
GO
DROP SCHEMA Forums;
GO
```

3. Type the following script into the second query window:

```
--Connection 2
USE [tempdb];
GO

DECLARE @RetryCount INT
SET @RetryCount = 5
WHILE (@RetryCount > 0)
BEGIN
    BEGIN TRY
        BEGIN TRANSACTION

        UPDATE Forums.tblPosts SET Title = N'Session 2 Post 2'
            WHERE PostID = 2
        WAITFOR DELAY '00:00:10'
        UPDATE Forums.tblPosts SET Title = N'Session 2 Post 1'
            WHERE PostID = 1
        SET @RetryCount = -1 --Update successful, break
    END TRY
```

```
BEGIN CATCH
   IF (ERROR_NUMBER() = 1205)
      SET @RetryCount = @RetryCount-1 --retry
   ELSE --Some other error, break
      SET @RetryCount = -1


   IF (@@TRANCOUNT > 0)
         ROLLBACK TRANSACTION
   END CATCH
END


IF (@@TRANCOUNT > 0)
   COMMIT TRANSACTION
```

4. Start SQL Server 2005 Profiler.

5. Click the New Trace toolbar button or select File | New Trace and connect to the same SQL Server 2005 instance as in step 1.

6. On the General tab of the Trace Properties dialog that appears, select Blank from the Use the Template combo box.

7. Click the Events Selection tab. Expand the Locks event class and then check the Deadlock Graph event.

8. Click the Run button on the Trace Properties dialog.

9. Switch back to the Management Studio query windows.

10. Run the entire batch in the first query window and immediately switch to the second query window and run that batch also.

11. Switch back to the Profiler window. Wait about 12 or 15 seconds, and you should see a Deadlock Graph entry in the Profiler window, with a picture shown in the bottom part of that Profiler window and deadlock XML data in the TextData column.

12. The first query window updates the record that has a PostID of 1, and the second query window updates the record that has a PostID of 2. Each waits for 10 seconds and then tries to update the record that is updated by the other query window. Because this all happens within a transaction scope, it creates a deadlock scenario. Close the query windows and Profiler.

XML Showplans
One of the techniques used to troubleshoot query performance issues is to obtain the detailed query execution plan and study it to find about which query components can be optimized. SQL Server 2000 provides SET statements such as SET SHOWPLAN_TEXT and SET SHOWPLAN_ALL that can be used to obtain query execution plan details. When you turn on

these options and then execute the query batch, SQL Server does not actually run the queries, but it returns the execution plan details for the queries.

SQL Server 2005 introduces a new SET SHOWPLAN statement option, SET SHOWPLAN_XML, which can be used to obtain the query execution plan as XML text. Let's try it out:

1. Start a new query window in Management Studio and connect to a SQL Server 2005 instance.

2. Run the SET SHOWPLAN_XML ON statement and then run any query. Instead of executing that query, the Query Editor result window contains execution plan details as XML text.

3. If you are viewing the results in the grid mode, click XML Showplan, and Management Studio launches a new editor window to show the XML results. Save this XML into a text file and give .sqlplan as the file extension.

4. Double-click the .sqlplan file, and the file opens through Management Studio, which shows the execution plan graphically, without even connecting to any server.

This can be very useful in tuning queries.

You can obtain the same XML showplan by using SQL Server 2005 Profiler. The Profiler also shows the execution plan graphically and also allows viewing and saving the showplan as XML. Here are the steps for obtaining an XML showplan by using Profiler and then viewing the execution plan graphically by using Management Studio:

1. Start SQL Server Management Studio; open a query window by connecting to a SQL Server 2005 instance.

2. Type the following script into the query window:

```
USE AdventureWorks;
GO

DECLARE @countRows INT
SET @countRows = 10
SELECT TOP(@countRows) * FROM Production.Product;
GO
```

3. Start SQL Server 2005 Profiler.

4. Click the New Trace toolbar button or select File | New Trace.

5. Connect to a SQL Server 2005 instance.

6. On the General tab of the Trace Properties dialog that appears, select Blank from the Use the Template combo box.

7. Click the Events Selection tab and select Showplan XML under the Performance event class. Check Show Only Selected Events and make sure only one entry is listed.

8. As soon as you click the Showplan XML event, you should see a third tab called Events Extraction Settings on the Trace Properties dialog. Select this tab and check the Save XML Showplan Events Separately check box.

9. Select the path and type a filename in the Save As dialog. The XML Showplan details will be saved in this file. The file will have .SQLPlan as the file extension. Leave the All XML Showplan Batches in a Single File option checked and click the Run button to begin tracing.

10. Switch back to the query window in Management Studio and execute the query batch.

11. Switch back to the Profiler window and stop the trace by clicking the Stop Selected Trace toolbar button or by selecting File | Stop Trace.

12. Start Windows Explorer and browse to the folder that contains the .showplan file generated by the Profiler. Double-click the file to have the file opened in Management Studio. Notice how Management Studio reads the showplan XML file and graphically displays the execution plan.

New Performance Monitor Counters

Performance Monitor (PerfMon.exe), also known as System Monitor, is a tool that is provided with Windows and can be used to identify bottlenecks in application, database, and resource utilizations. Compared to previous releases, SQL Server 2005 installs several new counters to monitor new subsystems, such as Service Broker, Database Mirroring, HTTP Web Services, Notification Services, Reporting Services, and Database Mail, and it also provides additional information for existing components. The sys.dm_os_performance_counters dynamic management view can be used to see a list of SQL Server performance counters and their current values. You start PerfMon and press Ctrl+I or click the Add toolbar button (the plus sign) to launch the Add Counters dialog. Then you expand the Performance Object combo box to see the new SQL Server 2005 counters.

If you have a named instance, then the counters' object names for the relational engine will start with MSSQL$<instance_name>, and SQLAgent$<instance_name> for Agent counters, MSOLAP$<instance_name> for Analysis Server counters, and MSFTESQL$<instance_name> for Full-Text Search counters, and for the default instance, the counter object names will start with SQLServer for Relational Server and Analysis Server for Analysis Services. For each instance of the Notification Services application, PerfMon provides a set of counters that can be used to monitor subscriptions, events, notifications, and so on. All the Notification Services counter object names begin with NS$<app_instance_name>. The Reporting Services counters are provided under the RS Windows Service and RS Web Service objects. The SSIS performance counters are provided under the SQLServer:SSIS Pipeline and SQLServer:SSIS Service objects.

Database Engine Tuning Advisor

The physical database design is one of the crucial factors on which the performance and manageability of an enterprise database system depends. Therefore, Microsoft wanted to provide an automated physical design tool that DBAs can use to figure out things like what indexes should or should not exist, how and if the data should be partitioned, whether indexed views should be created, and so on. Some of this functionality was provided by the Index Tuning Wizard in SQL Server 2000.

In SQL Server 2005, the Index Tuning Wizard has been replaced with a full-fledged application called Database Engine Tuning Advisor (DTA). It's not just a direct replacement of a wizard with an application. Rather, the DTA has significant improvements and contains new features to make better and integrated recommendations for indexes, indexed views, and partitioning. Here are some of the enhancements introduced in the DTA:

- The DTA can be executed either from a graphical user interface (dtashell.exe) or from the command line (dta.exe). The command-line executable accepts several switches that can be used to configure the tuning settings.

- The DTA supports tuning multiple databases simultaneously.

- The DTA is designed to scale well with large databases and workloads, while maintaining good recommendation quality. The DTA achieves this scalability goal by using innovative techniques such as workload compression (looking for "similar" queries to templatize and partition the workload), intelligent algorithms to reduce the number of statistics created, and the ability to tune in a production/test server scenario, which enables tuning a production server while offloading most of the tuning load onto a test server, without actually having the data on the test server. The DTA copies the metadata, necessary statistics, views, stored procedures, triggers, and so on from the production server to the test server, and then it tunes the workload on the test server. When the what-if analysis and tuning are complete on the test server, the recommendation can be applied to the production server. This functionality is provided only via the -ix switch to the DTA command-line executable (dta.exe) and is not available in the DTA graphical user interface.

- The recommendations made by DTA are not solely based on performance. Rather, they can be based on both performance and manageability.

- The DTA supports more T-SQL constructs than the Index Tuning Wizard. For instance, your workload can now have table-valued functions and reference a temporary table, and the DTA will be able to consider that, analyze the workload, and make recommendations accordingly. In addition, the DTA can now tune triggers.

- The DTA allows you to evaluate recommendations and specify which recommendations to implement. You can immediately apply a selected recommendations or schedule it for later, or you can save recommendations to a script file.

- The input (databases to tune, query workload, and other constraints) and output (physical design recommendations) to the DTA are in XML format with a public schema. The use of XML makes scripting and customization easy and also enables other tools to build value-added functionality on top of the DTA. The XML schema file is named dtaschema.xsd, and it is available in the folder

```
%ProgramFiles%\Microsoft SQL
Server\90\Tools\Binn\schemas\sqlserver\2003\03\dta.
```

- The DTA provides richer user interface experience and contains a lot of usability enhancements.

- Unlike the Index Tuning Wizard, which only `sysadmin` server role members can use, the DTA can be executed by any members of the `db_owner` database role.

- The DTA works very closely with the Query Optimizer. This ensures that the recommendations made by the DTA will actually be effective when the Query Optimizer runs the same workload. Also, as the Query Optimizer's cost model evolves over time, the DTA will be able to automatically benefit from improvements to it.

- The DTA allows you to control whether the physical database design should be aligned. That is, a table and all its indexes can be partitioned identically, which simplifies the partition management.

- The DTA has been enhanced to take into consideration the new indexing options, such as online index, non-key columns with nonclustered indexes, and so on. In addition to providing recommendations regarding indexes and indexed views, the DTA can make several other recommendations, such as how to range partition the data, indexes, and indexed views; recommendations on including non-key columns with nonclustered indexes, implementing XML indexes, and index rebuilding/reorganizing suggestions to reduce the cost of index scans and seeks.

- The DTA provides the ability to limit the tuning time and have the tuning operation end at a particular time. The default is one hour for the graphical tool and `0` for the command-line `dta.exe`, which means unlimited time. This is useful if you are tuning the production server and want to make sure that the tuning finishes well before your maintenance window ends.

The input to the DTA is one or more user databases on a server, a workload to tune, which can be a SQL script file, a Profiler trace file saved as a `.trc` or `.xml` file, a table containing a Profiler trace, features to tune (indexes, indexed views, partitioning, and a combination of these), an optional alignment constraint, an optional time constraint indicating by when the tuning should end, and an optionally bound on the size of the physical design it recommends (for instance, a restriction on the size of indexes). The output of the DTA is a physical design recommendation consisting of indexes (online and offline), indexed views, and partitioning recommendations.

TIP

For best results, remove any index hints from the query statements in the workload.

Let's now see the DTA in action. Follow these steps to create a large table and optimize the query against this table by using the DTA:

1. Start SQL Server Management Studio and connect to a SQL Server 2005 instance in a Query Editor mode.

2. Execute the following script in Query Editor:

```
USE AdventureWorks;
GO

IF OBJECT_ID('dbo.TestOrderDetails') IS NOT NULL
    DROP TABLE dbo.TestOrderDetails;
GO

CREATE TABLE dbo.TestOrderDetails(
    [SalesOrderID] [int] NOT NULL,
    [SalesOrderDetailID] [int]  NOT NULL,
    [CarrierTrackingNumber] [nvarchar](25) ,
    [OrderQty] [smallint] NOT NULL,
    [ProductID] [int] NOT NULL,
    [SpecialOfferID] [int] NOT NULL,
    [UnitPrice] [money] NOT NULL,
    [UnitPriceDiscount] [money] NOT NULL,
    [LineTotal]  NUMERIC(17, 2) NULL,
    [rowguid] [uniqueidentifier],
    [ModifiedDate] [datetime] NOT NULL);
GO

DECLARE @counter INT;
SET @counter = 1;
WHILE @counter <= 10
BEGIN
    INSERT INTO dbo.TestOrderDetails
    SELECT * FROM Sales.SalesOrderDetail;
    SET @counter = @counter + 1;
END

SELECT COUNT(*) FROM dbo.TestOrderDetails;
GO

EXEC sys.sp_help 'TestOrderDetails';
GO
checkpoint;
dbcc freeproccache;
dbcc dropcleanbuffers;
GO
```

This script creates a table and copies rows in a loop from an existing table, Sales.SalesOrderDetail, in the AdventureWorks sample database. After you execute this script, you should have a table with about 1,213,170 rows in it.

3. The query workload is a single query to retrieve all orders that have a quantity greater than 20. Let's assume that the following query is available in a file named DTAWorkload.sql:

```
USE [AdventureWorks];
GO

SELECT SalesOrderID, SalesOrderDetailID, OrderQty
    FROM TestOrderDetails WHERE OrderQty > 20;
GO
```

Run this query and note the time it takes to finish. Also obtain the execution plan for the query by highlighting the query and selecting Query | Display Estimated Execution Plan or by pressing Ctrl+L. Because the table does not have any indexes, the execution plan should show Table Scan as the step taking 100% of the cost. Hover the mouse over the Table Scan icon and note the various parameters, such as I/O Cost, CPU Cost, and Operator Cost. You need to try to optimize this query by using DTA.

4. Start the DTA by running dtashell.exe or selecting Start | All Programs | Microsoft SQL Server 2005 | Performance Tools | Database Engine Tuning Advisor.

5. Connect to the same SQL Server instance as in step 1.

6. A new DTA session should be created by default. If it is not, select File | New Session to start a new DTA tuning session.

7. Type the session name as TestSession.

8. Select DTAWorkload.sql as the workload file.

9. Check AdventureWorks from the list of databases to tune.

10. Expand the Selected Tables list box for AdventureWorks and clear the top check box to unselect all tables. Select TestOrderDetails and click anywhere else on the DTA to close the Selected Tables list box. Ensure that the Selected Tables list box shows that only one table is selected.

11. Select the Tuning Options tab. Check the Indexes radio button from the Physical Design Structure (PDS) to use in database group. Check the No Partitioning radio button from the Partitioning strategy to employ group, and check Do Not Keep Any Existing PDS from the Physical Design Structures (PDS) to Keep in database group.

12. Click Advanced Options to see that the DTA provides options to limit the size of recommendations and that it recommends online or offline indexes. Close the dialog without changing anything.

13. Note the Limit Tuning Time option on the Tuning Options tab. If you would like, uncheck that option.

14. Click the green arrow on the toolbar or select Actions | Start Analysis or press F5 to begin analysis.

    After you start the analysis, you should see the Progress tab with the progress indicator. When the tuning is over, you should see two more tabs: Recommendations and Reports. Figure 5.9 shows the Recommendations tab after the analysis is over.

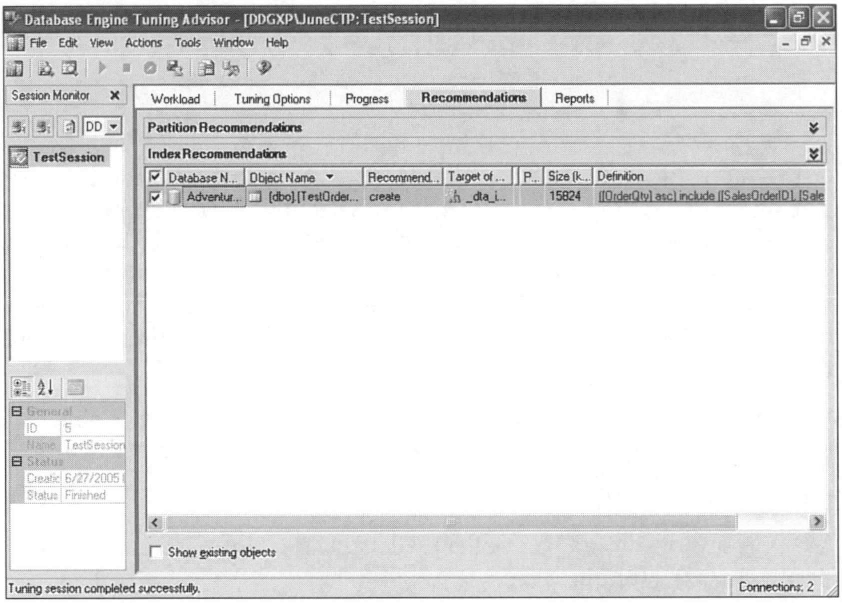

FIGURE 5.9   Based on the workload and other settings, the DTA recommends creating a nonclustered index with a few other non-key columns included in the index.

15. You can click the link under the Definition column to see the T-SQL script to implement that recommendation. The check box in the first column lets you choose which recommendations to apply. You can evaluate the recommendations by clicking Actions | Evaluate Recommendations or apply the recommendations by clicking Actions | Apply Recommendations. When you select to evaluate the recommendations, the DTA creates a new session and passes it the configuration XML file that contains the recommendation details. You can view the XML configuration text used for evaluating the recommendation by clicking the Click Here to See the Configuration Section link provided at the bottom of the Workload tab for the new session created for evaluation. You have to provide the session name, start the analysis, and review the reports to see the evaluation results. At this point, you need to just apply the recommendations instead of evaluating them.

16. Select Actions | Save Recommendations to save recommendations as a T-SQL script file. Then select Actions | Apply Recommendations to either apply the recommendations immediately or schedule them to run at a later time, which creates a job with one T-SQL step.

17. After you apply the recommendations, again run the SELECT query in the DTAWorkload.sql file and see how fast it runs. Also obtain the execution plan for the query by highlighting the query and selecting Query | Display Estimated Execution Plan or by pressing Ctrl+L. This time, the execution plan should show Index Seek instead of Table Scan. Hover the mouse over the Index Seek icon and note that parameters such as I/O Cost, CPU Cost, and Operator Cost have gone down significantly.

You can import or export the session details as XML by using the File | Import Session Definition and File | Export Session Definition menu items. You can export the analysis results as an XML file by using File | Export Session Results. You can duplicate the DTA session settings by selecting Actions | Clone Session. DTA uses the msdb system database to store session and tuning log result details. You can execute the following query to obtain a list of tables and stored procedures used by the DTA:

```
SELECT * FROM msdb.sys.all_objects
   WHERE ([name] LIKE 'dta%' OR [name] LIKE 'sp_DTA%') AND
         ([type] = 'U' OR [Type] = 'P')
   ORDER BY [name], [type];
GO
```

Operations and Configuration

This section focuses on the tools that you can use to configure and manage services, administer client and server network configurations, configure email support in SQL Server 2005, and run SQL Server scripts from the DOS command prompt.

SQL Server Configuration Manager

SQL Server Configuration Manager is yet another example of Microsoft's initiative to combine multiple tools into a single integrated tool. SQL Server Configuration Manager provides the functionality of three tools provided with SQL Server 2000: Service Manager, Server Network Utility, and Client Network Utility. SQL Server Configuration Manager is an MMC snap-in (%SystemRoot%\system32\SQLServerManager.msc) that provides the means to manage SQL Server services and connectivity settings. SQL Server Configuration Manager internally uses WMI to access and update SQL Server services and connectivity details.

Figure 5.10 shows the SQL Server Configuration Manager. The three top-level items on the tree on the left are SQL Server 2005 Services, SQL Server 2005 Network Configuration, and SQL Native Client Configuration. When you select SQL Server 2005 Services from the tree, the grid on the right shows various SQL Server 2005 services including Relational Engine, Analysis Services, Integration Services, Notification Services, Reporting Services, Agent, Full-Text, and the SQL Server Browser service. You can right-click a service and select Properties to view and change service settings. Figure 5.10 shows SQL Server Configuration Manager, listing various SQL Server 2005 services.

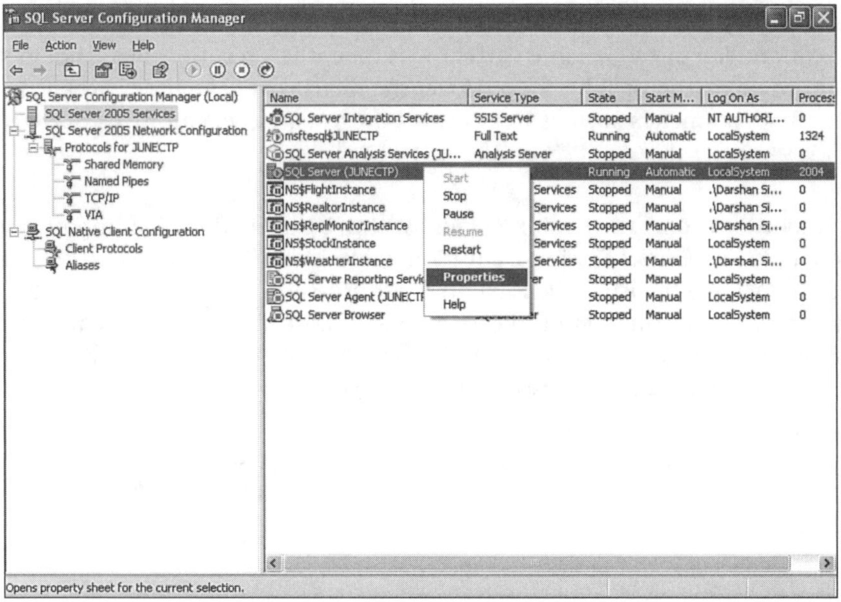

FIGURE 5.10   SQL Server Configuration Manager is an MMC snap-in application that helps you manage services and connectivity settings.

You can use SQL Server Configuration Manager to start, pause, resume, or stop services and to view and change service properties, such as service start mode (automatic, manual, or disabled) and the account name under which the service runs. If you would like to change the account under which the services should run, it is recommended that you use SQL Server Configuration Manager to do that. This ensures that the new account is assigned the required permissions on the disk folders and registry hives.

The SQL Server 2005 Network Configuration node in the SQL Server Configuration Manager tree can be used to configure network libraries that SQL Server listens on. If you expand this node in the tree, you should see items such as Shared Memory, Named Pipes, TCP/IP, and VIA for Virtual Interface Architecture, which is a network library designed to support highly reliable, fast, efficient data transfer between servers by using hardware from Giganet. You can right-click any network library and select Properties to view and configure network library settings or to enable or disable the protocol.

The SQL Native Client Configuration node can be used to manage the client net-libraries and define server alias names. Click Client Protocols and you should see all the client network libraries on the right hand side. You can right-click or double-click any entry to set the properties for the selected client network library. To create a new client alias, you expand the SQL Native Client Configuration node, right-click Aliases, and select New Alias.

The SQL Server Configuration Manager can also connect to a different server and manage services and connectivity settings for that server. To connect to a different server, you select the Start menu, right-click My Computer, and click Manage. In Computer Management, you right-click Computer Management (Local) and then select Connect to Another Computer. You connect to the remote server and under Services and Applications, you should see SQL Server Configuration Manager, which you can use to control SQL Server services and network settings on that server.

SQL Server Configuration Manager ships with all SQL Server 2005 editions, including SQL Server 2005 Express Edition.

The SQLCMD Utility

SQLCMD is a new DOS command-line utility introduced in SQL Server 2005 to interactively execute T-SQL statements and also to execute scripts from the command line.

SQL Server 2005 no longer ships the DB-library–based `isql.exe`, and it discourages the use of the ODBC-based `osql.exe`. `SQLCMD.exe` uses the SQL native client, which is OLE DB based, to communicate with SQL Server. SQLCMD doesn't just replace `osql.exe`, but it also contains various enhancements that make it more robust and usable.

SQLCMD Basics

SQLCMD accepts several command-line switches, similarly to `osql.exe`. Also as with `osql.exe`, the SQLCMD command-line parameters are case sensitive. You can pass the `-?` or `/?` command-line switch to get a list of all the parameters that SQLCMD accepts. If you pass the `-S` parameter along with the server name, such as `MyServer` or `MyServer\InstanceName`, SQLCMD connects to the specified SQL Server instance by using Windows authentication.

Let's look at some basic SQLCMD examples.

The following statement connects to an instance named `YUKON` on the server `DDGXP` (`-S`) by using a trusted connection (`-E`); update the statement to connect to your SQL Server 2005 instance. It defaults to a database named `AdventureWorks`, and the `-p` switch tells SQLCMD to print performance statistics after every query is executed:

```
SQLCMD -S DDGXP\YUKON -E -d AdventureWorks -p
```

After you run this statement from a DOS command prompt, you should see the `1>` prompt, where you can type T-SQL commands, press Enter, type `GO`, and press Enter to execute the query. You can type `EXIT` to end the SQLCMD session.

You use the `-Q` switch to execute the specified query and exit:

```
SQLCMD -S DDGXP\YUKON -E -d AdventureWorks -Q "SELECT Name FROM Sales.Store"
```

If you pass the -q switch, SQLCMD executes the query and stays in interactive query mode, and you have to type EXIT to end the SQLCMD session.

You can use the -Z switch to change the SQL Server password:

```
SQLCMD -S DDGXP\YUKON -U sa -P OldPassword2005 -Z NewPWD1234
```

If you pass the -z switch, SQLCMD changes the password and stays in interactive query mode, and you have to type EXIT to end the SQLCMD session.

One of the nice enhancements introduced in SQLCMD is the ability to provide multiple input script files. The following statement asks SQLCMD to connect to a SQL Server 2005 instance named YUKON, run the script files c:\1.sql and c:\2.sql, save the output results in a file called results.txt, separate the columns using the tilde character (~), and save the results.txt file as a Unicode file (-u switch) instead of using the default ANSI file format:

```
SQLCMD -S DDGXP\YUKON -i c:\1.sql,c:\2.sql -o results.txt -s~ -u
```

The -L switch is for getting a list of local and other remote SQL Server machines that are broadcasting on the network:

```
SQLCMD -L
```

If you pass -Lc instead of -L, SQLCMD generates "clean" output, which does not have the Servers: heading line or any formatting spaces in front of the listed server names.

Table 5.3 lists all the SQLCMD switches.

TABLE 5.3   SQLCMD.exe **Command-Line Switches**

Switch	Description
-S	Specifies the SQL Server instance to connect.
-U	Specifies the SQL Server login ID, if using SQL authentication to connect.
-P	Specifies the SQL server password, if using SQL authentication to connect.
-E	Specifies to use trusted or Windows authentication to connect.
-d	Specifies the default database to connect to.
-i	Specifies one or more input script files to execute.
-o	Specifies the output file to which results should be redirected.
-c	Specifies the batch terminator string. The default is GO.
-A	Logs in to SQL Server with a dedicated administrator connection (DAC), described later in this chapter.
-L or -Lc	Lists the servers.
-Q	Executes the specified query and exits.
-q	Executes the query and stays in interactive query mode.
-Z	Changes the SQL Server password for the login specified with -U and exits.

TABLE 5.3   Continued

Switch	Description
z	Changes the SQL Server password for the login specified with -u and stays in interactive query mode.
-v	Passes variable values, as discussed later in this chapter.
-s	Specifies a column separator.
-h-1	Specifies to avoid printing column headers in the output.
-W	Removes trailing spaces from column values.
-k1 or -k2	Replaces each control character, such as a tab or a newline character, with a single space (-k1) or replaces each and consecutive control characters with a single space. In other words, if you have two consecutive tabs in the data, -k1 causes the tabs to be replaced with two space characters; -k2 causes the tabs to be replaced with a single space.
-p or -p1	Prints statistics. If 1 is specified, prints colon-separated stats (for example 4096:1:1:1.00:1000.00, which signifies, network packet size in bytes : number of transactions : clock time total in ms. : clock time avg. in ms.: transactions per second).
-I	Turns on the QUOTED_IDENTIFIER option.
-H	Specifies the name that is shown in the hostname column of the sys.processes catalog view.
-l	Specifies the login timeout, in seconds.
-t	Specifies the query timeout, in seconds.
-w	Specifies the screen width, a number between 9 and 65535. The default is 80.
-a	Specifies the packet size, a number between 512 and 32767.
-e	Prints the input script to standard output.
-f	Inputs and/or outputs a code page.
-R	Specifies to use client regional settings.
-u	Specifies to use Unicode output.
-m	Customizes the display of error messages. If an error occurs in a T-SQL script, SQLCMD shows the message number, the state, and the error level only if the T-SQL error severity level is greater than or equal to value specified with -m switch.
-V	Specifies the lowest severity level that SQLCMD reports. If an error occurs in a T-SQL script, SQLCMD reports the severity level only if the T-SQL error severity level is greater than or equal to value specified with -V switch. You can use %ERRORLEVEL% at the DOS command prompt or in a batch file to find out the severity level when it is reported.
-b	Specifies that if an error occurs in a T-SQL script, SQLCMD aborts the batch and exits, returning 1 as %ERRORLEVEL% if T-SQL error has a severity level greater than 10; else, %ERRORLEVEL% is 0.

TABLE 5.3   Continued

Switch	Description
-X or -X1	Disables the SQLCMD commands ED and !!. If 1 is passed, and if the script contains either ED or !! command, SQLCMD exits while showing a warning.
-r or -r0 or -r1	Redirects all error messages (-r1) or error messages with severity 17 or higher (-r or -r0) to stderr.
-y	Limits the number of characters that are returned for varchar(max), nvarchar(max), varbinary(max), xml, text, ntext, image, and user-defined data types.
-Y	Limits the number of characters that are returned for char, nchar, varchar(n) (where 1≤n≤8000), nvarchar(n) (where 1≤n≤4000), and sqlvariant.

SQLCMD and Environment Variables

One way to instruct SQLCMD about the server and database to connect to, the authentication method to use, the network packet size, and other settings, is by passing the appropriate command-line switches, as described in the previous section. The other method is to set some environment variables. For instance, if you set an environment variable named SQLCMDDBNAME to a database name string, either by using a SET statement at the command prompt or in a batch file or by using the Environment Variables button on the Advanced tab of System Properties dialog (which you open by selecting Control Panel | System), SQLCMD connects to the database specified by the environment variable, provided that the -d switch is not passed to it. Similarly, if you set the SQLCMDSERVER environment variable and you don't pass the -S parameter to SQLCMD, SQLCMD connects to the server specified by the environment variable. In other words, when you run SQLCMD, in addition to command-line switches, SQLCMD also looks at certain environment variables. If an environment variable is set to some value, and if an overriding switch is not provided on the command line, SQLCMD honors the environment variable. Here is how it works:

```
C:\>SET SQLCMDSERVER=DDGXP\YUKON
C:\>SET SQLCMDDBNAME=AdventureWorks
C:\>SET SQLCMDPACKETSIZE=8192
C:\>SQLCMD -p1
1>SELECT TOP 1 Name FROM Sales.Store;
2>GO
Name
-------------------------------------------------
A Bike Store
(1 rows affected)
8192:1:1:1.00:1000.00
```

These statements at the DOS command prompt set environment variables for server, database, and network packet size and then run SQLCMD with -p1 to have colon statistics printed after each line. Note that SQLCMD automatically connects to a SQL Server 2005 instance, makes AdventureWorks the current database, and sets the packet size to 8192.

You can use the :setvar SQLCMD command to change the SQLCMD environment variable value. SQLCMD commands such as :setvar are discussed in the next section.

The following DOS command-prompt statements connect to a SQL Server 2005 instance and set ~ as the column separator:

```
C:\>SQLCMD -S DDGXP\YUKON -E -dAdventureWorks -s~
1> SELECT TOP(1) LEFT(Name, 15) Name, SalesPersonID FROM Sales.Store;
2> GO
Name            ~SalesPersonID
--------------------~---------------
A Bike Store    ~          280
1> :setvar SQLCMDCOLSEP ","
2> SELECT TOP(1) LEFT(Name, 15) Name, SalesPersonID FROM Sales.Store;
3> GO
Name            ,SalesPersonID
----------------,------------
A Bike Store    ,          280
1> :setvar SQLCMDCOLSEP ";"
2> SELECT TOP(1) LEFT(Name, 15) Name, SalesPersonID FROM Sales.Store;
3> GO
Name            ;SalesPersonID
----------------;------------
A Bike Store    ;          280
```

After executing one SELECT statement, this script sets SQLCMDCOLSEP to a comma (,), and the results returned by a subsequent SELECT statement separate the columns by using a comma instead of a tilde. This is repeated again to change the column separator to a semicolon (;).

Table 5.4 lists the SQLCMD-specific environment variables and their command-line switch equivalents.

TABLE 5.4   SQLCMD-Specific Environment Variables

Variable	Switch
SQLCMDSERVER	-S
SQLCMDUSER	-U
SQLCMDPASSWORD	-P
SQLCMDDBNAME	-d
SQLCMDPACKETSIZE	-a
SQLCMDLOGINTIMEOUT	-l
SQLCMDSTATTIMEOUT	-t
SQLCMDHEADERS	-h

TABLE 5.4   Continued

Variable	Switch
SQLCMDWORKSTATION	-H
SQLCMDCOLSEP	-s
SQLCMDCOLWIDTH	-w
SQLCMDERRORLEVEL	-m
SQLCMDMAXVARTYPEWIDTH	-y
SQLCMDMAXFIXEDTYPEWIDTH	-Y
SQLCMDEDITOR	Not applicable (Determines which application to launch when the !!ED SQLCMD command is run.)
SQLCMDINI	Not applicable (Used to set a startup script, which is a script that is executed when SQLCMD is started.)

SQLCMD Commands

In addition to T-SQL commands, SQLCMD supports few other commands that you can run in interactive mode or inside T-SQL scripts executed using SQLCMD. The previous section shows an example of this—using the setvar command to set environment and scripting variables.

Every SQLCMD command must be preceded with a colon character. For backward compatibility with osql.exe, a colon is not required before EXIT, QUIT, ED, !!, and RESET, but it is recommended that you use the colon in front of all SQLCMD commands except GO. The !! is used to execute operating system commands, much like xp_cmdshell in SQL Server 2000 extended stored procedures.

Try out the following:

```
C:\>SQLCMD -S DDGXP\YUKON -E -dAdventureWorks
1> :Help
<Output omitted for brevity; shows help on all SQLCMD commands>
1> :ServerList
<Output omitted for brevity; List of servers, output similar to -L switch>
1> !!DIR
<Output omitted for brevity; Runs Operating System command>
1> :!!CLS
<Runs Operating System command; clears the screen>
1> INSERT INTO tblTest VALUES (10);
2> GO 100
< Output omitted for brevity; Runs the INSERT statement 100 times>
1> :r c:\1.sql
< Output omitted for brevity; Runs another script file>
```

The final command in this example can be particularly very helpful. You can use the :r command to execute some other script from within your T-SQL script. Also note the command before the :r line. The number 100 is passed with the GO statement, which leads to executing the batch—the INSERT statement, in this case—100 times.

Table 5.5 lists the available SQLCMD commands.

TABLE 5.5   SQLCMD Commands

SQLCMD Command	Description
:Help	Lists SQLCMD commands along with a short description of each command.
GO [number]	Executes the T-SQL batch in statement cache the specified number of times. The default is 1.
:RESET	Clears the statement cache.
:ED	Launches the script editor. It defaults to the DOS command prompt utility EDIT.exe. You can cause the editor to launch by setting the SQLCMDEDITOR environment variable. The statement SET SQLCMDEDITOR=sqlwb sets SQL Server Management Studio as the script editor when the ED SQLCMD command is run. Note that if the statement cache is empty, the :ED command does nothing.
:!!	Executes an operating system command, much like the xp_cmdshell extended stored procedure in SQL Server 2000.
:QUIT	Ends the SQLCMD session.
:EXIT [(statement)]	Ends the SQLCMD session. You can execute a SQL statement and return a number that can be captured in a batch file or at the command prompt by using the %ERRORLEVEL% variable: 1>:EXIT (SELECT 0) C:\>ECHO %ERRORLEVEL% The EXIT statement in the SQLCMD session returns 0, and then on the DOS command prompt, the %ERRORLEVEL% variable prints the value returned by the EXIT statement.
:ServerList	Lists the locally configured servers and the names of the servers broadcasting on the network. The output is similar to that of the -L switch.
:List	Prints the content of the statement cache.
:Listvar	Displays a list of the variables that are currently set, using :setvar command.
:Error <filename>|stderr|stdout	Redirects all error output to the file specified by <filename> to stderr or to stdout.

TABLE 5.5   Continued

SQLCMD Command	Description
`:Out <filename>¦stderr¦stdout`	Redirects all query results to the file specified by `<filename>` to `stderr` or to `stdout`.
`:Perftrace <filename>¦stderr¦stdout`	Redirects all performance trace information to the file specified by `<filename>` to `stderr` or to `stdout`.

`:Connect`	Connects to an instance of SQL Server, closing the current connection.
	
	The following example first connects to a SQL Server 2005 named instance and then uses the `:connect` SQLCMD command to connect to a SQL Server 2000 default instance on the machine, using trusted connection:
	
	`C:\>SQLCMD -E -S DDGXP\YUKON`
	`1> :connect DDGXP`
	`Sqlcmd: Successfully connected to server 'DDGXP'.`
	`2> SELECT @@Version`
	`3> GO`
	`-------------------------------`
	`Microsoft SQL Server  2000 - 8.00.760 (Intel X86)`
	`<Output truncated for brevity>`
	
	You can pass the server and instance name, the timeout, and SQL Server authentication details with the `:connect` command.

`:On Error[ exit¦ignore]`	Tells SQLCMD what to do in case of a T-SQL script error in the batch. The `exit` option causes the SQLCMD session to end, returning the appropriate error value; the `ignore` option causes SQLCMD to disregard the T-SQL script error and continue executing the batch or script.
`:XML [ON¦OFF]`	Specifies whether the results are returned as a binary stream (in hex format) or as text. If your script makes use of the `FOR XML` clause and you would like the results to be returned as XML text, you should turn on the XML SQLCMD option by running `:XML ON`. By default this option is `OFF`, and with that the `FOR XML` results are returned as binary stream in hex format. When this option is ON, even the error messages are returned as XML streams.

TIP

The Query Editor in SQL Server Management Studio supports SQLCMD mode, which can be useful for authoring, editing, and executing T-SQL scripts that use SQLCMD features, such as SQLCMD commands and variables. You can use the SQLCMD Mode button on the SQL Editor toolbar or the Query | SQLCMD Mode menu item to turn on or off the SQLCMD mode.

SQLCMD and Variables

The support for using variables with SQLCMD script enables you to write generic scripts so that one script can be used for multiple scenarios. Your T-SQL scripts can use $(VariableName) syntax in the T-SQL statements, and then you can pass the variable values from the command line (by using the -v switch), by using the :setvar SQLCMD command, or by setting their values as environment variables, using the SET statement.

Let's say that the following text is available in a script file called SQLCMDVariables.sql:

```
EXEC master.dbo.sp_addumpdevice
    @devtype = N'disk',
    @logicalname = '$(DeviceLogicalName)',
    @physicalname = '$(DevicePhysicalName)';
GO


BACKUP DATABASE
    $(DBName) TO
    $(DeviceLogicalName)
GO
```

This script creates a new backup device and then performs a full database backup. The logical device name, physical file location, and database to back up are variables that can be set by using the :setvar command in the script (which is not done in this case), or they can be environment variables that are set by using the SET statement or by using the Control Panel, or they can be passed to SQLCMD by using the -v switch. Here is how to pass variables by using the -v switch:

```
SQLCMD -E -S DDGXP\YUKON
➥-v DeviceLogicalName="AW1" DevicePhysicalName="c:\AW1.bkp"
➥DBName="AdventureWorks" -i "c:\SQLCMDVariables.sql"
```

Instead of passing the variable values on the command line by using the -v switch, you can set an environment variable with the same name as the variable name in the script, and SQLCMD uses the environment variable value if the variable value is not passed using -v:

```
C:\>SET DeviceLogicalName=AW2
C:\>SET DevicePhysicalName=c:\AW2.bkp
C:\>SET DBName=AdventureWorks
C:\>SQLCMD -E -S DDGXP\YUKON -i "c:\SQLCMDVariables.sql"
```

The third way to set variable values is by using the :setvar SQLCMD command, as illustrated earlier.

You can also use the $(VariableName) syntax to access environment variables:

```
1> SELECT '$(NUMBER_OF_PROCESSORS)'
2> GO
```

These statements, when executed in a SQLCMD session, return the value of the NUMBER_OF_PROCESSORS environment variable, indicating the number of processors on the local machine.

Startup Scripts

You can set the SQLCMDINI environment variable to a SQL script file that will be run every time SQLCMD is started. Assume that the following text is available in the c:\SQLCMDStartup.sql file:

```
SET NOCOUNT ON
PRINT ''
PRINT @@SERVERNAME
PRINT @@VERSION
PRINT GETDATE()
PRINT SYSTEM_USER
PRINT USER
PRINT DB_NAME()
PRINT ''
```

Now, if you set the SQLCMDINI environment variable to the c:\SQLCMDStartup.sql file, this script will be run every time you start SQLCMD:

```
C:\>SET SQLCMDINI=c:\SQLCMDStartup.sql
C:\>SQLCMD -E -S DDGXP\YUKON
<executes script c:\SQLCMDStartup.sql; output omitted for brevity>
```

Using a Dedicated Administrator Connection

In situations where SQL Server is locked or running in an abnormal state and not responding when you try to connect to it, the members of sysadmin server role can connect to a local or remote SQL Server 2005 instance over TCP/IP by using SQLCMD and the -A switch to troubleshoot problems on the SQL Server machine. This feature is called *dedicated administrator connection (DAC)*. SQL Server allows only one DAC per instance. When you connect to SQL Server by using the -A switch, it is strongly recommended that you restrict your usage to certain diagnostic and troubleshooting commands only and set the isolation level to READ UNCOMMITTED to avoid any blocking. The 'remote admin connections' sp_configure option must be turned on in order to allow remote connections using DAC. If you are connecting to a named instance, the SQL Browser service must be started.

Introducing Database Mail

SQL Server 2005 introduces a highly scalable, reliable, and secure method of sending emails from within T-SQL code. This new feature, called Database Mail, uses Simple Mail Transfer Protocol (SMTP) to send email messages. Unlike the SQL Mail feature in SQL Server 2000, Database Mail does not require Microsoft Outlook or MAPI to be installed on the server.

Database Mail scales well because it uses Service Broker to asynchronously send email messages. Service Broker in turn activates an external process (DatabaseMail90.exe) to send email messages. This external Database Mail process uses a standard ADO.NET connection to communicate with SQL Server. This process isolation increases server reliability because even if the external process stops or fails, it does not affect the SQL Server process. The other reliability feature introduced in Database Mail is the ability to specify a failover SMTP server. If Database Mail cannot send by using one SMTP server, it tries to use another specified SMTP server to send emails. Unlike SQL Mail in SQL Server 2000, Database Mail is cluster aware and is fully supported on a cluster. Database Mail is fully supported on 64-bit SQL Server 2005 installations.

Some of the ways in which Database Mail offers a secure emailing solution are the MaxFileSize (to limit the size of email attachments) and ProhibitedExtensions (to restrict attachment file types) configuration settings, the fact that it does not require Outlook or MAPI on the SQL Server machine, and auditing and logging.

> **NOTE**
>
> Database Mail only supports sending emails. Unlike SQL Mail in SQL Server 2000, Database Mail in this release cannot be used to read emails. MAPI-based SQL Mail is still available in SQL Server 2005 and can still be used to read and send emails.

Configuring Database Mail

Following the "secure by default" principal, SQL Server 2005 does not enable Database Mail support by default. You have to configure Database Mail before you can use msdb.dbo.sp_send_dbmail stored procedure to send emails. You can enable and configure Database Mail by using the Database Mail Configuration Wizard. You can launch the Database Mail Configuration Wizard from within Management Studio by right-clicking the Database Mail node under Management folder in Object Explorer and selecting the Configure Database Mail menu item.

> **NOTE**
>
> Because Database Mail depends on Service Broker to send email messages, Service Broker must be enabled in the msdb database.

The Database Mail Configuration Wizard allows you to perform multiple tasks. You can use this wizard to enable and install Database Mail, to manage Database Mail profiles and accounts, to manage Database Mail security settings, and to configure Database Mail system parameters, such as MaxFileSize and ProhibitedExtensions.

The msdb database is the Database Mail host database. It contains the stored procedures and messaging objects for Database Mail. Database Mail stores the SMTP server information, profiles, accounts, security, and system parameters in the msdb system database.

Figure 5.11 shows various things that you can do by using the Database Mail Configuration Wizard.

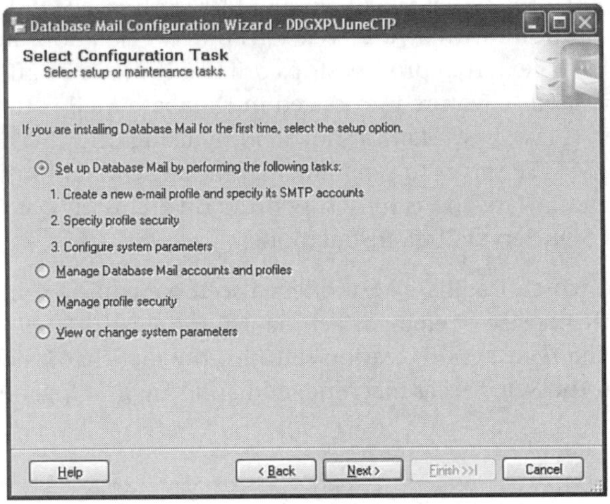

FIGURE 5.11   The Database Mail Configuration Wizard can be used to enable and configure Database Mail.

The msdb.dbo. sp_send_dbmail stored procedure posts the email message in a Service Broker queue. The Service Broker activation feature launches an external application (DatabaseMail90.exe) when there is a message in the queue. This external process reads the messages from the Service Broker queue and the SMTP account and profile setting, including the SMTP server settings, from the msdb mail host database; and sends messages to the email server. The SMTP server is then responsible for actually delivering the messages.

Here are the steps for enabling Database Mail and sending an email by using Database Mail. These steps assume that you have an SMTP server installed and working. These steps use the local SMTP service installed as part of an IIS Web server. The SMTP virtual server is configured to grant connection and relay access to the IP address on which SQL Server 2005 is installed (local, in this case):

1. Launch SQL Server Management Studio. Connect Object Explorer to a SQL Server 2005 instance.

2. Expand the Management folder, right-click Database Mail, and select Configure Database Mail.

3. The Database Mail Configuration Wizard appears. Click Next on the Welcome screen.

4. Select the first option, Set up Database Mail by performing the following tasks, and then click Next.

5. Set the Profile Name to TestProfile. Click the Add button next to the SMTP Accounts heading and provide the SMTP account details. Type the account name as TestAccount; specify outgoing and reply-to email addresses, and specify the SMTP server. For a local IIS SMTP service, specify localhost. Provide SMTP authentication information if needed. Click OK and then click Next on the New Profile screen.

6. Make TestProfile a public profile by selecting the check box next to it. Also make it the default profile. Click Next.

7. The next wizard screen is Configure System Parameters. This is where you can specify things like the maximum file size for attachments, prohibited file extensions, and so on. For this demo, leave the defaults and click Next.

8. Verify the Database Mail configuration settings and click Finish when you're done reviewing. When the wizard finishes, click Close to end the wizard. Database Mail is now configured.

9. Send an email by using Database Mail:

```
EXEC msdb.dbo.sp_send_dbmail
     @profile_name = 'TestProfile',
     @recipients = 'someonw@somewhere.com',
     @body = 'Simple Database Mail Message',
     @subject = 'Database Mail';
```

When you run these statements, you should get the "Mail queued." message, and the recipient should get an email if the SMTP server is configured properly.

The msdb.dbo.sp_send_dbmail stored procedure takes various parameters, which you can use, for instance, to send results of a query in text or HTML format, attach files, and specify CC recipients, importance, sensitivity, and so on. Refer to SQL Server 2005 Books Online for details on other parameters.

Monitoring and Troubleshooting Database Mail

You can monitor and troubleshoot Database Mail by using the auditing and logging tables in the msdb mail host database.

For each outgoing email, Database Mail adds a status/logging record to the sysmail_log table, and the actual mail details are saved in the sysmail_mailitems table. You need to run a SELECT query on these two tables to find out whether Service Broker was able to activate the DatabaseMail90.exe application, whether DatabaseMail90.exe encountered problems while sending messages, and the status of each outgoing email. The event_type and description fields in the sysmail_log table and the sent_status field in the sysmail_mailitems table can be used to determine the success or failure for each

outgoing email. The value of 0 for the sent_status field means that the
DatabaseMail90.exe application is yet to process the message; 1 means success, indicating
DatabaseMail90.exe was able to deliver message to the SMTP server; and 2 means that
DatabaseMail90.exe received an error while delivering the message to the SMTP server, and
in this case you should look at the sysmail_log table for more details about the failure.

In addition to the above-mentioned two tables, you can also access other Database Mail
tables also in the msdb mail host database to verify the profile, SMTP account, security,
and other system configuration settings. Table 5.6 lists these Database Mail-related tables
in the msdb database.

TABLE 5.6   Database Mail-Specific Tables in the msdb System Database

Table Name	Description
sysmail_attachments	Contains one record for each attachment in every email message sent.
sysmail_profile	Contains Database Mail SMTP profile details.
sysmail_principalprofile	Contains profile security details.
sysmail_account	Contains SMTP account details, including email address, display name, and reply email address.
sysmail_profileaccount	Associates account(s) with a profile.
sysmail_servertype	Contains a row that indicates whether a server is incoming, outgoing, or both. In this release, Database Mail does not support reading emails.
sysmail_server	Contains SMTP server information, including name, port, and credentials.
sysmail_configuration	Contains the server configuration settings, such as MaxFileSize and ProhibitedExtensions.

In addition to tables mentioned in Table 5.6, you should also check the system and application event log (eventvwr.exe) entries for any errors related to Database Mail or SMTP.
You should also check the folders under the C:\Inetpub\mailroot directory to see
whether emails are being queued.

Management APIs

Earlier in this chapter you saw how to register a server in SQL Server Management Studio.
What if you have to register hundreds of servers? You can certainly do it through the user
interface or create an XML file by hand and import it into the user interface, but that is
still a lot of work. You are likely to run into a similar situation when managing a large
number of servers, databases, or database objects. For situations like this, you need the
ability to automate common management tasks.

SQL Server 6.5 first introduced a COM-based application programming interface (API)
called SQL-DMO, which allowed automating management tasks using languages such
as VBScript, C++, and Visual Basic. This API was further extended in SQL Server 7.

SQL Server 2000 continued supporting SQL-DMO to automate all the tasks that you can do by using SQL Server Enterprise Manager. SQL Server 2005 still ships SQL-DMO COM libraries, but it is not upgraded to support newer features, such as Service Broker, Database Mail, Database Mirroring, and so on.

SQL-DMO is now being superseded by a .NET-based object library called SQL Server Management Objects (SMO). In addition to SMO, SQL Server 2005 introduces other .NET object libraries to automate replication tasks (Replication Management Objects [RMO]) and to automate Analysis Services management tasks (Analysis Management Objects [AMO]). This chapter provides details on SMO and WMI support in SQL Server 2005. Refer to Chapter 4 for an overview of WMI.

SQL Server Management Objects (SMO)

The SMO API's primary goal is to provide a powerful yet easy-to-use programming interface to automate administration, deployment, and maintenance of SQL Server. In addition to providing maximum coverage of SQL Server 2005 features, the SMO API contains several other improvements over SQL-DMO. SMO is designed from the ground up so that the API can perform better, scale well, and increases flexibility. The SQL Server Management Studio internally uses the SMO API to interact with SQL Server. Therefore, anything you can do by using Management Studio, you can automate by using SMO. You can use SMO from any .NET programming language, such as Visual Basic .NET or C#. In addition, SQL Server 2005 provides a COM wrapper over this .NET library so that you can use SMO from scripting and unmanaged languages to automate management tasks.

TIP

You can use SMO to manage SQL Server versions 2000 and 2005. SMO does not support databases with the compatibility level set to 60 or 65.

The following are some of the improvements introduced in the SMO API:

- **Delayed instantiation**—If you access any of the instance class objects, SQL-DMO retrieves all the properties up front. On one hand, this might reduce the roundtrips to the server, but on the other hand, it requires more memory and also does not scale well. SMO gives developers the option to determine whether they want to retrieve objects and properties as needed (delayed instantiation), prefetch entire collections, or retrieve objects by using a set of predefined properties. In other words, SMO gives developers a fine level of control over how data is retrieved from the server.

- **Cached object model**—Unlike SQL-DMO, SMO does not propagate object changes to the server immediately. It caches the changes until you decide to apply or discard the changes, and hence it reduces the roundtrips to the server by sending updates in batches.

- **WMI provider**—If using WMI API seems complex to you, SMO has an answer for you. SMO provides a simple programming interface for performing tasks that you can do by using WMI API. Things that you can do using SQL Server Configuration Manager, such as managing service accounts, network protocols, and so on can now be easily done by using the SMO API.

- **COM wrappers**—The fact that SMO is a .NET-based object library does not mean you can use it only from .NET applications. SMO ships with a COM wrapper that can be used from scripting languages such as VBScript and JScript, and from other unmanaged programming languages, such as Visual Basic and Visual C++.

- **Capture mode**—Earlier in this chapter you learned that all the management dialogs in SQL Server Management Studio are scriptable. That means that a T-SQL script can be generated for the changes you perform in the dialog. The management dialogs provide this functionality by using the capture mode feature in SMO, which lets you record or capture changes made to SMO objects and generate a T-SQL script for those changes.

- **Exception hierarchy**—SMO exceptions are almost always chained, providing context at every level. This means that if there is an error, you can find out about the entire error chain.

- **Releasable state**—The SQL-DMO object model consists of a static object named `Application` as the root, and this object is a starting point for accessing SQL Server objects. SQL-DMO does not allow releasing this object. With SMO, the `Application` object is gone; the new top-level class in the SMO object hierarchy is `Server`, which can be released (set to `null`) at any time, freeing the memory.

- **XPath-style syntax**—Let's say you would like to find out the total number of rows in a table. You can first get the `Server` object, then the `Database` object, and then the `Table` object, and then you can access the `RowCount` properties. SMO provides an alternative, simpler, and more efficient syntax to do this. This syntax, which looks like folder hierarchy syntax or like the unique resource name (URN) syntax, allows you to specify the path of the object you want to access.

- **Advanced scripting support**—With SQL-DMO, scripting was deeply embedded in SQL-DMO classes, each having a `Script` method. SMO continues to support this approach for backward compatibility, but it also introduces a standalone object, a class called `Scripter` that provides advanced scripting support such as discovering object dependencies.

The SMO API provides three types of classes:

- **Instance classes**—These classes provide access to all SQL Server objects and their properties. Examples of instance classes include `Server`, `Database`, `Table`, `View`, and `StoredProcedure`.

- **Utility classes**—These classes can be used for management and administration tasks such as backup/restore, jobs, Database Mail, and Service Broker management.

- **Scripter class**—This class provides advanced scripting functionality.

NOTE

Because SMO is a .NET-based object library, you need the Microsoft .NET Framework version 2.0 or higher installed on the machine in order for your SMO application to work. SQL Server 2005 provides an MSI setup for SMO, SQL-DMO, and SMO COM wrappers that you can redistribute with your application.

Here is an example of using SMO in VBScript:

```
Dim smoSvr
Dim svrName
Dim smoDB


svrName = "DDGXP\YUKON"

Set smoSvr = CreateObject("Microsoft.SqlServer.Management.Smo.Server")

smoSvr.ConnectionContext.ServerInstance  = svrName

For Each smoDB in smoSvr.Databases
    WScript.Echo smoDB.Name
Next
Set smoSvr = Nothing
```

This script lists all the databases on a server. You can update the svrName variable with your SQL Server 2005 instance name, save the script, and run it. The script displays a message box that lists each database on the specified server.

Here is another example of using SMO in VBScript. This VBScript creates a new database on the specified server.

```
Dim smoSvr
Dim smoDB

Dim svrName
Dim dbName

svrName = "DDGXP\YUKON"
dbName = "TestDatabase"

Set smoSvr = CreateObject("Microsoft.SqlServer.Management.Smo.Server")

smoSvr.ConnectionContext.ServerInstance  = svrName

'Create the database
Set smoDB = CreateObject("Microsoft.SqlServer.Management.Smo.Database")
smoDB.Parent = smoSvr
```

```
smoDB.Name = dbName
smoDB.Create()
WScript.Echo "Done! Database created successfully."

Set smoSvr = Nothing
Set smoDB = Nothing
```

Before concluding this chapter, let's see an example of WMI support in SQL Server 2005.

Windows Management Instrumentation (WMI)

As described in Chapter 4, WMI provides an industry-standard programming interface for managing an enterprise environment. WMI provides a consistent way of managing hardware such as disk drives and software such as IIS Web server and SQL Server. (Refer to Chapter 4 for an overview of WMI.)

WMI support in SQL Server 2005 primarily allows you to do the following:

- Manage SQL Server services, service accounts, and network protocols. SQL Server Configuration Manager uses WMI and hence anything that you can do using SQL Server Configuration Manager can be programmed using WMI API.

- Monitor SQL Server events. As you will see in an example later in this section, you can write VBScript or code in some other language, use WMI, and monitor the events in SQL Server. In the example provided in this chapter, the VBScript monitors any DDL events, such as creating a table or dropping a table.

- Generate SQL Server Agent alerts in response to WMI events. This is essentially a counterpart to the previous point. You can write T-SQL code to raise an Agent alert in response to a WMI event. You can use the new @wmi_namespace and @wmi_query parameters added to the msdb.dbo.sp_add_alert stored procedure to implement this functionality.

Not enough time to work on this one! It's ok. Here is a VBScript example that uses WMI to monitor DDL events in SQL Server 2005:

```
Dim evtToMonitor
Dim currentEvent
Set evtToMonitor = GetObject("winmgmts:{impersonationLevel=impersonate}!
➥//./root/Microsoft/SqlServer/ServerEvents/YUKON").
➥ExecNotificationQuery("select * from DDL_EVENTS")

WScript.Echo "Running...Click OK to continue..."

Do
Set currentEvent = evtToMonitor.NextEvent
```

```
If Err <> 0 then
 WScript.Echo Err.Number, Err.Description, Err.Source
 Exit Do
Else
 WScript.Echo "DDL Event in database '" & _
      currentEvent.DatabaseName & "' for object '" & _
      currentEvent.ObjectName & "'" & vbNewLine & vbNewLine & _
      currentEvent.TSQLCommand & vbNewLine & vbNewLine
 End If
Loop
```

Type this VBScript text into a text file or use the `WMIEventMonitor.vbs` script file provided with the code download, update the WMI namespace to include your SQL Server 2005 instance name in place of `YUKON`, and then run the VBScript file by double-clicking it in File Explorer.

The period (.) in the WMI namespace indicates the local server. If you want to monitor SQL Server on a different machine, you type the machine name instead of a period. Also, the word `YUKON` in the WMI namespace is the SQL Server 2005 instance name. You should change it to your named instance; for default or unnamed instance, you can replace `YUKON` with the word `MSSQLSERVER`.

After you launch the VBScript file, click OK, and then start SQL Server Management Studio or a SQLCMD session and connect to the server specified in the WMI script. Then you should create a table by using the `CREATE TABLE` DDL or by using Object Explorer. Or you can alter or drop a table, and for each DDL action you perform on this server, the script shows a message box showing the database in which DDL action is performed, the object name in context, and the XML formatted DDL action. To end the monitoring, you launch Windows Task Manager and end the `wscript.exe` process.

Summary

In this chapter, you have learned about the new suite of graphical and command-line tools introduced in SQL Server 2005.

The new SQL Server Management Studio consolidates the functionality provided by Enterprise Manager, Query Analyzer, and Analysis Manager. The new Business Intelligence Development Studio supports the complete business intelligence development life cycle by providing integrated tools to integrate, analyze, and report. The free SQL Server edition, SQL Server 2005 Express Edition, now bundles graphical tools such as Express Manager that can be used to manage server and author queries.

SQL Profiler is enhanced to support SQL Server 2005 features and also to provide better information to aid in troubleshooting performance issues. The Index Tuning Wizard from the previous release has now been replaced with a brand-new application called the Database Engine Tuning Advisor that assists in physical database design by recommending indexes, indexed views, and partitioning.

The new SQL Server Configuration Manager integrates Service Manager, Server Network Utility, and Client Network Utility into one application. SQLCMD is the new command-prompt utility that replaces `osql.exe` and also contains better scripting support. SQL Server 2005 introduces a SMTP-based emailing solution called Database Mail that provides a scalable, reliable, and secure method of sending emails.

The final section in this chapter shows you how to automate management tasks by using SMO and WMI. Chapter 6, "Transact-SQL Enhancements," describes the new features and enhancements introduced in the T-SQL language.

Transact-SQL Enhancements

Even though SQL Server 2005 supports writing stored procedure, functions, and triggers using .NET languages such as C#, Transact-SQL (T-SQL) will still be the primary language that database developers and DBAs will use to write scripts and procedural code. SQLCLR integration is provided as a supplement to help in writing business logic or complex computational tasks, or to perform functions that cannot easily be done by using T-SQL. SQLCLR is not a replacement for T-SQL. In fact, SQL Server 2005 introduces several new enhancements to the T-SQL language, as you will learn in this chapter.

The first section in this chapter compares .NET integration support with T-SQL, and the rest of the chapter details the new and improved T-SQL features.

T-SQL Versus SQLCLR

SQL Server has traditionally shipped with the ability to support one native programming language, T-SQL. With the release of SQL Server 2005, a big enhancement to the SQL Server 2005 engine is the ability to host the .NET common language runtime (CLR). This enables the writing of procedural code, such as stored procedures, functions, and triggers, using any of the .NET languages, such as Visual Basic .NET or C#. The addition of CLR support in SQL Server 2005 does not mean that T-SQL is no longer supported or that T-SQL should no longer be used. It is important to recognize that SQL Server database applications should use T-SQL as much as possible. Database applications should take advantage of the set-oriented query processor and resort to procedural programming only for expressing logic that cannot be expressed within the query language. This remains true with CLR support in SQL Server. The CLR should not be used to write procedural code that can be expressed in a single SELECT statement.

You should think of the CLR as an alternative for logic that cannot be expressed in T-SQL. A good point of reference is that the CLR should be considered to replace extended stored procedures in SQL Server or to build user-defined functions that perform logic not easily performed in T-SQL. The CLR is a complement to T-SQL, not a replacement for it.

The SQLCLR code benefits from the large number of classes and functions available as part of the .NET Framework base class library. The .NET Framework class library is much richer than the built-in functions supported in T-SQL. In addition, CLR programming languages provide rich constructs, such as arrays and lists, that are lacking in T-SQL.

The SQLCLR code is compiled code, whereas T-SQL is an interpreted language. Therefore, SQLCLR code yields better performance in certain scenarios.

Database administrators have the ability to enable or disable CLR integration in SQL Server 2005. By default, it is disabled. A new sp_configure advanced option has been added to SQL Server 2005 to control this setting. The following script enables the SQLCLR integration:

```
--Show advanced options
EXEC sys.sp_configure 'Show Advanced Options', 1;
RECONFIGURE WITH OVERRIDE
GO
--You can check the current value of CLR before setting
EXEC sys.sp_configure 'clr enabled';
GO
--Change CLR configuration
EXEC sys.sp_configure 'clr enabled', 1;
RECONFIGURE WITH OVERRIDE
GO
--Check the updated value
EXEC sys.sp_configure 'clr enabled';
GO
```

You can also enable or disable CLR integration by using the SQL Server Surface Area Configuration tool. After the server is configured to allow CLR integration, the functions in a .NET assembly can be mapped to a SQL Server stored procedure, function, or trigger, which can then be called like any other T-SQL module. SQL Server verifies the clr enabled setting when a SQLCLR method is invoked and not when it is mapped to a T-SQL module. When a SQLCLR method is executed, if the clr enabled option is turned off, SQL Server raises an error.

When you have a .NET assembly that contains SQLCLR functions, the first step in using these functions from within T-SQL code is to import the .NET assembly by using the CREATE ASSEMBLY statement. Next, you use the AS EXTERNAL NAME clause with a CREATE PROCEDURE/FUNCTION/TRIGGER DDL statement to map a T-SQL stored procedure or function or trigger to the specified .NET method. Let's assume that you have a SQLCLR .NET assembly called Test.dll, which contains a method that you want to use as a stored procedure from T-SQL code. Here is how you register the assembly, map the stored procedure, and invoke the SQLCLR code:

```
CREATE ASSEMBLY DotNetSQLServerSProc
FROM 'C:\Dev\Test.dll'
WITH PERMISSION_SET = SAFE;
GO
--Create procedure and map it to a method in the assembly
CREATE PROCEDURE dbo.sqlclr_HelloWorld @Message NVARCHAR(255)
AS EXTERNAL NAME DotNetSQLServerSProc.StoredProcedures.PrintMessage;
GO
--Execute the stored procedure
EXEC dbo.sqlclr_HelloWorld N'Hello to the DotNet world!';
GO
```

The important things to note in this batch are the WITH PERMISSION_SET clause in the CREATE ASSEMBLY DDL statement and the AS EXTERNAL NAME clause in the CREATE PROCEDURE DDL statement. SQLCLR integration is discussed in great detail in Chapter 11, "SQL Server 2005 and .NET Integration."

The following section describes the T-SQL enhancements introduced in SQL Server 2005.

The TOP Operator

Although the TOP operator has been around since SQL Server 7.0, in the past it only accepted a constant as the number of rows to return or as the percentage of the rows to return. The TOP statement in SQL Server 7.0 and SQL Server 2000 was also limited to SELECT statements. Thanks to improvements in the TOP operator for SQL Server 2005, the TOP statement can now accept variables and subqueries for the number of rows to return or the percentage of the rows to return. The TOP operator has also been enhanced so that it can be used with INSERT, UPDATE, and DELETE statements in addition to the SELECT statement.

Traditionally, developers utilized the TOP operator to reduce the number of rows returned by a query. When developers needed to page the results from a SQL Server query, they would either have to just return a static number of rows each time or build a dynamic query in which they could control the actual number of rows being returned by the query. The following query returns only 10 rows of data, and by changing the value of the variable, you could essentially page through a large result set:

```
USE AdventureWorks;
GO
DECLARE @startAfter INTEGER;
SET @startAfter = 0;
SELECT TOP (10) * FROM HumanResources.Employee
    WHERE EmployeeID > @startAfter
    ORDER BY EmployeeID;
GO
```

You could then return the result set to the client, and when you needed to page down, you would just reset the variable to the largest `EmployeeID` value (for example, `10`) returned in the current set of data:

```
DECLARE @startAfter INTEGER;
SET @startAfter = 10;
SELECT TOP (10) * FROM HumanResources.Employee
    WHERE EmployeeID > @startAfter
    ORDER BY EmployeeID;
GO
```

Most of the time, this method is fine, but what if there were only two rows left in the table? Would you really want to incur an additional network trip to return only two rows? You could get around this issue with the use of dynamic SQL statements to change the number of rows returned by the query to include those two additional rows, as shown here:

```
DECLARE @strSQL NVARCHAR(1000);
DECLARE @intRows INTEGER;
DECLARE @startAfter INTEGER;
SET @intRows = 10 ;
SET @startAfter = 0;
SET @strSQL = 'SELECT TOP (' + CAST(@intRows AS VARCHAR(3)) + ') *
    FROM HumanResources.Employee
    WHERE EmployeeID > ' + CAST(@startAfter AS VARCHAR(3)) + '
    ORDER BY EmployeeID';
EXEC sys.sp_executesql @strSQL;
GO
```

For the next result set, if 12 rows should be returned, you can set `@intRows` to 12, and the dynamic SQL execution will take care of returning the requested number of rows. This way, you can prevent a third stored procedure call and an additional network trip.

With SQL Server 2005, the ability to pass an expression with the `TOP` operator enables the application to simply state how many rows of data it requires; this prevents the need for dynamic SQL and the problems associated with using dynamic SQL:

```
DECLARE @intRows INTEGER;
DECLARE @startAfter INTEGER;
SET @intRows = 12 ;
SET @startAfter = 10;
SELECT TOP (@intRows) * FROM HumanResources.Employee
   WHERE EmployeeID > @startAfter
   ORDER BY EmployeeID;
GO
```

You can still use the PERCENT keyword to return a percentage of rows instead of a fixed number of rows:

```
DECLARE @intPercRows INTEGER
DECLARE @intPage INTEGER
SET @intPercRows = 12
SET @intPage = 10
SELECT TOP (@intPercRows) PERCENT * FROM HumanResources.Employee
   WHERE EmployeeID > @intPage
   ORDER BY EmployeeID;
GO
```

In addition to passing an expression, you can also use a subquery to satisfy the TOP statement value requirement. Here is an example of passing a subquery with the TOP operator:

```
DECLARE @startAfter INTEGER;
SET @startAfter = 0;
SELECT TOP (SELECT COUNT(*)/11 FROM HumanResources.Employee) *
  FROM HumanResources.Employee
  WHERE EmployeeID > @startAfter
  ORDER BY EmployeeID;
GO
```

Considering that the HumanResources.Employee table has 290 rows, you can use this script to retrieve 11 batches of 26 rows, and the remaining 12th batch of 4 rows, by changing the value of the @startAfter variable.

The TABLESAMPLE Clause

The previous section illustrates one way of limiting a result set by using the TOP operator. SQL Server 2005 introduces a new clause, TABLESAMPLE, that you can use in a SELECT statement to restrict a result set to a randomly selected row. This clause is useful when you don't necessarily need to process all the rows and when you don't need the exact results—you just need to work on a sample of rows from a table that contains millions of rows. For instance, if a sales table contains a few million rows and you need to find out the *approximate* average order quantity, using TABLESAMPLE will yield better performance than processing all the rows in the table.

You can specify a number that indicates how many rows or what percentage of rows should be sampled. If you specify a number instead of a percentage, SQL Server calculates a percentage value based on the total number of rows and uses that percentage value for sampling. Let's assume that this percentage number is 30. SQL Server will then return all the rows from 30% of the specified table's data pages. If a table consists of a single page, either all rows on the page are returned or none of the rows are returned.

NOTE

TABLESAMPLE **cannot be used with views or table variables. Also, before you can use** TABLESAMPLE**, the database's compatibility level must be set to** 90**.**

Let's look at an example of using the TABLESAMPLE clause to find out the approximate average line total from the Sales.SalesOrderDetail table in the AdventureWorks sample database:

```
USE AdventureWorks;
GO
SELECT AVG(LineTotal) FROM Sales.SalesOrderDetail;
GO
SELECT AVG(LineTotal) FROM Sales.SalesOrderDetail
    TABLESAMPLE (30 PERCENT);
GO
```

The first SELECT statement finds the exact average value by processing all the rows in the table, and on my machine it returns 905.449206. If you execute this SELECT statement multiple times, you will notice that every time it returns a different value, which shows that SQL Server 2005 selects rows from a 30% set of random pages to calculate the average. You should get values such as 919.500875, 913.139024, 907.427679, 922.164805, and so on. If you want to get the same results every time, you can use the REPEATABLE clause and specify a seed value. As long as the same seed value is passed and the data is unchanged, you should get the same result:

```
SELECT AVG(LineTotal) FROM Sales.SalesOrderDetail
    TABLESAMPLE (30 PERCENT) REPEATABLE(2);
GO
```

The ISO SQL-2003 standard includes two sampling methods: BERNOULLI and SYSTEM. SQL Server 2005 supports only the SYSTEM sampling method. The other sampling method might be supported in the future. You can be specific and provide the SYSTEM method as an algorithm name in the TABLESAMPLE statement, as shown here:

```
SELECT AVG(LineTotal) FROM Sales.SalesOrderDetail
    TABLESAMPLE SYSTEM (50000 ROWS);
GO
```

This query also illustrates how you specify the number of rows instead of a percentage value.

Common Table Expressions (CTEs)

A new T-SQL enhancement in SQL Server 2005 that will have a dramatic effect on future queries is common table expressions (CTEs), which are defined in SQL-99. CTEs can be thought of as a type of derived table, but unlike with derived tables, the result set of CTEs can be defined once and used multiple times in the defining query. With this capability to define once and use it several times, CTEs can even reference themselves, making CTEs superior to other methods for defining hierarchies with a SQL Server query.

Here is the simplistic CTE syntax:

```
WITH <cte_alias>(<column_aliases>)
AS
(
     <cte_query>
)
SELECT * FROM <cte_alias>;
```

SQL Server 2005 supports two different types of CTEs: non-recursive and recursive. CTEs that do not have self-references are non-recursive, whereas recursive CTEs have self-references. Here is an example of simple non-recursive and recursive CTEs:

```
USE AdventureWorks;
GO
--Non-recursive CTE
WITH NonRecCTE (cnt) AS
(
    SELECT COUNT(EmployeeID) AS cnt
    FROM HumanResources.Employee
    GROUP BY ManagerID
)
SELECT AVG(cnt) AS AvgDirectReports
FROM NonRecCTE;

--Recursive CTE
WITH RecCTE(ManagerID, EmployeeID, EmployeeLevel) AS
(
    SELECT ManagerID, EmployeeID, 0 AS EmployeeLevel
       FROM HumanResources.Employee
       WHERE ManagerID IS NULL

    UNION ALL

    SELECT e.ManagerID, e.EmployeeID, EmployeeLevel + 1
       FROM HumanResources.Employee e
```

```
        INNER JOIN RecCTE r
        ON e.ManagerID = r.EmployeeID
)
SELECT EmployeeID, ManagerID, EmployeeLevel
FROM RecCTE;
GO
```

In the non-recursive CTE query in this example, the inner query groups the employees by `ManagerID` and returns the count. The outer query in this non-recursive CTE then performs an average on this count column and returns a number indicating the average number of direct reports in the `Employee` table.

A recursive CTE always contains at least two queries combined using a `UNION ALL` clause. The first query, called the *anchor member*, is the starting point (usually the first row in the result set). In the second query, the called recursive member follows the `UNION ALL` clause, and in this query the CTE refers to itself. The preceding recursive CTE query returns the `EmployeeID`, the `ManagerID`, and the level of the employee in the hierarchy.

The most common problem with recursion is infinite loops. SQL Server solves this problem by defining a serverwide recursion level limit setting, called `MAXRECURSION`, which defaults to `100`. You can also specify the `MAXRECURSION` hint in your outer query to limit the recursion level for that query.

A CTE can refer to another CTE, as illustrated in the following query:

```
WITH YearlyOrderAmtCTE(OrderYear, TotalAmount)
AS
(
    SELECT YEAR(OrderDate), SUM(OrderQty*UnitPrice)
    FROM Sales.SalesOrderHeader AS H JOIN Sales.SalesOrderDetail AS D
        ON H.SalesOrderID = D.SalesOrderID
    GROUP BY YEAR(OrderDate)
),
SalesTrendCTE(OrderYear, Amount, AmtYearBefore, AmtDifference, DiffPerc)
AS
(
 SELECT thisYear.OrderYear, thisYear.TotalAmount,
        lastYear.TotalAmount,
        thisYear.TotalAmount - lastYear.TotalAmount,
        (thisYear.TotalAmount/lastYear.TotalAmount - 1) * 100
 FROM YearlyOrderAmtCTE AS thisYear
      LEFT OUTER JOIN YearlyOrderAmtCTE AS lastYear
      ON thisYear.OrderYear = lastYear.OrderYear + 1
)
SELECT * FROM SalesTrendCTE;
GO
```

This query defines two non-recursive CTEs. The first CTE, called `YearlyOrderAmtCTE`, groups the total sales by year. This CTE is then used in the second CTE, called `SalesTrendCTE`, and the outer or main query selects all the rows from `SalesTrendCTE`. The preceding query returns the following results:

OrderYear	Amount	AmtYearBefore	AmtDifference	DiffPerc
2001	11336135.376	NULL	NULL	NULL
2002	30859192.305	11336135.376	19523056.929	172.21
2003	42308575.2263	30859192.305	11449382.9213	37.10
2004	25869986.4061	42308575.2263	-16438588.8202	-38.86

NOTE

When a CTE is used in a statement that is part of a batch, the preceding statement in the batch must be followed by a semicolon.

Neither recursive nor non-recursive CTEs can include the following clauses in the defining, or inner, query for the CTE:

- COMPUTE or COMPUTE BY

- ORDER BY (except when a TOP clause is specified)

- INTO

- OPTION clause with query hints

- FOR XML

- FOR BROWSE

Recursive CTEs have the additional following restrictions:

- The FROM clause of the recursive member must refer only once to the CTE expression_name.

- The recursive member CTE_query_definitions does not allow SELECT DISTINCT, GROUP BY, HAVING, scalar aggregation, TOP, LEFT or RIGHT OUTER JOIN (INNER JOIN is allowed), functions with input or output parameters, or subqueries.

Let's look at the power of CTEs, using a simple example. In this example, a report is created to show each manager, his or her direct reports, and the employees under each manager's direct reports—kind of an organization chart:

```
WITH OrgChart
  (FirstName, LastName, Title, ManagerID, EmployeeID, EmpLevel, SortValue)
AS
(
```

```
    SELECT ct.FirstName, ct.LastName, emp.Title, emp.ManagerID,
           emp.EmployeeID, 0 AS EmpLevel,
        CAST(emp.EmployeeID AS VARBINARY(900))
    FROM HumanResources.Employee emp INNER JOIN Person.Contact ct
           ON ct.ContactID = emp.ContactID
    WHERE emp.ManagerID IS NULL

    UNION ALL

    SELECT ct.FirstName, ct.LastName, emp.Title, emp.ManagerID,
           emp.EmployeeID, EmpLevel + 1,
           CAST(SortValue + CAST(emp.EmployeeID AS BINARY(4))
                AS VARBINARY(900))
    FROM HumanResources.Employee emp JOIN Person.Contact AS ct
           ON ct.ContactID = emp.ContactID
        JOIN OrgChart org
           ON emp.ManagerID = org.EmployeeID
)
SELECT
    EmpLevel, REPLICATE('        ', EmpLevel) + FirstName + ' ' + LastName
    AS 'Employee Name', Title
FROM OrgChart
ORDER BY SortValue;
GO
```

The anchor member in this recursive CTE query finds out about an employee who does not have a manager (`ManagerID IS NULL`). Then the recursive member finds out the topmost manager's direct reports, and then in recursion it finds out about employees reporting to direct reports. The outer `SELECT` statement uses the `REPLICATE` function and `EmpLevel` and `SortValue` columns to generate a formatted organization chart of employees. The query produces the following results (some rows have been omitted for brevity):

```
EmpLevel  Employee Name                Title
--------  ---------------------------  ---------------------------
0         Ken Sánchez                  Chief Executive Officer
1           David Bradley              Marketing Manager
2             Kevin Brown              Marketing Assistant
2             Sariya Harnpadoungsataya Marketing Specialist
2             Mary Gibson              Marketing Specialist
2             Jill Williams            Marketing Specialist
2             Terry Eminhizer          Marketing Specialist
2             Wanida Benshoof          Marketing Assistant
2             John Wood                Marketing Specialist
2             Mary Dempsey             Marketing Assistant
1           Terri Duffy                Vice President of Engineering
2             Roberto Tamburello       Engineering Manager
```

TIP

Notice the use of the semicolon (;) as the statement separator in the scripts throughout this chapter. SQL Server 2005 recommends using the semicolon as a statement termina-tor. In addition, the semicolon is required at the end of the preceding statement when the CTE or Service Broker statement (for example, SEND or RECEIVE) is not the first state-ment in a batch or module.

Large Object Data Type Enhancements

Often when working with large strings in SQL Server 2000, developers were forced to use a text, image, or ntext data type. Most developers quickly realized that working with these large object data types was cumbersome. Some of the limitations with text, image, and ntext data types include are as follows:

- You cannot declare a variable of these types.

- Many string functions, such as LEFT, RIGHT, and so on, do not work with these types.

- These data types often require special handling, by using functions such as TEXTPTR and TEXTVALID and T-SQL statements such as WRITETEXT and UPDATETEXT.

SQL Server 2005 fixes this problem by introducing enhancements to the varchar, varbinary, and nvarchar data types to allow for increased storage. The max option now allows varchar, nvarchar, and varbinary to hold up to 2GB in this release. max may refer to a new maximum in a future release.

The types using the max specifier do not require any special handling, as do text, ntext, and image types. You can treat the max large object types as regular varchar, nvarchar, and varbinary types, and you can use them in joins, in subqueries, to order by, to group by, with distinct clauses, with aggregates, for comparison, for concatenation, and with string functions such as LEFT, RIGHT, SUBSTRING, and so on. You can define variables and parameters of large object types with the max specifier, and you can store up to 2GB of data in the variable or parameter.

NOTE

Because the max specifier allows storing up to 2GB of data and at the same time offers the flexibility to use the type as traditional varchar, varbinary, or nvarchar types, you might be inclined to use the max specifier for all string or binary columns. However, you should consider the performance implications of I/O and CPU costs involved with rows spanning multiple pages. You should use the max specifier only when large storage (more that 8000 bytes) is desired for the column.

Here is an example of using the max specifier in a table column and a variable declaration:

```
USE AdventureWorks;
GO
```

```
IF OBJECT_ID('HumanResources.EmployeeNotes') IS NOT NULL
   DROP TABLE HumanResources.EmployeeNotes;
GO
CREATE TABLE HumanResources.EmployeeNotes
 (EmployeeID INT PRIMARY KEY IDENTITY(1,1) NOT NULL,
  Notes NVARCHAR(MAX));
GO


DECLARE @varNotes NVARCHAR(MAX)
SET @varNotes = N'New Hire 4/11/2005'
INSERT INTO HumanResources.EmployeeNotes SELECT @varNotes;
GO


SELECT * FROM HumanResources.EmployeeNotes ;
GO
```

This script illustrates declaring a column and a variable of type nvarchar(max).

Often when you store a large amount of data in a max type column, you might want to update just part of the column or variable data instead of completely replacing the value. The legacy large object types (text, ntext, and image) provided the UPDATETEXT T-SQL statement to change only a portion of data. For max types, SQL Server 2005 provides similar functionality via the .write(expression, @offset, @length) clause, which can be used in a SET statement for variables and in an UPDATE statement for a column, as illustrated in the following script:

```
UPDATE HumanResources.EmployeeNotes
SET Notes.write('; Orientation and training complete 4/13/2005', NULL, NULL);


SELECT * FROM HumanResources.EmployeeNotes ;
GO


- - - - - - - - - - - - - - - - -


DECLARE @varNotes NVARCHAR(MAX)
DECLARE @yearIndex INT

SELECT TOP(1) @varNotes = Notes FROM HumanResources.EmployeeNotes;
SET @yearIndex = CHARINDEX('2005', @varNotes)
SET @varNotes.write('2004', @yearIndex - 1, 4);
SET @yearIndex = CHARINDEX('2005', @varNotes)
SET @varNotes.write('2004', @yearIndex - 1, 4);
PRINT @varNotes;
GO
```

The first batch in this script runs an UPDATE statement and passes @offset and @length as NULL in the .write() clause, which indicates that you want to append the first parameter to the existing value. The second batch in this script illustrates updating parts of the nvarchar(max) variable data by using the .write() clause—in this case replacing 2005 with 2004 in the variable string.

> **TIP**
>
> In addition to previously mentioned enhancement to the varchar, varbinary, and nvarchar types, SQL Server 2005 also introduces a new data type, xml, which can be used to store XML documents and fragments in a table column, variable, or parameter. SQL Server provides several methods on this data type that can be used to query and update the XML data. The new xml data type and T-SQL constructs related to this type are discussed in Chapter 10, "XML and Web Services Support in SQL Server 2005."

T-SQL Error Handling

T-SQL developers often used the combination of the @@ERROR global variable and the RETURN or GOTO statement inside a batch or a stored procedure to handle errors. Because SQL Server clears or resets @@ERROR after every statement, in order to catch the error, it is required to check for @@ERROR immediately after the statement. SQL Server did not provide any other useful information besides @@ERROR on what went wrong.

SQL Server 2005 adopts the modern error-handling paradigm and introduces support for TRY...CATCH blocks. You can place multiple statements in a TRY block and catch any error in the CATCH block. Within the CATCH block, you can invoke functions such as ERROR_MESSAGE(), ERROR_NUMBER(), ERROR_SEVERITY(), ERROR_STATE(), ERROR_LINE(), and ERROR_PROCEDURE() to get more information on the error. Here's an example:

```
USE AdventureWorks
GO
IF OBJECT_ID('Production.tblTry_Catch_Audit') IS NOT NULL
    DROP TABLE Production.tblTry_Catch_Audit;
GO
CREATE TABLE Production.tblTry_Catch_Audit
( ErrCode INT, ErrMessage NVARCHAR(4000),
  ErrUser NVARCHAR(100) DEFAULT SYSTEM_USER NOT NULL,
  ErrDate DATETIME DEFAULT GETDATE() NOT NULL);
GO


IF OBJECT_ID('Production.spTRY_CATCH') IS NOT NULL
    DROP PROCEDURE Production.spTRY_CATCH
GO
CREATE PROCEDURE Production.spTRY_CATCH (@ProductID INT)
AS
BEGIN
    SET NOCOUNT ON
    DECLARE @errorString  NVARCHAR(4000)
    DECLARE @rowcount      INTEGER
```

```
BEGIN TRY
   DELETE FROM Production.Product
      WHERE ProductID = @ProductID;
END TRY
BEGIN CATCH
   SELECT @errorString = 'ERROR '
            + CONVERT(NVARCHAR(100), ERROR_NUMBER())
            + ' in procedure ''' + ERROR_PROCEDURE()
            + ''' while deleting the product.'
            + CHAR(13) + ERROR_MESSAGE();

   INSERT INTO tblTry_Catch_Audit (ErrCode, ErrMessage)
      VALUES(ERROR_NUMBER(), @errorString);

   RAISERROR(@errorString, 10, 1);
   RETURN ERROR_NUMBER();
   END CATCH
   RETURN 0
END;
GO


EXEC Production.spTRY_CATCH @ProductID = 1;
GO


SELECT * FROM Production.tblTry_Catch_Audit;
GO
```

In this example, deleting a product creates a referential integrity error, which is captured by the TRY...CATCH block. The CATCH block generates a more descriptive error string, saves that into an error audit table, and returns that, along with the actual error message and error number, to the caller.

You should keep in mind the following when writing TRY...CATCH blocks:

- The END TRY statement in a TRY...CATCH block must be immediately followed by a BEGIN CATCH statement. A syntax error is reported if you put anything between END TRY and BEGIN CATCH.

- A TRY...CATCH construct cannot span multiple batches.

- If the code in the CATCH block raises an error, the error is sent back to the caller, unless you have a nested TRY...CATCH block in the CATCH block itself. SQL Server 2005 allows nested TRY...CATCH blocks. You can have a TRY...CATCH block within another BEGIN TRY...END TRY block or BEGIN CATCH...END CATCH block.

- The GOTO statement can be used to jump within the same TRY or CATCH block or to jump out of a TRY or CATCH block, but it cannot be used to enter a TRY or CATCH block.

- TRY...CATCH blocks cannot be used to capture all T-SQL errors. For example, the TRY...CATCH block will not capture any syntax errors or any warning below severity level 11 or errors above severity level 20, and so on.

- If the code in a TRY block generates a trappable error, the control goes to the first line in the CATCH block. If you want to return the error information to the caller, you can use either SELECT, RAISERROR, or PRINT to do that, as illustrated in the preceding example.

DDL Triggers

The concept of triggers is not new in SQL Server 2005. Almost every RDBMS supports a procedural T-SQL code, called a *trigger*, that is invoked when a Data Modification Language (DML) statement, such as INSERT, UPDATE, or DELETE, is executed. SQL Server 2005 expands this support, however, and now you can have a procedural T-SQL code executed when a DDL statement, such as CREATE TABLE, ALTER TABLE, DROP TABLE, and so on, is executed.

A DDL trigger can be defined at the database level or at the server level. A database-level DDL trigger allows you to capture events such as CREATE/ALTER/DROP TABLE, VIEW, USER, ROLE, and other DDL statements. A server-level DDL trigger allows you to respond to events such as CREATE/ALTER/DROP LOGIN, CERTIFICATE, and other server-level DDL statements. The syntax to create a DDL trigger is similar to that for creating a DML trigger, except that you specify whether it is a database-scoped (the ON DATABASE clause) or a server-scoped (the ON ALL SERVER clause) DDL trigger.

Here is an example of a script that creates a database-level DDL trigger to audit and prevent dropping of a table:

```
USE AdventureWorks;
GO
IF OBJECT_ID('dbo.tblDDLActions') IS NOT NULL
   DROP TABLE dbo.tblDDLActions;
GO
CREATE TABLE dbo.tblDDLActions
 (RecordID INT PRIMARY KEY IDENTITY(1,1) NOT NULL,
  Action XML,
  ActiveUser NVARCHAR(100) DEFAULT SYSTEM_USER,
  ActionDate DATETIME DEFAULT GETDATE());
GO

IF EXISTS (SELECT name FROM sys.triggers
           WHERE parent_class = 0 AND name = 'trgTest1')
   DROP TRIGGER trgTest1
   ON DATABASE;
GO
```

```
IF OBJECT_ID('dbo.tblTest') IS NOT NULL
    DROP TABLE dbo.tblTest;
GO

CREATE TRIGGER trgTest1
ON DATABASE
FOR DROP_TABLE
AS
BEGIN
    DECLARE @eventData XML
    SET @eventData = EVENTDATA();
    ROLLBACK;
    SET NOCOUNT ON;
    INSERT INTO dbo.tblDDLActions (Action) VALUES (@eventData);
    PRINT 'Dropping a table is not allowed';END;
GO

--Test the trigger
CREATE TABLE dbo.tblTest(col1 int);
GO
BEGIN TRY
    DROP TABLE tblTest;
END TRY
BEGIN CATCH
    PRINT ERROR_MESSAGE();
END CATCH
GO

SELECT * FROM dbo.tblDDLActions;
GO

--Clean up
DROP TRIGGER trgTest1 ON DATABASE;
DROP TABLE dbo.tblTest;
DROP TABLE dbo.tblDDLActions;
```

This script creates an audit table that is used to store details about who performed the DDL action and when, and what action (dropping a table in this case).

The **EVENTDATA()** function can be used inside a DDL trigger to find complete details about an action that led to the firing of the trigger. This function returns a value of xml data type. Here is an example of the XML document returned by the EVENTDATA() function for the DROP_TABLE database-level event:

```
<EVENT_INSTANCE>
    <EventType>DROP_TABLE</EventType>
    <PostTime>2005-02-25T16:36:12.313</PostTime>
```

```
    <SPID>51</SPID>
    <ServerName>DDGXP\DECCTP</ServerName>
    <LoginName>DDGXP\Darshan Singh</LoginName>
    <UserName>dbo</UserName>
    <DatabaseName>AdventureWorks</DatabaseName>
    <SchemaName>dbo</SchemaName>
    <ObjectName>tblTest</ObjectName>
    <ObjectType>TABLE</ObjectType>
    <TSQLCommand>
        <SetOptions ANSI_NULLS="ON" ANSI_NULL_DEFAULT="ON" ANSI_PADDING="ON"
                    QUOTED_IDENTIFIER="ON" ENCRYPTED="FALSE" />
        <CommandText>DROP TABLE tblTest;</CommandText>
    </TSQLCommand>
</EVENT_INSTANCE>
```

You can save the XML returned by EVENTDATA() into a table, as is done in the preceding example, or directly execute XQuery queries on the value returned. XML data types and XQuery are discussed in detail in Chapter 10.

Here is an example of a server-level DDL trigger that prevents the creation of a SQL Server login. It allows the creation of Windows NT authenticated logins, but if it finds out that the login being created uses SQL authentication, it executes the ROLLBACK statement to abort the statement that fired the trigger:

```
IF EXISTS (SELECT name FROM sys.server_triggers
           WHERE parent_class = 100 AND name = 'trgTest2')
   DROP TRIGGER trgTest2
   ON ALL SERVER;
GO

CREATE TRIGGER trgTest2
ON ALL SERVER
FOR CREATE_LOGIN
AS
BEGIN
   SET NOCOUNT ON;
   IF 'SQL Login' =
     EVENTDATA().value('(/EVENT_INSTANCE/LoginType)[1]',
                       'varchar(100)')
   BEGIN
     ROLLBACK;
     PRINT 'Creating a SQL login is not allowed.';
   END
   ELSE
   BEGIN
     PRINT 'Creating Windows NT Authenticated logins is allowed.';
   END
```

```
END;
GO

--Test the trigger, should print error message
BEGIN TRY
    CREATE LOGIN DarshanSingh WITH PASSWORD = 'WjKkWjKf1234'
END TRY
BEGIN CATCH
    PRINT ERROR_MESSAGE();
END CATCH
GO

--Test the trigger, should work fine
BEGIN TRY
    --Change the NT Login in the following statement
    CREATE LOGIN [DDGXP\Guest] FROM WINDOWS;
END TRY
BEGIN CATCH
    PRINT ERROR_MESSAGE();
END CATCH
GO

--Clean up
DROP TRIGGER trgTest2 ON ALL SERVER;
GO
--Change the NT Login in the following statement
DROP LOGIN [DDGXP\Guest];
GO
```

This script creates a server-scoped DDL trigger to handle the CREATE_LOGIN event. The trigger code uses the EVENTDATA() function to get an xml type value that contains the event information. It then uses the value() XML method and an XQuery expression to see if the login being created uses SQL authentication. If it does, it rolls back the transaction and prints an error message. The rest of the statements in this batch test the trigger by first trying to create a SQL authenticated login, which should fail, and a Windows NT authenticated login, which should succeed. Remember to change the NT login name in the preceding script to match your machine or domain in place of DDGXP.

TIP

You can use the sys.triggers catalog view to see database-level DDL triggers. The parent_class column in this catalog view has 0 as the value for DDL triggers. You can use the sys.server_triggers catalog view to get a list of server-level DDL triggers. The sys.trigger_events and sys.server_trigger_events catalog views contain a row for each time a database-level and **server-level trigger was fired, respectively. Database-level DDL triggers are listed in the** `Programmability\Database Triggers` **folder in Object Explorer. The server-level triggers are listed under the** `Server Objects\Triggers` **folder in Object Explorer.**

The `ON DATABASE` or `ON ALL SERVER` clause can be used with `DROP TRIGGER` to delete a DDL trigger, `ALTER TRIGGER` to modify a DDL trigger definition, `DISABLE TRIGGER` to disable a DDL trigger, and `ENABLE TRIGGER` to enable a DDL trigger. The `CONTROL SERVER` permission is required to create a DDL trigger at the server scope, and `ALTER ANY TRIGGER` permission is required to create a DDL trigger at the database scope.

For simplicity, SQL Server 2005 groups the related events into event groups on which you can define the triggers. For instance, instead of specifying `FOR CREATE TABLE, ALTER TABLE`, and `DROP TABLE` in the `CREATE TRIGGER` statement, you can just specify `FOR DDL_TABLE_EVENTS`, which includes the three table DDL statements.

In addition to having different purpose, DDL triggers differ from DML triggers in some ways. You cannot define an `INSTEAD OF` DDL trigger. The virtual `inserted` and `deleted` tables are not available and cannot be accessed inside the DDL trigger code; rather, the `EVENTDATA()` function is used to get the triggering event information, as illustrated previously.

Both DML triggers and DDL triggers are executed synchronously. This means that the action that leads to execution of a trigger waits until the trigger finishes executing. This is the reason DDL events such as `CREATE DATABASE` cannot be captured using DDL triggers: Such events are meant for asynchronous, non-transacted statements only.

SQL Server 2005 provides an alternative to DDL triggers—a mechanism called *event notifications*, which can be used to handle DDL events asynchronously. In addition to DDL events, event notification can also be used to handle profiler trace events, as discussed in the following section.

Event Notifications

The previous section illustrates how you can use DDL triggers to capture server and database events. DDL triggers have two limitations. First, the trigger code is executed synchronously and hence it does not yield a scalable solution. Second, it does not allow capturing some DDL events (such as `CREATE DATABASE`). In addition, let's say you wanted to have the DDL trigger handler code executed on a different server. You could not do that by just using DDL triggers.

Event notifications allow you to handle database, server, and subsets of SQL trace events asynchronously. The `CREATE EVENT NOTIFICATION` T-SQL statement can be used to create an event notification object. You might wonder how the events are handled asynchronously. The answer involves Service Broker. With the `CREATE EVENT NOTIFICATION` statement, you provide the name of a Service Broker service to which the specified database, server, or SQL trace events will be posted. The events or messages posted to the Service Broker queue are then handled asynchronously. The event information is posted as XML to the specified Service Broker queue. Service Broker is a new technology introduced in SQL Server 2005 that brings the reliable and asynchronous messaging platform closer to the database engine. It is discussed in detail in Chapter 14, "SQL Server 2005 Service Broker."

Here is a summary of how event notifications differs from DDL triggers:

- DDL triggers execute in the scope of the transaction of the action that causes them to fire and trigger code executes synchronously. If required, a DDL trigger can roll back the entire transaction. Event notifications, on the other hand, do not execute in the scope of the transaction of the action that causes them to fire, and hence they cannot roll back the transaction. Event notifications are processed asynchronously, using the Service Broker technology.

- In addition to database and server events, event notifications also support responding to a subset of SQL trace events.

- DDL triggers execute on the same server. Because event notifications are based on Service Broker, the events may be processed on a different server.

The following is the CREATE EVENT NOTIFICATION syntax:

```
CREATE EVENT NOTIFICATION event_notification_name
ON { SERVER ¦ DATABASEQUEUE <queue_name>
[ WITH FAN_IN ]
FOR { event_type ¦ event_group } [ ,...n ]
TO SERVICE <'broker_service'> ,
        {<'broker_instance_specifier'> ¦ 'current database' } [;]
```

With the ON clause, you specify whether you want to handle database or server events or events on specified queue. With the FOR clause, you specify which events or event groups you want to listen on. With the TO SERVICE clause, you specify the name of the Service Broker service to which the event XML messages should be posted. The service and queue should already be created. If the Service Broker service uses the activation feature to execute a stored procedure when a message is posted in the queue, the stored procedure should also be already created, as you will see in the following example. If the WITH FAN_IN option is specified, SQL Server will group the same events and send them all together as a single event.

```
SET NOCOUNT ON
GO

USE [AdventureWorks];
GO

-- 1.Create the audit table
IF OBJECT_ID('dbo.tblAudit') IS NOT NULL
    DROP TABLE dbo.tblAudit;
```

```
GO
CREATE TABLE dbo.tblAudit
  (eventXMLData XML null);
GO


-- 2. Create the stored procedure
IF OBJECT_ID('dbo.sproc_Audit') IS NOT NULL
BEGIN
   DROP PROCEDURE dbo.sproc_Audit;
END
GO


CREATE PROCEDURE dbo.sproc_Audit
AS
BEGIN
   DECLARE @eventDataXML  varbinary(max);
   RECEIVE TOP(1) @eventDataXML = message_body
    FROM [AdventureWorks].dbo.AuditQueue

   IF CAST(@eventDataXML as XML) IS NOT NULL
   BEGIN
      INSERT INTO dbo.tblAudit (eventXMLData)
         VALUES (CAST(@eventDataXML as XML));
   END
END
GO


-- 3. Create the service broker queue and service
IF EXISTS(SELECT * FROM sys.services WHERE name = 'AuditService')
   DROP SERVICE AuditService;
GO
IF OBJECT_ID('dbo.AuditQueue') IS NOT NULL AND
   EXISTS(SELECT * FROM sys.service_queues WHERE name = 'AuditQueue')
  DROP QUEUE dbo.AuditQueue;
GO


CREATE QUEUE dbo.AuditQueue
   -- Activation turned on
   WITH STATUS = ON,
   ACTIVATION (
      -- The name of the proc to process messages for this queue
      PROCEDURE_NAME = AdventureWorks.dbo.sproc_Audit,
      -- The maximum number of copies of the proc to start
      MAX_QUEUE_READERS = 1,
      -- Start the procedure as the user who created the queue.
      EXECUTE AS SELF )
```

```
   ON [DEFAULT] ;
GO

CREATE SERVICE
   AuditService ON QUEUE AuditQueue
   ([http://schemas.microsoft.com/SQL/Notifications/PostEventNotification]);
GO

-- 4. Setup event notification
CREATE EVENT NOTIFICATION ENDBAudit
ON SERVER
FOR CREATE_DATABASE, DROP_DATABASE
TO SERVICE 'AuditService', 'current database';
GO

-- 5. Try out the event notification
IF EXISTS (SELECT [name]
           FROM [master].[sys].[databases] WHERE [name] = N'TestDB1')
BEGIN
    DROP DATABASE TestDB1;
END
GO

CREATE DATABASE TestDB1;
GO

IF EXISTS (SELECT [name]
           FROM [master].[sys].[databases] WHERE [name] = N'TestDB1')
BEGIN
    DROP DATABASE TestDB1;
END
GO

--WAITFOR few seconds
WAITFOR DELAY '00:00:05';
GO

SELECT * FROM dbo.tblAudit;
GO

-- 6. Cleanup
DROP EVENT NOTIFICATION ENDBAudit ON SERVER ;
GO

IF OBJECT_ID('dbo.tblAudit') IS NOT NULL
   DROP TABLE dbo.tblAudit;
```

```
GO

IF EXISTS(SELECT * FROM sys.services WHERE name = 'AuditService')
    DROP SERVICE AuditService;
GO
IF OBJECT_ID('dbo.AuditQueue') IS NOT NULL AND
   EXISTS(SELECT * FROM sys.service_queues WHERE name = 'AuditQueue')
  DROP QUEUE dbo.AuditQueue;
GO
```

The script first creates an audit table and then a stored procedure that will be activated whenever an event message is posted to the Service Broker queue. This stored procedure retrieves the message from the queue, casts it as XML, and inserts a row into the audit table. Next, a Service Broker queue and service is created. The CREATE EVENT NOTIFICATION statement then uses this service to monitor CREATE_DATABASE and DROP_DATABASE server events. To try out the event notification mechanism, the script then creates and drops a test database. The SELECT statement on the audit table should show the two rows, containing the event data as XML documents. The last step in the script does the clean-up and removes the objects created. When you run this script, you see two records in the audit table, containing the following XML document:

```xml
<EVENT_INSTANCE>
  <EventType>CREATE_DATABASE</EventType>
  <PostTime>2005-06-26T17:44:38.077</PostTime>
  <SPID>53</SPID>
  <ServerName>DDGXP\JUNECTP</ServerName>
  <LoginName>DDGXP\Darshan Singh</LoginName>
  <DatabaseName>TestDB1</DatabaseName>
  <TSQLCommand>
    <SetOptions ANSI_NULLS="ON" ANSI_NULL_DEFAULT="ON" ANSI_PADDING="ON"
                QUOTED_IDENTIFIER="ON" ENCRYPTED="FALSE" />
    <CommandText>CREATE DATABASE TestDB1;</CommandText>
  </TSQLCommand>
</EVENT_INSTANCE>

<EVENT_INSTANCE>
  <EventType>DROP_DATABASE</EventType>
  <PostTime>2005-06-26T17:44:38.127</PostTime>
  <SPID>53</SPID>
  <ServerName>DDGXP\JUNECTP</ServerName>
  <LoginName>DDGXP\Darshan Singh</LoginName>
  <DatabaseName>TestDB1</DatabaseName>
  <TSQLCommand>
    <SetOptions ANSI_NULLS="ON" ANSI_NULL_DEFAULT="ON" ANSI_PADDING="ON"
                QUOTED_IDENTIFIER="ON" ENCRYPTED="FALSE" />
    <CommandText>DROP DATABASE TestDB1;</CommandText>
```

```
  </TSQLCommand>
</EVENT_INSTANCE>
```

You can view the metadata for database, object, or assembly event notifications by using the `sys.event_notifications` catalog view; and you can view the metadata for server event notifications by using the `sys.server_event_notifications` catalog view. Some other catalog views related to event notifications include `sys.event_notification_event_types`, `sys.trace_events`, `sys.events`, and `sys.server_events`.

Snapshot Isolation

SQL Server 2005 introduces a new isolation level called *snapshot isolation*, which, like REPEATABLE READ, avoids dirty reads and non-repeatable reads, but unlike with REPEATABLE READ, with snapshot isolation, readers don't block writers. Snapshot isolation is based on a technique called *as row versioning*, which makes use of the `tempdb` system database to keep a version of updated rows. With snapshot isolation, if a transaction updates or deletes a row that is already read by another transaction, SQL Server copies the original version of the row to the `tempdb` database. If the transaction tries to read the row again, instead of reading the row from the user database, SQL Server reads the row from the `tempdb` database, and hence avoids the non-repeatable read issue; at the same time, it avoids the blocking. This increases the concurrency and data availability and reduces the locking and deadlocking.

Snapshot isolation in SQL Server 2005 is exposed in two ways:

- By turning on the READ_COMMITTED_SNAPSHOT database option. Then the default READ COMMITTED isolation level makes use of row versioning instead of locks to protect transactions from dirty reads and to support repeatable reads. Once the READ_COMMITTED_SNAPSHOT database option is turned on, all the READ COMMITTED transactions in that database use row versioning to run in snapshot isolation mode.

- By turning on the ALLOW_SNAPSHOT_ISOLATION database option. Then you set the session's isolation level to snapshot isolation by running the SET TRANSACTION ISOLATION LEVEL SNAPSHOT T-SQL statement. With this, only the transactions in the current session are run in snapshot isolation mode.

NOTE

The ALLOW_SNAPSHOT_ISOLATION database option is by default turned off. Even if this option is off, SET TRANSACTION ISOLATION LEVEL SNAPSHOT will succeed, but as soon as you try to perform any DML or SELECT operation, SQL Server raises an error indicating that the database is not enabled for snapshot isolation.

Snapshot isolation is discussed in great detail, including its pros and cons and examples, in Chapter 9, " Performance Analysis and Tuning."

Ranking Functions

SQL Server 2005 introduces a new category of built-in functions: analytical ranking functions. This category consists of four functions—ROW_NUMBER(), RANK(), DENSE_RANK(), and NTILE()—that you can use to generate a sequence number or a sequential number for each row or to rank rows based on some partition criteria. The main idea behind providing these functions is to reduce the complexity and amount of query code that you have to write in order to efficiently calculate row numbers or rank the rows. Let's look at an example of this and then examine each function in detail.

The goal of this example is to output a column containing a sequential number based on a unique combination of ProductID and LocationID columns in the Production.ProductInventory table in the AdventureWorks sample database. Here is how you would do it without using any ranking function:

```
USE AdventureWorks;
GO
SELECT
  ( SELECT COUNT(*)
    FROM Production.ProductInventory AS pi2
    WHERE
        pi2.ProductID < pi1.ProductID OR
        (
        pi2.ProductID = pi1.ProductID AND
        pi2.LocationID <= pi1.LocationID
        )
  ) AS SequenceNo, *
FROM Production.ProductInventory AS pi1
ORDER BY ProductID, LocationID;
GO
```

This query produces the following output (some columns and rows have been omitted for brevity):

SequenceNo	ProductID	LocationID	Shelf	Bin	Quantity
1	1	1	A	1	408
2	1	6	B	5	324
3	1	50	A	5	353
4	2	1	A	2	427
5	2	6	B	1	318
6	2	50	A	6	364

Here is how you can obtain the same results by using the new ROW_NUMBER() ranking function:

```
SELECT ROW_NUMBER() OVER (ORDER BY ProductID, LocationID) as SequenceNo, *
FROM Production.ProductInventory;
GO
```

Let's assume that you want to reset the sequence number and start over from number 1 when the ProductID changes. Here is how you would do it without using any ranking function:

```
SELECT
  ( SELECT COUNT(*)
    FROM Production.ProductInventory AS pi2
    WHERE pi2.ProductID = pi1.ProductID AND
        (pi2.ProductID < pi1.ProductID OR
          (pi2.ProductID = pi1.ProductID AND
            pi2.LocationID <= pi1.LocationID)
        )
  ) AS SequenceNo, *
FROM Production.ProductInventory AS pi1
ORDER BY ProductID, LocationID;
GO
```

This query produces the following output (some columns and rows have been omitted for brevity):

SequenceNo	ProductID	LocationID	Shelf	Bin	Quantity
1	1	1	A	1	408
2	1	6	B	5	324
3	1	50	A	5	353
1	2	1	A	2	427
2	2	6	B	1	318
3	2	50	A	6	364
1	3	1	A	7	585
2	3	6	B	9	443

You can obtain the same results by using the new ROW_NUMBER() ranking function as shown here:

```
SELECT ROW_NUMBER() OVER
 (PARTITION BY ProductID ORDER BY ProductID, LocationID) as SequenceNo, *
FROM Production.ProductInventory;
GO
```

As you can see in these two examples, you write less code when you use the ranking functions, the queries are simple to understand and maintain. And if you study the execution plan for these queries, you notice that ranking functions perform better than the traditional approach.

The ROW_NUMBER Ranking Function

As illustrated in the preceding section, the ROW_NUMBER ranking function can be used to sequentially number starting at 1 for the first row. You can partition the result set and restart the sequential numbering by using the PARTITION BY clause, also illustrated in the preceding section.

One common application where ROW_NUMBER can be very valuable is when you are building a web application and need to implement the paging in the result set:

```
SELECT * FROM
    (SELECT ROW_NUMBER() OVER (ORDER BY ProductID, LocationID) as SequenceNo, *
     FROM Production.ProductInventory) AS tblRows
WHERE SequenceNo BETWEEN 101 and 120;
GO
```

Note that you can directly use the alias for the ROW_NUMBER function; you simply have to nest the query as shown here to use the ROW_NUMBER column alias (SequenceNo in this case) in the WHERE condition.

The RANK and DENSE_RANK Ranking Functions

The RANK and DENSE_RANK ranking functions are similar to the ROW_NUMBER function as they also produce ranking values according to sorting criteria, optionally partitioned into groups of rows. However, unlike the ROW_NUMBER function, which generates a different value for each row, the RANK and DENSE_RANK functions output the same value for all rows that have the same values in the sort column. The RANK and DENSE_RANK functions differ in the way the rank number value is generated when the sort order column value changes. The following example illustrates this:

```
SELECT RANK() OVER (ORDER BY ProductID) as Rank,
       DENSE_RANK() OVER (ORDER BY ProductID) as DenseRank,
       *
FROM Production.ProductInventory;
```

This query produces the following output (some columns and rows have been omitted for brevity):

Rank	DenseRank	ProductID	LocationID	Shelf	Bin	Quantity
1	1	1	1	A	1	408
1	1	1	6	B	5	324
1	1	1	50	A	5	353
4	2	2	1	A	2	427
4	2	2	6	B	1	318
4	2	2	50	A	6	364
7	3	3	1	A	7	585
7	3	3	6	B	9	443
7	3	3	50	A	10	324
10	4	4	1	A	6	512

When `ProductID` changes, the `DENSE_RANK` function increments the rank value by 1. However, the `RANK` function increments the rank value by the number of rows for the preceding rank.

The `NTILE` Ranking Function

The fourth and final ranking function introduced in SQL Server 2005, `NTILE` can be used to assemble rows into a desired number of buckets according to specified sorting criteria, optionally within partitions. This function takes an integer value that indicates how many groups you want:

```
SELECT NTILE(3) OVER (ORDER BY ShipMethodID) AS Bucket, *
FROM Purchasing.ShipMethod;
```

The `Purchasing.ShipMethod` table contains five rows. `NTILE(3)` divides those five rows into three buckets, returning values 1 through 3 in the first column, named `Bucket`, as the output of preceding query (some columns have been omitted for brevity):

Bucket	ShipMethodID	Name
1	1	XRQ - TRUCK GROUND
1	2	ZY - EXPRESS
2	3	OVERSEAS - DELUXE
2	4	OVERNIGHT J-FAST
3	5	CARGO TRANSPORT 5

Note how the `NTILE` function handles the situation when even distribution of rows is not possible. It puts two rows into the first group, two rows into the second group, and the remaining one row into the third group. When even distribution is not possible, larger groups precede smaller groups. Implementing this functionality in SQL Server 2000 is possible but a little complex, and it requires more code.

New Relational Operators: `PIVOT`, `UNPIVOT`, and `APPLY`

If you have ever worked with Microsoft Access, you might have used the `TRANSFORM` statement to create a crosstab query. Similar functionality is provided by SQL Server 2005 via the `PIVOT` operator with the `SELECT` statement. The `PIVOT` operator can be used to transform a set of rows into columns. The `UNPIVOT` operator complements the `PIVOT` operator by allowing you to turn columns into rows.

The following simple example illustrates the use of the `PIVOT` and `UNPIVOT` operators:

```
USE AdventureWorks;
GO
IF OBJECT_ID('dbo.tblCars') IS NOT NULL
    DROP TABLE dbo.tblCars;
GO
```

```
CREATE TABLE dbo.tblCars
   (RecordID INT IDENTITY(1,1) PRIMARY KEY NOT NULL,
    DealerID INT NOT NULL,
    Make NVARCHAR(50),
    MakeYear SMALLINT,
    CarsSold INT);
GO


INSERT INTO dbo.tblCars SELECT 1, 'Honda', 2003, 100;
INSERT INTO dbo.tblCars SELECT 2, 'Toyota', 2003, 500;
INSERT INTO dbo.tblCars SELECT 2, 'Honda', 2003, 200;
INSERT INTO dbo.tblCars SELECT 1, 'Honda', 2004, 200;
INSERT INTO dbo.tblCars SELECT 1, 'Toyota', 2004, 600;
INSERT INTO dbo.tblCars SELECT 2, 'Honda', 2004, 300;
INSERT INTO dbo.tblCars SELECT 2, 'Toyota', 2005, 50;
GO
SELECT * FROM dbo.tblCars;
GO


SELECT Make, [2003], [2004], [2005] FROM
   (
       SELECT Make, CarsSold, MakeYear FROM dbo.tblCars
   ) tblCars
   PIVOT (SUM(CarsSold) FOR MakeYear IN ([2003],[2004], [2005])) tblPivot;
GO
```

This script creates a sample table to store car sales data. It then inserts some sample data into that table, as shown here:

```
RecordID    DealerID    Make    MakeYear CarsSold
----------- ----------- ------- -------- ---------

1           1           Honda   2003     100
2           2           Toyota  2003     500
3           2           Honda   2003     200
4           1           Honda   2004     200
5           1           Toyota  2004     600
6           2           Honda   2004     300
7           2           Toyota  2005     50
```

The PIVOT statement transforms rows into columns, at the same time calculating the total sales per year. It produces the following results:

```
Make     2003   2004   2005
-------  -----  -----  -----

Honda    300    500    NULL
Toyota   500    600    50
```

Here's how you save this pivoted data into a table and then use UNPIVOT to transform columns into rows:

```
IF OBJECT_ID('dbo.tblPivotData') IS NOT NULL
    DROP TABLE dbo.tblPivotData;
GO


SELECT Make, [2003], [2004], [2005] INTO dbo.tblPivotData FROM
    (
        SELECT Make, CarsSold, MakeYear FROM dbo.tblCars
    ) tblCars
    PIVOT (SUM(CarsSold) FOR MakeYear IN ([2003],[2004], [2005])) tblPivot;
GO


SELECT Make, tblUnPivot.MakeYear, tblUnPivot.CarsSold
FROM dbo.tblPivotData
    UNPIVOT
    (CarsSold for MakeYear  in ([2003],[2004], [2005])) tblUnPivot;
GO
```

Using the UNPIVOT clause results in the following output:

```
Make       MakeYear    CarsSold
-------    ----------  ----------
Honda      2003        300
Honda      2004        500
Toyota     2003        500
Toyota     2004        600
Toyota     2005        50
```

Refer to the pivoted data shown earlier (with 2003, 2004, and 2005 as the columns). All UNPIVOT does is convert columns into rows.

The two common applications of the PIVOT operator are to create an analytical view of the data, as illustrated previously, and to implement an open schema, as illustrated here:

```
IF OBJECT_ID('dbo.tblServers') IS NOT NULL
    DROP TABLE dbo.tblServers;
GO


CREATE TABLE dbo.tblServers(
 ServerID INT IDENTITY(1,1),
 ServerName VARCHAR(50));
GO


INSERT INTO dbo.tblServers SELECT 'Server_1';
INSERT INTO dbo.tblServers SELECT 'Server_2';
```

```
INSERT INTO dbo.tblServers SELECT 'Server_3';
GO

IF OBJECT_ID('dbo.tblServerEquip') IS NOT NULL
    DROP TABLE dbo.tblServerEquip;
GO

CREATE TABLE dbo.tblServerEquip(
    ServerID INT,
    EquipmentType VARCHAR(30),
    Description VARCHAR(100));
GO

INSERT INTO dbo.tblServerEquip SELECT 1,'Hard Drive','40GB';
INSERT INTO dbo.tblServerEquip SELECT 1,'Memory Stick','512MB';
INSERT INTO dbo.tblServerEquip SELECT 2,'Memory Stick','512MB';
INSERT INTO dbo.tblServerEquip SELECT 2,'Hard Drive','40GB';
INSERT INTO dbo.tblServerEquip SELECT 2,'NIC','10 MBPS';
INSERT INTO dbo.tblServerEquip SELECT 3,'Memory Stick','512MB';
INSERT INTO dbo.tblServerEquip SELECT 3,'Hard Drive','40GB';
INSERT INTO dbo.tblServerEquip SELECT 1,'Hard Drive','100GB';
INSERT INTO dbo.tblServerEquip SELECT 1,'NIC','10 MBPS';I
INSERT INTO dbo.tblServerEquip SELECT 1,'NIC','1GB Fibre Channel';
GO

SELECT * FROM
    ( SELECT s.ServerName, se.EquipmentType, se.Description
      FROM dbo.tblServers s
      INNER JOIN dbo.tblServerEquip se
      ON s.ServerID = se.ServerID
    ) AS pnt
    PIVOT
    (
      COUNT(Description)
      FOR EquipmentType IN([Hard Drive], [Memory Stick], [NIC])
    ) AS pvt;
GO
```

Using the PIVOT command produces the following output:

```
ServerName    Hard Drive  Memory Stick  NIC
-----------   ----------  ------------  ----------
Server_1      2           1             2
Server_2      1           1             1
Server_3      1           1             0
```

This script creates a table to store all the servers in a production environment and another table to store server equipment type. The PIVOT operator is used to join these two tables to create a simplified view that shows the server name and counts of the equipment in that server.

The third new operator, APPLY, can be used to invoke a table-valued function for each row in the rowset. A table-valued function is a function that returns a rowset (that is, a table) as a return value.

For each row in the outer query in which the APPLY operator is used, the table-value function is called, and the columns returned by the function are appended to the right of the columns in the outer query, to produce a combined final output. You can pass the columns from the outer query as the parameters to the table-valued function specified with the APPLY operator. Here is an example of using the APPLY operator:

```
IF OBJECT_ID('dbo.GetEmpHierarchy') IS NOT NULL
    DROP FUNCTION dbo.GetEmpHierarchy;
GO


CREATE FUNCTION dbo.GetEmpHierarchy (@EmployeeID AS INT) RETURNS TABLE
AS
    RETURN
        WITH RecCTE(ManagerID, EmployeeID, EmployeeLevel) AS
        (
            SELECT ManagerID, EmployeeID, 0 AS EmployeeLevel
                FROM HumanResources.Employee
                WHERE EmployeeID = @EmployeeID

            UNION ALL

            SELECT e.ManagerID, e.EmployeeID, EmployeeLevel + 1
                FROM HumanResources.Employee e
                INNER JOIN RecCTE r
                ON e.ManagerID = r.EmployeeID
        )
        SELECT EmployeeID, ManagerID, EmployeeLevel
        FROM RecCTE;
GO


SELECT s.SalesPersonID, s.SalesOrderID, s.CustomerID, s.TotalDue, tvf.*
FROM Sales.SalesOrderHeader AS s
    CROSS APPLY dbo.GetEmpHierarchy(s.SalesPersonID) AS tvf
ORDER BY TotalDue DESC;
GO
```

This script defines a table-valued function that accepts EmployeeID as an input parameter and returns a table by using a recursive CTE (as discussed earlier in this chapter, in the section "Common Table Expressions (CTEs)") to return the hierarchy for that employee. The APPLY operator is used in the SELECT statement so that for each row in the Sales.SalesOrderHeader table, the query returns the employees directly or indirectly reporting to the current SalesPersonID. If you run the script in the AdventureWorks sample database and scroll down in the result set grid, you see some Sales.SalesOrderHeader rows repeated with the employee hierarchy shown, using the three columns on the right side.

APPLY can take two forms: CROSS APPLY and OUTER APPLY. With CROSS APPLY, if the table-valued function returns an empty set for a given outer row, that outer row is not returned in the result. On the other hand, OUTER APPLY also returns rows from the outer table for which the table-valued function returned an empty set. As with OUTER JOINs, NULL values are returned as the column values that correspond to the columns of the table-valued function.

The OUTPUT Clause

SQL Server 2005 introduces the OUTPUT clause to capture the data rows changed when a DML statement—that is, INSERT, UPDATE, or DELETE—is executed. The OUTPUT clause can be specified with any of the DML operations; you can use the inserted and deleted virtual tables with the OUTPUT statement and copy the affected rows into a table variable.

Here is an example of using the OUTPUT clause to capture the rows updated:

```
USE AdventureWorks;
GO
BEGIN TRANSACTION;
DECLARE @varOriginalRows AS TABLE
  (
    CustomerID INT,
    Name NVARCHAR(50),
    SalesPersonID INT,
    Demographics XML,
    rowguid uniqueidentifier,
    ModifiedDate datetime
  );

UPDATE Sales.Store
SET SalesPersonID = 280
OUTPUT deleted.* INTO @varOriginalRows
WHERE SalesPersonID = 282;

SELECT * FROM @varOriginalRows;

ROLLBACK TRANSACTION;
GO
```

The preceding script declares a table variable that has the same schema as `Sales.Store` because you want to capture all the columns with the `OUTPUT` clause. The `UPDATE` DML statement uses the `OUTPUT` clause to capture all the rows that are affected and saves them into the `@varOriginalRows` table variable. The script is executed in a transaction scope, which is rolled back toward the end to avoid making any changes to the table.

The `BULK` Rowset Provider

SQL Server 2005 enhances the `OPENROWSET` function by providing a `BULK` rowset provider that can be used to read a file and return the file contents as a rowset, which can then be bulk loaded into a table. You can optionally specify an XML or non-XML format file, using the same format file structure as the `bcp.exe` utility.

The `SINGLE_BLOB` option tells the `BULK` rowset provider to return the contents of a file as a single-row, single-column rowset of type `varbinary(max)`. With the `SINGLE_CLOB` option, the `BULK` rowset provider returns the contents of the file as a single-row, single-column rowset of type `varchar(max)`, and with `SINGLE_NCLOB` it returns a single-row, single-column rowset of type `nvarchar(max)`. `SINGLE_NCLOB` requires that the input file to be saved in Unicode (widechar) format.

Let's look at an example of `BULK` rowset provider. Let's assume that the following text is available in a text file called `c:\property.txt`:

```
This charming almost new home offers glistening hardwood floors and a formal
living and dining room. The Great Room is two story and is basked in sunshine
and opens onto the breakfast room and huge kitchen. Upstairs, an outstanding
master suite boasts a luxury bath w/ separate shower! Nestled into a
cul de sac high on a knoll, this wonderful home is available for immediate
occupancy.
```

Here is how you would bulk load this text into a table, using the `OPENROWSET` function and the `BULK` rowset provider:

```
USE AdventureWorks;
GO
IF OBJECT_ID('dbo.tblProperty') IS NOT NULL
   DROP TABLE dbo.tblProperty;
GO
CREATE TABLE dbo.tblProperty
   (MLSID INT PRIMARY KEY NOT NULL,
    Description VARCHAR(max));
GO

INSERT INTO dbo.tblProperty
     SELECT 12345, txt.*
     FROM OPENROWSET(BULK N'C:\Property.txt',
             SINGLE_CLOB) AS txt;

SELECT * FROM dbo.tblProperty;
GO
```

If you run the preceding script, you should notice that data from the text file is inserted into the Description column.

New Declarative Referential Integrity Actions

The two declarative referential integrity (DRI) actions available in SQL Server 2000 are NO ACTION and CASCADE. When you create or alter a table, you can define the DRI actions on foreign key columns to tell SQL Server what to do when the referenced row is deleted from the parent table. For example, when defining the ContactDetails table, you can specify CASCADE to delete the rows when the referred row is deleted from the Customer table, or you can specify NO ACTION, in which case SQL Server raises an error indicating that you cannot delete the rows from Customer table because they are being referenced in the ContactDetails table.

SQL Server 2005 introduces two new DRI actions: SET NULL and SET DEFAULT. When SET NULL is specified, first you have to make sure that the foreign key column is nullable, and then, when rows from the parent table are deleted, SQL Server puts NULL in the referenced foreign key column. When SET DEFAULT is specified, first you have to make sure that the column is either nullable or has a default definition, and then when rows from the parent table are deleted, SQL Server puts the default value in the referenced foreign key column. If a default constraint is not defined on the column and the column is nullable, SQL Server puts NULL in that column.

In addition to using the delete operation, you can also specify SET NULL and SET DEFAULT actions for the instances when the referenced row is updated in the parent table.

Here is an example of the new SET NULL and SET DEFAULT actions:

```
CREATE TABLE dbo.tblMaster
    (CustomerID INT PRIMARY KEY NOT NULL,
     Name VARCHAR(100));
GO


CREATE TABLE dbo.tblChild1
    (AddressID INT IDENTITY(1,1) PRIMARY KEY NOT NULL,
     CustomerID INT NULL FOREIGN KEY REFERENCES dbo.tblMaster (CustomerID)
     ON DELETE SET NULL,
     AddressLine1 VARCHAR(100));
GO

CREATE TABLE dbo.tblChild2
    (AddressID INT IDENTITY(1,1) PRIMARY KEY NOT NULL,
     CustomerID INT NOT NULL DEFAULT -1
     FOREIGN KEY REFERENCES dbo.tblMaster (CustomerID)
     ON DELETE SET DEFAULT,
     AddressLine1 VARCHAR(100));
GO
```

```
INSERT INTO dbo.tblMaster SELECT 1, 'Customer1';
INSERT INTO dbo.tblMaster SELECT 2, 'Customer2';
INSERT INTO dbo.tblMaster SELECT 3, 'Customer3';
INSERT INTO dbo.tblMaster SELECT -1, 'Invalid Customer';

INSERT INTO dbo.tblChild1 SELECT 1, 'Customer1Address';
INSERT INTO dbo.tblChild1 SELECT 2, 'Customer2Address';
INSERT INTO dbo.tblChild1 SELECT 3, 'Customer3Address';

INSERT INTO dbo.tblChild2 SELECT 1, 'Customer1Address';
INSERT INTO dbo.tblChild2 SELECT 2, 'Customer2Address';
INSERT INTO dbo.tblChild2 SELECT 3, 'Customer3Address';

DELETE dbo.tblMaster WHERE CustomerID = 2;
GO

SELECT * FROM dbo.tblChild1;
SELECT * FROM dbo.tblChild2;
GO
```

This script creates a table that is referenced by two other tables. For the first referenced table, tblChild1, you specify the DRI action to set the foreign key column to NULL if the row is deleted from the parent table. For the second referenced table, tblChild2, you specify the DRI action to set the foreign key column to a default value of -1 if the row is deleted from the parent table. In the case of the default value, the value must be present in the parent table (Customer, with -1 as the CustomerID in this case). When the customer with CustomerID as 2 is deleted, the corresponding CustomerID foreign key column in tblChild1 is set to NULL, and the corresponding CustomerID foreign key in the tblChid12 table is set to the default value of -1.

Metadata Views and Dynamic Management Views

With SQL Server 2000, T-SQL developers often used system tables, system stored procedures, and SQL-99 INFORMATION_SCHEMA views to access system metadata to get answers about things such as numbers and names of tables in a database; find out about constraints, indexes, and keys defined for a table; determine the number of columns in a table or the number and names of databases on a server; and so on.

The SQL-99 INFORMATION_SCHEMA views are still available in SQL Server 2005, but system tables are no longer directly accessible. SQL Server 2005 introduces the concept of *catalog views*, which is a recommended way to access the system metadata. The catalog views provide a consistent and secure interface to access system metadata in SQL Server 2005. All the catalog views are defined in the sys schema. For backward compatibility with previous releases, SQL Server 2005 also provides the *compatibility views*, which have the same names and return the same data as the system tables. However, using the compatibility views is discouraged, and accessing catalog views is the recommended option if you need to access the system metadata. The INFORMATION_SCHEMA views are not updated to cover all the new features, such as Service Broker, introduced in SQL Server 2005. The catalog views are the only metadata-access interface that covers all the new SQL Server 2005 features. The catalog views are also more efficient than compatibility views and INFORMATION_SCHEMA views.

Table 6.1 lists the catalog view categories and examples of catalog views in each category.

TABLE 6.1   SQL Server 2005 Catalog Views

Catalog View Category	Example
Object	sys.columns, sys.procedures, sys.objects, sys.indexes, sys.triggers, sys.xml_indexes, sys.synonyms, and so on
Database and file	sys.databases, sys.database_files, sys.backup_devices, and so on
Scalar types	sys.types and sys.assembly_types
Schema	sys.schemas
Security	sys.certificates, sys.sql_logins, sys.database_principals, sys.credentials, and so on
Database mirroring	sys.database_mirroring_witnesses
Linked server	sys.servers, sys.linked_logins, and sys.remote_logins
Error message	sys.messages
Partition function	sys.partition_functions and so on
SQLCLR integration	sys.assemblies, sys.assembly_files, and so on
Service Broker	sys.services, sys.routes, sys.transmission_queue, and so on
Endpoint	sys.endpoints, sys.tcp_endpoints, sys.http_endpoints, and so on
XML	sys.xml_indexes, sys.xml_schema_collections, and so on
Data space and Full-Text	sys.data_spaces, sys.filegroups, sys.fulltext_catalogs, and so on
Configuration	sys.configurations and sys.fulltext_languages

Dynamic management views (DMVs) are one more type of view provided with SQL Server 2005. DMVs can be used to view the current state of the SQL Server 2005 system. In other words, DMVs provide a real-time snapshot of internal memory structures that indicate the server state. This means that instead of using sp_who, you can now use the sys.dm_exec_sessions DMV to effectively get more current details on users logged in. Like catalog views, DMVs are also defined in the sys schema. All DMV names begin with dm_, and the next word in the name indicates the DMV category (for example, sys.dm_exec_sessions refers to the execution category). SQL Server 2005 contains several DMVs to get current memory, I/O, an index, a full-text index, Service Broker information, and transaction activity. DMVs are discussed in more detail in Chapter 9.

Miscellaneous T-SQL Enhancements

Before concluding this chapter, let's look at some other enhancements made to T-SQL in SQL Server 2005 release.

The ALTER INDEX Statement

The ALTER INDEX statement, which is new in SQL Server 2005, can be used to disable, rebuild, or reorganize the XML and relational indexes. This statement can also be used to set the index options, such as whether row locks or page locks are allowed when accessing the index, whether index statistics should be automatically recomputed, and so on.

> **NOTE**
>
> You cannot use ALTER INDEX to add or remove columns or change the column order in an index or to repartition or move an index to a different file group. For such operations, you still have to use the CREATE INDEX statement with the DROP_EXISTING clause.

Here is an example of using ALTER INDEX to disable and enable an index:

```
USE AdventureWorks;
GO

ALTER INDEX AK_SalesOrderHeader_rowguid ON Sales.SalesOrderHeader
DISABLE;
GO

SELECT is_disabled, * FROM sys.indexes
WHERE name = 'AK_SalesOrderHeader_rowguid';
GO

ALTER INDEX AK_SalesOrderHeader_rowguid ON Sales.SalesOrderHeader
REBUILD;
GO

SELECT is_disabled, * FROM sys.indexes
WHERE name = 'AK_SalesOrderHeader_rowguid';
GO
```

> **CAUTION**
>
> If you disable a clustered index on a table, SQL Server might have to disable a clustered index's dependent indexes. Also, access to the underlying table will be denied until the index is either dropped or enabled using the REBUILD clause.

Statement-Level Recompilation

In SQL Server 2000, when schema changes were made to the objects referenced in a stored procedure, when SET options were changed, or when statistics were changed, SQL Server would recompile the entire stored procedure. SQL Server 2005 introduces a new optimization technique in which only the statement that caused the recompilation, instead of entire stored procedure, is compiled. This results in faster recompile times, fewer compile locks, less CPU and memory utilization, and overall better performance in a T-SQL module. In addition to this built-in enhancement, a new query hint, OPTIMIZE FOR, is provided that you can use to instruct SQL Server to use a particular value for a local variable when the query is compiled and optimized.

New Server Configuration Options

The security-related changes in SQL Server 2005 might break your existing T-SQL scripts. For instance, by default, the xp_cmdshell extended stored procedure and SQL Mail stored procedures are disabled in SQL Server 2005. An error is raised when xp_cmdshell or SQL Mail procedures are executed. You can use the new security tool, SQL Server Surface Area Configuration, or the sp_configure statement to enable or disable features such as the xp_cmdshell extended stored procedure, SQL Mail procedures, Web Assistant stored procedures, and OLE Automation extended stored procedures. To view these options using sp_configure, you have to first enable the show advanced options server configuration option.

Synonyms

SQL Server 2005 permits creating synonyms that serve as alternative names for another database object, referred to as the *base object*. The base object can exist on a local or remote server. Synonyms can also be used to create a layer of abstraction that protects the client application from changes made to the name or location of the base object.

> **NOTE**
>
> A synonym cannot be the base object for another synonym, and a synonym cannot reference a user-defined aggregate function.

You can create a synonym by using the CREATE SYNONYM DDL statement, and you can remove it by using the DROP SYNONYM statement, as illustrated in the following example:

```
USE AdventureWorks;
GO
IF OBJECT_ID('edh') IS NOT NULL
    DROP SYNONYM edh;
GO
CREATE SYNONYM edh FOR HumanResources.EmployeeDepartmentHistory;
GO
SELECT * FROM edh;
```

```
GO
SELECT * FROM sys.synonyms;
GO
IF OBJECT_ID('edh') IS NOT NULL
   DROP SYNONYM edh;
GO
```

You can use the sys.synonyms catalog view to view the metadata, including the base table name, for the synonym. When you run the CREATE SYNONYM statement, it is not required for the base object to exist at that time, and no permissions on the base object are checked. When the synonym is accessed, the base object existence and permission check is done. If base object and synonym owners are the same, SQL Server just ensures that the user accessing the synonym has sufficient permissions on the synonym. If the synonym and base object owners are different, SQL Server ensures that the user accessing the synonym has sufficient permissions on both the synonym and the base object.

The EXCEPT and INTERSECT Operators

The EXCEPT and INTERSECT operators allow you to compare the results of two or more SELECT statements and return distinct values. The EXCEPT operator returns any distinct values from the query on the left side of the EXCEPT operator that are not returned by the query on the right side. INTERSECT returns any distinct values that are returned by both the query on the left and right sides of the INTERSECT operator.

Result sets that are compared using EXCEPT or INTERSECT must all have the same structure. They must have the same number of columns, and the corresponding result set columns must have compatible data types.

Here is an example of the EXCEPT and INTERSECT operators:

```
USE [tempdb];
GO

IF OBJECT_ID('dbo.t1') IS NOT NULL
   DROP TABLE dbo.t1;
GO
IF OBJECT_ID('dbo.t2') IS NOT NULL
   DROP TABLE dbo.t2;
GO

CREATE TABLE dbo.t1(col1 int, col2 int);
GO
CREATE TABLE dbo.t2(col1 int, col2 int);
GO

INSERT INTO dbo.t1 SELECT 1, 1;
INSERT INTO dbo.t1 SELECT 2, 2;
INSERT INTO dbo.t1 SELECT 3, 3;
```

```
INSERT INTO dbo.t2 SELECT 1, 1;
INSERT INTO dbo.t2 SELECT 2, 2;
GO


SELECT * FROM dbo.t1 EXCEPT SELECT * FROM dbo.t2;
GO


SELECT * FROM dbo.t1 INTERSECT SELECT * FROM dbo.t2;
GO
```

The first SELECT statement in this script returns a row with col1 and col2 as 3 because this is the row that is present in dbo.t1 and not in the dbo.t2 table. The second SELECT statement returns the first two rows because they are present in both the tables.

The SET SHOWPLAN_XML and SET STATISTICS XML Statements

SQL Server 2005 provides two new SET statements—SET SHOWPLAN_XML and SET STATISTICS XML—that can be used to obtain a query showplan and statistics as an XML document. These XML results can then be processed in many ways, and they also open up the opportunity for third-party application vendors to provide add-on tools to optimize and compare performance results. Here is an example of these two statements:

```
USE AdventureWorks;
GO
SET SHOWPLAN_XML ON;
GO
SELECT * FROM Sales.Store;
GO
SET SHOWPLAN_XML OFF;
GO
SET STATISTICS XML ON;
SELECT * FROM Sales.Store;
SET STATISTICS XML OFF;
GO
```

If you run the queries, you can see how the showplan and query statistics are returned as XML values. You can run the preceding script in Management Studio and view the results in grid mode. The showplan XML appears as a hyperlink. You can click the showplan XML hyperlink to view the XML text in a new window. You can copy and paste the showplan XML text into a text file that has the extension .sqlplan. Then you can start Windows Explorer and double-click the .sqlplan file or select File, Open (Ctrl+O) from Management Studio and open the .sqlplan file that you just created. You should notice that Management Studio reads the XML showplan and shows the execution plan graphically.

Summary

This chapter highlights the new and improved T-SQL language features in SQL Server 2005. It begins with a comparison of T-SQL with SQLCLR to help you decide where to use which option. T-SQL is still the primary language that DBAs and developers should use for any kind of data access and scripting.

The rest of the chapter discusses the T-SQL enhancements in SQL Server 2005. SQL Server 2005 has enhanced the TOP operator and introduces a new TABLESAMPLE keyword that you can use to restrict the result set. The chapter next talks about a very cool T-SQL feature, CTE, which can be used instead of derived tables to produce simpler and efficient queries. The real power of CTEs can be seen when they are used recursively.

The other features discussed in this chapter include the max specifier to store 2GB of character or binary data in varchar, nvarchar, or varbinary columns; structural error handling using TRY...CATCH blocks; DDL triggers to handle database- and server-level DDL events; event notifications to asynchronously handled database, server, and SQL trace events; the new snapshot isolation level to reduce locking and increase concurrency and scalability; analytical ranking functions; new relational operators, including PIVOT, UNPIVOT, and APPLY; the OUTPUT clause to capture changes made by DML statements; enhancements to the OPENROWSET function to bulk load data; and metadata views, index enhancements, and the XML showplan.

Chapter 7, "SQL Server 2005 Security," covers the security-related features in SQL Server 2005.

SQL Server 2005 Security

On January 24, 2003, a worm named Sapphire or W32.Slammer attacked the computers running SQL Server 2000 and MSDE 2000, propagating via UDP Port 1434 and causing a dramatic increase in network traffic. This incident reinforced the importance of the ongoing Trustworthy Computing initiative. In the past two years, Microsoft has invested significant time and resources in enhancing the security in each of its products, including SQL Server 2005.

SQL Server 2005 redefines the server's security framework by introducing several new features and enhancements that offer developers and administrators greater control over access to sensitive data while simplifying their routine tasks. A lot of work has been done to address weaknesses in previous releases, to simplify security management and administration, to strengthen SQL Authentication, to provide granular permissions, to secure system metadata, to improve auditing capabilities, and to secure various subsystems. This chapter discusses these security enhancements to assure you that SQL Server 2005 is secure by design, secure by default, and secure in deployment.

An Introduction to Security in SQL Server 2005

The security features in SQL Server 2005 fall into five categories:

- Authentication

- Authorization

- Auditing

- Cryptography Support

- Surface Area Configuration (SAC)

In addition, each new subsystem is designed with security in mind. For instance, SQLCLR security features help ensure that the .NET CLR code running inside SQL Server is secure and reliable; Service Broker provides multiple layers of security to dialog messages by authenticating and authorizing dialog initiators and targets, by preserving the message integrity, and by securing the transport; and Reporting Services security follows the role-based security model to determine who can perform operations and access items on a report server.

This chapter covers the new security features in each of the five categories and also provides an overview of security features in new subsystems such as SQLCLR and Service Broker. Detailed discussions on subsystems' security features can be found in later chapters.

Let's begin by looking at new security features in the authentication arena.

Authentication

Authentication is the process of validating that someone is who they say they are. In other words, authentication is the process of verifying someone's identity based on things like login name and password, security token, or certificate.

Like previous releases, SQL Server 2005 continues to support two authentication modes: SQL Authentication and Windows Authentication. The latter is still the recommended way of connecting to SQL Server. The authentication model in SQL Server is enhanced to strengthen the SQL Authentication mode. Before we look at this, let's first look at two new security features related to how a connection is made to a SQL Server instance: endpoint-based authentication and the role of the SQL Browser service.

Endpoint-Based Authentication

SQL Server 2000 allows clients to connect over network protocols such as TCP/IP and named pipes. The only application-level protocol supported by SQL Server 2000 is the Tabular Data Stream (TDS), which is used to send SQL statements from the client to the server and result sets from the server to the client. The TDS packets are encapsulated in the packets built for the underlying network protocol, such as TCP/IP packets. SQL Server 2005 extends this framework by introducing the concept of endpoints.

An *endpoint* can be thought of as an entry point into a SQL Server instance. You can create multiple endpoints per instance by using the CREATE ENDPOINT Transact-SQL (T-SQL) statement. When you create an endpoint, you have to specify what transport protocol it will be accessed over and what kind of payload it will accept. For instance, you can create an endpoint to work with TDS payload over the TCP/IP network protocol. In other words, an endpoint binds a transport protocol to payload.

The benefit of this approach is that you can manage permissions on a per-endpoint basis. Endpoint security comes in the form of permissions such as CONNECT that can be granted, revoked, or denied to database users. For instance, using endpoints, you can implement a scenario where certain users can access SQL Server over named pipes or shared memory, but not over HTTP, a transport protocol that is now supported by SQL Server 2005. SQL Server 2005 introduces support for HTTP, which can work with XML/SOAP payload and can be used to implement XML web services or Service Oriented Architecture (SOA) in SQL Server 2005. This is discussed in more detail in Chapter 10, "XML and Web Services Support in SQL Server 2005." In addition, an endpoint can also be created to implement database mirroring and work with Service Broker. Database Mirroring is discussed in Chapter 8, "Reliability and High Availability in the Database Engine," and Service Broker is discussed in Chapter 14, "SQL Server 2005 Service Broker."

The other benefit with the endpoint approach is that you can start, stop, or disable an endpoint to have SQL Server listen or not listen on that endpoint. When you create an endpoint and do not specify the STATE = STARTED clause, for security reasons the endpoint is stopped by default.

When SQL Server 2005 is installed, it creates an endpoint for every enabled transport protocol, such as named pipes, TCP/IP, shared memory, and so on. Each authenticated login is assigned the CONNECT endpoint permission on these endpoints, which can be denied on a per-endpoint basis. For security reasons, SQL Server 2005 does not create any HTTP endpoints out of the box. If you need to enable XML web services in SQL Server 2005, you can create HTTP endpoints by using the CREATE ENDPOINT statement.

With the endpoint-based authentication model, when a user connects to a SQL Server instance, in addition to verifying the login credentials, SQL Server also verifies that the login is authorized to connect via the endpoint.

SQL Browser Service and the New Security Model

SQL Server 2000 enables up to 16 instances to be installed on a machine. SQL Server 2005 raises this number to 50. When a client tries to connect to a named instance or an instance listening on a non-default static or dynamic port, the client has no knowledge of where to connect. The instance resolution protocol in previous SQL Server releases was an answer to this problem. With this approach, a client could connect to the SQL Server machine over UDP port 1434 and enquire about all the instances listening on that machine. This open port 1434 was exploited by hackers, and this led to the W32.Slammer attack described at the beginning of this chapter.

This functionality of translating an instance name passed in from the client to the appropriate TCP/IP port or pipe is now separated into a Windows service called SQL Browser. In SQL Server 2005 you can stop or disable the SQL Browser service to turn off the UDP 1434 traffic instead of relying on the firewall.

When the SQL Browser service is running and clients query over UDP 1434, the SQL Browser service returns a list of SQL Server machines (SQL Server 7.0 and above, clustered and non-clustered), Analysis Server machines, Report Server machines, and SQL Mobile databases, along with version numbers for all the servers.

> **CAUTION**
>
> It is recommended that the SQL Browser service be run in the security context of a low-privileged account because all it does is accept unauthenticated requests and map instances to a TCP/IP port or a named pipe. Running this service under a low-privileged account reduces the exposure to malicious attacks.

When the client knows about the TCP/IP port or the named pipe to connect to, the next step is login authentication. For Windows logins, the token from the domain controller is presented to the SQL Server machine, and for SQL logins, the login name and the password hash are presented to the SQL Server machine. After establishing the login credentials, SQL Server 2005 ensures that the login has access over the endpoint through which it is trying to connect. When this is verified, SQL Server switches to the database to obtain the user context, which is then used for database permissions for the most part.

In summary, SQL Server 2005 separates the functionality of listening over UDP 1434 and responding to anonymous clients with instance information or mapping instance names into TCP/IP port or named pipe into a separate service called SQL Browser, which can be turned on or off to control the UDP 1434 traffic. And the notion of endpoints allows you to control access to the server based on transport and payload, as well as the ability to start, stop, or disable individual endpoints to better control access to the server.

Let's now look at how SQL Server strengthens the SQL Authentication mode.

Strengthening SQL Authentication

Windows Authentication is still the recommended approach for connecting to SQL Server because it can leverage the domain password policy and other security infrastructure and is based on NTLM and Kerberos protocols, which are much stronger than the SQL Authentication. However, Microsoft recognizes that customers may need to continue to use SQL Server authentication. Hence, SQL Server 2005 strengthens the SQL Authentication to make it more secure. The following are some of the limitations of SQL Authentication in SQL Server 2000:

- When clients connect to a server by using SQL Authentication, the channel is not secured, and anyone can figure out the login and password used to connect to SQL Server. The only way to secure the client/server channel is to install a certificate from the Certificate Authority on the server and client machines and then use Super Socket Net-Library (`Dbnetlib.dll` and `Ssnetlib.dll`) to encrypt the communication. In other words, the channel is not secure by default; extra administrative steps have to be performed to secure it.

- It is not possible to enable or disable logins.

- SQL Server 2000 does not support any password policy or account lockout or expiration rules.

SQL Server 2005 fixes these limitations. SQL Server 2005 contains built-in support for securing the channel for SQL Authentication. It first checks whether an SSL certificate is installed for the server communication, and if a certificate exists, SQL Server 2005 uses it to secure the communication. If not, SQL Server 2005 automatically generates a 512-bit certificate that it uses to encrypt the credentials. Note that you don't have to make any changes in your SQL Server 2005 applications to use this feature, and SQL Server 2005 continues to provide support for old-style authentication for down-level clients.

SQL Server 2005 introduces a new DDL statement, `ALTER LOGIN`, that can be used to enable or disable a login.

Now let's look at the new password policy feature in SQL Server 2005 that fixes the third limitation mentioned earlier.

Password Policy Support

Windows network administrators almost always use the following security features to secure the domain logins and thereby in some way secure their networks:

- Enforce password policies to ensure that domain users make use of strong passwords.

- Enforce account lockouts so that if someone tries the brute-force approach to breaking in using a particular login, that account gets locked out or disabled after a certain number of failed tries.

- Enforce password expiration so that domain users change their passwords periodically.

- Force users to change their passwords on first login.

All this functionality is now available for SQL Authenticated logins. SQL Server 2005 makes use of the Windows 2003 Server API to enforce the Windows password policies of the computer on which SQL Server is running on the SQL Authenticated logins. Because this API is not available on Windows 2000 Server, SQL Server 2005 only supports native password complexity. The native password complexity feature disallows blank or null password and certain words, such as password, admin, sa, administrator, sysadmin, the name of machine, or the same string as the login name.

The `sp_addlogin` system stored procedure for creating new SQL Server logins is being deprecated in SQL Server 2005. Using the new DDL statement `CREATE LOGIN` is the recommended approach for creating new logins. For each new SQL Authenticated login that you create, SQL Server by default enforces the password policy.

There are three important options with the `CREATE LOGIN` DDL statement for SQL authenticated logins:

- **`CHECK_POLICY`**—ON by default, this option enables the Windows password and lockout policy on SQL logins. For security reasons, it is not recommended to set this option to OFF. Turning off the `CHECK_POLICY` option puts you back to SQL Server 2000 behavior, where SQL Server does not enforce password complexity or lockout rules. The account lockout mechanism ensures that if there are X number of bad password attempts within Y window of time, the account is locked out for a Z period of time, where X, Y, and Z are the parameters controlled by the policy. It is important to note that the CHECK_POLICY option controls both password complexity and account lockout. Just password complexity is not sufficient to protect against brute-force attack.

- **CHECK_EXPIRATION**—ON by default, this option specifies whether the password expiration policy should be enforced on the SQL login being created. If you set the CHECK_POLICY option to OFF, the CHECK_EXPIRATION option is also turned off. In other words, you can enable CHECK_POLICY without enabling CHECK_EXPIRATION, but you cannot enable CHECK_EXPIRATION without enabling the CHECK_POLICY option. CHECK_EXPIRATION and CHECK_POLICY are enforced only on Windows 2003 Server and above. On other operating systems, SQL Server 2005 supports only native password complexity.

- **MUST_CHANGE**—This option is only supported on Windows Server 2003, and when it is specified, SQL Server prompts the user for a new password when the login is used to connect to SQL Server. If MUST_CHANGE is specified, CHECK_EXPIRATION and CHECK_POLICY must be set to ON. Otherwise, the CREATE LOGIN statement will fail.

The is_policy_checked and is_expiration_checked fields in the sys.sql_logins catalog view can be used to determine whether the CHECK_POLICY and CHECK_EXPIRATION options are ON or OFF. This catalog view derives from the sys.server_principals view, which contains fields such as is_disabled, which can be used to figure out whether the account is enabled or disabled.

In addition, you can associate an existing credential with a SQL Authenticated login. SQL Server 2005 uses such credentials when connecting outside the server. The credential can be created by using the CREATE CREDENTIAL DDL statement. One credential can be associated with multiple logins, but a login can have only one credential associated with it.

When specifying the password for SQL Authenticated login, you can use the HASHED option to tell SQL Server that the password string is already hashed and SQL Server should store the string as it is in the database, without hashing it again.

The following is an example of using the CREATE LOGIN and ALTER LOGIN statements to create and alter SQL Authenticated logins:

```
USE master;
GO


CREATE LOGIN Bob WITH PASSWORD = 'Bob';
GO
CREATE LOGIN Bob WITH PASSWORD = 'Admin';
GO
CREATE LOGIN Bob WITH PASSWORD = 'Admin',
   CHECK_POLICY = OFF,
   CHECK_EXPIRATION = ON;
GO
```

```
CREATE LOGIN Bob WITH PASSWORD = 'Admin', CHECK_POLICY = OFF;
GO
CREATE LOGIN Rob WITH PASSWORD = 'WjkKWjkF', CHECK_EXPIRATION = OFF;
GO

ALTER LOGIN Rob DISABLE;
GO

SELECT * FROM sys.server_principals;
SELECT * FROM sys.sql_logins;
GO

DROP LOGIN Bob;
DROP LOGIN Rob;
```

The first three CREATE LOGIN statements in this script fail because the first two statements do not specify the strong password, and the third statement tries to keep password expiration on without keeping policy check on, which is not allowed.

The fourth CREATE LOGIN statement succeeds even though it is using a weak password string because it turns off the CHECK_POLICY option. The next login creation succeeds, too, because it uses a strong password and requests to turn off password expiration, while keeping policy check on, which is allowed. The ALTER LOGIN statement illustrates disabling a login.

TIP

The LoginProperty built-in function can be used to determine the state of an account with regard to the password policy:

```
CREATE LOGIN Robert WITH PASSWORD = 'WjKkWjKf';
SELECT LoginProperty('Robert', 'IsLocked');
SELECT LoginProperty('Robert', 'IsMustChange');
SELECT LoginProperty('Robert', 'IsExpired');
SELECT LoginProperty('Robert', 'LastSetTime');
DROP LOGIN Robert;
```

This concludes the discussion on authentication-related security features in SQL Server 2005. Let's now look at authorization-related enhancements introduced in SQL Server 2005.

Authorization

After SQL Server has authenticated the user and has verified that someone trying to access the SQL Server resource is who they say they are, the next step is to authorize the user to determine what resource can or cannot be accessed and what actions can or cannot be performed by that user. The authorization process essentially verifies the permissions and access rights granted to the user.

SQL Server 2005 introduces several interesting features in the authorization arena, as you will learn in this section. However, let's first look at some terms introduced in SQL Server 2005.

SQL Server 2005 Security Terminology

The following are some important terms in SQL Server 2005:

- **Principal**—*Principal* is a generic term that can be used to refer to an individual Windows login or a Windows group, a SQL login, a database user, an application role, or a database role, which is used for authentication and authorization purposes in SQL Server. The sa SQL Server login and BUILTIN\Administrators Windows group are examples of principals. Each principal has a unique SID. The sys.server_principals and sys.database_principals catalog views can be used to view a list of server-level and database-level principals, respectively.

- **Securable**—*Securables* are items like endpoints, databases, the Full-Text catalog, Service Broker contracts, tables, views, functions, procedures, and so on that you can secure at the server level, database level, or schema level.

- **Grantor**—The *grantor* is the principal that grants a permission.

- **Grantee**—The *grantee* is the principal to whom the permission is granted.

Let's now look at how SQL Server 2005 simplifies the management of permissions and incorporates support for the principle of least privileges.

Granular Permissions Control

SQL Server 2000 provided the ability to manage statement-level permission for a few statements such as CREATE DATABASE; object-level permissions such as SELECT, INSERT, DELETE, REFERENCES, or UPDATE on objects; and permissions based on fixed server-level and database-level roles. The problem with fixed roles is that they do not follow the principle of least privileges. For instance, with SQL Server 2000, a user has to be a member of a sysadmin fixed server role to run the Profiler or SQL trace. However, when you make someone part of sysadmin, that person has full control of the server and can do whatever he or she chooses to. According to the principle of least privileges, if you want grant permission to a user to perform an action, you should be able to grant the permission just for that action—nothing more, nothing less. This is what SQL Server 2005 is trying to achieve by introducing several new permission verbs and allowing you to grant permissions at multiple scopes. SQL Server 2005 provides granular permissions at the server level, database level, schema level, object level, and principal level. The SQL Server 2005 security model is hierarchical. For instance, if you grant some permission at a schema level, the principal will get that permission on all objects in the specified schema.

Examples of *server*-scoped permission include permissions to run a trace or create endpoints. Examples of *database*-scoped permissions include permissions to create tables, views, procedures, functions, a Service Broker queue, contracts and services, synonyms, schemas, XML Schema collections, and so on. Examples of *schema*-scoped permissions include permissions to alter any objects in a particular schema, execute any procedure or function in a particular schema, and so on. Examples of *object*-scoped permissions include permissions to alter a specific table, view, procedure, function, or synonym. SQL Server 2005 not only allows assigning permissions *to* a principal (such as a login or user), but it also defines a set of permissions *on* principals itself, and these permissions can in turn be granted *to* other principals. For instance, you can grant IMPERSONATE permission on login X to the other login Y, allowing the login Y to impersonate and run commands as login X.

Permissions in SQL Server 2005 are still managed using the familiar T-SQL constructs GRANT, DENY, and REVOKE. The GRANT statement gives permission to perform the action, DENY prevents from performing the action, and REVOKE brings to the original "unassigned" state by removing the granted or denied permission. SQL Server 2005 extends these statements and introduces several new permission verbs, such as CONTROL, IMPERSONATE, ALTER TRACE, and ALTER SERVER STATE, to provide granular control over managing permissions at multiple scopes.

Here is the syntax of a simple GRANT statement:

```
GRANT < permission > [ ON < scope > ]
        TO < principal >


< permission >::=  ALL [ PRIVILEGES ] ¦ permission_name
    [ ( column [ ,...n ] ) ]


< scope >::= [ securable_class :: ] securable_name


< securable_class >::= APPLICATION ROLE ¦ ASSEMBLY ¦ ASYMMETRIC KEY
    ¦ CERTIFICATE ¦ CONTRACT ¦ DATABASE ¦ ENDPOINT ¦ FULLTEXT CATALOG
    ¦ LOGIN ¦ MESSAGE TYPE ¦ OBJECT ¦ REMOTE SERVICE BINDING ¦ ROLE
    ¦ ROUTE ¦ SCHEMA ¦ SERVER ¦ SERVICE ¦ SYMMETRIC KEY ¦ TYPE
    ¦ USER ¦ XML SCHEMA COLLECTION


< principal >::= Windows_login ¦ SQL_Server_login
    ¦ SQL_Server_login_mapped_to_certificate
    ¦ SQL_Server_login_mapped_to_asymmetric_key
    ¦ Database_user ¦ Database_role ¦ Application_role
    ¦ Database_user_mapped_to_certificate
    ¦ Database_user_mapped_to_asymmetric_key
```

Before looking at examples of the GRANT statement, let's look at some of the new permission verbs introduced by SQL Server 2005:

- **CONTROL**—With CONTROL permission, the grantee can do everything that the owner can do. For instance, if you grant CONTROL permission on a schema to someone, the grantee can do everything that the schema owner can do. However, note that you are only giving owner-like permissions to the grantee; you are not making the grantee the owner. You can use CONTROL permission to implement a subtractive model, where you start with maximum, owner-like permissions and then take away certain specific permissions.

- **ALTER**—The ALTER permissions gives the grantee the ability to alter the properties of a particular securable and a securable contained within that scope. For instance, ALTER on a procedure gives the user permission to change the procedure text, and ALTER on a schema gives user permission to create, alter, and drop objects from the schema.

- **ALTER ANY <server securable> ¦ <database securable>**—This permission grants the ability to create, alter, and drop individual instances of server securables, such as logins, endpoints, and so on, or database securables, such as schemas.

- **TAKE OWNERSHIP**—This verb is yet another great example of granular permission control in SQL Server 2005. In previous releases, you had to be a member of the sysadmin server role to change the database owner, and you had to be a member of the sysadmin server role or both the db_ddladmin and db_securityadmin database roles in order to change the object ownership. With SQL Server 2005, if you are assigned TAKE OWNERSHIP permission, you can take the ownership of the securable on which it is granted.

- **IMPERSONATE <login> ¦ <user>**—This is one more example of granular permission control in SQL Server 2005. Previously, only the members of the sysadmin server role or the db_owner database role could use SETUSER to impersonate another user. Now, if you are assigned IMPERSONATE permission, you can impersonate a login or user by using the EXECUTE AS and REVERT statements.

SQL Server 2000 provided the db_datareader and db_datawriter database roles, which allowed a user to read from or write to any table in the database. However, if you wanted to give EXECUTE permission on all the stored procedures and functions in the database, it was required to execute a GRANT statement for each stored procedure and function. There was no role called db_procexecutor that allowed executing any procedure in the database. The hierarchical permission model in SQL Server 2005 fixes this problem by allowing you to grant EXECUTE permission at the schema level or database level to allow users to execute any procedure within the specified schema or database, respectively. You can create your own role by using the CREATE ROLE statement and then grant EXECUTE permission to that role. Now, whoever is part of that database role will have EXECUTE permissions on the stored procedures.

Let's now look at some examples of granular permission control and the hierarchical permission model in SQL Server 2005. Let's begin by creating two users in the AdventureWorks sample database:

```
USE AdventureWorks;
GO
CREATE LOGIN Test1 WITH PASSWORD = 'PWD1';
GO
CREATE USER Test1;
GO
CREATE LOGIN Test2 WITH PASSWORD = 'PWD2';
GO
CREATE USER Test2;
GO
```

These lines create the logins Test1 and Test2 and add them as users in the AdventureWorks sample database. Let's now grant some permissions to user Test2:

```
GRANT CONTROL  ON  OBJECT::Person.Address TO Test2;
GRANT SELECT   ON  SCHEMA::Person TO Test2;
GRANT EXECUTE  ON  DATABASE::AdventureWorks TO Test2;

USE master;
GRANT ALTER TRACE TO Test2;
```

These GRANT statements allow the Test2 user to have full control on the Person.Address table, much like the owner of the table; query any object in the Person schema; and execute any procedure or function in the AdventureWorks database. The ALTER TRACE permission allows Test2 to run Profiler to trace SQL Server. Because ALTER TRACE is a server-scoped permission, the statement has to be run in the master database.

The following statement illustrates principal-scoped permission and the new IMPERSONATE permission verb to allow user Test1 to impersonate user Test2:

```
USE AdventureWorks;
GRANT IMPERSONATE ON USER::Test2 TO Test1;
```

TIP

You can use the sys.server_permissions and sys.database_permissions catalog views to view server-level and database-level permission details.

You can start a new query window, connect as Test1, and run following statements:

```
USE AdventureWorks;
SELECT * FROM Person.Contact;
GO
ALTER TABLE Person.Address ADD col1 int NULL;
GO
ALTER TABLE Person.Address DROP COLUMN col1;
GO
```

```
EXEC dbo.uspGetEmployeeManagers 1;
GO
```

You should notice that all the four statements fail because user Test1 does not have permission to select from the Person.Contact table or change the Person.Address table or execute the stored procedure.

You can run the following line to impersonate the Test2 user and then run the preceding four statements. This time, the batch succeeds without any error messages because Test2 user has the required permissions:

```
EXECUTE AS USER='Test2';
GO
SELECT USER_NAME()
GO
--Run the earlier batch again
```

You can run the REVERT statement to switch back to the Test1 user execution context. Close this query window.

Next, you should start the Profiler tool and connect as user Test2. You should then be able to run SQL trace even though Test2 is not part of the sysadmin server role but has ALTER TRACE server-level permission. After you have verified that you can run Profiler trace by connecting using the Test2 login, close the Profiler and return to original query window in Management Studio, where you should execute the following lines to clean up:

```
USE AdventureWorks;
GO
DROP USER Test1;
GO
DROP USER Test2;
GO

DROP LOGIN Test1;
GO
DROP LOGIN Test2;
GO
```

TIP

You can use the sys.fn_builtin_permissions function to see SQL Server's built-in permission hierarchy. You can pass DEFAULT or a securable classname, such as SERVER, DATABASE, SCHEMA, OBJECT, and so on, as a parameter. This is a table-valued function, so you can use it in a SELECT statement as shown here:

```
SELECT * FROM sys.fn_builtin_permissions(DEFAULT);
```

Within the SQL Server 2005 permissions hierarchy, granting a particular permission may convey the rights of other permissions by implication. High-level permissions may be described as "covering" the more granular, low-level permissions that they "imply." SQL Server 2005 Books Online contains a user-defined function called `ImplyingPermissions` that uses the `sys.fn_builtin_permissions` function to obtain a list of list of permissions that include the specified permission by implication. This function accepts the name of a class of securable (such as `schema` or `object`) and the name of a permission (such as `alter` or `execute`) and returns a list of permissions that include the specified permission by implication. You can search for the word "ImplyingPermissions" in Books Online for more details on this.

Module Execution Context

As described in the previous section, the SQL Server 2005 security model allows granting permissions *to* users and logins and also granting permissions *on* users and logins (principals in general). One such principal-level permission is IMPERSONATE, which allows a user or login to change the execution context and perform actions as an impersonated user or login. As illustrated earlier, once the IMPERSONATE permission is granted, the EXECUTE AS statement can be used to switch the execution context, and the REVERT statement can be used to revert to the previous execution context.

SQL Server 2005 introduces a concept called module execution context that allows you to specify the execution context under which to execute a module, such as a stored procedure, a function (except an inline table-valued function), or a trigger. You can specify the EXECUTE AS clause with DDL statements such as CREATE PROCEDURE, CREATE FUNCTION, and CREATE TRIGGER to implicitly define the execution context of these user-defined modules. You can just grant the EXECUTE permission on the module to the users, and when the module is actually executed, the database engine will use the account specified with EXECUTE AS to validate permissions on objects referenced in the module. This way, you don't have to separately give permissions on the referenced objects to users of the module.

This might seem somewhat similar to the concept of ownership chaining that was available in previous releases. As a matter of fact, module execution context is designed to fix some of the limitations of ownership chaining.

Ownership Chaining and Its Limitations

The notion of ownership chaining simplifies permissions management and also yields small performance gains. The term *chain* refers to a virtual link that is established when an object, such as a stored procedure or a function, accesses other objects, such as tables and views.

For instance, if UserX executes the procedure UserY.Proc1, SQL Server first checks whether UserX has EXECUTE permission on UserY.Proc1. Once that is verified, if UserY.Proc1 queries the table UserY.Table1, SQL Server does not check whether UserX has permissions on UserY.Table1 because the procedure owner and object owner are the same (that is, `UserY`), forming an ownership chain. This way, you don't have to grant permissions on referenced objects—just the `EXECUTE` permission on stored procedures. By avoiding the extra permission check, SQL Server provides a small performance gain. However, if the procedure `UserY.Proc1` queries the table `UserZ.Table2`, SQL Server checks whether the caller, `UserX`, has permissions on `UserZ.Table2` because the referenced table owner (that is, `UserZ`) is different than the procedure owner (that is, `UserY`), breaking the ownership chain.

As you can see, ownership chaining is a very useful concept. However, it suffers from three limitations:

- The ownership chain works only for DML statements (`SELECT`, `INSERT`, `UPDATE`, and `DELETE`) and does not work for DDL statements. For instance, in the preceding example, if the stored procedure `UserY.Proc1` alters `UserY.Table1`, even though the executing object owner and referenced object owner are the same, SQL Server still checks permissions to ensure that `UserX` has sufficient permissions to alter the table.

- For security reasons, SQL Server explicitly blocks or disables ownership chaining for dynamic SQL.

- Ownership chaining relies on the fact that that the owners in the chain are the same. Ownership chaining is not designed to let you run a module under a different user context.

All these limitations are addressed by the module execution context feature introduced in SQL Server 2005. If you specify the `EXECUTE AS` clause with the module definition, SQL Server runs the entire module under the security context of the specified account, regardless of whether the ownership boundaries are crossed, the module contains DDL statements, or the module uses dynamic SQL. The concept of ownership chaining and module execution context is illustrated in Figure 7.1.

Let's now look at module execution context features and the `EXECUTE AS` clause in more detail.

The `EXECUTE AS` Clause

The `WITH EXECUTE AS` clause can be used to explicitly define the execution context of the user-defined modules, including stored procedure, functions, DML triggers, DDL triggers, and Service Broker queues. The `EXECUTE AS` clause can be specified with the `CREATE` or `ALTER` DDL statement for user-defined modules. You can specify one of the following four execution contexts for the module:

```
EXECUTE AS {CALLER | 'UserName' | SELF | OWNER}
```

The default is `CALLER` (except in Service Broker queues, where `SELF` is the default), which provides the same execution context behavior as in previous release—that is, the permission check is skipped if the referenced object owner and module owner are the same, forming the ownership chain. If the referenced object owner and the module owner are different, breaking the ownership chain, SQL Server ensures that the caller has the permissions on the referenced object. By specifying an execution context other than CALLER, you are telling SQL Server that you cannot rely on ownership chaining and that you would like to specify an account under which it should run the module.

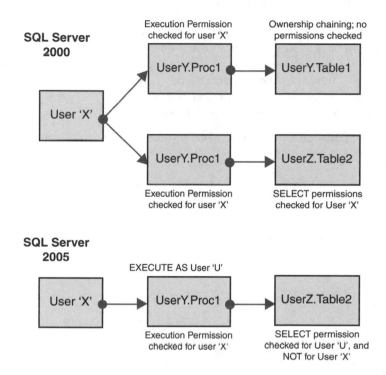

FIGURE 7.1 SQL Server 2005 introduces the EXECUTE AS clause, which you can use to implicitly specify the security context to be used while running a user-defined module.

In order to specify <UserName> with EXECUTE AS, you must have the IMPERSONATE permission on that user. The statements in the module are then executed in the security context of the specified account. For server-scoped DDL triggers, you have to specify a login name.

The SELF execution context indicates the user creating or altering the module. SELF is the default for Service Broker queues. SELF is essentially a shortcut to <UserName>, where SQL Server puts the name of the user creating or altering the procedure.

The OWNER execution context tells SQL Server 2005 to run the module under the security context of the *current* module owner at the time of execution. While creating the module, if you are specifying a different owner, you must have the IMPERSONATE permission on the module owner. The specified owner must be a singleton account, and it cannot be a role or a group.

NOTE

execute_as_principal_id **in the** sys.sql_modules **system catalog view can be used to find out about the module execution context. If this column contains** NULL, **it indicates the** CALLER **execution context,** -2 **indicates** OWNER, **and any other number indicates the principal ID of the user specified as** SELF **or** <principal>.

Let's now look at EXECUTE AS in action. In the following example, the user Sean is a DBA who would like to allow the user Erin to truncate a table but not do anything else with that table. Because TRUNCATE is not a grantable permission, Sean creates a stored procedure and specifies the EXECUTE AS SELF clause and grants the EXECUTE permission to user Erin. This way, the DBA creates his own new "permissions bucket."

You can begin working with this example by creating the users Sean and Erin:

```
USE AdventureWorks;
GO

CREATE LOGIN Sean WITH PASSWORD = '1234';
GO
CREATE LOGIN Erin WITH PASSWORD = 'pqrs';
GO

CREATE USER Sean;
CREATE USER Erin;

EXEC sp_addrolemember 'DB_OWNER', 'Sean';
GO
```

Next, you need to launch a new query window, connect as login Sean with password 1234, and run the following statements to create a table and the stored procedure to truncate the table:

```
USE AdventureWorks;
GO
CREATE TABLE dbo.tblTestData
 (col1 INT IDENTITY(1,1) NOT NULL PRIMARY KEY,
  col2 VARCHAR(10) DEFAULT 'Test');
GO
INSERT INTO dbo.tblTestData DEFAULT VALUES;
INSERT INTO dbo.tblTestData DEFAULT VALUES;
INSERT INTO dbo.tblTestData DEFAULT VALUES;
INSERT INTO dbo.tblTestData DEFAULT VALUES;
GO
SELECT * FROM dbo.tblTestData;
GO
```

```
CREATE PROCEDURE dbo.usp_TruncateTestData
WITH EXECUTE AS SELF
AS
    SELECT USER_NAME();
    TRUNCATE TABLE dbo.tblTestData;
GO

GRANT EXECUTE ON dbo.usp_TruncateTestData TO Erin;
GO
```

Then you need to launch one more query editor window. This time connect as user Erin with password pqrs and run the following script:

```
USE AdventureWorks;
GO

SELECT * FROM sys.all_objects WHERE type = 'U';
GO

SELECT * FROM dbo.tblTestData;
GO

EXEC dbo.usp_TruncateTestData;
GO
```

Because the user Erin does not have permission on any user table, the query on the sys.all_objects catalog view returns an empty set, even though there are many user tables in the database. This is because of the new metadata security feature introduced in SQL Server 2005, which is discussed later in this chapter.

Let's say that somehow user Erin found out that there is a table called tblTestData. If she tries to run the SELECT statement on this table, the operation fails because Erin does not have permission to query the table. However, when Erin runs the stored procedure, SQL Server runs the procedure under the security context of user Sean, as shown by the SELECT USER_NAME() statement inside the procedure. And because user Sean has full control on the table, the truncate statement inside the usp_TruncateTestData stored procedure succeeds.

Next, you need to close the query window connections made using the logins Sean and Erin and return to the original query window, where you can run the following statements to clean up:

```
DROP TABLE dbo.tblTestData;
DROP PROCEDURE dbo.usp_TruncateTestData;

DROP USER Sean;
DROP USER Erin;
```

```
DROP LOGIN Sean ;
DROP LOGIN Erin ;
GO
```

If you comment the WITH EXECUTE AS clause while creating the stored procedure, and if you follow the preceding demo steps again, you notice that when Erin executes the stored procedure, it fails because it is executing under her security context, and she does not have any permission on the table. If the procedure had the SELECT statement instead of the TRUNCATE statement, the stored procedure would work because of ownership chaining (the procedure owner and table owner are the same). However, ownership chaining works only for SELECT, INSERT, UPDATE, and DELETE statements, and not for TRUNCATE or any DDL statements, so this procedure fails if EXECUTE AS is commented. This example illustrates that EXECUTE AS works, regardless of the type of statements in a module.

User–Schema Separation

In SQL Server 2000, a fully qualified object name consists of four parts—server name, database name, owner name, and object name—and can be specified by using the following format:

```
[[[server.][database].][owner_name].]object_name
```

The objects can have the same name, as long as they have a different owner. In other words, you can have two tables named tblTest, as long as they are owned by different users. In that case, the applications qualify the object as User1.tblTest or User2.tblTest, depending on which table they wants to access. As you can see, here the username is used to avoid duplicates and to avoid name collisions. As per the ANSI SQL-92 standard, this is the job of a schema. SQL Server 2000 treated the schema and user the same. In other words, the schema and user were tightly coupled; they were one and the same. As per the ANSI SQL-92 standard, the purpose of schemas is to act like a namespace to club related objects and to avoid name collisions. With SQL Server 2000, the usernames were used for this purpose, and there was no true support for schemas.

Although this approach worked, there are a few problems. Let's say UserX created a bunch of tables, stored procedure, functions, views, and so on. And the application accessed the objects as UserX.object_name. Now, let's say for some reason that you wanted the drop UserX after the application went into production. You cannot drop a user unless all the objects the user owns are dropped or the ownership is assigned to a different user. Dropping the objects in almost all cases is not possible. And changing the owner requires that the application change. After the ownership is assigned to UserY, for example, the application has to access the objects as UserY.object_name instead of UserX.object_name.

Application developers often use dbo as the object owner to avoid the problem just described and also to avoid any name resolution issues. If the object is not fully qualified, SQL Server first tries to find an object with the specified name that is owned by the currently logged-in user. If not found, SQL Server tries to find dbo.object_name. For example, if UserX is trying to access table tblTest, and the table name is not fully quali-fied with the owner name, SQL Server first tries to find UserX.tblTest, and if it is not found, SQL Server tries to find a table named dbo.tblTest. This is the reason it is recom-mended that you fully qualify objects to avoid this extra name resolution check. Using dbo to group objects works fine until an application needs to create the objects and even the new objects have to be under the dbo ownership to aid name resolution. Just the CREATE TABLE permission is not sufficient to create a table in the dbo namespace. You have to be a member of either the sysadmin fixed server role or the db_dbowner or db_ddladmin fixed database role to create an object with dbo as the owner.

SQL Server 2005 decouples users (or principals in general) from schemas by changing the four-part naming convention to this:

[[[server.][database].][**schema_name**].]object_name

As you can see, with SQL Server 2005, the schema is the third part of the fully qualified object name. Schemas in SQL Server 2005 provide the notion of namespaces, allowing you to club the related objects together under a single name. In SQL Server 2000, objects were owned by users, whereas in SQL Server 2005, objects are contained in a schema that is owned by a user. Because a user does not own the objects directly, a user can be dropped without the objects needing to be dropped. By just assigning the schema owner to some other user, you can drop the user. Changing the schema owner does not require changing the application because the application continues to access the object as schema_name.object_name, regardless of who the schema owner is. This is illustrated in Figure 7.2.

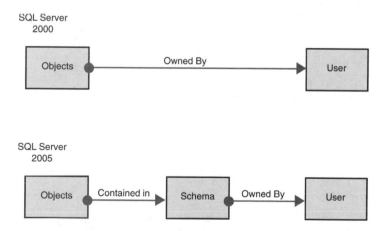

FIGURE 7.2   SQL Server 2005 decouples users from the schema to simplify the security management and for ANSI SQL-92 compliance.

Schema can be created by using the CREATE SCHEMA DDL statement. The sys.schemas catalog view can be used to view a list of schemas in the current database.

NOTE

The CREATE SCHEMA T-SQL statement was available in SQL Server 2000. However, it did not actually create a schema as SQL Server 2005 does. In SQL Server 2000, using CREATE SCHEMA was merely a way to create objects and grant permissions in a single statement and to aid system administrators in managing object dependencies.

Here is a simple example of how to create a schema and create objects in that schema:

```
USE AdventureWorks;
GO

CREATE SCHEMA Inventory;
GO

CREATE TABLE Inventory.tblReportData
    (col1 INT PRIMARY KEY NOT NULL IDENTITY(1,1),
     col2 XML DEFAULT '<Report />');
GO

INSERT INTO Inventory.tblReportData DEFAULT VALUES;
SELECT * FROM Inventory.tblReportData;
GO

SELECT name AS SchemaOwner FROM sys.database_principals
    WHERE principal_id =
    (SELECT principal_id FROM sys.schemas
        WHERE name = 'Inventory');
GO

SELECT * FROM sys.all_objects WHERE schema_id =
    (SELECT schema_id FROM sys.schemas
        WHERE name = 'Inventory');

DROP TABLE Inventory.tblReportData;
GO

DROP SCHEMA Inventory;
GO
```

This script creates a schema named Inventory and then creates a table in that schema. Note how this new table is accessed by INSERT and SELECT statements, using the schema_name.table_name convention, rather than user_name.table_name. This script uses the sys.schemas, sys.database_principals, and sys.all_objects catalog views to find out about the schema owner and the objects in the schema. The schema owner depends on the account you are logged in as while running the script. To drop the user, all you have to do is assign the schema ownership to some other user, and the application can continue to access the object as `Inventory.tblReportData`.

Multiple objects can still have the same name, as long as they are in different schemas. Because objects are not owned by users anymore, you might ask how name resolution works. How does SQL Server 2005 determine which object to access when a fully qualified name is not provided? The answer to this question is a new concept called default schemas.

Default Schemas

When you create or alter a user by using a CREATE USER or ALTER USER DDL statement, SQL Server 2005 gives you an option to provide a default schema for that user. You can use the WITH DEFAULT_SCHEMA = schema_name construct to specify the default schema for that user. If you do not make use of this construct while creating the user, by default SQL Server 2005 makes dbo as the user's default schema. The notion of default schemas is used for name resolution when an object is not fully qualified. SQL Server looks for the default schema for the user trying to access the object, and if the object is not found in user's default schema, SQL Server searches for the object in the dbo schema.

Here's an example of a default schema:

```
USE AdventureWorks;
GO


CREATE LOGIN demoLogin WITH PASSWORD = '1234';
CREATE USER demoLogin WITH DEFAULT_SCHEMA = Sales;
GRANT SELECT ON OBJECT::Sales.Store TO demoLogin;
GRANT EXECUTE ON XML SCHEMA COLLECTION::Sales.StoreSurveySchemaCollection
    TO demoLogin;
GO


EXECUTE AS USER = 'demoLogin';
GO


SELECT * FROM Store;
GO
SELECT * FROM Sales.Store;
GO


REVERT;
GO


ALTER USER demoLogin WITH DEFAULT_SCHEMA = Production;
GO


EXECUTE AS USER = 'demoLogin';
GO
```

```
SELECT * FROM Store;
GO
SELECT * FROM Sales.Store;
GO

REVERT;
GO

DROP USER demoLogin;
DROP LOGIN demoLogin;
GO
```

This script creates a login named demoLogin and a user with the same name in the AdventureWorks sample database. While creating the user, a schema named Sales is made as the default schema for the user. The script then grants permissions so that this user can run SELECT queries on the Sales.Store table. The security execution context is then changed by using an EXECUTE AS statement to run the next SELECT statement under the demoLogin user's context. Both the SELECT statements succeed because the user's default schema is Sales. When an object is not fully qualified, SQL Server looks for an object in user's default schema. If it is not found, SQL Server looks in the dbo schema namespace. In this case, it finds the Store table in the user's default schema. The script then changes the user's default schema to Production. The same SELECT then fails because it does not find the Store table either in the Production schema or in the dbo namespace.

NOTE

Notice that the sp_addlogin and sp_adduser system stored procedures are not used in the preceding script. They are deprecated in this release, and their use is strongly discouraged. The new T-SQL statements CREATE LOGIN and CREATE USER should be used instead. When you run CREATE USER, you have an option to provide the user's default schema, and if it is not provided, it defaults to dbo. However, if you create a user by using the sp_adduser stored procedure, SQL Server 2005 creates a schema with the same name as the username. This schema is then set as the default schema for this user, and the user is marked as the owner of this schema. The sp_dropuser stored procedure is updated to remove the schema created by sp_adduser. The sp_grantdbaccess and sp_revokedbaccess stored procedures are also updated to create and drop the schema with the same name as the username. Like sp_adduser and sp_dropuser, the sp_grantdbaccess and sp_revokedbaccess stored procedures are deprecated, and you should use the CREATE USER and DROP USER statements instead.

The notion of default schemas allows applications to not fully qualify objects but still guarantees to find the objects. As described earlier, in SQL Server 2000 this was achieved by having dbo as the owner. However, as alluded to earlier, creating objects to have dbo as the owner required high privileges, such as being part of the sysadmin, db_dbowner, or db_ddladmin roles. The default schema notion also fixes this problem. You can create a schema and have that as the default schema for all your users. Users can now create objects in this schema without requiring high privileges, and they can access the objects without fully qualifying the objects.

> **NOTE**
>
> If you look at rows in the sys.schemas catalog view, you see an entry for every fixed database role. For instance, there are schemas named db_owner, db_ddladmin, and so on. SQL Server 2005 creates these schemas in every new database to provide backward compatibility with SQL Server 2000. In previous releases, you could create an object in the form *fixed_db_role.object_name*. Although not very common, some developers might have created objects owned by fixed database roles. To provide backward compatibility, SQL Server 2005 creates a schema name for every fixed database role. However, there is no requirement or system reason to use these schemas.

A SQL Server 2005 database may consist of many schemas. Each schema has an owner. A user can *own* multiple schemas; however, there is always a single owner per schema. Each user has a single default schema that aids SQL Server in name resolution. In order to create objects in a schema, the user must have the CREATE permission and also ALTER or CONTROL permission on the schema.

Secure Metadata

SQL Server 2005 disallows direct access to system tables and exposes persistent metadata in the form of catalog views. SQL Server 2005 implements a security layer on top of the catalog views to restrict access to metadata and to make it visible only on a need-to-know basis. Row-level filtering on a catalog view ensures that if the user is not the owner or does not have permission to view the metadata, the catalog view row is not returned.

SQL Server 2005 defines a new permission, VIEW DEFINITION, which can be granted to a user to allow access to the metadata. Like other permissions, the VIEW DEFINITION permission can be granted at multiple scopes such as at database, schema, or object level.

> **NOTE**
>
> The database metadata (that is, the content of sys.databases catalog view) is never hidden from any database user. The system administrator has access to the entire server metadata, and the database owner has access to the entire database metadata.

Here is an example of catalog security in action:

```
USE AdventureWorks;
GO
CREATE LOGIN login1 WITH PASSWORD = 'WjkKWjkF';
GO
CREATE USER user1 FOR LOGIN login1;
GO
```

```
EXECUTE AS USER = 'user1';
GO
EXEC sp_helptext 'dbo.uspGetBillOfMaterials';
GO
SELECT OBJECT_DEFINITION(OBJECT_ID('dbo.uspGetBillOfMaterials'));
GO
SELECT * FROM sys.objects WHERE type = 'U';
GO
SELECT * FROM INFORMATION_SCHEMA.TABLES;
GO
REVERT;
GO

GRANT VIEW DEFINITION ON OBJECT::dbo.uspGetBillOfMaterials TO user1;
GRANT VIEW DEFINITION ON SCHEMA::HumanResources TO user1;
GO

EXECUTE AS USER = 'user1';
GO
EXEC sp_helptext 'dbo.uspGetBillOfMaterials';
GO
SELECT OBJECT_DEFINITION(OBJECT_ID('dbo.uspGetBillOfMaterials'));
GO
SELECT * FROM sys.objects WHERE type = 'U';
GO
SELECT * FROM INFORMATION_SCHEMA.TABLES;
GO
REVERT;
GO

DROP USER user1;
DROP LOGIN login1;
GO
```

This script creates a user who initially does not have any permission. When this user tries to see the stored procedure text by using sp_helptext, SQL Server 2005 returns an error, and OBJECT_DEFINITION returns NULL. When this user tries to obtain a list of user tables by using the sys.objects catalog view or by using the INFORMATION_SCHEMA view, SQL Server 2005 returns an empty result set because the user does not have permission on any of the tables and also does not have VIEW_DEFINITION permission. When the VIEW_DEFINITION permission is granted, the user can see the stored procedure text and can see all the tables in the schema on which the VIEW_DEFINITION permission is granted. The script uses EXECUTE AS and REVERT statements to change the security execution context.

Auditing Enhancements

SQL Server 2005 continues to support auditing successful and failed logins as previous releases did. In SQL Server Management Studio, you right-click the server instance in Object Explorer, select Properties to launch the Server Properties dialog, and on this dialog, you use the Security page to turn on or off auditing of successful or failed logins.

In addition to login auditing of the database engine, SQL Server 2005 now also supports auditing of Analysis Services. The Security Audit event class in the SQL Profiler tool can be used to audit login and logout actions. To see this in action, you can launch Profiler, connect to an Analysis Services instance, and select the Security Audit event class.

When you connect to a SQL Server 2005 instance by using Profiler, you see a lot of new events under the Security Audit class. Examples of these new security audit events include `Audit Schema Object GDR Event`, `Audit Database Object Take Ownership Event`, `Audit Server Principal Impersonation Event`, `Audit Broker Conversation`, `Audit Broker Login`, and so on.

Using triggers is one of the ways in which developers implement a custom auditing solution to track DML events, such as `INSERT`, `UPDATE`, and `DELETE`. SQL Server 2005 extends this model, and now you can use the new DDL triggers or event notification features to implement custom auditing solutions to track DDL events, such as altering a table, dropping a view, and so on. DDL triggers and event notifications are discussed in great detail in Chapter 6, "Transact-SQL Enhancements."

Cryptography Support

In previous releases, if you were to encrypt and decrypt data, you had to either implement your own custom solution or rely on third-party vendor solutions that integrated with SQL Server to provide cryptography support. Listening to the feedback from SQL Server developers, Microsoft decided to add native support for encryption capabilities, including the key management infrastructure in SQL Server 2005. Functions such as `EncryptByKey`, `EncryptByAsmKey`, `EncryptByCert`, and `EncryptByPassPhrase`, as well as their decryption equivalents can be used to encrypt and decrypt data. The following sections show you how to encrypt/decrypt data and how to manage keys and certificates, and then it discusses signed modules, which are an alternative to the module execution context feature described earlier. Let's begin with the data encryption feature introduced in SQL Server 2005.

Data Encryption

Encryption is a technique for securing data by converting clear or plain text into scrambled text or ciphertext. Encryption algorithms require an entity that they can use to encrypt or decrypt the text. This entity is known as the *key*. If the same key is used for encryption and decryption, such a key is termed a *symmetric key*. If one key is used for encryption and a different key is used for decryption, this key is termed an *asymmetric key*. An asymmetric key is generally a pair of public and private keys. SQL Server 2005 supports both symmetric and asymmetric keys. Asymmetric keys offer more robust security than symmetric keys, but encryption and decryption using asymmetric keys can be a very costly operation and should be restricted to small datasets. In addition to using symmetric and asymmetric keys, you can use a certificate or a passphrase to encrypt and decrypt data. You can think of a certificate as an entity that wraps the public key and is associated with a private key. A symmetric key can be created by using the CREATE SYMMETRIC KEY DDL statement, an asymmetric key can be created by using the CREATE ASYMMETRIC KEY DDL statement, and a certificate can created by using the CREATE CERTIFICATE statement, which can load a certificate from a file into SQL Server or have SQL Server generate a certificate.

Encrypting and decrypting using keys and certificates is discussed later in this chapter. To see cryptography in action, here's a simple example of encrypting and decrypting data by using a passphrase:

```
USE AdventureWorks;
GO
CREATE TABLE dbo.tblAccount
  (RecordID int IDENTITY(1,1) NOT NULL PRIMARY KEY,
   AccountNo VARBINARY(100) NOT NULL,
   BusinessName VARBINARY(512) NOT NULL,
   Balance MONEY NOT NULL);
GO

INSERT INTO dbo.tblAccount VALUES
  (EncryptByPassPhrase('WjkKWjkF_1', '001'),
   EncryptByPassPhrase('WjkKWjkF_2', 'Progressive Sports'),
   1000);

INSERT INTO dbo.tblAccount VALUES
  (EncryptByPassPhrase('WjkKWjkF_1', '002'),
   EncryptByPassPhrase('WjkKWjkF_2', 'Metropolitan Sports Supply'),
   5000);

SELECT * FROM dbo.tblAccount;
GO

SELECT RecordID,
       CONVERT(VARCHAR(15),
               DecryptByPassPhrase('WjkKWjkF_1', AccountNo)) AS AccountNo,
       CONVERT(VARCHAR(255),
               DecryptByPassPhrase('WjkKWjkF_2', BusinessName)) AS BusinessName,
       Balance
FROM dbo.tblAccount;
GO

DROP TABLE dbo.tblAccount;
GO
```

This script creates a table to store some financial data. The requirement is to encrypt two fields: the account number and the business name. The script uses the EncryptByPassPhase function during the INSERT operation and the DecryptByPassPhrase function while querying the data from this table. After you run the INSERT statements, the account number and business name columns appear as varbinary encrypted data in the table. The DecryptByPassPhrase function, along with the same passphrase used for encryption, is used to turn the ciphertext into plain text.

NOTE

The EncryptByPassPhase and DecryptByPassPhrase functions use the 3DES encryption algorithm in Cipher Block Chaining (CBC) mode.

Let's now look at what it takes to implement encryption by using keys and certificates.

Key Management

As mentioned earlier, you need a key or a certificate to encrypt and decrypt data. The SQL Server 2005 team realized that it is critical to secure the keys and certificates used for encryption. If someone gets access to a key/certificate, he or she can easily decrypt the data, and you lose the purpose behind encrypting the data. Therefore, how keys are managed and secured is very important.

SQL Server stores keys in the database. Symmetric keys (where the same key is used for encrypting and decrypting the data) and the private key (the secret part of an asymmetric key) are always stored encrypted in a database. Also, when symmetric keys and private keys are being used and are in memory, they are encrypted in memory, too.

There are three ways to secure symmetric keys and private keys. The first method allows you to specify a password that only you know. SQL Server uses this password to encrypt the key. With this method, it is your responsibility to secure the password. The second method for securing a key is to encrypt it by using a certificate. The third method is to encrypt a key by using another key, which is secured by a password, certificate, or yet another key.

As mentioned earlier, a *certificate* is nothing but an entity that wraps the public key and is associated with the private key. If a key is secured by using a certificate, it is important that the private key associated with the certificate be secured. The private key associated with the certificate can be secured by using a password or by using a *database master key*. You can create a single database master key per database by using the CREATE MASTER KEY DDL statement. The database master key itself is secured by using a DPAPI (Windows Data Protection API)-based instance-level secure key called a *service master key*. The service master key is generated per instance during the installation process and is the root of the SQL Server encryption hierarchy.

Figure 7.3 shows the key management concepts discussed here.

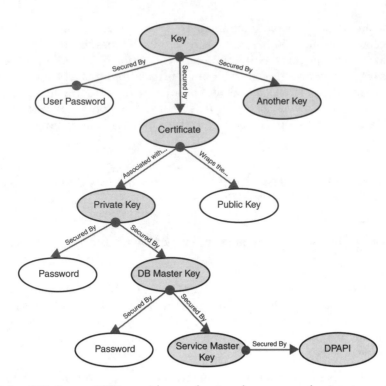

FIGURE 7.3   SQL Server 2005 provides a robust and secure mechanism to protect the keys and certificates used for encryption.

Let's now look at an example of encrypting data by using a symmetric key. In this example, the key itself will be secured by using a certificate. The certificate will be secured by using a database master key, which will be secured by using a password.

The following code creates a sample database and a table to store encrypted data:

```
USE master;
GO
CREATE DATABASE BankDB;
GO
USE BankDB;
GO
CREATE TABLE dbo.tblAccount
  (RecordID int IDENTITY(1,1) NOT NULL PRIMARY KEY,
   AccountNo VARBINARY(100) NOT NULL,
   BusinessName VARBINARY(512) NOT NULL,
   Balance MONEY NOT NULL);
GO
```

NOTE

You can use the following formula to determine the size of a column that will store the encrypted data:

```
Cipher_Col_Size (in bytes) = (FLOOR((8+PT)/BLOCK)+1) *
                                      BLOCK + 16 + BLOCK
```

In this formula, BLOCK is 8 for 8-bit ciphers, such as RC2, DES, TRIPLE_DES, DESX; it is 16 for 16-bit ciphers such as AES_128, AES_192, and AES_256; and PT is the size of plain text, in bytes.

Now you should create a symmetric key to be used for encrypting the data. The symmetric key will be secured by using a certificate, which in turn will be secured by using a database master key. As shown here, you need to create a database master key, and then you need to create a certificate and a symmetric master key:

```
--Step 1
CREATE MASTER KEY
   ENCRYPTION BY PASSWORD = 'WjkKWjKF';
GO
--Step 2
CREATE CERTIFICATE certAccount
   WITH SUBJECT  = 'certAccount';
GO
--Step 3
CREATE SYMMETRIC KEY keyAccount
   WITH ALGORITHM = TRIPLE_DES
   ENCRYPTION BY CERTIFICATE certAccount;
GO

SELECT * FROM sys.symmetric_keys;
SELECT * FROM sys.certificates;
GO
```

The sys.symmetric_keys and sys.certificates catalog views can be used to view the keys and certificates metadata. The sys.key_encryptions catalog view information related to encryptions of symmetric keys. For instance, the following query could be used to get a list of symmetric keys encrypted using the certificate named certAccount:

```
SELECT [sk].[name] FROM
   sys.symmetric_keys AS [sk] JOIN
   sys.key_encryptions AS [ke]
       ON [ke].key_id = [sk].symmetric_key_id
   JOIN sys.certificates AS [c]
       ON [ke].thumbprint = [c].thumbprint
WHERE [c].[name] = 'certAccount';
```

After the symmetric key is created, the data can be encrypted by using the EncryptByKey function. But before you use the key, you need to open the key by using the OPEN SYMMETRIC KEY statement, which prepares the key to be used for encryption or decryption. Once the key is open, it can be used until it is closed or until the session is active. You can execute the following statements to open the symmetric key and use it for encrypting the data.

```
OPEN SYMMETRIC KEY keyAccount DECRYPTION BY CERTIFICATE certAccount;
GO


INSERT INTO dbo.tblAccount VALUES
  (EncryptByKey(KEY_GUID('keyAccount'), '001'),
   EncryptByKey(KEY_GUID('keyAccount'), 'Progressive Sports'),
   1000);

INSERT INTO dbo.tblAccount VALUES
  (EncryptByKey(KEY_GUID('keyAccount'), '002'),
   EncryptByKey(KEY_GUID('keyAccount'), 'Metropolitan Sports Supply'),
   5000);
--Close Symmetric Key
CLOSE ALL SYMMETRIC KEYS;
GO
```

If you now look at the rows in the table, you see that the account number and business name columns appear as encrypted data:

```
SELECT * FROM dbo.tblAccount;
GO
```

To decrypt the data, the key needs to be opened again:

```
OPEN SYMMETRIC KEY keyAccount DECRYPTION BY CERTIFICATE certAccount;
GO


SELECT RecordID,
       CONVERT(VARCHAR(15), DecryptByKey(AccountNo)) AS AccountNo,
       CONVERT(VARCHAR(255), DecryptByKey(BusinessName)) AS BusinessName,
       Balance
FROM dbo.tblAccount;
GO


--Close Symmetric Key
CLOSE ALL SYMMETRIC KEYS;
GO


--Cleanup
USE master;
```

```
GO
DROP DATABASE BankDB;
GO
```

This time you see the account number and business name columns appear decrypted as plain text.

When a database master key is created by using the CREATE MASTER KEY statement, SQL Server encrypts it by using the specified password and stores it in a system table in the user database, which can be viewed by using the sys.symmetric_keys catalog view. At the same time, SQL Server encrypts the database master key by using the instance-level service master key and stores it in the master database. SQL Server uses this encrypted user database master key in the master database for key management, without relying on the user password used to encrypt the database master key. You can change the password used for encrypting the database master key by using the ALTER MASTER KEY DDL statement and specifying the REGENERATE WITH ENCRYPTION BY PASSWORD option. Regenerating the database key leads to decrypting all the keys generated using this database master key and re-encrypting them by using the new database master key. This process can be resource intensive and should be run during off-peak hours.

During the installation, the service master key is generated by using DPAPI, which derives the key from the service account under which the SQL Server service is running. You can regenerate the service master key by using ALTER SERVICE MASTER KEY, which results in decrypting all keys generated using the current service master key and re-encrypting them by using the new service master key. This is a resource-intensive operation and should only be performed during off-peak hours. You can back up and restore the service master key by using the BACKUP SERVICE MASTER KEY and RESTORE SERVICE MASTER KEY statements.

In this section, you have learned how to encrypt data by using passphrases and keys and how key management and security work in SQL Server 2005. The next section illustrates use of certificates to sign a module, which is an alternative technique to implement the module execution context feature described earlier.

Signed Modules

Earlier in this chapter, you learned about the EXECUTE AS clause, which can be used to change the security execution context. This clause, when specified with the modules, fixes the issues with ownership chaining, allowing you to explicitly specify the execution context under which the module should run. This greatly simplifies permission management because you don't have to individually grant and manage permission on the objects referenced in the module. However, this approach has one limitation. Because the module execution context changes to the one specified by using the EXECUTE AS clause, there is no way you can find out who from the list of users having the EXECUTE permission on the module *actually* executed the procedure. The example provided in the section "The EXECUTE AS Clause," earlier in this chapter, illustrates this by outputting the value returned by USER_NAME().

In summary, if you want to grant access to a resource but only when it is accessed through a particular module, the problem with EXECUTE AS is that it changes the module execution context, which may interfere with your auditing process. If you want to preserve the execution context, you can use a *signed module*.

To implement signed modules, you have to create a certificate, create a "logical" user associated with the certificate, grant permissions on referenced objects to this logical user, and then use the ADD SIGNATURE T-SQL construct to associate the certificate with a stored procedure, a function, a trigger, or an event notification.

As long as the certificate is associated with the module and the logical user associated with the certificate has permissions on the referenced objects, the users having EXECUTE permissions should be able to successfully execute the module and access the referenced objects through the module. When SQL Server 2005 executes the module and it finds out that a certificate is associated with the module, it adds the certificate to the security token, and by virtue of the presence of the certificate in the token, access to referenced objects is granted for the duration of module.

Let's now look at a signed module in action. The goal is to restrict direct access to a table but allow access to the table via a stored procedure.

You can begin working with a signed module by creating a login and a user named tableOwner, who will have permission to create schemas and tables in the AdventureWorks sample database. The EXECUTE AS statement is then used in the script to change the security context to the tableOwner login, and in this context, a schema and table are created, and a few rows are added to the table. The REVERT statement at the end changes the execution context back to the original login used to connect to SQL Server. You can execute the following script by using Management Studio or SQLCMD:

```
USE AdventureWorks;
GO
CREATE LOGIN tableOwner WITH PASSWORD = 'pwd';
GO
CREATE USER tableOwner;
GO
GRANT CREATE SCHEMA TO tableOwner;
GRANT CREATE TABLE TO tableOwner;
GO

EXECUTE AS LOGIN = 'tableOwner';
GO
CREATE SCHEMA tableOwner;
GO
CREATE TABLE tableOwner.tblTest
   (col1 INT IDENTITY(1,1) NOT NULL PRIMARY KEY,
    col2 DATETIME DEFAULT GETDATE(),
    col3 UNIQUEIDENTIFIER DEFAULT NEWID());
GO
INSERT INTO tableOwner.tblTest DEFAULT VALUES;
INSERT INTO tableOwner.tblTest DEFAULT VALUES;
INSERT INTO tableOwner.tblTest DEFAULT VALUES;
GO
SELECT * FROM tableOwner.tblTest;
GO
REVERT;
GO
```

In this example, a user named `tableOwner` owns a table on which the DBA wants to give access to a user, but only if this table is accessed via a stored procedure. The DBA creates a stored procedure and signs it with a certificate:

```
CREATE PROCEDURE dbo.sproc_Test
AS
BEGIN
   SELECT USER_NAME();
   SELECT SYSTEM_USER;
   SELECT * FROM tableOwner.tblTest;
END;
GO

CREATE CERTIFICATE crt_Demo
   ENCRYPTION BY PASSWORD  = 'JbSSSA'
   WITH SUBJECT = 'Certificate to use for signing modules';
GO
```

```
ADD SIGNATURE TO dbo.sproc_Test
  BY CERTIFICATE crt_Demo
  WITH PASSWORD = 'JbSSSA';
GO
```

Now that the module is signed, you can create a logical user associated with the certificate and grant SELECT permission on the table to this user:

```
CREATE USER userCert FOR CERTIFICATE crt_Demo;
GO
GRANT SELECT ON tableOwner.tblTest TO userCert;
GO
```

You can now create the user to whom the DBA does not want to give direct table access—only access through a stored procedure:

```
CREATE LOGIN demoLogin WITH PASSWORD = 'WjkKWjkF';
GO
CREATE USER demoUser FOR LOGIN demoLogin
GO
GRANT EXECUTE ON dbo.sproc_Test TO demoUser;
GO
```

The user is granted EXECUTE permission on the signed stored procedure that accesses the table. Now you can change the security context to the demoLogin principal and then try to access the table directly and by running the stored procedure:

```
EXECUTE AS LOGIN = 'demoLogin';
GO
SELECT * FROM tableOwner.tblTest;
GO
EXECUTE dbo.sproc_Test;
GO
REVERT;
```

Here the SELECT statement fails, but the user can see the data through the stored procedure. Now you can revoke the permission from the certificate (that is, the certificate-mapped user), and you should notice that demoLogin now can't see the data, even through the stored procedure:

```
REVOKE SELECT ON tableOwner.tblTest FROM userCert;
GO

EXECUTE AS LOGIN = 'demoLogin';
GO
```

```
SELECT * FROM tableOwner.tblTest;
GO
EXECUTE dbo.sproc_Test;
GO
REVERT;
GO

DROP TABLE tableOwner.tblTest;
DROP PROCEDURE dbo.sproc_Test;
DROP USER demoUser;
DROP LOGIN demoLogin;
DROP SCHEMA tableOwner;
DROP USER tableOwner;
DROP LOGIN tableOwner;
DROP USER userCert;
DROP CERTIFICATE crt_Demo;
GO
```

This time, even the stored procedure fails because the certificate-mapped user does not have permission to use SELECT on the table. The DROP statement toward the end performs the cleanup by removing the users, logins, schemas, and table.

An important thing to note in this script is the result of the USER_NAME() function in the stored procedure. Unlike as with the EXECUTE AS clause, the security execution context remains unchanged while using signed modules, and USER_NAME() returns demoUser as the user trying to run the stored procedure. This way, you can avoid changing security execution context and still overcome the ownership chaining limitations.

Surface Area Configuration (SAC)

Surface Area Configuration (SAC) is an example of Microsoft's commitment to security initiatives in SQL Server 2005. SAC refers to two things: the features and components that are not implicitly installed or activated during setup and a new tool that you can use to enable or disable features, services, and network protocols. By having you selectively install or activate the components and by providing the SAC tool, SQL Server 2005 lets you protect your SQL Server 2005 environment by reducing the attackable area of a system.

When you install SQL Server 2005, components such as Analysis Services, Reporting Services, Notification Services, Full-Text Search, and Integration Services are not implicitly selected. You can explicitly select to install these components.

SQL Server 2005 by default disables several engine features, such as CLR integration, execution of xp_cmdshell extended stored procedures, SQLMail, Database Mail, execution of OLE automation stored procedures, ad hoc distributed queries using OPENDATASET and

OPENDATASOURCE, Web Assistant stored procedures, and so on. You can turn these features on or off by using the sp_configure stored procedure or by using the SAC tool. As in the database engine, certain Analysis Services features are also turned off. These include ad hoc data mining queries using OPENROWSET, anonymous connections, user-defined functions written using .NET CLR or COM, and linked objects. You can use the SAC tool (which you open by selecting Start | All Programs | Microsoft SQL Server 2005 | Configuration Tools | SQL Server Surface Area Configuration) to enable or disable these features as well. The sys.system_components_surface_area_configuration security catalog view can be used to obtain a list of executable system objects that can be enabled or disabled by SAC.

Figure 7.4 shows the SAC tool to configure services and network protocols.

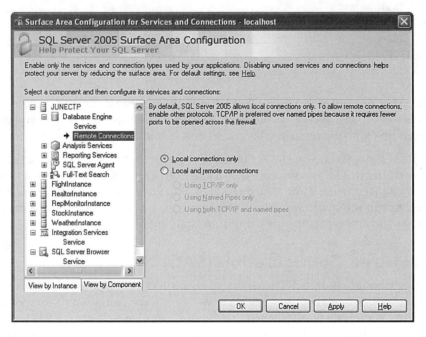

FIGURE 7.4   SAC is a new tool dedicated to protecting SQL Server 2005 systems by reducing the attackable surface area.

Figure 7.5 shows the SAC tool for configuring database engine and Analysis Services features.

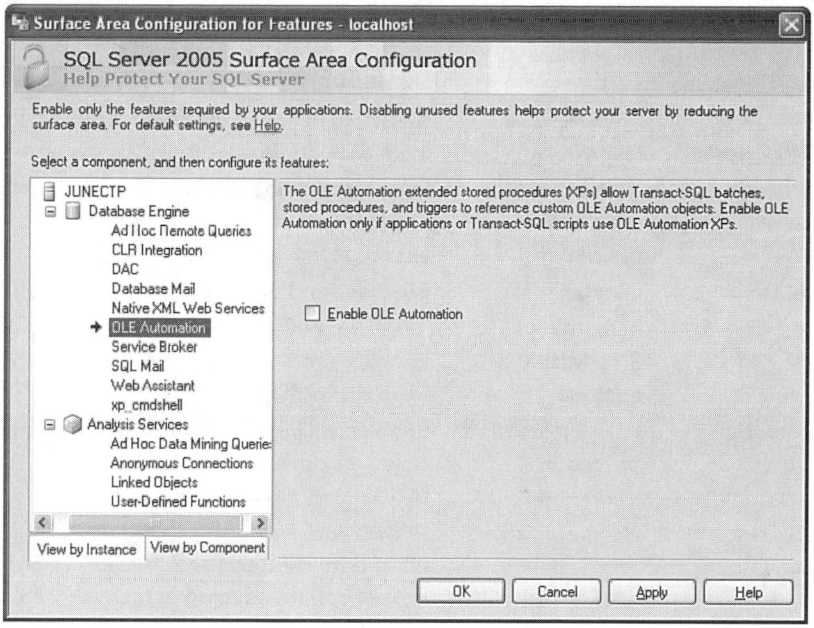

FIGURE 7.5   In addition to services and network connections, SAC can also be used to enable and disable database engine and Analysis Services features.

Table 7.1 lists the engine features that can be turned on or off.

TABLE 7.1   SQL Server 2005 Database Engine Features

Feature	sp_configure Option	Description	Default
CLR Integration	clr enabled	Enables executing .NET CLR stored procedures, triggers, user-defined types, and user-defined functions.	Off
HTTP Access	Not applicable	The tool lists all the current HTTP endpoints and allows you to start or stop an HTTP endpoint.	No HTTP endpoints are created by default.
xp_cmdshell	xp_cmdshell	Enables running an xp_cmdshell extended stored procedure, which allows running operating system commands from within SQL Server.	Off

TABLE 7.1   **Continued**

Feature	sp_configure Option	Description	Default
Web Assistant Stored Procedures	Web Assistant Procedures	Allows generating HTML files from SQL Server databases.	Off
OPENROWSET and OPENDATASOURCE Support	Ad hoc distributed queries	Supports ad hoc connections to remote data sources without linked or remote servers.	Off
Database Mail	Database Mail XPs	Enables sending emails over SMTP by using Database Mail.	Off
SQL Mail	SQL Mail XPs enabled	Enables sending emails by using MAPI-based SQL Mail.	Off
OLE Automation	OLE automation procedures	Enables calling COM automation objects from within T-SQL code by using sp_OAxxx procedures.	Off
Service Broker Endpoints	Not applicable	Allows enabling or disabling endpoints created for Service Broker communication across instances.	No Service Broker Endpoints created by default.
SMO and DMO Extended Stored Procedures	SMO and DMO XPs	Enables access to SMO and DMO.	On
Remote Dedicated Administrator Connection (DAC)	Remote admin connections	Enables DAC from a remote computer.	Off
SQL Server Agent Extended Stored Procedures	Agent XPs	Enables executing SQL Server Agent extended stored procedures.	On
Replication Extended Stored Procedures	Replication XPs	Enables executing Replication extended stored procedures.	Off

SQL Server Agent Security Overview

The Agent security enhancements in SQL Server 2005 include the two new database roles in the msdb system database and an ability to use multiple proxy accounts. Administrators can use the new database role named SQLAgentUserRole to manage users who can create or execute SQL Server agent jobs. By default, no user is a member of the SQLAgentUserRole role.

<u>**NOTE**</u>

Except for members of the `sysadmin` **server role, users are not able to see the SQL Server Agent folder in Object Explorer in Management Studio unless they are part of the** `SQLAgentUserRole msdb` **database role.**

SQL Server 2000 allowed one proxy account. A *proxy* essentially defines the security context for a job step. SQL Server changes that by allowing you to have any number of proxy accounts. You as a system administrator can allow logins, `msdb` roles, and system roles to access one or more proxy accounts. You can also assign proxy accounts to access one or more subsystems such as SQL Server Integration Services (SSIS; formerly DTS) package execution, Replication Distributor, Replication Transaction Log Reader, and so on. Members of the `sysadmin` server role can use the `sp_add_proxy` stored procedure to create a new SQL Agent proxy account and `sp_grant_login_to_proxy` to grant access on a proxy to a principal.

SQLCLR Security Overview

Microsoft knew that allowing .NET code to run inside the SQL Server 2005 engine would raise security-related concerns among database administrators. SQL Server 2005 addresses this concern by introducing a security architecture that combines SQL Server's user-based model with the .NET Framework's code-access–based security model. You as an administrator have complete control over what the SQLCLR can and cannot do.

The code access security in .NET is based on permissions defined in the configurable Runtime Security Policy (which you access by selecting Start | Programs | Administrator Tools | .NET Framework 2.0 Configuration). Based on where the .NET assembly originated and the user running the assembly, the administrator can determine what that assembly can or cannot do. The .NET Framework security is provided via four configurable policy levels: Enterprise, Machine, User, and Host. The assembly receives the permissions based on the intersection of permissions defined in these policies. The highest level is Enterprise, which describes the policy for an entire application. The next level is the Machine policy, which affects all .NET assemblies running on the machine. For instance, if you define Machine policy that disallows writing or creating new entries in the registry under the HKLM hive, then all assemblies running on that machine will not be able to create entries or write into the HKLM hive in the registry. The User policy allows assigning different permissions to the same assembly based on the users executing it. In the case of SQL Server 2005, it is the account under which SQL Server 2005 service is running. The Host policy is defined by the host of the .NET CLR—in this case, SQL Server 2005.

SQL Server 2005 Host policy allows you to put user assemblies into one of following three permissions buckets:

- **SAFE**—This is the most restrictive and recommended permission set. It allows the assembly to perform internal computations and data access, and nothing else. An assembly with the SAFE permission set cannot access external system resources such as files. This is the default permission set.

- **EXTERNAL_ACCESS**—This is the next level after SAFE, and it adds the ability to access external resources, such as files.

- **UNSAFE**—The UNSAFE permission set allows assemblies unrestricted access to resources, both within and outside SQL Server. Assemblies can even call unmanaged code. Assemblies should be put in the UNSAFE permission bucket after thorough consideration and analysis. Only sysadmin role members can import assemblies by using this permission set.

When you import a .NET assembly by using the CREATE ASSEMBLY DDL statement, you can put that assembly in one of the three permissions buckets by using the WITH PERMISSION_SET = clause, as illustrated here:

```
CREATE ASSEMBLY sqlclrXMLHelper
FROM 'E:\Dev\sqlclrXMLHelper.dll'
WITH PERMISSION_SET = EXTERNAL_ACCESS;
```

When the SQLCLR .NET code is executed, the intersection of permissions defined in Machine policy, User policy, and Host policy (the permissions bucket) determine what the code can or cannot do. The .NET integration in SQL Server 2005 and security considerations are further discussed in Chapter 11, "SQL Server 2005 and .NET Integration."

Service Broker Security Overview

Service Broker is a new technology introduced in SQL Server 2005 that brings asynchronous messaging services closer to the database engine, allowing you to build reliable, asynchronous queued database applications. A message can originate at one instance and can possibly be received at another SQL Server 2005 instance. The security features in Service Broker guarantee that the conversation is secure and that the unauthorized databases are not able to send Service Broker messages.

When you create an endpoint to be used for Service Broker communication, the default value for the ENCRYPTION option is REQUIRED, which indicates that endpoint must use encryption. Therefore, to connect to this endpoint, another endpoint must have ENCRYPTION set to either SUPPORTED or REQUIRED. The Service Broker transport authentication can be based on certificates or SSPI.

Service Broker security is based on certificates. A certificate is used to verify the identity of a remote database and to identify the local database principal for the operation. Service Broker uses the public key associated with the local database principal to decrypt the information received from the remote server. If it is able to decrypt the information, the remote database contains the private key that corresponds to the public key in the local certificate associated with the principal. After this verification, the remote database can act with the permissions of the local database principal that owns the certificate that contains the public key for the remote database.

SQL Server Service Broker and its security features are described in Chapter 14.

Summary

The goal of this chapter is to introduce you to the security enhancements in SQL Server 2005. The SQL Server 2005 team has done everything possible to ensure that this release provides the most secure and robust environment possible to build database applications. Following the Trustworthy Computing initiative, SQL Server 2005 is secure by design, secure by default, and secure in deployment.

SQL Server 2005 contains significant enhancements to authentication, authorization, metadata access, and auditing schemes. This chapter also discusses the built-in cryptography support that you can use to easily encrypt and decrypt data and secure the keys used for encryption. SQL Server 2005 provides tools and technologies that can be used to protect the SQL Server environment by disabling unused features, protocols, and services and thereby reducing the attackable surface area.

The final section in this chapter briefly discusses security initiatives in various SQL Server 2005 subsystems, such as Service Broker and .NET CLR integration. Chapter 8 discusses the new reliability and high availability features introduced in SQL Server 2005.

Reliability and High Availability in the Database Engine

The term *reliability* refers to a system's support for maintaining stability and integrity. *High availability* can be thought of as the ability of a system to continue serving client connections in the event of a hardware, software, or system failure. A highly available system is almost always operational and accessible to clients.

Reliability and availability are two important characteristics that define the level of quality of service offered by a database system. This chapter introduces SQL Server 2005 database engine features that make database solutions reliable and highly available.

Reliability Enhancements

Database backups are a key component of any disaster recovery plan. In most IT environments, backups are the last line of defense against data loss. A well-designed and tested backup and restoration strategy can minimize data loss and downtime in case of a loss of data access due to human error, system malfunction, or some other system failure. SQL Server 2005 introduces enhancements that allow you to reliably and efficiently back up your databases and reduce the downtime by using features such as instant file initialization and online restorations.

Mirrored Backup Media

Redundancy is one of the common techniques used to increase the reliability of a system. SQL Server 2005 uses this technique and allows writing, or *mirroring*, of data to multiple backup devices simultaneously. Mirroring a media set increases backup reliability by reducing the impact of backup-device malfunctions. Mirrored backup media support is provided via the new MIRROR TO clause with the BACKUP T-SQL statement. A single BACKUP statement can contain up to three MIRROR TO clauses, for a total of four mirrors (including the mirror created by the TO clause). Let's look at a couple examples of performing database and log backups, using mirrored backup media.

The following statement performs a full database backup, creating two additional mirrored backup copies on the E: and F: drives:

```
USE master;
GO
BACKUP DATABASE AdventureWorks
    TO DISK='C:\AWCopy1.bak'
    MIRROR TO DISK='E:\AWCopy2.bak'
    MIRROR TO DISK='F:\AWCopy3.bak'
WITH FORMAT;
GO
```

This backup set consists of a single backup media family having three media sets, each having a single backup media disk file, called a *device*.

The following statement performs a full database backup, creating an additional mirrored backup copy on the E: drive:

```
BACKUP DATABASE AdventureWorks
    TO DISK='C:\AWCopy1a.bak', DISK='C:\AWCopy1b.bak'
    MIRROR TO DISK='E:\AWCopy2a.bak', DISK='E:\AWCopy2b.bak'
WITH FORMAT, STATS = 5;
GO
```

This time, each media set consists of two backup media disk files, or *devices*. Each device (for example, C:\AWCopy1a.bak or C:\AWCopy1b.bak) holds approximately half of each backup set. Up to 64 devices may be specified with the TO clause or the MIRROR TO clause. If you specify *n* devices in the TO clause, then the same *n* number of devices must also be specified with each MIRROR TO clause.

The backup set created in the preceding example consists of two media families. The devices C:\AWCopy1a.bak and E:\AWCopy2a.bak form the first media family, and the devices C:\AWCopy1b.bak and E:\AWCopy2b.bak form the second media family.

You can access the following tables in the msdb system database to view the backup history and other details:

```
SELECT * FROM msdb.dbo.backupset;
SELECT * FROM msdb.dbo.backupmediaset;
SELECT * FROM msdb.dbo.backupmediafamily;
SELECT * FROM msdb.dbo.backupfilegroup;
SELECT * FROM msdb.dbo.backupfile;
```

The following BACKUP statement fails because the second MIRROR TO clause does not have two devices like the TO and the first MIRROR TO clause:

```
BACKUP DATABASE AdventureWorks
    TO DISK='C:\AWCopy1a.bak', DISK='C:\AWCopy1b.bak'
    MIRROR TO DISK='E:\AWCopy2a.bak', DISK='F:\AWCopy3b.bak'
    MIRROR TO DISK='F:\AWCopy3a.bak'
WITH FORMAT, STATS = 5;
GO
```

For mirrored backup media functionality, all the devices in a media family must be equivalent (for instance, tape drives with the same model number from the same manufacturer). Backup and restore operations impose different requirements on whether all the mirrors must be present. For a backup operation to write (that is, to create or extend) a mirrored media set, all the mirrors must be present. In contrast, a restore operation can read the media for only one mirror per media family at a time. In the presence of errors, however, having the other mirror(s) enables some restoration problems to be resolved quickly. This is because RESTORE and RESTORE VERIFYONLY support substitution of damaged media with the corresponding backup-media volume from another mirror.

Backup and Restore Media Checks

The BACKUP and RESTORE statements now support the CHECKSUM clause to enhance the reliability of the backup and restore operations. The CHECKSUM clause introduces an additional verification and error detection step during backup and restoration.

When the CHECKSUM clause is specified with the BACKUP statement, SQL Server computes a backup checksum on the backup stream and records it on the backup media. In addition, SQL Server also verifies the page-level information, such as page checksum or torn page detection, if either exists. If page checksum or torn page detection information is not available, BACKUP cannot verify the page and silently skips it. The has_backup_checksums column in the msdb..backupset table can be used to determine whether a backup checksum is present with the backup set.

NOTE

Generating and verifying backup checksum and page-level information may affect the performance and backup/restoration throughput. This is why the default setting for BACKUP and RESTORE is NO_CHECKSUM, which disables page validation and the generation or verification of backup checksums.

Similarly, the CHECKSUM clause can be specified with the RESTORE and RESTORE VERIFYONLY statements. If the CHECKSUM clause is specified, both the RESTORE and RESTORE VERIFYONLY operations verify the backup checksums and page checksums.

When the CHECKSUM clause is specified, if BACKUP encounters a page error during verification, the backup fails. You can specify CONTINUE_AFTER_ERROR to instruct BACKUP to continue despite encountering an invalid backup checksum. In such cases, BACKUP logs an entry in the SQL Server error log and to the msdb..backupset (is_damaged field) and msdb..suspect_pages tables. It also issues a message that the backup was successfully generated but contains page errors.

Unlike in previous releases, the RESTORE VERIFYONLY now performs a thorough analysis to ensure that the backup set is really good and reliable.

Checksum I/O Validation

You can use the new PAGE_VERIFY clause with the ALTER DATABASE statement to discover incomplete I/O transactions caused by disk I/O errors. Disk I/O errors can cause database corruption problems, and they are usually the result of power failures or disk hardware failures that occur at the time the page is actively being written to disk. The PAGE_VERIFY clause provides the following three options:

- **CHECKSUM**—This is the default PAGE_VERIFY option. A checksum is calculated using the contents of the entire page and stored in the page header when a page is written to disk. When the page is read from disk, the checksum is recomputed and compared to the checksum value stored in the page header. If the values do not match, error message 824 is reported to both the SQL Server error log and the Windows Event Viewer. The database engine distinguishes between an I/O error detected by the operating system (error 823) and an I/O error detected by the SQL Server PAGE_VERIFY CHECKSUM option (error 824). In addition, you can validate the page checksums during backup and restore operations by using the CHECKSUM clause with the BACKUP/RESTORE statement, as discussed earlier in this chapter.

- **TORN_PAGE_DETECTION**—With this option, a bit is reversed for each 512-byte sector in the 8KB database page when the page is written to disk. If a bit is in the wrong state when the page is later read, the page is assumed to be written incorrectly; a torn page is detected.

- **NONE**—You use this option to turn off the PAGE_VERIFY functionality. Future data page writes will not contain a checksum or torn page detection bit, and the page will not be verified at read time, even if a checksum or torn page detection bit is present.

Online, Piecemeal, and Page Restorations

Online restoration is a new feature available in SQL Server 2005 Enterprise, Evaluation, and Developer Editions. It can be used for the following:

- Databases containing multiple filegroups and using the full or bulk-logged recovery models

- Databases containing multiple read-only filegroups and using the simple recovery model

In earlier versions of SQL Server, the basic unit of availability during a restoration was the entire database. Such restorations are known as *offline restorations* because the database is not available while the restoration is in progress. In SQL Server 2005, filegroups are the basic unit of availability. During a restoration, a database can be online, but some file-groups may not be available. You first restore the primary filegroup, and it becomes avail-able immediately; you then restore other filegroups by priority, and each becomes available as it is restored. Only the filegroups in the process of being restored or that are not restored yet remain offline; the rest of database is online and available. If a client application tries to access data from an unavailable filegroup, it receives an error. This type of online restore operation is known as a *piecemeal restoration*. Data should be care-fully distributed on filegroups in order to make the best use of this feature. Piecemeal restorations can be considered an enhancement over SQL Server 2000 partial restorations. In addition to restoring critical data first, a piecemeal restoration can also be helpful in restoring a damaged file or set of files.

> **NOTE**
>
> SQL Server 2005 allows you to perform offline restorations of backups from SQL Server 7.0 and 2000. However, online restoration is not supported from backups from earlier versions of SQL Server. SQL Server 2005 does not support restorations of backups from SQL Server 6.x and earlier.

The other online restoration type introduced in SQL Server 2005 is *page restorations*. You can use the new PAGE clause with the RESTORE statement to restore and fix one or more pages that have been detected as corrupted by check-summing or a torn write. Like piece-meal filegroup restoration, a page restoration is by default an online restoration option, meaning that the database is online for the duration of the restore, and only the data that is being restored is offline. If you want a piecemeal or a page restoration to be an offline restoration, you can use the WITH NORECOVERY clause with the RESTORE statement.

> **NOTE**
>
> In SQL Server 2005, you can use the BACKUP and RESTORE statements to back up and restore full-text catalogs along with other database data. The backup operation treats full-text catalogs as files. During the backup, the catalog is put into a read-only mode so that the process of creating and maintaining a full-text index is suspended until the backup completes. To back up only the full-text catalog, and not the database data, you specify the FILE clause in the BACKUP command. To back up only the filegroup that stores multiple full-text catalogs, you specify the FILEGROUP clause in the BACKUP command.

The EMERGENCY Database State Option

In case of restoration errors due to damaged backups or trying to recover a corrupt database, you can change the database state to EMERGENCY by using the ALTER DATABASE statement. You can put a database in EMERGENCY state to gain limited access to the data as is. If database is marked as suspect, you can change the database state to EMERGENCY to either gain read-only access to the database or to detach a suspect database.

Emergency mode changes the database to a single-user and read-only database, disables logging, restricts access to members of the sysadmin fixed server role, and allows repair or restoration of the database.

The following script places the AdventureWorks sample database into EMERGENCY state by using the ALTER DATABASE statement:

```
--connect to an instance using a member of sysadmin fixed server role
USE master;
ALTER DATABASE [AdventureWorks] SET EMERGENCY;
GO
SELECT DATABASEPROPERTYEX('AdventureWorks', 'Status');
SELECT name, state, state_desc FROM sys.databases;
GO


USE AdventureWorks
GO
SELECT * FROM Sales.Store;
BEGIN TRAN
GO
--Following statement will fail
UPDATE Sales.Store SET [Name] = 'X' + [Name];
GO
ROLLBACK TRAN
GO
--following statement will also fail
BACKUP DATABASE [AdventureWorks] TO DISK='c:\temp\test.bak';
GO


USE master;
ALTER DATABASE [AdventureWorks] SET ONLINE;
GO
SELECT DATABASEPROPERTYEX('AdventureWorks', 'Status');
SELECT name, state, state_desc FROM sys.databases;
GO
```

You can use the DATABASEPROPERTYEX function or sys.databases catalog view to view the state of a database. The preceding script illustrates that updates and database backup are disallowed if a database is put in emergency mode. Also note that databases in emergency mode cannot be moved or copied by using the Copy Database Wizard.

The `ATTACH_REBUILD_LOG` Clause

Consider a scenario where you have an OLTP database with a very large log file(s), and you want to copy this database on another server for mostly or only read operations. In such a case, you can avoid copying the log file. You simply shut down the database properly, copy all the .mdf and .ndf files (there's no need to copy the log .ldf files), and run the `CREATE DATABASE` statement on another server, along with the `ATTACH_REBUILD_LOG` clause. The `ATTACH_REBUILD_LOG` clause instructs SQL Server to rebuild the log for the database being attached. Note that this operation breaks the log backup chain. It is recommended that a full database backup be performed after the operation is completed. The `sp_attach_single_file_db` system stored procedure available in previous releases to perform similar tasks is being deprecated, and it is recommended that you instead use `FOR ATTACH_REBUILD_LOG` with the `CREATE DATABASE` statement.

Availability Enhancements

High availability involves keeping your servers and their services up and running. Organizations running large enterprise applications, with users from all around the globe, demand a high-availability solution to assure 24x7 accessibility of the application by users. Continuous availability is essential to maintaining a successful online business. The need for a high-availability solution is easily justifiable by looking at the cost of unavailability, which in some instances can exceed the cost of the application and infrastructure.

The key to building highly available solutions is to minimize or eradicate the points of failures in the system architecture. The design of a highly available solution is focused on minimizing the points of failure within the available budget. Designing for availability involves anticipating, detecting, and automatically resolving hardware or software failures before they result in service errors, event faults, or data corruption—thereby minimizing downtime.

The following are the high-availability options in SQL Server 2000:

- **Failover clustering**—A *failover cluster* is a set of two or more independent computers that share resources so that if one of the servers fails, another server in the cluster will take over the resource and the processing load.

- **Replication**—SQL Server replication can be used for creating one or more synchronized, warm standby servers. The three replication configurations available in SQL Server 2000 are snapshot replication, transactional replication, and merge replication. A replication-based high-availability solution requires some downtime and is not as seamless and automatic as failover clustering. In addition, replication is generally a database-level high-availability solution, unlike clustering, which provides server-level high availability. Replication is a simpler and less expensive solution than failover clustering.

- **Log shipping**—Log shipping automatically synchronizes databases by continually backing up the transaction logs from the source database, copying and restoring the logs to the destination database. Like replication, log shipping is also easy to configure and provides a database-level availability solution.

SQL Server 2005 continues to support and enhance these three high-availability solutions. In addition, a lot of new features, such as database mirroring, database snapshots, online and parallel indexing, and early restore access, are provided to increase availability. Let's look at a new, interesting high-availability solution, called database mirroring, that has the potential of becoming the best high-availability solution for SQL Server–based applications.

Database Mirroring

Like replication and log shipping, database mirroring is a software solution for increasing the availability of a specific database. Database mirroring was originally called *real-time log-shipping*. However, database mirroring is the accurate and more appropriate term for this high availability technology. Mirroring maintains two copies of the database, only one of which is accessible by clients at a given time. The accessible database is known as the *principal database*, and its duplicate is known as the *mirror database*. The two server instances communicate and cooperate as partners in a database mirroring session. The principal and mirror databases must reside on different server instances, which are known as the *principal server* and the *mirror server*, respectively. In production environments, the principal and mirror servers are installed on different servers to enable the mirror server to operate as a "hot" standby server for the database. In typical mirroring configurations, if the principal server is lost, the mirror server is readily available as a failover partner.

In its simplest form, database mirroring involves only the principal and mirror servers. A third server instance, known as the *witness*, can be added to a mirroring session. The witness server enables automatic failover. Automatic failover causes the mirror server to roll forward its copy of the database until it is completely up-to-date and then switch principal role. The former mirror server becomes the principal server, and the former mirror database becomes the principal database. In addition to automatic failover, the mirror server also plays the tie-breaker role between the principal and mirror to prevent a *split-brain* scenario where both machines think they are the principal. For instance, if the principal and mirror servers come up at the same time and both think they are the principal, then the witness can break the tie.

NOTE

Database mirroring works only with databases that use the full recovery model. It does not work with databases that use the simple and bulk-logged recovery models. In addition, the master, `msdb`, `temp`, and `model` databases cannot be mirrored.

Figure 8.1 shows a typical database mirroring configuration.

Before we look at database mirroring in more detail, let's review some of the benefits offered by this high-availability solution and also compare it with failover clustering.

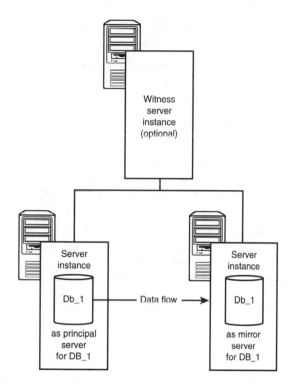

FIGURE 8.1   Database mirroring configuration consists of a principal server instance hosting the live database, a mirror server instance hosting the "hot" standby copy of the mirrored database, and, optionally, a witness server instance to be used for automatic failover.

Benefits of Database Mirroring

The following are some of the benefits offered by a database mirroring–based high-availability solution:

- Database mirroring offers an easy-to-manage alternative to failover clustering. Database mirroring provides zero-data-loss high availability for individual databases through complete or near-complete redundancy of data.

- Database failover is instantaneous (it takes less than 3 seconds). This is possible because of the new fast recovery technology in SQL Server 2005 (which is available only in the Enterprise Edition). When the original principal server is fixed, it can then rejoin the partnership, although when it does, it takes on the mirror server role. Role reversal or switching can be either automatic or performed manually.

- Database mirroring works with a standard computer and storage, and it does not require a special and identical hardware configuration, as failover clustering does. In addition, database mirroring does not rely on any shared storage components.

- Database mirroring provides an optional, self-monitoring configuration that allows automatic failover when a failure is detected.

- Clients can use the mirror database as a reporting server by creating one or more database snapshots on the mirror database.

- Servers can be in separate locations. A mirror server instance can be at a geographically remote location from the principal.

- Database mirroring differs from log shipping because changes are reflected in real-time on the mirror (standby) server, and failover is automatic in database mirroring.

- The data access API is enhanced to support database mirroring and facilitate automatic, transparent client redirection. In other words, when a database failover happens, clients can be automatically redirected to the new principal server. Clients can specify the name of the failover partner in the connection string while connecting to the principal server. All committed transactions remain intact; however, any uncommitted transactions are rolled back. The "Failover Partner = <partner_name>;" clause in the connection string instructs the client to connect to the specified partner, if it cannot connect to the principal. If the client can connect to the principal, it obtains the failover partner name from the principal server, ignores the failover partner value specified in the connection string, and caches the value that it obtained from the principal server. If the connection string does not specify the failover partner value, and if the client is not able to connect to the principal, the connection fails. Therefore, it is recommended that you always specify the failover partner value in the connection string.

- Database mirroring supports full-text catalogs. This means you can mirror a database that has a full-text catalog. Database mirroring synchronizes the catalog along with the database. Changes to a full-text catalog are logged, copied to the mirror server, and replayed there. You can add or drop the full-text catalog on the principal server, and the actions are repeated on the mirror server. Note that if the replay fails on the mirror server, the mirroring session is paused, and the DBA must fix the problem on the mirror server and resume the session.

- The impact of database mirroring on transaction throughput is zero to minimal.

Setting Up Database Mirroring

You can configure database mirroring by running T-SQL statements or by using Object Explorer in SQL Server Management Studio. The Mirroring page on the database properties dialog provides an interface to configure and monitor database mirroring. This section discusses the T-SQL approach.

Database mirroring requires SQL Server 2005 to be installed on the primary and the mirror instances and on the witness server instance (if present). After you have installed SQL Server 2005 on these servers and verified that the principal database is running in full recovery mode, you need to take these steps to set up database mirroring:

1. Use the CREATE ENDPOINT...FOR DATABASE_MIRRORING statement to create an endpoint over TCP to accept the database mirroring payload. With this step, you can specify that the transport security use Windows authentication or certificate-based authentication. In addition, you can specify one or more database mirroring

roles (that is, witness, partner, or all) that the endpoint supports. Create a database mirroring endpoint on the principal, mirror, and witness servers. Note that only one database mirroring endpoint can be created per server instance. Use the `sys.endpoints` catalog view to find out whether a database mirroring endpoint already exists on the server instance.

2. After the endpoints are created and started, create the mirror database by using `NORECOVERY` to restore a recent full backup of the principal database. The mirror database must have the same name as the principal database, and these databases cannot be renamed during a database mirroring session. You must restore all the log backups done since the full backup. The mirror database needs the last log backup from the principal database. The principal and mirror database names must be the same. It is also recommended that the path of the mirror database files be identical to the path of database files on the principal.

3. Ensure that logins exist on the mirror server for all the database users.

4. Use SQL Server Management Studio or the `ALTER DATABASE...SET PARTNER` and `ALTER DATABASE...SET WITNESS` T-SQL statements to configure database mirroring.

5. If the witness and partners are running in different (but trusted) domains, you should create a login on the witness server for the domain user account of partner instances and grant `CONNECT` permission on the witness endpoint to the login just created. Similarly, on each partner server instance, you should create a login for the domain user account of the witness instance and grant `CONNECT` permission on the partner endpoint to the login for the witness server instance just created. If the witness and partners are running in different (and not trusted) domains, you must use the certificates for authentication.

CAUTION

You can pause database mirroring by running the `ALTER DATABASE...SET PARTNER SUSPEND` statement. You can resume mirroring by running the `ALTER DATABASE...SET PARTNER RESUME` statement. You can stop mirroring by running `ALTER DATABASE...SET PARTNER OFF`.

Database Mirroring Operating Modes

A database mirroring session can operate in either synchronous or asynchronous mode. In *synchronous mode*, every transaction committed on the principal database is also committed on the mirror server, guaranteeing the protection of the data (that is, *high-protection mode*). This is achieved by waiting to commit a transaction on the principal database until the principal server receives a message from the mirror server stating that it has hardened the transaction's log to disk. In other words, synchronous mode forces the principal to not consider a transaction committed until the mirror has entered the transaction into its transaction log and sent back an acknowledgement. Note that the wait for this message increases the latency of the transaction. The time required for synchronization essentially depends on how far the mirror database was behind the principal database at the start of the session (as measured by the number of log records initially received from the principal server), the workload on the principal database, network latency, and the speed of the mirror system.

Synchronous operation is maintained in the following manner:

1. On receiving a transaction from a client, the principal server writes the transaction to the transaction log.

2. The principal server writes the transaction to the database, and concurrently sends the log record to the mirror server. The principal server waits for an acknowledgement from the mirror server before confirming any of the following to the client: a transaction, preparation to commit, a commit, or a rollback.

3. The mirror server hardens the log to disk and returns an acknowledgement to the principal server.

4. On receiving the acknowledgement from the mirror server, the principal server sends a confirmation message to the client.

In synchronous operation mode, if a witness server is present, the session supports both automatic and manual failover (that is, *high-availability* mode). In the absence of a witness, synchronous sessions run in *high-protection* mode, and only manual failover is supported. In other words, high-availability mode requires the presence of a witness, which ideally resides on a third computer.

If transaction safety is set to OFF (that is, ALTER DATABASE <database> SET PARTNER SAFETY OFF), the mirroring session operates in *asynchronous* mode, also known as *high-performance* mode. In *asynchronous mode*, as soon as the principal server sends the log for a transaction to the mirror server, the principal server sends a confirmation to the client, without waiting for an acknowledgement from the mirror server. The database is synchronized after the mirror server initially catches up to the principal server. However, transactions commit without waiting for the mirror server to harden the log. Asynchronous operation permits the principal server to run with minimal transaction latency. The mirror server attempts to keep up with the log records sent by the principal server. But the mirror database always lags somewhat behind the principal database, never quite catching up. The gap between the databases is typically small. However, the gap can become substantial if the principal server is under a heavy workload or the system of the mirror server is overloaded. If the witness server is absent in the mirroring configuration, it is not recommended that you turn off transaction safety and run in asynchronous mode. Such a configuration can lead to data loss and split-brain between the principal and mirror.

NOTE

Changing the transaction safety restarts the database, disconnecting all clients that are currently using the database.

Monitoring Database Mirroring

The following are some system catalog views, dynamic management views (DMVs), Profiler trace events, and PerfMon (that is, System Monitor) counters that you can use to monitor database mirroring:

- The sys.database_mirroring catalog view contains a row for each database present in the current instance. If a database does not participate in mirroring, all the columns prefixed with mirroring are NULL. This catalog view contains information such as the mirroring state, role, sequence, safety level, and connection timeout. The database mirroring state can be either synchronizing, synchronized, suspended, pending_failover, or disconnected.

- The sys.database_mirroring_endpoints catalog view contains one row for the database mirroring endpoint of the server instance.

- The sys.database_mirroring_witnesses catalog view contains a row for every witness role that a server plays in a database mirroring partnership.

- The sys.dm_database_mirroring_connections DMV returns a row for each database mirroring network connection and can be used to view mirroring activity, including connection time, authentication method, encryption details, total bytes sent on a connection, and so on.

- The Database Mirroring State Change event under Database Event Class in Profiler can be used to trace events when the state of a mirrored database changes.

- Database mirroring writes log messages into the Windows application event log (eventvwr.exe). You can use a third-party event log monitoring solution to filter and monitor database mirroring events.

- The database mirroring performance object ("SQLServer:Database Mirroring" for an unnamed instance, and "MSSQL$instance_name:Database Mirroring" for a named instance) contains about 11 counters that you can use to monitor database mirroring activity. For instance, the Transaction Delay counter displays the average delay in transaction termination waiting for acknowledgement; Bytes Sent/sec displays the number of bytes sent per second; and so on.

You might want to avoid using your OLTP system (that is, the principal server) for reporting; this helps you better utilize the mirror server resources. As mentioned earlier, to use a mirror database for reporting, you can create one or more database snapshots on the database. However, remember that creating snapshots and using the mirror server for reporting increases the load on the mirror server, and this performance hit can slow down the entire database mirroring solution. Let's take a detailed look at database snapshots feature.

Database Snapshots

The CREATE DATABASE statement now supports a new clause, AS SNAPSHOT OF, that can be used to create a static, read-only, transaction-consistent snapshot of a database as it existed at the moment of the snapshot's creation. The most common application of database snapshots is to create a snapshot of a mirror database so that clients can access the snapshot database for purposes such as reporting. In order to provide updated data to the clients, new snapshots must be created periodically, and new client connections must be directed to the most recent snapshot. Each database snapshot exists independently of any other database snapshots. Database snapshots on a mirror database may reduce performance on the principal database. Therefore, after all the clients have disconnected from an out-of-date snapshot, it should be deleted.

The other application of database snapshots is in the event of a user error on a source database. You can revert the source database to the state it was in when the snapshot was created. Data loss is confined to updates to the database since the snapshot's creation.

You cannot create a database snapshot graphically by using Management Studio. The only way to create a database snapshot is to run the CREATE DATABASE statement with the AS SNAPSHOT OF clause. SQL Server creates an NTFS sparse file to hold the snapshot. Snapshots cannot be created on FAT32 or RAW partitions.

NOTE

Database snapshots are available only in the Enterprise Edition of Microsoft SQL Server 2005.

The following is an example of creating a database snapshot:

```
SET NOCOUNT ON
USE master;
GO


IF EXISTS(SELECT database_id FROM sys.databases
    WHERE [name] = 'AW_05082005_SS1')
    DROP DATABASE AW_05082005_SS1;
GO


CREATE DATABASE AW_05082005_SS1 ON
    (NAME = AdventureWorks_Data, FILENAME='C:\AW_05082005_SS1.ss')
 AS SNAPSHOT OF AdventureWorks;
GO


SELECT * FROM sys.databases
    WHERE name = 'AW_05082005_SS1';
GO


USE AW_05082005_SS1;
GO


SELECT * FROM sys.database_files;
GO
```

This script checks whether a database named AW_05082005_SS1 exists. If it does, the script drops the database snapshot. Dropping a database snapshot is exactly the same as dropping any other user database. (Dropping a database snapshot deletes all the sparse files used by the snapshot.) Next, the preceding script creates a database snapshot by using the CREATE DATABASE statement. You can use the sys.databases, sys.master_files, and sys.database_files catalog views to see the database snapshot metadata. You can identify the source database for a snapshot by using the source_database_id column in the sys.databases catalog view. You can obtain the NTFS sparse filename for a database snapshot by using the physical_name column in the sys.master_files catalog view. You can use the fn_virtualfilestats function to determine the actual size and other statistics about the sparse file. The following SELECT statement uses the fn_virtualfilestats function to return the sparse file details for the database snapshot created in the preceding script:

```
SELECT * FROM
 fn_virtualfilestats(DB_ID('AW_05082005_SS1'),FILE_IDEX('AdventureWorks_Data'))
```

NOTE

A database snapshot must exist on the same instance as the source database. Multiple snapshots can exist on a source database, and they must always reside on the same server instance as the database.

Database snapshots operate at the data-page level. Before a page of the source database is modified for the first time, the original page is copied from the source database to the snapshot. This process is called a *copy-on-write* operation. The snapshot stores the original page, preserving the data records as they existed when the snapshot was created. Subsequent updates to records in a modified page do not affect the contents of the snapshot. The same process is repeated for every page that is being modified for the first time. In this way, the snapshot preserves the original pages for all data records that have ever been modified since the snapshot was taken.

To store the copied original pages, the snapshot uses one or more sparse files. Initially, a *sparse file* is an essentially empty file that contains no user data and has not yet been allocated disk space for user data. As more and more pages are updated in the source database, the size of the file grows. When a snapshot is taken, the sparse file takes up little disk space. As the database is updated over time, however, a sparse file can grow into a very large file. Figure 8.2 shows the properties of a sparse file used for a database snapshot just created on the AdventureWorks sample database. Note that the Size value is 165MB; however, the Size on Disk value is 128KB.

When users read data from a database snapshot, SQL Server always accesses the original data pages, regardless of where they reside. If the page has not yet been updated on the source database, a read operation on the snapshot reads the original page from the source database. After a page has been updated, a read operation on the snapshot still accesses the original page, which is now stored in a sparse file.

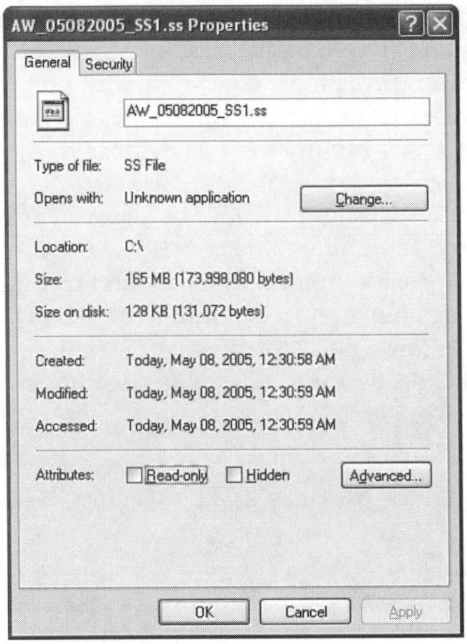

FIGURE 8.2   When a database snapshot is created, the sparse file reserves the space but does not use any space until the source database is updated.

Sparse files grow in 64KB increments; thus, the size of a sparse file on disk is always a multiple of 64KB. The latest 64KB increment holds from one to eight 8KB pages, depending on how many pages have been copied from the source database. This means that, on average, the size of a sparse file slightly exceeds the space actually filled by pages. It is important to remember that a snapshot is not an entire copy of the source database. The snapshot refers to the source database for data that has not changed. Therefore, if the source database goes into recovery mode or if the source database takes a file offline, some data might not be available in the snapshot. If a filegroup was offline when a snapshot was created and you bring the filegroup online later, it is still considered offline in the snapshot.

Here are some considerations to keep in mind when creating and using database snapshots:

- As long as a database snapshot exists, the source database cannot be dropped, detached, or restored. However, backing up the source database works normally; it is unaffected by database snapshots. The following SELECT statement shows an example of obtaining a list of database snapshots that use AdventureWorks as a source database:

```
SELECT name FROM sys.databases
  WHERE source_database_id = DB_ID('AdventureWorks');
```

- Performance is reduced, due to increased I/O on the source database resulting from a copy-on-write operation to the snapshot every time a page is updated.

- As long as a database snapshot exists, files cannot be dropped from the source database or from any snapshots.

- Snapshots of the model, master, and temp databases are prohibited.

- You cannot back up or restore and attach or detach snapshots.

- You cannot create snapshots on FAT32 file systems or RAW partitions.

- Full-text indexing is not supported on database snapshots, and full-text catalogs are not propagated from the source database.

- A database snapshot inherits the security constraints of its source database at the time of snapshot creation. Because snapshots are read-only, inherited permissions cannot be changed, and permission changes made to the source will not be reflected in existing snapshots.

As mentioned earlier, a database snapshot can sometimes be very helpful in recovering from user errors. The following script shows that a table is dropped from a database and then a database snapshot is used to recover that deleted table:

```
SET NOCOUNT ON
USE master;
GO

IF EXISTS(SELECT database_id FROM sys.databases
    WHERE [name] = 'AW_05082005_SS1')
    DROP DATABASE AW_05082005_SS1;
GO

CREATE DATABASE AW_05082005_SS1 ON
    (NAME = AdventureWorks_Data, FILENAME='C:\AW_05082005_SS1.ss')
 AS SNAPSHOT OF AdventureWorks;
GO

USE AdventureWorks;
GO

DROP TABLE dbo.DatabaseLog;
GO
--SELECT * FROM dbo.DatabaseLog
USE master;
GO

RESTORE DATABASE AdventureWorks
    FROM DATABASE_SNAPSHOT = 'AW_05082005_SS1';
```

```
GO

USE AdventureWorks;
GO

SELECT * FROM dbo.DatabaseLog;
GO
```

The RESTORE statement allows you to restore from a database snapshot, provided that the following are true:

- The source database does not contain any read-only or compressed filegroups.

- Filegroups that are online were not offline when the snapshot was created.

- Only one snapshot of the source database exists at the time of restoration.

- The database does not have any full-text catalog at the time of restoration. You can drop the full-text catalogs and then start the restoration.

You have now learned about two new availability solutions introduced in SQL Server 2005. In addition to these new capabilities, SQL Server improves the classic availability solutions. The next two sections provide an overview of enhancements made to failover clustering and replication.

Failover Clustering Enhancements

Earlier versions of SQL Server supported only two-node or four-node clusters. SQL Server 2005 now supports failover clusters with up to eight nodes on 32-bit and 64-bit systems. In addition, Analysis Services has been enhanced to be cluster aware. Similarly to the database engine, you can configure Analysis Services on a failover cluster with up to eight nodes on 32-bit systems and four nodes on 64-bit systems.

SQL Server 2005 on Windows Server 2003 now supports dynamic Address Windowing Extensions (AWE) memory management. In an active-active cluster scenario, when the failover happens, SQL Server can dynamically adjust the amount of memory use based on the current workloads on the instances. It is recommended that you set the minimum server memory configuration setting to achieve a better balance after failover.

SQL Server 2005 setup has been enhanced to provide a simpler and more robust installation experience. Setup now allows scripted installation and also allows you to select components that you want to install. In SQL 2000, setup log files were dispersed across nodes and in various directories. In addition, the logging behaved differently for non-cluster installations than for clustered installations. In SQL 2005, all logs are consolidated on the host computer. These logs use a standard naming convention that includes the machine name and the name of the component. The logs are placed by default into %ProgramFiles%\Microsoft SQL Server. Logging is now the same for clustered and non-clustered installations.

SQL Server 2005 now supports mount points. Clustered installations of SQL Server are limited to the number of available drive letters. Assuming that you use only one drive letter for the operating system, and all other drive letters are available as normal cluster drives or cluster drives hosting mount points, you are limited to a maximum of 25 instances of SQL Server per server. A mounted volume, or mount point, allows you to use a single drive letter to refer to many disks or volumes. If you have a drive letter G: that refers to a regular disk or volume, you can connect, or "mount," additional disks or volumes as directories under drive letter G: without the additional disks or volumes requiring drive letters of their own.

Replication Enhancements

SQL Server 2005 significantly enhances the replication support to allow you to implement a secure, easy-to-set up, easy-to-manage, and scalable enterprise data movement and availability solution. Complete description of these new features is beyond the scope of this chapter. However, the following are some of the replication enhancements introduced in SQL Server 2005:

- **Peer-to-peer transactional replication**—A new publication type for transactional replication has been designed to help improve application performance and system availability. Peer-to-peer transactional replication allows applications to read and modify the data at any of the databases participating in replication. All nodes in a peer-to-peer topology are peers: Each node publishes and subscribes to the same schema and data. Changes (that is, insertions, updates, and deletions) can be made at all nodes. Replication recognizes when a change has been applied to a given node, preventing changes from cycling through the nodes more than one time.

- **Replication of schema changes**—Replication is often considered a static schema environment. As applications evolve, they may require changes to the database schema. If a database is published, DBAs often find it challenging to have those schema changes propagated to all the subscribers with minimal downtime and effort. Previous SQL Server releases provided two special system stored procedures, sp_repladdcolumn and sp_repldropcolumn, to add a column to or remove a column from a published table. Use of these two stored procedures ensured that a table schema change was sent to all the subscribers. Basically, previous releases limited the schema changes on a published object to just adding and deleting a column and that, too, required use of special stored procedures. SQL Server 2005 fixes this by supporting a wide range of schema changes to published objects, without using any special stored procedures. You can continue to use statements such as ALTER TABLE, ALTER VIEW, ALTER PROCEDURE, ALTER FUNCTION, and ALTER TRIGGER on a published object, and SQL Server takes care of propagating the schema change to all SQL Server subscribers.

- **Publishing from Oracle databases to SQL Server 2005**—Snapshot and transactional replication topologies can now include an Oracle database as a publisher. Oracle version 8.0.5 and above on any Oracle supported hardware and operating system can be configured as a publisher. Oracle publishing does not require any special programming or the installation of any software on the Oracle side, nor does it require expertise in Oracle.

- **New Replication Monitor**—Replication Monitor has been completely redesigned for SQL Server 2005 and now runs as a separate application (`sqlmonitor.exe`). To start Replication Monitor, in Management Studio, you right-click the Replication folder in the Object Explorer and select Launch Replication Monitor. Replication Monitor allows you to monitor the overall health of a replication topology, providing detailed information about the status and performance of publications and subscriptions.

- **Initializing a transactional subscription from a backup**—By default, a subscription to a transactional publication is initialized with a snapshot, which is generated by the Snapshot Agent and applied by the Distribution Agent. With this behavior, setting up replication between databases that initially contain large volumes of data can be time-consuming and requires large amounts of storage. SQL Server 2005 provides a new publication option that allows any backup made after the creation of a publication to be restored at the subscriber, rather than by using a snapshot to initialize the subscription. When you configure replication by using Management Studio, the Subscription Options page of the Publication Properties - <Publication> dialog box provides the option "Allow Initialization from Backup Files, which you" can use to avoid initializing using a snapshot. Similarly, the `sp_addpublication` stored procedure now accepts a new parameter, `@allow_initialize_from_backup`, to provide the functionality of initializing a transactional subscription from a backup. Later, the `sp_addsubscription` stored procedure must be called with the `@sync_type` parameter having `'initialize with backup'` as its value, and backup details must be provided via parameters such as `@backupdevicetype`, `@backupdevicename`, and so on.

- **Replication Management Objects (RMO)**—SQL Server 2005 provides a .NET-based API to automate configuring, managing, and scripting of replication, and for synchronizing subscribers.

- **Transactional publications**—Transactional publications now allow up to 1,000 columns in each published table.

Online and Parallel Index Operations

SQL Server 2005 Enterprise Edition now supports index operations such as creating, altering, and dropping an index to be performed while users are still accessing the table data and using other indexes on the table. The CREATE INDEX, ALTER INDEX, DROP INDEX, and ALTER TABLE statements support the ONLINE option with a value of either ON or OFF (the default is OFF). The ONLINE option being set to ON specifies that underlying tables and associated indexes are available for queries and data modification during the index operation.

<u>**NOTE**</u>

ONLINE cannot be set to ON when an index is being created on a local temporary table, when an XML index is being created, while you're creating a clustered index of a table that contains large object data types, or while you're creating nonclustered index on a large object data type.

When the ONLINE option is set to ON, long-term table locks are not held for the duration of the index operation. During the main phase of the index operation, only an intent share (IS) lock is held on the source table. This enables queries or updates to the underlying table and indexes to proceed. At the start of the operation, a shared (S) lock is held on the source object for a very short period of time. At the end of the operation, for a short period of time, an S lock is acquired on the source if a nonclustered index is being created; or a schema modification (SCH-M) lock is acquired when a clustered index is created or dropped online and when a clustered or nonclustered index is being rebuilt.

The underlying table cannot be modified, truncated, or dropped while an online index operation is in process. Under certain circumstances, the online index operation can cause a deadlock when it interacts with database updates because of user or application activities. In these rare cases, the SQL Server 2005 database engine selects the user or application activity as a deadlock victim. Although online index operations permit concurrent user update activity, the index operations take longer if the update activity is very heavy. Typically, online index operations are slower than equivalent offline index operations, regardless of the concurrent update activity level.

Let's try an online index operation and at the same time monitor it by using the Profiler. You need to start SQL Server Management Studio and connect to a SQL Server instance, using Query Editor, and then type the following query:

```
USE AdventureWorks;
GO
ALTER INDEX ALL ON Sales.SalesOrderHeader
  REBUILD WITH (ONLINE = ON);
GO
```

Before you execute this query, you need to start SQL Profiler and connect to the same SQL Server instance. On the Trace Properties dialog, you need to select Blank from the Use the Template combo box. Then you should select the Events Selection tab, expand Progress Report, and check Progress Report: Online Index Operation. You can use this event to view the progress of an online index build while it is running. Then you click the Run button to begin the Profiler trace. Next, you execute the preceding query in Management Studio. Figure 8.3 shows an example of trace events that result from running this query.

In addition to online index operations, SQL Server 2005 Enterprise Edition also enables support for parallel index execution. The MAXDOP option can now be specified with the CREATE INDEX, ALTER INDEX REBUILD, DROP INDEX, and ALTER TABLE DDL statements. The MAXDOP index option cannot be specified in the ALTER INDEX REORGANIZE statement.

EventClass	DatabaseName	ObjectID	ObjectName	IndexID	EventSubClass
Progress Report: Online Index O...	AdventureWorks	642101...	PK_SalesOrderHeader_SalesOrderID	1	1 - Start
Progress Report: Online Index O...	AdventureWorks				2 - Stage 1 execution begin
Progress Report: Online Index O...	AdventureWorks	642101...		1	6 - Inserted row count
Progress Report: Online Index O...	AdventureWorks	642101...		1	6 - Inserted row count
Progress Report: Online Index O...	AdventureWorks	642101...		1	6 - Inserted row count
Progress Report: Online Index O...	AdventureWorks				3 - Stage 1 execution end
Progress Report: Online Index O...	AdventureWorks	642101...	PK_SalesOrderHeader_SalesOrderID	1	7 - Done
Progress Report: Online Index O...	AdventureWorks	642101...	AK_SalesOrderHeader_rowguid	2	1 - Start
Progress Report: Online Index O...	AdventureWorks	642101...	AK_SalesOrderHeader_SalesOrderNumber	3	1 - Start
Progress Report: Online Index O...	AdventureWorks	642101...	IX_SalesOrderHeader_CustomerID	5	1 - Start
Progress Report: Online Index O...	AdventureWorks	642101...	IX_SalesOrderHeader_SalesPersonID	6	1 - Start
Progress Report: Online Index O...	AdventureWorks				4 - Stage 2 execution begin
Progress Report: Online Index O...	AdventureWorks	642101...		2	6 - Inserted row count
Progress Report: Online Index O...	AdventureWorks	642101...		2	6 - Inserted row count
Progress Report: Online Index O...	AdventureWorks	642101...		3	6 - Inserted row count
Progress Report: Online Index O...	AdventureWorks	642101...		3	6 - Inserted row count
Progress Report: Online Index O...	AdventureWorks	642101...		5	6 - Inserted row count
Progress Report: Online Index O...	AdventureWorks	642101...		5	6 - Inserted row count
Progress Report: Online Index O...	AdventureWorks	642101...		6	6 - Inserted row count
Progress Report: Online Index O...	AdventureWorks	642101...		6	6 - Inserted row count
Progress Report: Online Index O...	AdventureWorks				5 - Stage 2 execution end
Progress Report: Online Index O...	AdventureWorks	642101...	AK_SalesOrderHeader_rowguid	2	7 - Done
Progress Report: Online Index O...	AdventureWorks	642101...	AK_SalesOrderHeader_SalesOrderNumber	3	7 - Done
Progress Report: Online Index O...	AdventureWorks	642101...	IX_SalesOrderHeader_CustomerID	5	7 - Done

FIGURE 8.3   You can use Profiler to track the progress of an online index build while it is running.

Enhanced Multi-instance Support

The SQL Server 2000 supported up to 16 instances of the relational engine per computer. SQL Server 2005 Enterprise Edition increases the number of instances supported to 50, making server consolidation a more viable option. Other SQL Server 2005 editions support up to 16 instances of the relational engine. When you install multiple instances, it is possible to install different editions of SQL Server 2005. For instance, you may have a few instances of Enterprise Edition and a few instances of Standard Edition on the same computer. One instance of the Microsoft search service MSSearch 3.0 (a full-text search engine) exists per instance of SQL Server.

In addition to the database engine, SQL Server 2005 Analysis Services now supports the notion of multi-instance installations. Previous releases did not support installing multiple instances of Analysis Services. With SQL Server 2005 Enterprise Edition, up to 50 instances of Analysis Services can be installed on a single computer. Other SQL Server 2005 editions support up to 16 instances of Analysis Services.

Dedicated Administrator Connection

In previous releases, when SQL Server appeared to be unresponsive or running in an abnormal state, administrators struggled to connect to that instance in order to terminate problematic processes and fix the problem. SQL Server failed to respond to client connections in such situations. This has been fixed in SQL Server 2005 by means of Dedicated Administrator Connection (DAC). The new command prompt utility SQLCMD.exe supports the -A switch, which you can use to connect to an instance of SQL Server even if the server appears to be locked or running in an abnormal state. Members of the sysadmin fixed server role can activate the dedicated administrator connection locally over TCP/IP. Because DAC is established over TCP/IP, you need to ensure that the SQL Browser service is running if you are connecting to a named SQL Server 2005 instance. The connection is only allowed from a client running on the server. No network connections are permitted.

When connected using DAC, to avoid any potential blocking scenarios, it is recommended that you run all diagnostic queries with the lowest transaction isolation level, READ UNCOMMITTED, and that you use the LOCK_TIMEOUT value to set to a short time-out period. You should run only diagnostic queries and avoid potentially long-running operations such as defragmenting or rebuilding indexes. You can also use SQL Server Management Studio to connect to an instance by using DAC, by prefixing the instance name with ADMIN:. However, note that any Management Studio activity that attempts a second connection fails. For instance, let's say you connect to a Query Editor window in Management Studio by using DAC. Now, if you try to change the database by using the Database combo box on the toolbar, the operation fails, and you get an error message.

Here is an example of using SQLCMD.exe to use DAC on a SQL Server 2005 instance:

```
SQLCMD -S DDGXP\SQL2005 -E -A
```

This command prompt statement connects to a SQL Server 2005 instance by using DAC over Windows authentication.

Early Restore Access

A restoration is a multi phase process. There are three possible phases of a restoration:

- **Data copy**—The data copy phase involves copying all the data, log, and index pages from the backup media of a database to the database files. The data copy phase initializes the contents of the database, files, or pages being restored. This phase is accomplished by restore database, restore file, and/or restore page operations, using full or differential backups. A restoration allows you to restore a subset of the data contained in a data backup; for example, you can restore one or more files from a full backup.

- **Redo (roll forward)**—The redo (roll forward) phase applies the logged transactions to the roll forward setup to the recovery point of the restore. The database engine processes log backups as they are restored, beginning with the log contained in data backups. At this point, a database might contain changes made by transactions that are uncommitted. End roll forward or redo phase brings the data to the point in time, called the *recovery point*, to which the user specifies that the set of data be recovered. Under the full or bulk-logged recovery model, you can specify the recovery point as a particular point in time or log record.

- **Undo (roll back)**—The undo (roll back) phase ends a restoration sequence by rolling back any uncommitted transactions and making the database available to users.

The database engine in SQL Server 2005 Enterprise Edition now lets users access a database after the redo, or roll forward, phase of a database restore operation completes. Earlier versions of SQL Server did not allow access to the database until completion of the roll back, or undo, phase. The other editions of SQL Server 2005 also do not let users access the database until recovery completes.

Instant File Initialization

If the database and transaction log files do not already exist, they must be created before data can be restored to them. The database and transaction log files are created, and the file contents are initialized to zero. Separate worker threads create and initialize the files in parallel. In addition to while creating a database, the file initialization process is also run when you add files to an existing database by using the ALTER DATABASE statement.

On Windows XP and Windows Server 2003 systems, SQL Server 2005 enables data files to be initialized instantaneously, which allows for fast execution of database or filegroup restore operations. Instant file initialization reclaims used disk space without filling that space with zeros. Instead, disk content is overwritten as new data is written to the files. To use instant file initialization, you must run the SQL Server service under an account that has the SE_MANAGE_VOLUME_NAME special Windows privilege. This privilege is assigned to the Windows Administrators group by default. If you have system administrator rights, you can assign this privilege by adding the Windows account to the Perform Volume Maintenance Tasks security policy.

> **NOTE**
>
> Instant file initialization works only for data files and not for log files. A *log file* is a circular chain of log blocks, and the log manager relies on a block parity bit change to detect the end of a log at startup. SQL needs to initialize the log files so that SQL can establish the initial parity bit to correctly detect the end of a log after a restart.

Summary

In case of system malfunctions, failures, and other errors, it is a DBA's responsibility to ensure that the database system can be recovered to its consistent state and made available as soon as possible. This chapter introduces reliability and high-availability features introduced in SQL Server 2005. You can use these features to perform reliable backups, increase system availability, and proactively detect disk I/O errors.

This chapter starts with a discussion of reliability enhancements, including mirrored backup media, use of checksums, and piecemeal and page restores. The second part of this chapter focuses on high-availability features and covers topics such as the new database mirroring and database snapshots, enhancement to existing availability solutions, online and parallel index operations, and dedicated administrator connection. Chapter 9, "Performance Analysis and Tuning," discusses performance monitoring and tuning enhancements in SQL Server 2005.

Performance Analysis and Tuning

Performance analysis and tuning is a challenging exercise that requires understanding of tools and techniques to measure and troubleshoot a performance issue. Some of the top performance killers include poor application design, inferior physical/logical database design, and costly/slow-running queries. Insufficient hardware resources and improper configurations of the operating system and the database system are some more causes of performance degradation.

SQL Server 2005 changes the performance analysis and tuning paradigm by introducing innovative features and tools that facilitate efficient physical database design, query optimization, locking and blocking avoidance, and so on. In this chapter, you will learn how to use these features and tools to proactively design, monitor, and tune a database application.

Let's begin by looking at some of the new techniques for optimizing the physical database design.

Physical Database Design, Analysis, and Tuning

Physical database design refers to specifying how on-disk data structures are stored and accessed. It plays an important role in maximizing the performance of and simplifying the management of databases. In general, physical database design involves where and what kind of indexes to use, how to partition the data, how to organize data and log in files and filegroups, and so on.

Imagine that you are working with developers to optimize the physical database design of a database that contains 50 tables. One of the tables has a million rows and grows at a rate of approximately 50,000 rows a weekday. There are about 1,500 users entering data into the system and about 50 users generating and viewing reports most of the time. Let's say you have gone through the index analysis process, but still the performance is not as expected. The following sections describe some new things that you can try in SQL Server 2005 to improve the physical database design.

Creating Indexes with Included Columns

One of the best recommendations for nonclustered indexes is to create a narrow and efficient index. For best performance, it is recommended that you avoid using too many columns in an index. A narrow index can accommodate more rows into an 8KB index page than a wide index, thereby reducing I/O, reducing storage requirements, and improving database caching.

On the other hand, database professionals often try to gain performance by creating a covering index. A *covering index* is a nonclustered index built upon all the columns required to satisfy a SQL query without going to the base table. However, the key size cannot exceed 900 bytes, and you can have up to 16 columns in an index.

SQL Server 2005 introduces the new concept of including columns with nonclustered indexes. It results in smaller, efficient, and narrow keys, and at the same time it provides the benefits of a covering index and removes the 900 bytes/16 columns key size restriction. When you create a nonclustered index by using a CREATE NONCLUSTERED INDEX DDL statement, you can use the INCLUDE clause to specify up to 1,023 columns that are non-key columns to be included to the leaf level of the index. The included columns are not part of the index key, which keeps the key size small and efficient. However, having them available at the leaf pages with the index means you can avoid querying the base table if the included columns can satisfy the query.

In a nutshell, including non-key columns helps keep the key size small and efficient, provides the benefit of a covering index to improve the performance, and removes the 900 bytes/16 columns key size restriction because the included columns are not considered part of the index key.

NOTE

Columns of data type `text`, `ntext`, and `image` are not allowed as non-key included columns.

Let's look at an example of how included non-key columns can be used to create efficient nonclustered indexes and to improve performance. The following statements create a sample table and insert some test data into the table:

```
SET NOCOUNT ON;
USE AdventureWorks;
GO
```

```
IF OBJECT_ID('dbo.tblTest') IS NOT NULL
    DROP TABLE dbo.tblTest;
GO
CREATE TABLE dbo.tblTest (C1 INT, C2 INT, C3 CHAR(255));
GO
DECLARE @counter INT;
SET @counter = 1;
WHILE @counter <= 99999
BEGIN
    INSERT INTO dbo.tblTest VALUES(@counter%500, @counter, @counter);
    SET @counter = @counter + 1;
END;
```

The table does not have any indexes yet. Next, you should query the table:

```
SET STATISTICS IO ON;
SELECT C1, C2, C3 FROM dbo.tblTest WHERE C1 = 2;
GO
```

After you run this query, you should notice that the number of logical reads is 3,449 and that the execution plan shows the table scan.

You can optimize the preceding query by creating a nonclustered index:

```
CREATE NONCLUSTERED INDEX idxtblTest ON dbo.tblTest(C1);
GO
```

```
SELECT index_type_desc, index_depth, index_level, page_count, record_count
FROM sys.dm_db_index_physical_stats (DB_ID(),
    OBJECT_ID('dbo.tblTest'), OBJECT_ID('idxtblTest'), NULL, 'DETAILED')
WHERE index_id > 1;
```

```
SELECT C1, C2, C3 FROM dbo.tblTest WHERE C1 = 2;
GO
```

These Transact-SQL (T-SQL) statements create a narrow nonclustered index on column C1. The first SELECT query here uses a dynamic management view (DMV) to find out the total number of pages used by the index. The index uses about 224 pages.

After you run the preceding query, you should notice that the number of logical reads comes down to 204 and that the execution plan shows the use of an index and avoids a table scan. The execution plan shows RID lookup, which is a bookmark lookup accompanied by a nested loop join.

You can further optimize the query by creating a covering index:

```
CREATE NONCLUSTERED INDEX idxtblTest ON dbo.tblTest(C1, C2, C3)
    WITH DROP_EXISTING;
GO
```

```
SELECT index_type_desc, index_depth, index_level, page_count, record_count
FROM sys.dm_db_index_physical_stats (DB_ID(),
   OBJECT_ID('dbo.tblTest'), OBJECT_ID('idxtblTest'), NULL, 'DETAILED')
WHERE index_id > 1;

SELECT C1, C2, C3 FROM dbo.tblTest WHERE C1 = 2;
GO
```

The index key now contains all the columns queried in the SELECT statement. Because the nonclustered index key now contains more columns, the index will use a higher number of pages. The DMV SELECT query proves this, and you should notice that the index now uses about 3,581 pages.

The SELECT query on the table is optimized, and you should notice that the number of logical rows has now come down to 12 and that the execution plan shows the index seek as 100% of the cost.

Here's what happens when you use non-key included columns instead of a covering index:

```
CREATE NONCLUSTERED INDEX idxtblTest ON dbo.tblTest(C1)
   INCLUDE (C2, C3)
   WITH DROP_EXISTING;
GO

SELECT index_type_desc, index_depth, index_level, page_count, record_count
FROM sys.dm_db_index_physical_stats (DB_ID(),
   OBJECT_ID('dbo.tblTest'), OBJECT_ID('idxtblTest'), NULL, 'DETAILED')
WHERE index_id > 1;

SELECT C1, C2, C3 FROM dbo.tblTest WHERE C1 = 2;
GO
```

Note that the index key contains only the C1 column; C2 and C3 are included non-key columns. The DMV SELECT statement indicates that the index is using 3,463 pages, and the SELECT query on the table shows 11 logical reads and shows the index seek as 100% of the cost. (Compare this with the 3,581 index pages and 12 logical reads in the covering index.) On top of this, the index key size is small and efficient, and you can also overcome the 900 bytes/16 columns index keys restriction by using non-key included columns.

The data for non-key columns resides in the base table data pages and is also duplicated in index leaf-level pages. Therefore, you should avoid including unnecessary columns as non-key index columns. Because the included column data is duplicated, an index with included columns consumes more disk space, especially if included columns are of the varchar(max), nvarchar(max), varbinary(max), or xml data type. Fewer index rows will fit on an index page, which might increase the I/O and decrease the database cache efficiency. Index maintenance may increase in terms of the time that it takes to perform modifications, inserts, updates, or deletions to the underlying table. You should do analysis and testing to determine whether the gains in query performance outweigh the effect on performance during data modification and the additional disk space requirements.

Creating Indexes on Computed Columns

A computed column's value is calculated from an expression by using other columns in the same table. With SQL Server 2000, computed columns are always virtual columns, not physically stored in the table. In order to create an index on such columns, the column expression must be deterministic and precise. In other words, an index cannot be created on a computed column if the column expression uses a nondeterministic function such as USER_ID() or CHARINDEX() or if the column expression results in an imprecise value such as a floating-point number.

SQL Server 2005 introduces the ability to persist the computed column values. In some situations, this can improve performance because the computed column value is already available in the data pages and is not calculated at runtime. In addition, having persisted computed columns allows you to create indexes on columns that are imprecise. Here's an example of this:

```
SET NOCOUNT ON;
USE AdventureWorks;
GO
IF OBJECT_ID('dbo.tblTest') IS NOT NULL
    DROP TABLE dbo.tblTest;
GO
CREATE TABLE dbo.tblTest
    (C1 float, C2 float, C3 AS C1*C2 PERSISTED, C4 AS C1*C2);
GO
CREATE INDEX idxTest ON dbo.tblTest(C3);
GO
--CREATE INDEX idxTest2 ON dbo.tblTest(C4);
GO
SELECT is_persisted, * FROM sys.computed_columns
    WHERE [object_id] = OBJECT_ID('dbo.tblTest');
GO
SELECT * FROM sys.indexes WHERE name = 'idxTest'
GO
```

This script creates a sample table with two computed columns. Column C3 is a persisted computed column, whereas C4 is a virtual computed column. Creating an index on an imprecise computed column succeeds if it is persisted; uncommenting and trying to create an index on C4 will fail. You can use the sys.columns system catalog view to find out whether the column is computed, and then you can use the sys.computed_columns catalog view to check whether the computed column is persisted.

Indexing XML Data

SQL Server 2005 introduces a new data type named xml that you can use to store XML documents inside a database. The data stored in xml type columns can be queried by using the XQuery syntax and xml type methods such as exist(), query(), and value(). The XML data is internally stored as binary large objects (BLOBs), and this internal binary representation of XML data cannot exceed 2GB. Without an index on such columns, these BLOBs are parsed and shredded at runtime to evaluate a query, which can have a significant adverse impact on the query performance.

You can use the CREATE XML INDEX DDL statement to create an index on an xml type column. Each table can have up to 249 XML indexes. Here is the T-SQL syntax for creating XML indexes:

```
CREATE [ PRIMARY ] XML INDEX index_name
    ON <object> ( xml_column_name )
    [ USING XML INDEX xml_index_name
        [ FOR { VALUE ¦ PATH ¦ PROPERTY } ]
    [ WITH ( <xml_index_option> [ ,...n ] ) ]
[ ; ]


        <xml_index_option> ::=
        {
            PAD_INDEX  = { ON ¦ OFF }
          ¦ FILLFACTOR = fillfactor
          ¦ SORT_IN_TEMPDB = { ON ¦ OFF }
          ¦ STATISTICS_NORECOMPUTE = { ON ¦ OFF }
          ¦ DROP_EXISTING = { ON ¦ OFF }
          ¦ ALLOW_ROW_LOCKS = { ON ¦ OFF }
          ¦ ALLOW_PAGE_LOCKS = { ON ¦ OFF }
          ¦ MAXDOP = max_degree_of_parallelism
        }
```

The primary XML index is a shredded and persisted representation of the XML BLOBs in the xml data type column. Using a primary XML index avoids the need to shred the XML BLOBs at runtime. After a primary XML index is created and when the shredded representation is available, the query performance can be further improved by creating secondary XML indexes on XML tags, values, and paths. Each xml column in a table can have one primary XML index and multiple secondary XML indexes. A primary XML index is required before any secondary index can be created. There are three types of secondary XML indexes—PATH, VALUE, and PROPERTY—and they are discussed later in this section.

A primary XML index requires a clustered index to be present on the primary key of the table. If you ever need to modify the primary key clustered index, then all XML indexes on the user table must be dropped first. When a primary XML index is created, SQL Server internally creates a clustered index, a B+ tree, with the clustered key formed from the clustering key of the user table and an XML node identifier. For each XML BLOB in the column, the index creates several rows of data.

Let's assume that the following XML instance is stored into an xml type column:

```
<book subject="Security" ISBN="0735615882">
    <title>Writing Secure Code</title>
    <author>
        <firstName>Michael</firstName>
        <lastName>Howard</lastName>
    </author>
    <price currency="USD">39.99</price>
</book>
```

When a primary XML index is created on a column containing this XML document, SQL Server internally creates a clustered index that contains the columns and rows listed in Table 9.1.

TABLE 9.1   Primary XML Index Internal Representation

PK	XID	NID (TAG)	TID	VALUE	HID
4	1	1 (book)	Element	Null	#1
4	1.1	2 (ISBN)	Attribute	"0735615882"	#2#1
4	1.5	4 (subject)	Attribute	"Security"	#4#1
4	1.7	5 (title)	Element	Null	#5#1
4	1.7.1	8 (text)	Text node	"Writing..."	#8#5#1
4	1.9	6 (author)	Element	Null	#6#1
4	1.9.1	7 (firstName)	Element	Null	#7#6#1
4	1.9.1.1	8 (text)	Text node	"Michael"	#8#7#6#1

Table 9.1 contains partial columns and rows indicating how the primary XML index is stored internally. The first column, PK, is the value of the primary key column in the base table. The second column, XID, is an internal identifier generated for each node in the XML tree. These first two columns (PK, XID) together form a clustered index key for the primary XML index. The third column is the node ID (NID) and the XML tag name (TAG), the fourth column (TID) indicates the node type, the fifth column (VALUE) contains the node value, and the last column (HID) shows the hierarchical ID, which is an internal tokenized representation of the reversed path from a node to the root of the tree.

After the primary XML index is created, you can further optimize query performance by creating secondary XML indexes. There are three types of secondary XML indexes:

- **PATH index**—Secondary indexes built on the paths are useful for path queries such as /person/address/zip. A PATH secondary XML index consists of the HID, VALUE, PK, and XID columns of the primary XML index.

- **VALUE index**—These secondary indexes are useful for queries where you know the node value but don't know the location of the node. A VALUE index is useful for queries such as //city[.="Dallas"] or /item/@*[.="NA"]. A VALUE secondary XML index consists of the VALUE, HID, PK, and XID columns of the primary XML index.

- **PROPERTY index**—These secondary indexes are useful for "property extraction" scenarios, where queries retrieve multiple, sometimes related, values from individual XML instances.

The following example shows how XML indexes can be used to optimize the queries on xml type columns. You need to first create a sample table and insert some test XML data into the table:

```
SET NOCOUNT ON;
USE AdventureWorks;
GO
IF OBJECT_ID('dbo.tblXMLTest') IS NOT NULL
    DROP TABLE dbo.tblXMLTest;
GO
CREATE TABLE dbo.tblXMLTest
    (c1 int IDENTITY(1, 1) NOT NULL PRIMARY KEY,
     c2 xml NOT NULL);
GO
DECLARE @counter INT;
SET @counter = 1
WHILE @counter < 1000
BEGIN
    INSERT INTO dbo.tblXMLTest (c2)
        VALUES ('<book id="1"><category>Security</category></book>');
    INSERT INTO dbo.tblXMLTest (c2)
        VALUES ('<book id="2"><category>Architecture</category></book>');
    INSERT INTO dbo.tblXMLTest (c2)
        VALUES ('<book id="3"><category>Design Patterns</category></book>');
    INSERT INTO dbo.tblXMLTest (c2)
        VALUES ('<book id="4"><category>Certification</category></book>');
    SET @counter = @counter + 1
END;
GO
```

The table yet does not have any index on the xml column. You can click "the Include Actual Execution Plan" toolbar button in Management Studio, run the following query, and study the execution plan:

```
SELECT * FROM dbo.tblXMLTest
    WHERE c2.exist('/book/@id[. = "3"]') = 1;
GO
```

SQL Server parses and shreds the XML BLOB data for each row, and it runs the XPath expression to filter rows where the id attribute value is 3. The execution plan shows the use of the "Table Valued Function XML Reader with XPath Filter" operator, and the estimated subtree cost for the SELECT operator (approximately 4,012) is significantly large.

Next, you should create a primary XML index to create a persisted, shredded representation of the XML data and then execute the same SELECT statement again:

```
CREATE PRIMARY XML INDEX pxmlidxTest ON dbo.tblXMLTest (c2);
GO

SELECT * FROM dbo.tblXMLTest
   WHERE c2.exist('/book/@id[. = "3"]') = 1;
GO
```

Now, the execution plan no longer contains the XML Reader operator, which proves that XML parsing and shredding is not required. Instead of the XML Reader operator, the execution plan now shows a clustered index scan using the primary XML index, and the estimated subtree cost for the SELECT operator (approximately 0.19) is significantly reduced.

You can further optimize the query by creating a PATH secondary index:

```
CREATE XML INDEX sxmlidxPathTest ON dbo.tblXMLTest (c2)
   USING XML INDEX pxmlidxTest FOR PATH;

SELECT * FROM dbo.tblXMLTest
   WHERE c2.exist('/book/@id[. = "3"]') = 1;
GO
```

You should notice that the PATH secondary XML index results in a further simplified execution plan with a clustered index seek, and the estimated subtree cost for the SELECT operator (approximately 0.06) is further reduced.

Figure 9.1 shows the preceding three execution plans.

You can find more details about XML support in SQL Server 2005 in Chapter 10, "XML and Web Services Support in SQL Server 2005."

Optimizing Physical Design Structures by Using Database Engine Tuning Advisor

As a database's workload, data, and application change over time, the existing indexes may not be entirely appropriate, and new indexes might be required. To help in this process, SQL Server 2000 provided a tool called Index Tuning Wizard (ITW) that could be used to identify an optimal set of indexes for a given workload. The workload could be a SQL trace saved to a trace file (.trc) or a SQL trace saved to a trace table or a SQL script file (.sql). ITW accepted workload as an input, used the query processor to determine the most effective indexes for the workload by simulating index configurations, and gave recommendations on deleting/adding indexes. These recommendations could be saved in a .sql script file to be analyzed and executed later.

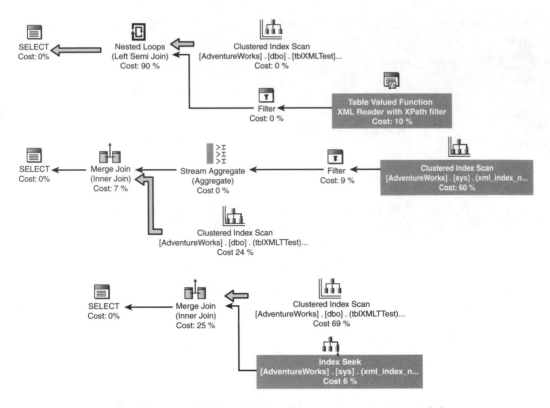

FIGURE 9.1   XML indexes avoid shredding and parsing XML BLOBs, and the PATH secondary XML index further optimizes the query.

SQL Server 2000 ITW had the following limitations:

- It could tune only one database during a tuning session.

- The wizard-based interface was not well suited for iterative tuning and analysis process.

- ITW recommendations were solely based on performance, and not on improving manageability. Therefore, ITW did not make recommendations on how tables/indexes should be partitioned.

- ITW did not provide the ability to limit the tuning time.

- ITW did not scale well with very large databases and workloads. In addition, ITW could not tune workloads that used T-SQL constructs, such as table-valued functions, temporary tables, or triggers.

- ITW allowed a developer to apply the recommendations immediately or at a later time, but it did not allow a developer to evaluate recommendations to perform "what-if" analysis.

- Only members of the sysadmin fixed server role could use the ITW to tune databases.

SQL Server 2005 introduces a new tool called Database Engine Tuning Advisor (DTA) that fixes the problems with ITW and offers recommendations on various physical design structures, including indexes, indexed views, and partitioning. Unlike ITW, which provided a wizard-based interface, DTA is a full-fledged application that provides a session-based analysis and tuning approach. DTA allows for the tuning of multiple databases per session and is designed to scale well with very large databases and workloads. You can find more details on DTA in Chapter 5, "SQL Server 2005 Tools and Utilities."

In addition to the physical database design enhancements discussed so far, SQL Server 2005 offers improvements in the way indexed views and partitioning work. The SQL Server 2005 query optimizer can match more queries to indexed views than in previous versions, including queries that contain scalar expressions, scalar aggregate and user-defined functions, and so on. The table and index partitioning feature is enhanced in SQL Server 2005 to simplify the administration, design, and development of a partitioned data set. A developer can optimize query performance by aligning tables and the associated index and also by aligning related tables. *Alignment* refers to SQL Server's ability to group rows that have the same partitioning key. With partitioned tables in SQL Server 2005, a table can be designed (using a function and a scheme) such that all rows that have the same partitioning key are placed directly on (and will always go to) a specific location. When multiple tables use the same function (but not necessarily the same scheme), rows that have the same partitioning key will be grouped similarly.

Troubleshooting Locking and Blocking

For a lot of database applications, performance degrades as the number of concurrent users increases. One of the common reasons for this behavior is blocking. Whenever two connections or system process IDs (SPIDs) try to access a common database resource in a conflicting way, the SQL Server lock manager ensures that the second SPID waits until the first SPID completes its work. This helps in maintaining data consistency. Poor query and transaction design can lead to excessive locking and blocking, significantly degrading system performance and affecting the scalability of the system.

Traditional techniques for blocking analysis include using sysprocesses and syslockinfo system tables, sp_lock and sp_who2 system stored procedures, the DBCC INPUTBUFFER statement, and Profiler trace. Microsoft released a sample script (see Knowledge Base article 271509) that uses these techniques to monitor blocking. Some of the techniques used to reduce blocking include keeping transactions short, optimizing queries by using indexes, using covering indexes, using a different (lower) isolation level, partitioning the data, and so on. In SQL Server 2005, you can continue to use these techniques to minimize the blocking and thereby increase the concurrency. The following sections outline some new techniques that you can implement in SQL Server 2005 to proactively monitor and troubleshoot blocking scenarios.

Using the Blocked Process Threshold Option

SQL Server 2005 introduces a new advanced system configuration (sp_configure) option called "blocked process threshold." You can use this option to proactively monitor blocking and deadlocking instances. You can use `sp_configure` to set the blocked process threshold to an integer value between 0 (the default) and 86400 (24 hours). Let's assume that you set the blocked process threshold configuration value to 10. Now, if there is a blocking for over 10 seconds, SQL Server will raise an event that can be captured by using the SQL Server event notification mechanism to perform an action, and the event can also be seen in SQL Profiler. The event is raised every 10 seconds after that until the blocking is resolved.

Let's look at an example of using the blocked process threshold configuration option to monitor blocking. In this example, the blocked process threshold is set to 10, and then a blocking scenario is created. In response to a blocking event generated by SQL Server, an entry is made into an audit table. You can handle the event differently and do things such as notify a DBA or do something to resolve the blocking. For simplicity, this example makes an entry into an audit table whenever the blocked process threshold event is raised.

The following code block shows how you set the blocked process threshold configuration option to 10 seconds:

```
USE master;
GO

EXEC master.dbo.sp_configure 'show advanced options', 1;
RECONFIGURE WITH OVERRIDE;
EXEC master.dbo.sp_configure 'blocked process threshold', 10;
RECONFIGURE WITH OVERRIDE;
EXEC master.dbo.sp_configure 'show advanced options', 0;
RECONFIGURE WITH OVERRIDE;
```

Next, you should create an audit table that will be used to record the blocking instances:

```
IF OBJECT_ID('dbo.tblBlocking') IS NOT NULL
    DROP TABLE dbo.tblBlocking;
GO

CREATE TABLE dbo.tblBlocking
    (id INT IDENTITY(1,1) NOT NULL PRIMARY KEY,
     server_name VARCHAR(100) NULL,
     blocker_spids VARCHAR(8000) NULL,
     event_info xml NULL,
     date_time DATETIME NOT NULL DEFAULT GETDATE());
GO
```

SQL Server raises the `BLOCKED_PROCESS_REPORT` event when there is a blocking for 10 seconds and every 10 seconds after that until blocking is resolved. This event can be captured by using the event notification mechanism introduced in SQL Server 2005. The event notification mechanism captures the event and notifies a Service Broker service by placing a message in the queue. In this example, a stored procedure is associated with the queue and activated whenever there is a message in the queue. Service Broker is discussed in great detail in Chapter 14, "SQL Server 2005 Service Broker."

In summary, SQL Server raises the BLOCKED_PROCESS_REPORT event, which is captured by the event notification mechanism, which places a message in the Service Broker queue, which in turn activates the stored procedure, which finally makes an entry into the audit table. Here is the stored procedure that is activated whenever there is a new message in the queue (created later in this example) in response to the BLOCKED_PROCESS_REPORT event:

```
IF OBJECT_ID('dbo.sp_NotifyBlocking') IS NOT NULL
    DROP PROCEDURE dbo.sp_NotifyBlocking;
GO


CREATE PROCEDURE dbo.sp_NotifyBlocking
AS
BEGIN
    --Find blocked process chain
    DECLARE @probclients TABLE(spid SMALLINT, ecid SMALLINT,
               blocked SMALLINT, waittype BINARY(2), dbid SMALLINT,
               PRIMARY KEY (blocked, spid, ecid));

    INSERT @probclients
        SELECT spid, ecid, blocked, waittype, dbid
        FROM master.dbo.sysprocesses
        WHERE blocked != 0 OR waittype != 0x0000;

    INSERT @probclients
        SELECT DISTINCT blocked, 0, 0, 0x0000, 0
           FROM @probclients
           WHERE blocked != 0 AND blocked NOT IN
            (SELECT spid FROM @probclients);

    DECLARE @HeadBlockerSPIDs varchar(4000)
    SELECT @HeadBlockerSPIDs =
        COALESCE(@HeadBlockerSPIDs + ', ', '') + CAST(spid AS varchar(5))
        FROM @probclients
        WHERE blocked = 0 AND
            spid in (SELECT blocked FROM @probclients WHERE spid != 0);

    --Receive message from the queue
    DECLARE @QMessage XML
    DECLARE @SBMessage TABLE (msgText XML);
    RECEIVE CAST(message_body AS XML) AS msgText
        FROM AdventureWorks.dbo.BlockingMonitoringQueue INTO @SBMessage;
    SELECT TOP 1 @QMessage = msgText FROM @SBMessage;
```

```
  --Insert into audit table
  INSERT INTO master.dbo.tblBlocking (server_name, blocker_spids, event_info)
    VALUES (@@SERVERNAME, @HeadBlockerSPIDs, @QMessage);
END;
GO
```

This stored procedure is activated in response to the blocking event. It uses the master.dbo.sysprocesses backward compatibility view to determine the blocking chain, including the head blocker process. Toward the end, the stored procedure retrieves the message from the Service Broker queue and inserts the queue message, along with blocked process chain information, into an audit table.

The final configuration step required is to enable Service Broker in the user database, create Service Broker objects such as the service and the queue, and set up the event notification to respond to the BLOCKED_PROCESS_REPORT event. Here's how you do that:

```
IF NOT EXISTS (SELECT * FROM sys.databases
               WHERE name = 'AdventureWorks'
               AND is_broker_enabled = 1)
   ALTER DATABASE AdventureWorks SET ENABLE_BROKER ;
GO


USE AdventureWorks;
GO


IF EXISTS(SELECT * FROM sys.services WHERE name = 'BlockingMonitoringService')
    DROP SERVICE BlockingMonitoringService ;
GO


IF OBJECT_ID('[dbo].BlockingMonitoringQueue') IS NOT NULL AND
   EXISTS(SELECT * FROM sys.service_queues
          WHERE name = 'BlockingMonitoringQueue')
  DROP QUEUE [dbo].BlockingMonitoringQueue;
GO


CREATE QUEUE dbo.BlockingMonitoringQueue
   -- Activation turned on
   WITH STATUS = ON,
   ACTIVATION (
      -- The name of the proc to process messages for this queue
      PROCEDURE_NAME = master.dbo.sp_NotifyBlocking,
      -- The maximum number of copies of the proc to start
      MAX_QUEUE_READERS = 5,
      -- Start the procedure as the user who created the queue.
      EXECUTE AS SELF )
   ON [DEFAULT] ;
GO
```

```
CREATE SERVICE
   [BlockingMonitoringService] ON QUEUE BlockingMonitoringQueue
   ([http://schemas.microsoft.com/SQL/Notifications/PostEventNotification]);
GO


IF EXISTS(SELECT * FROM sys.server_event_notifications
          WHERE name = 'EventNotifyBlocking')
  DROP EVENT NOTIFICATION EventNotifyBlocking ON SERVER ;
GO


CREATE EVENT NOTIFICATION EventNotifyBlocking
   ON SERVER
   FOR BLOCKED_PROCESS_REPORT
   TO SERVICE 'BlockingMonitoringService', 'current database';
GO
```

These statements first enable Service Broker in the `AdventureWorks` sample database, in which the blocking scenario will be created later in this example. Next, they create a Service Broker queue with activation enabled, as well as a service. Toward the end, an event notification mechanism is set up to monitor `BLOCKED_PROCESS_REPORT` and send the event notification to the `BlockingMonitoringService` Service Broker service in the current database.

You can run the preceding script statements to set up the blocking monitoring process. Next, you should open two query windows in SQL Server Management Studio and run the following two scripts simultaneously to create the blocking scenario:

Connection 1:

```
USE [AdventureWorks];
GO
SET TRANSACTION ISOLATION LEVEL READ COMMITTED;
GO
BEGIN TRANSACTION;
GO
```

Connection 2:

```
USE [AdventureWorks];
GO
SET TRANSACTION ISOLATION LEVEL READ COMMITTED;
GO
BEGIN TRANSACTION;
GO
UPDATE Production.ProductInventory SET Quantity = Quantity - 1
   WHERE ProductID = 1;
GO
```

Next, you should switch back to Connection 1, run the following SELECT statement, and notice that it is blocked by Connection 2 because Connection 2 updated the information inside a transaction that Connection 1 is trying to access:

Connection 1:

```
SELECT SUM(Quantity) FROM Production.ProductInventory
   WHERE ProductID = 1;
GO
```

> **NOTE**
>
> This SELECT statement does not cause blocking if row versioning (discussed next) is enabled. You should run the following statement and ensure that it returns 0:
>
> ```
> SELECT is_read_committed_snapshot_on
> FROM sys.databases
> WHERE name = 'AdventureWorks';
> ```
>
> If this statement returns 1, you know that row versioning is enabled, and in such cases, the preceding SELECT statement will run successfully, without any blocking. Then you should turn off the READ_COMMITTED_SNAPSHOT database option by using the ALTER DATABASE statement to disable row versioning.

You should let Connection 1 be blocked for about 40 to 50 seconds. Then you should switch to Connection 2 and run ROLLBACK TRANSACTION; after this, you should notice that Connection 1 is no longer blocked. You should run ROLLBACK TRANSACTION in Connection 1 as well to end the transaction. Then, when you select the rows from the master.dbo.tblBlocking audit table, you should see a few rows in this table indicating one or more processes in the chain that caused the blocking. While Connection 1 is blocked, you may also run Profiler and select "Blocked Process Report" under "Errors and Warning." Every time SQL Server raises the BLOCKED_PROCESS_REPORT event, you should then see an entry in Profiler, showing the blocking information in XML format.

When you're done with this example, you can reset "the blocked process threshold" sp_configure setting to 0 and drop the Service Broker objects, event notification, and audit table.

The blocked process threshold option is an example of how SQL Server 2005 is changing the performance monitoring and tuning paradigm for you to be *proactive* so that you no longer simply react to performance issues.

Row Versioning and Snapshot Isolation

The SQL Server 2005 row versioning feature can significantly reduce the occurrences of blocking and deadlocking. You can enable the row versioning feature for a database by doing either of the following:

- Setting the READ_COMMITTED_SNAPSHOT database option to ON while using the "read committed" transaction isolation level, which is the default isolation level

- Setting the ALLOW_SNAPSHOT_ISOLATION database option to ON while using the new "snapshot" transaction isolation level

When row versioning is enabled, whenever a transaction modifies a row, SQL Server uses the tempdb system database to maintain a copy of the original row (that is, a before image of the row). If multiple transactions modify a row, multiple versions of the row are stored in a version chain. For short-running transactions, a version of a modified row may get cached in the buffer pool without getting written into the tempdb database. If the need for the versioned row is short, the row will simply get dropped from the buffer pool. The read request is served by traversing the version link list to retrieve the last version of each row that was committed when the read transaction or statement started.

By keeping versions of updated rows, SQL Server avoids the need to lock the data, and it still maintains the data consistency. When row versioning is enabled, the number of deadlocks is reduced, and the number of locks required by a transaction is reduced, thereby reducing the system overhead required to manage locks; in this case, fewer lock escalations take place. If row versioning is enabled, you must ensure that there is adequate space in tempdb to maintain the rows version store.

Let's look at an example of how row versioning helps in reducing blocking and increasing concurrency. You should run the following statement to see whether row versioning is enabled for the AdventureWorks sample database:

```
SELECT is_read_committed_snapshot_on FROM sys.databases
    WHERE name = 'AdventureWorks';
```

If this statement returns 1, it indicates that transactions that use the READ COMMITTED (the default) isolation level will use row versioning to prevent readers from blocking the writers and vice versa, without locking any rows. If the preceding statement returns 0, you should run the following command to enable row versioning for the AdventureWorks sample database:

```
ALTER DATABASE AdventureWorks SET READ_COMMITTED_SNAPSHOT ON;
```

Before you run this statement, you need to make sure no users are connected to the AdventureWorks sample database. After you enable the READ_COMMITTED_SNAPSHOT option for the AdventureWorks database, you should run the preceding SELECT statement on the sys.databases catalog view to verify that row versioning is enabled.

Next, you should try to create the same blocking scenario explained earlier in this chapter, in the section "Using the Blocked Process Threshold Option." You will notice that, even though transactions are using the READ COMMITTED isolation level, readers are not blocking the writers and vice versa.

Analyzing Deadlocks by Using SQL Profiler

In SQL Server 2005, SQL Profiler has been enhanced to better assist in troubleshooting deadlock scenarios. You can use the new "Deadlock Graph" trace event under "the Locks" event class to view deadlock information graphically or as an XML document (see Figure 9.2).

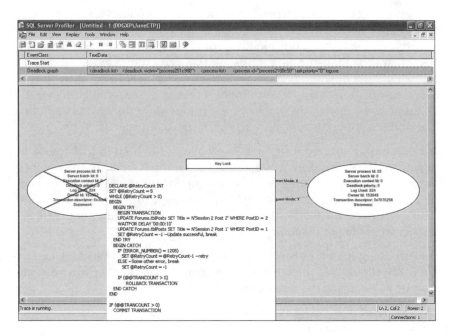

FIGURE 9.2   Profiler shows the deadlock information graphically and as an XML document.

Chapter 5 contains a script that can be used to simulate a deadlock scenario. As shown in Figure 9.2, Profiler shows the SPIDs involved in the deadlock. When you hover the mouse over each process (shown as a circle in a graph), Profiler shows the T-SQL statements that the process was executing when the deadlock happened. The circle with the blue X lines indicates the process that was selected as a deadlock victim. The TextData column contains the deadlock information as an XML document. You can right-click this column and select "Extract Event Data" to save the deadlock XML document to a disk file.

Locking and Blocking Monitoring Tools

In SQL Server 2005, Activity Monitor has been enhanced to support filtering and automatic refreshing. You can launch Activity Monitor from SQL Server Management Studio by connecting to a SQL Server instance by using Object Explorer, expanding the Management folder, and then double-clicking the Activity Monitor node. Figure 9.3 shows the redesigned Activity Monitor window:

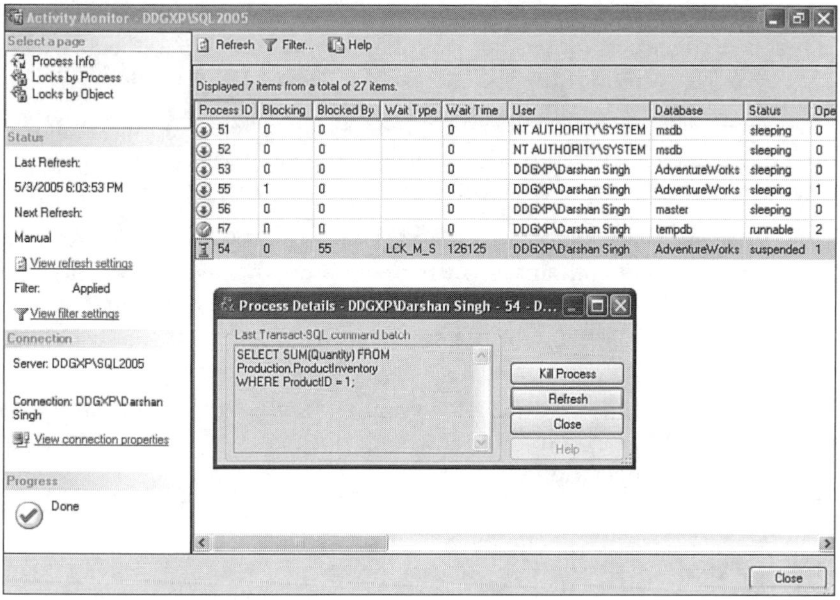

FIGURE 9.3   Activity Monitor now supports filtering and automatic refreshing.

You can continue to use the T-SQL constructs sp_who, sp_who2, sp_lock, DBCC INPUTBUFFER, and so on to monitor and troubleshoot blocking. You can also use the following DMVs and dynamic management functions (DMFs) to further obtain the information on processes and locks:

- **sys.dm_tran_locks**—You can use this DMV to obtain information about the current state of locking. Each row represents a currently active request to the lock manager that has either been granted or is waiting to be granted (that is, the request is blocked by an already granted request).

- **sys.dm_exec_connections**—This DMV contains a row describing each connection established to SQL Server.

- **sys.dm_exec_requests**—This DMV returns information about each request executing within SQL Server.

- **sys.dm_exec_sql_text**—The fn_get_sql() function is being deprecated in SQL Server 2005. The recommended approach is to use the sys.dm_exec_sql_text DMF. Like the fn_get_sql() function, the sys.dm_exec_sql_text DMF accepts a SQL handle as an input parameter and returns a result set that contains the database ID, the object ID, a number for numbered stored procedures, a flag indicating whether text is encrypted, and the query text itself. The SQL handle can be obtained by using the sql_handle column from the sys.dm_exec_requests DMV results.

- **sys.dm_exec_query_plan**—This DMF accepts the plan handle as an input parameter and returns a result set that contains the database ID, the object ID, a number for numbered stored procedures, a flag indicating whether text is encrypted, and the compile-time showplan representation in XML format of the query execution plan that is specified with `plan_handle`. The plan handle can be obtained by using `plan_handle` column from the sys.dm_exec_requests DMV results.

- **sys.dm_exec_query_stats**—This DMV returns aggregate performance statistics for cached query plans. The returned information includes logical and physical reads and writes, elapsed time, and CLR time.

- **sys.dm_exec_sessions**—Similar to the master.dbo.sysprocesses backward compatibility view, this DMV contains a row for each process (client or system) running on a current SQL Server 2005 instance. This DMV is available from any database, and it contains more information than the sysprocesses view.

Let's look at an example of using these DMVs and DMFs to obtain information about long-running queries. You can run the following script to create a stored procedure that performs a long-running operation:

Connection 1:

```
USE AdventureWorks;
GO
IF OBJECT_ID ('dbo.sprocTest') IS NOT NULL
    DROP PROCEDURE dbo.sprocTest;
GO
CREATE PROCEDURE dbo.sprocTest
AS
BEGIN
    DECLARE @i INT
    SET @i = 0
    WHILE @i < 5000
    BEGIN
        SELECT TOP (@i) Name FROM Sales.Store;
        SET @i = @i + 1;
    END;
END;
GO
```

Then you open another query window and type the following T-SQL batch, but don't run the following script yet:

Connection 2:

```
USE AdventureWorks;
GO

DECLARE @SessionID INT
DECLARE @SQLHandle varbinary(64)
DECLARE @PlanHandle varbinary(64)
```

```
SELECT TOP 1 @SessionID = session_id FROM sys.dm_exec_requests
   ORDER BY total_elapsed_time DESC;

SELECT @SQLHandle = sql_handle FROM sys.dm_exec_requests
   WHERE session_id = @SessionID;

SELECT @PlanHandle = plan_handle FROM sys.dm_exec_requests
   WHERE session_id = @SessionID;

SELECT @SQLHandle AS SQLHandle;
SELECT @PlanHandle AS PlanHandle;

SELECT DB_NAME(dbid) AS [db_name],
       OBJECT_NAME(objectid) AS obj_name,
       number, encrypted, [text]
   FROM sys.dm_exec_sql_text(@SQLHandle);

SELECT query_plan FROM sys.dm_exec_query_plan(@PlanHandle);

SELECT * FROM sys.dm_exec_query_stats
   WHERE plan_handle = @PlanHandle;

SELECT * FROM sys.dm_tran_locks
   WHERE request_session_id = @SessionID;
GO
```

This T-SQL script first uses the sys.dm_exec_requests DMV to obtain the SPID or session ID for the longest-running request. This session ID is then used to obtain the plan handle and SQL handle, which are then used to obtain the query text, query plan, and query stats information.

You need to now execute the stored procedure in Connection 1:

Connection 1:

```
EXEC dbo.sprocTest;
GO
```

Then you should run the T-SQL batch in Connection 2 to obtain the information about the longest-running request.

Query Performance Tuning

One of the common techniques for troubleshooting a performance issue is to use SQL Profiler to obtain the top *n* worse-performing queries. You can do this by looking at the Duration, CPU, Reads, and Writes columns in Profiler. After you identify such queries, some of the techniques you can use to tune the workload include generating and analyzing graphical and text query execution plans, obtaining statistics (such as STATIS-TICS PROFILE, STATISTICS IO, and STATISTICS TIME), changing the queries to effectively use the indexes and produce a better execution plan, providing query hints to the optimizer, rewriting stored procedures to avoid the use of cursors, avoiding recompilations, and so on. You can continue to use these techniques in SQL Server 2005. The following sections describe some new features introduced in this release that you can use for query performance tuning.

Plan Guides

As mentioned earlier in this chapter, one of the techniques you can use to improve query performance is to use the OPTION clause to specify query hints such as MAXDOP, LOOP JOIN, MERGE JOIN, and KEEP PLAN. As a general rule, you should avoid using optimizer hints because they overrule the decision-making process of the optimizer. The SQL Server 2005 query optimizer is smart enough to generate highly efficient execution plans, and therefore it is recommended that hints be used only as a last resort and only by experienced developers and DBAs.

Let's assume that you have a third-party vendor application that you are trying to tune and optimize. You used SQL Profiler to obtain some of the queries that are not performing well. After you identified such queries, you tried to tune the queries by using Management Studio, providing query hints and analyzing the query execution plans. Now assume that you are sure that one or more query hints can optimize the query or fix a problem. But what if you cannot change the query? What if the query is hard-coded into the application and there is no way to change the query to provide optimizer hints? Enter plan guides.

In the Standard and Enterprise Editions of SQL Server 2005, you can run the sp_create_plan_guide system stored procedure in order to create plan guides to optimize the performance of queries by providing hints at runtime to queries when it is not possible or desirable to change the text of the query directly. In other words, if you can create a plan guide for a query or a type of query and specify the query hints while creating a plan guide, whenever such queries are executed, SQL Server attaches the query hints to them. This way, you don't have to change the original query text, but you can still provide hints to the optimizer whenever such queries are executed. For plan guides to work, the query text executed on the server and specified with sp_create_plan_guide must match exactly character-by-character. If there is a difference of even a single character, the plan guide will not work, and the hints will not be attached with the query.

It is important to note that plan guides are not just for tuning third-party applications where you don't have access to source code to change the query. Even in scenarios where you have access to source code and could possibly change the query, it is recommended that you create a plan guide for the query instead of directly specifying the optimizer hints with the query. You should consider plan guides a recommended approach whenever you have to do optimizer hinting. This allows you to change the query behavior without changing the application and also simplifies application maintenance and future database upgrades.

Here is the T-SQL syntax for the `sp_create_plan_guide` stored procedure:

```
sp_create_plan_guide [ @name = ] N'plan_guide_name',
  [ @stmt = ] N'statement_text',
  [ @type = ] N' { OBJECT | SQL | TEMPLATE }',
  [ @module_or_batch = ]
    {
      N'[ schema_name.]object_name'
      | N'batch_text'
      | NULL
    },
  [ @params = ] { N'@parameter_name data_type [,...n ]' | NULL } ,
  [ @hints = ] { N'OPTION ( query_hint [,...n ] )' | NULL };
```

The `@type` parameter can have one of following three values:

- **OBJECT**—This value indicates that the specified `statement_text` appears in the context of a T-SQL stored procedure, scalar function, multistatement table-valued function, or T-SQL DML trigger in the current database.

- **SQL**—This value indicates that the specified `statement_text` appears in the context of a standalone statement or batch that can be submitted to SQL Server through any mechanism.

- **TEMPLATE**—This value indicates that the plan guide applies to any query that parameterizes to the form indicated in `statement_text`. If TEMPLATE is specified, then only the `PARAMETERIZATION { FORCED | SIMPLE }` query hint can be specified in the `@hints` argument.

Plan guides are database scoped, and you can use the `sys.plan_guides` catalog view to obtain a list of plan guides created in the current database. You can enable, disable, or drop plan guides by using the `sp_control_plan_guide` system stored procedure.

NOTE

Plan guides cannot be created against stored procedures, functions, or DML triggers that specify the `WITH ENCRYPTION` clause. Attempting to drop or alter a function, stored procedure, or DML trigger referenced by a plan guide, either enabled or disabled, results in an error. Attempting to drop a table with a trigger defined on it that is referenced by a plan guide also results in an error.

Let's look at an example of a plan guide for attaching MAXDOP and LOOP JOIN optimizer hints with a SQL statement at runtime. First, you need to start SQL Server Management Studio and connect to a SQL Server 2005 instance by using the Query Editor. Then you should click the" Include Actual Execution Plan" toolbar button and run the following T-SQL statements:

```
SET NOCOUNT ON;
USE AdventureWorks;
GO
SELECT h.SalesOrderID, h.OrderDate, h.DueDate, h.ShipDate,
       h.Status, h.SalesOrderNumber, c.FirstName, c.LastName, h.TotalDue,
       a.City, a.PostalCode
  FROM Sales.SalesOrderHeader h JOIN Person.Contact c
  ON c.ContactID = h.CustomerID
     LEFT OUTER JOIN Person.Address AS [a]
     ON [a].AddressID =
        (SELECT  TOP 1 AddressID FROM Sales.CustomerAddress
         WHERE CustomerID = h.CustomerID)
ORDER BY c.LastName, c.FirstName;
GO
```

Figure 9.4 shows the execution plan for above query. It shows that the query utilizes multiple processors on the server to execute the query in parallel. The query processor also uses hash match (inner join) operator.

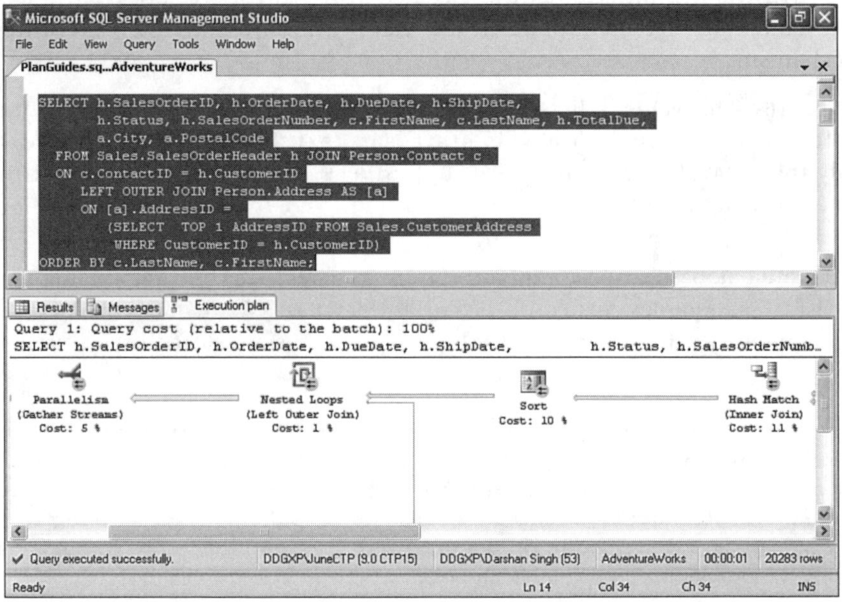

FIGURE 9.4   The execution plan for a sample query shows that the query is using parallelism and the hash match operator.

Let's assume that you want to disable parallelism and that you want the optimizer to use a loop join operator for the preceding query. You run the following T-SQL statement to create a plan guide to provide MAXDOP 1 and LOOP JOIN hints for the query:

```
IF EXISTS(SELECT * FROM sys.plan_guides WHERE name = 'planguideTest')
    EXEC sp_control_plan_guide N'DROP', N'planguideTest';
GO


EXEC sp_create_plan_guide
 @name = N'planguideTest',
 @stmt = N' SELECT h.SalesOrderID, h.OrderDate, h.DueDate, h.ShipDate,
        h.Status, h.SalesOrderNumber, c.FirstName, c.LastName, h.TotalDue,
        a.City, a.PostalCode
  FROM Sales.SalesOrderHeader h JOIN Person.Contact c
  ON c.ContactID = h.CustomerID
     LEFT OUTER JOIN Person.Address AS [a]
     ON [a].AddressID =
        (SELECT  TOP 1 AddressID FROM Sales.CustomerAddress
        WHERE CustomerID = h.CustomerID)
ORDER BY c.LastName, c.FirstName;',
 @type = N'SQL',
 @module_or_batch = NULL,
 @params = NULL,
 @hints = N'OPTION (LOOP JOIN, MAXDOP 1)';
GO


SELECT * FROM sys.plan_guides;
GO
```

This T-SQL script uses sys.plan_guides to check whether the named plan guide already exists. If it does, the script uses sp_control_plan_guide to drop the plan guide. Next, it creates a plan guide by using the sp_create_plan_guide system stored procedure.

Now if you run the same SELECT statement again, you should notice that at runtime, SQL Server attaches MAXDOP 1 and LOOP JOIN operator hints with the query. You can see this by looking at an execution plan generated for exactly the same query (see Figure 9.5).

In summary, plan guides are a powerful feature that you can use to address queries targeted for improved or stabilized performance.

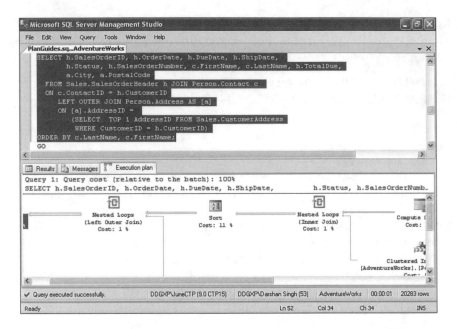

FIGURE 9.5   After you create a plan guide, the same query generates a different execution plan with no parallelism and also uses a loop join instead of a hash join.

New Query Hints

SQL Server 2005 introduces four new query hints that you can directly specify with the queries (not recommended) or specify by using plan guides (the recommended approach, discussed in the preceding section). These are the new query hints:

- **RECOMPILE**—SQL Server 2000 provided three ways to recompile a stored procedure: by using the sp_recompile stored procedure; by specifying the WITH RECOMPILE option while creating a stored procedure; and by specifying the WITH RECOMPILE option while executing the stored procedure. However, there was no way to recompile a subset of a stored procedure or just few queries inside the stored procedure. SQL Server 2005 fixes this by introducing a RECOMPILE hint that instructs SQL Server to discard the plan generated for the query after it executes, forcing the query optimizer to recompile a query plan the next time the same query is executed. By using this hint, you can implement a scenario where only a subset of a stored procedure is recompiled instead of the entire stored procedure.

- **OPTIMIZE FOR (@variable = value [,...n])**—If you know that a local variable will have a certain value or a certain range of values, you can specify the OPTIMIZE FOR hint with the query to instruct SQL Server to use the specified value during the query optimization process.

- **USE PLAN 'xml plan'**—You can use this query hint to force the query optimizer to use a specified query plan for a query. A common situation where this hint might be used is when a query plan chosen by the query optimizer in an earlier product version is preferred over the one chosen after the upgrade. You can obtain the 'xml plan' to specify with USE PLAN by either using the SET SHOWPLAN XML or SET STATISTICS XML statements, by using the plan column of the sys.dm_exec_query_plan DMV, or by using the SQL Profiler Showplan XML event class, the Showplan XML Statistics Profile event class, or the Showplan XML For Query Compile event class.

- **PARAMETERIZATION { SIMPLE | FORCED }**—Using parameters or parameter markers in T-SQL statements increases the ability of the relational engine to match new SQL statements with existing, unused execution plans. If a SQL statement is executed without parameters, SQL Server 2005 parameterizes the statement internally (similarly to sp_executesql) to increase the possibility of matching it against an existing execution plan. This process is called *simple parameterization*. SQL Server parameterizes a relatively small class of queries. If you want all queries in a database to be parameterized, subject to certain limitations, you can use the ALTER DATABASE statement and change the PARAMETERIZATION setting from the default SIMPLE to FORCED. However, if you want to keep the database PARAMETERIZATION setting at the default but would like a particular query to be forced to be parameterized, you can use the PARAMETERIZATION query hint.

New Database Options

The previous section discusses a new database option, PARAMETERIZATION, that you can use to choose between simple and forced query parameterization behavior. The following sections discuss some other database options that you can set by using the ALTER DATABASE statement and that you can use to tune databases.

The AUTO_UPDATE_STATISTICS_ASYNC Option

By default, the AUTO_UPDATE_STATISTICS_ASYNC database option is turned off, which means that if a plan at compile time sees that statistics are out-of-date, the query will wait until the statistics are updated so that a better query optimization plan can be generated based on up-to-date statistics. This can result in different response times for the same query. If you turn on this option, and then if a plan at compile time sees that statistics are out-of-date, the query will not wait until the statistics are updated. The query will continue to use the existing statistics and start a new thread to update the statistics in parallel. The next time the query is called, it may use the updated statistics. This results in stable and consistent query response times. The AUTO_UPDATE_STATISTICS option must be ON for the AUTO_UPDATE_STATISTICS_ASYNC option to work. In addition, the sampling formula for statistics update has changed; SQL Server 2005 makes sure that the optimizer samples at least 8MB of pages.

You can use the is_auto_update_stats_async_on column in the sys.databases catalog view to find out whether the AUTO_UPDATE_STATISTICS_ASYNC option is turned on or off.

The DATE_CORRELATION_OPTIMIZATION Option

By default, the DATE_CORRELATION_OPTIMIZATION database option is turned off, which means that SQL Server does not maintain any correlation statistics for tables in the database that are linked by a foreign key constraint and have datetime columns. You can turn on this database option to improve the performance of queries that perform an equi-join between two tables whose datetime columns are correlated and that specify a date restriction in the query predicate. For instance, the OrderDate column of the Purchasing.PurchaseOrderHeader table can be considered correlated with the DueDate column of the Purchasing.PurchaseOrderDetail table. If the application workload has queries on these tables, using equi-joins, and uses DueDate or OrderDate columns in the WHERE condition, turning on the DATE_CORRELATION_OPTIMIZATION option can increase the performance of such queries.

You can use the is_date_correlation_on column in the sys.databases catalog view to find out whether the DATE_CORRELATION_OPTIMIZATION option is turned on or off.

The ENABLE_BROKER Option

SQL Server 2005 introduces a new asynchronous messaging platform for creating scalable, queued, distributed database applications. You can set the ENABLE_BROKER database option for a database to allow Service Broker communication from and to that database. Service Broker is discussed in great detail in Chapter 14.

Statement-Level Recompilation

The SQL Server 2005 performance-related enhancements discussed so far in this chapter require you to make the right design decisions and use the right techniques to maximize performance. This section presents one example of enhancements that are built into the SQL Server 2005 database engine to improve query performance without you making any changes to your application.

As discussed in Chapter 2, "SQL Server 2005 Database Engine Architectural Changes," in order to optimize query execution performance, SQL Server uses a part of the memory buffer pool to cache the query execution plans. This space is called the *plan cache*. The execution plan consists of two main components:

- **Query plan**—The query plan is a read-only data structure that can be used by any number of users of a query. The query plan is reentrant (that is, all users share the plan, and no user context information is stored in the plan). SQL Server keeps only one copy of the plan for serial executions and, if needed, another plan for parallel executions.

- **Execution context**—With the execution context data structure, each user currently executing the query has a data structure that holds the data specific to their execution, such as parameter values.

When any SQL statement is executed in SQL Server 2005, the relational engine first looks through the plan cache to verify that an existing execution plan for the same SQL statement exists. SQL Server 2005 reuses any existing plan it finds, which saves the overhead of recompiling the SQL statement. If no existing execution plan exists, SQL Server 2005 generates a new execution plan for the query. Certain changes in a database can cause an execution plan to be either inefficient or invalid, given the new state of the database. SQL Server detects the changes that invalidate an execution plan and marks such a plan as invalid. A new plan must then be recompiled for the next connection that executes the query.

In SQL Server 2000, whenever a statement within a batch causes recompilation, the entire batch, whether submitted via a stored procedure, a trigger, an ad-hoc batch, or a prepared statement, is recompiled. In SQL Server 2005, only the statement inside the batch that causes recompilation is recompiled. Because of this "statement-level recompilation" feature, SQL Server 2005 spends less CPU time and memory on batch recompilations, and it obtains fewer compile locks, which increases the overall performance.

One other benefit of statement-level recompilations is that it is no longer necessary to break a long stored procedure into multiple short stored procedures just to reduce the recompilation penalty of the long stored procedure.

You can use a new Profiler event called SQL:StmtRecompile, which is under the TSQL event class, to trace statement-level recompilations. In addition, the existing SP:Recompile event under the Stored Procedures event class has been updated to show what query caused the recompilation in the TextData column on the SP:Recompile row.

The following is an example of statement-level recompilation:

```
IF OBJECT_ID('dbo.tblTest') IS NOT NULL
    DROP TABLE dbo.tblTest;
CREATE TABLE dbo.tblTest
    (C1 INT IDENTITY(1,1) NOT NULL PRIMARY KEY,
    C2 INT, C3 VARCHAR(20), C4 CHAR(5));

IF OBJECT_ID('dbo.sprocTest') IS NOT NULL
    DROP PROCEDURE dbo.sprocTest;
GO
CREATE PROCEDURE dbo.sprocTest
AS
BEGIN
    SELECT * FROM sysobjects WHERE 1 = 2;
    SELECT * FROM master.dbo.sysprocesses;

    SELECT * FROM dbo.tblTest WHERE C2 % 10 = 0 ORDER BY C4 DESC;
END;
GO

EXEC  dbo.sprocTest;
CREATE INDEX idxTest ON dbo.tblTest (C4);
EXEC  dbo.sprocTest;
DROP INDEX tblTest.idxTest;
EXEC  dbo.sprocTest;
```

This script creates a sample table that is accessed in the stored procedure. After the first time the stored procedure is executed, an index is created on column C4, and the stored procedure is executed again. In SQL Server 2000, the entire stored procedure was recompiled during the second execution, whereas in SQL Server 2005, only the SELECT statement on the tblTest is recompiled. To see this in action, you can start a SQL Server 2000 Profiler trace, select the Stored Procedures:SP Recompile event, and select a few columns, including the TextData column, from the Data Columns tab. Then you can run the preceding script in Query Analyzer. You should see an SP:Recompile entry in Profiler and note that the TextData column is empty. You have to select another Profiler event, such as SP:Starting or SP:Completed, to find out which stored procedure is being recompiled.

Next, you should start SQL Server 2005 Profiler and select the Stored Procedures:SP Recompile and TSQL:StmtRecompile events. Then you run the preceding script in a query window in Management Studio, and you should notice that Profiler shows that only the SELECT statement is recompiled. Profiler should list SP:Recompile followed by SQL:StmtRecompile, but the TextData for both the rows is the SELECT statement that caused the recompilation (because the schema for the table being accessed changed).

Designing Applications for Performance

As mentioned at the beginning of this chapter, poor application design is one of the top reasons applications run slowly and don't scale well. Application designers and architects should think about performance objectives early in the application life cycle. Designers should proactively make key design choices to maximize performance and scalability, while balancing other quality-of-service (QoS) considerations, such as availability, manageability, integrity, and security.

The following sections present a brief overview of new developer features introduced in SQL Server 2005 to create applications that perform and scale well.

Service Broker and Asynchronous Messaging

With just a few lines of T-SQL code, you can now build triggers that execute asynchronously, execute stored procedures in parallel, scale out with no or minimal change in an application, defer part of the processing to spread out the load evenly or for batch processing, increase the availability by distributing or splitting the server-side processing, and so on. The platform, or framework, that supports this inside SQL Server 2005 is Service Broker.

If you want to build scalable database applications, you should seriously consider using Service Broker in your applications. You can use T-SQL statements to create Service Broker queues, services, and routes; send and receive messages; and so on. Service Broker, which is built into the SQL Server 2005 database engine, provides the infrastructure required for queuing and communicating messages asynchronously, reliably, and securely. Refer to Chapter 14 for complete details on Service Broker.

.NET Runtime Integration

T-SQL is an interpreted language, and it is not well suited for complex computational and procedural tasks. The SQL Server 2005 database engine can host the .NET runtime to facilitate running compiled .NET code inside SQL Server. This feature is called the .NET Common Language Runtime (CLR) integration, or SQLCLR, and it can be used to write stored procedures, triggers, and user-defined functions, types, and aggregates, using any .NET programming language. You can use SQLCLR to implement computational and procedural tasks that may yield better performance than their T-SQL counterparts. SQLCLR is discussed in Chapter 11, "SQL Server 2005 and .NET Integration."

T-SQL Enhancements

The previous section describes that you can use .NET to extend T-SQL. If something is not possible using T-SQL, you can implement it by using .NET (as a stored procedure, a function, a trigger, a type, or an aggregate) and execute it inside SQL Server. For data access, T-SQL is still the premier and most optimal language. SQL Server 2005 introduces enhancements to the T-SQL languages that database professionals can leverage to write efficient and manageable queries. Common table expressions, PIVOT/UNPIVOT operators, and ranking functions are some examples of T-SQL enhancements. Refer to Chapter 6, "Transact-SQL Enhancements," for a detailed description of new T-SQL features in SQL Server 2005.

Multiple Active Result Sets

Before SQL Server 2005, a connection supported only a single request at any time. If there was a pending request or an open result set (that is, a fire hose cursor), the connection could not execute another statement until the first one finished. SQL Server 2005, along with the new SQL Native Client data access API, or .NET 2.0 SqlClient provider, changes this by introducing a feature called Multiple Active Result Sets (MARS). As the name suggests, MARS provides the ability to have more than one pending request under a given SQL Server connection. MARS involves enabling the interleaved execution of multiple requests within a single connection. It allows a batch to run and, within the execution, allows other requests to execute. Note, however, that MARS is defined in terms of interleaving, not in terms of parallel execution. In many situations, MARS may provide an alternative to server-side cursors and provide performance improvements.

Query Notifications

Query notifications are a new functionality introduced in SQL Server 2005 that allow an application to request a notification from SQL Server when the results of a query change. The most common scenario where this can be used is while caching a result set. Instead of polling the database periodically or refreshing the cache periodically, an application can enlist with SQL Server 2005 to be notified whenever there is a change in the cached result set. This can aid in reducing the number of round trips to the database and improving the overall system throughput. The database engine uses Service Broker to deliver query notification messages. Therefore, Service Broker must be enabled in the database where the application requests the subscription.

HTTP SOAP Support

The SQLXML add-on to SQL Server 2000 allows you to invoke stored procedures over HTTP as web service methods. However, this requires the Microsoft Internet Information Services (IIS) web server and an ISAPI extension DLL. This layering can have some impact on performance when web service methods are invoked.

HTTP SOAP web services support is now built into the SQL Server 2005 database engine, eliminating the need for any web server or any ISAPI extension DLL, resulting in better performance. The HTTP endpoints can be created, and web service methods can be mapped to stored procedures, by using the CREATE ENDPOINT T-SQL statement. Refer to Chapter 10 for more details on this.

Performance Monitoring and Tuning Tools

Tools play an important role in monitoring, troubleshooting, and tuning database performance. The basic performance monitoring toolset in SQL Server 2000 included System Monitor or Performance Monitor, SQL Profiler, the Current Activity folder in Enterprise Manager, system stored procedures and DBCC statements, and the showplan and statistics display in Query Analyzer. The ITW was the only tuning tool available in SQL Server 2000.

SQL Server 2005 continues to support and enhance SQL Profiler, Activity Monitor, showplan and statistics display, and Performance Monitor. In addition, the new dynamic management objects add a powerful capability to monitor the system state. In addition to graphical and textual execution plans, SQL Server 2005 supports using Profiler or SQL Server Management Studio to generate execution plans in XML format.

As mentioned earlier in this chapter, the ITW has been replaced with a more powerful, full-fledged application called DTA. Plan guides (by using sp_create_plan_guide) are a new tuning tool available in SQL Server 2005. Chapter 5 provides a detailed description of these tools.

SQL Server 2005 contains about 78 DMVs and about 9 dynamic management functions (DMFs). All the dynamic management objects belong to "the sys" schema, and at least two-part names are required to access these objects. DMVs can be referenced using two-part, three-part, or four-part names, and DMFs can be referenced using two-part or three-part names.

DMVs and DMFs are grouped into the following 12 categories:

- .NET CLR
- Execution
- Full-text services
- Index
- IO
- Query notifications
- Replication
- Service Broker
- SQLOS
- Database
- Database mirroring
- Transaction

DMV and DMF names begin with `"dm_"` and then are named consistently to identify the category they belong to. For instance, all the dynamic management objects in the .NET CLR category begin with `"dm_clr_"`, execution-related objects begin with `"dm_exec_"`, index-related objects begin with `"dm_index_"`, and I/O-related objects begin with `"dm_io_"`.

A complete description of all the dynamic management objects is beyond the scope of this chapter. However, Table 9.2 describes a few dynamic management objects that you can use to monitor and troubleshoot performance issues.

TABLE 9.2   Dynamic Management Objects

Dynamic Management Object	Description
dm_exec_cached_plans	Provides information about the query execution plans that are cached by SQL Server for faster query execution.
dm_exec_connections	Provides information about the connections established to SQL Server on various endpoints.
dm_exec_sessions	Contains one row per authenticated session on the SQL Server instance.
dm_exec_query_stats	Provides aggregate performance statistics for cached query plans.
dm_exec_query_optimizer_info	Provides detailed statistics about the operation of the SQL Server query optimizer.
dm_io_pending_io_requests	Contains a row for each pending I/O in the system.
dm_os_loaded_modules	Contains a row for each module loaded into the server address space.
dm_os_memory_cache_counters	Provides a general snapshot of the health of the cache.
dm_os_memory_cache_entries	Enables you to view all entries in caches and their statistics.
dm_os_performance_counters	Lists SQL Server 2005 Performance Monitor counters and their current value.
dm_os_waiting_tasks	Provides information on the wait queue of tasks that are waiting on some resource.
dm_tran_locks	Returns one row for every active request to the lock manager that has either been granted or is waiting to be granted (that is, the request is blocked by an already granted request).
dm_tran_current_transaction	Returns a single row that displays state information of the transaction in the current session.
dm_tran_active_transactions	Provides information about active transactions.
dm_clr_properties	If the CLR is enabled, provides information such as CLR version, directory, state, and so on.
dm_clr_appdomains	Returns a row for each CLR application domain in the server.
dm_clr_loaded_assemblies	Contains a row for each CLR user assembly loaded into the server address space.

To try out some of the dynamic management objects, you can start SQL Server Management Studio and run the following script in a query window:

```
SELECT SUM(pagesused) * 8 AS 'Plan Cache (KB)'
    FROM sys.dm_exec_cached_plans;

SELECT protocol_type, count(*) AS 'Total Connections'
FROM sys.dm_exec_connections
GROUP BY protocol_type;

SELECT login_name, client_interface_name, count(*) AS 'Total Sessions',
    sum(memory_usage) AS 'Memory Usage'
FROM sys.dm_exec_sessions
GROUP BY login_name, client_interface_name;

SELECT name, description, company, file_version, product_version
FROM sys.dm_os_loaded_modules;

SELECT [type], sum(single_pages_kb) AS 'Total Single Pages (KB)',
    sum(multi_pages_kb) AS 'Total Multi Pages (KB)',
    sum(virtual_memory_reserved_kb) AS 'Total Virtual Memory Reserved (KB)',
    sum(virtual_memory_committed_kb) AS 'Total Virtual Memory Committed (KB)',
    sum(awe_allocated_kb) AS 'Total AWE Allocated Memory (KB)'
  FROM sys.dm_os_memory_clerks
  GROUP BY [type]
  ORDER BY 2 DESC, 3 DESC;

SELECT * FROM sys.dm_os_performance_counters;

SELECT * FROM sys.dm_os_tasks
    ORDER BY context_switches_count DESC;

SELECT * FROM sys.dm_clr_properties;
```

The first SELECT statement uses the sys.dm_exec_cached_plans DMV to calculate total memory taken by the plan cache. The second SELECT statement uses the sys.dm_exec_connections DMV to total the connections to the SQL Server over each protocol. The third SELECT statement uses the sys.dm_exec_sessions DMV to group sessions by login name and displays total sessions and total memory used by each login. The next query displays all the loaded modules by using the sys.dm_os_loaded_modules DMV. The next SELECT statement uses the sys.dm_os_memory_clerks DMV to display the total single-page, multi-page, virtual, and AWE memory being managed by each clerk. The final three SELECT statements use the sys.dm_os_performance_counters, sys.dm_os_tasks, and sys.dm_clr_properties DMVs to display the current SQL Performance Monitor counter data, tasks, and CLR properties, respectively.

Summary

Performance tuning is often an iterative process in which you identify and fix bottle-necks, apply one set of configuration changes at a time, and test and collect data to see if the application meets its performance objective, and, if not, continue with the tuning-configuration-testing process. Proactive monitoring and tuning can save significant time, money, and resources. This chapter assumes that you are somewhat familiar with SQL Server 2000 performance monitoring and tuning, and it discusses the new techniques and features that you can use to proactively design, monitor, and tune database applications to maximize the performance.

The chapter begins with a discussion on optimizing physical database design, which is an important aspect of maximizing the performance and manageability of any database system. Next, some new techniques are presented to troubleshoot locking and blocking issues. The subsequent two sections describe techniques to optimize the queries and appli-cation design. Because Chapter 5 already contains a detailed description of SQL Server 2005 tools, including performance monitoring and tuning tools, this chapter discusses only DMVs in detail.

The next few chapters introduce you to developer and business intelligence features to show you how they affect you as a DBA. Chapter 10 starts with an overview of XML and web services support in SQL Server 2005.

XML and Web Services Support in SQL Server 2005

Extensible Markup Language (XML) is a set of guidelines for describing structured data in plain text. These guidelines are defined as a specification by the World Wide Web Consortium (W3C; www.w3.org), the body that sets the standards for the Web. Because of its textual nature, XML has been widely adopted as a platform-independent format for data representation. Some of the current applications of XML include exchange of data over the Internet, application integration, content management and document publishing, use as configuration files, news/weblog syndication (RSS), and use as a file format such as Word documents stored as XML.

With the increased use of XML for representing documents and forms, more and more developers want to store XML documents directly into databases and also be able to effectively query and retrieve the XML data. SQL Server 2005 is the first release that has native support for XML storage and querying. This chapter shows you how to store XML data in a database column, index it, modify it, and query it by using another W3C specification, called XQuery.

In addition to the new XML data type and XQuery querying capabilities, SQL Server 2005 also includes enhancements to the OPENROWSET function to allow bulk loading of XML data, as well as several enhancements to the existing FOR XML clause.

The other topic discussed in this chapter is HTTP SOAP or web services support in SQL Server 2005. HTTP SOAP support in SQL Server 2005 allows you to execute T-SQL batches, stored procedures, and scalar-valued user-defined functions over the Internet, from any client platform. For instance, a Unix client application can use Perl to post a SOAP request envelope over the Internet (via HTTP or HTTPS) to a SQL Server 2005 web service method, which in turn can execute a batch or a stored procedure or a function on the server side and return a SOAP response envelope, which is an XML document that contains the results, which can be then parsed by the client Perl application on the Unix machine. This enables cross-platform application integration. You do not need Microsoft Internet Information Server (IIS) or any web server to enable and use the web services support in SQL Server 2005. The second part of this chapter discusses this in great detail.

Before looking at XML support in SQL Server 2005, here is a quick introduction to XML.

XML Primer

If you have ever seen or worked with HTML, you will find an XML document very similar to it. Both HTML and XML are markup languages based on tags within angled bracket. But unlike HTML, XML does not have a fixed set of tags. You can create your own tags, as long as the tags adhere to the rules defined by the XML specification, and then include your data between those tags. Because of this extensibility feature, today more than 450 other markup languages or standards are based on XML, which means they use XML syntax (for example, Scalable Vector Graphics [SVG], VoiceXML, Wireless Markup Language [WML], NewsML).

Whereas HTML's primary focus is presentation, XML's main focus is data and its structure. You can use technologies such as XSL Transformations (XSLT) and XSL Formatting Objects (XSL-FO) to present the data in an XML document in different formats. This is one of the reasons XML is being used heavily in content management and document publishing applications.

NOTE

Unlike HTML, XML is case-sensitive.

The textual nature of XML makes data highly portable, enabling you to send data and integrate applications across platforms. The most common use of XML is for "data on move"—that is, transferring data from one machine to another, cross-platform, cross-networks, and over the Internet.

Let's now see what an XML document looks like.

Well-Formed XML Document

As mentioned earlier, an XML document might look very similar to an HTML document. However, XML has more strict syntax rules than HTML. An XML document must meet the following requirements:

- All tags must be closed.

- Tags are case-sensitive.

- An XML document must have a single top-level root element.

- Elements must be nested properly, without overlap.

- No element may have two attributes with the same name.

- Attribute values must be enclosed in either single or double quotes.

If an XML document meets all these requirements, it is considered a well-formed XML document. Here is an example of a well-formed XML document that contains some details from a survey form:

```
<IndividualSurvey xmlns="http://schemas.microsoft.com/AW/IndividualSurvey">
  <TotalPurchaseYTD>8248.99</TotalPurchaseYTD>
  <DateFirstPurchase>2001-07-22Z</DateFirstPurchase>
  <BirthDate>1966-04-08Z</BirthDate>
  <MaritalStatus>M</MaritalStatus>
  <YearlyIncome>75001-100000</YearlyIncome>
  <Gender>M</Gender>
  <TotalChildren>2</TotalChildren>
  <NumberChildrenAtHome>0</NumberChildrenAtHome>
  <Education>Bachelors &amp; Masters</Education>
  <Occupation>Professional</Occupation>
  <HomeOwnerFlag>1</HomeOwnerFlag>
  <NumberCarsOwned>0</NumberCarsOwned>
  <CommuteDistance>&lt; 4 Miles</CommuteDistance>
</IndividualSurvey>
```

The XML specification identifies five characters (that is, <, >, &, ', and ") that have special meanings. If any of these characters is required, the alternative entity references (that is, <, >, &, ', and ") must be used in its place in an XML document.

In addition to elements and attributes, an XML document may contain other special-purpose tags, such as comments (enclosed in <!-- ... -->), processing instructions (enclosed in <? ... ?>) to provide some instructions to the XML parser, and CDATA sections (enclosed in <![CDATA[...]]>). Everything inside a CDATA section is ignored by the parser, so you can include special characters such as <, >, and & within a CDATA section without escaping them as <, >, and &.

Valid XML Documents

One of the primary goals of XML is to enable exchange of data between organizations and applications. To do this, the XML document format that is used for the exchange of information must first be defined and agreed upon. W3C provides a specification called

XML Schema Definition (XSD) that can be used to define the structure of an XML document, the data types of elements and attributes, and other rules and constraints that an XML document should follow. If a well-formed XML document adheres to the structure and rules defined by a XSD schema document, that XML document is considered a valid XML document. You can find more details on XSD at www.w3.org/XML/Schema.

XML Namespaces

Namespaces are generally used for two purposes:

- To group related information under one umbrella

- To avoid name collisions between groups

XML namespaces also serve these two purposes. The following sample XML document declares two namespaces, and for each namespace, it defines a prefix (s1 and s2), which is a convenient name for the lengthy namespace URI. The first three child elements are in the s1 namespace, and the others are in the s2 namespace (see Listing 10.1).

LISTING 10.1   Survey XML Document

```
<?xml version="1.0" encoding="UTF-8"?>
<StoreSurvey xmlns:s1="http://schemas.microsoft.com/Survey1"
             xmlns:s2="http://schemas.microsoft.com/Survey2">
  <s1:AnnualSales>300000</s1:AnnualSales>
  <s1:AnnualRevenue>30000</s1:AnnualRevenue>
  <s1:BankName>International Bank</s1:BankName>

  <s2:AnnualSales currency="USD">320000</s2:AnnualSales>
  <s2:AnnualSales currency="Euro">2000</s2:AnnualSales>
  <s2:AnnualRevenue>29000</s2:AnnualRevenue>
  <s2:BankName>National Bank</s2:BankName>

</StoreSurvey>
```

XML does not enforce the use of namespaces, and it is totally legal for elements to have the same name. So you could have AnnualSales or BankName elements repeated without using the namespace, but how would you identify in your code which one is which? This is where namespaces come handy. Note in Listing 10.1 that the root element (StoreSurvey) is in no namespace, which is the default namespace here.

Also note the use of a processing instruction, an XML declaration line at the top of Listing 10.1, which tells the XML parser about the XML specification version that the document is based on and the text encoding used for the document.

Navigating XML by Using XPath

XML Path (XPath) is yet another W3C specification (see www.w3.org/TR/xpath), and it is widely used to search through XML documents and to retrieve specific parts of an XML document. XPath is based on the notion that every XML document can be visualized as a hierarchical tree. XPath is a language for expressing paths through such trees, from one node to another. XPath query syntax is similar to the syntax you would use to locate a file or files on a Unix file system (that is, using forward slashes to indicate levels of hierarchy). In addition, XPath enables you to retrieve elements or attributes that satisfy a given set of criteria.

For instance, the following XPath expression can be used to retrieve the annual revenue element in the s2 namespace from Listing 10.1:

```
/StoreSurvey/s2:AnnualRevenue
```

The conditions are expressed in square brackets, and the attribute names are preceded with the @ symbol. For instance, the `//s2:AnnualSales[@currency="USD"]` XPath expression returns annual sales elements that have the currency attribute value USD.

In the following sections, you'll see how SQL Server 2005 supports XML.

The xml Data Type

SQL Server 2005 introduces a new data type, xml, to store XML data inside a relational database. The xml data type can be used for a column in a table, as a variable, as a parameter to a stored procedure or function, and as a function return value. The SQL Server 2005 xml data type implements the ISO SQL-2003 standard xml data type. You can store an entire XML document or XML fragments (XML data without single top-level element) in xml data type columns and variables. By default, SQL Server does not enforce the storing of well-formed or valid XML documents, and it allows the storing of XML fragments in xml data type columns and variables.

As with other data types, you can assign defaults, define column-level and table-level constraints, create XML indexes, and define full-text indexes on xml data type columns. However, there are few restrictions:

- SQL Server internally stores XML data as a binary large object (BLOB), and hence the internal representation of XML in a column cannot exceed 2GB. The depth of the XML hierarchy is limited to 128 levels in SQL Server 2005.

- The xml data type column cannot be defined as a primary key or foreign key; in addition, the UNIQUE, COLLATE, and RULE constraints cannot be used on xml data type columns.

- The xml data type cannot be compared or sorted, except with the IS NULL operator. Hence, you cannot use an xml data type column with an ORDER BY or GROUP BY clause.

- An xml data type column cannot be part of a clustered or a nonclustered index. You can define XML indexes on xml type columns, as discussed later in this chapter.

- The XML declaration processing instruction (<?xml ... ?>) is not preserved when the instance is stored in the database. XML data is always stored and retrieved using UTF-16 encoding. If an XML document has other processing instructions besides the XML declaration line, they all are preserved.

- The order of attributes and insignificant whitespace is not preserved. Also, the single or double quotes around attributes are not preserved; SQL Server always returns attributes enclosed in double quotes.

- You cannot cast an xml data type column to either text or ntext. You can cast or convert an xml data type to varchar or nvarchar, including to varchar(max) and nvarchar(max), and then use that to implicitly or explicitly cast to text or ntext.

- Only ISNULL, COALESCE, and DATALENGTH scalar functions are supported with xml data type columns.

- xml data type columns cannot be used in distributed partitioned views.

CAUTION

The xml data type is not supported on SQL Server 2005 Mobile Edition. If xml data type columns are synced to the SQL Server Mobile database, they will be converted to the ntext type.

Here is an example of using the xml data type in a table:

```
USE [AdventureWorks];
GO

--User-defined functions used later while creating a table
IF OBJECT_ID('dbo.IsXMLFragment') IS NOT NULL
   DROP FUNCTION dbo.IsXMLFragment;
GO
CREATE FUNCTION dbo.IsXMLFragment(@xmlData xml) returns bit
BEGIN
   RETURN
      CASE @xmlData.value('count(/*)', 'bigint')
         WHEN 1 THEN (@xmlData.exist('/text()'))
         ELSE 1
      END
END;
GO

IF OBJECT_ID('dbo.EmpIDPresent') IS NOT NULL
   DROP FUNCTION dbo.EmpIDPresent;
```

```
GO
CREATE FUNCTION dbo.EmpIDPresent(@xmlData xml) returns bit
BEGIN
   RETURN
     @xmlData.exist('/Employee/@ID')
END;
GO


IF OBJECT_ID('dbo.tblXMLTest') IS NOT NULL
   DROP TABLE dbo.tblXMLTest;
GO
CREATE TABLE dbo.tblXMLTest
   (id INT IDENTITY(1,1) PRIMARY KEY,
    col1 XML,
    col2 XML NOT NULL,
    col3 XML DEFAULT N'<Person />',
    col4 XML NOT NULL DEFAULT N'<Address />',
    col5 XML CHECK(dbo.IsXMLFragment(col5) = 0),
    col6 XML NULL CHECK(dbo.EmpIDPresent(col6) = 1) );
GO
```

This script is available in the file XMLDataTypeDemo.sql in the code download for this book. This script creates a table with six columns of xml data type. The second column, col2, specifies the NOT NULL constraint; the third column, col3, specifies the column default; the fifth column, col5, specifies a check constraint and uses a user-defined function to ensure that only well-formed XML documents are inserted into the column; and the sixth column, col6, also specifies a check condition and uses a user-defined function to ensure that the XML document or fragment has a top-level element called Employee and an attribute called ID. The exist() and value() methods used inside the user-defined functions, as well as other methods available with the xml data type, are discussed later in this chapter.

In the following script, the first three INSERT statements succeed, and the other four INSERTs fail:

```
INSERT INTO dbo.tblXMLTest(col2, col5) VALUES
 (N'<col2Data />', N'<col5Data />');
INSERT INTO dbo.tblXMLTest(col2, col5, col6) VALUES
 (N'<col2Data />', N'<col5Data />', N'<Employee ID="123" />');
INSERT INTO dbo.tblXMLTest(col2, col5, col6) VALUES
 ('<col2Data />', '<col5Data />', '<Employee ID="1"/><Employee ID="2"/>');
GO


SELECT * FROM dbo.tblXMLTest;
GO
```

```
INSERT INTO dbo.tblXMLTest(col5, col6) VALUES
  (N'<col5Data />', N'<Employee ID="123" />');
INSERT INTO dbo.tblXMLTest(col2, col5, col6) VALUES
  (N'<col2Data />', N'<col5Data /><col5Data />', N'<Employee ID="123" />');
INSERT INTO dbo.tblXMLTest(col2, col5, col6) VALUES
  (N'<col2Data />', N'<col5Data />', N'<Employee/>');
INSERT INTO dbo.tblXMLTest(col2, col4, col5) VALUES
  (N'<col2Data />', NULL, N'<col5Data />');
GO
```

Of the four failed INSERTs toward the end, the first one fails because col2 does not allow
NULLs, the second INSERT fails because col5 does not allow XML fragments, the third one
fails because col6 does not have XML with the Employee top-level element having an ID
attribute, and the final one fails because col4 is non-NULLable.

The following script shows how to declare a variable of the xml data type:

```
DECLARE @var1 XML
SET @var1 = '<TestVariables />'

INSERT INTO dbo.tblXMLTest(col2, col5) VALUES
  (@var1, @var1);

SELECT * FROM dbo.tblXMLTest;
GO
```

The following script block illustrates how to pass an xml data type as a function parameter
to implement a technique called *property promotion,* where some value from XML is
copied to a separate table column, so that you don't have to necessarily access and parse
XML to access that value:

```
CREATE FUNCTION dbo.fn_GetID (@empData XML)
RETURNS INT
AS
BEGIN
    DECLARE @retVal INT
    -- do some more things here on the input XML
    SELECT @retVal = @empData.value('(/Employee/@ID)[1]', 'INT')
    RETURN @retVal
END;
GO

SELECT dbo.fn_GetID(col6) FROM dbo.tblXMLTest;
```

```
ALTER TABLE dbo.tblXMLTest ADD empNo AS dbo.fn_GetID(col6);

INSERT INTO dbo.tblXMLTest(col2, col5, col6) VALUES
  ('<col2Data />', '<col5Data />', '<Employee ID="999"/>');
GO


SELECT * FROM dbo.tblXMLTest;
GO


IF OBJECT_ID('dbo.tblXMLTest') IS NOT NULL
   DROP TABLE dbo.tblXMLTest;
GO
IF OBJECT_ID('dbo.fn_GetID') IS NOT NULL
   DROP FUNCTION dbo.fn_GetID;
GO
IF OBJECT_ID('dbo.IsXMLFragment') IS NOT NULL
   DROP FUNCTION dbo.IsXMLFragment;
GO
IF OBJECT_ID('dbo.EmpIDPresent') IS NOT NULL
   DROP FUNCTION dbo.EmpIDPresent;
GO
```

This script begins with a user-defined function that accepts an xml data type parameter, uses the value function on the input XML parameter, and returns an integer value. Next, the ALTER TABLE statement adds a new computed column whose value is the integer returned by the fn_GetID function, passing the col6 column to it.

Validating XML Data by Using Typed XML

So far you have seen examples of storing untyped XML documents and XML fragments into xml data type columns, variables, and parameters. SQL Server 2005 supports associating XSD schemas with the xml data type so that the XML value for the column, variable, or parameter adheres to the structure and data types defined by the associated XSD schema. Having SQL Server validate the xml data type column, variable, or parameter by associating it with an XML schema collection is known as typed XML.

With typed XML, you can associate an XSD schema collection with the xml data type column, and the engine validates against the associated schema and generates an error if the validation fails. The typed XML has two main benefits. First, it ensures that the XML data in the column, variable, or parameter is according to the schema you desire. Second, it helps the engine to optimize storage and query processing. Also, when declaring the typed XML, you can specify the DOCUMENT clause, which ensures that the XML has only one top-level element and hence XML fragments are disallowed. The default is CONTENT, which allows XML fragments.

TIP

For performance reasons, it is recommended that you use typed XML. With untyped XML, the node values are stored as strings, and hence the engine has to do the data conversion when you extract the XML values or use node values in the predicate (for example, /person/age < 50); on the other hand, with typed XML, no data conversion takes place because the XML data values are internally stored based on types declared in the XSD schema. Typed XML makes parsing more efficient and avoids any runtime conversions.

Here's an example of creating typed XML:

1. Make sure you have an XSD schema in a XML schema collection. SQL Server 2005 provides the CREATE, ALTER, and DROP XML SCHEMA COLLECTION DDL statements, which can be used to manage the XML schema collections in a database. When you have your XSD schema in the database as part of an XML schema collection, it can be associated with any number of xml data type columns or variables to create typed XML.

The following T-SQL statements create a schema collection called SampleXSDs that contains an XSD schema which defines the purchase order:

```
USE AdventureWorks;
GO

IF EXISTS
  (SELECT schema_id FROM sys.xml_schema_collections
   WHERE name = 'SampleXSDs')
BEGIN
    RAISERROR('Schema collection named SampleXSDs already exists.',
            16, 1);
    RETURN
END;

CREATE XML SCHEMA COLLECTION SampleXSDs AS
N'<?xml version="1.0" encoding="UTF-16"?>
<xsd:schema xmlns:xsd = "http://www.w3.org/2001/XMLSchema"
          targetNamespace = "http://schemas.sams.com/PO"
          elementFormDefault="qualified"
          attributeFormDefault="unqualified"
          xmlns = "http://schemas.sams.com/PO">

    <xsd:complexType name="USAddress">
      <xsd:sequence>
        <xsd:element name="name"   type="xsd:string"/>
        <xsd:element name="street" type="xsd:string"/>
        <xsd:element name="city"   type="xsd:string"/>
        <xsd:element name="state"  type="xsd:string"/>
```

```
      <xsd:element name="zip"     type="xsd:decimal"/>
    </xsd:sequence>
    <xsd:attribute name="country" type="xsd:NMTOKEN"
                    fixed="US"/>
  </xsd:complexType>

  <xsd:complexType name="Items">
    <xsd:sequence>
      <xsd:element name="item" minOccurs="0" maxOccurs="unbounded">
        <xsd:complexType>
          <xsd:sequence>
            <xsd:element name="productName" type="xsd:string"/>
            <xsd:element name="quantity">
              <xsd:simpleType>
                <xsd:restriction base="xsd:positiveInteger">
                  <xsd:maxExclusive value="100"/>
                </xsd:restriction>
              </xsd:simpleType>
            </xsd:element>
            <xsd:element name="USPrice"  type="xsd:decimal"/>
            <xsd:element name="shipDate" type="xsd:date"
                          minOccurs="0"/>
          </xsd:sequence>
        </xsd:complexType>
      </xsd:element>
    </xsd:sequence>
  </xsd:complexType>

  <xsd:complexType name="PurchaseOrderType">
    <xsd:sequence>
      <xsd:element name="shipTo" type="USAddress"/>
      <xsd:element name="billTo" type="USAddress"/>
      <xsd:element name="items"  type="Items"/>
    </xsd:sequence>
    <xsd:attribute name="orderDate" type="xsd:date"/>
  </xsd:complexType>

  <xsd:element name="purchaseOrder" type="PurchaseOrderType"/>

</xsd:schema>'
```

The XSD schema first defines a type called USAddress, and then it defines a type
called Items, and finally it defines a type called PurchaseOrderType, which makes
use of the USAddress and Items types. The XSD schema defines a single root
element called purchaseOrder that is of type PurchaseOrderType. Before creating a
new schema collection, the script uses the sys.xml_schema_collections catalog

view to check whether a schema collection with that name already exists. In this example, it raises an error and returns; alternatively, you can run ALTER XML SCHEMA COLLECTION and add an XSD schema to this existing schema collection.

2. After you register an XSD schema in a schema collection, SQL Server 2005 stores the schema metadata in various system tables. You can use the XML catalog views to view the XSD schema collection details. Execute the following T-SQL batch to see the details of an XSD schema in the XML schema collection created in step 1:

```
DECLARE @collection_id INT
SELECT @collection_id = xml_collection_id
FROM sys.xml_schema_collections
WHERE name = 'SampleXSDs';

SELECT * FROM sys.xml_schema_namespaces
WHERE xml_collection_id = @collection_id;

SELECT * FROM sys.xml_schema_elements
WHERE xml_collection_id = @collection_id;

SELECT * FROM sys.xml_ schema_attributes
WHERE xml_collection_id = @collection_id;

SELECT * FROM sys.xml_ schema_types
WHERE xml_collection_id = @collection_id;

SELECT XML_SCHEMA_NAMESPACE('dbo', 'SampleXSDs');
```

For each XML schema collection, there is an entry in the sys.xml_schema_ collections catalog view. One schema collection can contain multiple XSD schemas that have different target namespaces. For each such schema, there is an entry in the sys.xml_schema_namespaces catalog view. The types, elements, attributes, and so on are available via the catalog views sys.xml_schema_types, sys.xml_schema_elements, sys.xml_schema_attributes, and so on. The last statement shows how to view the registered XSD schema by using the XML_SCHEMA_ NAMESPACE function. Other schema collection catalog views include sys.xml_schema_components, sys.xml_schema_facets, sys.xml_schema_model_groups, sys.xml_schema_wildcards, and sys.xml_schema_wildcard_namespaces.

3. When an XSD schema is available in an XML schema collection, associate the schema with the XML column to yield typed XML:

```
IF OBJECT_ID('dbo.tblTypedXML') IS NOT NULL
    DROP TABLE dbo.tblTypedXML;
GO
```

```
CREATE TABLE dbo.tblTypedXML
    (id int IDENTITY(1,1) PRIMARY KEY,
     col1 XML (dbo.SampleXSDs));
GO
```

The first INSERT statement in the following T-SQL batch succeeds because it validates with the XSD schema specified for the typed XML column, but the second INSERT fails because it is missing the `billTo` element:

```
INSERT INTO dbo.tblTypedXML (col1) VALUES
(N'<purchaseOrder orderDate="2005-03-03Z"
                       xmlns="http://schemas.sams.com/PO">
    <shipTo country="US">
       <name>Alice Smith</name>
       <street>123 Maple Street</street>
       <city>Mill Valley</city>
       <state>CA</state>
       <zip>90952</zip>
    </shipTo>
    <billTo country="US">
       <name>Robert Smith</name>
       <street>8 Oak Avenue</street>
       <city>Old Town</city>
       <state>PA</state>
       <zip>95819</zip>
    </billTo>
    <items>
       <item>
          <productName>Lawnmower</productName>
          <quantity>1</quantity>
          <USPrice>148.95</USPrice>
       </item>
    </items>
</purchaseOrder>
');
```

```
PRINT 'Following statement will fail:'
INSERT INTO dbo.tblTypedXML (col1) VALUES
(N'<purchaseOrder orderDate="2005-03-03Z"
                     xmlns="http://schemas.sams.com/PO">
    <shipTo country="US">
        <name>Alice Smith</name>
        <street>123 Maple Street</street>
        <city>Mill Valley</city>
        <state>CA</state>
        <zip>90952</zip>
    </shipTo>

    <items>
        <item>
            <productName>Lawnmower</productName>
            <quantity>1</quantity>
            <USPrice>148.95</USPrice>
        </item>
    </items>
</purchaseOrder>
');
GO
```

4. Finally, clean up:

```
IF OBJECT_ID('dbo.tblTypedXML') IS NOT NULL
    DROP TABLE dbo.tblTypedXML;
GO

IF EXISTS
  (SELECT schema_id FROM sys.xml_schema_collections
            WHERE name = 'SampleXSDs')
BEGIN
    DROP XML SCHEMA COLLECTION SampleXSDs
END;
```

Bulk Loading XML Data

If you have XML data in a disk file and would like to load it into an xml data type
column, you can use the BULK rowset provider with the OPENROWSET function and specify
the SINGLE_CLOB option to read the entire file as a single-row, single-varchar(max)
column value.

Let's assume that you have the following XML text saved into a disk file called "c:\PO.xml" on the SQL Server machine:

```
<purchaseOrder orderDate="1999-10-20" xmlns="http://schemas.sams.com/PO">
    <shipTo country="US">
        <name>Alice Smith</name>
        <street>123 Maple Street</street>
        <city>Mill Valley</city>
        <state>CA</state>
        <zip>90952</zip>
    </shipTo>
    <billTo country="US">
        <name>Robert Smith</name>
        <street>8 Oak Avenue</street>
        <city>Old Town</city>
        <state>PA</state>
        <zip>95819</zip>
    </billTo>
    <items>
        <item>
            <productName>Lawnmower</productName>
            <quantity>1</quantity>
            <USPrice>148.95</USPrice>
        </item>
    </items>
</purchaseOrder>
```

The following T-SQL statements illustrate creating a table with an untyped xml data type column and bulk loading the preceding XML file into this column:

```
USE AdventureWorks;
GO
IF OBJECT_ID('dbo.tblBulkLoadXML') IS NOT NULL
    DROP TABLE dbo.tblBulkLoadXML;
GO
CREATE TABLE dbo.tblBulkLoadXML
 (id INT IDENTITY(1,1)  NOT NULL PRIMARY KEY,
  POData XML NOT NULL);
GO
INSERT INTO dbo.tblBulkLoadXML (POData)
    SELECT * FROM
    OPENROWSET(BULK 'c:\PO.xml', SINGLE_CLOB) AS POData;
GO
SELECT * FROM dbo.tblBulkLoadXML;
```

Before we look at other functions to query and modify the xml data type columns and variables, let's first take a look at a quick overview of the XQuery specification.

Introduction to XQuery

If SQL is used to query relational data, XQuery is a language that is used to query data that is either physically stored as XML or virtualized as XML. In addition, XQuery also allows general processing of XML (such as creating nodes). XQuery borrows a lot of features from XPath. XQuery 1.0 is said to be an extension to XPath 2.0, adding support for better iteration, sorting of results, and construction (that is, the ability to construct the shape of the desired XML). In summary, XQuery is an expression-based declarative query language that is used to efficiently extract data from XML documents. In SQL Server 2005, the data stored in xml data type columns and variables can be queried using XQuery. SQL Server 2005 partially implements the W3C XQuery specification (see www.w3.org/TR/xquery) and is aligned with the July 2004 working draft (see www.w3.org/TR/2004/WD-xquery-20040723/).

An XQuery query consists of two parts: the prolog and the query body. The optional prolog section is used to declare the namespaces used in the query, and the required query body consists of an expression that is evaluated by the SQL Server 2005 engine to produce the desired output. Each XQuery prolog entry must end with a semicolon (;).

These are the three most common expression types used in XQuery queries:

- **Path expressions**—Exactly as in XPath, the path expressions are used to locate nodes within an XML tree. The path expression (for example, /purchaseOrder/items/item[5]/text()) may consists of steps (separated by / or //), filter steps, axis steps, predicates, a node test, and a name test.

- **FLWOR expressions**—FLWOR, which stands for "for-let-where-order by-return," is pronounced "flower," and it is the core XQuery expression that allows looping, variable binding, sorting, filtering, and returning of results. SQL Server 2005 does not support the LET construct.

- **Constructors**—As mentioned earlier, in addition to querying XML data, XQuery allows the creating of XML nodes. There are two approaches to creating XML nodes in XQuery. The "direct" approach involves directly writing XML text or using expressions that produce XML inside curly braces ({}). The other approach, called "computed," involves the use of keywords such as element, attribute, document, text, processing-instruction, comment, or namespace to create the respective nodes. SQL Server 2005 supports both approaches.

SQL Server 2005 primarily provides three xml data type methods that can be used to run XQuery queries. These methods are query(), value(), and exist(). The other two xml type methods are nodes(), which is used to shred xml type instance into relational data, much like OPENXML, and the modify() method, which is used to modify the content of an xml type column or a variable.

XML Type Methods

The xml data type supports five methods that you can use to manipulate XML instances; you can call these methods by using xmltype.method() syntax:

- The query() method allows users to run an XQuery expression to obtain a list of XML nodes as an instance of untyped XML.

- The value() method is useful for extracting scalar values from XML documents.

- The exist() method is useful for evaluating XQuery expressions to determine whether the expression results in an empty or nonempty set. This method returns 1 for a nonempty result, 0 for an empty result, and NULL if the XML instance itself is NULL.

- The modify() method is useful for modifying the content of an XML document.

- The nodes() method is useful for decomposing an XML document into relational data.

Let's begin with an example of the query() method:

```
USE AdventureWorks;
GO
SELECT Name, Demographics.query('
    declare namespace d=
  "http://schemas.microsoft.com/sqlserver/2004/07/adventure-works/StoreSurvey";
    d:StoreSurvey/d:AnnualSales')
    AS AnnualSales
FROM Sales.Store;
GO
```

This T-SQL statement illustrates the query() method. The parameter to the query() method is an XQuery query that begins with a namespace declaration in the prolog section and a path expression as the query body. This SELECT statement queries the Demographics xml data type column to find out each store's annual sales. Note that the query() method returns the untyped XML as the result.

You can also declare namespaces by using the WITH XMLNAMESPACES clause, as shown here:

```
WITH XMLNAMESPACES (
  'http://schemas.microsoft.com/sqlserver/2004/07/adventure-works/StoreSurvey'
  AS "d")
```

```
SELECT Name, Demographics.query('d:StoreSurvey/d:AnnualSales') AS AnnualSales
FROM Sales.Store;
GO
```

You can use the `value()` method to get the node data as a scalar value:

```
SELECT Name, Demographics.value('
    declare namespace d=
   (d:StoreSurvey/d:AnnualSales)[1]', 'decimal(18,2)')
    AS AnnualSales
FROM Sales.Store;
GO
```

The `value()` method takes two parameters: an XQuery expression string and a string that indicates the type of returned scalar value (`decimal(18,2)`, in this example). The second parameter cannot be specified as an `xml` data type, a CLR user-defined type, or an `image`, `text`, `ntext`, `timestamp`, or `sql_variant` data type. The XQuery expression must return a singleton or an empty sequence.

The `exist()` method takes just one parameter—the XQuery expression—and returns either 1 (indicating TRUE), 0 (indicating FALSE), or NULL (indicating that the xml data type instance was NULL). This method is generally used in the WHERE clause. Let's say you want to get a list of stores that have T3 internet lines. One of the ways in which you can do this is by running the following query:

```
SELECT * FROM Sales.Store
WHERE Demographics.value('
declare namespace d=
"http://schemas.microsoft.com/sqlserver/2004/07/adventure-works/StoreSurvey";
""
  (/d:StoreSurvey/d:Internet)[1]', 'varchar(20)') = 'T3';
GO
```

However, this is not an efficient approach because SQL Server has to retrieve the node value, do the conversion (Unicode to ANSI, in this case), and then do the comparison. An alternate and better approach is to use the `exist()` method as shown here:

```
SELECT * FROM Sales.Store
WHERE Demographics.exist('
declare namespace d=
  "http://schemas.microsoft.com/sqlserver/2004/07/adventure-works/StoreSurvey";
""
  /d:StoreSurvey[d:Internet = "T3"]') = 1;
GO
```

The `exist()` method exploits the PATH and other XML indexes (discussed later in this chapter) more effectively and can yield better performance than the `value()` method.

Before concluding this section, here are some more examples that show the capabilities of XQuery. The first two queries illustrate the FLWOR expressions, and the next two queries illustrate constructing XML using XQuery:

```
--FLWOR Example 1
SELECT EmployeeID, Resume.query('
   declare namespace
    r="http://schemas.microsoft.com/sqlserver/2004/07/adventure-works/Resume";""
   for $emp in /r:Resume/r:Employment
   order by $emp/r:Emp.OrgName
   return concat(string($emp/r:Emp.OrgName), "~")
') AS PrevEmployers
FROM HumanResources.JobCandidate
WHERE EmployeeID IS NOT NULL


--FLWOR Example 2
SELECT name,
   Instructions.query('
   declare namespace i="http://schemas.microsoft.com/sqlserver/
➡2004/07/adventure-works/ProductModelManuInstructions";
   for $step in //i:step
   where count($step/i:tool) > 0 and count($step/i:material) > 0
   return $step
   ') AS StepWithToolAndMaterialReq
FROM Production.ProductModel
WHERE Instructions IS NOT NULL


--Constructing XML - direct approach
SELECT FirstName, LastName, AdditionalContactInfo.query('
declare namespace a=
"http://schemas.microsoft.com/sqlserver/2004/07/adventure-works/ContactTypes";""

 <PhoneNumbers>
 {
   for $p in //a:number
   return <Number>{string($p)}</Number>
 }
 </PhoneNumbers>
') AS AdditionalPhoneNumbers
FROM Person.Contact
WHERE AdditionalContactInfo IS NOT NULL;


--Constructing XML - computed approach
SELECT FirstName, LastName, AdditionalContactInfo.query('
declare namespace a=
"http://schemas.microsoft.com/sqlserver/2004/07/adventure-works/ContactTypes";""
```

```
 element PhoneNumbers
 {
    for $p in //a:number
    return
     element Number {string($p)}
 }
') AS AdditionalPhoneNumbers
FROM Person.Contact
WHERE AdditionalContactInfo IS NOT NULL;
```

The first query in this batch illustrates the FLWOR expression. The $emp looping variable is bound to the Employment elements under the Resume top-level elements, and for each such element, the XQuery expression sorts and returns the organization names, separated by tilde characters (~). The second FLWOR example, which illustrates the where clause, and returns the steps that have both material and tool nodes. The final two examples show constructing XML directly and by using computed approach.

XQuery in SQL Server 2005 supports various types of functions and operators, including arithmetic, comparison, and logical operators and the string manipulation, data accessors, and aggregate functions. XQuery expressions also support the if-then-else construct that you can use to perform operations based on the value of a conditional expression. The sql:column() and sql:variable() functions can be used inside XQuery expressions to access a non-XML relational column and an external variable.

SQL Profiler includes a trace event called XQuery Static Type under the TSQL event category that you can use to trace XQuery activity. The event provides a method name, including the column on which the method was executed and the static type of the XQuery expression. To use it, you run Profiler, select the XQuery Static Type event, and run the preceding queries. If you do not see the events in Profiler, you can run DBCC FREEPROCCACHE and then run the XQuery queries again.

In summary, XQuery can be used for querying and reshaping the data stored in xml data type columns and variables. Processing XML at the server by using XQuery can result in reduced network traffic, better maintainability, reduced risk, and increased performance.

Indexes on XML Type Columns

Properly designed indexes are the key to improving query performance. At the same time, you need to consider the cost of maintaining indexes in measuring the overall benefits of the indexes created. As mentioned earlier, SQL Server 2005 stores XML data as a BLOB, and every time an XML column is queried, SQL Server parses and shreds the XML BLOB at runtime to evaluate the query. This can be quite an expensive operation, especially if you have large XML data stored in the column or if you have a large number of rows. To improve the performance of queries on xml data type columns, SQL Server 2005 provides two new types of indexes: primary XML indexes and secondary XML indexes. You can create XML indexes on typed or untyped XML columns.

You can create primary XML indexes by using the `CREATE PRIMARY XML INDEX` DDL statement. This type of index is essentially a shredded and persisted representation of XML BLOB data. For each XML BLOB in the column, the primary index creates several rows of data in an internal table. This results in improved performance during query execution time because there is no shredding and parsing involved at runtime. The primary XML index requires a clustered index on the primary key of the base table in which the XML column is defined. If the base table is partitioned, the primary XML index is also partitioned the same way, using the same partitioning function and partitioning scheme. After a primary XML index is created on a table, you cannot change the primary key for that table unless you drop all the XML indexes on that table.

All the primary XML index does is avoid the runtime shredding. After you analyze your workload, you can create secondary XML indexes to further improve the performance of an XML query.

A secondary XML index cannot be created unless you have a primary XML index. There are three types of secondary XML indexes—`PATH`, `VALUE`, and `PROPERTY`—each designed for improving the response time for the respective type of query. You can create secondary XML indexes by using the `CREATE XML INDEX` DDL statement.

If your XML queries make use of path expressions, such as `/Production/Product/Material`, the `PATH` secondary XML index can improve the performance of such queries. In most cases, the `exist()` method on XML columns in a `WHERE` clause benefits the most from the `PATH` indexes. The `PATH` index builds a B+ tree on the path/value pair of each XML node in the document order across all XML instances in the column.

If your XML queries are based on node values and do not necessarily specify the full path or use wildcards in the path (for example, `//Sales[@amount > 10000]` or `//Catalog[@* = "No"]`), the `VALUE` secondary XML index can improve the performance of such queries. The `VALUE` index creates a B+ tree on the value/path pair of each node in the document order across all XML instances in the XML column.

If your XML queries retrieve multiple values from individual XML instances, the `PROPERTY` XML index might benefit from using such queries because it groups the properties for each XML together.

TIP

You can include the word `Primary`, `Path`, `Property`, or `Value` in the name of a primary or secondary XML index that you create to quickly identify the type of XML index.

The following T-SQL batch illustrates creating primary and secondary XML indexes and then using the catalog views and functions to view the XML index details:

```
USE AdventureWorks;
GO
IF OBJECT_ID('dbo.tblIndexDemo') IS NOT NULL
    DROP TABLE dbo.tblIndexDemo;
```

```
GO
CREATE TABLE dbo.tblIndexDemo
  (ID INT IDENTITY(1,1) PRIMARY KEY NOT NULL,
    col1 XML NOT NULL);
GO

CREATE PRIMARY XML INDEX PrimaryXMLIdx_col1
ON dbo.tblIndexDemo(col1);
GO

CREATE XML INDEX PathXMLIdx_col1
ON dbo.tblIndexDemo(col1)
USING XML INDEX PrimaryXMLIdx_col1
FOR PATH;
GO

CREATE XML INDEX PropertyXMLIdx_col1
ON dbo.tblIndexDemo(col1)
USING XML INDEX PrimaryXMLIdx_col1
FOR PROPERTY;
GO

CREATE XML INDEX ValueXMLIdx_col1
ON dbo.tblIndexDemo(col1)
USING XML INDEX PrimaryXMLIdx_col1
FOR VALUE;
GO

--Get Index Information
SELECT * FROM sys.xml_indexes
   WHERE [object_id] = OBJECT_ID('dbo.tblIndexDemo');

--Cleanup
IF OBJECT_ID('dbo.tblIndexDemo') IS NOT NULL
   DROP TABLE dbo.tblIndexDemo;
GO
```

This script creates a table that has a column of xml data type. It then creates a primary
XML index on this column, followed by all three types of secondary indexes on the same
column. You can use the sys.xml_indexes catalog view to view the details on XML
indexes. This catalog view indicates whether an XML index is a primary or secondary
index; if it is secondary, the view indicates what primary index it is based on and what
type (PATH, PROPERTY, or VALUE) of secondary index it is.

SQL Server 2005 allows you to create full-text indexes on xml data type columns. You can combine a full-text search with XML index usage in some scenarios to first use full-text indexes to filter the rows and then use XML indexes on those filtered rows, in order to improve the query response time. However, note that attribute values are not full-text indexed as they are considered part of the markup, which is not full-text indexed.

Modifying XML Data

SQL Server 2005 provides the modify() method, which you can use to change parts of XML content stored in an xml data type column or variable. When you change the xml type table column, the modify() method can only be called within a SET clause in an UPDATE statement; when you change the xml type variable, the modify() method can only be called by using the SET T-SQL statement. The modify() function can be used to insert one or more nodes, to delete nodes, or to update the value of a node. This function takes an XML Data Modification Language (XML DML) expression, which is an extension to the XQuery specification. XQuery 1.0 does not support the update functionality. Hence, SQL Server 2005 introduces an extension to XQuery 1.0 by including three new case-sensitive keywords—"insert", "delete", and "replace value of"—that you can use inside an XQuery query to change parts of the XML data.

The following T-SQL script shows an example of the modify() method and XML DML:

```
DECLARE @xmlVar xml
SET @xmlVar = N'
  <Person>
    <Phone type="h">111-111-1111</Phone>
    <Phone type="c">222-222-2222</Phone>
  </Person>
';
SELECT @xmlVar;

--insert
SET @xmlVar.modify(
  'insert <Phone type="w">333-333-3333</Phone>
   into (/Person)[1]');

--delete
SET @xmlVar.modify(
  'delete /Person/Phone[@type="c"]');

--change node value
SET @xmlVar.modify(
  'replace value of (/Person/Phone[@type="h"]/text())[1]
   with "444-444-4444"');
```

```
SELECT @xmlVar;
GO
```

At the end, the @xmlVar XML variable has the following value:

```
<Person>
  <Phone type="h">444-444-4444</Phone>
  <Phone type="w">333-333-3333</Phone>
</Person>
```

FOR XML Enhancements

The native XML support in SQL Server 2000 was introduced by providing the FOR XML clause and the OPENXML function. The FOR XML clause can be used in a SELECT statement to convert a relational rowset into an XML stream. On the other hand, the OPENXML function does the reverse: It provides the rowset view over an XML document. SQL Server 2005 enhances these two constructs to fix some of the limitations from previous releases and also to add support for the new xml data type.

The following FOR XML clause enhancements have been introduced in SQL Server 2005:

- The new TYPE modifier can be used to generate an instance of an xml data type that can be assigned to a variable or can be directly used in a query. The following query uses the TYPE modifier with a FOR XML clause and saves the generated XML fragment in an xml data type variable, on which the XQuery query is executed later on:

```
USE AdventureWorks;
GO
DECLARE @Contacts xml
SET @Contacts =
  (SELECT TOP 10 FirstName, MiddleName, LastName, EmailAddress, Phone
   FROM Person.Contact ORDER BY LastName
   FOR XML AUTO, TYPE);

SELECT @Contacts.query('
<Contacts>
{
 for $c in /Person.Contact
 return
   <Contact>
     <Name>{data($c/@LastName)}{data(" ")}{data($c/@FirstName)}
     </Name>
     <Phone>{data($c/@Phone)}</Phone>
     <Email>{data($c/@EmailAddress)}</Email>
   </Contact>
}
```

```
</Contacts>
');
GO
```

- The FOR XML queries can now be nested. It is important to use the TYPE directive with the internal query; otherwise, the XML generated by the internal query will be entitized (that is, < will be replaced with < and so on). Many complex queries that were written using FOR XML EXPLICIT can now be replaced with nested FOR XML queries, which are simple to write and manage. Here is an example of nesting the FOR XML clause:

```
SELECT SalesOrderNumber, PurchaseOrderNumber,
  (SELECT AddressLine1, AddressLine2, City, PostalCode
   FROM Person.Address
   WHERE AddressID =
     (SELECT AddressID FROM Sales.CustomerAddress
      WHERE CustomerID = s.CustomerID AND AddressTypeID = 3)
   FOR XML AUTO, ELEMENTS, TYPE
   )
FROM Sales.SalesOrderHeader s
WHERE PurchaseOrderNumber IS NOT NULL
FOR XML AUTO
```

- The FOR XML clause in SQL Server 2000 could only generate XML Data Reduced (XDR) schemas. (XDR is Microsoft's proprietary XML schema format.) The new XMLSCHEMA directive in SQL Server 2005 allows you to generate inline XSD schemas, which are based on the W3C standard. The optional input to the XMLSCHEMA directive is the target namespace URI, as in the following example:

```
SELECT * FROM HumanResources.Department
FOR XML AUTO, XMLSCHEMA('urn:test.com');
```

  The default namespace URL is auto-generated in a format such as urn:schemas-microsoft-com:sql:SqlRowSet1.

- The new ROOT directive allows you to generate a well-formed XML document with a single root element. The optional input to the ROOT directive is the name of the topmost element. By default, the top-level element is called root when the ROOT directive is specified:

```
SELECT * FROM HumanResources.Department
FOR XML AUTO, ROOT('Departments');
```

- The RAW mode now supports the ELEMENTS directive so that the generated XML stream contains elements instead of attributes for columns. The first SELECT statement is without the ELEMENTS clause, and the next one uses the ELEMENTS clause with FOR XML RAW. In addition, you can now pass the name of an element that is generated for each record, instead of the default element, called row. Try the following two SELECT statements to see the RAW mode enhancements:

```
SELECT * FROM HumanResources.Department
FOR XML RAW, ROOT('Departments');

SELECT * FROM HumanResources.Department
FOR XML RAW('Department'), ELEMENTS, ROOT('Departments');
```

- In SQL Server 2000, the EXPLICIT mode provided the most control over the structure of the XML document generated. However, it is not easy to write queries by using the EXPLICIT mode. SQL Server 2005 simplifies this by providing a new mode called PATH that allows you to use XPath and specify where and how in the hierarchy the column should appear. The PATH mode provides a simpler way to mix elements and attributes and control the hierarchy of generated XML. An optional argument with the PATH mode is the element name for each record. By default, it is called row. Here is an example of the PATH mode:

```
SELECT
    DepartmentID "@id",
    ModifiedDate "@updated",
    Name        "Name",
    GroupName   "Group"
FROM HumanResources.Department
FOR XML PATH ('Department'), ROOT('Departments');
```

- The ELEMENTS directive now provides an XSINIL option to map NULL values to an element with an attribute of xsi:nil="true" instead of completely omitting the element. If you execute the following batch in SQL Server 2000, you notice that for first row, the col2 element is completely missing:

```
USE [tempdb];
GO

CREATE TABLE tblTest
 (col1 INT IDENTITY(1,1) NOT NULL,
   col2 VARCHAR(20) NULL);
GO

INSERT INTO tblTest DEFAULT VALUES;
INSERT INTO tblTest (col2) VALUES ('Value2');
GO

SELECT * FROM tblTest FOR XML AUTO, ELEMENTS;
GO
```

```
--SELECT * FROM tblTest FOR XML AUTO, ELEMENTS XSINIL;
GO

DROP TABLE tblTest;
GO
```

If you execute the script in SQL Server 2005, you notice the same thing. If you uncomment the statement containing the XSINIL option and run it in SQL Server 2005, you notice that for col2 having the NULL value, an element is generated with an xsi:nil="true" attribute.

Native XML Web Services Support

After SQL Server 2000 shipped, Microsoft released SQLXML web releases to update and enhance the XML support in SQL Server 2000. SQLXML release 3.0 introduced support for SOAP web services, allowing stored procedure and user-defined functions to be invoked over HTTP as web service methods. The similar XML web services support is now built into SQL Server 2005.

SQLXML provided the web services support via an Internet Services API (ISAPI) DLL running under Microsoft's IIS web server. The fact that the ability to expose stored procedures and functions as web service methods is natively built into SQL Server 2005 eliminates the dependency on IIS and also means there is no need to install SQLXML to use the web services functionality. Shortly you'll learn about the native HTTP SOAP support introduced in SQL Server 2005. But first, here is a quick introduction to SOAP, web services, and WSDL.

> **NOTE**
>
> Native HTTP SOAP support is not a complete replacement for SQLXML—only for the web services support. SQLXML contains a lot more functionality, including support for URL queries, templates, updategrams, and bulk loading, which is available only via SQLXML.

Introduction to SOAP, Web Services, and WSDL

XML web services is a technology based on HTTP, SOAP, and XML that allows one application on one platform to invoke a method in another application, possibly running on a totally different platform, over the Internet.

The most common application of web services is application-to-application integration over the Internet. The client application posts an XML package, called a SOAP request envelope, over HTTP to a web server where the web service is located. On the server side, the web service method is invoked, and it returns another XML package, called a SOAP response envelope, which is received and parsed by the client to see the method execution results. In case of an error, the web service method returns a SOAP fault message.

Web services are platform and language independent. This means you can develop web services by using any programming language, deploy them on any platform, and then invoke a web API from any platform, using any programming language. As long as the client can generate and post SOAP request XML text, the server can parse the posted XML and reply back with the SOAP response XML text. Finally, the client can parse and process that response XML. This is all you need in order to implement and utilize XML web services.

Web Services Building Blocks

The four primary building blocks of today's XML web services are XML, SOAP, HTTP, and WSDL.

XML is the key to application interoperability and cross-platform integration. Its flexibility (XML defines the syntax, and it is a meta-language that can be used to create other languages), extensibility (XML does not have a fixed set of tags), and portability (XML is text) makes XML a perfect choice for sending and receiving messages over the Internet. Web services use XML as the marshaling format.

The W3C created the SOAP standard, which defines the format of messages sent to implement web services. SOAP was originally an acronym for Simple Object Access Protocol, but now this messaging format specification is no longer an acronym but is simply called SOAP. SOAP uses XML syntax to define the request and response payloads. In other words, the SOAP specification defines how the request and response XML payloads should look, how the web service should report errors, how to send additional information via SOAP headers, and so on. Standardizing on the web services request and response payloads enables you to write web services by using technology from one vendor and consume web services by using technology from a different vendor.

Here is what the SOAP request payload, including the SOAP-specific HTTP headers and the request envelope, looks like:

```
POST /StockQuote HTTP/1.1
Host: www.stockquoteserver.com
Content-Type: text/xml; charset="utf-8"
Content-Length: nnnn
SOAPAction: "Some-URI"

<SOAP-ENV:Envelope
  xmlns:SOAP-ENV="http://schemas.xmlsoap.org/soap/envelope/"
  SOAP-ENV:encodingStyle="http://schemas.xmlsoap.org/soap/encoding/">
  <SOAP-ENV:Body>
      <m:GetLastTradePrice xmlns:m="Some-URI">
          <symbol>DIS</symbol>
      </m:GetLastTradePrice>
  </SOAP-ENV:Body>
</SOAP-ENV:Envelope>
```

And here is what the SOAP response payload, including the SOAP-specific HTTP headers and the response envelope, looks like:

```
HTTP/1.1 200 OK
Content-Type: text/xml; charset="utf-8"
Content-Length: nnnn

<SOAP-ENV:Envelope
  xmlns:SOAP-ENV="http://schemas.xmlsoap.org/soap/envelope/"
  SOAP-ENV:encodingStyle="http://schemas.xmlsoap.org/soap/encoding/"/>
   <SOAP-ENV:Body>
       <m:GetLastTradePriceResponse xmlns:m="Some-URI">
           <Price>34.5</Price>
       </m:GetLastTradePriceResponse>
   </SOAP-ENV:Body>
</SOAP-ENV:Envelope>
```

The SOAP request and response can be sent over any protocol (HTTP, SMTP, and so on). As an analogy, if you have a package that you want to send somewhere, you can ship it by using FedEx, UPS, USPS, or another carrier. The most commonly used transport protocol for today's web services, and the only one supported by SQL Server 2005, is HTTP. The native web services support in SQL Server 2005 is available on only two platforms: Windows Server 2003 and Windows XP SP2. This is because only on these two platforms is the HTTP stack part of the operating system kernel, which is used by SQL Server 2005 to provide HTTP SOAP support without requiring IIS. As a matter of fact, having the HTTP stack (http.sys) in the operating system kernel allows faster execution of HTTP requests. Hence, the native HTTP SOAP support in SQL Server 2005 performs better than ISAPI and IIS-based SQLXML. Prior to HTTP SOAP support in SQL Server 2005, the only network protocol that could be used to access SQL Server was Tabular Data Stream (TDS). The HTTP SOAP support now enables HTTP as an alternate protocol over which SQL Server can be accessed from any platform, without installation of any client or SQL Server network library components. For instance, you can now access SQL Server 2005 over HTTP from a Perl client running on a Unix machine or a C++ or .NET application running on a Pocket PC or smart phone, without requiring any client components such as MDAC.

The fourth and final primary building block for web services is Web Services Description Language (WSDL). WSDL, like SOAP and XML, is a specification defined by the W3C (see www.w3.org/TR/wsdl). WSDL is essentially an XML-based format that describes the complete set of interfaces exposed by a web service. WSDL defines the set of operations and messages that can be sent to and received from a given web service. A WSDL document serves as a contract between web services consumers and the server. A WSDL document describes what functionality a web service offers, how it communicates, and where to find it. In summary, WSDL provides the information necessary for a client to interact with a web service. SQL Server 2005 can dynamically auto-generate the WSDL, or you can write a stored procedure that spits out a custom WSDL document, or you can disable availability of a WSDL document for a web service created by using native HTTP SOAP support.

Creating HTTP Endpoints

To have SQL Server listen on HTTP for SOAP requests, the first step is to create an HTTP endpoint by using the CREATE ENDPOINT T-SQL statement. The CREATE ENDPOINT statement allows you to create a new web service and, optionally, to define the methods that the endpoint exposes. The ALTER ENDPOINT statement can be used to change the web service settings and to add or remove web methods.

When you create an HTTP endpoint, you have to provide a unique URL, which may include a port number, that SQL Server uses to listen for incoming SOAP requests. When requests are submitted to this URL, the http.sys kernel HTTP stack routes the posted message to the SQL Server endpoint associated with the URL. SQL Server then executes the stored procedure or function, depending on the web method referred in the posted SOAP request envelope, serializes the stored procedure or function results as XML, and replies with the SOAP response envelope.

Although not recommended for security reasons, SQL Server 2005 does allow you to execute ad hoc T-SQL batches over HTTP. You can use the BATCHES=ENABLED option with the CREATE ENDPOINT statement to enable execution of ad hoc T-SQL batches on the endpoint. When this option is enabled, the web service adds a method called sqlbatch in the sql namespace, which clients can invoke to execute ad hoc batches.

CREATE ENDPOINT is a generic statement that is used to create HTTP SOAP endpoints, or to create a TCP-based endpoint to accept T-SQL requests, or to create an endpoint for service broker or database mirroring functionality. With this statement, you provide the name of the endpoint, the authorization details, and a collection of other options, depending on the type of endpoint being created.

__NOTE__

The CREATE ENDPOINT statement cannot be executed within the scope of a user transaction. That is, if you have started a transaction by using the BEGIN TRANSACTION statement, you cannot execute CREATE ENDPOINT in that session unless you commit or roll back the transaction.

The following is an example of using a CREATE ENDPOINT statement to create an HTTP SOAP web service that exposes the following stored procedure as a web service method:

```
USE AdventureWorks;
GO


IF OBJECT_ID('dbo.GetEmployees') IS NOT NULL
    DROP PROCEDURE dbo.GetEmployees;
```

```
GO

CREATE PROCEDURE dbo.GetEmployees
AS
BEGIN
    SELECT c.FirstName, c.LastName, c.EmailAddress, c.Phone,
            e.NationalIDNumber, e.LoginID, e.Title, e.BirthDate,
            e.MaritalStatus, e.Gender, e.HireDate
    FROM HumanResources.Employee e JOIN Person.Contact c
    ON e.ContactID = c.ContactID;
END;
```

Let's now use the CREATE ENDPOINT statement to expose the preceding stored procedure as a web service method that can be invoked over HTTP to get a list of employees in the AdventureWorks sample database:

```
IF EXISTS (SELECT endpoint_id FROM sys.endpoints WHERE name = 'AWEmployees')
    DROP ENDPOINT AWEmployees;
GO

CREATE ENDPOINT AWEmployees
    STATE = STARTED
    AS HTTP
        ( AUTHENTICATION = (INTEGRATED),
          PATH = '/SQLWebSvcs/AW',
          PORTS = (CLEAR)
        )
    FOR SOAP
        ( WEBMETHOD 'GetEmployees'
          ( NAME = 'AdventureWorks.dbo.GetEmployees'),
          WSDL = DEFAULT,
          DATABASE = 'AdventureWorks'
        );
GO
```

This batch first uses the sys.endpoints catalog view to check whether the endpoint named AWEmployees already exists. If it does, the batch drops the endpoint by using the DROP ENDPOINT DDL statement. Next, the CREATE ENDPOINT statement defines an HTTP endpoint and a web method that maps to the GetEmployees stored procedure created earlier.

CAUTION

If you are executing the preceding T-SQL statements on Windows XP SP2 and have IIS running, you might get error 0x80070020 and have CREATE ENDPOINT fail. In this case, either you can stop IIS or use a different port to create the HTTP SOAP endpoint. If you have an HTTP SOAP endpoint on port 80 (that is, with PORTS = (CLEAR)), and if IIS is also listening on the same port, starting IIS fails. You have to either drop the HTTP SOAP endpoint or use a different port for the endpoint. Note that this problem does not occur on Windows Server 2003 because IIS 6.0 on that platform is `http.sys` based, whereas IIS 5.1 on Windows XP SP2 is not `http.sys` based.

The web service is available at `http://localhost/SQLWebSvcs/AW`. After you successfully create the HTTP SOAP endpoint by using the preceding statement, you can start Internet Explorer and type `http://localhost/SQLWebSvcs/AW?wsdl` in the address bar. Internet Explorer should return an XML document, the WSDL for the web service, and it should contain one web method called `GetEmployees`. To consume this web service, you can try using Visual Studio .NET to add a web reference to `http://localhost/SQLWebSvcs/AW?wsdl`, which creates the proxy class for the web service, which you can use to invoke web service methods. The code download for this book includes a C# client application that uses the web service created in this section.

Administering HTTP SOAP Endpoints

Following the "secure by default" principle, SQL Server 2005 does not include any HTTP SOAP endpoint out of the box. Members of the `sysadmin` role and the users who have `CREATE ENDPOINT` permissions can create HTTP SOAP endpoints. The endpoints are stopped by default, and the `STATE = STARTED` options can be used with `CREATE ENDPOINT` or `ALTER ENDPOINT` to start HTTP SOAP access.

SQL Server 2005 includes Secure Sockets Layer (SSL) support to accept incoming requests and send responses on a secure (`https://`) channel.

To control access to the endpoint, the `AUTHENTICATION` option can have one or more of five values: `BASIC`, `DIGEST`, `INTEGRATED`, `NTLM`, or `KERBEROS`. `BASIC` authentication mode requires SSL and consists of an authentication header containing the Base 64–encoded username and password, separated by a colon. In `DIGEST` authentication mode, the username and password are hashed using a one-way hashing algorithm (MD5) before the request is sent to the server. The server has access to either the raw password or a stored MD5 hash created at the time the password was set. It can then compare the stored calculated value to the one provided by the client. This way, the client can prove that it knows the password without actually giving it to the server. In `INTEGRATED` authentication mode, the server first tries to authenticate by using Kerberos, and if it is not supported by the client, or if negotiation is not possible, authentication falls back to NTLM. NTLM is the authentication mechanism supported by Windows 95, Windows 98, and Windows NT 4.0 (client and server). This authentication mechanism is a challenge-response protocol that offers stronger authentication than either basic or digest. NTLM is implemented in Windows 2000 and later versions by a Security Support Provider Interface (SSPI). Kerberos authentication is an Internet standard authentication mechanism. Kerberos authentication is supported in Windows 2000 and later versions by an SSPI. After a user is authorized, the user can be routed to a specific database by using the `DATABASE=` parameter in the `CREATE ENDPOINT` statement.

An endpoint is a server-level securable. The owner of an endpoint or a sysadmin role member can use GRANT, REVOKE, or DENY for the ALTER, EXECUTE, CONNECT, TAKE OWNERSHIP, and VIEW DEFINITION endpoint permissions regarding a specified principal.

Table 10.1 lists the four catalog views that you can access to view HTTP SOAP endpoint metadata.

TABLE 10.1   HTTP SOAP-Specific Catalog Views

Catalog View	Description
sys.endpoints	This table contains one row per endpoint. The protocol and protocol_desc columns indicate what type (TCP, VIA, HTTP, and so on) of endpoint it is, and the state column indicates whether the endpoint is started, stopped, or disabled. The principal_id column indicates the endpoint owner.
sys.http_endpoints	This catalog view lists the endpoints that use HTTP. In includes columns to show the site, URL, port, authentication method, and compression setting.
sys.soap_endpoints	This catalog view contains one row for each endpoint in the server that is defined to carry a SOAP-type payload. It shows the name of the stored procedure used to generate the WSDL document, the default namespace, the default database for the endpoint, and other settings, such as the session timeout.
sys.endpoint_webmethods	This catalog view contains a row-per-SOAP-method defined on a SOAP-enabled HTTP endpoint. It lists the web method name, the object (stored procedure or function) that the web method maps to, and the result format.

SQL Server:General Statistics (or MSSQL$InstanceName:General Statistics, for a named SQL Server 2005 instance) contains several Performance Monitor counters that you can use to monitor things such as HTTP authenticated requests, SOAP batch SQL requests, SOAP method invocations, SOAP WSDL requests, failed SOAP requests, execution of SOAP requests, and successful SOAP requests.

Summary

This chapter presents the new XML and web services support introduced in SQL Server 2005. The new xml data type allows you to save XML documents and fragments into a relational database. This gives you a consistent way to save structured and unstructured data inside a relational database.

You can associate XSD schemas with an XML type column or variable to yield typed XML. For a typed XML column or variable, SQL Server makes sure that the XML content validates with the structure and type defined in the associated XSD document from the schema collection.

SQL Server 2005 partially implements the XQuery W3C specification to allow querying of XML data. You can create indexes based on XML type to improve the query response time. The XML DML extension to the XQuery specification allows you to update parts of XML data.

This chapter also presents an overview of improvements made to the FOR XML clause from SQL Server 2000.

The final section in this chapter introduces the concept of SOAP and web services and then shows how SQL Server 2005 natively supports mapping of stored procedures and functions to web service methods.

Chapter 11 presents details on another big developer productivity feature introduced in SQL Server 2005—.NET integration with the SQL Server 2005 engine.

SQL Server 2005 and .NET Integration

On June 22, 2000, Microsoft announced a new development platform named ".NET" (pronounced "dot-net") at the Forum 2000 conference in Redmond, Washington. The .NET platform vision was then shared with around 6,500 developers at the eighth Microsoft Professional Developer Conference (PDC) in Orlando, Florida, in July 2000. Bill Gates addressed the developers by saying, "The transition to .NET is as dramatic a transition as the move from MS-DOS to Windows." Announcements about a new programming language, C# (pronounced "c-sharp"); a new development toolkit, Visual Studio .NET; and several other features of the .NET Framework were made around the same time. Since then, Microsoft .NET has become the premier platform for building Windows, web-based, and mobile applications. For the past five years, developers have leveraged the Visual Studio .NET toolkit and the object-oriented classes provided by the .NET Framework library to build Windows Forms applications, ASP.NET web applications, mobile applications, and XML web services. As a matter of fact, almost all GUI tools provided with SQL Server 2005 are built using the Microsoft .NET Framework.

The .NET Framework is now integrated with the SQL Server 2005 database engine, allowing developers to write stored procedures, functions, triggers, user-defined aggregates, and user-defined types by using .NET languages such as C# and Visual Basic .NET. This chapter explores the .NET integration feature in detail from a database administrator's perspective. In this chapter you will learn about the benefits and challenges of allowing .NET code to run inside SQL Server 2005. Two examples in the final section of this chapter illustrate how to write stored procedure and functions using C#.

Let's begin with an overview of the .NET Framework and the common language runtime (CLR). If you are not familiar with .NET, then carefully read the following pages in order to better understand the integration of the .NET Framework with SQL Server 2005.

What Is the .NET Framework?

Introduced in June 2000, the Microsoft .NET Framework is the next-generation, revolutionary development platform for building Windows, web, and mobile applications.

Prior to the introduction of the .NET platform, developers used programming languages such as C++ and Visual Basic to build Windows applications using the non-object-oriented Win32 API and object-oriented APIs such as the Microsoft Foundation Class (MFC) library. Web applications were built using Active Server Pages (ASP) in the VBScript and JScript programming languages. There was not good support for building XML web services or mobile applications. The Component Object Model (COM) was used as a cross-language component-based development platform. This generation of developer technologies combined with the limited cross-language development and debugging facility restricted developers' productivity. Microsoft .NET changes this by introducing the next generation of tools, infrastructure, and technologies to significantly improve developers' productivity.

Here are some of the benefits offered by the .NET Framework:

- **Cross-language development and language interoperability**—Regardless of what .NET language you use to write the code, the compiler generates Microsoft Intermediate Language (MSIL) at the compile time. The MSIL instructions are then compiled to native platform language code at execution time. While building .NET solutions, you can write code using your choice of language, such as VB .NET, inherit from or make use of classes written by some other developer, possibly in a different .NET language, such as C#, and still be able to debug across languages by using Visual Studio .NET. The Common Type System (CTS) and Common Language Specification (CLS) defined by the .NET Framework facilitate cross-language development and debugging.

- **.NET Framework base class library**—The .NET Framework comes with a unified object-oriented class library that provides the functionality earlier provided by the Win32 API and more. This extensive library provides consistent and very easy-to-use classes for data access, XML processing, graphical device interface (GDI), I/O, security and cryptography, network programming, serialization, distributed applications, web applications and web services, collections, and more.

- **Garbage collection**—As discussed in the next section, the CLR takes care of de-allocating objects, freeing memory, and hence avoiding the memory leaks common in C/C++ programming. CLR tracks the code's use of objects and ensures that objects are not freed while still in use and that objects are freed when no longer in use. Memory management is one of the primary benefits of the CLR's managed execution mode, which greatly simplifies the writing of .NET code because the developer does not have to worry about releasing the memory. The garbage collection algorithm intelligently frees objects and manages the memory.

- **Code access security and type verification**—Based on the security policies or permissions defined at the enterprise level, machine level, and user level, the same .NET code can or cannot perform an action, depending on the origin or identity of the code. For instance, a .NET assembly executed from a local drive can perform a particular action, but the same assembly if downloaded and executed from a network or an Internet location cannot perform the same action. During the MSIL-to-native code compilation at runtime, the .NET Framework can verify the code to ensure that it is accessing the types in a safe manner (that is, the objects are used the way they were intended to be used, preventing an object's state from being corrupted). Type safety ensures that memory structures are accessed only in well-defined ways. Code access security and type verification are two important features that aid in building secure and reliable applications.

- **Self-describing assemblies**—Assemblies in the .NET Framework are .dll and .exe files that are the fundamental unit for packaging, deployment, and versioning. Assemblies are also important in .NET with respect to security because many of the security restrictions are enforced at the assembly boundary. In addition to MSIL code, every .NET assembly contains metadata, which is information that describes the assembly. This includes version, culture, and public key information; referenced assemblies; information about classes and class members and their visibility; and so on. By looking at assembly metadata, the CLR knows exactly what other assemblies are required by the assembly. An assembly may consist of multiple files, including resource files for internationalization.

- **Interoperability with Win32 and COM code**—Microsoft realized that it is critical to allow the calling of classic Win32 or COM objects from within .NET. Although not recommended, it is possible to call a Win32 API from within .NET managed code by using a technique known as PInvoke and to call a COM object from within .NET managed code by using a technique known as COM Interop.

- **Object-oriented programming**—A .NET assembly consists of one or more classes or *types*. Every type in the .NET Framework is directly or indirectly derived from the Object class in the System namespace. A .NET Framework application can implement object-oriented programming features such as encapsulation, inheritance, and polymorphism.

The .NET Framework bundles everything you need to build and execute .NET applications. It includes the Framework Class Library, CLR, and language compilers, such as the C# compiler (csc.exe) and the VB .NET compiler (vbc.exe), which you can use to turn your source code into an assembly that contains MSIL instructions, metadata, and resources. Visual Studio .NET is an integrated development environment (IDE) for building and debugging .NET applications. The .NET Framework is free and is already installed with operating systems such as Windows XP SP2 and Windows Server 2003. However, Visual Studio .NET is a commercial development tool that must be purchased. The next version of this tool, Visual Studio .NET 2005, codenamed "Whidbey," includes the templates that allow you to create SQL Server 2005 stored procedures, functions, aggregates, triggers, and types, using managed languages such as C# and VB .NET.

Let's now look at the CLR in a little more detail.

What Is the CLR?

At the heart of the .NET Framework is the execution environment called the CLR. The CLR provides several important services to the hosting application. It is responsible for memory management, object lifetime management, thread management, type safety, security, and I/O management. Any code running under the CLR execution environment is termed *managed code*. If you call a Win32 function or a COM object from within .NET code, it is referred to as *unmanaged code* because the CLR does not control Win32 API or COM object code.

The CLR architecture allows it to be *hosted* by another program. A process can load (that is, host) the .NET runtime and use it to run code in a managed environment. Internet Explorer, ASP.NET, and SQL Server 2005 are examples of processes that host the CLR. The CLR hosting facility offers several options that the host can provide to control the behavior of CLR functions, such as garbage collection and assembly loading. The CLR 2.0 hosting facility has undergone a major overhaul to support the security, stability, reliability, and performance requirements of the SQL Server 2005 host. This is discussed in the following section.

.NET Framework Integration

With SQL Server 2000, Transact-SQL (T-SQL) was the primary language that database administrators and developers used to interact with SQL Server. Stored procedure, triggers, user-defined functions, batches, and so on are written using the T-SQL language. If something was not possible using T-SQL, developers had an option of writing an extended stored procedure by using C++ and the Open Data Services (ODS) API. However, writing extended stored procedure is not a trivial task. On top of that, because an extended stored procedure ran directly in SQL Server 2000 process space, it could possibly compromise the reliability and stability of the server. Memory leaks were other common problems with extended stored procedures, including those from Microsoft (for example, see Microsoft Knowledge Base articles 300414 and 164523).

T-SQL is still the primary language that database administrators and developers use to interact with SQL Server 2005. However, this release now provides a simpler, secure, reliable, and efficient way of extending the T-SQL language. The .NET integration with SQL Server 2005 allows developers to write stored procedures, functions, triggers, aggregates, and types, using any of the .NET languages, such as C# or Visual Basic .NET. As explained earlier, the .NET code is executed under the CLR execution environment. Therefore, in order to allow stored procedures, functions, and triggers written using .NET to run from within the database engine, SQL Server 2005 hosts the CLR, which in turn runs the managed code.

Extending the T-SQL Language

Developers can use any .NET programming language, such as Visual Basic .NET or C#, and any SQL Server project template in Visual Studio .NET 2005 to create a CLR assembly that contains methods decorated to be mapped to stored procedures, functions, or triggers.

This assembly is then imported into a SQL Server 2005 database by using the CREATE ASSEMBLY DDL statement. CREATE ASSEMBLY permission defaults to members of the sysadmin fixed server role and the db_owner and db_ddladmin fixed database roles, as well as to users with CREATE ASSEMBLY permission. The Windows login of the user executing CREATE ASSEMBLY must have read permission on the share and the files being loaded in the statement.

NOTE
_____

The current release does not support assembly encryption or obfuscation.

After the assembly is imported into the database, the assembly .dll file on the disk is no longer required. It is recommended that you import into the database the source code and other files required for the assembly by using the ALTER ASSEMBLY...ADD FILE statement. While creating the assembly using the CREATE ASSEMBLY statement or re-importing the assembly using the ALTER ASSEMBLY statement, you can specify what an assembly can and cannot do. For example, you can use the WITH PERMISSION_SET clause with the CREATE or ALTER ASSEMBLY statement to put the assembly in one of following three permission buckets:

- **SAFE**—This is the most restrictive, recommended, and default permission set. It allows an assembly to perform internal computations and data access—and nothing else.

- **EXTERNAL_ACCESS**—This is the next level after SAFE, and it adds the ability to access external resources, such as files. Members of the sysadmin server role and principals who have login-level EXTERNAL_ACCESS permission can put assemblies in the EXTERNAL_ACCESS permission bucket.

- **UNSAFE**—The UNSAFE permission set allows assemblies unrestricted access to resources, both within and outside SQL Server. Assemblies can even call unmanaged code. Assemblies should be put in the UNSAFE permission bucket only after thorough consideration and analysis. Only the sysadmin role members can import assemblies with this permission set.

When the assembly bits are available in the database, you can create a stored procedure or a function or a trigger and use the AS EXTERNAL NAME clause with the CREATE PROCEDURE, FUNCTION, or TRIGGER DDL statement and specify the assembly name, class name, and method name to which the module maps. After the stored procedure, function, or trigger is created, it can be invoked like any other T-SQL module.

When you call a managed stored procedure, function, or trigger, SQL Server 2005 first checks whether clr enabled systemwide configuration is enabled. If it is disabled, you see an error message similar to the following:

```
Msg 6263, Level 16, State 1, Line 3
Execution of user code in the .NET Framework is disabled.
Use sp_configure "clr enabled" to enable execution of user code in the
.NET Framework.
```

clr enabled is an advanced option, and you need to enable the show advanced options option and then run RECONFIGURE to see the clr enabled option. After you change the clr enabled option, you must run RECONFIGURE to activate the option. If the clr enabled option is enabled, SQL Server checks whether the assembly containing the mapped method is already loaded in memory. If it is not, the assembly is loaded from the bits imported in the database, and the method is invoked. The .NET CLR code access security integrated with the SQL Server authentication- and authorization-based security model ensures that the method can perform only the operations for which it is granted permissions.

You can drop an assembly from the database by using the DROP ASSEMBLY statement. You cannot drop an assembly unless all the objects (stored procedures, functions, triggers, types, and aggregates) that depend on the assembly are dropped and all the other assemblies that reference this assembly are dropped.

You can use the ALTER ASSEMBLY statement to modify the properties of an assembly, to refresh it to the latest or current version, or to add or remove files associated with the assembly. ALTER ASSEMBLY and DROP ASSEMBLY permissions default to the assembly owners and members of the sysadmin fixed server role and the db_ddladmin and db_owner fixed database roles. These permissions are not transferable.

The Programmability folder under the database in the Object Explorer tree in Management Studio lists the assemblies and modules such as procedures and functions. You can right-click an assembly and select View Dependencies to see objects that depend on the selected assembly and objects on which the selected assembly depends. The Object Dependencies dialog is shown in Figure 11.1.

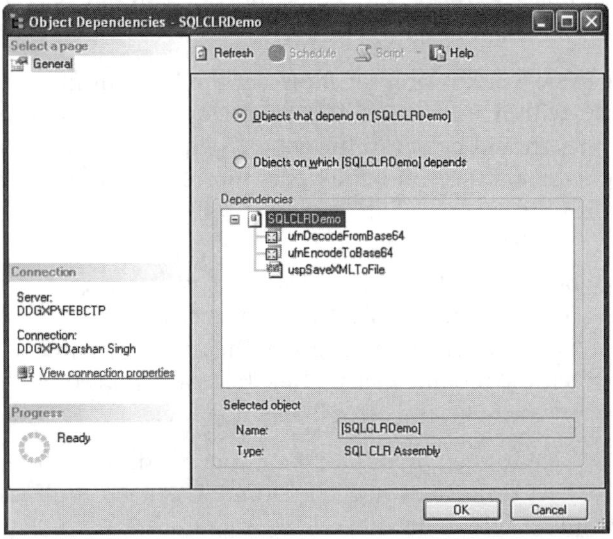

FIGURE 11.1   SQL Server Management Studio allows you to view objects that depend on an imported assembly and objects on which the assembly depends.

Similarly, you can right-click an object, such as a stored procedure or a function, and select View Dependencies to see the assemblies and other objects on which the selected object depends.

SQLCLR Design Goals

CLR hosting in SQL Server 2005 is architected to meet the following design goals:

- **Security**—The .NET code running inside SQL Server must follow authentication and authorization rules when accessing database objects such as tables and columns. In addition, database administrators should be able to control access to operating system resources such as files and the network from the .NET code running in the database. Database administrators should be able to enable or disable running .NET code from the database engine.

- **Reliability**—The .NET code running inside SQL Server should not be allowed to perform operations that compromise data integrity and transactional correctness. It should not be allowed to perform operations such as popping up a message box requesting a user response, exiting the process, overwriting DBMS memory buffers or internal data structures, causing stack overflow, and so on.

- **Performance and scalability**—The .NET code running inside SQL Server must perform as well as or better than an equivalent implementation through T-SQL. The .NET code should be restricted from calling APIs for threading, memory, and synchronization primitives to ensure the scalability of the system.

Meeting the above design goals was not easy because SQL Server 2005 and the CLR have different internal models for security, memory management, thread scheduling, and management schemes. To make SQL Server and the CLR work together, while achieving these design goals, the hosting API in .NET Framework 2.0 is enhanced to enable the runtime host, such as SQL Server 2005, to either control or make recommendation on how the resource should be managed.

SQL Server 2005 as a host has control over memory. It can reject the CLR memory request and ask the CLR to reduce its memory use if required. The .NET runtime calls SQL Server for allocating and de-allocating the memory. Because the memory used by the CLR is accounted for in the total memory usage of the system, SQL Server can stay within its configured memory limits and ensure that the CLR and SQL Server are not competing against each other for memory.

As explained in detail in Chapter 2, "SQL Server 2005 Database Engine Architectural Changes," to minimize context switching, SQL Server uses cooperative thread scheduling, where a thread must voluntarily give up control of the processor. On the other hand, the CLR supports the preemptive threading model, where the processor takes control back from the thread when the time slice is over. To ensure stability, the CLR calls SQL Server APIs for creating threads, both for running user code and for its own internal use. In order to synchronize between multiple threads, the CLR calls SQL Server synchronization objects. This allows the SQL Server scheduler to schedule other tasks when a thread is waiting on a synchronization object.

The CLR defines the notion of application domain (*appdomain*), which can be thought of as a lightweight process. Unlike Win32 processes, which are isolated by having different memory address spaces, the isolation in appdomains is achieved by .NET keeping control over the use of memory. The .NET CLR ensures that appdomains do not access each other's memory. One Win32 process may include multiple CLR appdomains. SQLCLR leverages the notion of appdomains to make the SQLCLR integration reliable when running inside a SQL Server host. Programmers and database administrators do not have control over when and how appdomains are created. The sys.dm_clr_appdomains dynamic management view (DMV) can be used to view a list of appdomains in the SQL Server process space.

To increase the reliability of the .NET code running inside SQL Server, the classes and functions in the .NET Framework base class library have been updated to include attributes called *host protection attributes*, which can be used by hosts such as SQL Server 2005 to indicate which API can or cannot be called by the .NET code running in the host.

In summary, the SQL Server engine performs all the memory and thread or task management for the hosted CLR programs. The notion of appdomains and host protection attributes increases the reliability of SQLCLR code.

Figure 11.2 shows the SQLCLR architecture.

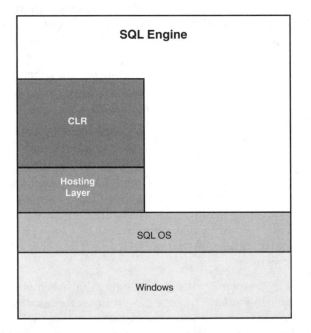

FIGURE 11.2   SQLOS and hosting layer components inside the SQL Server 2005 engine ensure the reliability, safety, and performance of the hosted CLR code.

The SQLOS is responsible for connection management, memory management, thread management, and synchronization services. The hosting layer provides coordination of assembly loading, deadlock detection, execution context, security, and memory management. This is explained in detail in Chapter 2.

Before looking at some SQLCLR examples, let's quickly review the benefits and challenges of integrating SQL Server 2005 and the CLR.

SQLCLR Integration Benefits

Here are some of the advantages of allowing .NET code to run inside the database engine:

- **Enhanced programming model**—The SQLCLR integration allows you to use any .NET programming language and the familiar ADO.NET data access methods to extend the T-SQL language. .NET features such as the object-oriented programming model and structural exception handling facilitate writing code that is manageable and robust.

- **Access to the .NET Framework base class library**—Managed modules (stored procedure, functions, and so on) have access to hundreds of classes in the .NET Framework base class library to performs tasks related to mathematical or statistical calculation, cryptography, disk I/O, XML and string manipulation, and so on.

- **Performance**—T-SQL is an interpreted language, whereas .NET code is just-in-time compiled the first time it is run. The compiled code is cached until the appdomain resides in memory. Several innovative techniques, such as fast transitions between SQL and CLR, the new streaming table-valued functions, binary format normalization of SQLCLR user-defined types, and so on, have been implemented to ensure that SQLCLR code performs as well as or better than an equivalent implementation through T-SQL.

- **A replacement for extended stored procedures**—As mentioned earlier, SQLCLR is an excellent replacement for extended stored procedure. You as a database administrator have control over what a SQLCLR module can and cannot do. The SAFE and EXTERNAL_ACCESS permission buckets guarantee that there will not be any memory leaks and that the module cannot compromise the stability and integrity of the database.

- **Security and reliability**—The SQLCLR integration feature is turned off by default. The .NET CLR code-access security integrated with SQL Server authentication- and authorization-based security gives you complete control over what a SQLCLR module can and cannot do. SQL Server 2005 as a host controls access to memory, thread management, and synchronization. This, in addition to the use of appdomains and host protection attributes, increase the reliability of SQLCLR code. SQL Server 2005 provides several catalog views, DMVs, profiler events, and Performance Monitor counters that you can use to track and trace SQLCLR activity. The ability to create external access or an unsafe SQLCLR module is restricted to few server and database roles or to principals that are granted permission to do so. In summary, SQL Server 2005 goes to great lengths to ensure the safety and reliability of the server.

- **Extending type systems and aggregates**—If SQL Server 2005 does not contain a built-in type or aggregate that you need, you can use SQLCLR to implement your own type or aggregate.

- **Developing and debugging using Visual Studio .NET**—The Visual Studio .NET 2005 IDE has been enhanced to simplify the development, debugging, and deployment of SQLCLR objects. The SQL Server Project template simplifies creating assemblies that you can import into SQL Server. Visual Studio .NET allows cross-language debugging. The deployment feature in Visual Studio .NET 2005 allows you to deploy managed modules directly to the database with a single click. It takes care of dropping existing object, re-importing the assembly, and re-creating the objects.

SQLCLR Integration Challenges

Here are some of the challenges of allowing .NET code to run inside the database engine:

- **Deciding between T-SQL and .NET**—T-SQL is best suited for data access with little or no procedural logic. SQLCLR is best suited for computational, procedural, CPU-intensive logic. Another reason to use SQLCLR is to make use of classes and functions that are available in the .NET Framework base class library. SQL Server 2005 introduces several significant improvements to the T-SQL language, such as recursive common table expression (CTE) queries, ranking functions, and new relational operators. You should be sure to consider these enhancements and see if you can implement the task at hand efficiently by using T-SQL before you start writing stored a procedure, trigger, or function using .NET managed code. You should continue to leverage T-SQL's set-oriented processing wherever possible. And you should consider writing CLR code as an efficient alternative for logic that cannot be expressed declaratively in query language. The CLR can be used to replace server-side cursors and in some such situation, it can gain performance improvements.

- **Deciding between the middle or client tier and the server tier**—If you want to centralize data validation or avoid frequent round-trips to the database server, or if you need to process large amounts of data while needing a small portion of it for application use, it makes sense to move the code from the middle or client tier to the server tier. However, you must consider the increased load on the server, which might affect the overall performance and scalability of the server.

SQLCLR Integration Examples

The following sections illustrate how to write stored procedures and functions using C#. You need Visual Studio .NET 2005 "in order" to compile and build the code, or you can use the .dll files available with the code download for this book.

The following sections also highlight the use of Performance Monitor, Profiler, catalog views, and DMVs to track and trace SQLCLR activity.

Saving XML Data to a File

SQL Server 2005 allows you to read XML data from a file by using the OPENROWSET T-SQL function, but it does not offer a functionality to save XML type data into a disk file. Here's how you implement that by using a C# managed stored procedure:

> ### NOTE
> The clr enabled sp_configure **option should be enabled for this example to work. You can run the** sp_configure **command or use SQL Server Surface Area Configuration tool to enable the** clr enabled **option.**

1. Start Visual Studio .NET 2005 and create a new C# SQL Server project by selecting File | New | Project and then selecting the Database Project types under Visual C#. Name the project SQLCLRDemo.

2. When Visual Studio .NET 2005 prompt you to define a SQL Server 2005 database connection where the managed objects is deployed, do so. This connection information is used for deploying and debugging managed objects. You can click the Add New Reference button and specify the database connection or click Cancel. You can later specify or change this connection by selecting Project | Properties and then using the Database tab.

3. Right-click the SQLCLRDemo project in the Solution Explorer window, select Add | Stored Procedure, and name the file SaveXMLToFile.cs. Then click Add button.

4. Type the following C# source code for the stored procedure:

```csharp
using System;
using System.Data;
using System.Data.Sql;
using Microsoft.SqlServer.Server;
using System.Data.SqlTypes;

using System.IO;

public partial class StoredProcedures
{
    [SqlProcedure]
    public static void SaveXMLToFile(SqlXml XMLData, String DestFile,
                                     Boolean Append)
    {
        StreamWriter writer = new StreamWriter(DestFile, Append);
        writer.Write(XMLData.Value);
        writer.Close();
```

```
        SqlContext.Pipe.Send(String.Format
            ("XML text successfully saved to file '{0}'", DestFile));
    }
};
```

This C# code uses the `StreamWriter` class from the `System.IO` namespace to write input XML text to the specified file.

5. Build the solution by pressing Ctrl+Shift+B. The `SqlProcedure` attribute with the `SaveXMLToFile` function indicates that this function will be mapped to a T-SQL stored procedure. This function is present in a class named `StoredProcedures`. You can change the classname to anything you would like.

6. Import the previously created assembly into a SQL Server 2005 database and map a T-SQL stored procedure to the `SaveXMLToFile` method in the assembly. Developers can then deploy the assembly to a SQL Server 2005 database by using the Build | Deploy Solution menu item in the Visual Studio .NET 2005 IDE. This option runs a script that drops any existing stored procedures, triggers, functions, types, and aggregates in the assembly; drops the assembly; re-imports the assembly; and then re-creates the modules defined in the assembly. In addition to importing the binary assembly, the deployment option in Visual Studio 2005 also imports the source code files and a `.pdb` file that is used by the Visual Studio .NET 2005 debugger. You can look at the `sys.assembly_files` catalog view to see all the files imported into the database by the Visual Studio .NET 2005 IDE. The other option is to manually run T-SQL statements by using SQL Server Management Studio or using `SQLCMD.exe` to import the assembly and create the T-SQL modules, mapping them to methods in the assembly. You should use the second approach here.

7. Start SQL Server Management Studio and launch Query Editor to connect to a SQL Server 2005 instance by using a Windows NT authenticated login or sa. Run the following T-SQL statements (being sure to update the path to assembly file):

```
USE AdventureWorks;
GO

CREATE ASSEMBLY SQLCLRDemo
FROM 'E:\SQLCLRDemo\SQLCLRDemo\bin\Debug\SQLCLRDemo.dll'
WITH PERMISSION_SET = EXTERNAL_ACCESS;
GO

CREATE SCHEMA SqlClr;
GO

CREATE PROCEDURE SqlClr.uspSaveXMLToFile
    @XMLData  XML,
    @DestFile NVARCHAR(255),
    @Append BIT
```

```
AS EXTERNAL NAME [SQLCLRDemo].[StoredProcedures].[SaveXMLToFile];
GO
```

8. Try to invoke the managed stored procedure from step 7. To do so, launch a new Query Editor window and run the following T-SQL commands to save XML type data into a disk file:

```
USE AdventureWorks;
GO


DECLARE @XMLData xml;
SELECT @XMLData = Demographics FROM Sales.Store
    WHERE CustomerID = 9
EXEC SqlClr.uspSaveXMLToFile @XMLData, N'C:\1.xml', 0;
GO
```

These T-SQL statements extract the XML data from a table into a variable that is then passed to the managed stored procedure. The C# code then saves the XML data into a disk file.

9. After running the statements in step 8, open the c:\1.xml file to see the XML column value saved into the file. Note that invoking a managed C# stored procedure is no different from invoking a T-SQL stored procedure.

Let's look at one more example of executing .NET managed code from within SQL Server. This time, you are going to write two user-defined functions that can be used to encode a string using base64 encoding and decode a base64encoded string to plain text.

Base-64 Encoding and Decoding

In this section you'll continue to use the SQLCLRDemo C# project you created in the previous section. You follow these steps to implement base-64 encoding and decoding functions, using C# and calling them from within a T-SQL batch:

1. Right-click the SQLCLRDemo project in Visual Studio .NET 2005 and select Add | User Defined Function. Name the class Base64Helper.cs. This class will generate a function named Base64Helper, change that to EncodeToBase64, and add one more function called DecodeFromBase64 in the same class. Write the EncodeToBase64 and DecodeFromBase64 methods, as shown here:

```
using System;
using System.Data;
using System.Data.Sql;
using System.Data.SqlTypes;
using Microsoft.SqlServer.Server;

using System.Text;
using System.Security.Cryptography;
```

```
public partial class UserDefinedFunctions
{
    [SqlFunction]
    public static SqlString EncodeToBase64(String PlainText)
    {
        Byte[] byteData = new Byte[PlainText.Length];
        ASCIIEncoding enc = new ASCIIEncoding();
        byteData = enc.GetBytes(PlainText);

        return (SqlString)Convert.ToBase64String(byteData);
    }

    [SqlFunction]
    public static SqlString DecodeFromBase64(String EncodedString)
    {
        Byte[] byteData = Convert.FromBase64String(EncodedString);
        ASCIIEncoding enc = new ASCIIEncoding();
        return enc.GetString(byteData);
    }
};
```

2. Build the solution by pressing Ctrl+Shift+B and then run the following DDL statement in Management Studio to refresh the assembly in the database:

```
ALTER ASSEMBLY SQLCLRDemo
FROM 'E:\SQLCLRDemo\SQLCLRDemo\bin\Debug\SQLCLRDemo.dll'
WITH PERMISSION_SET = EXTERNAL_ACCESS;
GO
```

3. Create the scalar-valued user-defined functions and map them to the CLR methods just created:

```
USE AdventureWorks;
GO
CREATE FUNCTION SqlClr.ufnEncodeToBase64(@PlainText NVARCHAR(MAX))
    RETURNS NVARCHAR(MAX)
    AS EXTERNAL NAME
      [SQLCLRDemo].[UserDefinedFunctions].[EncodeToBase64];
GO
CREATE FUNCTION SqlClr.ufnDecodeFromBase64
                    (@EncodedString NVARCHAR(MAX))
    RETURNS NVARCHAR(MAX)
    AS EXTERNAL NAME
      [SQLCLRDemo].[UserDefinedFunctions].[DecodeFromBase64];
GO
```

4. Try out the SQLCLR functions from step 3. The following T-SQL statements add a column to the Sales.CreditCard table, use the SqlClr.ufnEncodeToBase64 function to encode the data in the existing column named CardNumber, save the encoded data into the new column, and use the SqlClr.ufnDecodeFromBase64 function to decode the new column data:

```
ALTER TABLE Sales.CreditCard ADD EncryptedCC VARCHAR(255);
GO
UPDATE Sales.CreditCard
    SET EncryptedCC = SqlClr.ufnEncodeToBase64(CardNumber);
GO
SELECT * FROM Sales.CreditCard;
GO
SELECT CardNumber, SqlClr.ufnDecodeFromBase64(EncryptedCC)
    FROM Sales.CreditCard;
GO
ALTER TABLE Sales.CreditCard DROP COLUMN EncryptedCC;
GO
```

SQLCLR Metadata

SQL Server 2005 provides several catalog views that you can use to obtain information about imported CLR assemblies and objects. Table 11.1 shows some of these catalog views.

TABLE 11.1   SQLCLR Catalog Views

Catalog View	Description
sys.assemblies	This view contains a row for each .NET assembly imported into the database. The columns indicate the assembly permission bucket (safe, external access, or unsafe), the visibility, the CLR name that uniquely identifies the assembly, and the date when the assembly was imported into the database.
sys.assembly_files	This view contains a row for each file that makes up an assembly. At a minimum, it contains one entry per assembly for the .dll file. If you deploy using Visual Studio .NET 2005, you see additional files, including a .pdb debugger file and source code (.cs or .vb) files. The content varbinary column contains the contents of the assembly file.
sys.assembly_modules	This view contains a row for each stored procedure, function, or trigger that is created and associated with a method in an assembly. object_id identifies the stored procedure, trigger, or function; the assembly_class and assembly_method columns identify the exact method in the assembly identified by the assembly_id column that the object maps to.

TABLE 11.1   Continued

Catalog View	Description
sys.assembly_references	If an assembly references another assembly, this information is available via the sys.assembly_references catalog view. The view contains only two columns, assembly_id and referenced_assembly_id.
sys.assembly_types	This view contains a row for each user-defined type that is defined by a CLR assembly.

Monitoring SQLCLR Activity

You can use various DMVs, Profiler trace, and Performance Monitor counters to monitor SQLCLR activity. For instance, you can use the sys.dm_os_loaded_modules and sys.dm_os_memory_clerks DMVs as illustrated in the following code to find out about all the .NET DLLs loaded in the SQL Server address space and the amount of memory allocated by the .NET CLR:

```
SELECT name, description, * FROM sys.dm_os_loaded_modules
   WHERE description LIKE '%.NET%';


SELECT * FROM sys.dm_os_memory_clerks
   WHERE TYPE LIKE '%CLR%';
```

Table 11.2 lists some other DMVs that you can access to track SQLCLR activity.

TABLE 11.2   SQLCLR DMVs

DMV	Description
sys.dm_clr_properties	Provides details such as whether the CLR is initialized, and if it is, indicates the CLR version and the CLR directory.
sys.dm_clr_tasks	Returns a row for every CLR task that is currently running. A T-SQL batch that contains a reference to a CLR routine creates a separate task for execution of all the managed code in that batch. Multiple statements in the batch that require managed code execution use the same CLR task. The CLR task is responsible for maintaining objects and state pertaining to managed code execution, as well as transitions between SQL Server and the CLR.
sys.dm_clr_appdomains	Returns a row for each CLR appdomain in the SQL Server process. As described earlier, appdomain is a .NET Framework CLR construct that is the unit of isolation for an application.
sys.dm_clr_loaded_assemblies	Contains a row for each CLR assembly loaded into memory.

SQL Profiler provides a new event class called CLR that can be used to trace events such as loading a .NET assembly. Here is how you can use Profiler to trace SQLCLR activity:

1. Start SQL Profiler, connect to a SQL Server 2005 instance, and select "Blank" from the "Use the Template" box.

2. Select the Event Selections tab, scroll to the bottom of the tab, select "the Assembly Load" event under the CLR event class, and click the Run button to begin tracing.

3. Execute any CLR procedure or functions, and you should see the Assembly Load event in the Profiler. If this event is not raised in the Profiler, the assembly is already loaded. You can use the sys.dm_clr_loaded_assemblies DMV and the sys.assemblies catalog view to determine whether an assembly is already loaded. You can drop the objects, drop the assembly, re-import the assembly, and run the stored procedure or functions. Alternatively, you can start the Profiler trace and run the SQLCLRDemo.sql script provided with the code download for this book. This script contains the T-SQL code to import an assembly and create and execute CLR procedures and functions. In this case, you should see the assembly load event in the Profiler.

You can use several .NET and SQLCLR Performance Monitor counters to track .NET activity. The SQLServer:CLR or MSSQL$Instance_name:CLR performance objects provide counters such as CLR Execution that you can use to determine total execution time (milliseconds) in the CLR.

Summary

The .NET integration with SQL Server 2005 is one of the top developer productivity features introduced in SQL Server 2005. It allows you to write stored procedures, functions, and triggers, using any .NET managed language, such as C# or Visual Basic .NET. In addition, you can create your own type or aggregate by using the .NET Framework. SQL Server 2005 does everything possible to ensure that SQLCLR code does not compromise the reliability and safety of the database engine. You have complete control over enabling or disabling the running of .NET code inside SQL Server and determining what a managed module can and cannot do.

This chapter starts with an overview of the .NET Framework and the CLR. Next, you learned about CLR hosting in SQL Server 2005 and the integration design goals. The examples provided illustrate how to write procedures and functions by using C# and calling them from a T-SQL script. You also saw how to trace and track SQLCLR activity by using catalog views, DMVs, Profiler, and Performance Monitor.

Chapter 12, "SQL Server Integration Services Overview," shifts the focus from programming features to business intelligence features and discusses the first step in the BI process: integrating data by using SQL Server Integration Services (SSIS; formerly known as Data Transformation Services [DTS]).

SQL Server Integration Services Overview

In a typical enterprise environment, data is often stored in different formats and schemas in disparate sources. It is often necessary to extract and convert this data from different data types and formats into a unified format to be stored in a single destination or processed further for reporting. This task of moving, manipulating, integrating, cleaning, validating, and summarizing data in SQL Server 2005 can be achieved by using the technology called SQL Server Integration Services (SSIS). Formerly known as Data Transformation Services (DTS), SSIS has undergone a complete overhaul to improve performance, to provide better control over data flow, and to introduce conditional flow and looping. The basic architecture and programming object model have changed in SSIS to separate the different processes, such as management, the runtime, and data flow.

This chapter explores the SSIS platform by introducing you to the new SSIS architecture, the new control flow and data flow tasks, the new package authoring environment (the designer and wizards), and SSIS command-prompt utilities. Let's begin with an overview of new features introduced in SSIS.

New SSIS Features

SSIS includes a complete set of data transformation and integration services, graphical tools, programmable objects, and APIs. You can use SSIS to perform tasks such as integrating data from varied data stores, cleansing data, refreshing data into business intelligence data warehouses and data marts, automating administrative functions, and so on. Some of this functionality was available with DTS in SQL Server 2000. The current release takes the DTS functionality to the next level by introducing the following new features:

- **Architectural enhancements**—The new SSIS architecture is divided into four core components: clients, the SSIS service, the runtime engine, and the data flow engine. The SSIS client component includes the graphical and command-line tools and wizards that can be used for package design and creation. The SSIS service is responsible for managing the storage of packages and tracking packages that are running. The SSIS runtime engine manages and sets appropriate properties during runtime and provides support for logging and debugging. The SSIS data flow engine controls the flow of data from source to destination. The SSIS data flow components include source adapters, transformations, and destination adapters. The separation of the different components to be managed by different services allows for more manageability and efficiency. The new architecture allows you to extract data from multiple sources and write data to multiple destinations.

- **Performance enhancements**—The new SSIS architecture uses in-memory buffers as much as possible to move data from the source to the destination. SSIS is designed to leverage the increased amount of the memory. For example, in the case of a table lookup task, the lookups are stored in the memory cache to avoid expensive trips to the disk. This results in improved performance of the task execution.

- **New transformations and tasks**—SSIS introduces several new tasks that aid in data cleansing and transformation. Examples of these new tasks include Derived Column, Data Conversion, File Extractor, and File Inserter. In addition, different tasks such as Multicast, Conditional Split, Sort, Aggregation, Merge, and Merge Join have been introduced, and they can be very useful for redirecting output based on defined conditions and to perform various functions on the data. The new tasks specific to Analysis Services and data mining include Slowly Changing Dimensions, Data Mining Query, and so on. The new looping containers, such as the For Loop and Foreach Loop, allow you to iterate over files in a folder iterate over an items list, and so on. The new Script tasks allow you to use .NET languages such as C# or Visual Basic .NET to author scripts.

- **SSIS designer**—The new graphical designer includes better tools and templates to enable easy creation of packages. The designer offers better project management, new tasks and templates for easier package creation, tools for better deployment, and storage and debugging tools to monitor package execution. The designer includes Package Explorer, which allows you to browse and access different features of the package; Solution Explorer, to access projects and their associated packages; and different debugging windows, such as output windows, breakpoints, watches, and so on. The designer separates control flow, data flow, and event handling onto multiple tabs/screens, allowing complete control and flexibility to author complex packages and to provide better control flow semantics.

- **Extensibility**—If none of the built-in components satisfy your needs, you can create your own custom source, transformation, enumerators, and other control flow and data flow elements by using the SSIS extensibility object model and any .NET programming language, such as Visual Basic .NET or C#.

- **Import/Export Wizard enhancement**—The mport/Export Wizard has been enhanced to include better support for data in flat files, including the ability to manipulate data at the column level. The wizard allows you to create a new database if the destination database does not exist and allows you to map the source and destination columns. You can even omit the columns that are not required. In addition, the wizard allows you to preview the data in real time.

Let's now take a closer look at the new SSIS architecture.

The SSIS Architecture

With DTS in SQL Server 2000, control flow and data flow were tightly coupled, making it difficult to create and manage complex packages. The new SSIS architecture breaks this tight coupling and separates control flow from data flow. You will see this change when you start designing packages in SSIS designer inside Business Intelligence Development Studio. Control Flow and Data Flow are two tabs or screens in the SSIS package designer. The other change in the SSIS architecture is the division of package creation, storage, execution, and data flow into four core components: clients, the SSIS service, the runtime engine, and data flow engine.

Before further exploring these four core components, here are some SSIS terms that you should become familiar with:

- **Task**—A package contains one or more *tasks*, which perform various data manipulation and management functions.

- **Container**—Tasks are grouped by entities known as *containers*. Containers support iterative control flow in packages and group tasks into meaningful units of work. The SSIS architecture is based on containers. The package container organizes containers, tasks, connections, transformations, variables, configurations, and precedence constraints into an executable unit of work. Containers, except for the TaskHost container, can hold other containers, and they provide scope for variables, transactions, and events.

- **Precedence constraint**—*Precedence constraints* organize the tasks and containers in a package workflow and specify the conditions for execution of the tasks.

- **Data Flow task**—Tasks that extract data from different sources, provide the facility to transform, cleanse and modify data, and store data in the appropriate destination are known as *Data Flow tasks*.

- **Package**—A collection of different tasks and containers, connections, precedence constraints controlling data flow, variables, and different configurations is combined together into a unit of work called a *package*. The different components of SSIS manage, store, and execute this unit of work.

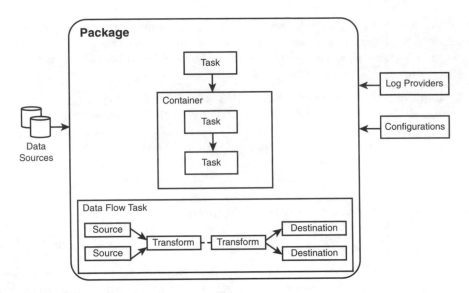

FIGURE 12.1   An SSIS package is a collection of components such as tasks, containers, connections, variables, and configurations.

The following sections look at the core SSIS components in more detail.

SSIS Clients

The SSIS clients include the built-in tools, wizards, and command-line utilities, as well the custom applications that you create for designing and creation of packages. The SSIS designer graphical tool allows you to create SSIS packages without writing a single line of code. The designer contains a collection of built-in tasks to choose from, or you can program a custom task by using .NET managed or native code. In addition to the designer, SSIS contains several wizards and command prompt utilities that assist in configuring the packages by creating configuration files, deploying packages, and creating package dependencies. These are discussed later in this chapter.

SSIS Service

SSIS has separated the management and design of packages for better manageability into a Windows service (`MsDtsSrvr.exe`). This service provides management support for SSIS package storage and execution. This service is off by default, and the startup type is set as disabled but is automatically started when the first DTS package runs. You can manage this service by using the SQL Server Configuration Manager tool. In addition to monitoring local and remote running packages, this service also controls the storage of packages. Packages can be stored either in the `sysdtspackages90` table in the `msdb` SQL Server system database or as XML files (`.dtsx`) on the file system.

NOTE

Business Intelligence Development Studio allows you to save SSIS packages to disk files only as .dtsx XML-formatted files. You can export the packages to the msdb database by using SQL Server Management Studio.

The SSIS Runtime Engine

The DTS runtime engine executes packages and provides support for logging, debugging, configuration, connections, and transactions. It provides support for the following:

- Execution of each task specified by the workflow and consideration of different properties, such as concurrent execution of multiple tasks.

- Handling of the scope and namespace of the variables passed between tasks, containers, or packages.

- Logging of events raised during package execution. Table 12.1 lists the SSIS events raised during package execution.

TABLE 12.1   SSIS Events

Event Handler	Description
OnError	This event is raised when an error occurs.
OnExecStatusChanged	This event is raised when its execution status changes.
OnInformation	This event is used for reporting purposes during the validation and execution of an executable. The report does not contain errors or warnings.
OnPostExecute	This event is raised by an executable immediately after it completes.
OnPostValidate	This event is raised by an executable when its validation completes.
OnPreExecute	This event is raised by an executable immediately before it runs.
OnPreValidate	This event is raised by an executable when its validation begins.
OnProgress	When the executable makes measurable progress, it raises this event.
OnQueryCancel	This event is raised by an executable to determine whether it should stop running.
OnTaskFailed	This event is raised by a task when it fails.
OnVariableValueChanged	This event is raised when the value of a variable is changed by the executable that defines this variable. This event is not raised if you set the RaiseChangeEvent property for the variable to False.
OnWarning	This event is raised by an executable when a warning occurs.

- Debugging of packages by storing information about enabled breakpoints.

The runtime engine is also responsible for establishing the connection to any external data source used by the package.

The Data Flow Engine

The SSIS data flow engine manages the tasks that move data between the source and destination. SSIS uses in-memory buffers for better performance. The Data Flow task provides and manages these buffers, calls the appropriate data flow components, and provides transformations to modify and cleanse data. The Data Flow task is a set of connected data flow components consisting of data adapters and pipelines. These are the different data flow components (see Figure 12.2):

- **Source adapters to extract the data**—Source adapters are usually the first components in a data flow and do not usually have an input but can have one or more outputs.

- **Transformations**—These are the pipeline processes that are used to modify and cleanse data. They have an input and output to receive data from upstream and send processed data to downstream. Transformations can be synchronous or asynchronous. For synchronous transformation task, every input has an associated output; in an asynchronous task, there can be multiple outputs for a single input.

- **Destination adapters**—These are used to connect and store data in the data sources. They have at least one input and are usually the last component in the graph.

- **Pipeline paths**—The components are connected together by pipeline paths. Paths connect the output of one component to the input of the second. They are different from precedence constraints because they only connect the components and do not constrain the next data flow component.

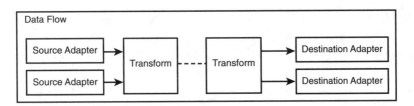

FIGURE 12.2   The Data Flow task is a set of connected data flow components consisting of source adapters, transforms, destination adapters, and pipelines.

As shown in Figure 12.2, the data flow task can contain one or more source adapters to read the data, one or more transformations to process and cleanse the data, and one or more destinations to store the data.

The data flow engine manages interdependency between the different components of a data flow task and also supports parallel execution of the non-connected tasks. The data flow engine supports merging, splitting, and multicasting of data in a data flow and can also be used to redirect an error to a destination output.

The SSIS Toolkit

SSIS offers a user-friendly integrated environment called Business Intelligence Development Studio (BIDS), which can be used to create, debug, and deploy SSIS packages. This tool leverages the Visual Studio .NET GUI foundation to offer features such as tabbed windows, solution and project management, enhanced designer interfaces, debugging, SourceSafe integration, help integration, and so on. BIDS combines a graphical editor to design packages and several tools and templates to create and debug packages. Several built-in tasks are available in BIDS to allow you to create complex packages without writing a single line of code. The SQL Server Management Studio tool, on the other hand, offers an environment to manage the existing packages.

Let's now look at some built-in containers and tasks that you can use while designing SSIS packages.

Containers

Containers provide structure and meaning to a package by grouping various tasks and containers together. Containers can include other containers in addition to tasks. Packages use containers for purposes such as to group tasks and containers that must succeed or fail as a unit, to repeat tasks for each element in a collection (such as files in a folder), and to repeat tasks until a specified expression evaluates to `false`.

SSIS provides four types of containers for building packages: the Foreach Loop container, the For Loop container, the Sequence container, and the Task Host container. Let's look at each of these types in little more detail.

The Foreach Loop Container

The Foreach Loop container allows a package to loop repetitively, based on an enumerator. The following different enumerator types are available:

- **Foreach File Enumerator**—This type is used to traverse files and subfolders on the disk drive.

- **Foreach ADO Enumerator**—This type is used to traverse rows in an ADO rowset.

- **Foreach ADO.NET Schema Rowset Enumerator**—This type is used to enumerate the data source in a schema.

- **Foreach Item Enumerator**—This type is used to traverse items in a collection such as documents.

- **Foreach From Variable Enumerator**—This type is used to traverse the values of a variable.

- **Foreach Nodelist Enumerator**—This type is used to enumerate the resultset of an XML Path Language (XPath) expression.

- **Foreach SMO Enumerator**— This type is used to enumerate SQL Server Management Objects (SMO) objects such as tables and databases in a SQL Server instance.

The For Loop Container

The For Loop container evaluates a specified expression, and the repetitive flow is continued until the expression evaluates to `false`. The loop is defined by an initial expression that is optional, an evaluating expression that should result in `false` for the loop to stop, and an optional iterative expression to increment or decrement the loop counter.

As shown in Figure 12.3, the initial expression sets the variable @var to 0. The tasks in the For Loop container are executed in a loop until @var is less than 10. `AssignExpression` increments the @var variable each time the loop is run.

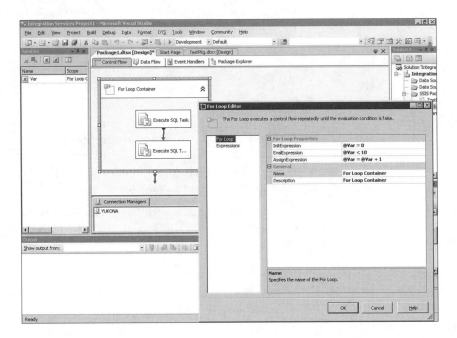

FIGURE 12.3   The For Loop container defines a repeating control flow in a package.

The Sequence Container

While designing SSIS packages, often it is necessary to run multiple tasks in parallel or to group together several tasks in a collection such that the collective property of all the tasks in the collection affects the next task downstream. Such tasks and containers can be grouped in the Sequence container. The Sequence container creates a subset of the package control flow to allow you to manage properties on multiple tasks by grouping them in a single container and allows debugging the tasks as a single unit of work. In addition, you can define scope on the variables over the entire Sequence container. An example of the Sequence container is shown in Figure 12.4.

The Task Host Container

The Task Host container essentially encapsulates a single task. Setting the properties of the encapsulated task automatically sets the properties of the Task Host Container. This container is useful when you're creating SSIS tasks programmatically.

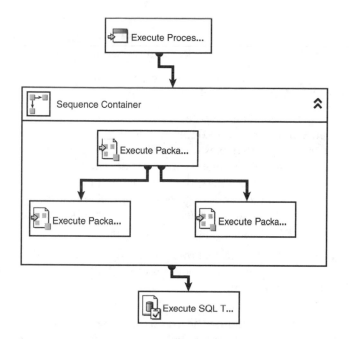

FIGURE 12.4 Sequence containers group a package into multiple separate control flows, each containing one or more tasks and containers that run within the overall package control flow.

Tasks

Tasks define the units of work to be performed as part of a package for process communication and data flow. The tasks in SSIS can be divided into the following categories:

- **Control-flow tasks**—These tasks are used for process-oriented tasks such as communicating with other processes, preparing data for the data flow, working with SQL or Analysis Services objects, or extending package functionality through programming.

- **Data flow tasks**—These tasks are used for data control and manipulation (for example, extracting, transforming, and loading data from a source to a destination).

- **Database maintenance tasks**—These tasks are used to perform administrative and maintenance processes for SQL Server to ensure performance, high availability, and disaster recovery.

- **Custom tasks**—If the required functionality is not available in the three other kinds of tasks, you can extend the functionality by implementing custom tasks. The SSIS programming model exposes a set of APIs and base classes for implementing custom tasks. You can inherit from these classes and override the required methods to achieve the desired functionality.

Let's now look at each of these task types in a little more detail.

Control-Flow Tasks

The different control-flow tasks can be further divided into SQL Server tasks, process-oriented workflow tasks, data-oriented tasks, Analysis Services tasks, and scripting tasks.

SQL Server Tasks   SQL Server tasks allow access, configuration, and administration of SQL Server objects. SQL Server tasks include the following:

- **The Execute SQL task**—The Execute SQL task allows execution of Transact-SQL (T-SQL) statements and stored procedures. In addition, it allows the running of parameterized queries. Input variables for stored procedures and queries are mapped to the value of ? at runtime. Parameters are order dependent. In the case of a stored procedure with several parameters, the SSIS engine follows the order in which the input variables are assigned and maps accordingly. The first input variable is mapped to the first ?, and so on. The return values can be a single row, multiple rows, or XML.

- **The Bulk Insert task**—This task allows you to copy data from flat files to SQL Server tables. It provides various properties of the bulk cinsert format file, such as format, batch size, and so on.

The other SQL Server tasks—including the Transfer SQL Server Objects task, the Transfer Database task, the Transfer Error Messages task, the Transfer Jobs task, the Transfer Logins task, and the Transfer Master Stored Procedures task—allow you to transfer different SQL Server objects to different database instances.

Process-Oriented Workflow Tasks   The process-oriented workflow tasks include the following:

- **The Execute Package task**—This task allows the execution of other SSIS packages as part of the workflow.

- **The Execute DTS 2000 Package task**—This task allows the execution of DTS packages developed in SQL Server 2000 as is, without migration to SSIS. Not all the tasks available to the DTS packages in SQL Server 2000 are available in SSIS. In addition, the architecture and object model have changed tremendously. Hence, not all DTS tasks can be migrated to SQL Server 2005 SSIS. This is discussed in more detail in the section "Migrating DTS 2000 Packages to SSIS," later in this chapter.

    A DTS 2000 Execute package requires the DTS 2000 Runtime to be present. The DTS runtime is part of SQL Server 2000. However, if SQL Server 2000 is not installed on the server, you can install the DTS 2000 runtime while installing SQL Server 2005. During the SQL Server 2005 setup, you click the Advanced Options button and select for DTS 2000 to be installed. The connections associated with packages to be executed by the Execute DTS 2000 Package task are maintained in the SQL Server 2000 format and are not migrated. Figure 12.5 shows the Execute DTS 2000 Package Task Editor window.

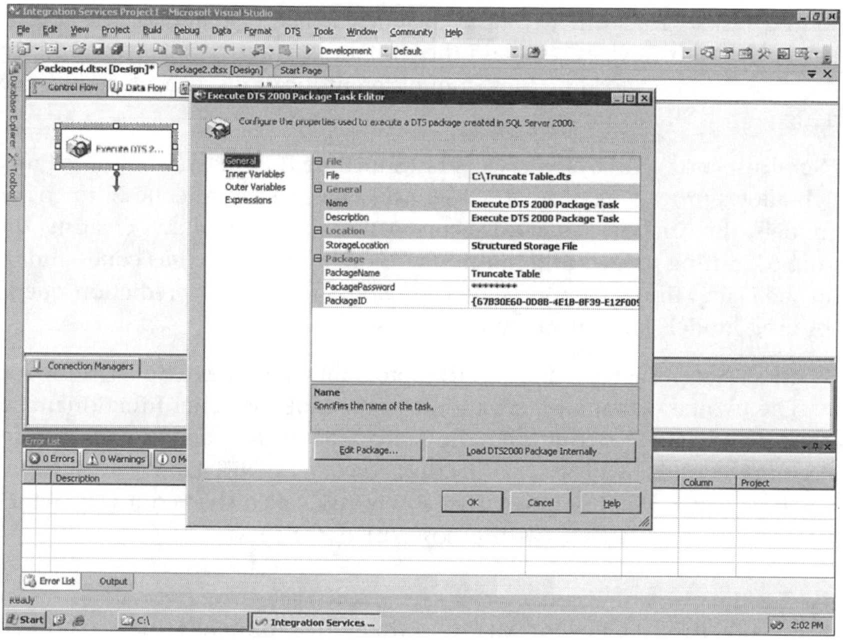

FIGURE 12.5 The Execute DTS 2000 Package task runs packages that were developed by using SQL Server 2000 tools.

- **The Execute Process task**—This task allows execution of applications and Windows batch files as part of the SSIS workflow.

- **The Message Queue task**—This task allows you to use message queuing to send and receive messages between SSIS packages or to send a message to an external application queue.

- **The Send Mail task**—As the name suggests, this task can be used to send email messages over SMTP. You can use this task to send an email message if tasks in the package workflow succeed or fail or in response to an event that the package raises at runtime. The task uses an SMTP connection manager to connect to a mail server.

- **The WMI Data Reader task**—This task runs Windows Management Instrumentation (WMI) Query Languages queries to retrieve information from windows event logs, application or performance information about the different server resources including hardware, and so on. The WMI Data Reader task uses a WMI connection manager to connect to the server from which it reads WMI information.

- **The WMI Event Watcher task**—The WMI Event Watcher task watches for specific configured WMI events. The alert events raised could be an application installation on a production server or degrading performance of hardware resources.

Data-Oriented Tasks   Data-oriented tasks include the File System task, the File Transfer Protocol task, the Web Services task, and the XML task. These tasks are used for copying and modifying files, downloading files from different locations, executing web methods, and working with XML documents.

Analysis Services Tasks   Analysis Services tasks include the Analysis Services Processing task, which allows processing of Analysis Services objects such as cubes, dimensions, and mining models; the Analysis Services Execute DDL task, which allows creating, dropping, and altering of mining models and multidimensional objects such as cubes and dimensions; and the Data Mining Query task, which allows running of prediction queries based on data mining models built in Analysis Services.

Scripting Tasks   Scripting tasks allow you to program code to extend the functionality of a package. The two tasks that allow you to program code for better functionality are the Script task and the ActiveX Script task. The ActiveX Script task allows you to code in scripting languages such as VBScript or JScript. To code in .NET languages such as Visual Basic. NET or C# .NET, SSIS has introduced a new task called the Script task, which allows you to perform complex tasks by writing VB .NET or C# code.

Data Flow Tasks

Data flow tasks control the flow of data from the source to the destination and allow you to cleanse and transform data and redirect portions of the data to different destinations.

The data flow tasks are divided into source adapters, transformations, and destination adapters.

Source Adapters   Source adapters allow you to connect to different data sources, using different connection managers, and to extract and read data. The different connections that you are allowed to connect to are OLE DB, flat files, Excel files, raw files, XML files, and data reader.

Transformations   Different transformation can be applied to cleanse, modify, and transform data. These are the different transformations:

- **The Conditional Split transformation**—This transformation can redirect data rows to different outputs based on certain conditions. Each input row is redirected to an output based on an expression.

- **The Multicast transformation**—The Multicast transformation is similar to the Conditional Split transformation but directs every row to every output. This task is useful when multiple sets of transformations need to be applied to the same data and logical copies of the data need to be created to be processed further, using different transformations.

- **The Derived transformation**—This transformation is useful for cleansing and modifying data because it replaces old columns or creates new column values by applying user-defined expression to the column values. You can also use it to create new columns based on expressions applied to variables.

- **The Data Conversion transformation**—This transformation converts the data type of a column to a different data type, so it is similar to the Cast/Convert function in T-SQL.

- **The Merge transformation**—The Merge transformation provides an output by merging two sorted datasets based on the values in their key columns, resulting in sorted merged output.

- **The Merge Join transformation**—Similarly to the Merge transformation, this transformation merges two datasets but joins them by using FULL, LEFT, or INNER joins.

- **The Aggregate transformation**—You can use this transformation to perform aggregation operations such as an average, a sum, or a count.

- **The Character Map transformation**—You can use this transformation to apply string functions against character data.

- **The Copy/Map transformation**—You can use this transformation to create new columns by copying input columns and adding the new columns to the transformation output.

- **The File Extractor transformation**—You can use this transformation to insert data from data flow into a file. This transformation is useful in moving data of specific formats to separate files.

- **The File Inserter transformation**—This transformation reads data from a file and adds it to a data flow. This transformation is useful for adding more information to processed data.

- **The OLE DB Command transformation**—This transformation executes a SQL command for each row in a data flow.

- **The Data Mining Model Training transformation**—This transformation trains data mining models on the data received from the data mining model algorithms.

- **The Data Mining Query transformation**—You can use this transformation to run data mining prediction queries.

- **The Dimension Processing transformation**—As the name suggests, you can use this transformation to process Analysis Services dimensions.

- **The Fuzzy Grouping transformation**—This transformation performs data cleansing tasks by identifying rows of data that are likely to be duplicates and choosing a canonical row of data to use in standardizing the data.

- **The Fuzzy Lookup transformation**—This transformation performs data cleansing tasks such as standardizing data, correcting data, and providing missing values by looking up values in a reference table, using a fuzzy match.

- **The Logged Lineage transformation**—This transformation allows extraction of environmental variable values and includes them as a part of the data flow.

- **The Lookup transformation**—You can use this transformation to perform lookups in a reference dataset, which can be an existing table or view, a new table, or the result of a SQL statement.

- **The Partition Processing transformation**—You can use this transformation to process Analysis Services partitions.

- **The Row Count transformation**—This transformation counts rows and stores the total in a variable.

- **The Row Sampling transformation**—You can use this transformation to create a sample dataset by selecting a specified number of the transformation input rows.

- **The Script Component**—This transformation uses script to extract, transform, or load data.

- **The Slowly Changing Dimension transformation**—You can use this transformation to coordinate the updating and inserting of records in data warehouse dimension tables.

- **The Sort transformation**—You can use this transformation to sort data in ascending or descending order.

- **The Union All transformation**—As the name suggests, this transformation merges multiple datasets.

- **The UnPivot transformation**—You can use this transformation to create a normalized version of an unnormalized table.

Destination Adapters   Destination adapters allow you to load processed data into different destinations. The different destination adapters available in the Toolbox are the Flat File destination adapter, the OLE DB Destination adapter, the Raw File destination adapter, the Recordset destination adapter, the SQL Mobile destination adapter, and the SQL Server destination adapter.

Database Maintenance Tasks

Maintenance tasks, such as backing up the database, monitoring index fragmentation, checking database integrity, and executing custom scripts to monitor database performance and high availability, are some of the common tasks that database administrators perform on a regular basis. SSIS offers several useful database maintenance tasks for DBAs to include in a maintenance plan without writing custom scripts or coding. The different database maintenance tasks available in the Toolbox include those described in the following sections.

The Backup Database Task   The Backup Database task allows you to back up a single or multiple databases. You can perform a full backup, a differential backup, or a transaction log backup based on the recovery model. In addition, this task also allows you to create a file and filegroup backup for a database with multiple filegroups and data files. The backup device can be specified or created in this task, and it contains all the properties associated with backup creation using T-SQL or SQL Server Management Studio.

The Reorganize Index Task   You use the Reorganize Index task to defragment fragmented indexes in a single or multiple databases. The task also includes an option to defrag large object data such as `text`, `ntext`, `varchar(max)`, `nvarchar(max)`, `varbinary(max)`, or `xml` data. To configure defragmentation of large objects, you check Compact Large Objects in the task dialog box or set the `CompactLargeObjects` option to `True` in the task properties box. This option is off by default.

The Check Database Integrity Task   The Check Database Integrity task encapsulates the DBCC `CHECKDB` T-SQL command to check the allocation and structural integrity of all the objects in a single or multiple databases. To check the integrity of indexes, you select Include Indexes in the dialog or the `IncludeIndexes` custom property in the properties box.

The Rebuild Index Task   The Rebuild Index task allows you to rebuild indexes on SQL Server objects such as tables and views. The task contain different custom properties, such as allocation of `free space`, `FillFactor` percentage, `PAD_INDEX` to allocate free space specified by the fill factor, `SORT_IN_TEMPDB` to store intermediate results in `TempDB`, and `IGNORE_DUP_KEY` to allow multiple-row index operations. In addition, it provides the option to release table locks by setting the `ONLINE` option to `ON`.

Other database maintenance tasks available in the Toolbox include the following:

- **The History Cleanup task**—You use this task to delete history tables in the `msdb` database.

- **The Execute SQL Server Agent task**—You use this task to run SQL Server Agent jobs.

- **The Notify Operator task**—You use this task to send notification messages

- **The Maintenance Cleanup task**—You use this task to remove old files related to maintenance plans.

- **The Notify Operator task**—You use this task to send notification messages via email, pager, or net send to SQL Server Agent operators.

- **The Shrink Database task**—You use this task to shrink the size of the database and logs to a user-defined size.

- **The Update Statistics task**—You use this task to update statistics by distributing the key values for one or more statistics groups.

Business Intelligence Development Studio

Business Intelligence Development Studio (BIDS) is an integrated environment for designing, building, and deploying business intelligence applications. BIDS integrates the features previously available in Analysis Manager and DTS in SQL Server 2000. BIDS contains windows described in the following sections.

Solution Explorer

The Solution Explorer provides a solution- and project-based organized view of packages, data sources, data source views, and other files. You can use it to view the various packages and access their properties. In addition, the Solution Explorer allows versioning of packages using Microsoft Visual SourceSafe.

The SSIS Designer Window

The SSIS designer window provides a nice graphical view of packages. It allows you to create, modify, debug, and save packages. The designer contains the following tabs:

- **Control Flow**—This tab contains the process-oriented tasks of the SSIS package, in the order of execution and the looping structures that allow repetitive execution of tasks.

- **Data Flow**—This tab contains the data-oriented part of the SSIS package and allows you to create packages that control the flow of data from the source to the destination.

- **Event Handlers**—This tab allows you to create custom event handlers to manage errors and other events raised during package execution. Error handlers can be created to send emails, retrieve system information, clean up after a particular task completion, and so on.

- **Package Explorer**—This tab displays package objects, including variables, executables, precedence constraints, event handlers, connection managers, and log providers, in a hierarchical view. The Package Explorer tab reflects the SSIS object hierarchy, with the package container being the top of the hierarchy. As this container is expanded, you can view and access the variables, executables, precedence constraints, event handlers, connection managers, and log providers associated with the package. The Package Explorer allows you to view and delete package objects.

- **Execution Results**—This tab displays the package execution results.

- **Connection Managers**—You can use the Connection Managers tab to create, edit, and delete various connection manager types, including OLE DB, ADO.NET, flat files, SMTP, WMI, and so on.

The Toolbox Window

The Toolbox contains all the built-in tasks, arranged in proper order and categorized by functionality. The Toolbox category and items change depending on the settings on the Control Flow and Data Flow tabs. For instance, if you are in the Control Flow tab, the Toolbox shows maintenance plan tasks and control flow items; however, if you are in the Data Flow tab, the Toolbox lists data flow source, transformation, and destination tasks.

The Properties Window

The Properties window contains the properties of each task selected. You can specify the custom properties associated with each task in this window.

The Debug Windows

The Debug windows give you the ability to set breakpoints and debug the SSIS package and watch the data as it flows through the package workflow. This provides tremendous value in catching and fixing errors and in troubleshooting SSIS packages. The following sections describe some of the debug windows available in BIDS.

The Breakpoint Window   A *breakpoint* suspends package execution at the point where the breakpoint is defined. Breakpoints can be set on the different tasks in the SSIS designer to suspend a package on the different event handlers specified in Table 12.1. You can customize breakpoint behavior by setting the hit count type. The hit count type can be specified as follows:

- **Always**—Execution is suspended when the breakpoint is hit.

- **Equals**—Execution is suspended when the breakpoints are equal to the hit count.

- **Greater or equal**—Execution is suspended when the breakpoint is equal to or greater than the hit count.

- **Multiple**—Execution is suspended when a multiple of the hit count occurs.

The enabled breakpoint can be viewed in the breakpoint window. It also displays the various supported breakpoints and allows you to enable or disable the breakpoints.

The Command Window   The Command window allows you to specify execution commands by bypassing the menu system.

The Immediate Window   The Immediate window allows you to debug, evaluate expressions, print variables, and so on.

Call Stack Window   The Call Stack window lists the SSIS containers that are currently running.

The Locals Window   The Locals window provides the status on the current executables and variables. It lists all the variables within the scope of the current context.

The Output Window   The Output window displays various status messages during the course of package compilation and execution. It displays validation errors when a package is opened, build errors when a package is compiled, and progress/status messages on execution of a package.

The Watch Window   The Watch window is used for viewing, editing, and saving variable values and expressions. It displays various variables and expressions with its associated data types and evaluated expressions.

Progress Reporting

SSIS uses two methods to report the progress of a package during the execution:

- The Progress tab

- Color-coding

The Progress tab displays the order of the task execution and the start and finish times of each task. In addition, it displays any errors encountered during the execution of the package.

Color-coding is also used to display the status of package execution. Depending on color, you can distinguish whether a package is running or whether it has successfully completed or failed. This color-coding is displayed only during package execution. Table 12.2 describes the color-coding.

TABLE 12.2   Execution Status Color-Coding

Color	Status
Gray	Waiting to run
Yellow	Executing
Green	Successful completion
Red	Completed with errors

SQL Server Management Studio

SQL Server Management Studio allows you to manage existing packages. It allows importing and exporting of packages saved from one kind of storage format to another. It allows storing of a package to either the file system in XML format, SQL Server, or the SSIS package store. Management Studio cannot be used for designing or debugging packages, but it can be used to execute a package, view running packages, and import and export packages. When the SSIS service is running, you can use Management Studio to connect to an SSIS instance in the Object Explorer window to see existing and running packages.

Command-Prompt Utilities

SQL Server 2005 includes several command-prompt utilities that you can use to manage and execute the SSIS packages. They include the following:

- **DTExecUI**—This utility allows execution of a package by opening a user interface to set the execution properties.

- **DTExec**—This utility allows execution of existing packages from the command line.

- **DTUtil**—This utility allows management of existing packages from the command line.

The following sections describe these utilities in more detail.

DTExecUI

You can invoke this utility from the command prompt by typing DTExecUI (see Figure 12.6). It opens up a user interface where you can set the properties to execute the package.

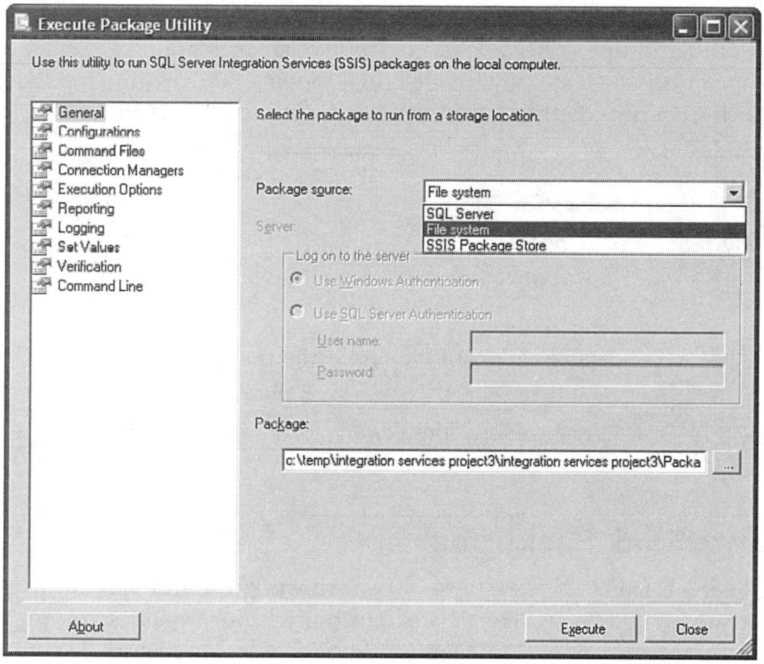

FIGURE 12.6   The DTExecUI utility can be used to run an SSIS package.

The DTExecUI utility allows execution of SSIS packages stored in SQL Server, the file system, or the SSIS package store. You can specify the configuration file to be loaded to set the object properties of the package during runtime, or you can set values of individual objects. In addition, you can specify the commands to load, and in what order, during runtime. You can set the connection properties if the package needs to connect to an external data source. You can also set different execution options, such as setting validation warnings or enabling package checkpoints. Log files can be specified to log the execution of a package or set package verification. Alternatively, you can choose to report execution information to the console, and you can specify the level of information to display.

DTExec

DTExec is similar to DTExecUI except that it does not contain a user interface. All the settings are passed as command-line parameters. Based on the exit code, the user can determine whether the command was executed successfully. Table 12.3 lists the return values for DTExec.

TABLE 12.3   Return Values for DTExec

Return Value	Description
0	Successful execution
2	Package failure
3	Package cancelled by the user
4	Unable to locate the requested package
5	Unable to load the requested package

DTUtil

The DTUtil command-line utility allows you to manage existing packages by allowing you to perform operations such as copying, deleting, moving, and signing a package. You can also use DTUtil to verify whether a package exists. Table 12.4 lists the return values for DTUtil.

TABLE 12.4   Return Values for DTUtil

Return Value	Description
0	Successful execution
1	Package failure
4	Unable to locate the requested package
5	Unable to load the requested package
6	Cannot resolve the command line because of errors

Designing SSIS Packages

As described earlier, SSIS bundles a suite of built-in workflow and data flow tasks that you can use to create SSIS packages. The SSIS extensibility feature enables you to create your own tasks and transformations. You can use the SSIS object model to execute a package programmatically or to change package properties dynamically at runtime. The following sections walk you through the process of designing and executing an SSIS package. But before that, let's look at the SSIS object model, expressions, and logging features.

The SSIS Object Model

As with DTS in SQL Server 2000, SSIS also includes an object model, which you can leveraged to do the following:

- Modify SSIS package properties at runtime

- Develop, load, and execute SSIS packages programmatically, in lieu of using the designer

- Extend SSIS by coding customized tasks, log providers, enumerators, connection managers, and data flow tasks

You can code against this object model inside a package itself by using the Script task or externally in .NET managed code. The Script task is preferably used for single-use, package-specific situations, such as modifying SSIS package properties during runtime. External .NET programs are usually implemented to create reusable customized code to be invoked in multiple SSIS packages, or to load, modify, or execute SSIS packages. The use of the object model to extend the functionality of SSIS (to create custom tasks and transformations) is beyond the scope of this book. An easy way to visualize the SSIS object model is to look at the Package Explorer in BIDS. The hierarchy should be traversed in code, much as it appears onscreen.

An SSIS Object Model Example

Let's look at an example of a simple package that loads the contents of a flat file into a SQL Server table. It is not uncommon for a flat file name, or even path, to change from one execution to another, or even within a loop in the same invocation. To resolve such issues, you can access the SSIS object model and assign task properties, using tasks such as the Script task. As shown in Figure 12.7, the tasks in this sample package include a Script task to change the source text file path, a SQL task to truncate the destination table, and a Data Flow task to copy the text file contents to the SQL Server table.

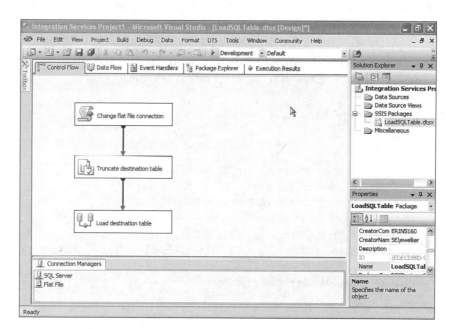

FIGURE 12.7   This simple package uses the Script task to change the source text file path to a value specified in a package variable.

You can follow these steps to try out this sample:

1. Unzip the ObjectModelExamplePackage.zip file provided with the source code download for this book.

2. Copy the testfile2.txt text file to C:.

3. Execute CreateTable.sql by using SQLCMD or Management Studio to create a table named dbo.TestTable in the tempdb database.

4. Double-click the Integration Services Project1.sln solution file to open it in BIDS.

5. Open the LoadSQLTable 1.dtsx package, if it is not already open in the designer.

6. Double-click the JUNECTP.tempdb connection on the Connection Managers tab and update the server name to connect to your SQL Server 2005 instance.

7. Double-click the Flat File connection and note the filename. It should be C:\TestSSIS.txt, a file that does not exist.

8. Right-click the package designer and select Variables. Ensure that the FilePath variable is set to C:\TestFile2.txt, a file that you copied to C: in step 2.

9. Execute the package by clicking the green arrow on the toolbar or by selecting Debug | Start Debugging. Notice that the Script task updates the Flat File connection to point to C:\TestFile2.txt instead of C:\TestSSIS.txt, the Execute SQL task truncates dbo.TestTable, and the Data Flow task copies the data from the flat file to the OLE DB destination (that is, into the dbo.TestTable table).

10. After the package executes successfully, view the data in the dbo.TestTable table by using Management Studio or SQLCMD. You should see the data from the flat file C:\TestFile2.txt inserted into the dbo.TestTable table.

The Script task code should appear as follows:

```
Public Sub Main()

    ' Modify the flat file connection string based on the value
    ' of the "FilePath" package variable.
    Dim DTSConnectionMgr As ConnectionManager

    DTSConnectionMgr = Dts.Connections("Flat File")
    DTSConnectionMgr.ConnectionString = CStr(Dts.Variables("FilePath").Value)

    Dts.TaskResult = Dts.Results.Success

End Sub
```

This script first declares a ConnectionManager variable and initializes it by referencing the name of the flat file connection manager in the Dts.Connections property. Next, it assigns the ConnectionString property of the ConnectionManager variable to the value of the FilePath package variable. The final statement returns the status of the task execution, much as was done in the ActiveX scripts used in DTS. During the package execution, the source filename is read from the package variable instead of what is currently designated in the connection property of the flat file connection manager. Other properties of an SSIS task can be modified dynamically at runtime in the same way.

SSIS Expressions

While creating packages, often it is necessary to combine variable values or constants to set a property value or to use functions to cleanse or extract a meaningful value from data before loading it to the destination. You can use expressions for such purposes.

An expression is a combination of operators, functions, and literals that yields a single data value. Here's an example of an expression on a variable with the string data type:

```
SUBSTRING (variable_name, 1, 4) = "SSIS"
```

This expression compares the first four characters of the string to SSIS and returns a Boolean value. Based on the return value, you can perform other operations.

The tasks that use expressions include Derived Column, Conditional Split, and For Loop Containers. The elements for which the SSIS expressions are useful include precedence constraints, variables, and property expressions. Property expressions are used to set the properties of tasks and containers at runtime by using expressions on variables and return values.

Logging

SSIS allows you to configure logging for quite an elaborate list of events, and it supports a diverse set of logging providers and commonly required information regarding package execution. You can configure logging from the SSIS designer and utilities such as the dtexecui.exe and dtexec.exe command-prompt utilities. The different log providers available include text files, the Profiler, the Windows Event log, SQL Server, and XML. In addition, you can write custom log providers. You can right-click the designer window in BIDS and select Logging to configure SSIS logs.

Log options can be set either at the package level, at the level of any of its task, or at the container level. You can tune the LoggingMode property at the package, container, and task levels to customize the logging behavior. A package can write to multiple logs. You can choose different events and logged information for different tasks and containers within a package. Hence, you can set logging at a granular level. The SSIS log schema defines the set of information that you are allowed for logging. You can select any event as specified in Table 12.1 to log information in the log file.

SSIS Package to Import Flat Files into Tables

Now let's look at designing and executing an SSIS package to import flat files into SQL Server tables. Here is the scenario: You have implemented a data warehouse database and need to load Sales and Product data into various dimensions tables. The Sales and Product data is available in flat files in respective folders. The Sales data contains a SalesID column, with the first three numbers representing the Sales category. The sales date field needs to be converted into the appropriate data type before it is loaded into the Sales table. Here is what needs to be done to load the Sales and Product data from the flat files into the database tables:

- **To load Sales data**—You need to implement a Data Flow task that will read the Sales data from the flat files, use the Derived Column transformation to transform and extract the required values using SSIS expressions, and load the data in the SQL Server table destination by using the OLE DB connection manager. Then you use the Foreach File enumerator to loop through the files. The file path can be stored to a variable. The variable value can be used to modify the connect string of the connection manager for the source adapter.

- **To load Product data**—Because no transformation is required on the data, you use the Bulk Insert task to load the data from the flat files in the Products table. Here also, you use the Foreach File enumerator to loop through the files.

Because the two preceding tasks are independent, they can be executed in parallel. You need to implement those processes as separate packages and execute both the packages in parallel in the main package.

Loading the Sales Data

You an unzip the `BookSample.zip` file provided with the source code download for this book and follow these steps to load the sales data:

1. Run the `Preparation.sql` SQL script file to create a database named `BookDW` and two tables, named `Sales` and `Products`, in this database.

2. Launch BIDS and create a new Integration Services project. Rename the default `Package.dtsx` file `LoadSalesData.dtsx`.

3. Drag and drop a Foreach Loop Container task from the Toolbox onto the Control Flow window. Double-click the Foreach Loop Container task to launch the Foreach Loop Editor dialog.

4. In the Foreach Loop Editor dialog, select the Collections page and ensure that the enumerator type is set to For Each File Enumerator. In the Enumerator Configuration panel, select the folder that contains the Sales data flat files and select all the files (`*.*`). Keep the Fully Qualified radio button selected to retrieve the fully qualified filenames. Click OK to close the Foreach Loop Editor dialog. Figure 12.8 shows the Collection page on the Foreach Loop Editor dialog.

5. Right-click anywhere on the Control Flow window and then select Variables to open the Variables window.

6. In the Variables window, add the variable `FileName` of data type `String` within the Foreach File Container scope. To add a variable in the Foreach Loop Container scope, select the container object in the designer and then click the Add Variable toolbar button on the Variables window.

7. Assign the collection value of the Foreach File to the new variable. To do this, double-click the Foreach Loop Container on the designer, select the Variable Mapping page, and select the `User::FileName` variable with the index `0`. Click OK to close the dialog.

8. Create a connection manager for the Sales data flat files. Right-click the Connection Manager window and select New Flat File Connection. Name the connection `SalesFileConnection` and point it to any text file under the `Sales` folder. Click the Columns page and then click the OK button. To assign the file path dynamically at runtime, you need to create a Script task to access the Flat File Connection Manager and set its properties programmatically.

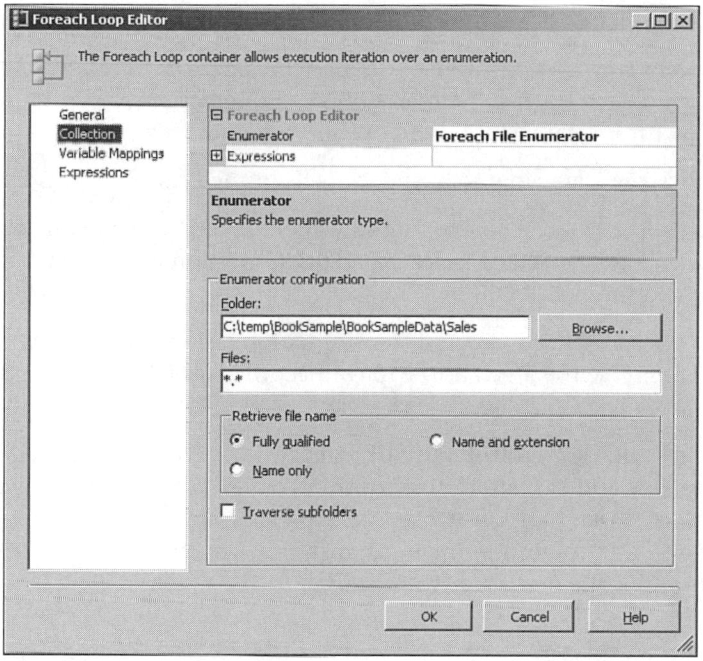

FIGURE 12.8   The Foreach Loop Container is used to iterate over all the files in the Sales folder.

9. Drag a Script task from the Toolbox onto the Foreach Loop Container. Double-click the Script task, select the Script page on the Script Task Editor dialog, and set ReadOnlyVariables to FileName.

10. Click the Design Script button to open the Microsoft Visual Studio for Applications script editor and write the following Visual Basic .NET script:

```vb
Imports System
Imports System.Data
Imports System.Math
Imports Microsoft.SqlServer.Dts.Runtime

Public Class ScriptMain
    Public Sub Main()

        Dim DTSConnectionMgr As ConnectionManager

        DTSConnectionMgr = Dts.Connections("SalesFileConnection")

        DTSConnectionMgr.ConnectionString = _
                CStr(Dts.Variables("FileName").Value)
        Dts.TaskResult = Dts.Results.Success

    End Sub
End Class
```

11. Save the script, close the script editor, and return to the package designer.

12. Create a Data Flow task to cleanse and load the data. Drag and drop the Data Flow task to the Foreach Loop Container. Connect the precedence constraint (that is, the green arrow) from the Script task to execute the Data Flow task.

13. Double-click the Data Flow task, and it opens in the Data Flow window.

14. Drag and drop a Flat File Source from the Toolbox to the Data Flow designer. Double-click Flat File Source, select SalesFileConnection as the Flat file connection manager, and then click OK.

15. Drag and drop a Derived Column transformation task from the Toolbox to the Data Flow designer. Use the green arrow to connect the Flat File Source to this Derived Column task.

16. Double-click the Derived Column task. Add two new columns named SalesCategory and SalesDate, as shown in Figure 12.9. The SalesCategory column uses the SUBSTRING([Column 0], 1, 3) expression to extract the first three characters from the first column in the input text files. The SalesDate column casts the third column to the date data type.

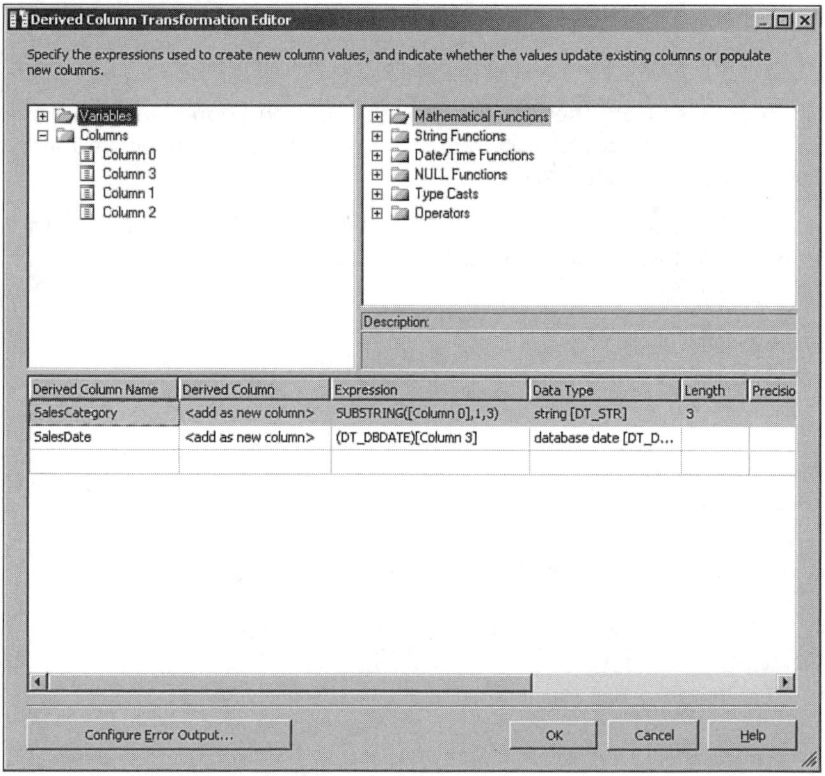

FIGURE 12.9 The Derived Column transformation task is used apply to expressions to transformation input columns.

17. To redirect the error rows to an error log file, click the Configure Error Output button on the Derived Column Transformation Editor dialog. For both the derived columns, change the Error column value from Fail component to Redirect row. Click OK to close the Configure Error Output dialog and the click OK to close the Derived Column Transformation Editor dialog. Figure 12.10 shows the Configure Error Output dialog.

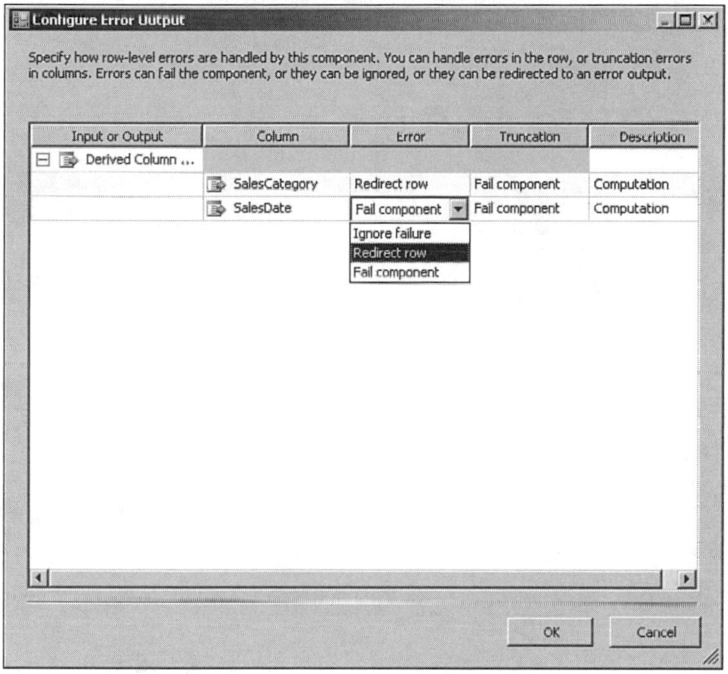

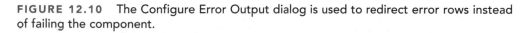

FIGURE 12.10 The Configure Error Output dialog is used to redirect error rows instead of failing the component.

18. Drag and drop a Flat File Destination component from the Toolbox to the Data Flow designer and link the error output (by using the red arrow) from the Derived Column to the flat file destination. Double-click the flat file destination and create a new flat file connection. Provide the path and name of the text file that will receive the error rows. After creating a new file connection, select the Mapping page on the Flat File Destination Editor and click OK.

19. To load the successful rows into the destination Sales table, drag and drop an OLE DB Destination adapter to the Data Flow designer. Link the Derived Column success path (by using the green arrow) to the OLE DB Destination. Next, double-click the OLE DB Destination and connect it to the BookDW database created in step 1. To do this, click the New button next to OLE DB Connection Manager and create a new connection manager that uses Native OLE DB/SQL Native Client to connect to SQL Server 2005 instance containing the BookDW database. Set Data Access Mode as Table or View and then select the Sales table from the Name of the Table or the View list. Click the Mappings page. Map Column 0 to Sales ID, Column 1 to TranID, Column 2 to Customer ID, and SalesCategory and SalesDate derived columns to table columns with the same names. Click OK.

20. Save the package. Figure 12.11 shows the package design in progress.

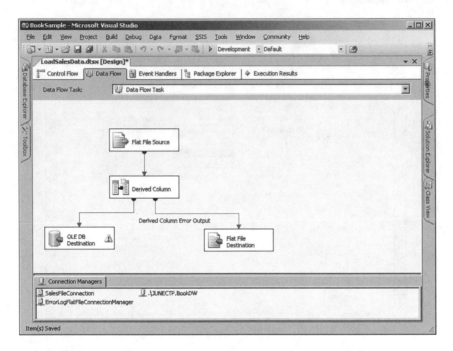

FIGURE 12.11   The package contains a flat file source, a derived column transformation, an OLE DB destination for successful rows, and a flat file destination for error rows.

21. In case you need to deploy this package to a remote machine, you need to define the file path for the Sales data directory and the destination SQL Server database connection when the package is loaded and the solution is to configure these properties in the configuration file. To configure the properties, right-click anywhere on the Control Flow window and select Package Configurations. Check the Enable Package Configurations box to enable to configurations. Click the Add button, and the Package Configuration Wizard starts. Click Next on the Welcome screen.

22. On the Select Configuration Type screen, select XML Configuration File type and specify the configuration file name. Click Next.

23. On the Select Properties to Export screen, for the `EnumeratorProperties` for the Foreach Loop Container task, select the Directory property. In the connection manager properties, select ServerName and Initial Catalog. Provide a name for the configuration and click Finish and then close the Package Configuration Organizer dialog. Figure 12.12 shows using the SSIS Package Configuration Wizard to export properties to a configuration file. Save the package.

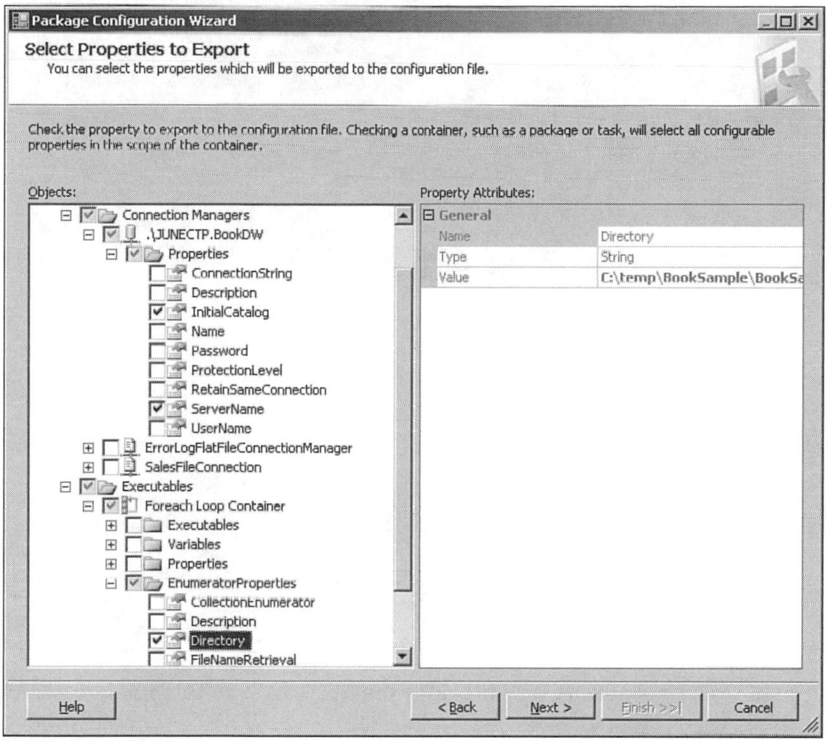

FIGURE 12.12   The Package Configuration Wizard can be used to export properties to a configuration file.

Let's now create another SSIS package to load product data from flat files to the table:

1. Open Solution Explorer, right-click SSIS Packages, and click New SSIS Package.

2. As with the Load Sales data package, use a Foreach Loop container to loop through the product directory and select the flat files to load. The initial steps for this package are similar to those of earlier package to load the sales data. Therefore, repeat the steps 3 through 11 from the earlier exercise to load the sales data, but specify the product directory and select a product flat file for the flat file connection.

3. Because no transformation needs to be applied to the data, use the Bulk Insert task to load the data to the destination SQL Server machine. Drag and drop the Bulk Insert task to the Foreach Loop container. Double-click the Bulk Insert task, select the Connection page, and specify the source and destination connection details as shown in Figure 12.13. Remember to change ColumnDelimiter to comma (,) instead of a tab.

Figure 12.14 shows how this package looks like in the designer.

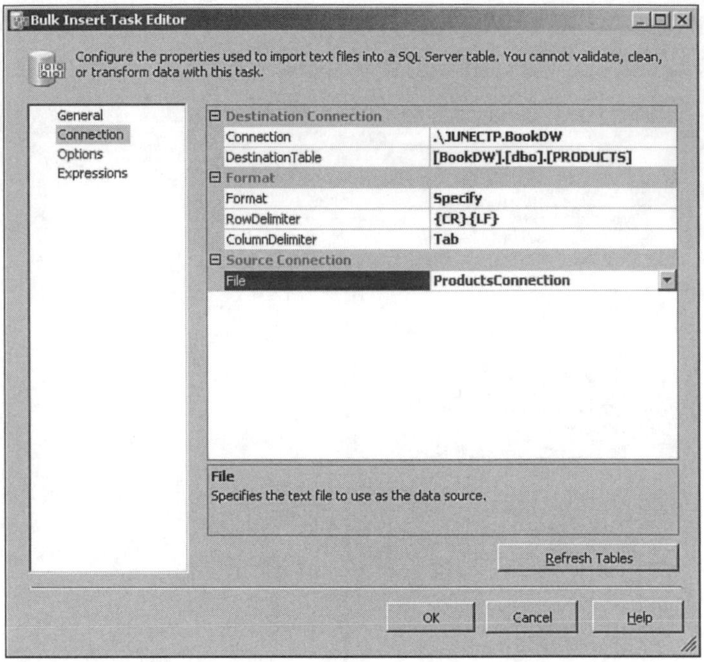

FIGURE 12.13   The Bulk Insert task provides the quickest way to copy large amounts of data into a SQL Server table or view.

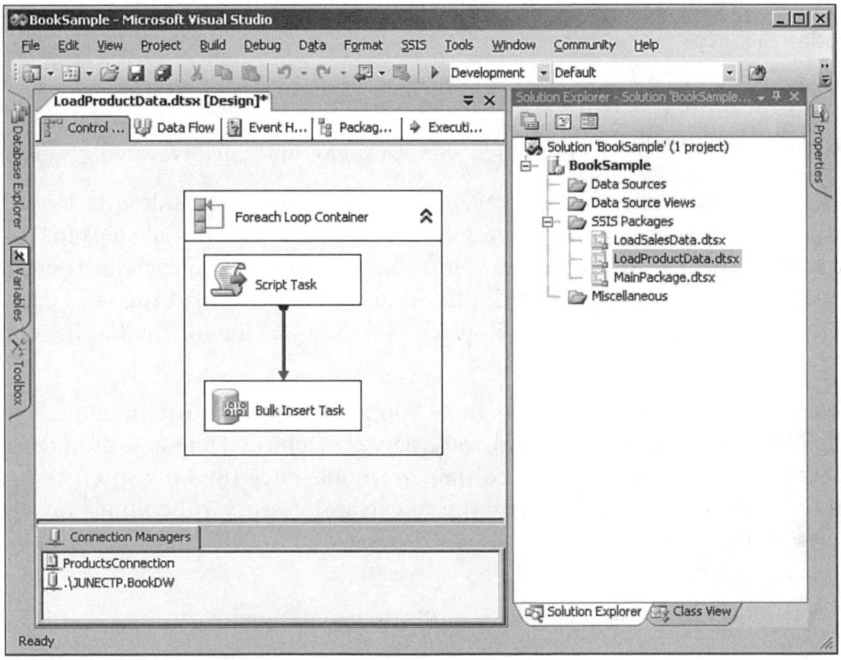

FIGURE 12.14   A Foreach Loop Container, a Script task, and a Bulk Insert task are used inside a package to bulk load data from files into SQL Server.

To execute these packages in parallel, you need to combine both the packages into a main package, like this:

1. Open Solution Explorer, right-click SSIS Packages, and click New SSIS Package.

2. Drag and drop an Execute Package task from the Toolbox to the Control Flow designer. Double-click the Execute Package task and select the Package page. Specify Location as File System and create a new connection that points to LoadSalesData.dtsx.

3. Repeat step 2 to add one more Execute Package task to the Control Flow window and point it to the LoadProductData.dtsx package.

4. To inform the administrator before the package is started, you need to use the Send Mail task. Drag and drop the Send Mail task to the Control Flow window. Double-click the Send Mail task and set the properties as shown in Figure 12.15.

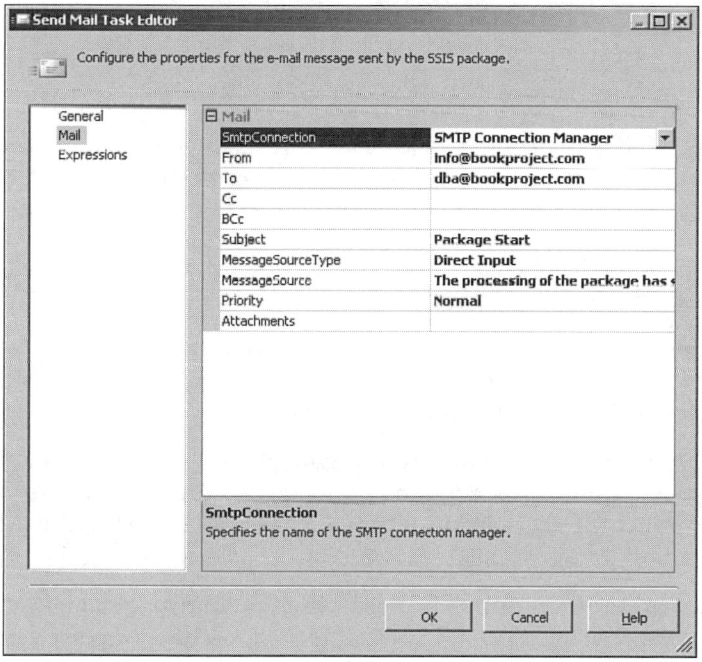

FIGURE 12.15   The Send Mail task is used to send an email message when the package starts.

5. Set the precedence constraints from the Send Mail task on success to execute the Load Sales data and Load Product data packages in parallel. Figure 12.16 shows what the main package looks like.

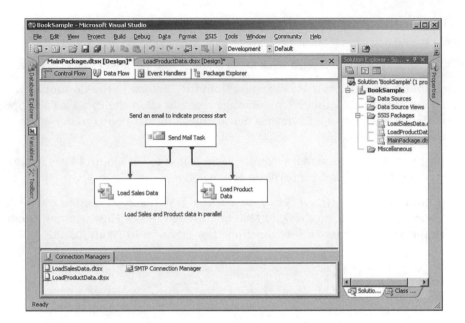

FIGURE 12.16   The main package uses the Execute Package task to run two other packages in parallel to load sales and product data, after sending an email using the Send Mail task.

6. Save the package. Right-click the package in Solution Explorer and select Set as StartUp Object.

7. To monitor execution, it is a good idea to log events and monitor the progress. To log the execution results, right-click the Control Flow window and select Logging. The Configure SSIS Logs window opens.

8. In the Configure SSIS Logs window, configure the events for each of the tasks as required (see Figure 12.17). You can also select the column details to be included while capturing the log events. To configure the columns, click the Advanced button on the Configure SSIS Logs window.

9. Select Debug | Start to start the package execution in debug mode. When the package is executing, based on the color of the tasks, you can determine whether the package execution is successful or fails. As shown in Figure 12.18, the two packages are executed in parallel.

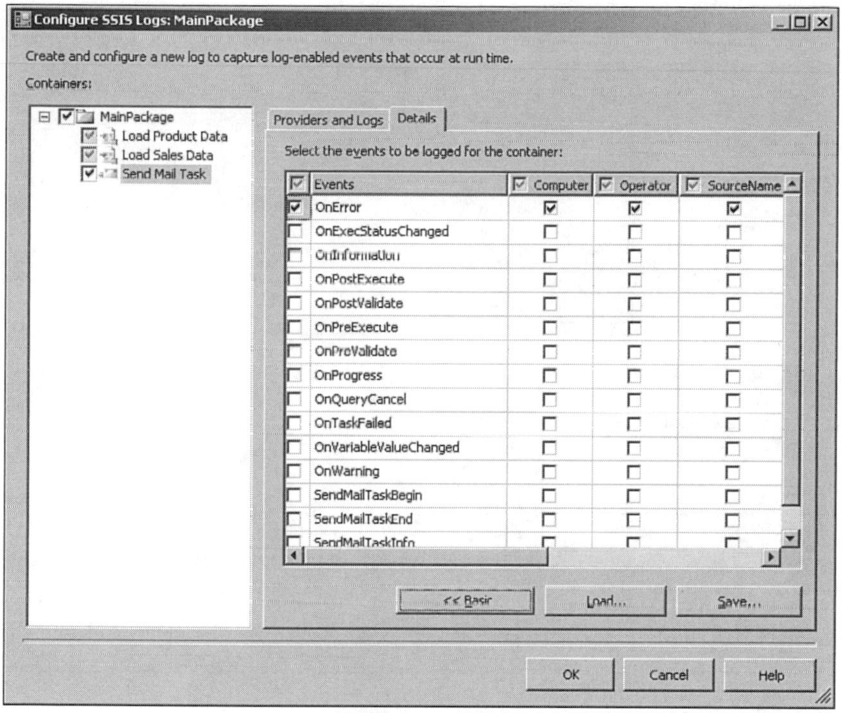

FIGURE 12.17 The Configure SSIS Logs dialog allows you to create and configure a new log to capture log-enabled events that occur at runtime.

10. In the Data Flow task, you can create data viewers on the data flow path to monitor the output rows. Open the LoadSalesData.dtsx package and select the Data Flow tab. Right-click the data path (that is, the green arrow) from Derived Column to OLE DB Destination and select Data Viewers, and add a new grid viewer. When the package is executing, SSIS shows a grid of rows being copied to the destination, as shown in Figure 12.19.

11. To check whether the error rows are written to the error log output file, change the dates in one of the sales data file such that it cannot be converted to the date data type and execute the package again. Before executing the package again, truncate the rows from the Sales and Products table.

    If the package is executed successfully, there will be green color-coding on all the tasks, indicating successful execution.

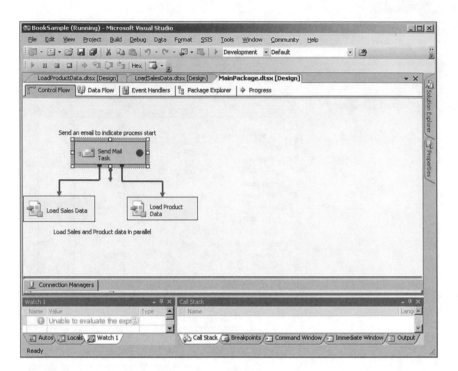

FIGURE 12.18   The Load Sales Data and Load Product Data packages are executed in parallel after an email message is sent.

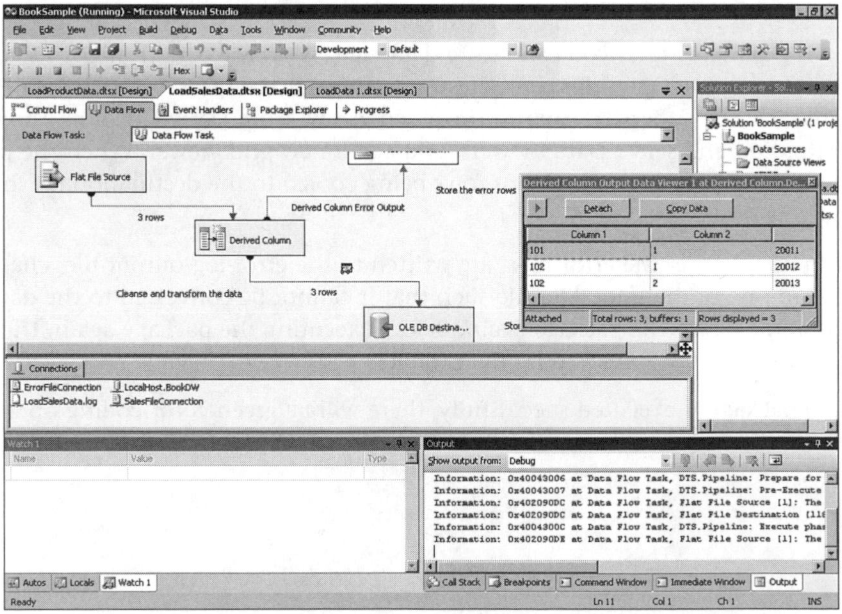

FIGURE 12.19   SSIS provides a powerful debugging capability called *data viewers* that can be used to display data between two data flow components during package execution.

The World of Wizards

As in previous releases of SQL Server, if you do not want to use the package designer, you can simply step through the Import/Export Wizard to create an SSIS package. The following sections discuss the Import/Export Wizard, the SSIS Configuration Wizard, the Package Installer Wizard, and the SSIS Migration Wizard.

The SSIS Import/Export Wizard

The SSIS Import/Export Wizard guides you through the steps to copy data between different data sources. It guides you to connect to the source and destination and allows different properties, such as copying constraints and copying data results from SQL query. You can access this wizard from BIDS, and the command prompt. To launch the wizard from BIDS, you open the Solution Explorer window, right-click the SSIS Packages folder, and select the Import and Export Wizard menu item. To launch the Import/Export Wizard from the command prompt, you run DTSWizard.exe.

This wizard allows you to select the source and destination data sources. The data sources supported are Microsoft SQL Server, flat files, Microsoft Office Access, Microsoft Office Excel, and other OLE DB providers. You are prompted to copy all the data or a portion of the data, based on a user-defined query from one or more tables or view. The wizard gives you the option to either execute the package immediately or save the package. The package can be saved either in the msdb database in SQL Server storage or in the XML format, as .dtsx file storage.

The SSIS Configuration Wizard

Configurations are loaded at the start of process runtime to dynamically set the values of variables and object properties. This feature is useful if the same package has to be deployed on different servers and you want to assign the properties automatically when the package starts running. The SSIS Configuration Wizard guides you in configuring the configurations to be deployed. To launch the SSIS Configuration Wizard from BIDS, you open the package in the designer and then select SSIS | Package Configurations to launch the Package Configurations Organizer. Then you check the Enable Package Configurations check box and click Add to start the Configuration Wizard.

On the first page of the wizard, you are prompted to select the configuration type. The different types of configurations available are the XML configuration type, environmental variables, registry entries, parent package variables, INI files, and SQL Server.

On the Select Objects to Export page, you are prompted to include the package objects to set the properties. Based on the configuration properties, the configuration file is created. You can edit the file to edit the properties set, if required.

The SSIS Migration Wizard

The SSIS Migration Wizard allows migration of existing DTS packages in SQL Server 2000 to SSIS in SQL Server 2005. In SQL Server 2000, the packages could be stored in structured storage, SQL Server databases, and the metadata services. Though the format of the package storage has changed in SSIS (files are now stored in XML format on the disk drive), the wizard allows you to migrate and store these packages to the disk by using the .dtsx XML format or to SQL Server databases. Not all DTS 2000 packages can be migrated to SSIS because some of the tasks are not available in SSIS or have been changed significantly. Even the DTS object model has changed, so packages created using the DTS object model cannot be migrated. Before looking at Migration Wizard details, let's discuss what can and cannot be migrated to SSIS.

Migrating DTS 2000 Packages to SSIS

SSIS provides the option to migrate your existing DTS 2000 packages to SSIS either manually (by re-creating the packages from scratch) or by using the SSIS Migration Wizard. Due to the changes in the SSIS architecture , not all the tasks can be migrated to SSIS. Also, some of the tasks have been removed from SSIS, and some of the tasks have changed, making migration a possibility in only some cases. You can also choose to leave a package as it is in DTS 2000, and can use the Execute DTS 2000 Package task to execute it in SSIS.

> **NOTE**
>
> The DTS 2000 runtime engine must be installed on the computer to run DTS packages by using the Execute DTS 2000 Package task.

The following tasks from DTS 2000 cannot be mapped to SQL Server 2005 tasks:

- Custom tasks—because the DTS object model and architecture have changed in SSIS
- Data Pump tasks such as the Data Driven Query task, the Transform Data task, and the Parallel Data Pump task
- SQL Server tasks such as Copy SQL Server Object, Transfer Databases, Transfer Jobs, Transfer Master Stored Procedure, and Transfer Logins
- Analysis Services tasks such as Analysis Services Processing and Data Mining Prediction
- Other tasks, such as Dynamic Properties and Transfer Error Messages
- Copy Database Wizard tasks

The tasks that can migrate without any issues include the following:

- The Execute SQL task
- The Bulk Insert task
- The File Transfer Protocol task
- The Execute Process task
- The Send Mail task
- The Message Queue task

Although there is an equivalent ActiveX script task in SSIS, an ActiveX script that contains code based on the old DTS 2000 object model cannot migrate because the new SSIS object model has changed. In addition, if the script contains or refers to global variables, the task cannot be migrated successfully. The tasks that cannot be mapped to SSIS are encapsulated into a SQL Server package task by the SSIS Migration Wizard and executed by the Execute DTS 2000 Package task.

Although package passwords are not migrated with the packages to the SSIS format, the SQL Server Package task maintains its password. The Execute DTS 2000 Package task contains the property to specify the passwords.

In DTS 2000, there was no direct method to implement looping; the user could hack into the DTS object model to work around this. If you have implemented DTS 2000 packages with looping, it is better if you re-design those packages to make use of the new looping container in SSIS.

Elements such as precedence constraints are migrated easily to their equivalent SSIS elements. After migration, a precedence constraint can be extended to include or over-write the result of the precedence with conditions under which the task can run or to combine multiple precedence constraints on a single condition.

In case of connections, the connections associated with tasks that can be migrated are also migrated to the equivalent OLE DB or ODBC connection manager, and properties that are not set in the connection manager are set to their defaults. For tasks that cannot be migrated, such as the Transform Data task, the connections remain part of the inter-mediate SQL Server package.

DTS 2000 does not define scope for variables, but it considers all the variables as global variables with the package as the scope. All the global variables can be migrated to SSIS and are added to the variables collection of the package in the User namespace. You can extend the functionality of these variables by creating additional namespaces, using expressions to set variable values, or raising events based on a variable's value.

Migration of transactions to SSIS is supported, but because of the difference in how the transactions are defined in DTS 2000 and SSIS, the successful migration of transactions depends on certain conditions. In DTS 2000, the transaction is tied to steps, which are the combination of the task and its associated precedence constraint. There was no concept of containers in DTS 2000. In SQL Server 2005, the transactions in the package scope follow the container hierarchy. These are the rules that govern transaction migration:

- If the step in the DTS 2000 package is configured to join a transaction, the transaction attribute on the migrated task is configured to support a transaction.

- If the DTS 2000 package is configured to use transactions, the transaction attribute on the migrated package is configured to require a transaction.

- If the DTS 2000 package does not use transactions, then the transaction attribute on the migrated task is configured to support a transaction.

Considering the architectural and performance enhancements in SSIS, the introduction of new tasks and containers, and the fact that not all DTS 2000 tasks can be successfully migrated to SSIS, it is recommended that you consider re-designing old packages from SQL Server 2000 to the SSIS model instead of migrating the old packages.

If you decide to migrate old packages to SSIS instead of re-designing them, the easiest way to do so is to use the SSIS Migration Wizard, as discussed in the next section.

Using the SSIS Migration Wizard

To start the SSIS Migration Wizard, you right-click the SSIS Packages folder in the Solution Explorer in BIDS and select Migrate DTS 2000 Package. Alternatively, you can run dtsmigrationwizard.exe.

The wizard guides you through the following steps in order to migrate the package:

1. **Select package source**—The wizard allows migration of packages stored in structured storage files, SQL Server databases, and the SQL Server metadata services. Packages saved in Visual Basic cannot be migrated. For packages saved in structured storage files, you can migrate some or all of the packages and versions saved in the file.

2. **Select package destination**—The packages can be migrated either to XML format as .dtsx files or to SQL Server 2005. You need to provide proper authentication and should have appropriate priveleges in order for the wizard to save the package to the choosen storage destination.

3. **Select packages to migrate**—The wizard prompts you to select the packages to migrate to SSIS. You can either choose to change the package names in the wizard or to do that after the migration, in BIDS or SQL Server Management Studio. During the package migration, you are prompted to supply the password if the packages are password protected.

4. **Specify Log file**—The wizard prompts you to specify a log file location. After running the SSIS Migration Wizard, you should always review this log file so that you can understand any warnings or errors that are encountered.

Based on the parameters you provide in the wizard, the SSIS Migration Wizard tries to migrate the packages to SSIS. The wizard displays the migration progress for each of the packages selected for migration. If the wizard is unable to migrate a package, it prompts you to either continue migrating the other packages or end the migration process.

As discussed earlier, not all the tasks in DTS 2000 packages can be migrated. For tasks that cannot be migrated to SSIS, such as Data Pump tasks, custom tasks, Transfer Database Object tasks, and so on, a SQL Server 2000 package is created to maintain the SQL Server 2000 format. The SQL Server 2000 package is then executed by the Execute DTS 2000 Package task. But a package that contains such tasks cannot be migrated to SSIS as a single package. A SQL Server 2000 package is created for each task, and each of these tasks executed by the Execute DTS 2000 Package task is encapsulated within the main package. For example, if there are two Data Pump tasks in a package, each task is converted into equivalent SQL Server 2000 package, resulting in three packages. Inside the main package, these two packages are called by the Execute DTS 2000 Package task to execute these packages.

The SSIS Migration Wizard issues a warning if the package choosen for migration contains the Dynamic Properties task. If you choose to migrate the package, the task is replaced by a Script task, which lists the property-value pair defined in the Dynamic Properties task, and this script is commented out.T

SSIS and Data Warehousing

Extraction, transformation, and loading (ETL) is a process that is common to data warehousing. It includes the process of extracting data from various data sources throughout an organization and manipulating it to conform to the standards of the data warehouse prior to populating the relational data warehouse. The manipulation falls into two basic categories:

- **Cleansing or scrubbing**—This involves removing or correcting incorrect, incomplete, or duplicate data.

- **Transforming**—This involves conforming data, translating data types, and/or looking up surrogate keys. In most cases, the data conformation and data type translation are done implicitly in the process. For instance, a dimension table may contain all possible business keys for a dimension member. The state of Alabama may be represented as AL in the Human Resources system and as 01 in the Financial system. Both should be represented in the dimension member, but the foreign key would be an unrelated surrogate key.

This chapter focuses on the T (transformation) step in ETL because it is traditionally the most challenging and low-performing part of the ETL process. In fact, in SQL Server 2000's DTS, ETL was often referred to as ELT (or more appropriately, ELTL). It was far more efficient to bulk-load the data extracted from the source into a staging area, perform the transformation, and then load it into the destination star schema format. Fact table transformations, in their purest form, consisted of dimension surrogate key lookups based on business keys. The most useful means of doing this was by using T-SQL to perform an INSERT from the fact table joined to the various dimension tables using the business keys. It was possible to use DTS's Data Transformation task for this purpose and use the Lookup feature within that task. This is the equivalent of using many SELECT statements to perform the table lookup for each dimension of each fact table row!

SSIS ETL Concepts

SSIS includes the *data adapters* and *pipelines* for dealing with ETL. A source data adapter provides access to an external data source and converts the native data types to SSIS data types. The pipeline is an in-memory series of tasks that operate on the data from the source to transform it to the desired values and format. The destination data adapter then converts data from the SSIS data types to the destination data types and sends the data to the connection string identified therein. The key to transforming data in SSIS is the fact that it occurs in memory. This results in increased performance, and tasks such as Lookup Table Reference, which really slowed down the ETL process, now occur in a few seconds. This is because the lookup tables are each referenced once, causing all the data to be pulled into memory, where subsequent lookups are performed. The resulting performance improvement leads back to the pure ETL process and potentially eliminates the need for an intermediate staging area.

What impact does this have on memory on the SSIS server? This is an important question to consider. Memory-intensive tasks have advanced settings that can moderate these effects. Memory availability is something to consider with this type of processing, though.

Data Source Views

Data source views (DSVs) are another new component of SQL Server 2005. They provide a means of defining particular tables of interest in a potentially complex underlying data model. In the ETL process, this can be used, for example, to focus on one subject area. Table drop-down lists in the SSIS designers can be simplified in this way, displaying only the tables defined in the DSV. This also has a positive performance impact on the time it takes to populate these dialog boxes. DSVs provide a layer of abstraction between the SSIS packages and the actual underlying data sources. Therefore, they can be used to provide disconnected package development capabilities. DSVs are defined within a BIDS solution and can be shared between SSIS and Analysis Services projects in the same solution.

In addition, you can use the Import and Export Wizard as explained in the "World of Wizards" section to transfer data from one data source to another.

Summary

SQL Server replaces DTS by introducing a revolutionary, completely redesigned ETL and integration platform, called SSIS. This platform facilitates the first step in the business intelligence life cycle: integrating, cleansing, transforming, validating, and aggregating data from various sources.

This chapter introduces you to SSIS concepts by discussing enhancements introduced in SSIS, SSIS architecture, and the SSIS toolset. BIDS and other command-line utilities are discussed, as is the step-by-step process to design, execute, and log SSIS packages. The final sections in the chapter talk about SSIS wizards, migration issues, and SSIS's role in data warehousing.

Chapter 13, "What's New in SQL Server Analysis Services 2005," focuses on the second step in business intelligence solution development—analysis—and discusses Analysis Services 2005 in great detail.

What's New in SQL Server Analysis Services 2005

M icrosoft SQL Server entered the business intelligence market when it introduced a new component with SQL Server 7 called *OLAP Services*. OLAP Services, in conjunction with Data Transformation Services (DTS), allowed information workers to combine data from disparate sources into a single, multidimensional repository, called the *data warehouse* or *data mart*. OLAP Services allowed storing, processing, and preparing of the multidimensional data warehouse, which is a pre-aggregated, summarized, de-normalized data store optimized for reporting, analysis, and decision making.

SQL Server 2000 extended the business intelligence support by introducing several enhancements to its analytical or OLAP engine and support for a new technology called *data mining*, which is used to determine patterns between two or more pieces of information. OLAP Services from SQL Server 7 was renamed Analysis Services in SQL Server 2000. The new OLAP features introduced in Analysis Services 2000 combined with DTS, the robust Extraction, transformation, and loading (ETL) tool, and the introduction of the Reporting Services add-on for SQL Server 2000, made SQL Server a clear leader in the business intelligence market.

Analysis Services 2005 builds on the solid foundation of business intelligence support in SQL Server 2000 and introduces new features, tools, and functionality to build and deploy end-to-end business intelligence solutions. In addition to introducing new features, Analysis Services 2005 addresses several limitations that were present in the previous releases.

The business intelligence support in SQL Server 2005 is based on the theme "integrate, analyze, and report." Chapter 12, "SQL Server Integration Services Overview," shows how to integrate data from various sources by using SQL Server Integration Services (SSIS); this chapter describes the new features introduced in Analysis Services to prepare your data for analysis, and also contains an overview of SQL Server 2005 Reporting Services.

Before looking at some of the most important new features in Analysis Services 2005, let's take a quick overview of OLAP, data warehousing, business intelligence, and data mining.

OLAP, Data Warehousing, Business Intelligence, and Data Mining

A relational database can either be designed for real-time business operations, such as order processing, or optimized to support the decision-making process. The former is referred as *an online transaction processing (OLTP) database*; the later is called *online analytical processing (OLAP)*. Data in an OLAP database is organized to support analysis rather than to process real-time transactions, as in an OLTP database. An ETL tool such as DTS is often used to extract, transform, and load data from various sources, including OLTP databases, into an OLAP database. OLTP databases are generally designed to support a much higher number of concurrent users than OLAP databases.

An OLAP database, also known as a data mart, consolidates and organizes data from varied sources, including the operational data from OLTP databases. This data is processed and pre-aggregated to provide superior performance for ad hoc queries submitted to provide actionable business insights and to aid in the business decision-making process. In other words, a data warehouse is a data store that is built using a more systematic approach to combine data from various sources, cleanse it for accuracy and consistency, and organize it in a way that favors queries that request thousands or millions of rows at a time versus one that requests limited rowsets, like the ones found in an OLTP system. A data warehouse may also help in segregating expensive reporting queries from the OLTP system. A data warehouse often contains historical and summarized data that supports business decisions at many levels.

Let's say you wanted to find out about local, regional, national, and worldwide sales per year for the past five years for a particular set of products. To obtain this information from an OLTP database, the query might have to process millions of records and could take a long time to come back with results. In contrast, because an OLAP data warehouse already stores the summarized data in a multidimensional fashion, it yields the desired results a lot faster than the relational database.

Business intelligence is a generic term that means different things to different people. Business intelligence refers to sets of tools and applications that query OLAP data and provide reports and information to enterprise decision makers. Business intelligence tools and applications allow the leveraging of the organization's internal and external information assets for making better business decisions. Business intelligence capabilities include data transformation (ETL), OLAP, data mining, and reporting.

Data mining is an activity that operates on a data warehouse to ferret out trending patterns in the data. A common example of data mining is exhibited on the Amazon.com website. If you have ever received an email from Amazon that recommends a new book or DVD based on your past purchases, you have experienced data mining at work. Data mining involves exploring large quantities of data, using patterns and rules, in order to discover meaningful information about the data. A data mining component allows you to define data mining models based on existing data to discover trends and predict outcomes.

OLAP Terminology

Before you read the rest of this chapter, it's important that you be familiar with some terms related to OLAP.

A table that contains columns and rows is a basic object in a two-dimensional database system. The equivalent to this in a multidimensional OLAP database is a cube. A *cube* is a conceptual container of detailed values consisting of dimensions and measures. The term *measures* refers to facts available in any data store that are interesting to the business user. Some common measures are sales amount, sales quantity, hourly rate, current inventory amount, total expenses, and cost. In other words, a measure is a summarizable numerical value used to monitor business activity. A *dimension* is an aspect of the business through which measures are analyzed. In other words, a dimension is a descriptive category, such as date, product, location, or customer. Dimensions may have multiple hierarchies, each hierarchy may have multiple levels, and each level may have multiple members. For instance, the location dimension may have country, states, and city as the hierarchy.

Measures are aggregated based on the members of a dimension. A *member* is a particular instance of a dimension. Examples of members of a date dimension might be 2005, Quarter 1, January, and 1/1/2005. A *level* provides a grouping of members at a level of a hierarchy. In the preceding example, the levels that correspond to the example members might be Year, Quarter, Month, and Day. Dimension attributes are pieces of information about a member that are interesting for reporting or analysis, such as customer name, day of week, SKU, store hours, and so on.

The term *fact table* refers to a relational database table that is a central table in a data warehouse schema. A fact table usually contains a large number of rows, sometimes in the hundreds of millions of records. A fact table's columns include numeric values for one or more measures and primary keys from dimension tables as the foreign key columns. An example of a fact table could be a table with the columns product_id, time_id, customer_id, promotion_id, store_id, store_sales, store_cost, and unit_sales. Note that a fact table contains primary keys from all the dimension tables as foreign keys, and the rest of the columns are the measures.

The two common schema design strategies for data warehouses include the star schema and the snowflake schema. The entity relationship diagram of the *star schema* resembles a star, with one fact table at the center and several dimension tables as the points of the star. The *snowflake schema* is an extension of a star schema such that one or more dimensions are defined by multiple tables. In a snowflake schema, only primary dimension tables are joined to the fact table. Additional dimension tables are joined to primary dimension tables. Snowflake schemas are more normalized than star schemas.

OLAP Storage Modes

There are three modes in which you can store dimensional data. Each choice has its own characteristic data storage requirement and can greatly affect both processing and querying performance:

- **Multidimensional OLAP (MOLAP)**—MOLAP stores both the underlying data used to create the cube and the aggregations created for the cube in a multidimensional structure maintained on the OLAP engine, such as an Analysis Services server. Because the OLAP engine can answer all queries directly from this multidimensional structure without further accessing the relational or any other store, the MOLAP storage mode presents the best overall querying performance of all three storage modes. However, because the data used to create the cube is copied from the relational database to this multidimensional structure, even though the OLAP engine might compress this data, the storage requirement needed to support MOLAP is still the largest of the three storage modes. Another important consideration with the MOLAP strategy is the time it takes to process the cubes.

- **Relational OLAP (ROLAP)**—With ROLAP storage mode, both the underlying data for the cube and the aggregates created for the cube are stored in a common relational database. Because the OLAP engine (the Analysis Server) must query the relational database to retrieve all cube data, this storage mode provides the slowest querying performance of the three storage modes.

- **Hybrid OLAP (HOLAP)**—HOLAP combines elements from both MOLAP and ROLAP. With HOLAP, the aggregations are stored on the OLAP engine (the Analysis Services server) in multidimensional storage. However, the underlying data for the cube remains in relational database and is not copied into multidimensional storage. HOLAP provides the best processing performance and uses the least additional storage. Query performance is typically better in HOLAP than in ROLAP but not good as in MOLAP, depending on the aggregation design.

Analysis Services 2005 supports all three of these storage modes.

Analysis Services Fundamentals

Analysis Services is Microsoft's OLAP engine. It stores multidimensional data in a way that facilitates the performance and flexibility of OLAP. Analysis Services 2000 was already the market leader in OLAP, and Analysis Services 2005 promises to even further increase the appeal of the product in the OLAP market space. Two large differentiating factors between Analysis Services and other products on the market are the way it deals with *data explosion* and *data sparsity*.

Data Explosion and Data Sparsity Handling

To explain data explosion, we first need to explore the power of OLAP engines in general. Most OLAP engines provide high-performance, flexible analytical environments by pre-storing aggregations across several dimension levels. To better understand this, let's look at a very simplistic example of a sales cube with two measures—sales amount and sales quantity—and two dimensions—product (category and SKU) and date (year, month, and day). Queries can request this data in a variety of different ways. Here are some sample requests that can be answered from the sample cube:

"How many widgets were sold in December of last year?"

"What is the average number of gadgets sold on Saturdays?"

"What were the total sales for last year?"

"How do the total sales for March of last year compare to the total sales for March of this year?"

OLAP engines provide quick answers by pre-calculating the answers to these and other questions. Given our simplistic example, there would be a total of 12 possible aggregations, as shown here:

Time Dimension Level	Product Dimension Level
All days	All products
All days	Product Category
All days	Product
Year	All products
Year	Product Category
Year	Product
Month	All products
Month	Product Category
Month	Product
Day	All products
Day	Product Category
Day	Product

The number of actual pre-calculations depends on the number of members at the given level of a category. For instance, if we are storing 5 years and we have a total of 40,000 products, there would be 200,000 pre-calculations for the "Year/Product" aggregation.

Data explosion occurs when additional dimensions or levels are added, especially those with a large number of members, such as customers. If each combination of dimension/level is precalculated, the number of aggregations can easily reach into the billions or higher. An efficient indexing strategy would be needed in order to parse through such a large set of data to find the relevant calculations!

Analysis Services solves this problem by selectively aggregating data. Taking the example above, Analysis Services might choose to store the "Month/Product" aggregation but not the "Year/Product" aggregation. A request for the total number of widgets sold last year could be easily resolved by adding the 12 "Month/Product" pre-calculations to obtain the total for the year. This is still far better than adding each product sale for the year.

One problem with this random, selective aggregation in Analysis Services is that all dimensions/levels are considered as equal candidates for aggregation. Analysis Services does not know to favor commonly queried dimension levels unless you tell it to. You can tell the Aggregation Design Wizard to eliminate some dimension levels from consideration for pre-aggregation. This takes the form of a property on the measure group to assign the levels that should be removed from consideration. Another way to influence the aggregation design is to feed the wizard a query load that has occurred on the cube or measure group. This is referred to as *usage-based optimization*. These methods do not concretely direct the Aggregation Design Wizard to create one aggregation over another. They are simply means of influencing the wizard to do so more intelligently. When using these methods, you can actually aggregate at a higher level (that is, create more aggregations) because there are fewer available possibilities.

Another prevalent issue in OLAP is data sparsity. For any given cube, a number of dimension intersections will not be populated. In the preceding example, let's say the store didn't start selling a particular product until this year. This means that all the intersection points for this product in previous years would return empty cells. Cubes, by their very nature, tend to be highly sparse. A dense cube would mean nearly every combination of dimension levels would be active. This is not so hard to believe in our simplistic example, but in a more realistic cube, where we have Date, Product, Location, Customer, Discount Type, Promotion Type and more, you can see where sparsity comes into play. In many other OLAP products, a placeholder is stored even for empty cells. Analysis Services compacts its cubes by not reserving space when there are no values for the intersection. Space saving can be in the neighborhood of 50% to 90%. This results, also, in a more efficient cube because there is less to manage and examine when queries are issued.

These two inherent features of Analysis Services have been integral to propelling it to its current position in the market. With this introduction to OLAP concepts and Analysis Services capabilities, let's now see what's new in Analysis Services 2005.

Analysis Services 2005 Enhancements

The enhancements to Analysis Services are extreme, enough to warrant multiple books of their own. This chapter focuses on the enhancements that are relevant to Analysis Services administrators and are mostly addressed at a very high level. Details are presented in specific cases where they provide critical insight to the new paradigms introduced in this new, dramatically improved version of the product. Specific changes to front-end development, such as the many language enhancements to Multidimensional Expressions (MDX), are not addressed in this chapter.

Integrated Tools and the Enhanced User Interface Experience

Business Intelligence Development Studio (BIDS) and SQL Server Management Studio (SSMS) are the two biggest tools introduced as part of the SQL Server 2005 toolset. BIDS provides an integrated environment for developing and deploying business intelligence solutions, and SSMS provides an administration and management interface for maintaining already deployed business intelligence solutions. SSMS also provides the ability to author and execute Multidimensional Expressions (MDX), Data Mining Extensions (DMX), and XML for Analysis (XMLA) queries. BIDS enables you to create SSIS packages, build Analysis Services objects such as cubes and data mining models, and author Reporting Services reports.

BIDS provides a lot of templates to accelerate the development of cubes, dimensions, and so on. SSMS also provides a bunch of templates to give you a head start in authoring MDX and DMX queries. Each management dialog in SSMS (such as the Analysis Server Properties dialog) contains a Script button that you can click to generate XMLA script for the actions performed by that dialog. XMLA is discussed later in this chapter.

SSMS and BIDS are discussed in great detail in Chapter 5, "SQL Server 2005 Tools and Utilities."

You can use the SQL Server Configuration Manager tool to start and stop the Analysis Services instance and to view or edit service properties, such as the account under which the service runs.

Profiler Support

The SQL Profiler tool can now be used to trace Analysis Services events. You can use it to view both administrative commands and query requests. The DDL commands are displayed as XMLA scripts, and the queries are displayed as either MDX or DMX. Using Profiler is a great way to learn about MDX, DMX, and XMLA queries. You can perform various operations, such as browse a cube, in SSMS or BIDS and use Profiler to see the commands executed by these tools. Profiler also exposes events to show whether data was read from cache or disk and which aggregations were used to satisfy the query. Figure 13.1 shows SQL Profiler in action, capturing the queries and commands submitted to an Analysis Services instance.

Multiple Instance Support

Analysis Services 2000 did not support the installation of multiple instances. SQL Server 2005 fixes that problem by enabling up to 50 instances of the Analysis Services engine from SQL Server 2005 Enterprise Edition or 16 instances of the Analysis Services engine from other editions to be installed on the same machine.

By default, Analysis Services listens on port 2383. Additional instances can be assigned specific ports or can use a dynamic port configuration. In the latter scenario, Analysis Services attempts to use port 2383. If that port is not available, it looks for the first available port in a range of port numbers. The Analysis Services redirector, a part of the SQL Browser Windows service, is responsible for redirecting connections to the appropriate ports by using instance names in the connection string. Therefore, the Analysis Services redirector port, 2382, must be open to any external traffic that does not explicitly specify port information.

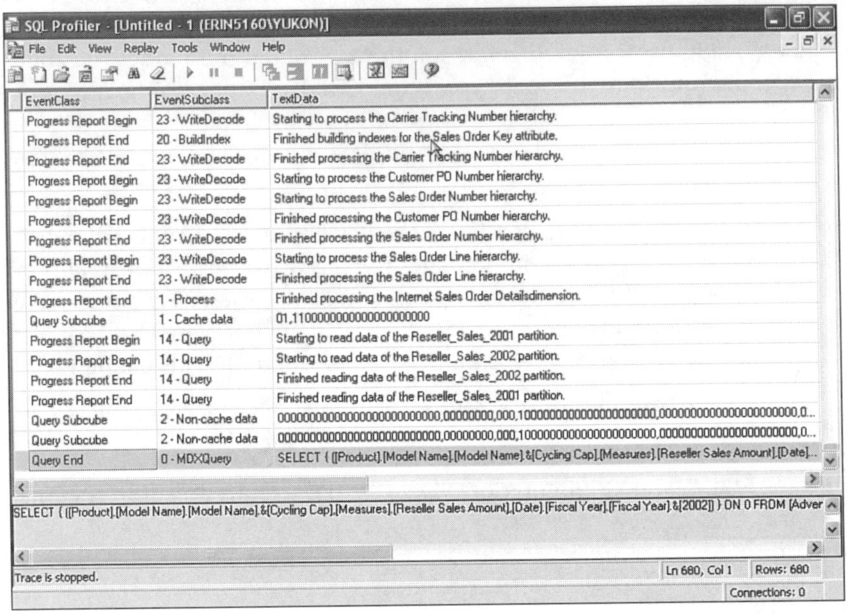

FIGURE 13.1   Profiler in SQL Server 2005 can be used to trace commands and queries submitted to Analysis Services 2005.

Failover Clustering Support

Analysis Services 2000 did not support failover clustering. Analysis Services 2005 adds this high-availability support and allows Analysis Services to be installed in an 8-node failover cluster on 32-bit systems and in a 4-node failover cluster on 64-bit platforms. The SQL Server 2005 setup is cluster aware and can seamlessly install Analysis Services on cluster nodes.

Unified Dimension Model (UDM) and Proactive Caching

The unified dimensional model (UDM) is arguably the most significant feature in Analysis Services 2005. The UDM provides a layer of abstraction between the source database and the data model that is presented to the querying user. The ultimate goal is to provide the best of OLAP and relational reporting.

Table 13.1 shows that the high-level benefits of relational reporting are not available in OLAP and vice versa. The UDM introduces a revolutionary platform for providing all these reporting features and more.

TABLE 13.1   Relational Reporting Versus OLAP Reporting

Feature	Relational Reporting	OLAP Reporting
Real-time data access	Yes	No
Detailed reporting	Yes	No
High performance	No	Yes
Flexible analysis	No	Yes

The UDM combines the best aspects of traditional OLAP-based analysis and relational reporting into one dimensional model. In its most simple form, the UDM could be used to provide user-friendly names to a querying client. Many OLTP applications have very cryptic column names that would not make sense to a business user, or even a developer, who tries to create queries on the information. You could simply define the UDM to provide a mapping to these underlying columns that renames them to more understandable names, such as changing CustID to Customer Identifier or CustFN to Customer First Name.

As mentioned previously, this is a highly simplified view of what the UDM provides; a UDM is far more powerful than that. The power of the UDM can best be demonstrated by walking through an implementation.

The UDM begins with the definition of one or more *data sources*. These are defined by using BIDS. These data sources can be any data store that is accessible via an OLE DB connection. This means that the UDM can actually be a combination of tables from various sources, such as SQL Server 2000, SQL Server 2005, Oracle, and DB2.

A *data source view* is then created to define a subset of information to be gathered from each data source. This data source view can then be manipulated to create relationships, rename tables or columns, add calculated columns, and more. The result is a logical data store that can be queried just as if it were physically stored in a single database. And, in fact, it can be physically stored. This is where the concept of proactive cache comes into play.

Proactive caching manages the local MOLAP data cache and can be configured to provide real-time, high-performance access to the information in the UDM at any point in time. This latency definition is literally represented as a slider bar in Analysis Services, as Figure 13.2 shows.

On one end of the slider bar, there is no latency. When changes have been made to the underlying data store, queries against the affected data revert to ROLAP until a new copy of the cache is rebuilt. At the other end of the slider bar is MOLAP. This means that the information is stored in Analysis Services and is updated within a period that is explicitly managed. Intermediate settings determine how often the MOLAP cache is rebuilt and whether the MOLAP cache can continue to be queried (instead of reverting to ROLAP) while the new cache is being built.

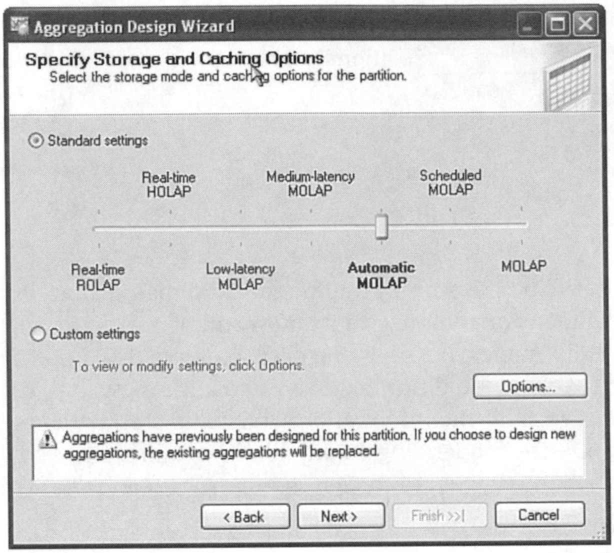

FIGURE 13.2 The Aggregation Design Wizard allows you to specify the storage mode and the caching options.

The beauty of proactive caching and the UDM is that it is fully configurable by the Analysis Services administrator. An experienced administrator knows that nothing comes without a price. It is rare that a business user does not say that he or she wants to receive information in real-time. It is up to administrators and developers to ascertain whether that is truly a requirement. The performance impact of real-time data should be taken into consideration. This impact does not change entirely with the UDM. Using MOLAP, which is on the other end of the spectrum, results in prestored, pre-calculated information that provides much better performance. MOLAP, however, does not give you the auto-processing functionality or the up-to-date information that you get with real-time or near-real-time analysis.

As you can see, the UDM does not remove all the real-world considerations of the past. However, it does provide a very easy mechanism of combining and presenting information for one or more source systems at a point in time that is completely configurable. Previously, such a solution would have required an extensive effort in architecting and programming.

Cube Enhancements

Analysis Services 2005 introduces several enhancements and new features related to designing and managing cubes. The following sections present some of the improvements introduced in Analysis Services 2005.

Multiple Fact Tables

You can use multiple fact tables in a single cube to consolidate related information. Measure groups are loosely equivalent to the concept of cubes in the previous versions of Analysis Services. These multiple-fact table cubes more closely resemble virtual cubes from Analysis Services 2000.

Intellicube

In Analysis Services 2000, an intimate knowledge of the underlying source database was required prior to the setup of dimensions and cubes. Each dimension had to be set up separately and added, explicitly, to a new cube. The Intellicube feature is invoked automatically when you create a new cube and check the Auto Build box in the Cube Wizard. It examines the tables in the designated data source view and determines what appear to be dimension and fact tables. These can be accepted or changed during the cube-building process. This functionality is very accurate, particularly if the source tables follow traditional multidimensional design techniques (using the star schema). This saves considerable time and effort in developing a new cube.

Key Performance Indicators (KPIs)

The term *key performance indicator (KPI)* refers to an indicator that measures how a business is doing in a given area. A simple example could be sales per day per retail square foot. For instance, for a given store, a KPI could be defined to include the following definition:

$\geq \$10,000$	Top performer
$\geq \$5,000$ and $< \$10,000$	Average performer
$< \$5,000$	Poor performer

You could define this KPI as a part of a cube and easily have any application reference it. A KPI consists of a value, a goal, a status, and the trend. Several user-friendly graphics give a visual representation of the values, such as a gauge, traffic light, road sign, or thermometer. Figure 13.3 shows the KPIs tab inside BIDS.

Translations

Translations are a globalization feature that provides the ability to display metadata (that is, dimension and measure labels) and data in alternate languages. This is all controlled at the cube definition level, again removing complexity from the underlying applications. Figure 13.4 shows some sample label strings and their respective translation strings in Spanish and French.

Perspectives

Perspectives provide a means of presenting alternate views of a cube to users to remove some of the underlying complexity. This is similar to creating a view in SQL Server that includes only a subset of the columns from the underlying tables.

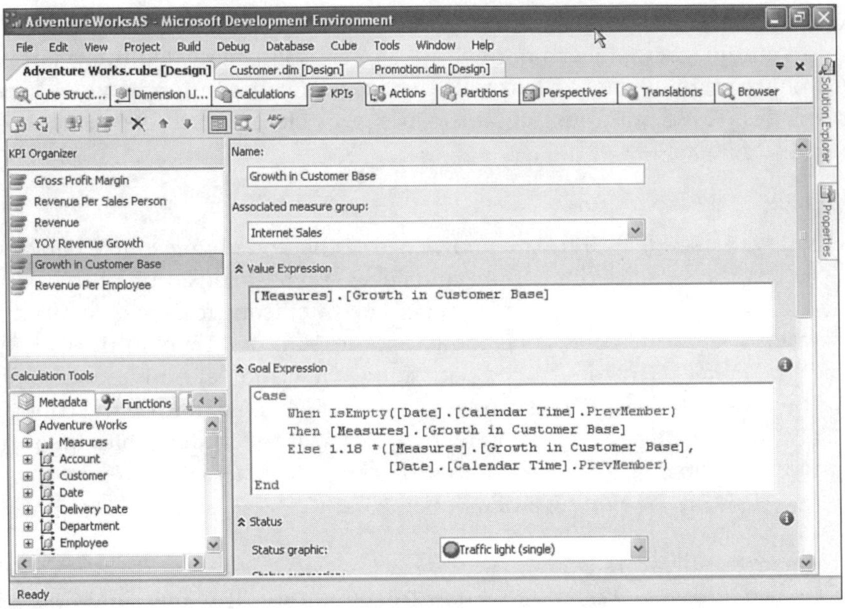

FIGURE 13.3   The Cube Designer in BIDS allows you to define KPIs and associate visual representational graphics such as traffic lights, gauges, and so on with them.

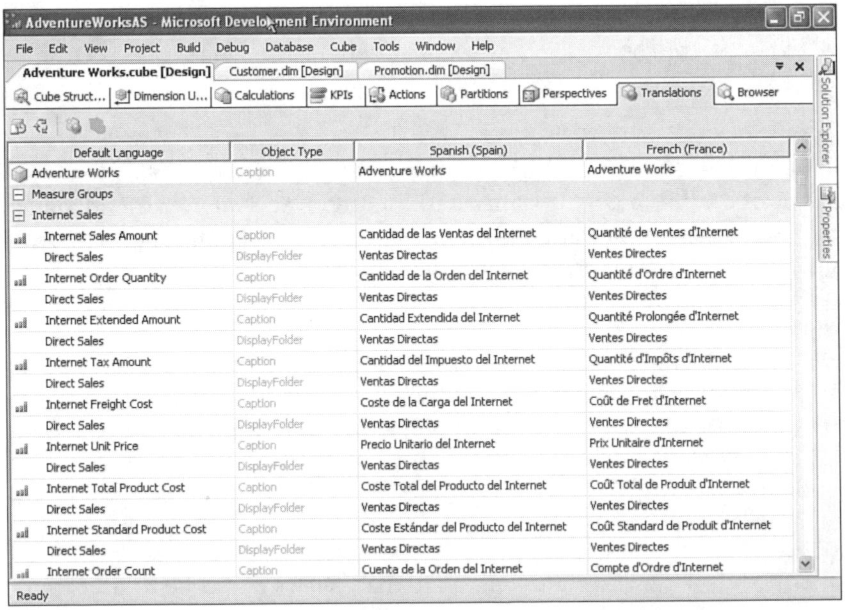

FIGURE 13.4   The Translations tab allows you to define dimension and measure labels in multiple languages.

Dimension Enhancements

At a high level, the concept of dimensions has changed in Analysis Services 2005. In Analysis Services 2000, dimensions were highly hierarchical structures. Dimension attributes, called *member properties,* could be used to create a separate dimension, called a *virtual dimension.* This greatly limited the navigational capabilities of business users.

Dimensions in Analysis Services 2005 are attribute based and are visible by default. They can be used for filtering and analysis, just like formal dimension structures were in Analysis Services 2000. This greatly expands the analytical capabilities of data analysts. Attributes correspond to the columns in the tables of a dimension. In addition to this extremely powerful aspect of dimension analysis, the following dimension enhancements are available in Analysis Services 2005.

No More 64,000 Limit

Analysis Services 2000 required that no member could have more than 64,000 children. This could be overcome by using member groups or introducing an explicit intermediate level that was invisible to the end user. This limitation is no longer present in Analysis Services 2005, and, therefore, no workaround is needed.

Role-Playing Dimensions

In Analysis Services 2000, any sourced dimension table could be used only once for a cube. This issue came up regularly if there were two date dimensions on the fact table that referenced a single date dimension. An example is when the fact table has an OrderDate and a ShipmentDate. Analysis Services 2000 required that a separate date dimension table be created to source the second dimension. In Analysis Services 2005, the same date dimension can be used for multiple foreign key columns in a fact table.

Reference Dimensions

A reference dimension table is one that is indirectly related to a fact table. Reference dimensions are readily apparent in snowflake designs, but Analysis Services 2005 provides the capability to separate out reference dimension with or without an underlying snowflake design. These dimensions can be used as part of a dimension hierarchy or created as a separate dimension in their own right. An example might be a case where a Product dimension is related directly to a Sales fact table. A Vendor table may then be related to the Product table but not directly to the Sales fact table. In this case, Vendor could be a level above Product in the same dimension, and/or it could be segregated into its own explicit dimension, even though it is not directly related to the Sales fact table.

Fact Dimension Relationships

A fact dimension is a dimension whose attributes are drawn from a fact table. This provides a means of implementing degenerate dimensions in Analysis Services without explicitly creating and populating the dimension in the star schema. Due to their large size, degenerate dimensions were difficult and expensive to load and manage.

Many-to-Many Dimensions

Analysis Services 2005 provides a solution to the age-old problem of many-to-many dimensions. An example could be a product that exists in multiple categories. The relational model would typically have a `ProductCategory` bridge table between the `Product` dimension and the `Sales` fact table. Analysis Services allows you to specify this type of relationship when defining the relationships between dimension tables and fact tables. Analysis Services handles the rest, making sure each view of the data shows the correct totals.

Multiple Hierarchy Dimensions

The concept of multiple hierarchies existed in Analysis Services 2000 in name only. In essence, dimensions with multiple hierarchies were actually separate dimensions that shared a high-level name. In fact, these dimensions are migrated as separate dimensions when you use the Migration Wizard because that's exactly what they are. In Analysis Services 2005, dimensions don't have this formal hierarchical structure. Many hierarchies are supported through the use of attribute dimensions, which is implicit within the product.

Data Mining Enhancements

Data mining can be used to provide tremendous insight into data without having to manually perform in-depth manual analysis. It can be used to determine patterns between two or more pieces of information (for instance, buying patterns based on age, gender, and years of education). Without the proper tools, the task of mining data can be very tedious and requires expertise in statistical analysis. Analysis Services provides data mining algorithms to circumvent this requirement and allow for easy definition of mining models in order to accomplish this task.

Analysis Services 2000 provided two data mining algorithms: clustering and decision trees. Data mining gets a significant boost in Analysis Services 2005, with the introduction of five new mining models. Here is a brief explanation of each of these new data mining algorithms:

- **Naïve Bayes**—This is a relatively simple algorithm that works well for predictive behavior analysis. Because it requires less computational activity, it is faster than most other models.

- **Association**—As its name implies, the Association algorithm associates items that are likely to appear together in a single unit, such as a transaction. This makes it ideal for market-basket analysis for the purposes of cross-selling.

- **Sequence clustering**—This algorithm can be used to analyze the sequence of events in a unit. It makes it an excellent tool for click-stream analysis.

- **Time series**—This is a forecasting algorithm that can be used to predict future sales trends based on historical data.

- **Neural network**—This algorithm is similar to decision trees (available in Analysis Services 2000) but can define a three-dimensional node structure to analyze larger amounts of data.

In addition to these new algorithms, the decision trees algorithm has been enhanced to allow an additional, continuous attribute as a predictable column.

The small number of data mining algorithms in Analysis Services 2000 is only partially the reason that data mining was a largely unused part of the product. Another was the difficulty in setup, maintenance, and presentation of the resulting findings of data modeling. Several new enhancements in Analysis Services 2005 have made data mining more accessible.

The Data Mining Wizard guides both novice and experienced users through the process of creating a data mining structures and models. SSIS has been enhanced with new tasks that create and process mining models and can subsequently run queries against them. Reporting Services also includes the ability to build reports on top of mining models.

XMLA Support

As previously mentioned, Analysis Services communication is now based exclusively on XMLA. XMLA is a standard protocol for communicating with multidimensional data stores. It is the result of a consortium between Microsoft and two other leading OLAP vendors, Hyperion and SAS. The specification can be found at www.xmla.org.

According to xmla.org, XMLA provides an "open industry-standard web service interface designed specifically for online analytical processing (OLAP) and data-mining functions." XMLA has actually been around since 2001 and was available for use in Analysis Services 2000, but it required the installation of the XML for Analysis Services Development Kit and the subsequent setup of a virtual directory in IIS. XMLA is the native language protocol in Analysis Services 2005 and is installed with the product. It can be integrated with SOAP to make Analysis Services a universally accessible web service.

Microsoft has further extended XMLA to include a specification for managing an instance of Analysis Services and to manage Analysis Services objects such as cubes, dimensions, data sources, and mining models. These extensions are comprehensively referred to as the *Analysis Services Scripting Language (ASSL)*. These objects can be scripted in either BIDS or SSMS. These objects can then be checked into a source code management system to provide a database versioning system. XMLA code can also be executed in SSMS.

Figure 13.5 shows an example of the XMLA script to create a new data source.

XMLA consists of two methods: `Discover` and `Execute`. The `Discover` method provides a means of examining metadata, such as enumerating through databases, data sources, cubes, and data models on an Analysis Services instance. Properties can be examined and used to construct a subsequent query request in the form of MDX or DMX. These are sent to the Analysis Services instance by using the `Execute` method.

As mentioned earlier, all Analysis Services objects are scripted and saved in the Data directories. XMLA code can be scripted or viewed in various ways. One way is to find the `.xml` scripts throughout the data directory. Another is to select the View Code option in BIDS when viewing the object to be scripted. Probably the most intuitive method is to script the objects directly within SSMS. You can script virtually any object at any point in the

Analysis Services hierarchy by right-clicking the object in Object Explorer and selecting the appropriate scripting menu option. These scripts can even be scripted to an XMLA query window, where text can be globally replaced and run to create a replica of the source object. This approach is useful for copying cubes and for creating additional partitions on a measure group.

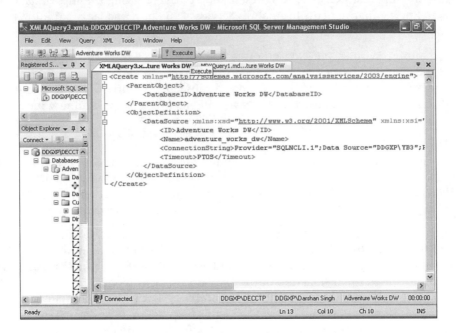

FIGURE 13.5   XMLA scripts can be authored and executed in SSMS. This script is for creating a data source in a database named Adventure Works DW.

In summary, XMLA support in SQL Server 2000 was provided as an add-on, whereas XMLA is natively built into Analysis Services 2005. XMLA with Analysis Services 2000 required clients to send HTTP/SOAP requests, which were processed by IIS, the XMLA SDK, and the Pivot Table Service on the middle tier. The middle-tier components then communicated with Analysis Services 2000 to execute the XMLA commands and obtain the results. With Analysis Services 2005, the client can submit the XMLA commands to Analysis Services 2005 directly over TCP/IP or over HTTP by using IIS.

TIP

There are four ways to learn XMLA: (1) by using SQL Profiler and tracing the server activity to see XMLA queries submitted to the server; (2) by right-clicking Analysis Services objects in Object Explorer in SSMS and selecting the appropriate scripting option; (3) by right-clicking Analysis Services objects in Solution Explorer in BIDS and selecting View Code; and (4) by clicking the Script button on the management dialogs in SSMS.

For instance, you can right-click an Analysis Server instance in Object Explorer, select Properties, and click the Script button to generate XMLA script to alter the server properties. Because AMO (discussed next) is based on XMLA, you can write an AMO script, execute it while Profiler is running, and see the XMLA that it submits to the server to perform the action. For example, if you write the AMO code to end, or kill, a long-running or a ghosted connection, you see an XMLA command similar to the following in Profiler:

```
<Cancel xmlns=
 "http://schemas.microsoft.com/analysisservices/2003/engine">
  <SPID>1453</SPID>
</Cancel>
```

If XMLA seems complicated to you, you can use a .NET-based API called Analysis Management Objects (AMO) from .NET code or scripting languages such as VBScript to manage Analysis Services 2005 objects. AMO is discussed in the following section.

Analysis Management Objects (AMO)

AMO provides a programmer-friendly layer on top of XMLA. It is exposed as a .NET object model and can be coded using any .NET programming language, such as Visual Basic .NET or C#. It replaces its predecessor, Decision Support Objects (DSO). DSO is still available in Analysis Services 2005 for backward compatibility, but it has not been enhanced to support any of the new functionality. Therefore, cubes that have been changed to use any of the new features in Analysis Services 2005 are no longer manageable by DSO.

AMO provides a more logical view of the Analysis Services environment than DSO. DSO inevitably required the use of the universal MDStores interface in order to reference databases, cubes, partitions, and aggregations. This was certainly confusing to anyone new to the object model, and it resulted in code that was sometimes difficult to interpret. MDStores had a list of possible properties that could be interpreted differently and were optionally available, depending on the object being referenced.

AMO has its own complexities, but they are related to the new Analysis Services architecture. When you understand the new architecture, the AMO object model becomes very intuitive. UDM, measure groups, and perspectives are just some of the new functionality that changes the way you traverse the object hierarchy to implement code. For instance, in Analysis Services 2000, the natural hierarchy from server to partition looked like this:

Server → Database → Cube → Partition

The DSO code to traverse this hierarchy looked something like this:

```
Set dsoServer = New DSO.Server
dsoServer.Connect ("localhost")
```

```
Set dsoDB = dsoServer.MDStores("Foodmart 2000")
Set dsoCube = dsoDB.MDStores("Sales")
Set dsoPartition = dsoCube.MDStores(1)
```

In Analysis Services 2005, the natural hierarchies have changed somewhat. In the preceding example, the roughly equivalent Analysis Services 2005 hierarchy is as follows:

Server → Database → Cube → Measure Group → Partition

A code segment to navigate this hierarchy would look something like this:

```
Server.Connect("LocalHost")
Database = Server.Databases("Foodmart 2000")
Cube = Database.Cubes("Sales")
MeasureGroup = Cube.MeasureGroups("Sales")
Partition = MeasureGroup.Partition(0)
```

AMO can be used to automate numerous tasks in Analysis Services, such as backing up all databases on a server, creating new partitions during incremental processing, and running reports to list metadata information and check for best practices. Virtually anything that can be done manually in Analysis Services can be coded in a .NET program, VBScript, or a script task in SSIS. This chapter focuses on SSIS because that is often the method of choice by system administrators. The SSIS script task is especially a good choice when using AMO to perform tasks such as adding partitions, performing backups, and so on because these tasks are often part of the end-to-end process of loading the data warehouse, which is usually performed in an ETL tool such as SSIS.

Using AMO Inside an SSIS Script Task

SSIS includes a new task that can be used to script managed code by using a .NET language. This has many advantages over VBScript, not the least of which is usability. The scripting environment offers many of the browse and help features of the Visual Studio .NET environment. You can use Visual Studio .NET to examine the objects, methods, and properties throughout the AMO model.

The first hurdle to implementing AMO, however, is referencing the object libraries. A limitation in Visual Basic for Applications (VBA), which is used in SSIS, requires that the AMO-related assemblies (`Microsoft.AnalysisServices.DLL` and `Microsoft.DataWarehouse.Interfaces.DLL`) be copied from the `%ProgramFiles%\Microsoft SQL Server\90\SDK\Assemblies` folder to the .NET folder in the Windows directory (for example, `%windir%\Microsoft.NET\Framework\v2.0.50215`). After you do this, the assemblies are accessible from the scripting task in SSIS. You can also right-click the script folder under Class View in the Microsoft Visual Studio for Applications script editor, select Add Reference, and then select Analysis Management Objects and `Microsoft.DataWarehouse. Interfaces` from the list. Figure 13.6 highlights the assembly references that are required for any basic AMO programming.

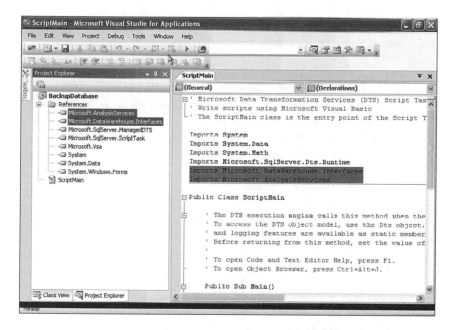

FIGURE 13.6 .NET assemblies are required to use AMO API.

To see AMO in action from an SSIS script task, you can launch BIDS, select File | Open | Project/Solution or press Ctrl+Shift+O, and open the `Backup Sample Project.sln` solution file. Then you can double-click the `BackupDatabase.dtsx` SSIS package, double-click the `BackupDatabase` script task, and on the Script page click the Design Script button to view the script.

Here is how the Visual Basic .NET script that uses AMO to back up an Analysis Services database looks:

```vb
Imports System
Imports System.Data
Imports System.Math
Imports Microsoft.SqlServer.Dts.Runtime

Imports Microsoft.DataWarehouse.Interfaces
Imports Microsoft.AnalysisServices

Public Class ScriptMain

    Public Sub Main()
        Dim server As New Server
        Dim database As Database
        Dim databaseName As String
        Dim serverName As String
```

```
    Dim backupFolderName As String
    Dim backupInfo As New BackupInfo

    serverName = Dts.Variables("ServerName").Value.ToString()
    databaseName = Dts.Variables("DatabaseName").Value.ToString()
    backupFolderName = Dts.Variables("BackupDirectory").Value.ToString()

    server.Connect(serverName)
    database = server.Databases(databaseName)

    backupInfo.AllowOverwrite = True
    backupInfo.ApplyCompression = True
    backupInfo.File = backupFolderName & databaseName & ".abf"


    database.Backup(backupInfo)

    server.Disconnect()

    Dts.TaskResult = Dts.Results.Success
  End Sub

End Class
```

Three SSIS variables are created to pass the name of the Analysis Services server, a database name, and a backup directory. You should right-click the Workflow designer area and select Variables. Then you should provide the values for these three variables, save the package, and execute it. If the package execution fails, you need to make sure that you have copied the Microsoft.AnalysisServices.DLL and Microsoft.DataWarehouse.Interfaces.DLL AMO assemblies from the %ProgramFiles%\Microsoft SQL Server\90\SDK\Assemblies folder into the .NET folder as mentioned previously; you also need to make sure you have updated the variable values and have the correct server name, database name, and backup folder path, as well as ensure that the specified backup folder already exists on the server.

AMO also allows you to create and maintain data mining objects, including model security, processing, and backup and restore.

ADOMD.NET

With SQL Server 2000, using the ADO MD and XMLA add-ons are the two ways to run queries against Analysis Server from a client application. ADO MD (MD for multidimensional) is a COM-based API created around OLE DB for OLAP. Much as all COM-based APIs are being replaced with .NET-based object libraries in SQL Server 2005, the ADO MD is being replaced with ADOMD.NET.

ADOMD.NET is a .NET-based object model for querying the Analysis Services server. Like AMO, ADOMD.NET is also based on XMLA. When you use the ADOMD.NET object model, behind the scene it generates XMLA that is submitted over TCP/IP or HTTP to the Analysis Server to retrieve data and metadata information from the server.

Performance Tuning for Analysis Services

There are two primary aspects to tuning Analysis Services: tuning processing performance and tuning query performance. This is often a balancing act because improving one often has a negative impact on the other. In a well-tuned Analysis Services instance, increasing aggregation improves query performance. This has a negative impact on processing times. The goal is to intelligently aggregate based on what is known about query requests.

Usage-Based Optimization (UBO)

When no additional information is given, Analysis Services creates aggregations randomly, with no knowledge of what aggregations will be most used. This is similar to indiscriminately creating indexes on all columns of a SQL Server table, without thinking about what columns will most frequently be searched on. One difference in a data warehouse is that it must be assumed that any piece of information may be used as a filter. Nonetheless, there will certainly be dimension levels that will be far more active than others. As previously mentioned, aggregation design can be influenced by setting properties at various levels in a dimension or by implementing usage-based optimization (UBO). UBO takes a workload from Analysis Services and designs aggregations based on the queries that were logged. You'll learn more about the implementation of UBO later in this chapter, in the section "Administering Analysis Services."

Partitioning Enhancements

Partitioning continues to be a performance-enhancing technique in Analysis Services 2005. Partitioning can improve the performance of queries against cubes by minimizing the amount of data that needs to be interrogated. A common partitioning strategy in Analysis Services uses a date as the partitioning key. Dates are an integral part of most analysis across industry verticals, providing feedback on trends and comparisons to historical segments in time. Partitioning by date has the side benefit of facilitating administration of the OLAP cubes. As new data is loaded into cubes, only the affected partitions require any type of processing. This can significantly diminish the batch window required for MOLAP and HOLAP processing. In addition, you can easily archive data out of an active cube by simply deleting older partitions. Otherwise, the data would need to be removed from the underlying source tables, and the entire cube/measure group would have to be reprocessed to remove the older data.

The implementation of partitioning in Analysis Services 2005 has been enhanced in a couple ways. First, data slices are no longer necessary if the aggregation design will be MOLAP. With MOLAP, Analysis Services keeps heuristics on the data stored in the partitions and can quickly examine that data to determine what partitions contain data relevant to the query. This does not apply to other aggregation storage levels. Second, partitions are processed in parallel by default. In Analysis Services 2000, this behavior required the use of a DSO application.

The Optimize Schema Option

One of the primary options used in Analysis Services 2000 and earlier implementations was Optimize Schema. By default, Analysis Services 2000 was pessimistic about the underlying integrity of the star schema tables. When processing a cube, it would issue a SQL query that joined the fact table to each associated dimension table as defined in the cube. This greatly slowed cube processing. Because the foreign key in the fact table is usually the same as the cube's member key, these joins could be removed by using the Optimize Schema option in the Cube Editor. This assumed that referential integrity was checked through foreign key relationships in the fact table or as part of the star schema loading process. Analysis Services 2005 uses the fact table's member key instead of joining to the dimension table by default. The Optimize Schema option was unknown by many users of Analysis Services, so the fact that this is now automatically implemented will speed up processing by default.

Administering Analysis Services

Now let's take a look at some of the changes in the administration of Analysis Services. Almost every aspect of administration has some noteworthy changes in SQL Server 2005.

One of the first notable areas is the location of the server/instance configuration properties. The properties associated with Analysis Services are more accessible than in previous implementations. Some were previously available only through registry entries. Now you can right-click the Analysis Services instance in Object Explorer and select Properties to launch the Analysis Server Properties dialog. The configurations display now closely resembles that in SQL Server, with a display of the current value, default value, and whether a restart of the service is required. The Show Advanced (All) Properties check box at the bottom of the screen exposes additional configuration values. Figure 13.7 shows the Analysis Server Properties dialog.

Full explanation of all available properties is beyond the scope of this chapter, but the following sections describe what you need to do in order to implement UBO.

Implementing UBO

UBO is mentioned previously as a means of designing custom aggregations based on a workload. The first step is to provide a workload to Analysis Services. You accomplish this by turning on the query log. Several properties are available for controlling query log behavior. Best practice continues to indicate placing the query log in a SQL Server database. To do this, you must enter a connection string in the Log\QueryLog\ QueryLogConnectionString property by using the Analysis Server Properties dialog. You select the Value cell and click the ellipsis (...) button to specify the server connection details. The name of the SQL Server table is controlled by the Log\QueryLog\ QueryLogTableName property. You need to modify the Log\QueryLog\QueryLogSampling property for the duration of the query sampling period in order to sample queries more frequently. This property defaults to 10, but you can lower this value to sample every *n*th query instead of every 10th. There is a slight performance hit involved with this, so it is good to set the property back to the original value or higher when sampling is complete.

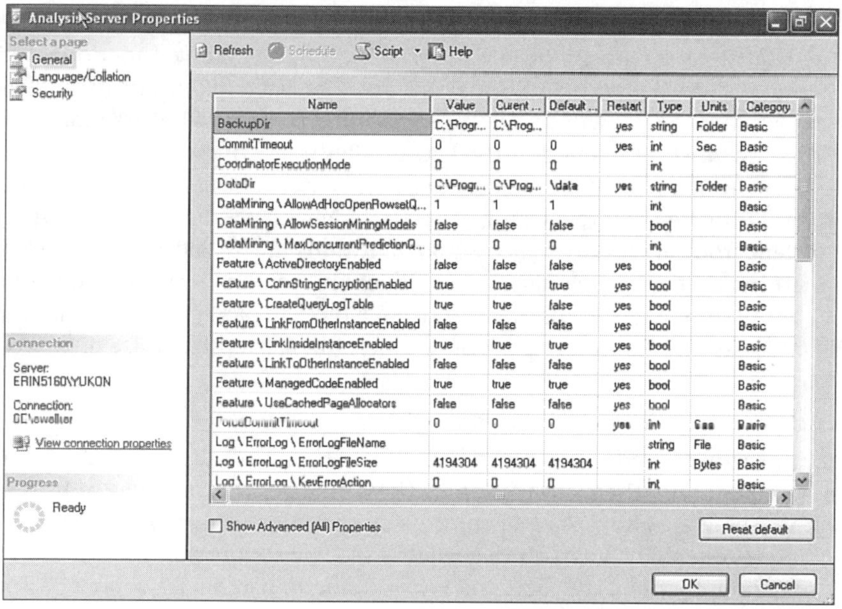

FIGURE 13.7   The Analysis Server Properties dialog provides a convenient way to view and edit Analysis Services instance configuration properties.

One final step is necessary in order to have Analysis Services create the log table in SQL Server. You need to check the Show Advanced (All) Properties check box to expose the Feature\CreateQueryLogTable property. Then you need to set this property value to true. When you look at the Restart column for this property, you should see that this requires a restart of Analysis Services in order to take effect. After you restart, your table is created in SQL Server, and you see rows appear in the log after Analysis Services cubes have been queried.

The UBO Wizard has not changed significantly since Analysis Services 2000. It can be invoked through SSMS. If you have sampled a workload by following the steps just outlined, the UBO Wizard allows you to filter on information, such as queries run by a specific user or queries that exceeded a specified duration, and it attempts to design new aggregations from which those queries would benefit. Note that UBO aggregation design still follows the rules for good aggregation design, which weigh the cost of an aggregation versus the benefit.

In Analysis Services 2000, you could automate UBO by using the DSO COM API via the CubeAnalyzer and PartitionAnalyzer objects. This continues to be true in Analysis Services 2005 but is made easier by the fact that SSIS can now expand beyond ActiveX scripting. Some of the limitations of VBScript required that the NextAnalysisStep method be invoked externally in a Visual Basic wrapper. This is not the case when you're using the Script task in SSIS.

Analysis Services Database Backup

You can back up Analysis Services databases to an operating system file to create a snapshot of the database at a point in time. This is similar to the archive functionality in Analysis Services 2000, but with additional options. The backup options include an indication as to whether to overwrite the destination file if it exists, whether to apply compression, and whether to encrypt the backup file. You can also indicate whether to include security information with the backup. This is useful on production backups, but you can turn it off when you're backing up a database with the intent to restore it on a different system. You can also indicate remote partitions in the Backup Database dialog. This is something that had to be handled separately in Analysis Services 2000. You connect to an Analysis Services instance by using Object Explorer in SSMS. Then you right-click any database and select Back Up to open the Backup Database dialog.

Cube and Mining Model Processing

Cube and mining model processing is the same in concept in SQL Server 2005 as in earlier implementations. The introduction of UDM changes this in terms of how manual a process it is. There are also a few new processing options, such as Process Index, Process Data, and Unprocess, that allow you to get more specific about what information is to be acted on. Also note that object processing is now done in parallel by default. For instance, when you process a cube, all partitions in all measure groups in the cube are processed in parallel. There are also new tasks in SSIS to more specifically define and perform the processing of cubes, dimensions, and mining models.

Analysis Services Security Overview

In the summer of 2003, Microsoft took a timeout to review the security vulnerabilities of literally every product it delivers. This is often referred to as Microsoft's Trustworthy Computing initiative, and it resulted in a "secure by design, secure by default, and secure by deployment" approach. Many product configurations are shut off by default as a way of protecting consumers from potential security vulnerabilities that they might not even be aware of. This is certainly true of Analysis Services. Several options that were either not available in Analysis Services 2000 or were inactive by default are implemented in such a way as to make Analysis Services 2005 more secure with the default installation. Examples include disallowing anonymous access and encrypting authentication. You can change most of these options, but any such changes could make your server more vulnerable, so you should closely evaluate them to make sure you understand possible repercussions.

Analysis Services authentication works much the way that it did in previous versions. There are two authentication schemes: integrated security and HTTP (IIS). When you use integrated security, Analysis Services leverages Windows authentication and all the associated robustness. Analysis Services can be configured to allow anonymous access, but, as mentioned previously, that is not the default. It is recommended that you retain the defaults.

You can use HTTP for connecting to Analysis Services over the Internet. Various middle-tier scenarios can be implemented to provide manageability for scenarios when the users are connecting from outside a trusted domain.

Granular Permissions

Authorization within Analysis Services has changed to be more granular and to more closely resemble what is found in the SQL Server relational engine. Previous versions of Analysis Services provided a single, all-or-nothing administrative role. This meant that anyone who had permissions to perform administrative functions on one database had the same, all-inclusive access to every other database on the server. That user also had access to the server-level attributes. For instance, he or she could modify the memory settings or change logging characteristics.

Like Analysis Services 2000, Analysis Services 2005 has a single, serverwide role that enables its members to perform any activity within Analysis Services. This is similar to the System Administrator role in SQL Server. Any members of the local System Administrators group are automatically added as members of this group. A user in this role does not require any additional permission in order to perform administrative functions or to access any objects in any database on the relative server instance. This is the only means of gaining access to Analysis Services databases, unless explicit database access is granted through database roles.

In Analysis Services 2005, individual database roles more granularly define access within an individual database. Logins can be given access to the Full Control role to be given full access to the database. Much like the database owner role in SQL Server, no further permissions need to be granted to such a login. More granular permissions can be granted by using one of these database roles:

- Process database

- Read definition

- Access a Data Source (Read/Write or None)

- Access a Cube (Read, Read/Write, or None)

- Access a Cell Data (Read, Read-contingent, Read/Write or None)

- Access a Dimension (Read, Read/Write, or None)

- Access a Mining Structure (Read or None)

- Access a Mining Model (Read, Read/Write, or None)

More defined permissions can be granted to individual objects within a database. If a user is a member of the Analysis Services administrator role or has Full Control access within a database, he or she needs no further permissions to access any objects within the database. All other users require explicit access to objects.

Analysis Services objects can be secured at a number of levels, down to the cell data level. A user can be a member of more than one role and has access to objects based on the union of all access from all roles. For instance, if a user has Read permissions to the HR cube through membership in the Human Resources role and has Read/Write permissions to the HR cube through membership in the HR Admin role, that user has Read/Write permissions to this cube.

Dimension-Level Security

Probably the most integral aspects of end-user security have to do with access to dimensions. In Analysis Services 2000, this access was based on access to dimension members in the dimension hierarchy. In Analysis Services 2005, the concept of hierarchy has been dismantled, and security is granted to attributes because any attribute can participate in a dimension view. MDX is used to define AllowedSet and DeniedSet properties. As the names imply, an AllowedSet property defines a set of members that can be accessed, and a DeniedSet property defines a set of members to which access is denied. An additional property, ApplyDenied, is available on the DeniedSet property, and it defaults to True. The ApplyDenied property specifies whether additional members of the attribute hierarchy are denied based on the members specified in the DeniedSet property. For instance, if a role is denied access to the United States member of the Country attribute, having ApplyDenied set to true would also deny access to all members that were descendents to this member in this attribute hierarchy.

One of the primary issues with Analysis Services 2000 had to do with memory usage when dimension-level security was implemented. Dimension-level security controls the members to which a user has access. So, if a user is a member of the SouthCentral Sales role, he or she may be limited to sales information for the states of Texas, Louisiana, and Oklahoma. In Analysis Services 2000, this resulted in a replica dimension when any user with access to a different combination of dimension access connected to Analysis Services. Dimension-level security uses memory much more conservatively in Analysis Services 2005, so concerns about memory utilization should not be an issue when determining whether to use dimension-level security.

Role-Based Security

Analysis Services provides role-based security. The middle-tier application is responsible for authenticating the user and simply passes the roles to be used when determining authorization to objects in SSAS. The disadvantage to this scenario is that the session has no username, and dynamic security cannot be implemented. Two other connection string properties are EffectiveUser and EffectiveRoles. The EffectiveUser property provides the name of a user to impersonate. Authorization is determined based on the roles of which that user is a member. The EffectiveRoles property can provide a subset of the user's roles that are defined within SSAS.

Migrating from SQL Server 2000 Analysis Services to SQL Server 2005 Analysis Services

As should be apparent from reading the previous sections in this chapter, Analysis Services 2005 introduces a big paradigm shift from previous versions. There are two options for migrating to Analysis Services 2005: using the Migration Wizard and starting all over and manually creating cubes from scratch.

> **NOTE**
>
> Analysis Services 2005 does not support migrating OLAP Services (the OLAP engine in SQL Server 7) databases.

Using the Migration Wizard

You can migrate Analysis Services 2000 databases to Analysis Services 2005 by using the Migration Wizard, which you can access by selecting Start | All Programs | Microsoft SQL Server 2005 | Analysis Services. You need to consider a number of issues when using this facility. The goal of the Migration Wizard is to migrate Analysis Services 2000 objects exactly. If you take this route, the new features of Analysis Services cannot be realized without some manual work. The following information should help you determine some of the compatibility issues with objects in previous versions and how to immediately leverage some of the new functionality in Analysis Services 2005.

An easy migration could be just that: You could migrate one or more databases and reprocess the objects. Applications should be validated to make sure that no functionality has been lost as a result of the migration. Drill-through settings, linked objects, and remote partitions are not migrated. Table 13.2 shows a list of object types in Analysis Services 2000 and how they appear in Analysis Services 2005.

TABLE 13.2 Analysis Services 2005 Migration Outcomes

Analysis Services 2000 Object	Analysis Services 2005 Object
Cube	Cube
Virtual cube	Cube with linked measure groups
Dimension	Dimension with one hierarchy
Virtual dimension	Dimension attributes and hierarchies
Calc member	MDX script
Calc cell	MDX script
Named Set	MDX script
Mining model	Mining structure with one model
Drill-through	Not migrated
Linked cube	Not migrated

After you run the Migration Wizard, all objects need to be reprocessed. Any changes to incorporate any of the many new features in Analysis Services 2005 need to be performed manually.

Starting from Scratch

Rather than use the Migration Wizard and manually update the features that need it, it might be more desirable to manually create cubes from scratch. This requires less effort than it might seem it would due to the new Intellicube technology. If you know your underlying schema well and it is in a star or snowflake schema format, the Cube Wizard can make a very accurate determination about which of the tables should become dimensions and which should become fact tables to feed the cubes when it invokes Intellicube. Because all cubes need to be reprocessed with either the Migration Wizard or the Cube Wizard, the latter option is worth considering.

SQL Server 2005 Reporting Services (SSRS) Overview

Reporting is an integral part of business intelligence development life cycle. Considering this, SQL Server 2005 includes a scalable and secure, enterprise reporting platform, called SQL Server 2005 Reporting Services. SSRS is a revolutionary reporting paradigm that can be used to author, manage, and deliver various kinds of reports containing data from relational or multi-dimensional data sources. Reporting Services was originally released as an add-on to SQL Server 2000. It is now natively integrated in SQL Server 2005 and also contains several enhancements over Reporting Services 2000. Before looking at these enhancements and new features, let's review some of the core components and tools that make up the reporting services platform.

Reporting Services Components and Tools

Reporting Services architecture consists of various components and tools that you can use to manage Reporting Services application. Here is an overview of these components and tools:

- At the core of Reporting Services architecture is a component called **Report Server**. Report Server is responsible for data and report processing and report delivery. Report Server itself consists of other sub-components including a Windows service and a web service. The Windows service provides scheduling and delivery infrastructure and the web service provides processing and rendering programming interfaces. The Report Server interacts with a SQL Server database that is used to store information and metadata of published reports, report models, and folder hierarchy. All access to this database must be handled through the Report Server by using management tools (such as Report Manager and SQL Server Management Studio, discussed next), or programmatic interfaces such as URL access, Report Server web service, or the Windows Management Instrumentation (WMI) provider.

- The web-based **Report Manager** tool can be used to access and manage reports, perform administrative tasks such as managing reports, folders, security, scheduling, subscription, and to launch Report Builder (which is discussed later). An alternative way to administer reports is to use Object Explorer in SQL Server Management Studio by connecting to a Report Services instance.

- SQL Server **Business Intelligence Development Studio** can be used to author and deploy reports. The report designer in BIDS is a full-featured report authoring tool that can be used to create both simple and complex reports. BIDS provides three SSRS project types, Report Server Project Wizard, Report Server Project, and Report Model Project. The Wizard can be used to quickly create a report and then modify it; Report Server Project can be used to build a report from the ground up using the designer and the Report Model Project can be used to create data sources, data source views, and report models that can be used by business uses to create ad-hoc reports by using by Report Builder (which is discussed next). A report model is an additional layer of information that maps database tables and views into concepts that are meaningful to business users.

- **Report Builder** is another report authoring tool available in SQL Server 2005. It is intended for business users who know their data and want to create ad-hoc reports. Report Builder is the result of the Microsoft's purchase of a company named ActiveViews in March 2004. Report Builder is a lightweight reporting tool that allows a business user to design and build reports without knowledge of SQL or MDX and without using complex tools such as BIDS. Report Builder provides an interface similar to those of Microsoft Office tools such as Excel. After a user defines his or her connection information to access a cube, the interface exposes the cubes, dimensions, and measures that are accessible by the user. The user then drags and drops the dimensions and measures that he or she wants to analyze. The user can then build a report that can be deployed and managed like any other report. A report that is built using Report Builder could be further embellished, however, through BIDS. In this scenario, a business user could define reports for one-time analysis, or he or she could decide that the report he or she has designed will have ongoing benefits to himself or herself as well as to additional users. The user could then request a more formalized report, based on the report definition, from a formal report writing department in the organization. Report Builder is a ClickOnce application, which means when the a user clicks Report Builder link inside Report Manager website, the application gets downloaded from the report server to a user's local computer. ClickOnce facilitates centralized management of the application.

- The reports created using BIDS and Report Builder are saved in an XML format called **Report Definition Language** (RDL). Once a report is created, it can be made available to other users by publishing or deploying a report project in BIDS or by saving a report in Report Builder.

- Users can view the reports by browsing to Report Manager website. Developers can present the reports in their custom applications by using new ReportViewer controls or on SharePoint sites by using report viewer web part. BIDS and Report Builder both allow previewing the reports. Reporting Services allows exporting reports to various formats such as XML, PDF, CSV, TIFF, Web archive (.mht), and Excel. Developers can extend the Reporting Services functionality by leveraging the WMI and SOAP web services programming APIs provided by SSRS.

- SSRS provides three **command line utilities** that can be used to administer a report server, rsconfig.exe, rskeymgmt.exe, and rs.exe. The rsconfig.exe utility is used to set configuration information for the specified report server. The configuration values are stored into RSReportServer.config file under %ProgramFiles%\Microsoft SQL Server\MSSQL.instance_id\Reporting Services\ReportServer folder. For security reasons, some configuration values are encrypted before saving. The rskeymgmt.exe utility is an encryption key management tool that can be used to back up, apply, and recreate symmetric keys. The rs.exe utility is provided to allow administrators to automate report server deployment and administration tasks. This utility can be used to execute Visual Basic .NET scripts against the specified Report Server.

- The new Reporting Services Configuration Manager tool allows configuring a local or remote Reporting Services installation. This tool allows managing Reporting Services virtual directories, Windows and web services credentials, report server database, encryption keys, and SMTP e-mail delivery settings.

Figure 13.8 shows the various configuration options provided by the Reporting Services Configuration Manager.

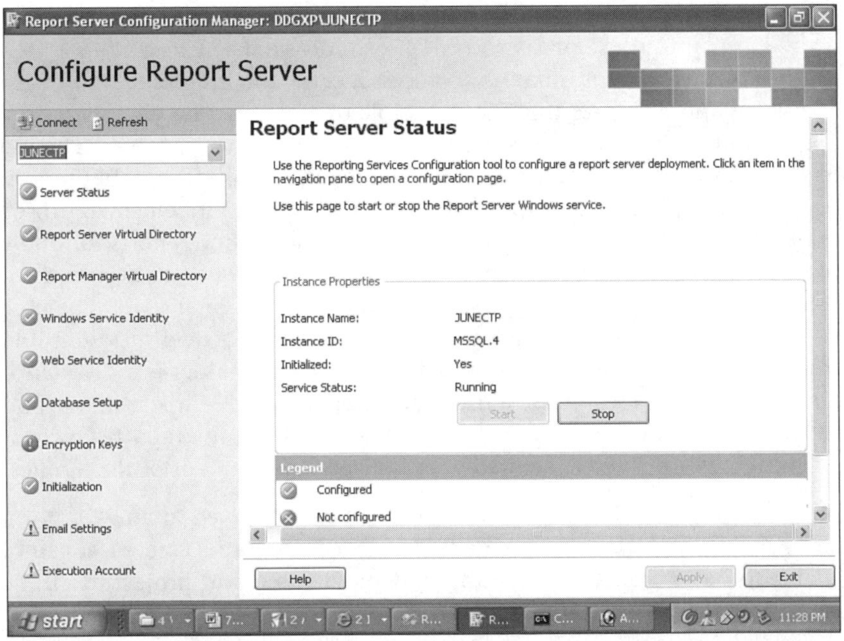

FIGURE 13.8   Reporting Services Configuration Manager allows configuring a report server deployment.

Reporting Services 2005 Enhancements

SQL Server 2005 Reporting Services builds on the solid foundation of Reporting Services 2000, providing a deep integration with other SQL Server 2005 components and SharePoint, core product enhancements, improved development productivity, and new tools. Here are some of the new features and enhancements introduced by SQL Server 2005 Reporting Services:

- Setup and deployment enhancements: SQL Server 2005 setup has been enhanced to decouple setup and configuration. Setup provides a files-only installation option that copies the program files to disk. And later, Reporting Services Configuration Manager tool can be used to complete the configuration step. Setup also provides a default configuration option that installs a ready-to-use report server. Independent of which setup option was chosen, the Reporting Services Configuration Manager tool can be used to configure and customize a Reporting Services installation. In addition, the new SQL Server 2005 Surface Area Configuration tool provides options to quickly enable or disable Report Server Windows service (and hence enable or disable scheduled events and report delivery), and web service (and hence enable or disable HTTP SOAP access).

- Management Studio integration: SQL Server Management Studio is enhanced to allow administering one or more report server instances. In addition, the scripting support allows generating a Visual Basic .NET script for report server objects. This script can be optionally updated, and then executed by rs.exe utility discussed earlier.

- Report Builder: As discussed earlier, SQL Server 2005 includes a new tool for business uses to create ad hoc reports based on the report models created and published by the model designers or developers. BIDS introduces a new project type called a Report Model that can be used to create the report models to be used by the Report Builder client.

- Report functionality enhancements: Responding to the feedback received on SQL Server 2000 Reporting Services, Microsoft has added several improvements to enhance the report functionality. The examples of these enhancements include ability to specify multiple values for a parameter, enhanced printing support, inter-active sorting in reporting, SharePoint integration, and improved RDL. Various report authoring enhancements have been made to report designer inside BIDS including a new graphical MDX query builder, enhanced expression builder, and SSIS integration.

- Programmability enhancements: Reporting Services 2005 introduces two new web services interfaces to manage objects on report server and to control the report processing and rendering. In addition, Visual Studio 2005 includes a set of freely redistributable report viewer controls that you can embed in your custom Reporting Services client application.

Summary

Analysis Services 2000 was already a leader in business intelligence. SQL Server 2005 continues this leadership by introducing the model "integrate, analyze, and report." The new tools and features introduced in this release make SQL Server 2005 an obvious choice for designing, developing, and deploying BI solutions. This chapter focuses on the "analyze" part of the new BI model and describes the latest and greatest features in Analysis Services 2005.

The chapter starts with an overview of OLAP, data warehousing, and BI concepts. Then it talks about some of the strengths of the Analysis Services 2000 release, the foundation on which Analysis Services 2005 is built. The chapter then discusses the new features in Analysis Services 2005, including the new UDM, cube and dimension enhancements, multiple-instance and clustering support, XMLA and AMO support, and data mining enhancements. The subsequent sections in the chapter provide an overview of Analysis Services 2005 performance tuning, administration, security, and migration-related topics. The chapter concludes with an overview of SQL Server 2005 Reporting Service, an integral part of the BI development lifecycle in SQL Server 2005.

This chapter concludes the discussion on business intelligence support in SQL Server 2005. Chapter 14 discusses Service Broker, a very interesting feature introduced in SQL Server 2005 that allows developers to build scalable applications by using asynchronous messaging within the database.

SQL Server Service Broker

Scalability, which refers to a system's ability to maintain the performance as the load increases, is one of the key characteristics of an enterprise application. The increased load can be due to a larger number of users, a larger number of transactions, more complex queries, or a larger volume of data. SQL Server 2005 introduces several new features to aid you in building scalable and distributed database applications. Service Broker is one such new feature that allows you to build scalable, reliable, secure, asynchronous, message-based, loosely coupled, distributed database applications.

Scalable application architectures often implement techniques such as performing parts of processing asynchronously, queuing the tasks for deferred or batch processing, and breaking tight coupling to distribute the load and to scale out. For instance, when an order record is inserted, the order fulfillment tasks can be queued, performed asynchronously, or performed on a different machine to increase the overall throughput of the order-accepting application and to shorten the interactive response time. Service Broker, a new component in the SQL Server 2005 database engine, provides the infrastructure and services for building such asynchronous, queued, distributed database applications. New DDL and DML statements have been introduced to create queues, send messages, receive messages, and so on. In other words, Service Broker acts as a framework and extensions to Transact-SQL (T-SQL) that you use to create message-based applications. SQL Server 2005 itself makes use of Service Broker to support various new features, such as

Database Mail (to asynchronously send emails), Query Notification (to asynchronously inform the client about change in the data), Event Notification (to asynchronously send DDL and trace event notifications), and so on.

This chapter introduces Service Broker concepts and explores ways to configure, administer, monitor, and troubleshoot Service Broker applications.

An Introduction to Asynchronous Messaging

Asynchronous messaging is not a new concept. Developers often use message queuing products such as Microsoft Message Queuing (MSMQ) to post a message to a queue and defer parts of processing to create scalable applications.

Asynchronous messaging offers the following benefits:

- **Improved performance and shortened interactive response time—** Responsiveness and overall throughput of the system is improved because much of the work is now done asynchronously, so the user doesn't have to wait for it to complete before receiving a response. Queuing and asynchronous messaging also allow developers to design an application to scale when the load increases.

- **Load distribution—**An application can send a message in a queue, which can be asynchronously received and processed by another application on a different machine to complete the rest of the processing.

- **Batch or deferred processing—**An application can send a message in a queue, which can be later received by an end-of-day batch process to complete the rest of the processing.

- **Scale out—**An application can send a message, which can be received and processed at different servers.

- **Parallelism—**Asynchronous messaging can also provide opportunities for increased parallelism. For instance, if you need to check inventory and verify a customer's credit, you can post messages to two queues. The queue messages can be processed asynchronously and in parallel to perform both tasks and to improve overall response time.

- **Loose coupling—**Messaging can be used to integrate applications. For instance, one application can post a message to a queue on which another application is listening. In addition, loose coupling (which involves breaking an application into sets of independent tasks) can also simplify deployment and upgrade scenarios.

At first it might seem simple to build your own asynchronous and queued messaging solution: Just post a message in a queue and then receive and parse the message to determine what processing needs to be done. However, it is not as simple as it seems. Asynchronous messaging frameworks such as MSMQ provide a lot of services to application developers, enabling them to focus on solving business problems. Messaging frameworks such as MSMQ have to guarantee the message delivery, ensure the message integrity, make sure that each message is received only once and received in the order sent, manage message routing and security, and handle situations where there are multiple queues and multiple readers or a single queue and multiple readers, and so on.

Asynchronous Messaging in a Database

Having an asynchronous messaging platform built into the database system offers following benefits:

- **Integrated management, deployment, and operations**—You do not have to worry about deploying, configuring, and administering two separate systems for data and messages. With SQL Server 2005, administration of messaging applications is part of the routine administration of the database. The high-availability solutions (such as clustering) protect the database and messages from failures. Familiar T-SQL and XQuery syntax can be used to query and find out things like total number of messages in a queue, the message text, what messages have not been delivered yet, and so on. Familiar trace events (from Profiler) can be used to monitor and debug the messages. The same connection can be used to manipulate data and to send/receive messages.

- **Unified programming model**—The same T-SQL language is used for data access and messaging. Database programmers find it convenient to use the same language (T-SQL) and tools to access data and to implement messaging.

- **Transactional distributed processing without the need for a complex two-phase commit**—Asynchronous messaging within a database can use message acknowledgements to provide reliable and transactional messaging without distributed (that is, two-phase commit) transactions.

- **Performance advantages**—By avoiding the use of external messaging system, which includes avoiding the two-phase commit requirement and optimizing in-instance messaging (the sender and receiver database are in the same instance), developers can get a significant performance advantage.

The asynchronous reliable messaging functionality is now built in to the SQL Server 2005 database engine in the form of Service Broker. You can use Service Broker technology in applications to send messages within the same database, between different databases on the same instance, between different instances on the same machine, or to a different server. Note that Service Broker is not based on MSMQ, and there are differences between the two technologies. Service Broker is compared with other messaging platforms later in this chapter, in the section "Service Broker and Other Messaging Technologies."

Understanding Service Broker

Service Broker helps developers to create database applications that can scale up and scale out. Developers can write a T-SQL script that creates Service Broker message types, queues, services, and stored procedures to be activated; begins and ends dialog conversations; sends and receives messages; and configures Service Broker networking (routing) and security settings. Your job as a DBA is to review the scripts; configure required security principals, certificates, endpoints, and so on; and execute the scripts to install the Service Broker application. Once the Service Broker application is installed, most administrative tasks are part of the normal administration for the database. As discussed later in this chapter, SQL Server provides several catalog views, dynamic management views, Profiler trace events, and Performance Monitor counters that you can use to maintain and optimize Service Broker applications.

The following sections explain the concepts by providing a glossary of Service Broker terms followed by T-SQL syntax for performing some common Service Broker tasks. Finally, you'll see a few scenarios where Service Broker can be used.

Service Broker Terminology

Service Broker applications consist of Service Broker objects such as messages, queues, services, and so on, and stored procedures and applications that use those objects. Messages, dialog conversations, and conversation groups are the basis of the conversation architecture for Service Broker. Message types, contracts, services, and queues are the basis of the service architecture for Service Broker. Routes, endpoints, and remote service bindings define the networking and security architecture for Service Broker. The following sections explain all these terms and how they play a role in the Service Broker application.

Messages

Messages are the information exchanged between applications that use Service Broker. Messages refer to blocks of data moved around a Service Broker application. Each message is a part of a conversation. Each message has a unique identity, as well as a sequence number within the conversation. The SEND T-SQL statement is used to send a message on an existing queue, and the RECEIVE T-SQL statement is used to retrieve one or more messages from a queue.

Service Broker uses two distinct categories of message:

- **Sequenced message**—A *sequenced message* is a message that must be delivered to an application exactly once, in order. All user-defined message types, end dialog messages, and error messages created by an application are sequenced messages.

- **Unsequenced message**—An *unsequenced message* is a message that can be processed immediately, regardless of the sequence in which the it arrives. Service Broker uses unsequenced messages for dedicated acknowledgement messages and error messages created by Service Broker.

Message Types

Message types define the content of messages. In other words, a message type is a definition of the format of a message. The CREATE MESSAGE TYPE DDL statement can be used to create a message type. A message type is stored in SQL Server, and it states what a message looks like.

The participants in a Service Broker conversation must agree on the name and content of each message. A message type object defines a name for a message type and defines the type of data that the message contains. If multiple databases participate in a Service Broker conversation, an identical message type has to be created in each database. Message type is used to validate incoming messages. If an incoming message does not conform to the message type specified for that conversation, Service Broker discards the invalid message and returns an error message to the service that sent the message.

NOTE

Regardless of the message type, SQL Server stores the content of the message as type `varbinary(max)`. Therefore, a message can contain any data that can be converted to `varbinary(max)`. The Service Broker message size is limited to 2GB.

Queues

Queues are database objects used for storing messages. These named database objects hold the messages in the order in which they were received while the messages await the processing. Like a table, a queue contains rows. Each Service Broker message is a row in a queue. Each queue row contains information such as message type, sequence number, conversation, service, validation, and contract details.

The `CREATE QUEUE` DDL statement can be used to create a queue. The `SEND` and `RECEIVE` statements (and not the `INSERT`, `UPDATE`, `DELETE`, or `TRUNCATE` statements) are used to manipulate queues. While creating a queue, you can associate a stored procedure by using the `ACTIVATION` clause. SQL Server runs, or *activates*, this stored procedure when there are messages in the queue to be processed. To catch up with the messages in the queue, Service Broker can activate multiple instances of the associated stored procedure. You use the `MAX_QUEUE_READERS` option specified with the `CREATE QUEUE` or `ALTER QUEUE` statement to specify the maximum number of stored procedure instances that Service Broker starts for this queue.

Services

A *service* is a named entity that is used to deliver messages to the correct queue within a database, to route messages, to enforce a contract for a conversation, and to determine the remote security for a new conversation. Services are endpoints for conversations.

You use the `CREATE SERVICE` DDL statement to create a new service. Each service is associated with a single queue. If you want a service to be a target in a dialog, you must specify one or more contracts for which this service may be a target.

Contracts

A *contract*, which is created by using the `CREATE CONTRACT` DDL statement, is an agreement that defines the message types used in a Service Broker conversation and also determines which side of the conversation can send messages of that type. Each Service Broker conversation follows a contract. In summary, a contract specifies the *direction* and *type* of messages in a given conversation.

Service Program

AA *service program* is normally a stored procedure—but can be an external program—that processes Service Broker messages. The stored procedure associated with a queue that uses the ACTIVATION clause is an example of a service program.

Dialog Conversation

A *dialog conversation*, or dialog, is a reliable, persistent stream of messages Abetween two services. It is a conversation between two services that guarantees exactly once-in-order delivery of messages.

A dialog conversation has two participants: an *initiator* that begins the conversation using the BEGIN DIALOG CONVERSATION T-SQL statement and ends the conversation using END CONVERSION statement; and a *target* that accepts a conversation begun by the initiator. A dialog incorporates automatic message receipt acknowledgement to ensure reliable delivery. Note that an instance that forwards a message does not acknowledge the message to the sender. Only the final destination acknowledges the message. If the sender does not receive an acknowledgement from the destination after a period of time, the sender retries the message.

Service Broker saves each outgoing message in the transmission queue until the message is acknowledged by the remote service. In cases where both sides of the conversation are in the same instance, Service Broker may optimize message delivery by placing the message directly on the destination queue. Where possible, acknowledgement messages are included as part of return messages for the dialog.

NOTE

Acknowledgement messages are handled internally by the database engine, and they do not appear in a queue or visible to the application. Service Broker does not consider it an error for a remote service to become unreachable. When a remote service is unreachable, Service Broker holds messages for that service until the service becomes reachable or the dialog lifetime expires.

Service Broker never ends a dialog automatically. Applications are responsible for indicating when they are done with a dialog by explicitly ending the dialog. The dialog remains in the database until an application explicitly ends the conversation by calling END CONVERSATION.

NOTE

SQL Server Service Broker architecture defines two types of conversations: dialog and monolog. *Dialog* is a two-way, reliable, ordered exchange of messages, and *monolog* is a one-way, reliable, ordered publication of messages from one endpoint to any number of endpoints. However, monolog conversation is not available in SQL Server 2005, but is a planned feature for a future release. In this release, the terms *dialog* and *conversation* are synonymous. This is the reason you begin a dialog (by using BEGIN DIALOG CONVERSATION), but end a conversation (by using END CONVERSATION). Throughout this chapter, *conversation* refers to either a dialog or a monolog.

Messages exchanged with services on different SQL Server instances are by default encrypted. Messages exchanged with services in the same SQL Server instance are never encrypted.

Conversation Groups

Service Broker internally creates a *conversation group* to group together related conversations and to provide exactly once-in-order access to messages that are related to a specific business task. SQL Server manages the lifetime of the conversation group. Each time an application sends or receives a message, SQL Server locks the conversation group, preventing another program from updating the same state data at the same time. Application developers can use conversation groups for state management and to orchestrate conversations. The sys.conversation_groups system catalog view can be used to obtain a list of active conversation groups.

Routes

A *route* specifies the location of the Service Broker service and the database that contains the service. Service Broker uses routes to deliver messages. By default, each database contains a route named AutoCreatedLocal which specifies that services with no other route defined are delivered within the current instance. Routes provide an abstraction over instances of SQL Server used in Service Broker communication, so that instances can be moved without changing any of the service programs. The basic components of a route are the service name, a broker instance identifier, and a network address.

When a dialog conversation is started using BEGIN DIALOG CONVERSATION, SQL Server uses the specified service name and broker instance identifier to determine the route for the conversation. After the target acknowledges the first message, all subsequent messages on that conversation are routed to the same database.

You can use the sys.routes catalog view to view a list of routes present in the current database. You can use the CREATE ROUTE DDL statement to create a new Service Broker route.

> **NOTE**
>
> Service Broker checks the routes defined in the msdb database (msdb.sys.routes) for messages on conversations that originate in another instance, including messages to be forwarded. The routing table in the local database is used only for the outgoing messages that originate in the current instance.

Service Broker message forwarding tracks the number of times a message has been forwarded to protect against endless routing loops.

In summary, a route maps a service name to a physical network address. It is possible to define multiple routes with the same service name for load balancing.

Service Broker Endpoints

As explained in Chapter 7, "SQL Server 2005 Security," an *endpoint* can be thought of as an entry point into a SQL Server instance. Service Broker communication outside the SQL Server instance requires a Service Broker endpoint to be created by using the CREATE ENDPOINT T-SQL statement. By default, an instance of SQL Server does not contain a Service Broker endpoint.

TCP is the only allowed protocol for Service Broker. In order for two SQL Server instances to exchange Service Broker messages, each instance must be able to send TCP/IP traffic to the port that the other instance uses for Service Broker communication. By convention, Service Broker uses port 4022 for broker-to-broker communication. You can specify a different port by using the LISTENER_PORT clause with the CREATE ENDPOINT statement. A Service Broker endpoint listens on a specific TCP port number and provides options for transport security and message forwarding. You can use the sys.service_broker_endpoints catalog view to see a list of Service Broker endpoints.

Remote Service Binding

Service Broker dialog security is based on certificates. A certificate is used to verify the identity of a remote database and to identify the local database principal for the operation. In other words, a certificate is used to establish the credentials of a remote database and then map operations from the remote database to a local user. The permissions for the local user apply to any operation on behalf of the remote service. The certificate is shared between databases. No other information for the user is shared. A remote service binding, which you can create by using the CREATE REMOTE SERVICE BINDING T-SQL statement, establishes a relationship between a local database user, the certificate for the user, and the name of a remote service. Service Broker uses the remote service binding to provide dialog security for conversations that target the remote service. A remote service binding is necessary only for initiating services that communicate with target services outside the SQL Server instance.

Poison Messages

If a service program such as an activated stored procedure rolls back the transaction that contains a RECEIVE statement because it cannot successfully process a message, that message is called a *poison message*. For instance, let's say that an application sends a message to withdraw a part from inventory in response to an order entry action. If the order is changed while the inventory message is being processed, the service program cannot successfully process the inventory change message because the new order does not contain the original part information. With these poison messages, the service program has to roll back the transaction because it cannot successfully process the message. If this happens five times, Service Broker disables all the queues from which the transaction received messages and raises the Broker:Queue Disabled trace event. Application developers can programmatically detect and handle poison messages, and administrators can create alerts on the Broker:Queue Disabled trace event.

Activation

Service Broker applications can optionally leverage a technique called *activation* that activates or starts a stored procedure (*internal activation*) or produces a SQL Server event that an external application can respond to (*external activation*), whenever there is a message in a Service Broker queue. You can use the sys.dm_broker_activated_tasks dynamic management view to see a list of stored procedures activated by Service Broker.

Message Forwarding

Service Broker *message forwarding* allows an instance of SQL Server to accept messages from an outside instance and send those messages to a different instance. It can be used in scenarios such as to provide connectivity between servers in different trust domains, to simplify administration by creating a single centralized instance that holds the routing information for a domain, to distribute work among several instances, and so on. You can use the CREATE/ALTER ENDPOINT statement to configure Service Broker message forwarding.

Figure 14.1 shows the basic Service Broker architecture and is a pictorial representation of terms explained in this section.

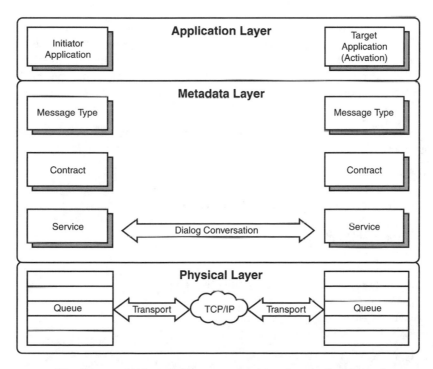

FIGURE 14.1 The Service Broker architecture consists of a physical layer (messages traverse between queues over TCP/IP in binary format), a metadata layer (services, contracts, and message types), and an application layer (initiator application and target application; target may optionally use activation).

Common Service Broker Tasks

The following sections show the T-SQL syntax for performing some common Service Broker tasks.

Enabling and Disabling Service Broker

SQL Server provides a database-level property to specify whether a database is enabled for Service Broker communication. When you create a new database, by default Service Broker is enabled for the new database. The is_broker_enabled flag is set to value 1 in the sys.databases catalog view to indicate that a database can send and receive Service Broker messages.

The DISABLE_BROKER option with the ALTER DATABASE statement deactivates Service Broker, and the ENABLE_BROKER option activates Service Broker in the database. When Service Broker is not active in the database, messages remain in the transmission queue. The sys.transmission_queue catalog view contains a row for each message in the transmission queue. As soon the Service Broker is activated, messages are delivered to the database.

Here is an example of enabling and disabling Service Broker in a database and using the sys.databases catalog to verify whether Service Broker is active in a database:

```
USE [master];
GO
ALTER DATABASE [AdventureWorks] SET DISABLE_BROKER;
GO
SELECT is_broker_enabled FROM sys.databases
   WHERE name = 'AdventureWorks';
GO
ALTER DATABASE [AdventureWorks] SET ENABLE_BROKER;
GO
SELECT is_broker_enabled FROM sys.databases
   WHERE name = 'AdventureWorks';
GO
```

CAUTION

By default, restored or attached databases have Service Broker disabled. The exception to this is Database Mirroring, in which Service Broker is enabled after failover.

Creating a Service Broker Endpoint

As mentioned previously, Service Broker communication outside a SQL Server instance requires a Service Broker endpoint to be created, by using the CREATE ENDPOINT T-SQL statement, as in this example:

```
USE [master];
GO
CREATE ENDPOINT testEndpoint
    STATE = STARTED
    AS TCP (LISTENER_PORT = 4022)
    FOR SERVICE_BROKER (AUTHENTICATION = WINDOWS);
GO
SELECT * FROM sys.service_broker_endpoints;
GO
ALTER ENDPOINT testEndPoint
    FOR SERVICE_BROKER (MESSAGE_FORWARDING = ENABLED);
GO
SELECT * FROM sys.service_broker_endpoints;
GO
DROP ENDPOINT testEndPoint;
GO
```

These statements create a Service Broker endpoint, use the sys.service_broker_endpoints catalog view to see metadata of the endpoint just created, enable message forwarding on the endpoint by using ALTER ENDPOINT, and finally drop the endpoint, preventing messages from arriving in the instance.

Creating a Message Type

You can use the CREATE MESSAGE TYPE DDL statement to create a Service Broker object that defines the format of messages. Here's an example:

```
USE [AdventureWorks];
GO
CREATE MESSAGE TYPE SBSampleMessageType
    VALIDATION = WELL_FORMED_XML;
GO
SELECT * FROM sys.service_message_types
    WHERE name = 'SBSampleMessageType';
GO
DROP MESSAGE TYPE SBSampleMessageType;
GO
```

These statements create a message type indicating that messages can contain well-formed XML documents.

NOTE

For XML messages, you can optionally specify the XML schema collection while creating the message type. When the message arrives at the target, Service Broker validates the XML message contents against the XML schema specified with the message type. If schema validation fails, an error message is sent back to the initiator. Note that XML validation imposes a fair amount of overhead.

Creating a Contract

You can use the CREATE CONTRACT DDL statement to create a Service Broker object that defines the direction and type of message in a Service Broker conversation. Here's an example:

```
USE [AdventureWorks];
GO
CREATE MESSAGE TYPE SBSampleMessageType
   VALIDATION = WELL_FORMED_XML;
GO
CREATE CONTRACT SBSampleContract
   (SBSampleMessageType SENT BY ANY);
GO
SELECT * FROM sys.service_contracts
   WHERE name = 'SBSampleContract';
GO
DROP CONTRACT SBSampleContract;
GO
DROP MESSAGE TYPE SBSampleMessageType;
GO
```

These T-SQL statements create a contract specifying that conversations can send well-formed XML documents and that both the initiator and target can send the message.

Creating a Queue

You can use the CREATE QUEUE DDL statement to create a new queue in the database to store Service Broker messages. While creating a queue, you can specify a name of a stored procedure that will be activated whenever there is a message in this queue. Here's an example:

```
USE [AdventureWorks];
GO
CREATE QUEUE dbo.SBSampleQueue
   WITH STATUS = ON,
        RETENTION = OFF,
     ACTIVATION (
       PROCEDURE_NAME = AdventureWorks.dbo.sproc_SBLengthyProcessing,
       MAX_QUEUE_READERS = 5,
```

```
        EXECUTE AS OWNER)
    ON [DEFAULT];
GO
SELECT * FROM sys.service_queues;
GO
DROP QUEUE dbo.SBSampleQueue;
GO
```

These statements create a queue and specify a stored procedure to be activated to process the messages in the queue. The CREATE QUEUE statement fails if the specified stored procedure does not exist.

Creating a Service

You can use the CREATE SERVICE DDL statement to create a service. Here's an example:

```
USE [AdventureWorks];
GO
CREATE SERVICE
    SBSampleService ON QUEUE SBSampleQueue
    (SBSampleContract);
GO
SELECT * FROM sys.services;
GO
DROP SERVICE SBSampleService;
GO
```

These statements create a service, associate it with a queue named SBSampleQueue, and specify that conversations must follow the agreement defined by the contract named SBSampleContract. Both the contract and queue must exist for the CREATE SERVICE statement to succeed.

NOTE

Service Broker objects, including services, queues, message types, and contracts, may not be temporary objects. Their names can begin with #, but they are still permanent database objects.

Starting a Dialog Conversation

You can use the BEGIN DIALOG CONVERSATION statement to begin a dialog from one service to another service. Here's an example:

```
DECLARE @dlgHandle UNIQUEIDENTIFIER;
BEGIN DIALOG CONVERSATION @dlgHandle
    FROM SERVICE SBSampleService
    TO SERVICE 'SBSampleService'
    ON CONTRACT SBSampleContract;
```

The dialog handle is then used to send the messages on this conversation. With BEGIN DIALOG CONVERSATION you can optionally specify the lifetime (in seconds) of the dialog, turn off encryption, and relate the dialog to an existing conversation or conversation group.

Sending and Receiving Messages

You use the SEND statement to post a message to a Service Broker queue. Here's an example:

```
SEND ON CONVERSATION @dlgHandle
    MESSAGE TYPE SBSampleMessageType (@InsertedData);
```

You use the RECEIVE statement, whose syntax is similar to SELECT statement, to retrieve the message from the queue, as in this example:

```
RECEIVE TOP (1) * FROM dbo.SBSampleQueue;
```

The RECEIVE statement is commonly used with the WAITFOR statement, as shown here:

```
WAITFOR (RECEIVE CAST(message_body AS XML) AS msgText
    FROM dbo.SBSampleQueue
    INTO @SBMessage), TIMEOUT 60000;
```

This statement blocks a thread until a message is available in a queue or until 60 seconds has elapsed. If a message is already present in the queue, the statement returns immediately, copying the message into the specified table variable (in this case, @SBMessage).

Ending Dialog Conversation

You use the END CONVERSATION statement to end an active conversation. Here's an example:

```
END CONVERSATION @dlgHandle;
```

Backing Up and Restoring Service Broker Applications

Because the Service Broker objects reside in the database in which the service runs, backing up the database takes care of the Service Broker components. The msdb database contains routes for incoming messages, and the master database contains the Service Broker endpoints and transport security configuration settings. These two system databases have to be backed up in case the Service Broker application communicates with other instances of SQL Server.

Service Broker Scenarios

Service Broker provides all the infrastructure and services required to reliably and securely queue and move the messages in a database, across databases, across instances, or across multiple servers. You can use some new T-SQL constructs to send and receive messages; everything else is handled by the Service Broker subsystem inside the SQL Server 2005 database engine.

SQL Server 2005 introduces new T-SQL DDL statements such as `CREATE SERVICE` and `CREATE QUEUE` and new DML statements such as `BEGIN DIALOG CONVERSATION`, `SEND`, `RECEIVE`, and `END CONVERSATION` that you can use to implement a Service Broker application. Any program that can run T-SQL statements can use Service Broker. A Service Broker application can be implemented as a program running outside SQL Server or as a stored procedure written in T-SQL or a .NET language.

The following sections look at a few typical scenarios where Service Broker can be used.

Asynchronous Triggers

Traditional triggers are executed synchronously. For instance, if a table has an associated `INSERT` trigger, then an `INSERT` operation on that table does not finish until the trigger completes. You can use Service Broker to change this. You can cause a trigger to simply post a message in a Service Broker queue and return. This message can be asynchronously received by a Service Broker application, such as a stored procedure, which can then asynchronously perform the tasks originally executed as part of the trigger.

Let's look at a traditional, synchronous trigger. Then let's use Service Broker to implement an asynchronous trigger. In the following example, when a row is inserted into a sample table, the trigger calls a stored procedure, which performs some lengthy processing:

```
SET NOCOUNT ON
GO


USE [AdventureWorks];
GO


IF OBJECT_ID('dbo.tblSBSample') IS NOT NULL
   DROP TABLE dbo.tblSBSample;
GO
CREATE TABLE dbo.tblSBSample
  (id INT NOT NULL IDENTITY(1,1) PRIMARY KEY);
GO


IF OBJECT_ID('dbo.sproc_LengthyProcessing') IS NOT NULL
   DROP PROCEDURE dbo.sproc_LengthyProcessing;
GO


CREATE PROCEDURE dbo.sproc_LengthyProcessing
AS
BEGIN
   SELECT GETDATE();
   DECLARE @var INT;
   SET @var = 1;

   WHILE @var < 9999999
   BEGIN
```

```
      SET @var = @var + 1;
   END
   SELECT GETDATE();
END
GO
IF OBJECT_ID('dbo.trgSBSampleSync') IS NOT NULL
   DROP TRIGGER dbo.trgSBSampleSync;
GO
CREATE TRIGGER dbo.trgSBSampleSync ON dbo.tblSBSample FOR INSERT AS
BEGIN
   PRINT 'Synchronous trigger started at:'
   EXEC sproc_LengthyProcessing;
   PRINT 'Synchronous trigger ended.'
END
GO

--Test the synchronous trigger by inserting a row
INSERT INTO dbo.tblSBSample DEFAULT VALUES;
GO

DROP TRIGGER dbo.trgSBSampleSync;
GO
```

This script (SynchTrigger.sql) creates a table, a stored procedure, and an INSERT trigger that simply invokes the stored procedure. An INSERT statement toward the end tests the trigger. You should run this script and notice how much time it takes to run the INSERT statement. When executed on a Pentium 4 3GHz machine, the INSERT statement (trigger) takes about 12 seconds to finish.

Let's now implement an asynchronous trigger that will simply post a message to an existing Service Broker queue and return (which means the INSERT statement should return quickly):

```
SET NOCOUNT ON
GO

USE [AdventureWorks];
GO

IF OBJECT_ID('dbo.tblSBSample') IS NOT NULL
   DROP TABLE dbo.tblSBSample;
GO
CREATE TABLE dbo.tblSBSample
  (id INT NOT NULL IDENTITY(1,1) PRIMARY KEY);
GO
```

```
IF OBJECT_ID('dbo.tblSBLog') IS NOT NULL
    DROP TABLE dbo.tblSBLog;
GO
CREATE TABLE dbo.tblSBLog
  (LogText XML);
GO


IF OBJECT_ID('dbo.sproc_SBLengthyProcessing') IS NOT NULL
    DROP PROCEDURE dbo.sproc_SBLengthyProcessing;
GO
CREATE PROCEDURE dbo.sproc_SBLengthyProcessing
AS
BEGIN
    DECLARE @SBMessage TABLE (msgText XML);

    WAITFOR (RECEIVE CAST(message_body AS XML) AS msgText
      FROM dbo.SBSampleQueue
      INTO @SBMessage), TIMEOUT 60000;

    INSERT INTO dbo.tblSBLog
      SELECT * FROM @SBMessage WHERE msgText IS NOT NULL;

    DECLARE @var INT;
    SET @var = 1;

    WHILE @var < 9999999
    BEGIN
      SET @var = @var + 1;
    END
END
GO
```

This script begins by creating a sample table on which an INSERT trigger will be created, another table to hold some logging information, and a stored procedure. This stored procedure will be activated whenever there is a message in the Service Broker queue. The stored procedure performs the same processing as in the previous script (which shows a synchronous trigger), except that it retrieves the message from the queue and saves it into a log table at the beginning.

Let's set up the Service Broker objects to send messages:

```
IF EXISTS(SELECT * FROM sys.services WHERE name = 'SBSampleService')
    DROP SERVICE SBSampleService;
GO
```

```
IF EXISTS(SELECT * FROM sys.service_contracts WHERE name = 'SBSampleContract')
    DROP CONTRACT SBSampleContract;
GO
IF EXISTS(SELECT * FROM sys.service_message_types
              WHERE name = 'SBSampleMessageType')
    DROP MESSAGE TYPE SBSampleMessageType;
GO
IF OBJECT_ID('dbo.SBSampleQueue') IS NOT NULL AND
    EXISTS(SELECT * FROM sys.service_queues WHERE name = 'SBSampleQueue')
  DROP QUEUE dbo.SBSampleQueue;
GO

CREATE MESSAGE TYPE SBSampleMessageType
    VALIDATION = WELL_FORMED_XML;
GO

CREATE CONTRACT SBSampleContract
    (SBSampleMessageType SENT BY ANY);
GO

CREATE QUEUE dbo.SBSampleQueue
    WITH STATUS = ON,
         RETENTION = OFF,
    ACTIVATION (
      PROCEDURE_NAME = AdventureWorks.dbo.sproc_SBLengthyProcessing,
      MAX_QUEUE_READERS = 5,
      EXECUTE AS OWNER)
    ON [DEFAULT];
GO
CREATE SERVICE
    SBSampleService ON QUEUE SBSampleQueue
    (SBSampleContract);
GO
```

These statements create a message type, a contract, a queue, and a service. The queue is associated with a stored procedure to be activated to process the messages.

Here is the trigger code that begins the dialog conversation, posts a message containing rows from an inserted virtual table as XML to the queue, and ends the conversation:

```
IF OBJECT_ID('dbo.trgSBSampleAsync') IS NOT NULL
    DROP TRIGGER dbo.trgSBSampleAsync;
GO
CREATE TRIGGER dbo.trgSBSampleAsync ON dbo.tblSBSample FOR INSERT AS
BEGIN
    PRINT 'Asynchronous trigger started at:'
```

```
SELECT GETDATE();

DECLARE @InsertedData XML

IF EXISTS(SELECT * FROM inserted)
BEGIN
   BEGIN TRANSACTION

   BEGIN TRY
      SELECT @InsertedData = (SELECT * FROM inserted FOR XML AUTO);

      DECLARE @dlgHandle UNIQUEIDENTIFIER

      BEGIN DIALOG CONVERSATION @dlgHandle
         FROM SERVICE SBSampleService
         TO SERVICE 'SBSampleService'
         ON CONTRACT SBSampleContract;

      SEND ON CONVERSATION @dlgHandle
         MESSAGE TYPE SBSampleMessageType (@InsertedData);

      --SELECT CAST(message_body as XML) FROM dbo.SBSampleQueue;

      SELECT * FROM sys.conversation_endpoints
         WHERE conversation_handle = @dlgHandle;

      IF EXISTS(SELECT * FROM sys.conversation_endpoints
         WHERE conversation_handle = @dlgHandle AND state = 'ER')
         BEGIN
            RAISERROR('Service Broker dialog in error state.', 18, 127);
         END
      ELSE
         BEGIN
            END CONVERSATION @dlgHandle;
            COMMIT TRAN;
         END
   END TRY
   BEGIN CATCH
      ROLLBACK TRANSACTION;
      DECLARE @error VARCHAR(max);
      SET @error = ERROR_MESSAGE();
      RAISERROR(@error, 18, 127);
   END CATCH
END
```

```
   PRINT 'Asynchronous trigger ended.'
   SELECT GETDATE()
END
GO


--Test the async trigger by inserting a row
INSERT INTO dbo.tblSBSample DEFAULT VALUES;
GO
```

The INSERT statement toward the end of this script tests the trigger. As soon as a message is posted to the queue, the stored procedure dbo.sproc_LengthyProcessing is activated, which retrieves the message from the queue, saves it into the log table dbo.tblSBLog, and does the lengthy processing as before. As you can see, this time the trigger—and hence the INSERT statement—returns immediately.

Parallel Processing

You can use Service Broker to improve overall response time and user experience by performing tasks in parallel. Consider a scenario where a user screen displays information that is retrieved from multiple databases. One option is to sequentially access each database, one after the other. This can significantly increase the response time. The other option is to post a message to a queue in each database and, as response becomes available, fill the screen with the information retrieved from the database.

Batch Processing

Applications can use Service Broker to take advantage of queuing, reliable messaging, and parallel processing to perform large-scale batch processing. The application stores information about data to be processed in a Service Broker queue, and then a program either periodically or off-hours reads from the queue and processes the data. Service Broker can also be used to offload batch processing to a computer other than the computer from which the request originates.

Increasing Availability by Distributing Server-Side Processing

Consider a scenario where order entry and order fulfillment are performed on two different computers. When an order is entered, a message is posted to a queue, which is routed to the order fulfillment computer. With this distributed OLTP system architecture, even if the order fulfillment computer is offline, the application can continue to accept orders. The messages will be held in the transmission queue until the order fulfillment server becomes available. In addition to increasing availability, this architecture facilitates scaling out, load distribution, and easy management and upgrading.

Data Collection

Service Broker security, reliability, and asynchronous messaging can be leveraged to implement applications that collect data from a large set of sources. For instance, a sales application with multiple sales offices can use Service Broker to send transaction information to a central data store.

Service Broker and Other Messaging Technologies

The following sections compare Service Broker with current messaging technologies, including MSMQ and BizTalk Server, and a future messaging technology code-named Indigo.

MSMQ

You can use MSMQ to create high-performance applications by leveraging MSMQ's guaranteed message delivery, efficient routing, security, and priority-based asynchronous and synchronous messaging.

Service Broker is built in to the SQL Server 2005 database engine and does not involve any additional installation requirements, whereas MSMQ has to be separately installed. Service Broker is not just for messaging; rather, it is a platform for building asynchronous database applications.

MSMQ supports a variety of messaging styles; Service Broker supports only transactional messaging. MSMQ supports messaging between machines running Windows, and Service Broker supports messaging between machines running SQL Server. With Service Broker, the initiator and target recipient of the message have to both be SQL Server. MSMQ offers an HTTP SOAP transport variant and can interoperate with other messaging products, such as IBM WebSphere MQ, but Service Broker works only on a proprietary binary protocol between SQL Server instances.

BizTalk Server

If an application requires transferring XML documents or binary messages between SQL Server instances, it can use Service Broker. However, if it has additional requirements, such as orchestrating workflow, managing state, converting message types, changing the message body; if it works on a variety of transports; or if it needs to integrate with other data sources, such as Exchange Server or Web services, the better option in such situations would be to use BizTalk Server.

Windows Communication Foundation

Windows Communication Foundation is the next-generation platform for building distributed application based on a service-oriented architecture. In addition to queued messaging, it supports distributed transactions, web services interoperability, .NET-to-.NET communication, and more. It is an extension to .NET Framework 2.0 and is scheduled for release in 2006. Unlike Service Broker, Windows Communication Foundation does not provide built-in asynchronous connectivity of SQL Server applications. However, Service Broker can be used to implement a custom channel to provide reliable messaging.

Service Broker Operations and Troubleshooting

This section provides a list of system catalog views, dynamic management views, Profiler trace events, and Performance Monitor counters that you can use to monitor and tune a Service Broker application.

Table 15.1 lists Service Broker catalog views.

TABLE 15.1   Service Broker Catalog Views

Catalog View	Description
sys.service_message_types	This catalog view contains one row per message type registered in the service broker.
sys.service_contracts	This catalog view contains one row for each contract in the database.
sys.services	This catalog view contains one row for each service in the database.
sys.service_broker_endpoints	This catalog view contains one row for the Service Broker endpoint.
sys.remote_service_bindings	This catalog view contains one row per remote service binding.
sys.transmission_queue	This catalog view contains one row for each message in the transmission queue.
sys.routes	This catalog views contains one row per route.
sys.service_queue_usages	This catalog view contains one row per (service, queue) pair.
sys.service_contract_message_usages	This catalog view contains one row per (contract, message type) pair.
sys.service_contract_usages	This catalog view contains one row per (service, contract) pair.
sys.conversation_groups	This catalog view contains one row for each conversation group.
sys.conversation_endpoints	Each side of a Service Broker conversation is represented by a conversation endpoint. This catalog view contains one row per conversation endpoint in the database.

Table 15.2 lists dynamic management views (DMVs) that are useful for monitoring Service Broker activity.

TIP

If you want to force-remove all the messages from the transmission queue, the quickest solution is to run the following T-SQL statement:

```
ALTER DATABASE db_name SET NEW_BROKER
```

However, be very careful in running this command as it unconditionally ends all dialogs. The specified database receives a new broker identifier, and all existing conversations in the database are immediately removed without producing end dialog messages. Instead, you should selectively get rid of the dialogs. For instance, the following T-SQL script creates a cursor over the sys.conversation_endpoints catalog view to end conversations that are in error states:

```
DECLARE @convHandle UNIQUEIDENTIFIER;
DECLARE cursorCE CURSOR FOR
    SELECT conversation_handle FROM sys.conversation_endpoints
    WHERE state = 'ER';

OPEN cursorCE;
FETCH NEXT FROM cursorCE INTO @convHandle;

WHILE @@FETCH_STATUS = 0
BEGIN
    END CONVERSATION @convHandle WITH CLEANUP;
    FETCH NEXT FROM cursorCE INTO @convHandle;
End

CLOSE cursorCE;
DEALLOCATE cursorCE;
GO
```

The state column in the sys.conversation_endpoints catalog view indicates the current state of the conversation, and it can have values such as SO for started outbound, SI for started inbound, CO for conversing, DI for disconnected inbound, DO for disconnected outbound, ER for error, and CD for closed.

TABLE 15.2   Service Broker DMVs

DMV	Description
sys.dm_broker_activated_tasks	This DMV contains a row for each stored procedure activated by Service Broker.
sys.dm_broker_connections	This DMV contains a row for each Service Broker network connection.
sys.dm_broker_forwarded_messages	This DMV contains a row for each Service Broker message that the SQL Server instance is in the process of forwarding.
sys.dm_broker_queue_monitors	This DMV contains a row for each queue monitor in the instance. A queue monitor manages activation for a queue.

Table 15.3 lists Profiler trace events that are useful for monitoring Service Broker activity.

TABLE 15.3   Service Broker Profiler Trace Events

ID	Trace Event	Description
163	Broker:Activation	Occurs when a queue monitor starts an activation stored procedure or sends a QUEUE_ACTIVATION notification, or when an activation stored procedure started by a queue monitor exits.
138	Broker:Connection	Reports the status of a transport connection managed by Service Broker.
124	Broker:Conversation	Reports the progress of a Service Broker conversation.
136	Broker:Conversation Group	Occurs when Service Broker creates a new conversation group or drops an existing conversation group.
161	Broker:Corrupted Message	Occurs when Service Broker receives a corrupted message.
140	Broker:Forwarded Message Dropped	Occurs when Service Broker drops a message that was intended to be forwarded.
139	Broker:Forwarded Message Sent	Occurs when Service Broker forwards a message.
141	Broker:Message Classify	Occurs when Service Broker determines the routing for a message. A message is classified for local, remote, or delayed delivery.
160	Broker:Message Undeliverable	Occurs when Service Broker is unable to retain a received message that should have been delivered to a service in this instance.
143	Broker:Queue Disabled	Indicates that a poison message was detected because there were five transaction rollbacks in a row on a Service Broker queue. The event contains the database ID and queue ID of the queue that contains the poison message.
149	Broker:Remote Message Acknowledgement	Indicates when an acknowledgement has been received.
142	Broker:Transmission	Indicates that errors have occurred in the Service Broker transport layer. The error number and state values indicate the source of the error.

Table 15.4 lists Performance Monitor counters that are useful for monitoring Service Broker activity. For a default instance, the Performance Monitor object name begins with *SQLServer:*, and for a named instance, the Performance Monitor object name begins with *MSSQL$<instance_name>:*.

TABLE 15.4   Service Broker Performance Monitor Counters

Performance Object	Description
Broker Activation	Contains Performance Monitor counters that report information about stored procedure activation, such as Stored Procedures Invoked/sec, Tasks Running, and so on.
Broker Statistics	Contains Performance Monitor counters that report general Service Broker information, such as SQL SENDs/sec, SQL SEND Total, SQL RECEIVEs/sec, SQL RECEIVE Total, Forwarded Messages/sec, and so on.
Broker / DBM Transport	Contains Performance Monitor counters that report information related to Service Broker and database mirroring network activity. This category includes counters such as Open Connection Count, Msg Fragment Send Size Avg, Message Fragment Send Total, and so on.

You can use the Object Explorer in SQL Server Management Studio to view message types, contracts, queues, services, routes, and remote service binding details. This information is available under the Service Broker folder for each database in the Object Explorer tree.

Troubleshooting Tips

You can use the catalog views and DMVs listed in Tables 15.1 and 15.2 to verify Service Broker configuration and execution. SQL Server writes Service Broker log and error messages to SQL Server error log files and the Windows event log. You can look in error log files and the event viewer for any errors that are interfering with Service Broker communication. For instance, if the database master key is missing, SQL Server logs the following message to the SQL Server error log:

```
Service Broker needs to access the master key in the database 'AdventureWorks'.
    Error code:25. The master key has to exist and the service master key
    encryption is required.
```

Here are some additional techniques you can use for troubleshooting Service Broker applications:

- You can debug an activated stored procedure by writing PRINT statements in it. Service Broker writes the output of the PRINT statement into the SQL Server error log file (ERRORLOG).

- If a stored procedure is not activated, you can use the sys.service_queues catalog view to review fields such as is_activation_enabled, activation_procedure, is_receive_enabled, execute_as_principal_id, and so on. You need to confirm that the security principal has EXECUTE permission on the stored procedure. You can review the SQL Server error log for any additional information.

- If messages remain in the transmission queue (sys.transmission_queue), you can use the is_broker_enabled column of the sys.databases catalog view to check whether Service Broker is enabled for the database. You should also check the transmission_status column in the sys.transmission_queue catalog view to see error text that describes the last error that occurred while trying to deliver messages for a specific dialog. If messages are exchanged across instances, you need to ensure that Service Broker is enabled in the msdb system database and that routes are configured correctly in this database.

Service Broker Security Overview

Service Broker messages may carry valuable business information. Therefore, it is important to ensure that their integrity is preserved, that messages are received from authenticated services, and that messages are sent to designated services. The Service Broker infrastructure ensures that only authorized databases send and receive the messages and that the message integrity is preserved.

Service Broker provides security at two levels:

- **Dialog**—*Dialog security* encrypts the messages, verifies the identities of participants, provides remote authorization, and performs message integrity checking. Therefore, dialog security helps protect data against inspection or modification in transit. Service Broker provides two types of dialog security: full security and anonymous security. *Full security* prevents the initiating service from sending messages to an untrusted database and protects the target service from receiving messages from an untrusted database. Service Broker encrypts messages transmitted over the network when the conversation uses full security. *Anonymous security* protects the initiating service against sending messages to an untrusted database. Service Broker encrypts messages transmitted over the network when the conversation uses anonymous security. Anonymous security identifies the target service to the initiating service, but it does not identify the initiating service to the target service. Full security requires the initiator to have a certificate and remote service binding with ANONYMOUS = OFF.

- **Transport**—*Transport security* prevents unauthorized databases from sending Service Broker messages to databases in the local instance. When transport security is enabled, authorization is required to connect to the Service Broker endpoint. Whether the network connection uses transport security depends on the AUTHENTICATION option for the broker endpoint and whether both databases contain a certificate for master.dbo.

Applications that send messages between SQL Server instances may use transport security, dialog security, or both. By default, all dialog conversations use dialog security. When you begin a dialog, you can explicitly allow the dialog to proceed without dialog security by including the ENCRYPTION = OFF clause on the BEGIN DIALOG CONVERSATION statement. However, if a remote service binding exists for the service that the conversation targets, the dialog uses security even when ENCRYPTION = OFF. For a dialog that uses security, Service Broker encrypts all messages sent outside a SQL Server instance. Messages that remain within a SQL Server instance are never encrypted.

Service Broker remote security, where more than one SQL Server instance participates in the dialog, is based on certificates. SQL Server uses certificates to verify the identity of a remote database and to identify the local database principal for the operation. You can create certificates by using the CREATE CERTIFICATE T-SQL statement. Service Broker uses the remote service bindings in the database that begins the conversation to determine the security for the conversation. Service Broker therefore uses the service name and, optionally, the contract name to determine the security for the service.

In addition to Service Broker dialog and transport security, SQL Server permissions are required to run Service Broker statements such as SEND, RECEIVE, CONNECT, and so on. The GRANT statement can be used to allow permissions on a Service Broker contract, message type, remote binding, route, or service.

Summary

Service Broker is one of the top developer features introduced in SQL Server 2005. It is a platform for building asynchronous database applications. It provides the infrastructure required for creating queued, asynchronous, reliable, and secure messaging applications. Application architectures based on Service Broker can scale up or scale out with minimal or no changes to the application code.

This chapter starts with an introduction to asynchronous messaging concepts and the benefits of integrating messaging into the database engine. The rest of the chapter discusses the Service Broker architecture, implementation, operation, troubleshooting, and security details.

Chapter 15, "SQL Server 2005 Support for 64-Bit Processors," discusses SQL Server 2005's support for the 64-bit processor architecture.

SQL Sever 2005 Support for 64-Bit Processors

One of the top reasons for insufficient performance and limited scalability is memory bottlenecks. A system's being low on memory stresses both the disk and the processor. Excessive paging results in very high CPU utilization, increased queuing, and slow response times. Adding more memory to the server is one option for improving performance in such scenarios. However, there is a limit to the amount of RAM supported by servers. A server with a 32-bit processor has a limit on the directly addressable memory space of 4GB. This is because a 32-bit pointer cannot hold a memory address larger than 4GB (that is, 2^{32}). The Address Windowing Extensions (AWE) API (discussed later in this chapter) is sometimes used to enable up to 64GB of memory support on 32-bit systems. However, AWE has some limitations and overhead associated with it, which makes AWE an impractical solution for a lot of memory-intensive, performance-critical enterprise applications.

When using AWE is impractical, you can consider using a 64-bit processor-based server that has support for up to 1024GB of directly addressable memory. Theoretically, a 64-bit processor supports up to 18 billion gigabytes (that is, 2^{64}) of flat or linear memory addressability. However, the maximum memory supported by the operating system is 1024GB on Windows Server 2003 Datacenter Edition. In addition to large memory support, the 64-bit processor architecture offers additional benefits, including enhanced parallelism, increased availability, and improved bus and I/O bandwidth architecture for faster and wider throughput.

Microsoft SQL Server 2000 was one of the first Microsoft enterprise product family members to leverage the 64-bit platform and provide true scalability to customer applications. In April 2003, Microsoft announced that Windows Server 2003 (64-bit) and SQL Server 2000 (64-bit) would enable SQL Server 2000 to run on the Intel Itanium 64-bit processor. The 64-bit version of SQL Server is functionally very similar to the 32-bit product. Essentially the same code base as SQL Server 2000 (32-bit) is compiled on the 64-bit platform to leverage the key improvements of the 64-bit operating system and processor architecture. The upgrade path from SQL Server 32-bit to SQL Server 64-bit is straightforward because the on-disk structure is the same on the two platforms; you can detach and attach or back up and restore the databases from a 32-bit to a 64-bit platform.

Intel Itanium Processor Family (IPF) is based on Explicitly Parallel Instruction Computing (EPIC) technology, which has a different architecture and instruction set than 32-bit x86 processors. On the other hand, x64 processors, such as the Intel EM64T or the AMD Opteron, extend the x86 instruction set to support running both 32-bit and 64-bit applications. SQL Server 2000 Service Pack 4 (SP4), released in May 2005, enables the running of SQL Server 2000 (32-bit) on x64 processors. In other words, now you can run SQL Server 2000 on either Itanium 2 or on x64 processors.

SQL Server 2005 is the first release to natively support Itanium 2 as well as x64 processors. SQL Server 2005 addresses some of the limitations of SQL Server 2000 (64-bit) and is designed and optimized to provide superior performance on 64-bit platforms. You can run SQL Server 2005 (64-bit) on 64-bit operating system such as Windows Server 2003 (64-bit) and 64-bit hardware from vendors such as Hewlett-Packard, Unisys, IBM, Dell, and NEC, in 4-way (that is, 4 processors) to 64-way (64 CPUs) configurations. This chapter introduces concepts related to the 64-bit processor and contains details on SQL Server 2005's support for 64-bit processors.

64-Bit Processor Usage Scenarios

The key architectural benefits of 64-bit processors include the following:

- **Very large memory addressability**—64-bit processors break the 4GB/64GB barrier and allow up to 1024GB of direct memory addressability, without any API layer such as AWE.

- **Enhanced parallel processing support**—64-bit chips include a number of features that enhance parallel processing performance.

- **Support for a large number of processors**—Improvements in parallel processing enable the 64-bit architecture to support a larger number of processors (up to 64). Having a larger number of processors enables SQL Server to scale up. In addition, the on-chip cache results in improved performance on 64-bit platforms.

- **Enhanced bus architecture**—The bus architecture on 64-bit chipsets is faster and wider, allowing more and faster data transfers between the cache and processor; this improves the overall system throughput.

These benefits can be leveraged in a number of scenarios, as described in the following sections.

Improving Performance of Memory-Constrained Applications

Industry benchmarks such as the TPC-C (see www.tpc.org) have shown that the 64-bit architecture can provide immediate performance improvements to applications that are currently memory-constrained on a 32-bit platform. For example, the latest TPC-C benchmark for SQL Server 2005 64-bit running on a HP Integrity Superdome 64-bit delivers two or three times greater TPC-C transaction throughput than any 32-bit–based system while maintaining a much lower total cost of ownership (TCO). Visit www.tpc.org/tpcc/results/tpcc_result_detail.asp?id=105060604 for more details.

As described earlier in this chapter, the 32-bit processor architecture restricts the directly addressable memory space to 4GB. Out of this 4GB of memory space, by default, 2GB is reserved for the operating system kernel, and the remaining 2GB can be used by applications such as SQL Server. Such small virtual address space could be a significant drawback for high-end servers manipulating gigabytes and terabytes of data.

If an application demands more virtual memory, you can put a /3gb switch in your system's boot.ini file. The /3gb switch reduces the kernel memory to 1GB and leaves remaining 3GB for user applications. Limiting kernel virtual address space to 1GB can cause effects from a drop in performance and memory allocation failures to system stalls. It is recommended that you avoid the use of the /3gb switch unless absolutely required and use it only after doing sufficient testing.

If even 3GB is not sufficient, and you are noticing excessive paging and disk or processor queuing, you can put the /pae switch in the boot.ini file. The /pae switch instructs the operating system to use AWE-mapped memory, allowing up to 64GB of addressable memory. The AWE API is based on Intel's Physical Addressing Extension (PAE), which allows Windows to *simulate* 36-bit memory addressing. Applications such as SQL Server can use the AWE API to scale memory up to 64GB RAM.

The AWE mechanism allocates physical memory and maps it to the given process's virtual address space (VAS). Once physical memory is allocated, the operating system cannot reclaim it until either the process is terminated or the process frees memory back to the operating system. An application can control and even avoid paging altogether for memory allocated by using AWE. In other words, by using AWE, applications can acquire physical memory as non-paged memory and then dynamically map views of the non-paged memory to the 32-bit address space. However, although AWE mapping is efficient, it still has mapping overhead. Also, the additional memory addressability is available only to the relational database engine, not to other engines, such as Analysis Services, Reporting Services, and Full-Text Search. In addition, the relational engine can use AWE-mapped memory only for the data buffer cache and not for other purposes, such as the procedure cache, the log cache, cursors, the sort area, hash memory, per-connection memory, or lock memory.

Many SQL Server resources, such as the procedure cache, per-connection memory, sort space, and so on are restricted to virtual memory only, which has a 3GB limit on 32-bit platforms and do not benefit from AWE. Moving to a 64-bit platform improves the performance of the applications experiencing memory-related problems, such as recompilation of stored procedures. Applications can benefit from massive in-memory caching of data as well as larger data structures for the procedure cache, sort space, lock memory, and connection memory. The 64-bit platform offers massively scalable performance for large, complex queries through large memory addressing, nearly unlimited virtual memory, and enhanced parallelism. On 64-bit systems, the /3gb and /pae switches and AWE are not required because the operating system can directly address up to 1024GB of memory.

Applications that generate complex query plans with a large number of joins, dozens of columns, a large number of open cursors, and an I/O-intensive workload can immediately benefit from a 64-bit processor's large addressable memory. In addition, a large data buffer pool can save considerable I/O costs, resulting in less CPU time spent on I/O and reduced latency spent waiting on I/O.

Server Consolidation

In the simplest terms, *consolidation* is the process of condensing multiple physical servers, applications, and workloads into a smaller number of physical servers providing an equal or better level of functionality and service.

Consolidation has two primary goals:

- To provide at least the same level of functionality and the service by using fewer servers to lower operational cost and management overhead

- To provide an architecture that can scale efficiently as the business grows

Server consolidation offers the following advantages:

- Centralized management

- Optimized hardware resources

- Standardization of platforms and processes

- Greater return on hardware investment

- Reduced operational costs

The support for very large directly addressable memory, enhanced parallelism, and the ability to scale up and handle a large number of concurrent users and transactions make 64-bit-based servers an ideal choice for large-scale server consolidation.

High-Performance Data Warehousing Applications

Analysis Services 2005 can always benefit from additional memory to provide better query and processing performance, to support very large dimensions, and to support a large number of concurrent users. However, because Analysis Services is unable to take advantage of the memory extensions of AWE, its memory is limited to 3GB in a 32-bit environment, even if more memory is actually available.

Analysis Services in a 64-bit system removes the 3GB memory limit and offers the following benefits:

- Greater parallelism in partition processing

- Faster aggregation processing

- Huge dimensions supported in memory

- Shorter load window

- Support for a large number of concurrent users running complex queries and processing cubes simultaneously

---

NOTE

It is important to note that things that could not be done on Analysis Services 2000 (32-bit) and required Analysis Services 2000 (64-bit), can now run successfully and efficiently on Analysis Services 2005 (32-bit). This is possible because of several new architectural enhancements made to Analysis Service 2005, including the new memory management architecture. However, the 3GB memory limit still exists in Analysis Services 2005.

In addition to the scenarios discussed here, the SQL Server 2005 (64-bit) platform can be a powerful alternative to traditional Unix systems for high-end database servers. A 64-bit-based solution can significantly improve overall performance and throughput of enterprise resource planning (ERP) (including supply chain), customer relationship management (CRM), and financial applications.

SQL Server 2005 (64-Bit) in Detail

SQL Server 2005 is the first SQL Server release to natively support Itanium and x64-based 64-bit processors. A single SQL Server 2005 source code base is compiled for three platforms: x86 (32-bit), Itanium (64-bit), and x64 (64-bit). SQL Server 2005 (64-bit) can run on Itanium-based servers with Windows Server 2003 Service Pack 1. SQL Server 2005 (64-bit) for the x64 platform can run on Windows XP x64 Professional 2003 (64-bit) or on Windows Server 2003 x64, which is based on the code for Windows Server 2003 SP1. In addition, you can run SQL Server 2005 (32-bit) on x64-based hardware and operating systems, such as Windows XP x64 Professional 2003 and Windows Server 2003 SP1 64-bit x64, in WOW64 mode.

NOTE

WOW64 mode, also known as *extended system support*, is a feature of 64-bit editions of Microsoft Windows that allows 32-bit applications to execute unmodified on a 64-bit system. Applications function normally in 32-bit mode even though the underlying operating system is running on the 64-bit platform.

SQL Server 2005 (32-bit) supports up to 32 processors, and SQL Server 2005 (64-bit) supports up to 64 processors.

Here are some of the enhancements in SQL Server 2005 (64-bit) compared to SQL Server 2000 (64-bit):

- SQL Server 2000 (64-bit) does not include management and monitoring tools such as Enterprise Manager, Query Analyzer, Profiler, Analysis Manager, and so on. SQL Server 2005 (64-bit) bundles all the management tools, including SQL Server Management Studio, Profiler, Database Engine Tuning Advisor, SQL Server Configuration Manager, and so on.

- Only Enterprise Edition of SQL Server 2000 (64-bit) is supported on 64-bit platforms, and SQL Server 2000 Service Pack 4 is required for x64 support. Both Standard and Enterprise Editions of SQL Server 2005 (64-bit) support 64-bit computing, which includes both the Intel Itanium 2 family of processors and the x64 family of processors from both Intel and AMD. In addition, Standard Edition does not have a memory limitation and is only limited to the level of memory supported by the version of Windows on which you run the product.

- SQL Server 2000 (64-bit) and SQL Server 2005 (64-bit) do not support MAPI-based SQL Mail. However, on SQL Server 2005 (64-bit) you can use SMTP-based Database Mail to send emails from T-SQL code.

- The SQL Server 2005 database engine and other subsystems are better aware of the 64-bit architecture than SQL Server 2000. Therefore, SQL Server 2005 can effectively make use of 64-bit computing to provide better performance and system throughput.

- SQL Server 2000 (64-bit) does not allow designing and running Data Transformation Services (DTS) packages. SQL Server 2005 (64-bit), on the other hand, fully supports SQL Server Integration Services (SSIS). You can use Business Intelligence Development Studio on a 64-bit machine to design, debug, and run an SSIS package. Also, because SSIS packages are saved as XML files (with the .dtsx file extension), you can create a package on one platform (for instance, on a 32-bit server) and then edit or run that package on another platform (for instance, on a 64-bit server).

- SQL Server 2000 Reporting Services and SQL Server 2000 Notification Services do not support 64-bit systems. SQL Server 2005 Notification Services is supported on both x64 and Itanium platforms. However, Notification Services Management Objects (NMO) is not supported in WOW64 mode on AMD and Intel x64 platforms. SQL Server 2005 Reporting Services is also supported on both x64 and Itanium platforms; however, a few things, such as the RSKeyMgmt.exe tool, subscription deliveries to reports in TIFF format, and so on, are not fully implemented.

NOTE

Side-by-side installation of 32-bit SQL Server 2000 SP4 on an x64 platform with SQL Server 2005 (64-bit) is not supported.

Summary

32-bit memory addressing is often limiting for performance-critical and memory-intensive enterprise applications that support thousands of concurrent users and run very complex queries. If memory bottlenecks are identified, one option to tackle performance and scalability issues is to add more RAM and enable AWE. However, as discussed in this chapter, AWE has some limitations, and the only way to gain performance and scalability in such situations is to consider moving to 64-bit computing. In addition to being used in memory-constrained scenarios, 64-bit systems are also being used in other scenarios, such as for server consolidation, data warehouse applications, Unix migration, and implementing ERP and CRM solutions.

This chapter begins with an introduction to 64-bit computing, including its benefits and a description of scenarios in which the 64-bit architecture can be helpful. The second part of the chapter describes SQL Server 2005's support for 64-bit systems. SQL Server 2005 natively supports Itanium and x64 platforms and fixes a lot of the limitations of SQL Server 2000 (64-bit).

Index

NUMBERS

A

B

breaking changes to SQL Server 2005, 48-49

Breakpoint window (BIDS), 365

breakpoints, 365

building blocks of XML web services, 324-325

bulk loading XML data, 310-312

BULK rowset provider, 186-187

business intelligence, 89-91, 390

Business Intelligence Development Studio.
See BIDS

business intelligence framework, 90

C

C#

base-64 cncoding and decoding, 343-345

stored procedures, saving XML data to file, 341-343

calculating query plan cost, 27-28

Call Stackwindow (BIDS), 365

calling xml data type methods, 313

capturing blocked process reports, 118-120

catalog security, 33-34

catalog views, 32-33, 64, 188, 345-346

for Service Broker, 441-442

HTTP SOAP, 329

certificates, 221, 234

Character Map transformation, 361

Check Database Integrity task, 363

checksum I/O transactions, validating, 240

cleansing data, 387

clients, SSIS, 352

CLR (common language runtime), 9, 62, 334

appdomains, 338

sys.dm clr, 338

as replacement for extended stored procedures, 9

hosting, design goals, 337

integration with SQL. *See also* SQLCLR integration

benefits of, 339-340

catalog views, 345-346

challenges, 340

examples, 341-345

monitoring activity, 346-347

CLS (Common Language Specification), 332

clusters, active-active, 87

code access security in .NET Framework, 233-234

color-coding of SSIS execution status, 366

columns

non-key, including in indices, 68

partition columns, 38

persisted computed columns, 68-70, 265

Q

T

operations and configuration

   Database Mail, 143-146

   SQL Server Configuration Manager, 131-133

   SQLCMD, 133-134, 136-138, 141-142

performance enhancement, 115

   DTA, 125-131

   Performance Monitor, counters, 125

   SQL Server 2005 Profiler, 116-125

features, 116-118

TOP operator, 155-157

TP-Lite, 11

tracing XQuery activity, 316

transactional publications, initializing subscriptions, 256

transactional replication, peer-to-peer, 89, 255

transactions, row versioning, 29

transformations, 360

translations, 399

transport protocols, endpoints, 197

transport security, 446

triggers, 167

   asynchronous, 68

      Service Broker solutions, 435-440

   DDL, 56

   T-SQL, 55

troubleshooting

   Database Mail, 145-146

   Service Broker, 445-446

Trustworthy Computing Initiative, 195

tuning performance

   AUTO UPDATE STATISTICs ASYNC option, 287

   DATE CORRELATION OPTIMIZATION ASYNC option, 287

   DTA, 84-85

   ENABLE BROKER option, 288

typed XML, 305

   columns, 59

   creating, 306-310

U

UBO (usage-based optimization), 409

   automating, 411

   implementing, 410

UBO Wizard, 411

UDM (unified dimensional model), 396-398

UMS (User Mode Scheduler), 16-17

Union All transformation, 362

unmanaged code, 62, 334

UNPIVOT keyword, 77-78

UNPIVOT relational operator, 180, 183

UnPivot transformation, 362

unreachable remote services, 426

unsequenced messages, 424

untyped XML, 59, 306

Upgrade Advisor, 49